WHY WAGES DON'T FALL DURING A RECESSION

Why Wages Don't Fall during a Recession

Truman F. Bewley

Harvard University Press

Cambridge, Massachusetts, and London, England   1999

Library of Congress Cataloging-in-Publication Data

Bewley, Truman F. (Truman Fassett), 1941–
   Why wages don't fall during a recession / Truman F. Bewley.
      p.   cm.
   Includes bibliographical references and index.
   ISBN 0-674-95241-3
   1. Wages.   2. Recessions.   3. Labor supply.   I. Title.
HD4909.B48   1999
331.2'1—dc21   99-16443

CONTENTS

ACKNOWLEDGMENTS

The work reported here began as a joint project with my colleague William Brainard, who did some of the initial interviews with me and who has advised me and patiently reviewed chapters of my book since then, making many important suggestions. I am very grateful to him as well as to a number of other people who have read and criticized parts or all of various drafts. These include Fischer Black, Moshe Buchinsky, Jonathan Conning, Ray Fair, Ernst Fehr, Werner Hildenbrand, Michael Jerison, Morton Kamien, David Levine, James Malcomson, George Milkovich, Andrew Oswald, Tomas Philipson, Marshall Pomer, Joseph Ritter, Oliver Williamson, Stanley Reiter, Joseph Ritter, James Robinson, Peter Sanfey, Hugh Schwartz, Robert Shiller, Martin Shubik, James Tobin, and Henry Tosi. James Robinson and Peter Sanfey have put particularly great effort into criticizing my manuscript, and Joseph Ritter made very helpful comments on Chapter 21. I have importuned a great many economists, psychologists, and sociologists for bibliographical information and am grateful for their help. These include Katharine Abraham, Eileen Appelbaum, George Baker, Robert Baron, John Barron, Bernard Bass, Rebecca Blank, Joel Brockner, William Wentworth Daniel, Walter Dolde, Gordon Donaldson, John Dunlop, Robert Folger, Jeffrey Fuhrer, Mark Granovetter, Jerald Greenberg, Richard Hackman, James Heckman, Harry Holzer, Glenn Hubbard, Casey Ichniowski, Bruce Kaufman, Brian Klaas, Edward Lawler, Guy A. Lofaro, Kenneth MacCrimmon, Bruce Meyer, Daniel Mitchell, Dale Mortensen, Brian Niehoff, William Nordhaus, Dennis Organ, Paul Osterman, Andrew Oswald, Judi McLean Parks, John Pencavel, Bruce Petersen, Phillip Podsakoff, James Rebitzer, Alvin Roth, Vida Scarpello, Henry Sims, Christopher Sims, René Stulz, Victor Vroom, and Hoyt Wheeler. I would like to thank the hundreds of people I interviewed for taking the time to meet with me, often in trying circumstances.

My administrative assistant when I began this project, Margaret Otzel, was extremely helpful, and I owe a great deal to my editor, Michael Aronson, for sage advice. I also appreciate the assistance of the New Haven Chamber of Commerce in obtaining interviews. I gratefully acknowledge support from NSF grant number SES-9110139 and from the Max-Planck-Forschungspreis, from the Deutsche Forschungsgemeinschaft (Sonderforschungsbereich 303), and from the Cowles Foundation of Yale University.

Some of the discussion in Chapter 21 appeared in the *Federal Reserve Bank of St. Louis Review*, 81, no. 3 (May–June 1999), in a paper of mine entitled "Work Motivation." Permission to use the material is gratefully acknowledged.

WHY WAGES DON'T FALL DURING A RECESSION

1

INTRODUCTION

Why have money wages and salaries seldom declined during post–World War II recessions in the United States and abroad, despite high unemployment and intense competition for jobs? Instead, market pay rates continue to rise during downturns, albeit at a slower rate than during economic booms. Why don't labor markets behave like competitive commodity markets, where prices fall or even plunge when supply exceeds demand? Why do few firms avoid layoffs by cutting pay and lowering product prices so as to increase sales? How can the frequency of layoffs be reconciled with the movement within the business community to treat workers humanely? The failure of pay rates to fall is termed wage stickiness, downward wage rigidity, or simply wage rigidity, and has puzzled economists for years.

I have sought explanations by interviewing more than 300 businesspeople, labor leaders, counselors of the unemployed, and business consultants in the Northeast of the United States during the recession of the early 1990s. It is unusual for economists to do surveys of any sort, and I undertook this one because I could think of no other way to answer my questions. From the interviews, I conclude that wage rigidity stems from a desire to encourage loyalty, a motive that superficially seems incompatible with layoffs. My findings support none of the existing economic theories of wage rigidity, except those emphasizing the impact of pay cuts on morale. Other theories fail in part because they are based on the unrealistic psychological assumptions that people's abilities do not depend on their state of mind and that they are rational in the simplistic sense that they maximize a utility that depends only on their own consumption and working conditions, not on the welfare of others. Wage rigidity is the product of more complicated employee behavior, in the face of which manager reluctance to cut pay is rational. Worker behavior, however, is not always completely rational, though reasonable and understandable. A model that captures the essence of wage rigidity must take into account the capacity of employees to identify with their firm and to internalize its objectives. This internalization and workers' mood have a strong impact on job performance and call for material, moral, and symbolic reciprocation from company leadership.

1.1 Clarification of the Question

The issue of wage rigidity should not be confused with the questions of why unemployment exists at all and why it increases during recessions. All students of the labor market accept as normal a minimal frictional level of unemployment. What is hard to understand is why increases in unemployment have so little impact on labor compensation.

Wage rigidity does not necessarily help explain why unemployment rises during recessions, for wage flexibility might not prevent it from doing so. Though a single firm might employ more workers at lower wages, it does not follow that the same is true for all firms together. This conclusion would involve the fallacy of composition, for, as John Maynard Keynes (1936, chap. 19) pointed out, wage cuts in response to high unemployment could have indirect effects that would decrease real aggregate demand and increase unemployment. For instance, deflation would increase the burden of debt, and sustained deflation could raise real interest rates enough to discourage investment.

1.2 The Topic Is Controversial

It is hard to take a detached view of wage rigidity, because it requires facing unpleasant truths; the world is imperfect, people often suffer for no good reason, and it is not clear what to do about it. Furthermore, the subject is central to intense controversy between Keynesian and neoclassical macroeconomists over whether government economic policy should be used to stabilize aggregate income and employment. The debate has important political implications, creating a highly charged atmosphere that colors thinking about wage formation and unemployment. Economists on the Keynesian side of the dispute claim that wage rigidity is confirmed by statistical evidence that pay rates almost never fall. They say that labor markets do not automatically adjust to eliminate excess unemployment and that joblessness is a grave misfortune forced on people, most of whom want to work, even at wages lower than those earned previously. Keynesians think recessions are caused by declines in aggregate demand and should be cured by expansionary economic policy.[1]

Those on the neoclassical side of the controversy assert that wage rigidity is an illusion, that wages and salaries are flexible, and that labor markets always clear.[2] A central tenet of these beliefs is that the existing rate of unemployment is the optimal outcome of market forces and should not or cannot be affected by government policy. The view is that during recessions pay rates fall below reservation levels, or the minimum at which people are willing to work, and this decline causes workers to leave their jobs and become unemployed. Neoclassicists also assert that anyone can find some job quickly and that people remain unemployed because they want higher pay than is available to them.[3] There are two main explanations of this behavior. According to the intertemporal substitution theory of Lucas and Rapping (1969), workers stop working because they want to enjoy leisure while it is unusually cheap in terms of forgone wage income. The market misperceptions theory of the same authors and of Lucas (1972) asserts that people leave their jobs to have more time to look for better-paying ones at other firms, believing incorrectly that pay is low only where they work. Opinions vary among neoclassicists as to the causes of recessions. One idea is that restrictive monetary policy precipitates decline. Another idea, associated with the names of David Lilien (1982) and Stephen Davis, John Haltiwanger, and Scott Schuh (1996), is that recessions are caused by waves of shocks, including productivity declines, to particular firms or industrial sectors. A similar idea, the real business cycle theory, is that economywide declines in productivity produce recessions. Some say that predictable macroeconomic policy cannot influence employment, but that only surprise changes in aggregate demand do so, and then just temporarily by producing unexpected fluctuations in nominal pay rates that confuse workers about the relation of their pay to what is normal. According to the neoclassical view, wage rates appear to be rigid downward only because workers prevent wages from declining noticeably by withdrawing labor as soon as they fall below reservation levels.[4] A current opinion is that unemployment always nearly equals a "natural rate" that fluctuates and cannot be influenced by macroeconomic policy. According to this view, chronically high unemployment, such as the rates of 12 percent or more seen in the mid-1990s in some European countries, is due solely to microeconomic problems, including generous unemployment insurance benefits, labor market rigidities, or the low skills of the unemployed.

Neoclassical economists describe unemployment as voluntary, whereas Keynesians claim it is involuntary. Although this difference is the core of the debate, I try to avoid applying the word "voluntary" to joblessness, for doing so leads to a logical ambiguity. If someone points a gun at you and says, "Give me your money," you surrender it voluntarily, but only because the alternative is dreadful. In the same sense, people are voluntarily unemployed if they would rather look for a job paying what they think they deserve than take a lower-paying one. Keynesians have tried to avoid this difficulty by labeling as involuntarily unemployed people who cannot find work at the prevailing wage at jobs they are willing and qualified to take. This definition involves a distracting difficulty; usually there is no such thing as a prevailing wage, because pay rates for the same kind of work vary widely among employers. This fiction is irrelevant, however, for in recessions most jobless people have difficulty locating any opening at the level of their qualifications, even one that pays little for their kind of work, and many gladly accept any position they find. They are likely to be rejected for positions at a level somewhat lower than that for which they are qualified, for reasons I will explain. They might have less difficulty finding and being accepted for very low level positions, but they would probably be ill-advised to take such jobs, unless faced with penury. Many do offer to take positions at a much lower level than they held previously, and those who refuse to do so could be said to be voluntarily unemployed because greater flexibility might enable them to find work more quickly. Nevertheless, they are involuntarily unemployed according to the everyday meaning of these words and according to the spirit of Keynes's usage. Judging from historical experience and what I have learned of the labor market, it seems probable that if aggregate demand for labor increased during a recession, fewer people would be jobless. This is the heart of what Keynes meant by "involuntary unemployment." I do not discuss the probable impact of changes in aggregate demand, however, for this question has to do with how the whole economic system functions and I gathered information only on microeconomic details. Among these were the flexibility of the unemployed and the difficulty they experienced finding work.

1.3 The Unsatisfactory State of Knowledge

Neoclassicists espouse a set of closely related logical explanations of why unemployment increases during recessions and why wages seem rigid downward, while actually flexible. Keynesians, in contrast, embrace no single theory of wage rigidity. Moreover, the lack of an accepted explanation is one of the neoclassicists' most persuasive arguments; labor markets must clear, because there is no compelling reason for them not to do so. They say that a convincing theory ought at least to explain why workers and employers do not exploit the gains from trade that would exist were there excess unemployment, for if workers were willing to work at wages at which employers could profitably employ them, then the two sides would agree on terms for exchanging labor for money.

Despite intense interest in wage rigidity, current understanding of the subject is highly unsatisfactory. Many explanations have been proposed, any or all of which could be valid, since they are not mutually contradictory. But little is known about which theories are correct or under what conditions. Such an abundance of competing, unrefuted theories indicates ignorance, not knowledge; greater abundance makes each theory less likely.[5]

1.4 Examples of Explanations

Some examples should give an idea of the variety of theories. Those of Lucas and Rapping (1969) and Lucas (1972) described above are accepted by many economists. Their models are inconsistent with the fact that during recessions layoffs increase and quits decline, and McLaughlin (1990, 1991) has suggested a way of resolving the discrepancy regarding layoffs. He assumes that firms offer workers a choice between layoff and continued work at lower pay, layoff occurring only when the lower pay is refused. Layoffs are compatible with the Lucas-Rapping model, because they are regarded as quits following refusal of pay cuts.

Search models start from the realistic observation that buyers and sellers of labor have imperfect knowledge of trading opportunities, so that both sides must spend time and money to find or fill jobs. In these models, unemployment is a natural consequence of delays in the matching of people to open positions. In most of the models, wage rates are the outcome either of bargaining between employers and individual employees or are set unilaterally by employers and adjusted so as to ensure an adequate supply of labor. There are two types of job search models, those which attribute downward wage rigidity to job hunters' misperceptions of market wages, and those of the transactions type in which there are no misperceptions, wages are completely flexible, and unemployment results from adjustment to change.[6] The Lucas-Rapping misperceptions model is of the first type.[7]

Another theory is that of Keynes (1936, chap. 2), who suggested that workers are so concerned about the relation of their wages to those of workers at other firms that no company dares cut pay. Resistance to wage cuts can be avoided only if all firms in an economy cut wages simultaneously so as to preserve traditional wage differentials. Since such reductions would be difficult to coordinate, nominal wages are rigid downward. Real wages can fall without meeting the same opposition, however, for inflation affects all workers, preserving wage differentials.

According to the implicit contract theory of Baily (1974), Gordon (1974), and Azariadis (1975), firms obtain labor most cheaply by guaranteeing that real wages will never decline, that is, by providing insurance against wage decline. If real wages do fall, employers have to pay more in the future than they would have otherwise in order to obtain or retain labor.

In the shirking theory of Eaton and White (1983) and Shapiro and Stiglitz

(1984), firms monitor workers randomly, firing those whose performance does not meet some standard. The higher are wages and salaries, the greater is the cost to workers of job loss, and hence the greater is their incentive to meet the standard. Increased pay, therefore, makes discipline more effective, raises productivity, and reduces labor monitoring costs. The theory implies that there must be some unemployment when the economy is in equilibrium, for if there were none any worker could find another job immediately after being dismissed, so that firms could control their workers only by paying them more than they would receive elsewhere. There can be no equilibrium under such conditions; very low unemployment would lead to rapid wage inflation as each firm tried to pay more than its labor market competitors. This theory does not necessarily imply either real or nominal downward wage rigidity, since higher unemployment increases the cost to workers of dismissal and so makes it possible to reduce pay. Wage flexibility may be slight, however. The theory is interesting, mainly because it typifies economists' thinking about how managers control workers. It is often assumed in economic models that managers order subordinates around and control them through threats, financial incentives, and monitoring.

According to the insider-outsider theory of Lindbeck and Snower (1988b), the resistance of an inner group of workers within each firm is responsible for wage rigidity. This group, the insiders, consists of employees who are well protected from layoff because of high seniority or special skills. They have no interest in giving up pay in order to save the jobs of recently hired employees, who are outsiders, or in order to encourage the hiring of unemployed workers. Insiders are able to prevent the firm from replacing employees with cheaper unemployed workers, who are outsiders.

A completely different explanation of wage rigidity is provided by the morale model of Solow (1979), espoused and elaborated by Akerlof (1982) and Akerlof and Yellen (1988, 1990). These authors assume that pay rates have a positive effect on productivity through their impact on morale. When setting pay, companies weigh labor costs against the impact of pay on productivity, and this trade-off determines a profit-maximizing wage. The models of Solow and of Akerlof and Yellen allow morale to depend on the wage level or on changes in it. If morale depends on the level, then the model can explain downward wage rigidity only if the profit maximizing wage exceeds what the firm must pay in order to recruit and retain workers. If morale depends on wage changes, then the theory can explain downward rigidity at any pay level.

1.5 The Dearth of Information

Each of these theories of wage rigidity depends critically on specific assumptions about the motives and behavior of workers or employers. Some of the suppositions may seem to conflict with common sense or to stem from the natural human tendency to blame the less fortunate for their suffering, yet to reject the theories on these grounds alone would be to base conclusions on opinion rather than on careful observation. Unfortunately, there are almost no published sources that give information detailed enough for verification of the assumptions in question. For instance, I found no reference showing whether McLaughlin is correct in asserting that firms offer employees the alternative of a pay cut before laying them off, though it is perhaps revealing that accounts of layoff procedures and surveys of unemployed people contain no reference to such proposals. The economics literature contains a great many tests of models of wage rigidity and unemployment, but most of these rely on indirect evidence, for economists usually obtain information only from introspection and from surveys made by public institutions that provide data on easily quantifiable variables. Surveys relevant to labor economics typically report wages, salaries, employment status, and perhaps the size and profitability of firms and the age, sex, and race of workers: insufficient information for discriminating among theories of wage rigidity. The feature that stands out in these data is that recessions increase unemployment and retard but do not stop the rate of growth of nominal wage averages. This is the pattern expressed by the Phillips curve, which shows the historical negative relation between unemployment and wage inflation (Phillips, 1958). This relation is roughly consistent with all well-known theories, since they were designed to explain it; often it is the main evidence cited to support them. The usual surveys contain other information, but every facet of the data seems consistent with several theories.

Nor is it possible to choose among the theories by appealing to introspection, which is used to justify both particular forms of irrational behavior and the assumption that economic behavior is rational. Many theories of wage rigidity assume that behavior is rational, so that they cannot be distinguished on these grounds. In any case, the rationality assumption is too general to be much help. It is a useful unifying principle in economics, but the implications of rationality depend on the conditions constraining decision makers, and often knowledge of these is precisely what is lacking. Furthermore, it may be naive to presume that all important forms of behavior are rational. Introspection does not necessarily give insight into the behavior of workers and employers, who react to complex and stressful circumstances at work that may be unfamiliar to academic economists, as they were to me. Indeed, some theories of wage determination reflect a mistaken extrapolation of the conditions of university life to business. Since standard sources of information do not provide a sound basis for choosing among explanations of wage rigidity, these will remain speculative until more enlightening sources are found.

1.6 The Utility of More Information

It is important to understand the mechanisms generating wage rigidity, both for scientific understanding and for the analysis of economic policy. In considering unemployment, it is vital to know to what extent it is a social evil. Joblessness is not a serious matter, if the models of Lucas and Rapping and of McLaughlin are accurate. They assume that layoff and unemployment are chosen by workers when wages fall or fall below expectation, so that the unemployed are just as well off as they would have been had they stayed with their jobs at their old pay or at the somewhat lower pay the employer offered. Layoff and unemployment are potentially much more harmful if they are forced on workers, as they are in Keynesian models. Another reason for understanding the microeconomic mechanisms creating unemployment is that they are critical for discovering how to reduce it. If the models of Lucas, Rapping, and McLaughlin are correct, then unemployment falls only when wages rise above expected levels, and since the public makes intelligent predictions about policy, it is hard for the government systematically to create the surprise increases in wages needed to reduce joblessness (Lucas, 1978). But suppose that during recessions wages do not decline and unemployment increases, because firms reduce employment as product demand declines. Then, it is possible that unemployment could be manipulated and even maintained at a low level by appropriate control of aggregate demand, and inflation would occur only if unemployment fell too low.

It is easy to think of policy implications of other microeconomic assumptions about unemployment. Keynes's theory of wage rigidity implies that workers would accept simultaneous wage cuts by most firms, if only the government could arrange them. The shirking model implies that laws increasing the disciplinary powers of firms would reduce wages and lead to a lower equilibrium level of unemployment. Whereas Keynes's model implies nominal wage rigidity, the implicit contract model implies that real wages are downwardly rigid, which in turn implies that employment might not respond to increases in aggregate demand.

1.7 Should Assumptions Be Verified Directly?

In "The Methodology of Positive Economics," Milton Friedman (1953) argues that it is pointless to verify a theory's assumptions directly. He asserts that the purpose of theories is to summarize principles that are useful for prediction and that the adequacy of predictions should be judged in terms of the uses made of them. A hypothesis should be accepted if its predictions are accurate enough to be useful. The realism of assumptions and the truth of a hypothesis are irrelevant to its acceptability. Friedman argues that assumptions help specify the circumstances in which a theory will predict successfully and help express principles chosen from the distracting details of reality. Such principles are needed, because reality is so confusing that it is impossible to perceive it without the aid of theories and their assumptions. Friedman stresses the distinction between the phenomena to be explained and other empirical information and he asserts that the sole usefulness of a theory is its ability to predict the phenomena to be explained. Although good tests of a hypothesis use data having to do with these phenomena, these data should have been unknown when it was formulated. Data should be used to verify the implications rather than the assumptions of a theory, where the words "prediction" and "implication" are used almost interchangeably. He argues that a theory should be designed so that its assumptions have to do with data other than the phenomena to be explained. It is impossible for assumptions to be accurate, since they must approximate and simplify reality in order to express simple rules useful for prediction. Carrying the argument a little further than he does, one might say that just as false premises can imply true conclusions, so false assumptions can lead to accurate predictions and hence the truth or accuracy of assumptions is irrelevant to the goal of a theory, which is prediction.

Friedman anticipates certain objections to his reasoning made later by Koopmans (1957). He recognizes that a theory's assumptions and implications cannot be distinguished logically, since the assumptions are themselves implications, one implication of a statement being the statement itself. Furthermore, hypotheses may be recast so that assumptions in one formulation are implications in another, deduced from still other assumptions. He even grants that among the tests of a theory is its ability to predict information bearing on assumptions.

Friedman handles these objections with his argument that a theory is judged only by its success in predicting data having to do with the phenomena to be explained. If a theory is formulated properly, its assumptions do not have to do with these phenomena, and weight is attached to direct empirical tests of assumptions, only if the data used relate to the phenomena to be explained.

To clarify his meaning, Friedman gives three examples. One is the physical law that the acceleration of a body is constant if it falls freely in a vacuum. He maintains that the applicability of this theory depends on whether its predictions are of practical use, not on how much air friction there is. Another example is the assumption that leaves are distributed on a tree so as to maximize sunlight exposure. He points out that the pertinence of the assumption depends on its predictions about leaf distribution, not on whether the leaves deliberately locate themselves so as to maximize light-gathering. His third example is the assumption that expert billiard players shoot as if they calculated precisely the ball's trajectory. Here, whether the theory applies depends on how well it predicts the path of the ball, not on whether billiard players actually make the calculations.

Friedman's argument is coherent if theories are understood merely to be instruments for making pragmatic predictions. Boland (1979) and Caldwell (1982) label this view an instrumentalist one. In the philosophy of science, this view contrasts with that of realists, who believe that there is a true theory, and conventionalists, who suspend judgment about whether there is a true theory, but agree to speak as if there were one. Realists believe that all aspects of theories, including assumptions, should be tested for consistency with empirical reality (Popper, 1957). For them, to ignore data about assumptions is to throw away useful information.

I find it difficult to choose between the three points of view, but believe that Friedman favors a too restricted use of instrumentalism. In my opinion, the weak point of his argument is his narrow view of the phenomena to be explained. From an instrumentalist perspective, we should want as complete as possible an explanation of the causes of these phenomena, so that we can learn what will happen when the circumstances creating the phenomena change, because of policy intervention or for other reasons. If we cannot make such changes experimentally, we cannot check the predictions we make against data and so cannot include them among the known phenomena to be explained. A false or unrealistic set of assumptions might by accident perfectly predict the known phenomena, but prove treacherous when conditions change. For this reason, it seems wisest to check as many aspects as possible of the mechanism generating the phenomena to be explained, including the realism of assumptions. Assumptions should be realistic in the sense that they correspond approximately to conditions under which the theory is applied, and how good the approximation should be depends on the mechanisms posited by the theory.[8]

There is a near circularity in Friedman's methodology, for the only evidence supporting explanations of the phenomena to be explained are these phenomena themselves. The circularity may be seen by considering the following nonsensical example. Someone tells you, "The stock market is rising, because Rapacitas, the demon of greed, is loose in the population." You answer, "How do I know this demon exists? What happens to him when the market falls?" The reply is, "Isn't the market rising and doesn't it always rise when Rapacitas is loose? When the market falls, his brother Timiditas, the demon of fear, takes his place."[9]

The circularity of the argument in this example is not a defect according to a literal interpretation of Friedman's reasoning, if stock market fluctuations are the only phenomenon to be explained. The flaws in the example's argument are not just that it names as a cause something that is ill defined and unobservable or that the theory cannot predict turning points in stock market averages. No theory does the latter, so that this deficiency is not much of a reproach. Another flaw is that the phenomenon selected to be explained is too narrow. We would like to have a theory that explains the effects of interest rates, inflation, economic forecasts, and other influences. There is empirical data on the impact of these factors, and we would make it harder to dream up a nonsense explanation by including their impact in the set of phenomena to be explained. A stronger check of a theory is consistency with data that are distinct from and unrelated to the phenomena to be explained, data Friedman would exclude and that are, as Friedman says, the kind of data used to test assumptions. It becomes especially important to use such data when you want to use the theory to predict phenomena previously unobserved, such as the impact on the stock market of a form of economic policy never tried before.

Friedman introduces aesthetic criteria, such as simplicity and fruitfulness, for choosing among theories that predict equally well the phenomena to be explained. These criteria are so subjective, however, that they may not guard effectively against believing what you want to believe, a key function of methodology. A pet theory might be declared to be fruitful because its principles explain many things, though little evidence supports these explanations and they may even be nonsensical. A theory should be called fruitful only if the other explanations it inspires are not contradicted by existing evidence. We see that fruitfulness does not provide an independent criterion for eliminating extraneous explanations; we cannot define fruitfulness without deciding what it means for theories to be consistent with observation.

The shift from the Ptolemaic to the Copernican view of the solar system is often cited as showing the power of aesthetic criteria. The Copernican model is certainly simpler and more fruitful; it may have helped stimulate Newton's theory of gravity. This example does not, however, bear on the choice of assumptions, for the Copernican and the Ptolemaic models have the same assumptions that are assertions about reality, namely, that the sun and the planets are bodies in relative motion. Both models are mathematical representations of the same phenomena, the movements of the planets. The models differ only in form; one uses a sun-centered coordinate system and the other, in effect, uses an earth-centered one. The choice of coordinate system is a mathematical device, not an assumption.

The task of this book is to explain wage rigidity, which has to do with unemployment and increases in it during recessions. For the purposes I have in mind, there is little interest in being able to predict these phenomena in the sense of mimicking time series of wages and unemployment. It seems reasonable to hope that a successful explanation of wage rigidity would contribute to understanding the extent of the welfare loss associated with unemployment and what can be done to reduce it. These issues are ultimate goals beyond those of this book. Many theories of wage rigidity and unemployment include partial answers to these questions as part of their assumptions, so that the phenomena of real interest, from my point of view, are described in the theories' assumptions. For instance, Lucas concludes that increased unemployment during recessions implies little welfare loss and that recessions can be minimized by avoiding unpredictable changes in monetary policy, and these judgments are immediate consequences of his assumptions that unemployed people choose to be unemployed because of unanticipated declines in wage rates (Lucas 1972, 1978). Theories of wage rigidity and unemployment typically are tested, however, as if their goal were to predict data on wages and unemployment.[10] If these predictions were the focus of inquiry, then it would hardly matter which of the many theories was used, since they all fit these data almost equally well. For this reason, Lucas's policy conclusions are not strongly supported by the fact that his model matches the historical relations among wages, employment, and other variables. Good support can come only from information that distinguishes his microeconomic assumptions from others yielding different policy recommendations.

A fanciful example may illustrate the danger of taking too narrow a view of instrumentalism. You are an explorer seeking contact with the Dafs, an isolated tribe about which almost nothing is known. You observe one of their villages through binoculars from far away, because these people might attack foreigners. You observe that every morning on sunny days, men wearing bright yellow hats stand in backyards and make sweeping gestures toward the sky. You conclude that these men are priests of a sun-worshiping religion, and therefore must be leaders. This theory predicts well the behavior of the men observed and even explains the color of their hats. When you finally arrange a meeting with some Dafs, you meet a few men with yellow hats and a few other plainer people. Believing the first to be leaders, you offer them presents, at which point all the Dafs are outraged and assault you. What you have not observed is that yellow hats mark slaves, who throw grain to the household chickens in the yard on sunny days and inside on rainy ones. The leaders are the plainer people. It would have been worth your while not to settle for treating arm waving and wearing yellow hats as the phenomena to be explained, but to test your assumptions about behavior by taking risks to sneak up closer and see precisely what the men were up to.

Spying on the Dafs would be not only a way of testing a theory, but would gather information that might make possible the formulation of a new one. My hope in studying the labor market has been to seek inspiration for new theories as well as to test existing ones. I have sought not to oppose economic theory, but to improve it.

1.8 Problems with Surveys

Despite negative attitudes in economics toward direct microeconomic investigations, a few economists have sought information about the causes of wage rigidity and unemployment by interviewing employers, and I have done the same, going further than previous investigators. Surveys involve serious difficulties, which perhaps make it understandable that few economists undertake them.[11] It can be hard to get businesspeople to cooperate, and this obstacle makes random sampling of companies nearly infeasible. The 15 to 35 percent of a randomly selected group who agree to participate is probably a very biased sample, for I learned from experience that those who agree most readily are often the least interesting, striving to make a good impression and revealing little. Other major difficulties are that respondents may hide or falsify information, may not understand their own intentions, and may have little incentive to give accurate answers, points that Fritz Machlup (1946) stresses. Consequently, the data collected are often thought of as "touchy-feely" rather than "hard."

I tried to avoid bias through my methods of sampling and interviewing, which I describe in Chapter 2. I believe this study could be repeated, and is therefore scientific in the sense of being approximately replicable. I have checked results by comparing my observations with other information, including U.S. statistics on wages and employment, econometric studies, surveys of various sorts, and experimental work. Some of the more important work has been done by researchers in fields other than economics, especially in psychology. Other surveys of businesspeople and of the unemployed are consistent with my own, as are experimental results. Some variation, of course, is to be expected. My conclusions are no doubt influenced by the time and place of the interviews, and by current fashions in management and in counseling. Nevertheless, there is reason to believe the basic results will apply for some time, for wage rigidity has been an enduring phenomenon. It was even mentioned by Malthus in 1798.[12] What is universal in the findings can be detected only by more field work in other regions.

There remains the question of whether the statements of businesspeople should be taken seriously, even if all say the same things to all investigators. Though probably few people lie systematically, it would be reassuring to check what they say. One check is to compare their statements with what they do, but I could not rely on this method, since I had few ways to verify actions. A control I did use was the relation between circumstances and claimed motivation. For instance, suppose that employers say that a condition, such as high labor turnover, causes a certain business policy. If this policy occurs in companies with high turnover and not in companies with low turnover, then the conclusion that turnover explains the policy is more convincing.

1.9 The Value of Surveys

Even if no controls were available, it would be presumptuous to ignore the testimony of people who make economic decisions and observe and participate in economic life. To do so would be to make economics a religion rather than a responsible analysis of experience. Good instincts about a subject can be developed only by contact with the phenomena studied.

Unfortunately, attitudes in the economics profession discourage the use of information other than well-known data. Among these attitudes are those articulated by Friedman and discussed above. An important one is the belief that nothing is seen if one looks too closely, that the forest is missed for the trees. It is true that remote views are useful, that aerial photographs disclose forest diseases. But it is also true that to understand forests, you should know something about trees.[13] A related idea is that knowledge can be obtained only through the systematic testing of hypotheses and that unstructured observation and checking of facts are pointless or even anti-intellectual, because reality is only imagined and nothing can be seen without a theory in mind. This view leaves unanswered the question of how to discover good hypotheses, one of the goals of this project.

Still another attitude discouraging surveys is the belief that people do not know their own motives. In order to defend this view, economists imitate Friedman and cite metaphors, such as that of baseball players, who catch a ball without mathematically calculating its trajectory, though they behave as if they do so. This argument may justify assuming that people act unconsciously in conformity with some complicated model, but it is also true that if you want to learn how to play baseball, you would do better consulting a Ted Williams or a Casey Stengel than a mathematician.[14] The businesspeople I talked to were articulate, had obviously thought a great deal about management problems, were able to analyze them clearly, and said they learned a great deal of what they knew from other managers. An outsider should also be able to learn from them how to run a business, and it is precisely knowledge of the personnel problems businesspeople face that is lacking in studies of wage rigidity. Although insight might be gained by interpreting such knowledge in terms of an optimization model, and I make suggestions in this direction, the main goal of this project is to uncover empirically the circumstances that give rise to wage rigidity.

Related to the idea that motives are unconscious is the notion that people may not be aware of principles governing their own behavior and that these are the proper objects of study. An example is implicit contracting; employers may not realize that they are insuring workers' income in exchange for lower pay. Such principles are, of course, precisely what any researcher should look for, and it is possible that people are not conscious of them. However, in order to discover or verify them, it is necessary to study behavior, and it is hard to know how to study business behavior without talking to people in business. I also doubt that people would be unaware of something as obvious as implicit insurance contracts, if they were real.

Skeptical attitudes lead some economists to treat economic life as almost unknowable, like distant galaxies, though it goes on all around us. In economics, variables not appearing in well-known data sets are often labeled as unobservable, even when they could be observed in principle. For instance, Heckman and MaCurdy (1988) argue that the assumption of labor market clearance cannot be contradicted because standard data sets do not contain key variables applying to unemployed job seekers, such as nonmarket opportunities for the use of time and job offers received and refused.[15] Although Heckman and MaCurdy admit the possibility of observing these variables, they stress that the unobservables make labor market equilibrium an irrefutable tautology. They do not point out that observation, difficult as it may be, is the obvious way to dispel the ambiguities. Someone just has to do the work. Why should economics differ from other sciences, where researchers spend much of their time collecting data? It is not healthy for a science to isolate itself from its subject of study, especially for a field that is highly contentious and where reality is constantly changing. In economics, it is all too easy to believe what one wants to believe, since theories become intertwined with political values and truly pertinent information is hard to obtain.

The utility of surveys is illustrated by my own experience. I have long wondered about wage rigidity. I was puzzled that firms and workers do not agree to cut wages and salaries during recessions when sales decline, for such cuts should benefit both sides by reducing costs and layoffs. I wasted years inventing theories describing impediments to pay cuts. Although none of my theories was convincing, I liked best one in which agreements to cut pay are difficult to negotiate because management and labor do not have the same information or opinions about the prospects of the company and the effects of pay reduction. I discounted surveys reporting that employers avoid cutting pay because of bad effects on morale, for this explanation seemed too easy and left too many questions unanswered. Why do not the obvious benefits of saving jobs overcome the bad effects on morale? Do not layoffs also hurt morale? Cannot the impact of pay cuts on morale be diminished by having them occur automatically when company sales or general economic conditions decline? Why do employers care about morale, since they can gain cooperation by threatening to fire workers who do not perform well? Why not hire new workers during recessions at a reduced pay scale? Frustrated, I turned to interviews, and the first of these shook my prejudices. I learned from an officer of a medium-sized, nonunion manufacturing firm that cutting pay would have almost no impact on company employment, that hiring new workers at reduced pay would antagonize them, that reducing the pay of existing employees was nearly unthinkable because of the impact on worker attitudes, and that the advantage of layoffs over pay reduction was that they "get the misery out the door." Furthermore, attitudes were important for performance, and by attending to them the company was able to maintain a loyal and productive work force despite paying considerably less than its main competitors in the labor market. Only gradually, after hearing similar comments many times, did I concede that what was said should be taken seriously. The origin of my puzzlement and mistaken theorizing had been incorrect intuition. For instance, I believed that an individual firm could save a significant number of jobs by reducing pay. This is seldom true, and the firms for which it is true are precisely the ones most likely to cut pay.

1.10 The Scope of the Study

This inquiry is intended to be exploratory, touching on many issues in order to test existing theories, to seek new hypotheses, and to see the overall shape of phenomena associated with wage rigidity and unemployment. I used an inductive approach, which had the advantage of revealing unsuspected phenomena and relationships. However, the resulting breadth of the study increased the difficulty of analyzing the data and of obtaining interviews, and consequently many of my conclusions are tentative, though I am confident of the main ones. The data were difficult to organize and interpret, because interviews covered varying topics and did not contain answers to standardized questions asked of all respondents. Partly for this reason, I avoid statistical methods. Some businesspeople refused to be interviewed because they felt that in loose conversation they might inadvertently divulge confidential information, a fear that was justified; some respondents did disclose matters that I thought it best not to record. The difficulty of obtaining interviews reduced the value of random sampling and led me to arrange many interviews through personal contacts. There is, I believe, a trade-off in fieldwork between the randomness of a sample and the quality of the interviews. Respondents were most informative when they talked freely and the discussion wandered, but businesspeople were reluctant to grant such interviews. I found that many of my best interviews were those arranged through intermediaries, who put respondents at ease. A sample obtained through friends and acquaintances, however, is hardly random.

1.11 Implications for Future Research

Surveys need not be as unstructured as this one. Narrowly focused inquiries can use a fixed list of specific questions, so that statistical methods can be applied to the responses. Businesspeople probably would be more willing to cooperate with such studies than they were with this one, making possible random sampling.[16] My hope is that economists will eventually make many narrow studies that will yield clear and firm conclusions.

The survey method could be used to shed light on urgent issues tangentially related to this inquiry, such as why large firms pay more for labor than small ones, why interindustry pay differentials are so large, why the distribution of earned income is becoming more unequal in many wealthy countries, whether higher unemployment in Europe than America is due to institutional differences or to more expansionary macroeconomic policies in the United States, whether wages are more flexible in Japan than in the United States, and if so why the difference exists and does Japan's greater flexibility explain its lower unemployment rate.

1.12 Findings

The main result of this inquiry is a commonsense explanation of downward wage rigidity in the private sector. The theory, summarized in the first section of Chapter 21, is an elaboration of that of Solow (1979) and Akerlof (1982). The investigation also yielded knowledge of the wage-setting process that may prove useful in thinking about macroeconomic policy. Unfortunately, it is not possible to go far in analyzing policy, because its effects depend on the interaction of wages and prices and little is known about price determination. Finally, I came upon hypotheses and phenomena that merit further exploration.

Though my findings contradict most theories of wage rigidity, the contradiction is not absolute, for each probably applies at any moment to certain individuals. Fieldwork makes obvious the enormous variety in the economic world. Many important decisions have no single correct resolution, because they depend on imponderables and on personal judgment. I interpret theories to be valid only if they apply often enough to be useful.

The results indicate that labor is in excess supply during recessions, so that the Keynesian side of the macroeconomic debate is the more accurate view, a view that contradicts the principle widely used in macroeconomics that economic equilibria maximize a social welfare function and so solve a dynamic optimization problem. This principle cannot apply even approximately if large amounts of labor are wasted. My observations are consistent with the Keynesian view that recessions are caused by declines in aggregate demand, though I did not focus on this question. Firms had layoffs because of financial setbacks, technical improvements, and declines in product demand, never because of declines in productivity. Wage demands were not a cause of unemployment. On the contrary, many unemployed workers became excessively flexible, in the eyes both of people who counseled them and of employers. As are all explanations of wage rigidity, mine is consistent with the Phillips curve.

1.13 Two Novel Findings

Two phenomena I observed, though commonplace in the business world, have not previously been well documented. These are the shunning of overqualified job applicants and behavioral differences between the primary and secondary sectors of the labor market. Job applicants are said to be overqualified if they are suitable for substantially better jobs than the one applied for, where "better" means better paid, more interesting, or with more responsibility. Unemployed overqualified applicants were common in the Northeast during the recession. The label applies to semiskilled and skilled manual workers as well as to technicians, professionals, and managers. Many employers were reluctant to hire overqualified applicants, because of concern they would quit to take better positions or might be unhappy or a threat to their supervisors (sections 15.2 and 17.6).

I find it helpful to distinguish between primary- and secondary-sector jobs. The latter are short-term positions that are often part-time, whereas primary-sector jobs are long-term and full-time.[17] Examples of secondary-sector workers are waiters and waitresses, floor crews in fast-food restaurants, sales clerks in most stores, taxi drivers, security guards, janitors, consultants, many telemarketers, and temporary, interim, or contract workers. Primary-sector personnel include most factory, clerical, and secretarial workers, technical, professional, and managerial employees with permanent positions, and salespeople in stores and restaurants with regular customers whom the staff should know on a first-name basis. Secondary-sector positions have high turnover because hiring and training costs are too low to make it worthwhile for firms to pay high enough wages to reduce quitting. Although pay is usually lower in the secondary than in the primary sector, this is not always so. Consultants are sometimes well paid, for instance, and some clerks and factory workers are poorly paid.

In contrast to the primary sector, in the secondary sector I found that the pay of new hires was more flexible downward and employers were more willing to hire overqualified workers, an attitude that made the sector a refuge for unemployed workers ready to take stopgap jobs (sections 17.2, 17.3, and 17.6). Low hiring and training costs here reduced concern about turnover among the overqualified. The greater flexibility of hiring pay derived from the lesser importance of internal pay equity. In both sectors, the pay of existing employees was rigid downward, but in the secondary sector the pay of new hires was less tied to that of existing employees. In contract labor, there are no comparable existing employees, for temporary workers usually do not relate their pay to that of permanent employees. In other secondary-sector jobs, confusion caused by part-time schedules and high turnover makes it difficult for workers to get to know one another and to learn one another's pay, and there is less resentment of pay inequities because jobs are seldom taken seriously as careers.

1.14 Goals

In this book I seek to give an accurate impression of what I observed, including the frequency of particular views, their variety, the intensity and manner with which they were expressed, and their logical structure. As I describe the findings, I relate them to published evidence, usually in chapter appendices. Only at the end do I integrate the material and relate it to economic theory. Naturally, the data can be interpreted in more than one way, and I believe I give enough information to enable readers to draw their own conclusions. Although I would like to influence their views, my main hope is to demonstrate that despite the considerable resources required, it is well worth the effort to get out of the office and face economic reality rather than invent it.

2

METHODS

This study grew from small beginnings. Seeking inspiration for theoretical models of wage rigidity, in 1992 I arranged a few interviews with businesspeople. I anticipated making no more than 15 interviews, but found myself drawn into doing more and more, for patterns quickly emerged and respondents were articulate and preoccupied with the questions that worried me. I persisted until I felt I had learned as much as I could, given my methods and the fact that I was working alone. My last interview was conducted in the spring of 1994.

The investigative approach I used differs sharply from the questionnaire method. The latter, however useful, inevitably imposes structure, and I was not sure which questions would be appropriate or which were the main issues confronting decision makers. I found that wage rigidity could be understood only in the context of hiring, layoffs, the structure and determination of pay, worker motivation, and the circumstances of the unemployed. I investigated all these topics.

The study revives methods used by institutional labor economists, mostly in the 1940s and 1950s. Although these authors did not focus on wage rigidity, there have been some recent questionnaire studies of the issue which reinforce findings reported here.

2.1 The Sampling Method

Initially I wished to interview executives of nonunion companies that had from 100 to 1,000 employees and were either hiring and expanding rapidly or shrinking and laying off employees. I asked the New Haven Chamber of Commerce for help in contacting companies, and it kindly sent me a list of member firms, from which I selected 35 in a variety of manufacturing and service industries. The chamber contacted the companies, and 16 of them agreed to interviews.

The interviews with officials from these 16 companies were interesting, but because I was discouraged by the refusals and afraid the sample might be biased toward socially responsible people, I turned to personal connections. These consisted of contacts through family, friends, acquaintances, and colleagues. I mentioned my project to everyone I knew and made a point of never refusing offers of help. People interviewed sometimes suggested others, often allowing me to use their names and sometimes placing a call to introduce me. The use of informants to obtain further contacts is known in sociology and cultural anthropology as snowball sampling. I also approached a number of companies without referral. I kept no record of my success rate in such cold calling, but I believe that it was about 40 percent. I found that if I was determined to gain access to a particular company, I almost always could do so by finding a person who knew someone there. If top officials refused, I could usually arrange an interview with a lower-ranking person.

As mentioned in Chapter 1, there was a trade-off between sample randomness and interview quality. If I had sought a random sample, it would have been representative only if I had a high response rate, and to obtain that I would have had to promise not to ask about delicate issues. I made no such promises, except that I declared I was not interested in "competitive information," which meant precise data on wages and salaries.

In selecting companies, I was guided by a desire to have as varied a sample as possible, for I hoped to see patterns in the relation between what people said and the circumstances they faced. I was looking for mechanisms governing labor relations and pay determination rather than conducting an opinion poll. For instance, among businesses, I sought companies that were growing despite depressed business conditions. Such firms would benefit most from reducing hiring pay, and I wanted to know whether companies cut hiring pay in response to a weak labor market and, if not, their reasons for not doing so. I looked for companies that had laid off a great many workers, since I wanted to know why firms typically lay off workers rather than cut pay. I went to great lengths to locate businesses that had cut or frozen pay or had reduced the pay of new hires while continuing to give raises to existing employees. I tried to gain access to firms in many different lines of business, of a full spectrum of sizes, in various states of prosperity or decline, of different forms of ownership, and in various stages of company life cycles. I looked for both union and nonunion companies and for both progressive, reform-minded management and managements that were known to be rough on their employees. Similarly, I strove for diversity when seeking interviews with labor leaders and counselors of unemployed people. It was difficult to know when to stop arranging interviews of a certain type, and my rule was to stop when what I heard sounded repetitive and I was confident of the patterns I saw. Initially, interviews were in the New Haven area, but as the study proceeded I went further afield, sometimes going to nearby states.

I tried to prevent bias by grouping companies into narrowly defined categories and then making sure that I exploited two or more disjoint networks in gaining access to each category. In this way, I avoided seeing only people from one group of friends. Examples of categories were small factories in poor neighborhoods and large insurance companies that had recently had mass layoffs. In addition, I sought respondents who might contradict whatever patterns I thought I discerned. This task was arduous, for atypical respondents usually worked for businesses that were in difficulty or had unsavory reputations. Managers of troubled companies typically were too busy to have time for me, while firms with bad reputations instructed employees not to grant interviews. The sample is not random and so does not provide accurate estimates of the incidence of occurrences such as pay cuts and layoffs, but the breadth of the sample yields a good idea of their consequences.

Within organizations, I tried to gain access to key decision makers for personnel policy, and these were not necessarily chief executives. I found that vice presidents of human resources or other high officials in human resource departments were good sources of information, but in large companies they did not always know the details of layoff procedures, hiring, and pay setting, which were handled by lower-ranking officials. In choosing labor leaders, I sought people who led strikes and organization drives and negotiated labor contracts. Appendix 2A contains a description of the sample.

2.2 Approaching and Interviewing

I learned how to do fieldwork primarily from experience. The key to success was to interest people in my project and to convince them they could trust me. Most people interviewed were extremely busy and had little time or patience for discussion. Just to make an initial contact often required many telephone calls, for messages went unanswered. Persistence in calling paid off and seldom seemed to annoy people; a few businesspeople even told me they answered only the third or fourth call from strangers. It was somewhat easier to arrange interviews at small businesses, especially restaurants and stores, where I often simply walked in and asked to see the manager. When I first reached someone by telephone, I identified myself and mentioned how I knew of him or her and then quickly explained the goal of the project, starting off with something like, "I am trying to learn why labor markets differ from commodity markets, such as the market for potatoes, in that the price does not decline when supply exceeds demand." Many people were intrigued by the topic. A few abruptly disagreed, saying they had cut pay or had reduced pay for new hires. Some said they wanted to help because they were concerned about the bad economic situation and the federal government's apparent lack of understanding. It was easier to arrange an interview if I gave the name of someone the person knew. Tone of voice was important. At first, often rejected, I became so fearful that my voice trembled and people simply cut me off, but eventually I learned to sound calm and eager and achieved greater success. I later heard that salesmen must also struggle with what they call "rejection shock."

Confidentiality was vital. A few businesspeople explained that they were afraid they would accidentally say something that could be used against them or their company. If necessary, I explained that I was not an investigative reporter, was promoting no cause, and would not interfere with the business in any way. Although I promised to be discreet, some people tested me, asking about other companies I had visited.

Before an interview, it proved helpful to send a list of questions along with a letter explaining the purpose of the project and promising confidentiality. The letter stated that the list was too long to be covered in one interview and simply indicated areas of interest that informants might discuss. Most people had such narrow areas of expertise that they could help with only certain topics. The lists evolved as I learned more, and there were different lists for different types of respondents.

Over the course of time, I changed the focus of interviews, for as I learned about certain subjects I moved to others, some of which occurred to me in the course of the study. For instance, the early interviews dealt a great deal with wage and salary structures; later on I guided the talk toward morale and overqualification, matters that had come up in the first interviews.

Most interviews lasted from an hour and a half to two hours, though I never requested more than an hour. Some lasted more than five hours, and in two cases, I returned a second time to conclude an interview. Even in long discussions, matters were left uncovered, so that often I later telephoned to clarify key points or obtain bits of missing information. Interviews took place in the office of the respondent or in a restaurant.

Interviews were best when I made it clear to people that they were in charge and that I wanted to hear what they thought I needed to know to understand wage rigidity. Many were articulate, had thought about the issues, and could make an organized presentation with little prompting once they understood the purpose of the project. They revealed most when speaking freely, with few interruptions from me. When I tried a more organized method, insisting on a fixed list of questions, answers were often inconsistent. Responses to direct questioning did not always match those given when the same topics later came up spontaneously. I eventually understood that close questioning failed because the issues discussed were emotionally charged and respondents had certain things they wanted to say. If interrupted, they tried to silence me either by saying what they thought I wanted to hear, or by argumentatively disagreeing, so that responses to queries that interfered with the flow of thought were not always consistent with what they said on their own initiative. After this realization, I let respondents choose the topics discussed during the body of the interview and spoke only enough to show interest and nudge the conversation toward new topics, saving questions until the respondent invited them. I then brought up new subjects and sought clarification of ambiguities and inconsistencies and elaboration of key points. I also found it useful to return to old topics from a different point of view in order to be sure we understood each other and to check for biases caused by context.

Though interviews were more interesting if I avoided suggestive prodding, I often asked for concrete examples when explanations became too general and I sometimes deliberately ruffled respondents to provoke discussion. For instance, I tried to avoid asking businesspeople whether cutting pay would hurt morale, but instead asked why they did not reduce wages and used what they came up with as the basis for further discussion. If the question was evaded, I might say, "What is the matter? Don't you want to make money? You say these are bad times and people have nowhere to go. What keeps you from cutting pay?"

I found it best to encourage people to speak in their own terms. Economic jargon stopped conversation, disheartening even those trained in economics. I found it unwise to ask for reactions to economic theories, except at the end of interviews. Many of the theories struck respondents as irritating and nonsensical. Another drawback of theories was that they injected an element of unreality, sometimes triggering political tirades, which could be fanciful and extreme and quite unlike respondents' down-to-earth attitude toward business. Theories' biggest disadvantage was their tendency to prompt people to try to understand or compete with me, rather than to explain their own thoughts. Retrospective or hypothetical questions—such as "Would it be easier to cut pay by 10 percent when there was no inflation or to have a pay freeze when there was 10 percent inflation?"—gave the impression that I was interested more in opinions than in reasoned arguments. The appropriate time for bringing up theories or abstract issues was at the end of the interview, when they were likely to provoke new discussion.

It proved wise to encourage respondents to talk only about their own experience and practices in their own organizations. When I asked people why they made certain decisions, I made it clear that I was interested in the important considerations they had in mind or discussed with associates, not in deep psychological causes.[1] General questions about labor relations or the functioning of the labor market usually led to empty talk. Respondents often lacked accurate knowledge of what happened beyond their area of responsibility. For instance, businesspeople usually had surprisingly erroneous impressions of personnel management practices at other companies.

I struggled with the fact that many of my questions struck respondents as naive. I heard indirectly of reactions to my interviews, and a typical one was, "Where has this guy been all these years?" Asking about theories seemed to add to the impression of naiveté.

Important was my general demeanor. Most of the people interviewed had excellent manners and expected the same of me. These manners did not appear to reflect social pretense, but rather showed the self-control and concern for others that are necessary for cooperation in business. This kind of good manners is revealed by details, such as ordering food quickly at a restaurant. Any expression of negative feelings was viewed suspiciously, as a sign that I might be a problem or a troublemaker. Job applicants can spoil their chances by complaining about former bosses, and I could spoil an interview by complaining about anything at all, even traffic or the weather.

A constant problem was that respondents tried at first to impress me. The best way to stop this was to focus attention on the project. I tried to show respect for them and their knowledge, and many were delighted, when thus reassured, to turn their attention to the topic at hand. They also were ready and willing to respect an academic, even if sarcastic about economists. To gain respect, it seemed sufficient to be friendly and open but not too friendly, to behave with dignity, and to show interest. Excessive familiarity or small talk spoiled interviews.

Personal contact is probably the main advantage of interviews over questionnaires. I might have obtained a higher response rate from questionnaires, but they are dull and can be resented by businesspeople and labor leaders already overburdened with paperwork. Explaining their vision of their world to an interested outsider and thinking about an important problem beyond the domain of their usual activities, in contrast, seemed worthwhile, even fun.

About 30 of the early interviews were followed by plant tours. These were eye opening, for they revealed the high pace and intensity of work. Sights I remember include a small room jammed with about 20 customer service agents in narrow booths with computer consoles, each agent constantly answering calls through a headset; rows of women working rapidly at sewing machines; a large kitchen with about 10 employees hurriedly preparing large quantities of food; a team of men pouring molten steel into molds; and large rooms full of men and women concentrating on metal-working machines. Some of the machine shops were dirty and crowded, others were spotless with glossy floors and white-gowned employees, each tending several widely separated and automated machines. How could all these people be induced to work so hard with little apparent supervision?

2.3 Recording

I took notes during interviews and wrote them up carefully as soon as possible, filling in missing information from memory. The notes were not perfectly accurate, but I did learn to write almost as fast as people talked and could record most of what was said. The quotes given in this book are from my notes, and for this reason their style is more abbreviated than actual speech. I avoided using a tape recorder, believing it might unnerve respondents.

2.4 Method of Analysis

The nature of the information collected required a form of analysis that is unusual in economics. Conventional statistical methods would be misleading, in part because the sample is not random. The sample of companies is probably biased toward diversity, and I no doubt oversampled companies that had layoffs or pay cuts as well as companies that were expanding. And not all respondents discussed the same issues, another possible source of bias. Tabulation of responses involved subjective interpretation, especially because responses were often not reactions to specific questions, but were offered spontaneously by informants as they raised topics themselves. When I did ask questions, wording varied. I treated factual and interpretative issues differently, usually asking directly only about facts such as whether a company paid severance benefits to workers who had been fired. An example of an interpretative issue is the likely impact of a pay cut.

I originally intended to relate what respondents said to their circumstances, and it was for this reason that I strove for a diverse sample. Diversity proved to be of less importance than expected, however, for views were astonishingly uniform. Regarding personnel management, the wisdom of a top executive at a huge corporation was not very different from that of a restaurant manager or machine-shop owner. The only interesting major distinction I detected was that between the primary and secondary sectors, and even there the divergence of opinion and experience was not dramatic. I therefore often lump together dissimilar sources, as if they were a random sample from a homogeneous population. In so doing, I do not mean to mislead the reader, but merely to describe the data.

In explaining conclusions, I treat each topic separately, giving an overview of what was said about it, usually expressed by tables, and then providing sample quotations. The tables show the frequency with which various views were expressed, and the quotations illustrate them. The relative numbers of quotations voicing particular opinions do not necessarily reflect the frequency of types of responses. When I give several similar quotations, I do so to make the meaning clear. For most topics, I could supply five to ten times as many quotations as I do. The quotations are the most important part of the data description, because they contain people's experience, the logical structure of their arguments, and the conviction of their expression. It is the underlying logic that gives coherence to the many things said. Each quotation is followed by a short description of the speaker. It is unique for everyone but advisers of the unemployed, making it possible to compare different statements by the same person.

People's perceptions, of course, are not necessarily accurate. For instance, although many managers believe that good morale brings high productivity and that employees tell one another how much they earn, it does not follow that these beliefs are correct. Managers may believe workers share pay information only because they remember complaints following rare cases of sharing. Even incorrect beliefs, however, can be important in motivating decisions.

In this book I do not use statistical methods, nor do I compute standard deviations for the various types of statements, though I provide the information needed to compute them. Suppose that a random sample of size N is drawn from a population and that a proportion, p, of the population would make a certain statement. If K people in the sample make the statement, then K/N is an unbiased estimate of p and the standard deviation of the estimate is

$$\sigma = \sqrt{\frac{(K/N)\ (1 - K/N)}{N}}.$$

Statistical theory says that the probability p has roughly a 95% chance of being between $K/N - 2\sigma$ and $K/N + 2\sigma$. Using this reasoning, I can say from Table 11.2 that 0.69 is an unbiased estimator of the probability that a businessperson would mention damage to morale as a likely consequence of a pay cut. Also, the true probability lies between 0.61 and 0.77 with probability 0.95. This interpretation, however, is not useful. The sample is nonrandom, after all; standard deviations draw attention to the precision of the tables and so distract from the central message, which is in the quotations.

If this formula for the standard deviation is applied, it is important to realize that the number N is not the total number of interviews, but the number covering a particular topic. This number is given in each table and when it is smaller than the total number of interviews, it reflects interview time constraints and my interviewing style, not people's reluctance or inability to answer questions.

Although it might seem appropriate to give more weight to statements by businesspeople from large than from small companies, I do not do so. Collectively, small businesses employ many more people than large ones, as may be seen in Table 2A.5. Moreover, businesspeople from large companies do not necessarily have more experience than those from small ones. Among my respondents, people running small companies tended to have more contact with personnel problems; executives of large companies were more preoccupied with administrative and strategic issues.

The tables are best used to gain a rough initial idea of the type of conclusions to be drawn. When views are unanimous or nearly so, the interpretation is clear. No employers said they offered workers a choice between layoff and continued work on the same job at lower pay. None said pay could be cut without causing employee reactions harmful to the business. In some cases, I can explain the minority of statements that contradict the majority. Consider, for example, the views of primary-sector employers on hiring overqualified job applicants (Table 15.4). Of the 126 who discussed this issue, 70 percent said they were totally unwilling to hire the overqualified. This is a high proportion, for refusal to hire the overqualified could be linked to illegal age discrimination and some employers probably denied a bias against the overqualified for this reason; some respondents were clearly uneasy when discussing the issue. Others who were willing to hire the overqualified explained that they could afford to do so because their companies were growing or were so large that overqualified new hires could soon be promoted to more appropriate positions. Regarding most issues, there is no such clear agreement. It should be kept in mind that the frequency of certain responses was reduced by my practice of not asking direct questions regarding interpretative issues. For example, though only 69 percent of employers discussing pay cuts mentioned morale, I am confident that everyone would have answered "yes" if asked whether a pay cut would hurt morale. This was the answer I heard when I slipped and asked this question, and I believe others omitted it as obvious. They spoke of other things, such as productivity and turnover, in a manner that implied worker disgust. The frequency of some types of responses may also have been reduced by the diversity of my sample. Since I looked for companies in extreme situations, I may have encountered a disproportionate number of people with unusual views.

Guarding against misrepresentation by respondents was a major concern. I doubt many lied, for too many said similar things. Nevertheless, respondents might have said what was correct according to some professional standard, rather than what they had found to be true by experience. Counselors of the unemployed might have described unemployment as terrible, because their function is to aid and protect the jobless. Similarly, conventional norms might lead businesspeople to express concern for the feelings of their workers, though they in fact treat them harshly. Although I lacked the resources to interview employees and unemployed people as well as business leaders, I could check for bias to some extent by comparing statements of businesspeople with those of labor leaders and counselors of the unemployed. However, the subjects covered by these categories of respondents did not fully overlap. Another check was to compare what was said with relevant existing surveys of employed and unemployed workers and businesspeople conducted by economists, psychologists, sociologists, management scientists, and government agencies. Unfortunately, some key issues, such as the use of punishment in business and the effects of inequity and of pay cuts, have not been dealt with adequately. I also make extensive use of relevant econometric studies, though the evidence they bring to bear is often indirect.

2.5 Comparison with Blinder's Survey on Price Rigidity

It is interesting to contrast this study with a recent survey on price rigidity organized by Alan Blinder and reported in Blinder (1990, 1991) and Blinder et al. (1998), for we made opposite decisions about key matters. Blinder wished to test existing economic theories of price rigidity and, as I did, he wished to know how businesspeople think about their problems. In order to achieve these goals, he took a poll of businesspeople's reactions to various theories of price rigidity. He sought a random sample, with the probability of selecting a given firm being proportional to its contribution to gross national product. He interviewed only sellers of goods and services, not buyers or intermediaries. Because there were many interviews, most of them were done by graduate students. In order to maintain control of the interviewing process and to have responses that could be analyzed statistically, most of the questions were standardized. The interviewer recorded reactions to theories by filling in a multiple-choice questionnaire, and each question was posed to all informants to whom it applied. In order to obtain a high response rate, Blinder avoided questions that might frighten businesspeople away, such as any hinting at interest in illegal price collusion (Blinder, 1990). For this reason, the study does not cover several well-known and likely theories, such as the kinked demand curve theory. He did succeed in obtaining a high response rate, 200 out of 330 or 61 percent.

The Blinder study is fascinating. I eschewed its methods not because I thought them misguided but because the objectives of my study differ sharply from Blinder's. Whereas he wished primarily to test existing theories, I gave other objectives higher priority. I was not sure any of the theories was accurate and so looked for other explanations. In addition, I wanted to understand the context in which businesspeople and labor leaders make personnel and compensation decisions. Because I wanted as complete a picture as possible of wage, salary, and employment determination, I talked to labor market intermediaries and to representatives of sellers of labor, as well as to its buyers. I asked few questions about economic theories and did not ask standardized questions, because I wanted informants to follow their own train of thought. I did all the interviewing myself, because interaction with respondents was paramount, despite my efforts to avoid intrusion. I had trouble getting interviews, in part, I believe, because my interview method was open-ended. I therefore often resorted to personal connections to obtain them. I made no effort to avoid delicate topics, such as those suggesting price collusion. Indeed, I heard several stories about the enforcement of price leadership and descriptions of behavior consistent with the kinked demand curve theory. It was clear that sensitive topics could be discussed, provided I stopped writing when they came up. Blinder's group also found that informants spoke freely, and I believe it is not necessary to avoid issues that touch on confidential matters, provided a good rapport is established with informants. It is pointless, however, to seek confidential information, since it cannot be used.

2.6 Summary

This study sought to gain an overview of the issues causing wage rigidity rather than to perform precise tests of specific theories. For this reason, efforts were made to obtain as broad a sample as possible and to induce informants to discuss freely concrete experiences and their interpretation of them. No attempt was made to sample randomly or to ask all respondents the same carefully worded questions. People were encouraged to come up with their own questions and explanations.

Appendix 2A The Sample

I here describe the sample statistically. There were 336 interviews with 374 people, more than one person being present at some interviews. Six of the interviews were by telephone, the rest in person. I count as one interview a discussion with one or more people, even if continued over two sessions. The interviewing was done from April 1, 1992, to April 20, 1994, though only 9 were conducted after July 30, 1993. Of the 336, 181 occurred in 1992. The distribution over broad categories is described in Table 2A.1. Of the 246 interviews in companies, 4 were in failed companies and 6 were in companies that had been founded during the recession.

Tables 2A.2 describes how the 336 total interviews came about, and Table 2A.3 describes the origins of a subset, the 246 interviews in nontemporary labor businesses. I label those arranged by friends, family, or acquaintances as "pri-

TABLE 2A.1   Types of interview

Type	Number of interviews
Companies, exclusive of temporary labor	246
Temporary labor services	13
Headhunters	15
Advisers of the unemployed	26
Labor leaders	19
Labor lawyers	4
Management consultants	13
Total	336

TABLE 2A.2   Origin of interview: all interviews

Origin	Number of interviews	Percentage of interviews
New Haven Chamber of Commerce	16	5
Private	75	22
Encounter	1	0
Snowball	48	14
Cold call–reference	88	26
Cold call	108	32
Total	336	100

vate" and those arranged by someone I had already interviewed as "snowball." "Cold call–reference" refers to interviews for which the respondents' names were obtained from other respondents, who gave me permission to use their names. There is little distinction between the snowball and cold call–reference categories. The "cold call" category refers to interviews I arranged by calling or visiting the business, with no reference or intermediary. The one "encounter" refers to a breakfast with a stranger I met by chance while traveling, a salesman for a California company who competed with some of the companies I had

TABLE 2A.3   Origin of interview: company interviews

Origin	Number of interviews	Percentage of interviews
New Haven Chamber of Commerce	16	7
Private	68	28
Encounter	1	0
Snowball	41	17
Cold call–reference	41	17
Cold call	79	32
Total	246	100

TABLE 2A.4   Types of businesses

Type	Number of businesses
Manufacturing	106
Services	65
Financial services	28
Nonfinancial services	37
Retail trade	37
Construction	15
Professional services	11
Wholesale trade	1
Total	235

studied and who knew a lot about their salespeople. I do not count his company as one studied, as he told me little about it.

Interviews were made in 13 temporary labor businesses and in 235 active businesses of other types. (In addition, as noted, interviews were made with leaders of 4 failed businesses.) Although temporary labor services are companies, I have not counted them as such because they are also labor market intermediaries. The 235 active businesses are categorized in table 2A.4. Fewer businesses were studied than there were interviews in companies, since in a few I interviewed two or more people at different levels in the hierarchy. Of the businesses listed in the table, a little more than a fifth were subsidiaries, divisions, or branches of larger companies, and the rest were independent. Some subsidiaries were themselves huge. There was a union presence in 26 of the manufacturing companies, in none of the financial service companies, in 4 of the nonfinancial service companies, in 3 retail chains, and in 2 stores. The manufacturing companies include a wide range of types of business, such as defense plants, gun companies, and machine shops as well as producers of pharmaceuticals, medical devices, chemicals, paper, food, apparel, books, newspapers, and many other commodities. Financial services include banks and other lenders, insurance companies, and brokerage houses; nonfinancial services include a great variety of businesses: trucking, stevedoring, hotels, laundries, janitorial services, security guard services, taxi companies, telecommunication companies, companies specializing in research and development, an HMO, a medical laboratory, an advertising agency, and others. Retail businesses include small stores, department stores, supermarkets, fast food restaurants, and ordinary restaurants. I talked to management of large retail chains as well as to owners or managers of individual stores and restaurants. Construction companies include general contractors as well as ones specializing in mechanical, electrical, or site work. Professional service companies include law, accounting, and architecture firms as well as associations of doctors.

The total of the number of employees in all active business units studied is 1,443,000, after elimination of multiple counting of parts of businesses covered in separate interviews. I consider employees to have been covered by an interview if they worked in the part of the company that the respondent understood well.

The sample of business units where I interviewed is not representative of the general population of businesses in that there is a disproportionate number of large ones, as may be seen by comparing the sample with data on the size distribution of U.S. business establishments. Table 2A.5 describes the size distribution in 1988, in terms of both the number of establishments and the number of their employees. Table 2A.6 gives the corresponding information for the sample.

The figures in Tables 2A.5 and 2A.6 are not strictly comparable, for what I call a business is not necessarily an establishment as defined by the U.S. Commerce Department. Also, Table 2A.5 includes agriculture and mining, and in my sample there are no companies from these industries.

It may be seen that in the U.S. economy small- and medium-sized businesses employ the bulk of the private-sector labor force. As I have explained, I sought a diverse sample, and sampled in one type of business until I discerned a pattern.

TABLE 2A.5   Size distribution of U.S. business establishments in 1988

Number of employees in establishment	Percentage of establishments in this range	Percentage of all employees employed by establishments in this range
1 to 9	74.93	15.6
10 to 49	20.17	27.7
50 to 99	2.78	13.1
100 to 499	1.89	24.2
500 to 999	0.15	6.9
1,000 or more	0.08	12.5

Source: Bureau of the Census (1990), p. 3.

TABLE 2A.6   Size distribution of sampled businesses

Number of employees in establishment	Percentage of establishments in this range	Percentage of all employees employed by sampled businesses in this range
1 to 9	4	0.00
10 to 49	27	0.11
50 to 99	13	0.15
100 to 499	26	1.01
500 to 999	6	0.56
1,000 or more	24	98.17

The undersampling of companies with one to nine employees occurred because I interviewed in such companies only by accident, when I mistakenly thought they employed at least ten people. The oversampling of large companies occurred because I needed a certain number in each size range for each line of business in order to see patterns. Once a few large companies are included in a sample, they inevitably account for most of the employees in it.

In the interests of variety, I sought, in particular, companies that were expanding or contracting and succeeded in interviewing in 75 business units that were shrinking and in 18 that were growing rapidly. In addition, I looked for companies with a variety of ownership forms. About half the companies were closely held by individuals or families. Most of the rest were publicly held joint stock companies, though 11 were ESOPs (employee owned), mutuals (customer owned), or nonprofit organizations. Most of the businesses studied were in Connecticut, though 24 had headquarters in neighboring states ranging from New Hampshire to Delaware.[2]

Table 2A.7 lists the positions of people interviewed in businesses of all types, including temporary labor companies. In small companies, I almost always talked with the person running the company, usually the owner and president, and that person made the main decisions regarding pay, hiring, layoffs, and other personnel matters. Since these decisions were made jointly by many people in larger companies, it was important to talk to people at several levels within the company hierarchy. Supervisors have a great deal of influence on hiring immediate subordinates, setting their pay, and choosing whom is laid off, so that low-level managers were good sources for the effects of these decisions and the processes governing them. High-level human resource officials were expert on overall personnel policy and budgetary decisions. The vice president of human resources would know about company policy regarding pay rates for new hires, but might not know whether these rates had fallen spontaneously, perhaps contrary to policy. The latter information could be obtained from a manager charged with recruiting for a particular department.

I interviewed 4 labor lawyers and 19 labor leaders from 18 different labor organizations. The labor lawyers had offices in Connecticut and specialized in labor negotiations. The labor organizations were parts of labor unions, such as locals or regional councils. Of the organizations, 7 were construction unions,

TABLE 2A.7   Businesspeople interviewed according to position

Position	Number of people	Percentage of people
Owner	81	29
Partner	7	3
President	9	3
Human resource manager or executive	120	43
Manager	43	16
Store or hotel manager	17	6
Total	277	100

8 were industrial unions, and 3 represented retail trade workers. The total number of union members represented by the leaders interviewed was 151,000. The numbers represented by respondents varied from 400 to 65,000. Of the 19 labor leaders interviewed, 3 were union local presidents, 2 were regional managers or directors, 11 were business managers or business representatives, 2 were general counsels, and 1 was solely an organizer.

There were 26 interviews with 44 advisers or counselors of the unemployed. Eight of these interviews were in outplacement companies, 13 were in state, city, or private employment offices, and 5 were with voluntary leaders of support groups for the unemployed. Outplacement companies are hired by corporations to counsel dismissed employees on their job search and on coping with unemployment. Outplacement counselors were usually best informed about unemployed professional people and executives, their main clients, with whom they met regularly until the clients found work. Counselors at other job and counseling centers saw a great many low-paid workers who were unemployed. Job center counselors usually met clients only once or twice. Support groups attracted mostly middle-class participants, and their leaders sometimes saw members regularly until they found work. Counselors and support group leaders seemed sincerely interested in the problems of unemployed people and tried to help them.

I conducted 15 interviews with headhunters in Connecticut and neighboring states. Headhunters are professional recruiters or labor market brokers, engaged by companies to find appropriate people for specific jobs. Headhunters seemed almost to dislike the unemployed, viewing them as competitors in the business of filling jobs. They did, however, find work for jobless people and so knew about the process of hiring them. Many headhunters specialize in particular types of labor, and in interviewing them I again strove for variety, finding recruiters who specialized in areas such as market research, engineering, computer programming, law, accountancy, human resources, or clerical help. Some were generalists, and some provided machinists, laborers, and clerical help. Another kind of labor market broker is an employment agency, which finds jobs for people rather than people for jobs. However, the agencies I contacted were doing almost no business during the recession and were surviving as temporary employment agencies or as headhunters.

I conducted 13 interviews with management consultants, whom I questioned about what they had learned from observing businesses and about the advice they gave on personnel and compensation management. Particularly interesting were consulting services that sold wage and salary surveys to client companies. These surveys contain a wealth of data on wage and salary levels and compensation practices.

Appendix 2B Related Literature

INTRODUCTION

Works by institutional labor economists include De Schweinitz (1932), Bakke (1933, 1940a, 1940b), Kerr (1942), Myers and MacLaurin (1943), Dunlop (1944), Lester (1948, 1954), Myers and Shultz (1951), Reynolds (1951), Palmer (1954), Rees and Shultz (1970), and Foulkes (1980). Recent questionnaire studies of wage rigidity include Kaufman (1984), Blinder and Choi (1990), Levine (1993a), Agell and Lundborg (1995), and Campbell and Kamlani (1997).

METHOD OF ANALYSIS (SECTION 2.4)

Many books describe field and survey research methods, including Schatzman and Strauss (1973), Kirk and Miller (1986), Babbie (1990), Johnson (1990), and Bernard (1994). Methods vary from random sampling and quantitative analysis of answers to questionnaires, techniques often used in sociology, to the looser style of some cultural anthropologists, who draw people out through conversation and obtain interviews through networks of contacts. There is controversy about method, though authors agree that the choice of one necessarily depends on circumstances. The method I used is considered most appropriate for initial investigation, hypothesis seeking, and learning how people think about certain questions, precisely my goals. Blinder (1990) makes a vigorous defense of the interview method and argues that econometric methods cannot distinguish among the main theories of wage and price rigidity. Callahan and Elliott (1996) advocate listening and conversation as ways of learning about economic motivation and about the ways in which individuals understand the economic decision problems they face, precisely my approach.

3

TIME AND LOCATION

This study coincided with a period of depressed business conditions during recovery from a jolting recession in the Northeast that followed a period of prosperity and labor scarcity. The contraction began in the summer of 1990 and ended in the spring of 1991. The region and timing were appropriate for the problems I wanted to investigate, for they were on people's minds.

3.1 The Recession

Most of my interviews took place in 1992 and 1993, which was a period of moderately high unemployment, low inflation, and economic recovery in the United States. I refer to this period as one of recession, though in the technical language of business cycle theory, a recession is a period of economic contraction. I follow the practice of the business community and use the word "recession" to refer to a period of high unemployment and a low level of economic activity, whether the economy is contracting or expanding. In this imprecise sense, the recession lasted from 1991 to sometime in 1993.

Although this recession was mild by historical standards with unemployment of about 7 percent, the period followed a boom that was especially marked in the Northeast and that had created a labor shortage in the opinion of local businesspeople. The rate of inflation was low (around 3 percent), but there had been periods of high inflation (11 to 13 percent) in the mid-1970s and the early 1980s.

In the opinion of many of the people interviewed, the recession of the early 1990s was severe and was the worst they had experienced at least since that of 1975. A common complaint was that the slowdown was long with no end in sight. Economic statistics do not reflect the severity, and I was never able to reconcile them with what I heard. Doubtless recessions are worse for those involved than is apparent from the statistics. Since no similar study exists, I cannot compare what I heard with reactions to past recessions. People probably exaggerate current displeasure when comparing the present with the past. Another possibility is that the recession of the early 1990s seemed vivid because it was especially hard on middle-class people. Counselors at the state unemployment offices were astonished by the number of normally well-paid people then unemployed. They claimed that professionals were especially hard hit, though the lower paid suffered as well. The majority of counselors believed that an unusually high proportion of layoffs were permanent. Businesspeople also asserted that relatively more well-paid, overtime-exempt employees were being laid off than in the past. These opinions may have been exaggerated, as I will explain in the first section of Appendix 18A.

3.2 Unionization

When I was looking for interviews, unionized companies seemed scarce. Union membership in the private sector was concentrated in old large companies in manufacturing, construction, transportation, and retail trade. No insurance companies or banks were unionized, nor were most of the small manufacturers with whom I had contact. The low incidence of unionization reflected national trends. Only 11 percent of private-sector U.S. workers were union members in 1992 and 1993, and in 1994 only 14 percent of private-sector manufacturing workers in Connecticut belonged to unions.[1]

3.3 Unemployment Insurance in Connecticut

In order to interpret what respondents said, it is important to understand basic facts about the unemployment insurance system. The benefits received by an eligible individual were 50 percent of his or her average pay in the best of the previous four quarters. During most of the period of the study, the ceiling on benefits was $306 per week plus $10 per dependent. Income taxes had to be paid on unemployment insurance benefits, but were not withheld. I was told by an official of the Connecticut Department of Labor that only 30 to 40 percent of those eligible for benefits actually applied for them.[2] He also asserted that the proportion of those applying was especially low among older white-collar workers. He believed they thought of unemployment insurance benefits as welfare and were ashamed to collect. Some believed they were not eligible because they were receiving severance benefits, though severance pay did not disqualify recipients if it had conditions. Typical conditions were that recipients work up to a certain date or that they not sue.

Part of the expense of unemployment insurance was paid for by a tax on employers. A company's tax depended on its unemployment insurance tax experience rating, which depended in turn on the amount that former employees collected in benefits. Workers were not qualified to collect benefits if they quit or were fired. Because of the experience rating system, employers had an incentive either to fire employees they wished to lay off or to pressure them into quitting. Being aware of the possibilities of abuse, the Department of Labor had a hearing procedure with rights of appeal. This procedure was intended to establish whether employees quit freely or were fired legitimately. According to Connecticut law, it was up to the employer to prove that a person either quit without pressure or was fired for a pattern of misconduct. A common complaint of Connecticut businesspeople was that enforcement of unemployment insurance eligibility was strongly biased against the employer.

In order to remain eligible, recipients of unemployment insurance benefits were supposed to be available for full-time employment and actively looking for work three out of five working days. The Department of Labor had a right to ask people for a record of their search effort, and the penalty for not searching was the loss of part of the unemployment benefit. For the first 26 weeks of unemployment benefit, people needed to accept only jobs that paid at least as much as their previous ones in order to remain eligible. When people received federal extensions of benefits beyond 26 weeks, they were allowed to refuse only jobs paying less than their unemployment insurance benefit. Beneficiaries who took part-time work had two-thirds of their pay deducted from their benefits, but the deduction prolonged the period in which they had a right to receive them.

3.4 The Minimum Wage

During the period of the study, the minimum wage in Connecticut was $4.27 per hour, and had been since April 1, 1991.

3.5 Summary

The study was performed in the Northeast during 1992 and 1993, which were years of depressed business conditions and followed a boom with locally low unemployment. At the time, a small proportion of the private-sector work force was unionized.

4

MORALE

Managers organize their thinking about their success in dealing with employees around the concept of morale. Good morale is thought to be vital for productivity, recruitment, and retention. The views of businesspeople contrast with the conclusions of many organizational psychologists, who after much study have found that morale has only a small impact on job performance. Recently, however, psychologists have been changing their views and finding that good morale improves the functioning of work groups.

4.1 What Is Morale?

I seldom asked respondents what they meant by the word "morale," but gathered its meaning from usage. Every sense in the dictionary applied. Morale meant emotional attitudes toward work, co-workers, and the organization. Good morale meant a sense of common purpose consistent with company goals and meant cooperativeness, happiness or tolerance of unpleasantness, and zest for the job. It meant moral behavior, mutual trust, and ease of communication with superiors and subordinates.

> Morale is having employees feel good about working for the company and respecting it. The employee with good morale likes his work and is willing to cooperate in moving from job to job. A positive attitude makes it possible to work out good teamwork.
> —Owner of a nonunion manufacturing company with 37 employees

> Morale equals motivation. . . . Morale in business is different from what it is in the army. In the army, you react at times on the basis of orders. Here, you have individual

thinkers. I want them to think. That has changed in the army too. As an officer,
I wanted to understand what my NCOs were thinking, for they had a lot to offer.

—General manager of a two-year-old, nonunion manufacturing company with 140 employees

Morale is feeling good about what you are doing on a daily basis and about the
direction of the company. I can't imagine being happy working for a company
where I disagreed with its basic strategy. Morale is partly an intellectual thing.

—High-level human resource official at a unionized manufacturing company with 19,000
employees

Companies differed in the importance attached to various aspects of morale.
Some emphasized happiness.

The company's philosophy is that it wants to have its employees enjoy working
here. It is more important to have people like the company than to get costs down.

—Officer of a nonunion consumer products manufacturing company with 600 employees

Others, downplaying happiness, stressed the ability to achieve.

Who cares about happiness? Nobody does here. People have to work together. If you
don't like someone, it is okay as long as you can work together. At this company, if
someone is in a bad mood, things still keep going. [The company] doesn't need
individuals so much. There is a big team to fill in the gaps. Moods aren't very good
around here anyway. [The chairman] is known for his moodiness. [The company] is
loosely organized and has a moody work force. It is very hard on its people. . . . A
frugal atmosphere prevails. There are no company cars, yachts, or houses.

—Human resource manager in a financial company with 24,000 employees

Some psychologists have suggested that there is a conflict between financial
incentives or extrinsic rewards and an aspect of morale, intrinsic rewards,
which are enjoyment of a task and belief in it (Notz, 1975; Deci and Ryan,
1985).[1] I imagine that many businesspeople would scoff at this suggestion,
though I did not ask about it. Managers made it clear that incentives can have
a tremendous impact on both motivation and morale. A few managers ridi-
culed attempts to belittle financial motivation.

Professors know nothing about business. At night school, an industrial psychologist
told us that pay is not a motivator. I thought, "What is he doing lecturing to me at
night if not to earn money. Who's he kidding?"

—Human resource officer of a manufacturing plant that had 2,000 employees a year earlier
but was closing

4.2 What Affects Morale?

According to businesspeople, morale is shaped by a sense of community, by understanding the purpose of company actions and policies, and by the belief that company actions are fair. Other important factors include employees' emotional state, ego satisfaction from work, and trust in co-workers and company leadership. As will be explained in Chapter 8, the managers I interviewed believed that personal contact and good communications with supervisors add to motivation and that threats are counterproductive.

In this section, I discuss the effect of management style on morale. Job security and pay are also important influences, affecting morale through their impact on egos and on private lives and through perceptions of fairness. Within a company, pay inequity offends (indeed, sometimes outrages) employees and destroys trust, as will be explained in Chapter 6. Raises assuage egos, and pay cuts hurt them and also bring on upsetting personal financial problems, matters discussed in Chapters 10 and 11. I explain in Chapter 7 that most employees have only imprecise knowledge of pay at other firms, so that long-run pay levels have little effect on morale as long as they are roughly in line with the market. Similarly, long-run pay levels have little impact on motivation, though incentives are thought to be effective because they make pay depend on performance.

Respondents stressed that building a sense of community and purpose was vital for good morale.

> People take more pride and interest in their work if they know what the part they are making will do.
> —General manager of a nonunion machine shop with 60 employees

> If people are paid well, that fact is lost on them after a while. People are paid well to attract them. It is necessary to pay competitively, but they can be motivated in other ways. The best way to motivate people is to give them important work to do and to recognize them for that. Their morale is good if they feel they are contributing.
> —The president of a community service organization with 80 employees

> In a business, you need a sense of community, . . . a team spirit, to keep score. It is a two-way relationship. It is not paternalistic. . . . Employees have to take care of themselves. Everyone has to pull together, like eight men in a shell. . . . Management is complicated by the fact the company's and the workers' goals are not the same. If the workers make more, the company makes less. The problem is to achieve goal congruence. This is accomplished to some extent by gainsharing. . . . I am careful not to flaunt my wealth. I drive a [low-priced car].
> —President and owner of a unionized manufacturing company with 150 employees

People work more effectively if they are self-incented. Lots of things can hurt morale. It could be financial, or a feeling that I don't count, that I am simply being manipulated and used, that bosses kick or cajole me. Rule by fear gives rise to a feeling of being manipulated. What is desired is a relationship of community.

—President of a nonunion manufacturing company and ESOP with 240 employees.

Managers commonly believed that company charities contribute to the sense of community, detaching people from narrow selfishness.

Philanthropic activity boosts morale. People get recognition or a pat on the back for what they give. When they contribute money, they always put their names on the envelopes. Everyone wants to feel special. Some employees have no family other than [the store], so that they get a thrill out of joining in its positive activities.

—Personnel manager of a department store with 300 employees

A sense of belonging and importance are created by personal direction and appreciation from supervisors. If such attention is given in a constructive spirit, it does not contradict the drive to decentralize decision making, mentioned in the next section.

I have done a lot of thinking about morale. I didn't believe in it until I got religion in the last few years. When I walk in in the morning, I try to talk to everyone. . . . I buy a cigarette from someone. That gives me something to talk about. They say, "Go on, take it. Don't give me money." But, I give them a quarter for it. This maintains support and creates better relations. I'm out there everyday in dirty jeans, loading a truck with them or in the dirt figuring out why something doesn't work. You need a family feeling from president to the guy on the loading dock. When I lose touch with a few of them, perhaps because I am too busy, I perceive a difference. It is more subtle than a loss of productivity. Their demeanor changes, and eventually that results in lower productivity. If they lose their comfort level with me, they'll lose it with the company.

—Owner of a nonunion manufacturing company with 25 employees

An individual's morale may depend on pay or relations with a supervisor. At an overall level, it depends on the general manager. I have seen three general managers in my two years here. Those who visit the plant every day and take an interest in everybody's job get more out of the men. People work to please both their supervisor and the general manager.

—Human resource manager of a nonunion manufacturing company with 80 employees

Morale was low when I first came. When I had my first store meeting, three people showed up. So, I offered coffee and donuts, said positive things, and tried to be fun. You have to communicate with employees. There used to be a saying that happiness was [the town] in your rearview mirror. There was no supervision. The ordinary employees ran the store. Now, they take more pride in what they do and work to keep the store neat and clean.

—Manager of a unionized department store with 125 employees

It is important that there be an atmosphere of seriousness capable of overriding other issues, such as personal problems.

Women going through divorce or having children out of wedlock can be stars at work, if they can feel they have a stable and secure environment. If they have emotional turmoil, they will make mistakes, but a good work environment makes them better able to leave their problems at the door. You have to set limits too, as with children. You may have to give some people days off to get their lives together.

—Part-owner and president of a medical laboratory with 85 employees

We have some piecework and are going to do more. . . . I don't like it when the high productivity people take some of their productivity as leisure, for this is bad for morale. I want 100% from everyone. I don't care about variation in output among employees. This variation can be up to 100%. Any slacking is bad for the plant's work atmosphere.

—The president and half-owner of a nonunion candy company employing 200 people

Managers recognized ego gratification as among employees' basic needs and important for the imaginative contribution desired, a theme to which I will return in Chapter 8.

If you train people well and entice them, they will work for you. You can't just order people around. People more and more realize that they are important and that they matter. The feeling of self-worth has become a major aspect of business. If you don't let people feel they are important, why would they work for you? The two-by-four approach works only as a last resort when all else fails. It gives the company a bad reputation and makes it hard for the company to recruit. People have no pride of ownership and productivity suffers. People want to be masters of their own destiny. . . . When the crunch comes, people can do the same thing they always did, only harder, or they can do something different. The company wants the second.

—Vice president of administration of a unionized manufacturing company with 900 employees

We are concerned about ego satisfaction. Some people function less well if they are offended. Morale and company culture are a very important part of any company. When I first came here, we did an attitude survey and found that employees complained about not knowing what was going on. So now, we have regular plant

meetings in which new products and initiatives are explained. If people feel they
know what is going on, they are happier and more productive.

—Human resource manager of a 3,500-employee research division of a large corporation

Good morale requires trust and fairness.

It is important for an employer to be viewed as fair and to communicate with the
employees regarding job assignments, promotions, and pay. People will leave if
not treated equitably. Young people are especially likely to leave. It is important
to have a reputation as a good place to work and not to lose credibility. . . . People
must trust you and have reasons for what you are doing before they will cooperate
fully.

—Human resource manager servicing 360 headquarters personnel of a large nonunion manufacturing company

Good morale means that they feel secure, that they are treated fairly, and that there
is some mechanism they can count on. Seniority helps here.

—Vice president of a supermarket chain with 30,000 employees

Employers did not pretend that managers always treat employees fairly and
respectfully. Though reluctant to relate specific stories of abuse, they made it
clear that the need for virtue was constantly learned from experience.

4.3 Fashions Affecting Management Attitudes toward Morale

Management interest in morale was colored by two somewhat contradictory
contemporary fashions in business reform, "participative" management and ruth-
less cost cutting. Participative management strove to increase communication in
all directions, upward, horizontally, and downward within the company chain
of command; to push decision making down to the level at which the appropriate
information was available; to have employees take initiatives to improve operations; to eliminate layers of middle management; and to have employees work
as near equals in teams with minimal supervision.[2] This management style attempted to soften the sense of hierarchy and to make employees feel that they
had a stake in the company's future. Proponents of the approach used slogans
such as "total quality management" and "empowerment" and sounded like writ-
ers of the human relations school of the 1960s such as McGregor (1960) and
Likert (1961). Cost cutters, in contrast, sounded tough. They sought to reduce
waste accumulated during the previous boom, in part by laying off unnecessary
employees. Layoffs interfered with participative management by creating both
fear of authority and fear of job loss, which diminished the stake employees
had in their company. (Loss of loyalty is well described in Heckscher, 1995.)

But layoffs actually fostered participative management to the extent that they eliminated middle management and forced employees to take over diverse responsibilities from those who had been dismissed. Both management fashions stimulated interest in morale, participative management because it required good morale and cost cutting because it damaged it.

These tendencies pervaded the business community, reaching even small companies. The flavor of participative reform may be gathered from the following.

We are in the process of organizing self-management teams and more horizontal contacts. If an assembler can't make something fit, he can go directly to the producer of the part and together they can figure something out, which they may explain to an engineer. This is exciting for them and gives them a sense of participation. Since middle management feels threatened by this, you have to start by convincing them. It is hard for the workmen to get used to taking the initiative and going to another building to discuss something. So, you start with volunteers and then they do so well that it becomes contagious. We are also starting self-checking quality control and doing away with inspectors. . . . Only a random sample is checked.

—Owner and founder of a nonunion manufacturing company with 500 employees

We are trying to shift more decisions downward to reduce the distance between those at the bottom doing the work and those at the top making policy decisions. Slogans are "customer-driven service" and "innovate to motivate." The company wants more unsupervised mutual consultation at the bottom. A change in corporate culture is occurring. We form local assemblies or focus groups to brainstorm on areas where there are problems. The group may select four problem areas. People low in the hierarchy are selected who are expert in these areas. Four subgroups are formed to study these problems and to come up with suggestions. Each proposes a solution to management, which has to give a yes or no answer immediately. If the solution is approved, the subgroup is responsible for carrying it out. This process is very exciting and improves morale 1,000 percent. People feel involved and see that little annoying things are getting fixed.

—Human resource manager for a group of 1,700 employees in a large insurance company

We have self-managed teams. All employees are given training in empowerment. More responsibility is given lower down in the organization. People are told that it is also their job to do what is right. Assembly lines got stopped by assemblers for the first time after this was done. Before, people were scared of the repercussions and of what the manager would say if they stopped the line. This amounted to upper management's giving lower employees a tool with which to fight middle management. Middle management will allow substandard output in order to keep their jobs.

—Human resource official of a nonunion manufacturing company with 9,500 employees

4.4 Why Care about Morale?

Managers were concerned about morale mainly because of its impact on productivity. They said that when morale is bad, workers distract one another with

TABLE 4.1   Why care about poor morale? (applies to 104 businesses)

Reasons	Number of businesses	Percentage of businesses
Low productivity	93	89
Low productivity not a concern	4	4
Poor customer service	15	14
Turnover[a]	13	13
Recruiting	7	7
Absenteeism	4	4
Unionization	3	3

a. As I will explain in Chapter 11, a great many employers believed that pay cuts would increase turnover in part because of bad morale. However, no statements about the connection between pay cuts and turnover are included in this table. The table refers to discussions of morale alone.

complaints and that good morale makes workers more willing to do extras, to stay late until a job is done, to encourage and help one another, to make suggestions for improvements, and to speak well of the company to outsiders. Psychologists refer to these actions as extrarole, prosocial, organizational citizenship behavior, or organizational spontaneity, and find these to be important for business success (section 4.6).

OVERVIEW OF INTERVIEW EVIDENCE

The impact of poor morale was discussed in interviews with managers in 104 companies. The most common concern was with low productivity or poor workmanship. Other important considerations were turnover, recruitment, and customer service. The effects on absenteeism and possible unionization were mentioned only a few times. Responses are summarized in Table 4.1.

I asked 13 of the 18 labor leaders interviewed for their views on morale, and 10 of these said they wanted their members to have good morale, 7 said that good morale made workers more productive, and only 1 asserted that morale had nothing to do with productivity.

MANAGERS' EXPLANATIONS

Managers believed almost universally that morale had an important impact on productivity, though the effect might be difficult to measure.

I care about morale because, in the case of my secretary, she could embezzle money easily. We don't yet have good financial controls in place. In the case of the pro-

fessional [psychotherapist], she has lots of independence. She is closeted with pa-
tients, and there is little supervision. If her morale were bad, she could take her
work less seriously and there would be more risk of litigation for malpractice, bad
work, and damage to the reputation of the firm.
—One of two partners owning a psychiatric clinic with 17 employees

The disadvantage of low morale has been inefficiency and lack of pride in work,
lack of punctuality, lack of follow-up. For instance, draftsmen don't check if customers have gotten drawings.
—Operations manager of a unionized architectural woodwork company with 20 employees

Morale is important. Once every two years or so, it collapses. Cooperativeness,
willingness to work, and productivity all deteriorate. You can't get anything done.
—Part-owner of a nonunion trucking company with 150 employees

An unhappy worker is not a good one. He may be unsafe. He might refuse to wear
the hand pulls while working with presses and lose a hand. . . . I have had lots of
experience with bad morale. Bad attitudes are regularly associated with bad performance.
—Personnel manager of a partly unionized manufacturing company with 365 employees

I know that morale affects productivity from output standards, made up by industrial
engineers and used in cost accounting. Certainly, when dealing with particular individuals, you can see a drop in productivity if a person feels he is being treated poorly.
—Vice president of human resources of a partially unionized manufacturing company with
5,500 employees

I pay attention to morale because it is assumed that poor morale goes with lower
productivity, though I don't know how I would measure this. In an office environment, this association is based on anecdotal evidence. . . . The judgment is subjective, but true.
—Human resource official at the headquarters of a unionized manufacturing company with
8,500 employees

A frequent comment was that unhappy employees wasted time complaining.

I want employees to be happy, because their happiness affects their productivity.
Worry interferes with their focusing on work. They talk too much if they worry
[about layoff].
—Owner of a nonunion manufacturing company with 35 employees

In the minds of some managers, poor morale especially affected the performance of workers who needed to be imaginative and creative.

Morale is important for productivity. The workman is no longer a pair of hands. People have to come in ready to use their minds and to innovate. They can't do that if they are unhappy and worried about their job description. I never want to go back to the old system. Everyone is working harder now and liking it more. The kick-ass foremen are having a hard time adjusting.

—Director of human resources of a nonunion manufacturing company with 1,000 employees

Knowledge workers have to have their heart and soul in their job or they won't work. There are pockets of the work force where we don't need their creativity, morale, and enthusiasm, because their work can be measured. For salesmen and engineers, you need enthusiasm.

—Vice president of human resources for a nonunion manufacturing company with 95,000 employees

Morale was important for employees who dealt with the public, because mood was likely to affect the way in which they treated customers.

Morale is important for performance. Employees need to enjoy coming to work. They need to be treated as individuals, and their ideas must be noticed and appreciated. They must be encouraged to take the initiative to make customers happy. Employees have to be happy to present a positive image to guests.

—Manager of a nonunion hotel with 60 employees

When I came, there were morale problems. Tellers were third-class citizens. I introduced a program to improve the egos, incentives, and performance of the tellers. I improved customer contact. Tellers were trained to smile. Your voice sounds better when you smile, and cheerfulness makes customers more friendly and this in turn makes the job more enjoyable.

—Human resource official of a bank with 200 employees that closed in 1991, a few months before the interview

According to my respondents, good morale meant that employees were likely to be more flexible about their assignments and to do extra tasks spontaneously. These comments were especially common among managers of small companies, people who were close to the work force.

Morale is very important to productivity. The company works as a family. People help each other and work together. If someone goes by and sees someone else struggling to lift a box down from a shelf, he will lend a hand. There is a good atmosphere and they feel relaxed. It is hard to explain. In a big company, or if there is a union, people take an "it's not my job" attitude. Here, everything is everyone's job. If a truck comes in with an emergency job which is needed the next day, the employees volunteer to work overtime until it gets done. They want to see the company succeed.

—Owner and founder of a new nonunion manufacturing company with 7 employees

A happy shop is a more efficient one. We do some emergency work and the work is seasonal, demand being strongest in spring and summer. People may have to work long hours and through weekends and they have the right to refuse overtime. Prompt service to customers is very important for our reputation. Last Christmas, someone had to go repair a tugboat in [an East Coast] harbor, leaving family, friends, and relatives who came to visit during Christmas break.

—Owner of a nonunion manufacturing firm with 40 employees

If we don't have a cohesive organization, if we have lots of petty disputes and resentments, we could have productivity problems. The work load is unevenly distributed across the firm over time, so that we need teamwork and to help each other out.

—Managing partner of a law firm with 70 employees

Employers also worried about the impact of morale on recruiting and turnover.

We are very concerned about morale. Though production may stay the same, there are other ways employees can contribute. . . . Employees can be a tremendous recruiting tool. The long-term impact of their dissatisfaction could be enormous.

—Vice president of human resources of a nonunion manufacturing company with 260 employees

We care about morale because we are a family. The company's reputation would affect recruiting and turnover. The first people to leave if morale is low are the better employees. There are places to go, even in bad times.

—Vice president of a nonunion manufacturing company with 5,000 employees

In the minds of some, turnover was linked with performance, because workers who were thinking of leaving would be less inclined to take the time to learn new skills.

If morale is bad, employees feel no loyalty and no desire to invest their efforts in learning more and improving. . . . Unhappy employees could leave after the recession is over, even if they wouldn't now. . . . If an employee is thinking of leaving, he is not going to be committed to learning how to do his job better. . . . If employees are sufficiently offended, they quit, even if there are no other opportunities for them.

—President and owner of a unionized manufacturing company with 150 employees

LABOR LEADERS' EXPLANATIONS

Labor leaders felt that good morale was in the interests of the union, because it made members cooperative and reasonable and it increased productivity and so made companies willing to pay more.

When morale is good, members feel better and productivity is higher. High productivity in turn affects our ability to negotiate good contracts.

—Regional manager of an industrial union with 6,500 active members

Morale is important to us. When layoffs occur, members can't strike back at the company, so they strike back at union leaders. They ask, "Why can't you save our jobs?"

—Head labor representative of an industrial union local with an active membership of 12,000

Morale is big in business. In stores, everyone is up front, and the customers come first. That requires a spirit. A manager could try to order employees to behave that way, but a smart manager has employees do it because they want to. The correct employee attitude is created by dignity and management's having made people feel they are important. Unions help give people dignity. . . . Morale is important to unions. They want members to be happy. It makes them better citizens.

—Business agent of a retail workers' union local with 16,000 members

Morale is a sense of a good relationship with the employer and is important to unions. . . . A happy employee is a better union member, one who speaks up at meetings, helps formulate a plan of action, and serves on committees. If someone is sore at the employer, he may be active with the union for that reason. But you try to turn it into something positive while solving the negative problem.

—Official in an umbrella organization of labor union locals, together representing 30,000 workers

4.5 Morale and Job Satisfaction

In interviews with 15 businesspeople, I challenged assertions that morale affected productivity by pointing out that psychologists had found little link between job satisfaction and performance. Seven of the respondents felt the findings were wrong and 8 argued that psychologists probably do not measure the appropriate aspects of morale or performance. Most of those who contradicted the findings reacted strongly.

Question: Are you aware of the psychological literature on job satisfaction, which asserts that there is little connection between job satisfaction and performance? *Answer:* No. *Question:* What do you think of the assertion? *Answer:* (A long laugh.) There's my answer. I put psychologists right down there with economists.

—Director of a community service organization with 150 employees

The attempts to distinguish morale from job satisfaction were interesting.

> Morale is always a factor. You want a crew that is striving for psychic and monetary rewards rather than complaining about management. But a happy newsman is not necessarily a good one. Reporters are complainers by nature. You want to channel their complaints. You want them focused on their beats and assignments or, for editors, their copy. The military is similar. If soldiers are completely happy, it is bad. You want constructive bitching. Bitching about hard work is tinged with pride. If they are bitching about NCO's, they won't follow them.
>
> —Newsroom editor of a local newspaper with 100 employees in the news department

4.6 Trends in the Study of Morale

There is a huge literature in organizational psychology, mostly cited in the appendix to this chapter, on the relation of morale to productivity. It is fairly well accepted that there is a small but significant negative correlation between morale, defined as positive job attitudes, and withdrawal behavior, that is, tardiness, absences, and quits. It is also accepted that there is a small and nearly insignificant positive relation between the morale of individuals and their job performance. There is a stronger positive relation between average morale in organizations and their performance. The difference between the strength of the effect at the individual and group levels may be explained by the effect of morale on forms of behavior that facilitate cooperation. There is good evidence that these are positively related to morale, and recent findings show that they increase the productivity of work groups. Trust among co-workers and between subordinates and superiors may also be an important link between individual job attitudes and group effectiveness.

The forms of behavior facilitating cooperation are innovative and spontaneous behavior (Katz and Kahn, 1966, p. 337; George and Brief, 1992), prosocial behavior (O'Reilly and Chatman, 1986), and organizational citizenship behavior (Organ, 1988), the concept which has been most studied. Organ (1988, pp. 4–6) describes it as having five aspects: altruism (mutual assistance), conscientiousness (doing more than the minimum required by a job and showing initiative), sportsmanship (not complaining), courtesy (politeness and exchanging information), and civic virtue (participating in organizational activities, such as meetings).[3]

One contrast stands out when comparing the literature and what the interviews revealed. Businesspeople were preoccupied with the consequences of bad morale among groups of employees, whereas no studies have been made of the impact of bad morale among entire groups. Another contrast is that businesspeople emphasized moral and personal values, whereas most of the literature ignores them.[4] A third contrast is that most businesspeople persist in believing that happiness increases productivity, despite evidence that this association is weak at the individual level. However, the literature on morale is not entirely unrelated to managers' perceptions, for the work on prosocial and organizational citizenship behaviors captures topics that were on the minds of employers. Perhaps fieldwork on the impact of moral values and on organizations suffering morale breakdowns would reveal what businesspeople believe they see. No such studies have been made, probably because it is difficult to gain access to companies in crisis, a time when employers want to hide their problems.

4.7 Summary

In the minds of business leaders, morale has to do with workers' mood and with the willingness to cooperate with company objectives. Happiness contributes to but is not sufficient for good morale. What is vital is to have efforts focused on company objectives. Many factors influence morale, including especially good personal contact with supervisors, a spirit of community within the business, and the perception that company policy is fair. Businesspeople value good morale because it fosters high productivity, low turnover, and ease in recruiting new workers.

Appendix 4A Related Literature

There is other evidence besides mine that the business community believes there is a positive relation between morale and performance. In a survey of businesspeople and labor leaders, Katzell and Yankelovich (1975, chap. 4) find that respondents see a positive association between productivity, loyalty, and punctuality on the one hand and positive worker attitudes on the other. James Lincoln (1946, 1951), a businessman, discusses motivational issues related to morale in the context of a highly successful incentive management system he created at his company, Lincoln Electric. He attaches importance to workers' idealism and desire for self-improvement.

A great many studies have been made of the relation between morale and withdrawal behaviors. These are reviewed in Brayfield and Crockett (1955), Herzberg et al. (1957, pp. 106–107), Vroom (1964, pp. 173–180), Locke (1976, pp. 1331–32), Price (1977, p. 79), Steers and Rhodes (1978), Mobley (1982, pp. 95–105), Staw (1984, pp. 638–645), and Mathieu and Zajac (1990). Telly, French, and Scott (1971) find a positive relation between turnover and unfair and inconsiderate treatment by supervisors.

Psychologists have obtained contradictory results when measuring the relation between the morale and job performance of individuals. Performance is measured through direct observation and supervisors' evaluations, and morale is measured from questionnaire evidence on job satisfaction and organizational commitment. Hundreds of papers have been written on the subject, and these have in turn been reviewed and analyzed by many (Brayfield and Crockett, 1955; Herzberg et al., 1957, chap. 4; Vroom, 1964, pp. 181–186; Locke, 1976, pp. 1330–34; Iaffaldano and Muchinsky, 1985; and Mathieu and Zajac, 1990, p. 184). Some suggest that performance may influence attitudes more than attitudes influence performance (Lawler and Porter, 1967; Locke, 1970), and Greene and Craft (1979) discuss evidence on the direction of causality. An individual's job satisfaction may not be a good indicator of morale, for job satisfaction is related to personality and therefore is not something that can be easily influenced by management (Staw, Bell, and Clausen, 1986).

Work on average worker job attitudes and the performance of work groups (Giese and Ruter, 1949; Blum, 1956, chap. 6; Angle and Perry, 1981; Ostroff, 1992; Schmit and Allscheid, 1995; and Ryan, Schmit, and Johnson, 1996) gives some weight to the conclusion that they are positively related, though the direction of causality is again not clear. Even stronger evidence of a relation between group attitudes and performance is contained in papers relating indicators of a group's morale to performance, examples of indicators being the incidence of grievances, disciplinary measures, strikes, absences, and quits (Pencavel, 1974, 1977; Katz, Kochan, and Gobeille, 1983; Katz, Kochan, and Weber, 1985; Norsworthy and Zabala, 1985; and Ichniowski, 1986).[5]

There is a body of interesting early research using experimental changes in management practices to determine the relation between group attitudes and performance (Viteles, 1953, chap. 8; Seashore, 1954; Whyte, 1955, 1961; and Likert, 1961, chap. 3). Main conclusions are that performance is positively associated with pride in the group and its achievements, but is not related to other attitudes, and that group cohesion does not help performance unless the group accepts the goals of the overall organization. Mathewson (1931) and Whyte (1955) document the restriction of output by cohesive but recalcitrant work groups.

Studies relating morale to organizational citizenship behavior and related forms of behavior include O'Reilly and Chatman (1986), Organ (1988), Organ and Konovsky (1989), Schnake (1991), Isen and Baron (1991), George and Brief (1992), Moorman (1993), Staw, Sutton, and Pelled (1994), Organ and Lingl (1995), and Organ and Ryan (1995). Many studies explore the link between organizational citizenship behavior and group performance (Karambayya, 1990; MacKenzie, Podsakoff, and Fetter, 1991, 1993; Podsakoff, MacKenzie, and Hui, 1993; Podsakoff and MacKenzie, 1994, 1997; and Podsakoff, Ahearne, and MacKenzie, 1997).

Trust plays an important role in some recent work on organizations. Trust in company leadership has been shown to foster organizational citizenship behavior and productivity (Podsakoff et al., 1990; Robinson and Morrison, 1995; and Robinson, 1996). In addition, there is literature in sociology and political science on the importance in business and government of networks of trusted personal connections, these being termed social capital (Loury, 1987; Coleman, 1990; Putnam, 1993; and Fukuyama, 1995).

There is abundant experimental evidence that reciprocity and even humanitarian feelings have an important impact on behavior, and these may be among the factors making morale important. The significance of reciprocity is substantiated by economic experiments in which subjects placed in the role of workers offer firms greater effort in exchange for higher pay (Fehr, Kirchsteiger, and Riedl, 1993, 1996; Fehr and Tougareva, 1995; Fehr, Gächter, and Kirchsteiger, 1996; Fehr and Falk, 1996; Fehr and Gächter, 1998a; and Fehr et al., 1998). (In the experiments, "effort" is a monetary sacrifice.) Humanitarian inclinations are revealed in cooperation experiments and especially those with public goods and voluntary contributions, for it is found that subjects do not "free ride" as much as they would if they were purely selfish (Goranson and Berkowitz, 1966; Greenberg, 1978; Kragt, Orbell, and Dawes, 1983; Kim and Walker, 1984; Andreoni, 1988; Isaac and Walker, 1988a, b; and Orbell, Dawes, and Kragt, 1988).

Students of military science have written a good deal about morale and have underscored its importance for performance. There have been debates about whether morale is fostered more by small-unit loyalties or by belief in the army's goals (Janowitz and Shils, 1948; Stouffer et al., 1949; Baynes, 1967; and Bartov, 1991). The first three of these works emphasize the importance of small-unit loyalties, whereas Bartov argues that the German army's cohesion was maintained by Nazi propaganda and extremely severe discipline.[6]

5

Company Risk Aversion

The interviews made it clear that budgetary or credit constraints influence company decisions regarding layoffs and pay. These restrictions make firms behave in ways I describe as reflecting risk aversion, though, strictly speaking, this term does not apply. It normally refers to the preferences of individuals, and a business is not a person and probably should not be thought of as having preferences. Furthermore, I apply the term to attitudes toward intertemporal choices rather than risky ones, though in normal usage people are said to be risk averse if they prefer receiving the expected value of monetary gambles to the gambles themselves and are risk neutral when indifferent between gambles and their expected values. However, a person who was risk averse in the usual sense would behave in the ways I label as risk averse. In the usual model of risk aversion, people attach a numerical utility to money or liquid wealth, and the marginal utility of money declines as money holdings increase, where the marginal utility of money is the utility of an additional dollar.[1] For risk-neutral people, the marginal utility of money is independent of wealth. An individual's utility of money is an indirect utility; it is derived from the satisfaction gained from money spent on goods and services. Companies, too, have an indirect "utility" for money in that it is useful for investing, paying wages and dividends, as a reserve for future contingencies, and so on. The usefulness of an additional dollar increases as company holdings of money or liquid assets decrease, because only the most urgent needs can be met when holdings are low. That is, companies are risk averse in the sense that the marginal "utility" of money increases as holdings of liquid assets decline; a decrease in liquid wealth increases the readiness to sacrifice for more money. The sacrifice could be of managerial effort, moral values, property, or of future income. A company may act like a person so short of money as to be hungry and therefore ready to sell a car worth $5,000 quickly for $2,000 rather than wait a few weeks to find a buyer willing to pay the full price. Entrepreneurs neutral toward risk in private life might act risk aversely in business, were their entire investment menaced by a cash shortage.

That companies are averse to risk is not surprising from the point of view of common sense, but is hard to reconcile with economic theory. Many explanations of credit constraints on businesses have been proposed, but, as with the many explanations of wage rigidity, the wealth of financial theories does not demonstrate understanding, for it is not clear which is correct. Most of the human resource officials and managers with whom I talked were not in a position to offer much insight, and therefore I did not explore with them which explanation might be most appropriate. Financial officers, stockbrokers, and bankers would have been more appropriate informants.

Most of the evidence of company risk aversion concerned the effect of company finances on matters interpretable as investments. Pay cuts, pay freezes, and some layoffs brought on by financial distress were a way of giving up future income in exchange for current cash.

5.1 The Theoretical Puzzle

In economic theory, it is often assumed that firms are risk neutral. The theoretical defense of this assumption is based on the idea that company owners should not be averse to risk on gambles or investments too small to affect significantly their liquid wealth and hence their marginal utility for it. If investors hold well-diversified portfolios, fluctuations in the wealth of one company should have little impact on their financial state. Since rational investors diversify, a company's wealth should hardly be correlated with that of its individual stockholders, except to the extent that their other sources of income and wealth move in sympathy with the company's finances. Because stockholders insist that companies be run for their benefit, publicly held firms should act as if they were risk neutral. Shareholders should also be willing to advance money to distressed corporations. Hence financial distress should not bring businesses to act as if they were risk averse.

This conclusion is probably invalid, for risk management is an important function in business. Many authors have noticed that even large companies' behavior is inconsistent with risk neutrality in that they often sacrifice future earnings to obtain cash when in financial distress. Although these observations do not imply that firms should be thought of as maximizing a concave function of profits, they do imply that financial distress increases the value of money to firms, so that they are risk averse in this narrow sense.

5.2 Manifestations of Company Risk Aversion

Evidence of company risk aversion came up incidentally in discussions of pay rates and layoffs, the topics central to my inquiries, and I never posed questions directly related to risk aversion. Had I done so, I would probably have heard more than I did about the difficulty of raising funds and the impact of financial stress on marketing, sales, research, development, and productive capacity.

OVERVIEW OF INTERVIEW EVIDENCE

Of the 235 businesses studied that were not temporary labor agencies, 165 acted in ways that reflected company risk aversion (Table 5.1). Actions included in the table were taken only because of financial problems. For instance, the majority of layoffs were made because of decreased need for labor, and such layoffs are not counted. Especially significant were 10 layoffs which, according to informants, led to the sacrifice of future profit in exchange for current gain. Similarly, I have not counted reductions in investment made because of decreases in projected future product demand. The impact of company finances on raises is not conclusive evidence of company risk aversion, for this relation is designed in part to stimulate employee interest in company success. Both large and small companies displayed risk aversion, though financial crises were more extreme in small companies. Only a few companies

TABLE 5.1   Actions taken during the recession reflecting company risk aversion (applies to 165 businesses)

Type of action taken to generate ready cash to relieve financial distress	Number of businesses
Reduced raises or bonuses	115
Froze pay	60
Cut the pay of some or all employees	31
Laid off employees	69
Did not buy enough materials to fill orders	4
Reduced expenditures on research and development	4
Reduced expenditures on marketing or sales	3
Reduced investment in plant, equipment, or employee training	3
Sold a profitable business	1

TABLE 5.2   Why do raises depend on profits? (applies to 53 businesses)

Reasons	Number of businesses	Percentage of businesses
The firm cannot afford to pay more	40	75
Employees expect pay to increase with profits	10	19
The company shares its prosperity and failures with workers in order to strengthen incentives	10	19
Wages are manipulated to achieve target profit levels	4	8

exhibited risk neutrality in that they did not cut back on marketing, investments, or raises despite financial reversals.

Table 5.2 summarizes the reasons given for why raises depended on company finances. The major reason was affordability, which implies company risk aversion.

I mention as an aside observations that may bear on the explanation for company risk aversion, a topic I do not address. In comparison with publicly owned firms, individually owned or family-owned businesses reacted to financial reversals in a manner displaying less risk aversion and as if they had a longer mental time horizon. This observation casts doubt on the idea that company risk aversion is merely a reflection of that of the owners. Some subsidiaries of huge and wealthy organizations, even small fast food restaurants, reacted with risk aversion to financial setbacks in the subsidiary alone, indicating that financial self-reliance is forced on units within large organizations as a way of maintaining discipline.

MANAGERS' EXPLANATIONS

Though I refrained from asking about the causes of company risk aversion, some managers and employers commented on increased pressures for financial performance brought on by hard times.

American companies have a quarter-to-quarter mentality, sacrificing the future for the present. This is one reason they lay off people. The company president is under pressure from the stockholders. They don't want their dividends to stop. Retired people in Florida depend on them. If the president does not maintain dividends, they will find a new president who will. For this reason, he does things he knows are not in the long-term interests of the company. Company executives worry about their stock options, and the value of the stock does not reflect the long-run prospects of the company.

—Human resource official in a bank with 800 employees

You get a short-term focus during periods of distress. This is only human nature. If you don't show progress now, you will be replaced by new management. The stockholders know that the business is cyclic, but you have to do well relative to your competitors.

—Vice president of human resources for a largely non-union manufacturing company with 125,000 employees

Sometimes, the need for savings stemmed from financial trickery, or what one executive called "paper games."

[The company's new owner] wants to take the company public in [nine months], so he needs a good year. He is doing all the cost cutting as a quick fix to make the company look profitable. [Heavy layoffs resulted.] He got rid of a lot of overhead executives, cut back on advertising and research and development. . . . He sacrificed the future. Advertising affects sales only nine months to a year from the time it is done. Human resources [i.e., the human resource department] makes a long-term contribution to a company too, through cost containment in benefits and through productivity improvements, which are affected by the environment, morale, attitude, and communication processes you set up.

—Head of human resources of a nonunion consumer products company with 1,500 employees

Executives and owners of small- and medium-sized companies expressed fear of indebtedness.

It has been hard to meet payments on the company's bank notes. . . . If we had a lot of debt, we would have gone under. [Our bank] is no longer honoring checks drawn on uncollected funds. . . . I sweat every payroll.

—Operations manager of a trucking company with 70 employees

We had a wage freeze in 1990. . . . The freeze was due to a severe drop in sales. I couldn't afford raises. . . . I didn't want to increase my debt. Going into debt will eventually put you out of business.

—Owner of a furniture store chain with 200 employees

The same fear was mentioned even by executives of large corporations.

If the pie gets smaller because the company is not making money, then we have to cut [research and development] programs. We can't just borrow money, or at least that decision has to be made at a very high level. Some programs are kept going, but at a slower pace. That is tough, because you need to have them in the marketplace.

—Director of human resources of a unionized manufacturing company with 30,000 employees

We are reluctant to fund losses for fear that our asset position will get out of control. In order to cut costs, you need capital for new technology, but the money is not there. It takes 18 months to two years to get new technology integrated into the system.

—High-level human resource official in an insurance company with 50,000 employees

Financial problems could bring loss of access to credit.

We raise capital directly in the capital market by selling commercial paper. [The chairman] drives people to have double-digit growth in net income in all lines of business all the time. All hell breaks loose if that is not achieved. If the company didn't do well, no one would want to buy its commercial paper and it would be cash short. Anticipating that, any hint of bad performance is immediately punished.

—Human resource manager in a financial company with 24,000 employees

Large debts also brought fear of financial reversals.

"High leveraging makes a company have a short-term outlook. It becomes preoccupied with the present." [The respondent said this in reference to his own company, owned by managers who borrowed heavily to buy it.]

—One of four owners of a nonunion manufacturing company with 200 employees

Some small companies simply could not hope for more capital.

In a start-up company, you are given a pot of money and told to do what you can with it. When it runs dry, you are finished.

—Founder and part-owner of a new nonunion manufacturing company with 10 employees

Most small companies had difficulty borrowing from banks during the recession. Some companies had so little working capital that they could not buy materials to fill orders and so had to lay off workers.

We had a line of credit with [a bank]. It got into trouble and called in our line of credit. I know a federal bank examiner, who told me that [the bank] was about to be examined by the FDIC on an emergency basis. The bank panicked and called in notes. As a result, we could no longer afford to buy materials, and our annual sales dropped to $1,900,000. We would have sold $3,000,000 if we could have bought parts. No other bank would extend credit. They wouldn't even factor a contract [lend money on the security of the amount due on a sales contract], which they used to do. They are all in trouble. Banks are horrendous to deal with. They won't lend on speculation or growth potential. . . . Buyers can't get funding either and they shop around to avoid paying one third up front. . . . We have twice been late with payrolls, once by two days, once by three.

—President of a nonunion electronics manufacturing firm with 25 employees

Our bank is far more attentive to our day-to-day activities now than five years ago. They apply pressure to be lean and mean and don't want personnel expenditure to go up too fast. We now go over our budget with them.

—Managing partner of a law firm with 70 employees

The recession has hurt us because it has financially weakened our customers [retail stores]. We have adequate production capacity and potential sales. The distribution channels are the problem. Most retailers depend on the profits of the last quarter of the year. The rest of the year, they usually lose money in all but a few months, when they break even. Usually, they buy spring merchandise in February and March, using bank loans to finance the purchases. These loans are repaid with the proceeds of the Christmas season. Now banks are not lending money to retailers for spring goods. So I have to extend credit, which I am not always able or willing to do, especially if the retailer is weak financially. . . . I borrow to lend.

—Owner of a nonunion apparel manufacturing company with 550 employees

In four businesses, cutbacks were precipitated in healthy, expanding divisions of large corporations by financial setbacks in the parent organizations.

The company is a division of . . . Corporation. . . . [The parent corporation] . . . is not doing very well, whereas we are doing extremely well and are expanding rapidly. [The parent corporation] is in financial trouble, and is holding us back. We could sell all we want to, but are held back by lack of funds for expansion. [The parent] has severe cash flow problems and tells us to skimp. For instance, I can't buy a new desk.

—Personnel manager of a partly unionized manufacturing company with 365 employees

Companies manifested risk aversion mainly through the effect of budget constraints on various investments. Most of the budgetary effects I heard about concerned layoffs, raises, pay cuts, and pay freezes. Raises were to some extent investments in employee goodwill and incentives, and some layoffs resulted from giving up activities that would bring in money only in the future. Many employers made it clear that financial problems were responsible for layoffs.

The layoffs were due to cash flow problems. I had to wait for payments to come in before I could pay people.

—Owner of a nonunion electronics manufacturing company with 15 employees

[When I reduced overhead staff], their total workload hadn't gone down. The extra time had always been there. *Question:* Why didn't you make the cost saving earlier? *Answer:* If a business is making $1,000,000 a year, making another $100,000 doesn't make much difference. You can spend only just so much.

—President and owner of a unionized manufacturing company with 135 employees

We run on research grants from corporate headquarters. When business is bad, grants are cut back. . . . The cuts are made just to save money for the parent company. [Layoffs occurred as a consequence.]

—Human resource official of a corporate research organization with 250 employees

We were under pressure from the FDIC to save money and rebuild capital. The FDIC said we were top heavy. So we looked over our departments to see what we could do without for now and decided to get rid of the business development area. These people try to obtain new loans and accounts. They are professional salesmen. They were let go and their tasks were turned over to the branch and department managers. The department will be brought back if times get better. For now, more is being asked of managers. Their workload has increased, as has that of everyone.

—Human resource officer of a bank with 400 employees

We are eliminating administrative support functions in order to make more money. We give up the future in this way. We are heavily influenced by short-term desires. We are not as profitable as we would like to be now.

—Human resource manager in a 21,500 employee subsidiary of a large insurance company

In some cases, the desire to please stockholders spurred the drive for quick savings through layoffs.

If we hit everyone now [i.e., lay off as many as possible] we can project the costs of severance and take all the losses in the current quarter. This is one reason current earnings are bad. In the next quarter, those costs won't be there and earnings will look good.

—Corporate director of human resources of a mostly nonunion manufacturing company with 5,000 employees

To some middle managers, layoffs seemed to result from financially motivated orders from top executives rather than from the situation within their group.

We laid off 20 people out of 580 in the news department. . . . We are trying to cut back on costs. This happens higher up. A mood is created up there, which says spend or don't spend. Budgets are determined there. You must live within the budget.

—Newsroom editor of a major newspaper with 580 employees in the news department

We had the largest downsizing in our history in April 1992. . . . Profitability was the issue. . . . [The parent company] said, "Do it now. Just do it. Don't give us reasons why you can't. Get twenty million dollars out of the cost structure."

—High-level human resource official in a 3,000-employee, largely nonunion division of a huge consumer products company

In many firms, financial setbacks reminded executives of their vulnerability and stimulated them to improve the efficiency of their operations, often making extensive layoffs while doing so. This reaction to adversity is probably not due to risk aversion and is discussed in section 13.2 under the rubric of organizational slack. In section 13.1, I explain that financially motivated layoffs often applied only to overhead personnel.

A large number of employers made it clear that the size of raises reflected company prosperity.

> Raises depend on individual performance and on how well the company is doing. They would be 4% in bad years, 7% in average years, and 15% in good years.
>
> —Manager of a nonunion manufacturing company with 65 employees

> When things are going well, we try to show our friendliness and goodwill by increasing pay. When things are going badly, we expect them to hold still and be patient. We are like one big family.
>
> —Owner of a nonunion manufacturing company with 1,500 employees

Indicating company risk aversion were many statements that financial needs forced companies to reduce raises.

> I went through a divorce in 1986 that cost me $1,000,000. As a result, I couldn't pay raises or bonuses in 1988 or 1989. Since then, I have paid regular raises, but because of the recession I have not paid bonuses.
>
> —Owner of a nonunion construction company with 10 employees

> Increases depend on profits because without them you'd be out of business.
>
> —Part-owner of a small chain of restaurants

Some companies deliberately traded-off expenditures on raises against investments in buildings and equipment, indicating a budget constraint.

> [Determining the increase budget] involves weighing compensation and the investment needs of the firm. The budget is the result of an interactive and iterative process among the managers. I tell them to put in a few dreams for equipment they would like, because if they don't try, they'll never get what they want.
>
> —Operations manager of a nonunion wholesale distribution company with 170 employees

Some corporations used the size of increases as a means of controlling profits, in order to impress stockholders or parent corporations.

> Our profitability has held back our pay recently. We use low merit increases to offset bad times. We have not reached the point where we have trouble retaining

employees. If we had, profits wouldn't have mattered. . . . There is a level of profit that [the parent corporation] wants. . . . I say what is needed for competitiveness. Management says what that does to profitability.

—Head of human resources of a nonunion manufacturing company with 1,200 employees

We want to deliver the profit number we have committed ourselves to. We develop the profit number before the merit budget. We have a responsibility to [our parent company]. . . . We want to be planful and in control. We want to be able to pre-scribe what is going to happen and meet it.

—High-level human resource official in a 3,000-employee, largely nonunion division of a huge consumer products company

The merit budget is affected by affordability. *Comment:* This leaves me puzzled since if the bank is maximizing profit, there should be one level of pay that maxi-mizes it. *Response:* Companies optimize rather than maximize profits. Pay increases are an investment and a reward which can be postponed. Increases attract people who make more money for you later.

—Human resource officer of a bank with 16,000 employees

Some employers said that the profit level could depress raises, but not in-crease them. Other said that prosperity lifted pay because it made management more generous and because management did not want to disappoint employees' expectations that they would benefit from company successes.

Profitability does not affect wages, theoretically, though it does in practice. The company is more willing to give if it is doing well.

—Human resource manager servicing 360 headquarters personnel of a large nonunion manu-facturing company

Increases are part of American culture. If you give no increase and have lots of profits, people will be upset and will eventually leave. The employees' interpretation of increases is important.

—Human resource manager of a unionized manufacturing company with 30,000 employees

Affordability is only a downward drag. . . . If profits surged, we wouldn't pay more than the market. The surge would just help us catch up.

—Vice president of human resources for a nonunion manufacturing company with 95,000 employees

A few comments by employers indicated that the link between raises and profits was in part a mechanism for creating collective incentives.

The dependence of pay on profits is not a specified program. But we want to instill the mind set that pay should depend on performance at all levels.

—Director of compensation of a nonunion manufacturing company with 18,000 employees

I say more about this matter in section 10.3 in connection with the relation between raises and the profits of operating units within larger companies.

The impact of company budgets on pay was especially clear when financial distress brought pay freezes or cuts, which were viewed as emergency sources of funds. Budgetary problems are viewed in the business community as a legitimate reason for obliging employees to share some of their company's financial risks.

> We didn't have the financial resources or the internal resources to develop the new products we needed. The company was in decline. We had the philosophy that everyone had an investment in the company. We could cut people. This would have impacted cash flow. But I needed them to get work done. I decided to keep everybody or most of them and to ask them to take a pay cut.
>
> —Former owner of a nonunion, 20-employee manufacturing company that closed in 1992

> A year ago, the officers gave up 10 percent of their pay because of cash flow problems. Customers, especially contractors, were not paying. Contractors are always behind. They aren't good financial people. They mix up cash flow and profit.
>
> —Vice president of a unionized manufacturing company with 90 employees

> In 1989, exempt employees got a 10 percent pay cut. This was done to protect the profits of the company after a drop in sales. The cut did nothing to promote the sales of the company. It simply protected its liquidity position.
>
> —Compensation manager for a nonunion manufacturing company with 1,750 employees

Financial difficulties leading to cuts or freezes were not always the result of reduced sales. Sometimes they were due to excessive borrowing or to problems in another division of the parent company.

> In 1987, the company was bought by another one. The new ownership went too much in debt and nearly went bankrupt. Pay was cut later in the year in order to keep the company afloat, with a promise of restoration after 6 months. . . . The cuts were explained to the work force as necessary to prevent bankruptcy.
>
> —Human resource manager of a nonunion printing company with 400 employees

> A wage freeze was imposed in the last week of August 1991. . . . The freeze was due to [the parent company's] problems. [This division] is doing fine.
>
> —Human resource officer of an 850-employee, nonunion division of a manufacturing company

5.3 Summary

Company policy is influenced by budget constraints. When companies are short of cash and this constraint binds, their implicit marginal utility of cash increases, just as if they were risk averse. This risk aversion has a major impact on layoffs and on pay raises, freezes, and cuts.

Appendix 5A Related Literature

A great many authors have produced evidence that companies are risk averse in the sense that money becomes more valuable to them in hard times, and Hubbard (1998) gives an excellent review of the literature. Most of the evidence is indirect and has to do with observations that firms restrict investment during hard times and manage risk at all times. There have also been a number of theoretical speculations about why firms show aversion to risk, but little evidence indicating which explanations apply. The key puzzle is why firms must compensate investors for diversifiable risk. The root cause of this phenomenon has never been explored empirically, as far as I know.

COMPANY LIQUIDITY AND INVESTMENT

Lamont (1997) and Shin and Stulz (1998) find that the capital expenditures of corporate divisions are strongly affected by the parent company's financial well-being. This is evidence that the parent is risk averse, since there is little reason to believe that there should be much correlation between the parent's financial state and the prospects of the divisions' investment opportunities. The evidence is consistent with my findings that layoffs and pay at divisions were influenced by the financial condition of the parent. Most studies relating companies' liquidity position to investment in productive capacity find a positive association, though there is controversy on the subject (Meyer and Kuh, 1959, chaps. 9, 10, 12; Fazzari, Hubbard, and Petersen, 1988, 1996; Devereux and Schiantarelli, 1990; Hoshi, Kashyap, and Scharfstein, 1990 and 1991; Reiss, 1990; Strong and Meyer, 1990; Calomiris and Hubbard, 1995; Hubbard, Kashyap, and Whited, 1995; and Kaplan and Zingales, 1997). Carpenter, Fazzari, and Petersen (1994) find in U.S. data that internal funds have a strong effect on inventory investment; Bronwyn Hall (1992) and Himmelberg and Petersen (1994) find that research and development expenditures are sensitive to the flow of internal finance.

Some executives told me they had cut back on marketing expenditures because of financial problems. An interesting unexplored question is whether expenditures on marketing and sales are sensitive to cash flow or other measures of company liquidity or distress.

COMPANY LIQUIDITY AND EMPLOYMENT

There is little work on the influence of company finances on layoffs and employment, but the few papers that exist on the subject are consistent with my observations that layoffs are sometimes used to relieve financial distress (Cantor, 1990; Nickell and Wadhwani, 1991; and Sharpe, 1994).

CORPORATE RISK MANAGEMENT

Numerous authors document the fact that corporations devote a great deal of attention and resources to reducing exposure to risk, itself important evidence of company risk aversion (Mayers and Smith, 1982; Dolde, 1985, 1993a, and 1993b; Bodnar et al., 1995; Phillips, 1995; Fenn, Post, and Sharpe, 1996; and Mian, 1996).

MEASUREMENT OF MANAGERIAL RISK AVERSION

Studies of business executives have found that they are risk averse as individuals and often financially conservative as managers (Donaldson, 1961; MacCrimmon and Wehrung, 1986).

THEORIES

Diverse theoretical explanations of company risk aversion have been provided by many authors. Barclay, Smith and Watts (1995) and Fite and Pfleiderer (1995) review the literature. Key contributors include Amihud and Lev (1981), Cragg and Malkiel (1982, section 2.1), Mayers and Smith (1982, 1987, 1990), Myers and Majluf (1984), Stulz (1984, 1996), Smith and Stulz (1985), Shapiro and Titman (1986), Campbell and Kracaw (1987), Greenwald and Stiglitz (1990), Bagwell (1991, 1992), Stiglitz (1992), Froot, Scharfstein, and Stein (1993), DeMarzo and Duffie (1995), and Tufano (1996).

6

INTERNAL PAY STRUCTURE

Employees' sensitivity to the relation of their pay to that of co-workers creates a need for standards of internal pay equity, which is both uniformity in the application of rules setting pay and a set of beliefs about fair relations between pay and its determinants. This sensitivity is greatest in the primary sector. The standards are established by a firm's internal pay structure, a system tying pay to individual output, qualifications, seniority, and position. These structures contribute to wage rigidity, for they make it difficult to reduce the pay of only some employees, such as the newly hired or those with skills in especially low demand. Internal pay structure would not be necessary if pay were determined tightly by the labor market, but the market is an imperfect guide. Pay varies widely among companies, even for the same type of work and people, and many jobs or skills specific to one or a few companies do not have market values.

6.1 Types of Internal Pay Structure

Many forms of internal pay structure exist. Why particular ones arise is not well understood, though certain tendencies can be seen in the relation between current circumstances and types of structure. Structures associate pay with the most easily verified characteristics of jobs or jobholders. Piece rates for factory workers and commissions for salespeople link pay directly to output, as is often done when output can be measured easily. As the ease of measuring product decreases, pay depends less on output and more on a description of the job and the qualifications of the jobholder. After output, the job itself is the next most objective basis for a pay scale, but when tasks are sufficiently varied the job becomes too amorphous a guide and the jobholder's abilities are all that remain.

Businesspeople have many objections to piecework, despite its incentives.

Piece rates are not practical for workers doing many tasks, because of the cost of establishing the rates and because piecework does not compensate workers for time spent switching tasks. Piece workers resist changing assignments, because they become expert at certain jobs and lose money while learning new ones. A need for high quality discourages use of piece rates, because quality is hard to quantify. Demands for quality can make commissioned pay systems equally impractical. For instance, most financial companies pay stockbrokers commissions, but one investment bank with extremely wealthy clients pays salaries because it does not want brokers to take unfair advantage of customers and spoil the bank's reputation among the world's small population of very rich people. For many or most workers, piece rates are infeasible, because it is not possible to identify the output of individual workers or groups of them, since total output is the joint product of varying groups of people.

Companies use grade and step systems for factory or clerical jobs that are simple but not suitable for piecework. In these systems, types of work are named and have precise duties. There are numbered steps or classes within each job, and jobs may also be assigned numbered grades, increasing with skill level. Pay depends on job or grade and step. New hires normally start at the step corresponding to their experience and progress upward. In some companies, the progression occurs automatically at fixed time intervals, provided the worker performs adequately. Elsewhere, progress may depend on mastery of certain skills. It usually takes six months to several years to reach a job's top step.

For work where tasks are varied and performance is difficult to measure, companies replace job steps with pay intervals called ranges, a job's pay being restricted to its range. Grade and range systems are common, especially in salaried jobs. Each level of pay within a range corresponds to a fixed level of skill or experience, however subjective the association between pay and accomplishment. New hires are normally paid at the minimum or in the bottom third of the range, and raises advance them through the range as they gain experience. Someone fully competent at a job is supposed to be paid at its midpoint. The upper half of the range is used to reward excellence and long service. People at the maximum are said to have "maxed out," for they are supposed to get a raise only when the maximum is increased. Compensation managers do not like to have too many workers at the maximum, for raises are an important incentive. Nevertheless, in many companies, regular raises push pay to the maximum, so that it is an important instrument for controlling labor costs. (Truly exceptional workers may be paid more than the maximum.)[1] Pay ranges are usually wide, the maximum often being one and a half times the minimum and sometimes much more. The relative width of ranges usually increases with grade, allowing room for rewarding performance. There is often considerable overlap between the ranges of successive job grades, for midpoints may increase by 8 percent or less from one grade to the next. The great width of the ranges does not imply that the pay structure is loose. On the contrary, the correspondence between pay and skill, performance, and experience can be quite regimented. Ranges are made wide to permit recognition of superior performance.

Despite the flexibility allowed by wide ranges, grade and range systems have the drawback that they interfere with job transfers. Some large companies use transfers to familiarize managers with diverse aspects of the organization. These "developmental lateral moves" sometimes involve switches to lower level jobs that employees resist as demotions, so a few companies attempted to reduce this artificial barrier by widening the ranges and diminishing the number of grades, giving rise to what was known as "broad banding."

Certain large companies tried to achieve greater flexibility through pay-for-knowledge schemes, which replace job descriptions and grades with bundles of skills that a person is certified as having mastered. As employees add new skills, they advance in grade and pay. The pay ranges for these schemes are often narrow. Because pay-for-knowledge schemes do not associate pay with particular jobs, they do not impede transfers.

The schemes I have described do not include all structures. For instance, those for retail salesclerks often specify a schedule of increases, but say nothing about wage levels. A clerk's pay is determined by the wage at the time of hire and subsequent raises. These systems are called "floating progressions" and are meant to accommodate flexible hiring pay, a matter discussed in Chapter 17. Many associations of lawyers, accountants, architects, or other professionals have a pay structure similar to that of academic departments. Tenure corresponds to partnership, which is the top grade, and grades for nonpartners (called associates) are defined by years since graduation from professional school. Some firms pay the same to all people in one grade; others differentiate according to merit or contribution. Partners earn the surplus remaining after all other employees are paid. Such a simple system is possible when the professionals in a firm all do similar work.

Many companies have separate pay structures for various classes of employees, such as executives, exempts, nonexempts, and hourly or production workers. Executives, of course, are the highest levels of management. Their total compensation is usually not downwardly rigid, as they share risks with company owners and are often themselves important owners. "Exempts" are employees who are not executives yet do not have to be paid the overtime premium required by the Federal Wages and Hours Statute of 1938. "Nonexempts" are salaried employees who must be paid the overtime premium. They are usually clerical or technical workers. Though common, the terminology is at first confusing, because executives are overtime exempt and production workers are nonexempt. In most large companies, the jobs of each class are graded, with 3 or more grades and with pay ranges for each grade. Companies may have from one to more than four classes, and there may be 30 or more grades in total.

Large corporations usually have a common structure for all high-level employees within the United States, in order to ease transfers among locations. Often each production facility within a large company has its own internal structure applying to all employees below top management. Companies separate the structures because they want pay to depend on local labor market conditions and on plant and divisional financial success. In a few corporations, I found that neighboring plants belonging to different divisions had distinct structures, causing tension between them.

A crucial element of most internal structures is the process of classifying jobs into grades, a sensitive issue given that grade influences pay and status. The grading process is vulnerable to manipulation and favoritism, since many jobs may be filled by only one person even in fairly large organizations. Some companies follow well-known systems published by professional and trade associations. Classification is supposed to order jobs according to labor market value and to assign similar status to jobs of similar value. Because many jobs are specific to one firm, classification systems must assign values to all jobs by extrapolating from "benchmark" jobs with verifiable average market prices. Some of the extrapolation methods apply statistical and mathematical methods.

6.2 Incidence of Types of Structure

Within my sample, a structure with pay grades and ranges was the most common (Table 6.1). Many companies had different types of structures for different categories of workers, and sometimes I did not learn about the structure for all categories. Most who used piece rates manufactured either guns or apparel. Grades and steps applied usually to factory workers. The companies with broad bands were large diversified corporations, and the bands applied to salaried workers.

The formality of pay structures depended on company size and whether employees were unionized. Labor unions imposed formal structures for their members in all the firms where I interviewed. Among nonunion firms, the formality of structure increased sharply with size. In small firms, the owner or boss knew everyone well enough to settle pay issues, and employees usually performed diverse tasks, so that jobs were vague. In larger organizations, jobs were usually narrower, and no one person could know everyone well. Supervisors knew their subordinates, but different supervisors might apply different standards. There was a critical company size, of about 75 employees, above which formal structure was essential. I base this conclusion mainly on managers' opinions, but

TABLE 6.1   Incidence of types of formal structure (applies to 159 businesses)

Type of structure	Number of businesses
Normal grades and ranges	140
Grades and steps	13
Grades and ranges with broad bands	10
Piece rates	8
Flat pay rates for each job	6
Floating progressions	5
Pay for knowledge	5
Professional associations with years since graduation as grades	4

TABLE 6.2   Size and formality of structure of nonunion firms

Type of structure	Number of businesses with			
	0–50 employees	51–100 employees	101–500 employees	More than 500 employees
Informal	28	8	3	1
Formal	9	8	31	38

another bit of evidence is Table 6.2, in which the number of employees is that of the overall company, not just of the business unit where I interviewed. I judge a structure to be formal if pay was governed by definite rules known to the personnel.[2]

6.3 Exempt Workers

The category of overtime exempt employees deserves explanation, for exempt workers are numerous and absorb a large proportion of the compensation budget in many firms. The qualifications for exempt status are specified by federal law and require, for instance, that workers receive a certain minimum salary, spend a certain amount of time on nonclerical work, or have a decision-making position with people reporting to them. Managers, salespeople, and scientists are usually exempt, as are many engineers. The category may be inflated artificially, for some companies take advantage of ambiguities in the legal definition to misclassify employees as exempt in order to circumvent the overtime rules. In many companies, 25 to 40 percent or more of the work force is exempt. The proportion varies widely and increases with company size. Table 6.3 gives an idea of the relation between the proportion of exempt employees and the size of the operating unit within my sample. Most of the companies in the table were in manufacturing and finance. The proportion of exempts was low in the retail sector, being less than 5 percent in two large supermarket chains.

Because the pay of salaried exempts does not depend on the number of hours they work, companies can reduce the hourly cost of exempt labor by laying off some and having the rest work longer hours. During the recession, many companies did just that (section 13.10).

6.4 Why Have Structure?

Many of my initial interviews were devoted to the rationale for internal structure, as I was not familiar with it and was surprised to learn that nonunion employers chose to impose bureaucratic constraints on their decision making. I here report what I learned from these early interviews. The material applies to the primary sector, for internal structure was less of an issue in the secondary sector (Chapter 17).

OVERVIEW OF INTERVIEW EVIDENCE

Employers stressed the importance of structure for internal equity. Inequities can be felt not only by employees doing the same job but by those at different levels within a company hierarchy. For instance, it is important for supervisors' authority and morale that they be paid more than subordinates.

The provision of incentives is another function of pay structures. Maintaining pay gaps between successive job levels encourages employees to seek promo-

TABLE 6.3 Proportion of exempt employees (applies to 57 businesses)

Firm size	Number of firms with			
	≤10% exempt	11%–30% exempt	31%–50% exempt	≥51% exempt
≤ 100 employees	3	2	2	2
101–1,000 employees	1	7	6	0
≥ 1,001 employees	2	13	7	12

TABLE 6.4   Frequency of reasons given for formal structure (applies to 51 businesses)

Reason	Number of businesses	Percentage of businesses
Internal equity, internal harmony, fairness, and good morale	35	69
External equity or comparison with market pay rates	10	20
Clarification of duties and promotion possibilities	8	16
Administrative control	5	10
Union avoidance	3	6
Avoidance of discrimination suits	3	6

tion. More broadly, structure defines and clarifies the organization of a firm, helping employees understand the promotion ladder and what they must do to succeed. Position on the ladder serves as a status symbol and reward. Some structures, such as piecework, contain explicit incentives.

Structure is also a powerful administrative tool. It instructs managers how much to pay and helps avoid favoritism and overpayment. It reduces strife and negotiation costs by determining pay differentials according to clear and generally accepted rules, which give an impression of fairness and objectivity. It makes it easier to identify the pool of candidates appropriate for promotion or transfer into an open job. Finally, structure gives standardized labels to those jobs that are common to many firms and so eases comparison of pay levels among companies. The relative importance of the various advantages of the system are reflected in Table 6.4.

MANAGERS' EXPLANATIONS

The most interesting comments on the rationale for structure were made by managers who had introduced their system fairly recently. Most focused on the virtues of fairness, objectivity, and internal equity.

> At one time, we had no such pay grades, and there was lots of dissension. There were questions about why is he making more than me. Arguments over small amounts of money took up too much time. This was all that was discussed during annual reviews, which distracted from what really should have been discussed, which was the quality of the work.
>
> —Founding partner of an architecture firm with 45 employees

When I arrived [five years ago], personnel administration was very haphazard. The managers would hire people for as little as they could. They would try to guess from an applicant's background how little they needed to pay to hire him. The result was a lot of inequity. . . . This was bad for morale. People had issues. They were discontent. This led to problems with productivity, attendance, turnover, and performance.

—Operations manager of a nonunion wholesale distribution company with 170 employees

You need objectivity to protect the manager and to give people the sense of control stemming from knowing what the [company's] objective is. An employee's objective should not be just to make the boss like him.

—President of a nonunion manufacturing company and ESOP with 240 employees

The jobs are in a fixed relationship with each other. The relationships have a history. The important thing is to pay consistently by some sort of yardstick. As soon as you change the system, you have a problem. The system was changed in 1967, when a factor was reinterpreted, changing the relationship among jobs. The shit hit the fan. The whole system was affected and had to be thrown out. There were grievances and uproar for a year. Productivity was affected. We wanted something simple and easily understood.

—Human resource officer of a 400-employee division of a large nonunion manufacturing company

The job grades and ranges are set nationally. People are often relocated. We worry about pay comparisons across the country, for people talk to each other. Inequities can lead to complaints and jealousy. . . . We want pay to be associated with accomplishment and contribution rather than favoritism.

—Director of compensation at the headquarters of a consumer products firm with 8,000 employees

Employers said that structure is useful when comparing internal with market pay rates.

We have job classifications with grades within them—milling machine operator with little experience, etc. We had an outside consultant help us with the classification scheme. We needed outside help for this because we wanted categories that correspond to general practices in industry. They make pay comparisons easier.

—Owner and founder of a nonunion manufacturing company with 500 employees

I have recently introduced a pay structure at an apparel company in North Carolina. . . . The company was worried about underpayment and internal equity. The reason for grades is internal and external equity. To make comparisons with the outside, you use benchmark positions and you look at average pay levels in the community for them.

—Head of human resources of a nonunion consumer products company with 1,500 employees

Other employers emphasized the importance to incentives of fairness and clear definitions of duties and of the promotion ladder.

> It is better to be structured and fair. If people know precisely what their job is, they will try to get their performance up.
>
> —Human resource officer of 270 headquarters staff of a unionized food products company with 1,000 employees

> The company has a system of job classifications. They serve in part to define the organization of the company by defining responsibilities and so avoiding having everyone try to do the same things.
>
> —Vice president of administration of a unionized manufacturing company with 900 employees

> Inequity has a tendency to lead to morale problems. But we are talking too much in terms of negatives. One of the positive benefits of a job evaluation and grade system is prestige—that you are able to say, "I've achieved X." We use the words "job content" too much in speaking of job evaluation. "I'm a 21" is a morale booster. You can take away title and pay, but not job grade. The job grade system also gives incentives, for you can aspire to the highest job.
>
> —Human resource manager of a nonunion manufacturing company with 6,000 employees

Employers valued structure as an administrative tool for controlling managers and costs.

> The purpose [of the structure introduced] was to eliminate inequities. Also, no one knew pay levels or even company averages. Pay had been haphazard and paternalistic. Some people were underpaid and many overpaid. We had assemblers earning $30,000 to $40,000 a year [about twice market value]. Because so many were overpaid, the company's average pay level was high by industry standards.
>
> —Human resource manager of a nonunion manufacturing company with 80 employees

> Grades . . . tell managers how to pay people. They also tell managers who within the company is qualified for an open position—those in the same grade or in nearby grades.
>
> —Human resource manager in a corporation in the service sector with 135,000 employees

Pay structure had drawbacks, mentioned mainly in connection with broad banding. Managers said that job grades encourage people to interpret their duties too narrowly, and to become preoccupied with grade as status, discouraging communication between different levels of the hierarchy, breeding jealousy, and interfering with teamwork. I have already mentioned that grades sometimes obstruct lateral job transfers. Although broad bands allow more flexibility, they too have disadvantages. For instance, they make it more difficult to compare pay levels between firms, and pay floats to the top of the bands, leading to overpayment. There seemed to be no single correct way to reconcile the conflicting objectives.

6.5 Why Have Internal Equity?

Managers claimed that internal equity was vital, since perceptions of inequity and favoritism embitter and antagonize employees. I suspect that the principal cause of managers' preoccupation with morale is experience with inequities.

OVERVIEW OF INTERVIEW EVIDENCE

Table 6.5 summarizes comments on the significance of internal equity made by managers of primary-sector workers.

Headhunters were an additional source of information about the value to companies of internal equity, for 12 of 15 headhunters interviewed stressed its importance. They were conscious of the force of internal pay comparisons because of their impact on the negotiation of clients' pay rates.

It might be thought that internal equity issues could be avoided by keeping pay secret. Some employers do reprimand or fire workers for revealing their pay to co-workers. Nevertheless, in many workplaces, workers tell one another how much they make. In a large majority of the companies where I inquired about this topic, managers believed that employees shared pay information freely, as Table 6.6 indicates. It is not clear whether employees actually knew one another's pay or managers only believed they did because occasional sharing led to complaints.

MANAGERS' EXPLANATIONS

I heard many descriptions of the consequences of inequity.

It just came out in the office that the MSW [an employee holding a master of social work degree] is earning less than one of the nurses. The nurse is paid $52,500

TABLE 6.5   Why internal pay equity is important, according to managers of primary-sector workers (applies to 41 businesses)

Reason	Number of businesses	Percentage of businesses
Internal harmony and morale	32	78
Job performance	20	49
Turnover	10	24
Avoidance of discrimination suits	7	17

TABLE 6.6 Managers' views of whether employees share pay information

Type of statement	Number of businesses	Percentage of businesses
Most or all employees know one another's pay	47	87
Few or no employees know one another's pay	6	11
Do not know	1	2
Total number of companies responding	54	100

without benefits, whereas the MSW started out at $45,000 and has come up to $50,000. I have paid her an additional $5,000, but she had to work extra for that. The MSW's reaction to this difference was tremendous. There was envy, suspicion, and a feeling of being devalued. "My work is as good as hers. I am better in some ways. Why am I being paid less?" I spent four hours talking with her about this.

—One of two partners owning a psychiatric clinic with 17 employees

I have had difficulties with people receiving different pay who had similar skills and worked in different parts of the building. . . . They felt underpaid and under-valued. It was partly a matter of ego. They felt gypped. Everyone feels underpaid anyway. They feel they are entitled to more. . . . Inequity is interpreted as cheating. Fairness is fairness. There is still a place for fairness in the business world.

—Director of a community service organization with 150 employees

People need self-respect, the feeling that the company needs them and cares about them. Internal equity is part of that. If people see that things are out of whack and that there is lack of uniformity, morale goes to hell as does the system, and whatever motivation there is from pay disappears. People want control over their working environment and to be connected to something bigger than themselves, something they can identify with in the most significant part of life. All that is broken by unfairness.

—Human resource officer of a 400-employee division of a large nonunion manufacturing company

Internal equity is very important, for you need to have your top people recognized as such. Word about pay rates gets out, and people know each other. People should feel that what they are paid relative to other people is in proportion to perfor-mance. . . . Turnover is the number one problem resulting from inequity. The next problem is poor productivity. There could be a lack of commitment to the job.

—Human resource officer of a bank with 16,000 employees

Unfairness can cause upheaval within an organization and lead to dysfunctional activities. People want to be treated fairly and to see that their contributions are recognized and that this is done on a consistent basis from one location to another and from one profession to another. We have had focus groups with employees to find out what was important to them and to locate flaws in the compensation system. Internal equity was found to be key.

—High-level human resource manager in a unionized manufacturing company with 27,000 employees

HEADHUNTERS' COMMENTS

Headhunters' business dealings brought them in contact with companies' internal structures.

Pay sometimes gets in the way of arranging job changes. Bigger companies have rigid pay structures. They will not bring in new people for more than comparable existing employees. If they did, five or six people might quit. Programmers can easily learn each other's pay through the computer. This rigidity can ruin a whole deal.

—Headhunter specializing in computer programmers

Inequity causes disharmony. Employees want more money if a new person is paid more than they are. If their requests are ignored, the company starts having complaints or people start looking to leave. They say, "I'm not appreciated." They disrupt the office. If someone is brought in for a lot less, the others are not threatened and the difference is ignored. Initially, the new employee is not disgruntled. He would be after three or four months.

—Headhunter specializing in international placement

6.6 Internal Equity and Wage Flattening

David Romer (1992) has formulated a theory to explain why companies do not restrict pay increases to the best workers (section 10.2). He proposes that companies cannot let pay fully reflect productivity differences, because workers do not take these into account when making internal pay comparisons. He claims his theory explains why firms prefer highly productive workers and try to enforce secrecy about pay. Researchers have found substantial evidence of egalitarian tendencies in pay administration (appendix to this chapter). Although I did not collect data on the relation of individual pay to productivity, I did hear a great deal related to the topic and report, as an aside, my conclusions.

Equality of the wage and marginal product applies to wages within one job or category of employee, not to individual workers, and is normally brought about by adjustment of the number of employees in a classification, not by changing pay rates. When making hiring and layoff decisions, employers sometimes compare marginal product with labor compensation plus the cost of severance benefits or of hiring and training (section 13.5). Although productivity differentials among individuals doing similar work are to some extent reflected in their pay, no attempt is made to equate pay and productivity differentials, nor is it necessary to do so, for workers do not normally know their marginal product. Even managers have difficulty estimating them. Pay differentials are determined by weighing their impact on incentives and internal equity, and these considerations normally lead to a flattening, relative to marginal products, of wages within one labor type. This flattening applies strictly to workers within one job or labor classification, not across jobs. It is normally not true that workers in low-level jobs are paid more than their marginal product, whereas workers in high-level jobs are paid less. Such disparities would induce employers to dismiss some low-level employees and hire more high-level ones.

6.7 Summary

Internal pay structures determine the relations among the pay of different workers within one establishment by fixing pay according to criteria that are accepted by the work force as reasonable and impartial. The main function of internal structure is to ensure internal pay equity, which is critical for good morale. In addition, structure is a tool of administrative control, makes clear lines of promotion and other incentives, and makes it easier to compare a company's pay levels with those of other firms. Internal structure makes it difficult for a firm to lower the pay of only some of its workers.

Appendix 6A Related Literature

TYPES OF INTERNAL PAY STRUCTURE (SECTION 6.1)

Institutional labor economists stressed internal pay structure, and their descriptions may be found in Dunlop (1957), Livernash (1957), Slichter, Healy, and Livernash (1960, chap. 20), and Doeringer and Piore (1971). A great deal of information on the subject also appears in Meij (1963), Osterman, (1984a, b), and Foulkes (1980). Dunlop applies the term "key job" to what are called benchmark jobs today, designating jobs that are well defined, are common to many firms, are held by enough employees within each firm to be noticeable, and so are used for making pay comparisons among firms. He claims these jobs are important because their holders have contact with many other employees, whereas today managers emphasize the fact that benchmark jobs have market valuations. Jacoby (1984, 1985) describes the history of internal labor markets and the pay structures they entail. Internal structure is described in detail in textbooks on compensation (Rock, 1972; Kochan and Barocci, 1985; Hills, 1987; and Milkovich and Newman, 1990), and Lazear (1995) discusses internal structure from the point of view of economic theory, with an emphasis on incentives.

Doeringer and Piore stress that most hiring is done into low-level jobs and that employees rise through the internal hierarchy. However, I noticed that some people are hired at all levels, especially into overtime-exempt positions, an impression substantiated by the work of Lazear (1992), Baker, Gibbs and Holmstrom (1993; 1994a, b), and Baker and Holmstrom (1995). Doeringer and Piore emphasize that pay rates are assigned to jobs rather than to people, which seems to imply a narrow association between pay and jobs. However, the pay ranges of grade and range systems are usually quite wide. These discrepancies may be due to the authors' focus on factory jobs. In many manufacturing companies, most experienced production workers are at the maximum for their position, so that their pay is indeed defined by the job. The situation is different for higher-level work, where individuals' pay is dispersed over the range. This observation is confirmed by Baker, Gibbs, and Holmstrom (1994a, b), who found that the pay for managerial workers varied widely in the same job category within the firm they studied. Similar observations were made by Wilson (1996) in a study of pay in two firms.

Levine (1993a) studies the response of internal structure to changes in relative market pay rates for different jobs. He finds that changes in market differentials have little impact on internal differentials for closely related jobs, but that the impact is greater for dissimilar jobs.

WHY HAVE STRUCTURE? (SECTION 6.4)

Reasons for structure are discussed in Dunlop (1957), Livernash (1957), Slichter, Healy, and Livernash (1960, chap. 20), Doeringer and Piore (1971), Foulkes (1980), and Frank (1985) and also in compensation textbooks, such as Rock (1972), Kochan and Barocci (1985), Hills (1987), and Milkovich and Newman (1990). The authors of the first three works emphasize the role of structure in dealing with labor unions. Doeringer and Piore emphasize the role of internal pay structure in reinforcing hierarchies within firms. Internal equity is stressed by Frank and in the texts of Hills, Kochan and Barocci, and Milkovich and Newman and is certainly not neglected by the other authors. Milgrom and Roberts (1988) discuss the importance of having rules govern compensation so as to reduce wasteful attempts by subordinates to cultivate good relations with superiors.

Baker and Holmstrom (1995, p. 259) find that the internal wage structure they study is sufficiently flexible to allow individual performance to be rewarded; Gibbs (1995) reports in detail on how this pay structure is used to provide incentives.

A great deal of empirical work has been done on the impact of internal inequity, most of it experimental tests of Adams's (1965) equity theory. Adams proposed that workers judge equity according to the ratio of rewards to inputs, where rewards are payments and other benefits and inputs are effort, contribution, and productivity. He said that differences in ratios among co-workers cause distress, which workers take steps to relieve. If the ratios differ among hourly wage or salaried workers, those with higher ratios work harder than those with lower ratios, narrowing the gaps by increasing inputs. Among piece-rate workers, those with higher ratios produce fewer and higher-quality items than people with lower ratios, reducing the gaps by reducing outputs. The large literature on tests of these implications is reviewed in Lawler (1971, chap. 8) and Martin (1981). The experimental literature provides strong support for the implications of the theory for piecework and less support for hourly or salaried work. I know of no field-work done on the subject, though Greenberg (1988) has done experiments on inequity among actual office workers, and Rees (1993) remarked that internal equity proved important in his studies of business. Although managers claim that inequity causes turmoil, I have found no published accounts of such strife.

Studies of two-tier wage systems, cited in Appendix 9A (section 9.4), bear on the effects of internal inequity and show that two-tier wage systems worsen job attitudes. The impact on productivity has been little studied.

There is a considerable body of evidence that group performance is improved by making pay more egalitarian. Experimental psychologists have found that greater equality improves the cooperation and productivity of work groups. It has also been found experimentally that people are egalitarian when they are told to distribute pay among a group so as to avoid conflict. This literature is reviewed in Greenberg (1982, pp. 418–422) and Deutsch (1985, 1986). There is some evidence that increases in equality improve the performance of actual organizations. Cowherd and Levine (1992) find a negative relation between product quality and the dispersion of pay within corporate business units. Pfeffer and Langton (1993) find that among college faculty, the greater the salary variation within departments, the lower is job satisfaction, research productivity, and research collaboration. Frank (1985), Lazear (1989), and Levine (1991) propose theoretical economic models in which greater uniformity of rewards increases productivity by encouraging cooperation.

Internal equity does not necessarily require that pay be proportional to contribution, despite Adams' theory. I found ample evidence that pay differentials often do not fully reflect differences in productivity. For instance, employers were concerned that if raises were inadequate or pay was cut, the best workers would leave, and this concern indicates that these employees contributed the most, relative to their pay. There has been little study of the extent to which actual pay reflects productivity. Bishop (1987) finds, in U.S. data, that pay rates and raises fall far short of fully compensating for productivity differentials. Frank (1984) uses as evidence of egalitarianism the fact that salespeople's commissions increase less rapidly than the net revenues they generate for firms. Campbell and Kamlani (1997) find that employers believe it would be unwise to make pay differentials fully reflect differences in productivity.

7

EXTERNAL PAY STRUCTURE

Pay levels in different firms are only loosely linked, unlike pay rates within company operating units. Whereas resentment and jealousy compel internal structure, the main ties among pay levels in different firms are the forces of supply and demand. Each company adjusts its overall pay level so as to be able to recruit and retain a labor force of adequate quality. External pay comparisons do not have the emotional impact that internal ones have. Jealousy arises mainly among workers in close contact who are evaluated by the same employer. Workers are usually not in close contact with employees doing similar work at other firms and do not have precise knowledge of pay levels outside their workplace. Company life isolates employees from the external labor market, for many jobs are so specific to one firm that market comparisons are difficult, and firms discourage employees from looking for work elsewhere and so learning their market value. I found that labor unions and close-knit communities overcame this isolation, but their influence extended to only a small fraction of the labor force. Furthermore, pay varies so widely among firms that full knowledge would not necessarily tell people how much they should be paid.

Market forces are not strong enough to tie pay rates of different firms tightly together. Employers I interviewed believed they had considerable discretion in choosing the pay of nonunion employees. They faced a trade-off between pay on the one hand and turnover, ease of hiring, and worker quality on the other, and the choice of pay level depended on a firm's needs and financial state and on management judgment. Despite the weakness of market forces, pay levels in different firms are roughly similar. Relations among these levels form an external pay structure, analogous to internal structure, though not nearly so restrictive.[1]

Although I did not inquire about the reasons for the weakness of labor market forces, this topic has been studied by institutional labor economists, such as Myers and MacLaurin (1943) and Reynolds (1951). Judging from what they say and the little information I gathered on the subject, the influence of supply and demand is blunted by differing internal structures, by strong ties between workers and their employers, and by the difficulty of finding new jobs and gaining acceptance in a new firm.

7.1 Forces Creating External Structure

I devoted considerable energy to learning what determines the overall level of a pay structure. The subject was difficult to broach in interviews, since only new companies are unrestricted by precedent in setting pay, and I never found a quick and effective way to inquire about the topic. The best approaches were to ask employers why they did not allow pay to drift lower relative to the market or why they collected information on pay at other firms. Employers were aware of where their pay stood in the market distribution, felt they had some choice in the matter, and could explain why they wanted their pay rates to be what they were. There was clearly a shift in emphasis between internal and external pay differentials. Managers feared internal inequities because of the uproar they caused, whereas underpayment relative to the external market implied high turnover and difficulties in attracting quality workers and usually prompted only vague references to a possible impact on morale.

The primary and secondary sectors differed in the relative importance of the various influences on overall pay levels. For primary-sector employers, turnover, hiring, and the quality of the work force were important and morale less significant, though a consideration. Secondary-sector employers hardly mentioned morale and turnover and saw the ability to hire as the main influence, since they expected high turnover and constantly hired people for short-term jobs.

It may seem perplexing that morale should have so little influence on the long-term level of pay, since fear of hurting morale is the main reason for not cutting pay during a recession. Probably if there were clear and precise market pay standards known to workers, below-standard pay would severely damage morale.

OVERVIEW OF INTERVIEW EVIDENCE

Tables 7.1 and 7.2 summarize nonunion employers' views of influences on pay levels.

I asked businesspeople whether they had ever paid a group of workers too little, and if so, what the consequences had been. Some had done so, and their experiences are summarized in tables 7.3 and 7.4. Underpayment resulted from

TABLE 7.1   Influences on the level of pay relative to that in other firms: nonunion primary-sector firms (applies to 99 businesses)

Influence	Number of businesses	Percentage of businesses
Turnover	57	58
Ability to hire	56	57
Quality of the work force	52	53
Morale	32	32
Fear of unionization	7	7

TABLE 7.2   Influences on the level of pay relative to that in other firms: nonunion secondary-sector firms (applies to 40 businesses)

Influence	Number of businesses	Percentage of businesses
Turnover	11	28
Ability to hire	39	98
Quality of the work force	20	50
Morale	1	3
Fear of unionization	0	0

TABLE 7.3   Consequences of underpayment in primary-sector firms (applies to 18 businesses)

Consequence	Number of businesses
Excessive turnover	11
Difficulty in hiring	5
Poor morale	5

TABLE 7.4   Consequences of underpayment in secondary-sector firms (applies to 4 businesses)

Consequence	Number of businesses
Excessive turnover	0
Difficulty in hiring	4
Poor morale	0

TABLE 7.5   The effect on productivity of the level of pay relative to that in other firms (applies to primary-sector businesses)

Effect	Number of businesses
No effect	14
Higher pay increases productivity	7
The effect cannot be measured and so is ignored	2
Total number of businesses	23

administrative error in the primary sector and in the secondary sector from experiments by retail companies with cuts in hiring pay.

Primary-sector employers were divided in their views on the effect of relative pay levels on productivity, as Table 7.5 indicates. The effect has to do with mood and motivation rather than the quality of the work force; I was careful to distinguish the two.

MANAGERS' EXPLANATIONS

The main emphasis in the discussion of pay levels was on the ability to recruit and retain high-quality employees.

> We pay higher than average starting pay because we want people to stay if they work out. By paying well, the company builds up loyalty. If we paid new hires a lot less, they might look for work elsewhere. You might keep them by matching outside offers, but you don't always get a chance to do that. Once people start looking, they are likely to leave no matter what you do. You don't want to put them in a frame of mind where they start looking.
>
> —Partner of an accounting firm with 8 employees

I now have a surplus of applicants. I could offer the minimum wage and do fine, but I offer a little more as starting pay, because I want a higher-quality employee than I would get for it.

—Manager of a fast-food restaurant with 20 employees

I feel through experience that the $12.50 pay rate is right. . . . If I paid $10.50, only bums would come in looking for work.

—Director of operations of a nonunion trucking company with 75 employees

We are not a high-paying company relative to the local competition. . . . If we fell too far behind, morale would suffer and good employees would start to quit. Some do anyway. Pay is not a key motivator nor necessarily the most important aspect of a job, but higher pay does attract people.

—Human resource manager of a nonunion machine shop with 225 employees

We pay well in part because we don't want employees to come in, gain skills and experience, and then leave for more money.

—Human resource manager of a nonunion consumer products manufacturer with 600 employees

The company has always been market driven. The object of being market driven is to recruit and retain the very best employees. For this reason, the company's pay level is above average, though not at the top in its industry. If another company really wants one of your employees, it will get him. For this reason, it is silly to be a top payer.

—Director of compensation of a nonunion manufacturing company with 18,000 employees

A few employers mentioned a tension between the strength of the internal structure and ties to the labor market.

Internal pay is important, probably too important. Now, the company is more externally focused. The internal focus leads to overpaying, because of the constant ratcheting effect of false comparisons. There is title inflation and grade creep and within-range pay creep. People get to the maximum in their grade and then have to be promoted.

—Director of compensation at a unionized manufacturing corporation with 180,000 employees

Some employers stressed the effect of pay on morale or the probability of unionization.

We are not eager to pay a lot, but we have to give a decent living standard. It is a matter of being decent and it helps morale. We prefer that employees be happy. If they are happy working here, they are more willing to be flexible about when they work, they are more likely to stay an extra five minutes to get stuff done, make suggestions, and help the company grow.

—Personnel officer of a nonunion manufacturing company with 80 employees

We do surveys to be sure that we are treating people fairly. External equity is for fairness, not for recruiting. . . . The fairness issue vis-à-vis the outside is good for human relations. It keeps the union out.

—Head of human resources of a nonunion manufacturing company with 1,200 employees

Incidents of underpayment led above all to high turnover and difficulties with hiring, though low morale was sometimes mentioned.

Earlier this year, I tried starting people at the minimum wage [of $4.27], but increased it to $4.75, because the minimum wage wasn't bringing people in and what it did bring didn't last.

—Manager of a fast-food restaurant with 28 employees

Pay was too low in the customer service department in 1985. We did not realize it, because we attached the wrong grades to jobs. This was discovered through a wage survey. A meltdown occurred. People left after working for only two weeks. There was an enormous amount of turnover, lots of complaining, and job performance was affected too. This situation was stopped by changing the job descriptions and grades.

—Human resource officer of 270 headquarters staff of a unionized food products company with 1,000 employees

All of the clerical positions were underpaid in 1987–88. . . . We got behind as [a Connecticut city] switched from manufacturing to service jobs. We had massive turnover, but did not have bad morale. Turnover among clerical employees went from 30 to 35 percent down to 20 to 22 percent after the correction.

—Head of human resources of a nonunion consumer products company with 1,500 employees

In the late 1970s and early 1980s, . . . computer systems people were in short supply and internal pay rates were low relative to the market. The company couldn't recruit, there was a morale problem as people came to realize they were underpaid, and people were distracted by looking for another job.

—Human resource official at a partially unionized manufacturing company with 12,000 employees

Managers had widely varying views on the link between pay level and productivity.

If my men felt they were being paid less than their market worth, they would say, "Why should I make the effort if he is not paying me enough?" and they would be less productive.

—Owner and founder of a nonunion manufacturing company with 40 employees

Our people are working hard—at peak efficiency. They would not be able to work harder if they were asked to do so. Cutting pay might demotivate them. Starting them out at lower pay would not demotivate them. Decreasing starting pay might mean that the firm would get fewer good people, but it would not get less effort. Increasing pay would not make them work harder.

—Managing partner of a law firm with 200 employees

The relationship between pay and productivity is unknown. Pay is determined by the need to attract and retain employees. You pay what you need to.

—Vice president of human resources for a nonunion manufacturing company with 95,000 employees

7.2 Sources of Information about Pay at Other Firms

Employers devoted considerable attention to learning about pay levels at other firms, in order to predict the impact of pay decisions on recruitment and retention of nonunion employees and to buttress arguments made during negotiations with labor unions.

The resources devoted to information gathering increased with firm size. Small companies usually relied on informal sources, such as word of mouth and what job applicants said they earned on previous jobs. Medium-sized companies with fifty to several hundred employees depended more on purchased survey data, and many large companies made their own surveys. Most medium and large companies shared general compensation information with labor market competitors.

The scope of a company's inquiries depended on their purpose. For unionized firms, the relevant comparison was usually the product market competition, since surveys were used to support arguments about the danger of losing market share. If the survey concerned nonunion employees, then the comparison group was usually the competition in the labor market. The geographic scope was usually national for executives and high-level professional and exempt employees, often recruited from all over the country; regional surveys were used for most other exempt employees; and surveys for nonexempt and hourly employees were usually local. The increase in geographic mobility with rank is relevant to the effect of unemployment on migration, a topic discussed in section 18.9.

TABLE 7.6   Sources of knowledge of external pay rates (applies to 155 businesses, of which 26 were in the secondary sector)

Number of employees	Number using informal sources	Number using formal sources
0 to 50	34	17
51 to 200	15	28
201 or more	10	67

OVERVIEW OF INTERVIEW EVIDENCE

Table 7.6 shows clearly the relation between firm size and methods used to collect information about pay at other firms. The larger the firm, the more thorough and formal the means. (Some firms used informal methods for management and formal methods for lower-level employees.) The table does not include temporary help agencies and similar companies. Temporary agencies and guard services did not consult one another about pay, since sharing pay information would help rivals bid against them. They depended on informal sources and on trickery. For instance, they might have their own employees apply for work at other agencies or make "marketing calls" to them while posing as potential clients.

MANAGERS' EXPLANATIONS

There was tremendous variation in the intensity of effort devoted to learning about pay rates. A few employers claimed they were isolated.

> Now, I don't know if I am above the competition, because I learn about pay from job applicants and I haven't hired lately. I don't use wage surveys and don't ask around about pay.
>
> —Nonunion, site-work contractor with 20 employees

> Entry-level wages are adjusted in a vacuum as far as the labor market goes. . . . What we pay is never important for getting people. . . . We don't use wage surveys. We get an idea of what others are paying from job applications. No one ever calls up to survey our wages.
>
> —Owner of a nonunion manufacturing company with 20 employees

Many small companies depended on experience and casual contacts for pay information.

We make no use of wage and salary surveys. We get information about pay from what applicants want. . . . We don't call around inquiring about pay rates either. We get an idea from applicants and what people who leave get.

—One of three partners owning an advertising agency with 9 employees

I don't keep track of what other companies pay. When I interview job applicants, I find out what they were paid. Also, I know drivers, and drivers talk. Pay levels become general knowledge.

—Part-owner of a nonunion trucking company with 14 drivers

I don't do wage surveys. I look at the number of my applicants to see if I am paying enough.

—Manager of a fast-food restaurant with 20 employees

Most intermediate and some small-sized companies bought survey information and some made informal inquiries among other employers.

I do wage shops. That is, I call up the competition in the area . . . and find out what they are paying as starting wages.

—Manager of a fast-food restaurant with 30 employees

Entry-level pay is wage-survey oriented. In order to set the pay of newly hired lawyers just out of law school, everyone watches a few big law firms to see how much they pay. I call other law firms and ask about the pay of new hires. You have to get networked. Not all firms will share such information. Starting salaries are also published in a book published by the Harvard Law School. . . . We also learn through interviews of job applicants about how much other firms pay older lawyers.

—Personnel director of a law firm with 60 employees

I use surveys from the CBIA, AAIM, and the Tool and Die Makers Association, and many others. I don't ask around or do my own survey. I also learn about pay levels from job applicants.

—Vice president of human resources of a nonunion manufacturing company with 260 employees

Large companies could afford to make formal surveys of their own as well as to buy the results of other surveys.

We go to the top 25 consumer products companies in the country and ask them in a blind survey, "What are you doing for range changes and the merit budget, what is your budget for promotions, what is your increase matrix, and so on?"

—High-level human resource official in a 3,000-employee, largely nonunion division of a huge consumer products company

We use a whole library of surveys, local, national, industry specific, and specific to a skill group, such as MIS [management information systems] professionals, human resource people, accountants, materials and logistics specialists, or engineers. We might call around to other companies for a unique position.

—High-level human resource manager in a unionized manufacturing company with 27,000 employees

Managers in 20 medium-sized and large companies mentioned that the relevant geographic scope for surveys increased with job rank.

We use both local and national surveys. On occasion, we conduct our own survey. Whether the survey is local or national depends on the nature of the job and where we recruit people for those jobs. The labor market is local for hourly and salaried nonexempt employees. These are the production people, the engineering assistants, and the secretaries. The national surveys are more for professional people. The bread and butter of the company are engineers, whom we recruit nationwide.

—Human resource manager of a unionized manufacturing firm with 1,800 employees

A few managers mentioned that dealings with labor unions made the product market especially relevant.

[In assessing pay], we work from the theory of competitiveness with the product competition. This is a more powerful argument in dealing with a union.

—Human resource official in a unionized manufacturing company with 250,000 employees

7.3 The Precision of Knowledge about Pay

Employers' and workers' knowledge of external pay rates was normally vague. Although the difficulty of obtaining information explained some of the imprecision, most of it stemmed from the wide variation of pay among companies. Employers spoke of the "market wage," but there was never anything like a single market price for any kind of labor.

The information on pay gathered by employers and surveyors was normally too rough to allow them to reconstruct the internal pay structure of other firms. Companies usually reported the wage or salary of current employees holding particular jobs. Ranges and starting pay were normally not reported, though I did hear of surveys of starting pay in the fast food industry. A few employers said they reported only average wages or salaries for employees at specific steps or stages for a job and did not report the number of employees at the various job levels, since that information might help product market competitors.

I have examined several surveys. Some listed the minimum, maximum, and average of the pay rates reported; others reported the 25th and 75th percentiles.

The differences between minima and maxima were typically enormous, the minima often being one-tenth to one-half the maxima. The gaps between the 25th and 75th percentiles were often large, as may be seen from Table 7.7. It is based on surveys made throughout Connecticut by a management consulting company in the years 1993, 1994, and 1995, for 42 salaried jobs and 38 jobs paid an hourly wage. The gap is defined to be the difference between the 75th and 25th percentiles divided by the 75th percentile.

The gaps reflect variation both within and among firms, where the variation within firms arises from differences in the pay of employees doing the same job. An idea of variation across firms can be gained by restricting attention to jobs typically filled by only one worker per firm. Table 7.8 applies to the same surveys used for Table 7.7 and describes the distribution of gaps for jobs for which the average number of employees per firm was no more than 1.3.[2] The jobs were salaried. The effects of the variation in pay rates were offset to some extent by a tendency for gaps to be narrow for standard or benchmark jobs that firms use in making comparisons.[3]

I did not systematically collect numerical information on pay rates, but learned

TABLE 7.7   Distribution of gaps

Salaried jobs	
Range of gap	Number of jobs with gaps in the given range
0 to 9%	3
10% to 19%	23
20% to 29%	62
30% to 39%	36
40% to 49%	2
Hourly jobs	
Range of gap	Number of jobs with gaps in the given range
0 to 9%	4
10% to 19%	39
20% to 29%	59
30% to 39%	9
40% to 49%	3

TABLE 7.8   Distribution of gaps for salaried jobs with no more than 1.3 workers per firm

Range of gap	Number of jobs with gaps in the given range
0 to 9%	0
10% to 19%	0
20% to 29%	19
30% to 39%	20
40% to 49%	1

incidentally that rates varied greatly. For instance, each of four nonunion trucking companies in the New Haven area paid top drivers $10.50, $11.25, $12.50, and $14.00 an hour, respectively.[4] Many employers mentioned the variation of pay among companies, a phenomenon well documented in the literature on labor economics.

Although employers used compensation surveys, many complained of their imprecision and especially of the difficulty of equating their own jobs with those listed in the surveys.

> In order to find out about going rates of pay, I call around. I participate in [a well-known] survey, but this is of questionable validity. People don't lie, but it is hard to fill out the questionnaires seriously. People doing them don't have the time.
>
> —Manager of a nonunion manufacturing company with 65 employees

> We get wage surveys and participate in [a well-known survey]. But these are not very helpful, for I can never find the jobs in the company among the survey classifications.
>
> —Vice president of a unionized manufacturing company with 90 employees

> There is a wide range of pay for the same job across companies and according to circumstances. For instance, cashiers start anywhere from the minimum wage to $7.50 an hour. We are intermediate in size between mom and pop shops and the big supermarkets, so that it is hard to find comparable companies, especially for salaried jobs. These involve more responsibility at bigger companies. We pay less than supermarkets, and the higher you go on the pay scale, the more this is true. [The minimum wage was then $4.25 in Massachusetts, where the chain was located.]
>
> —General manager of a nonunion cooperative food store chain with 250 employees

Most employers believed that workers did not have a precise idea of pay rates.

> Few [workers] understand the labor market. They always know someone who is making more and they pay little attention to those making less.
>
> —Human resource manager of a nonunion manufacturing company and ESOP with 250 employees

> Existing employees generally don't recognize how well they are paid. Those looking for work are more aware of pay levels at different companies. The main comparisons are internal.
>
> —Human resource manager servicing 360 headquarters personnel of a large nonunion manufacturing company

> People don't know accurately what other companies are paying. We do the surveys.
>
> —Human resource officer of a bank with 16,000 employees

Employers recognized that they had some latitude in setting pay levels, though the extent of this freedom was difficult to ascertain. To ask about it, I had to explain that I was interested in the long-run relation of pay to market levels. Although a few employers, discussed in section 7.5, felt tightly bound by the labor market, most indicated that they had real freedom in choosing pay levels.

> Pay rates are a guessing game. You put yourself in their position and ask what you would expect.
>
> —Manager in charge of telemarketing at a publishing company with 70 employees

> If you are cheap, it is harder to attract and keep people. It is judgmental as to where to put the pay scale. If it is too low, you get second-choice or low caliber people. You want to keep people from going to your competitors. People usually know when they are underpaid, but will give you time to correct it. . . . If you are making up for underpayment, you may split your raises into two hunks, so that you can say "thank you" twice and so that people don't get unreasonable expectations from having had a huge raise.
>
> —Head of human resources of a nonunion consumer products company with 1500 employees

> There is a big spread in the surveys, so that many rates of pay can be called competitive. . . . Those doing wage surveys are having difficulty now, for there is more and more broad banding and different organizations pay for different things and there are more teams. Job descriptions often describe people anyway.
>
> —Vice president of human resources for a largely nonunion manufacturing company with 125,000 employees

7.4 Isolating Effects of Company Life

Aspects of working life insulate employees from the labor market. They develop skills and knowledge useful only to their current employer, skills called firm-specific or nontransferable human capital in labor economics. Jobs are often unique to one or a few firms, and so do not have a market price. Employers encourage company loyalty and a clubby atmosphere and favor friends and relatives of employees when hiring (section 15.6), and this ambience separates employees from the world beyond the firm. Finally, many companies discourage workers from seeking outside offers. Although it is common for workers to solicit offers and leave, it is often dangerous to accept a counteroffer and stay, for the act of having entertained an offer will have antagonized the boss. Usually firms refuse to match outside offers, though companies may raise the pay of certain categories of employees in high demand.

The importance of firm-specific human capital became clear when workers lost their jobs. Most advisers of the unemployed emphasized the importance of identifying transferable or marketable skills. The difficulty of finding a good match for a person's skills was seen as one of the factors prolonging the job search.

> An obstacle to job search is that people may have very specific skills, useful only to their former employers. Sometimes, I have trouble figuring out what useful task my clients actually performed. People with general skills involving real knowledge, such as accountants and engineers, have an easier time getting work.
>
> —Outplacement counselor

OVERVIEW OF INTERVIEW EVIDENCE

In connection with my examination of influences on raises, I asked a number of primary-sector employers how they reacted to offers to their employees by other companies. Most said they made no counteroffers, or made them only rarely or to key people (Table 7.9). Managers believed that responding would encourage others to seek offers and would call into question the internal pay structure and the justice of the company's compensation. Outside offers were also resented as a form of disloyalty. Finally, many employers believed that employees who solicited offers were unhappy for reasons having nothing to do with pay and would eventually leave anyway. Employers were more tolerant of offers to people with special skills and marketable talents who were loyal to an outside community of professionals or craftspeople. Examples included cabinet makers, computer programmers, and research scientists. At corporate research facilities, the tolerant attitude toward outside offers was like that in

TABLE 7.9   Employer responses to outside offers (applies to 52 primary-sector businesses)

Reactions to outside offers	Number of businesses	Percentage of businesses
Never make counteroffers	21	40
Make counteroffers to crucial employees	14	27
Occasionally make counteroffers	12	23
Normally make counteroffers	3	6
Outside offers are frowned on	9	17
Employees are fired for looking for another job	3	6

TABLE 7.10   Headhunter experience with counteroffers (applies to 13 headhunters)

Employer reactions to outside offers	Number of headhunters	Percentage of headhunters
Never make counteroffers	0	0
Make counteroffers to crucial employees	3	21
Occasionally make counteroffers	10	71
Normally make counteroffers	0	0
Outside offers are frowned on	10	71

universities, for counteroffers were made to key people. Companies were willing to match outside offers to professionals who were star performers. Giving them large pay increases would not upset internal equity, since their high quality was widely recognized within the company.

The statements of businesspeople were confirmed by headhunters, who said that companies make counteroffers only sometimes or to key people (Table 7.10). Headhunters said that counteroffers were more common than employers admitted they were; several headhunters reported that people received counteroffers about 25 percent of the time. The discrepancy is probably explained by the fact that headhunters usually deal in those categories of employees most likely to receive counteroffers, namely, professionals with marketable skills. Recruiting agents earn commissions only when they fill a position and so do all they can to convince job candidates to refuse counteroffers.

MANAGERS' AND HEADHUNTERS' COMMENTS ON OUTSIDE OFFERS

An important reason for not responding to offers was the desire to discourage other workers from seeking them.

> If I matched outside offers, it would be open season. Everyone would start looking for them. They would leave, even if I did match. Matching would create an atmosphere of looking for jobs and would give people bad habits.
> —Owner and founder of a new nonunion manufacturing company with 7 employees

> There is almost a policy of not making counteroffers. Once you start doing that, there is no end to it.
> —Human resource manager of a unionized manufacturing firm with 1,800 employees

Responding to offers would also upset the internal pay structure.

> If someone gets an offer, we don't do anything. It would be unethical to do so. It would contextualize pay in a different way. It would be to say that we have been underpaying you. We couldn't promote such a person without disturbing the promotion process and internal equity.
> —Human resource officer of a 400-employee division of a large nonunion manufacturing company

> Only in very limited cases does the company match outside offers. Counteroffers do little for the company and the employees. . . . We don't want to set our entire pay policy in reaction to the possible loss of a few people.
> —Director of compensation at a unionized manufacturing corporation with 180,000 employees

Some employers said that a counteroffer would not solve the problems of those who wanted to leave.

> I generally advise managers not to make counteroffers. Even if you match, people generally leave within a year. The reasons for taking another job are usually still there and money is rarely the reason. The reason could be the work environment, co-workers, the work load, the type of work, location, and so on.
> —Human resource officer of a bank with 16,000 employees

Employers resented offers, though offers to professionals were better tolerated than those to managers.

> Outside offers work against you. Threats are frowned on. It is okay to ask for a raise if you stay within the system and say, "I've done a good job and deserve more."
> —Personnel officer of a nonunion manufacturing company with 80 employees

Our practice is that when we learn that people are talking outside, we feel that they are traitors, so that we don't try to convince them to stay. We do not match offers. Sometimes we are more subtle and say that their case is being looked at and that there are things in the future for them. . . . Professionals are loyal to a body of knowledge and managers are loyal to a company. The primary identity of a professional is as a professional. In business, nonprofessionals identify with the company. It is threatening to have someone look around. Someone who just mutters that they are at a dead end here is written off immediately. People say that they can't count on him.

—Corporate director of human resources of a mostly nonunion manufacturing company with 5,000 employees

A few employers fired employees for looking for new jobs.

I recently fired an estimator who was not satisfied and was looking for another job. He showed up for work in a suit, so that he was obviously going to an interview at lunchtime. I took the occasion to fire him. I simply brought things to a head. [Estimators know company secrets, namely, intended bids on new work, so that it is dangerous to have one leave for a competitor.]

—President and part-owner of a nonunion electrical contracting firm with 60 employees

If I find out that someone is trying to leave, I tell him to go immediately. This is for security purposes. You can't have someone with one foot out the door, because you don't want other firms to know who your clients are.

—Branch manager of a large financial brokerage firm

The people most likely to get counteroffers were those who were very hard to replace.

People, especially discovery managers, are approached, usually by agencies, or seek offers themselves. We handle these on a case-by-case basis. Often, we let people go. Crucial people we try to keep.

—Human resource manager for a corporate research facility with 2,000 employees

[The company] takes an arrogant attitude toward outside offers. If someone wants to leave, [the company] says good-bye, except in the case of very senior people. We may try to keep someone senior who is very important or has special knowledge. There is no policy toward employees who search for another job, though your boss may persecute you if he finds out.

—Human resource manager in a financial company with 24,000 employees

Production employees do not receive many counteroffers unless they have special skills.

We don't match outside offers made to hourly employees. If that starts happening, we can raise the ranges. We sometimes match outside offers made to salaried people, though that rarely happens.
—Head of human resources of a nonunion manufacturing company with 1,200 employees

Willingness to make counteroffers stemmed from boom conditions or from low wage-and-salary scales.

In the 1980s, there were lots of outside offers to my men in the shop. I matched. That is why I have high rates now.
—Owner of a unionized architectural woodwork firm with 40 employees

We make counteroffers to key people who get outside offers. It makes sense to do this, because our people are now paid below market as a result of the long freeze and we would have to pay more to replace the people who left. The low pay makes our employees more attractive to others. We have had raids on our people.
—Director of human resources of a bank with 380 employees

Although headhunters said that counteroffers were fairly common, they also spoke of company policies discouraging them.

Lots of companies have policies against counteroffers. They are permitted only in extreme cases and with the permission of senior management. Otherwise, everybody would start shopping and the situation would be chaotic.
—Headhunter dealing in diverse professionals

Headhunters stressed that it was dangerous to accept counteroffers because of the resentment caused by offer seeking.

People who accept counteroffers are, 80 percent of the time, not employed by the same company six months later. By accepting a counteroffer, you are giving long-term notice, but the company will decide when you leave. In middle- to small-sized companies, employees have a personal relation with the president. If you have put a gun to his head with an outside offer, he hates you and eventually gets even.
—Headhunter specializing in comptrollers

7.5 Examples of Tight External Structures

Although certain external structures were unusually tight, the tightness did not make wages rigid, which is evidence against Keynes's explanation of wage stickiness.

One example involved three neighboring stores in a small suburban town, each with 30 to 50 employees and all hiring students from the local high school. Because the students knew each other, the owners of the stores felt obliged to pay similar wages.

> It is very embarrassing to have someone come to you and say they are paying more at [one of the other two stores]. They will complain if they find out. There is a kid network, and they know what the pay rates are. We want them to come back for a second and third year and continue with us as they go through college. As they work for us, they mature and become more valuable. . . . If someone found out he could make more [at one of the other two stores], he wouldn't do less well on the job. But it wouldn't be fair for me to expect him to do a good job and not to pay him the market rate. His attitude might be that if I am not paid the market rate, why should I care if I am late? You want them to show up on time, well-dressed and with paper and pencil in their pockets. We want them to grow with us.
>
> —Owner of a local hardware store with 30 employees

I interviewed the owner of each of the three stores within a six-month time period, and all were paying similar wages. Starting pay for teenagers was $4.70, $5.25, and $5.50 an hour, respectively, in the stores. Despite the similarity, hourly starting pay had decreased during the recession in two of the stores, falling by a dollar in the store currently paying $5.25 and by $0.80 in the store paying $4.70. (The pay of existing employees was not cut.) The storekeepers' perceptions of the need for parity implied only approximate equality of pay and permitted an uncoordinated decline in starting wages.

Unusually tight external structures were also created by labor unions. Union leaders try to have all product market competitors pay nearly the same wages, since the highest-paying companies in a product market lose market share.

> The pay is about the same for [a competing company's plants]. The differences in pay are 20 cents an hour at most. Unions try to keep wages the same, so that companies can't play the unions off against each other, saying the other's costs are less.
>
> —Directing labor representative of an industrial union local with an active membership of 12,000

> When we took over the union, we had [two large retail chains]. They said, "What about [another chain]" and other nonunion [stores]. So we organized the competition. . . . As we organized them, we tried to make their rate of pay equal to that of [the two large chains].
>
> —President of a retail workers' union local with 16,000 members

Some unions allowed pay to depend on the product market rather than the type of work, taking advantage of differences in profitability and the elasticity of product demand. For instance, construction unions had work recovery programs according to which particular firms could pay lower wages in order to bid against nonunion competition. The fact that wage differentials could be created by product market conditions is evidence of the weak impact of external pay comparisons on wage determination.

> Contracts are done shop by shop. In the old local, all shops were under the same contract, but I changed that, because different plants had different needs. A company that is doing custom [products] for the local market can afford to pay more than a company producing standardized items for the national market. After I split them up, the pay in the custom [products] shops went up. Now, pay varies from $16 to $10 an hour for the same kind of person. It is true that custom shops require more skilled employees than do the industrial shops. . . . But the main difference is that the product market for the industrial shops is more competitive. The competition is from both nonunion and other union shops around the country.
>
> —Business agent for manufacturing workers in a union local with 3,400 active members

> Pay depends on what the traffic will bear. It depends on what kind of business you are in. . . . Employers tell you about what the competition is doing and to whom they are losing business.
>
> —President and business representative for a union local with a diversified industrial membership of 4,000

The union of the first of the two preceding quotations was particularly interesting. All its members were in the same industry, skilled in the same craft, and most worked for small companies with no more than 70 workers, the average being 18. The union business agent was a successful organizer and intent on imposing wage standards within the two branches of his industry, custom and standardized. Nevertheless, he was encouraging pay cuts at the time of the interview, so that Connecticut companies could survive out-of-state competition. This was another case where strong external structure did not prevent wage declines. The organization that created the external structure also coordinated pay cuts.

7.6 Summary

The term "external structure" applies to the relation among pay rates of different firms in the same geographic area. External structure is much looser than internal structure, except in unusual cases where a strong labor union or close social relations among workers impose a tight external structure. Normally, external structures are created by competitive forces in the labor market, and these are too weak to determine intercompany pay differentials completely. Concerns about morale, which generate the need for internal structure, have little to do with external structure. Workers usually know so little about pay levels at other firms that pay differences among firms have to be large before they affect worker attitudes. Companies promote ignorance of pay at other firms by not sharing wage and salary surveys with employees and by discouraging them from seeking outside offers.

Appendix 7A Related Literature

FORCES CREATING EXTERNAL STRUCTURE (SECTION 7.1)

There have been a few surveys of the motives and objectives of nonunion employers in setting the long-run level of pay. These surveys largely agree with my findings, and the disagreements are most likely explained by differences in the era or local circumstances. Lester (1948, chap. 2) found, as I did, that firms wished to keep up with firms with which they competed for labor. Reynolds (1951, pp. 159, 217) found that employers felt a moral obligation to respect general wage standards and were concerned about morale and productivity and the ability to recruit and retain a satisfactory work force. His respondents stressed morale and productivity more than did mine. Myers and Shultz (1951) found similar considerations to be important, though the nonunion employers they interviewed stressed avoidance of unionization. Foulkes (1980), in a field study of personnel policies in large American nonunion companies, also found that the desire to stay nonunion was an important consideration. Blinder and Choi (1990), in interviews with managers of 19 firms about wage policy, were told that workers attach great importance to wage differentials. However, their question did not distinguish internal from external wage differentials. In Agell and Lundborg's (1995) survey, Swedish employers said their employees were equally concerned about internal and external pay comparisons and that concern about external comparisons increased with rank. These respondents attached more importance to external comparisons than did mine, a difference which may be explained by the much greater degree of unionization in Sweden. Agell and Lundborg obtained mixed results from a question about whether workers reject wage cuts because these would change external wage differentials, which is Keynes's theory. Behrend (1984, p. 111) finds that managers believe wage levels have no effect on effort or on productivity, but that systems of incentive payments do.

There have been few surveys of workers' attitudes toward pay comparisons. Patchen (1961) conducted a survey in one company on this topic, and found that comparisons with similar workers earning higher pay cause greater discontent if the person one is compared with works for the same rather than another company (pp. 39–40), a conclusion relevant to this chapter. Andrews and Henry (1963) survey managers' attitudes toward pay and find that interest in external comparisons increases with job level, the tendency that employers reported to Agell and Lundborg. Gartrell (1982, 1985) finds that workers learn about others' pay primarily through word of mouth.

Econometric work has confirmed that turnover is indeed negatively related to the wage in cross-sectional and time series data, evidence consistent with a trade-off between pay and turnover (Ulman, 1965; Stoikov and Raimon, 1968; Burton and Parker, 1969; Pencavel, 1970, chap. 3, and 1972; MacKay, et al., 1971, chap. 6; and Campbell, 1993, 1995a, b). Campbell (1995b) finds that quit rates are even more negatively related to wage increases than wage levels.

The looseness of the external structure is a common theme in the writings of the institutional labor economists, who noticed that firms, especially nonunion ones, had a substantial range of discretion in setting pay rates (Reynolds, 1951, chaps. 7–8; Dunlop, 1957; Ross, 1957; and OECD, 1965). Doeringer and Piore (1971, p. 73) also remark on the vagueness of external constraints on pay. Reynolds observes that workers do not have precise knowledge of pay in other firms, and that their ignorance weakens the influence of competition. Freeman (1988, p. 218) asserts that Reynold's conclusion is contradicted by the findings of Freeman (1971) and Perella (1971) that job hunters have realistic wage expectations. However, their findings are consistent with the notion that workers do not have precise knowledge of pay for the specific jobs available to them. Rees and Shultz (1970) and many other labor economists argue that competitive forces determine wages, because in regressions of wages on variables determining supply or demand the coefficients usually have the right sign. However, these results do not contradict the idea that employers have some latitude in setting pay. Young and Kaufman (1997) discuss the coexistence of this latitude and labor market competition in a study of wages of crew workers in the fast food industry.

Although I have noted that external structure is not imposed by worries about morale, it should not be thought that external comparisons do not influence workers' state of mind. Rather, market pressures are more important than morale in determining external structure. Clark and Oswald (1996) find evidence that some sort of external comparison has a psychological impact, for they show that workers' self-declared level of happiness is positively related to the ratio of their income to the average income of others of the same age, sex, education, occupation, and region.

The issue of the importance of external pay comparisons is related to the efficiency wage theories of Solow (1979) and Akerlof (1982), which link productive effort to pay levels (section 20.4). Akerlof proposes that workers provide extra effort in return for wages that are high relative to some reference level that might be pay at other firms or might be a reservation wage. Reciprocity seems to be real and important, and has been confirmed by economic experiments (Appendix 4A). It is not clear that wages at other firms are reference points, however, since workers usually have little information about these wages.

SOURCES OF INFORMATION (SECTION 7.2)

The use of surveys is described in a few studies of compensation policy, including Lester (1948, chap. 2), Reynolds (1951, chap. 6), Doeringer and Piore (1971, chap. 4), and Foulkes (1980, chap. 8). Textbooks on compensation administration explain how to conduct and use surveys (Rock, 1972, chaps. 13–16; Hills, 1987, chap. 9; and Milkovich and Newman, 1990, chap. 7).

PRECISION OF KNOWLEDGE (SECTION 7.3)

There has been a great deal of work describing the dispersion of wages offered for one kind of labor in one area and the apparent inability of competitive forces to eliminate this variation. Early studies include Lester (1946, 1954), Slichter (1950), MacLaurin and Myers (1943), Myers and MacLaurin (1943), Myers and Shultz (1951, chap. 8), Reynolds (1951, chaps. 7–8), Dunlop (1957), Jarrell (1959), and OECD (1965). More recent work includes MacKay et al. (1971, chap. 4), Brown and Sisson (1975), Ward (1980), Nolan and Brown (1983), Foster (1985), Rynes and Milkovich (1986), and Leonard (1989), who finds that wage differentials among firms are transient, though fairly large. A number of recent studies of wage dispersion have been made in connection with efficiency wage models, cited in section 8.6.

ISOLATING EFFECTS OF COMPANY LIFE (SECTION 7.4)

Hills (1987, chap. 4) contains an interesting discussion of how a firm's internal labor market isolates employees from the external one. Lazear (1986) proposes that outside offers to employees play an important part in the determination of pay and the evaluation of workers. He assumes that firms make counteroffers to those they wish to retain and that those who fail to receive offers bear a stigma and are not paid as much as those who do receive them. The evidence I collected indicates that the effect of the offer process on the pay of individual employees is weakened by company policy against counteroffers, though general turnover does affect a firm's overall pay level. I found no evidence of the stigma Lazear describes, though I asked about it. On the contrary, there was a stigma associated with having received an offer.

EXAMPLES OF TIGHT EXTERNAL STRUCTURES (SECTION 7.5)

The union discussed in section 7.5 illustrates principles stressed by institutional labor economists, namely, that there is a negative relation between wages and

the price elasticity of product demand and that wage cuts are often a consequence of loss of control of product price. Dunlop (1944, pp. 131–132; 1988,
p. 66) finds that wage cuts during the Great Depression often followed declines
in product prices. The relation of wages to the elasticity of product demand is
a recurring theme in the writings of the institutional economists, such as Dunlop
(1957, p. 136) and Ross (1957, p. 197).

Institutional economists remarked that unions impose wage standards. Dunlop (1957) called the standards "wage contours" and Ross (1948) called them
"orbits of coercive comparison." The subject is also discussed in Lester (1948),
Reynolds and Taft (1956), Slichter, Healy, and Livernash (1960, chap. 20),
Brown and Sisson (1975), and Barsky and Personick (1981). Dunlop points
out that there can be several contours for similar labor in one geographical
area, with the wage in a given contour depending mainly on the elasticity of
demand for the output of workers in the contour. For this reason, contours
explain some of the dispersion in wages. Kerr (1988, p. 7) has an amusing
description of how he learned, while serving on the War Labor Board during
World War II, that going or market wage rates existed only in union controlled
labor markets, wages in competitive markets being widely dispersed.

8

THE SHIRKING THEORY

Managers responded negatively to requests for reactions to most theories, but the shirking model, summarized in Chapter 1, was an exception. It was easy to explain the idea that pay is kept high to make discipline and effort standards more enforceable. The theory provoked interest, and led to discussions of motivation that revealed much about management thinking relevant to wage rigidity. Most managers insisted that the theory did not describe their own behavior, but rather a form of bad management. They thought of punishment only as an extreme measure for dealing with antisocial behavior and said that the best results were obtained with a forthright and positive management style. Such a style is defeated by pay cuts, for they withdraw rewards and are interpreted as penalties.

A small amount of evidence suggested that the shirking theory may apply at the bottom end of the labor market, especially to the market for low-paid temporary labor, where wages are downwardly flexible (Chapter 17). This finding is contrary to the spirit of the theory, which is intended to explain high wages and wage rigidity.

8.1 Reactions to the Shirking Theory

My last request in many interviews with businesspeople was for a reaction to the shirking model, and almost all thought the theory inapplicable. Some informants were perhaps influenced by my presentation, which may have suggested an atmosphere of threats and blackmail and an emphasis on discipline and monetary rewards. It was difficult to avoid giving this impression, since these elements do underlie the theory. I usually explained that threats need only be implicit.

It was clear that most businesspeople do not think in the way described by the theory. A possible trade-off between productivity and pay level did not occur to them, except in connection with pay cuts or with the trade-off between pay and the quality of new hires. This reaction speaks against almost all efficiency wage theories, not just the shirking theory. Many managers doubted that the level of pay influences the productivity of a given work force (Table 7.5). I was told that all workers feel underpaid and soon forget raises. Employers believed that in good times most workers did not worry about losing their jobs. Recession and layoffs had awakened the fear, a change that managers did not always welcome, finding the anxiety paralyzing and provocative. Productivity issues regarding existing, as opposed to new, employees are said to have little influence on overall pay levels, which are determined by the need to stay abreast of the labor market. Productivity is obtained by good management, which means personal recognition as well as stern discipline and financial rewards. It means making clear to subordinates what is expected of them and when they are not meeting expectations, while presenting criticism in a constructive spirit. Supervisors should have personal contact with subordinates, encourage them, know what is going on, and create a sense of group identity, matters unrelated to the shirking theory. The spirit of the theory offended managers, and this seemed to be so because they believed that most workers want to do well and should have the right to do so. The theory seems to imply suspicion, repression, and blackmail, and employers do not expect a worker to be any more willing to accept blackmail than they themselves are willing to be coerced by outside offers to employees (section 7.4).

OVERVIEW OF INTERVIEW EVIDENCE

I asked managers in 118 companies about the shirking theory, and their reactions are summarized in Table 8.1. I asked the same question of three labor

TABLE 8.1   Overall reactions to the shirking theory

Type of reaction	Number of businesses	Percentage of those responding
Does not apply	103	87
Applies in some cases	10	8
Applies	4	4
No opinion	1	1
Total number of businesses responding	118	100

leaders, who all thought the model did not apply. The evidence that the model may apply to low paid temporary labor consists of comments by just a few agents for and users of interim labor.

The reactions of most managers revealed that the shirking theory was foreign to them.

> The theory doesn't make any sense. . . . I never heard of anyone talk of higher pay as a way of making discipline more effective.
>
> —Human resource official of a nonunion manufacturing company with 280 employees

> The thought process seems radical, given that the whole system is based on paying for education, experience, and skills. Also, we have certain limits within ourselves, regardless of what we are paid. Some people can't contend with their job. Money is then not the issue. . . . The whole way of thinking is alien. Managers don't order anyone to do anything.
>
> —Director of human resources of a bank with 380 employees

> Some people are stimulated by the fact that they cannot replace the job. But this is not discussed as a factor in the choice of pay level.
>
> —Human resource manager in a 21,500-employee subsidiary of a large insurance company

A common view, consistent with what was said about wage setting, was that pay rates were determined by factors other than those mentioned in the theory.

> People do work harder during a recession because they are concerned about their jobs, though this would be hard to measure. However, the logic does not imply that companies pay well for reasons of discipline. They do so in order to attract and retain employees.
>
> —Human resource officer of a nonunion manufacturing company with 350 employees

> [The theory] is not a working dynamic from the point of view of how the company is going to set pay. We look at competitive pressures and the value of output. Competitive pressures are the number one driving force. You cannot just tell people to perform or they will lose their job in today's enlightened world. We do think about the relation of pay to productivity. It is affected by pay because human nature is such that people respond to rewards. Rewards are given for being creative, for identifying a problem, finding a solution, and sharing the solution with others. . . . The company wants people to focus on their job, to think about it, learn about it, and sing about it in the shower.
>
> —Human resource manager in a corporation in the service sector with 135,000 employees

Some managers doubted that many workers feared job loss, except perhaps because of layoffs brought on by the recession.

I have trouble accepting the idea that people fear losing their jobs. People see an entitlement. They don't appreciate how well paid they are. People who rise wouldn't be where they are if they didn't have other motivations. . . . I never heard anyone talk about more productivity being induced by a higher merit budget. In order to get more productivity, you need gainsharing [a pay plan that rewards increases in productivity].

—Human resource manager of a unionized manufacturing company with 30,000 employees

Corporations don't normally fire people for unsatisfactory performance. They are doing so now only because of the bad times. They are cleaning house. So now, fear is probably motivating a lot of people. But in the long term, you may not get risk taking, innovation, and creativity [that way]. People would just be covering their asses.

—Director of compensation at a unionized manufacturing corporation with 180,000 employees

Some managers doubted that pay had anything to do with discipline, which derived more from choosing the right employees and establishing good relations with them.

I try to pay competitively in my labor market area, so that I can always replace people and so they have no incentive to leave. . . . At the time of labor shortage, I raised pay just to get people in. I had no discipline problem then. . . . Discipline problems are taken care of not by pay, but by management, by defining the job clearly and correctly.

—Owner of a nonunion manufacturing company with 35 employees

Pay has nothing to do with discipline. Performance is not obtained through the threat of firing. A termination occurs because you made a mistake about the character of a new hire. Usually, you can size people up during the 90-day probationary period. You feel each other out then. After that, you have a good relationship. Termination is a failure of management rather than [of] the employee. The key to obtaining performance is to establish that the employee is here because he has a good job and feels good about it.

—General manager of a nonunion hotel with 45 employees

Some managers said that any correlation between pay and productivity stemmed from the trade-off between employee quality and pay.

We don't try to elicit productivity through fear of job loss. You might get more out of people by paying more, but because you would get better people, especially professionals.

—High-level human resource manager in a unionized manufacturing company with 27,000 employees

Other managers questioned the correlation.

Lower pay brings higher turnover, but people won't work harder if they are paid above market rates. . . . Pay is not a big motivating factor.

—Human resource manager of a nonunion manufacturing company and ESOP with 250 employees

All employees, no matter how well paid, feel they are underpaid. A few weeks after every increase, people want more.

—Human resource official of a nonunion manufacturing company with 9,500 employees

A common theme was that productivity is best obtained simply by dealing effectively with subordinates at a personal level, engaging their interest, and taking advantage of the fact that most people naturally want to please and do well.

The whole logic is wrong. If people are underpaid, they may be dissatisfied and work less hard than they would otherwise. But it takes more than the threat of firing to motivate people. A rational discussion of their good and bad points is more important. They have to be made to face the difference between their actual performance and what they think their performance is. This requires explanation and patience. . . . If people are in a jam in their work habits, they may not know how to help themselves. . . . What people are looking for in a world that is not very fair is someplace that looks rational and fair.

—President and owner of a unionized manufacturing company with 150 employees

The carrot and stick don't work. The theory doesn't look at the individual as a human being. The best way to get people to work is to get them involved and interested in their work, to involve them in safety programs, and give them special responsibilities. This builds up loyalty. Christmas party plays, philanthropic activities, all such things help build a sense of community and organization.

—Vice president of human resources of a nonunion manufacturing company with 260 employees

You don't use compensation as a weapon. That breaks down the relationship with the employee. You don't want them working just for money. There are other reasons —a helping hand when in need, a sympathetic ear, sensitivity to their needs and welfare. Compensation is a weak weapon. If that is the only thing, the employee will jump ship at the first chance for more money.

—Owner of a unionized roofing company with 775 employees

The theory is bassackwards. It assumes that people don't want to work hard. Most people want to work hard. They want to be successful and to please their boss and they usually do work hard. Higher productivity comes from giving them the tools and skills and by removing the obstacles to productivity, such as having a jerk for a manager or having offices that are too hot or cold. Another obstacle would be having a new mission statement for the company every 12 months, so that people can't figure out what the right thing to do is. People hate that and find it unmotivating.

—Human resource official of a nonunion firm specializing in research and development with 1,800 employees

The carrot and the stick achieve only short-term goals. It is against human nature. You should encourage people, pat them on the back, point out what happens if all pull together, make buddy buddy. You also have to make sure of what happens. You have to work toward someone's pride in themselves, in the company, and in team effort. No big stick should ever be used. . . . People are motivated by personal things—by management's creating a positive environment with real goals and real participation in rewards. The rewards don't have to be spelled out explicitly. You need to have the entrepreneurial spirit—to show your face. One manager can make buddy buddy with hundreds of people. You have to get out and mix and share with employees the joys of success. . . . College-educated managers sit in their offices and try to create a bigger stick with systems and procedures.

—Part-owner of a small chain of restaurants

Many managers reacted to the theory by saying that a threatening atmosphere is bad for the workplace.

[A competing company] does it that way. They pay well and if you sneeze you are fired. Here, we pay less and people are more comfortable. I disagree with that type of management. People don't give you 100 percent when you treat them like that. They aren't giving you loyalty and telling you how to do things better. They are too scared to act on their own. They are afraid to do anything. People avoid saying anything at work if their livelihood is at stake. I tell people, "tell me what I need to do to improve." I tell people if they are not doing a good job. They want to know what they need to do to improve.

—General manager of a two-year-old, nonunion manufacturing company with 140 employees

My company wouldn't do it that way. I don't believe the stick works. I once worked for an electronics firm that managed in that way. Management was iron handed. People were paid well for the local labor market and worked to avoid losing their jobs. It was an unpleasant place to work. It was always a negative environment. People were always being forced to do things. The company used discipline and a competitive wage to get people to work. The system worked in Taiwan and Mexico, where a lot of production was done. Ultimately, it didn't work. The company wasn't successful. . . . The company ended up with supervisors who didn't develop as a team. They didn't contribute willingly to the company as it grew. The fear of losing a well-paying job kept them working. Fear didn't produce the quality and productivity gains the company wanted. People would leave and escape when they could and they didn't develop as a management team that could think on its own, become autonomous, set its own goals, and know how to achieve them, grow in responsibility, and take on higher responsibility.

—Officer of a nonunion consumer products manufacturing company with 600 employees

People don't work well if they are afraid of losing their job. The fear stifles them. This is not a positive way of getting things done. The fear of job loss is distracting.

—Human resource official of a unionized manufacturing company with 17,000 employees

A few labor leaders commented on the shirking model, and none liked it.

Pay rates are based on a more fundamental principle of supply and demand. . . . Layoffs occur all the time, so that firing wouldn't be much of a threat. It is a raw and cruel marketplace.

—The president of a construction union local with 3,400 active members

Employers are not consciously doing that. In a piecework environment, the incentive to get [more] productivity is to make more money. . . . They tend to work harder when mortgage payments are due or when they want to buy a new car. Productivity occurs in response to immediate needs, not to a distant threat of being fired.

—Regional manager of an industrial union with 6,500 active members

A few users and providers of temporary labor, however, spoke in ways consistent with the shirking theory.

On low-paying jobs, supervision costs are high to keep the level of terror where it should be.

—Owner of a temporary labor service specializing in light industrial, clerical, and technical help

You do your work or get out. My boss hates the word "morale." He says we are in the business of making products in exchange for wages, not making employees happy. [This comment refers to about 100 temporary workers doing light assembly work that required about 15 minutes of training.]

—Human resource manager servicing 360 headquarters personnel of a large nonunion manufacturing company

8.2 Performance Bonds and the Shirking Theory

According to the shirking theory, firms pay more than needed to hire and retain workers, the difference being what workers lose if fired. Some authors have pointed out that the same amount of pressure could be applied at a lower cost to the firm by having workers pledge a sum of money that they would forfeit to the firm if caught shirking. Proponents of the shirking theory must explain why such pledges are not made. This critique was made originally by Becker and Stigler (1974) and Salop and Salop (1976) and has been much discussed since (Carmichael, 1985, 1990; MacLeod and Malcomson, 1989, pp. 448–449; and Ritter and Taylor, 1994). Defenders of the shirking model have argued that workers would not have sufficient wealth to post such performance bonds, that employers would have an incentive to make false claims of shirking, and that performance bonds are illegal (Shapiro and Stiglitz, 1984; Akerlof and Katz, 1989; and Dickens et al., 1989). Such bonds are indeed illegal, in Connecticut at least.[1]

Performance bonds could be used to deal with other personnel management problems, such as turnover among overqualified workers, who could be required to forfeit a bond if they quit before a certain date. I asked employers about this possibility, but the idea was always quickly dismissed.[2] The reasons are summarized in Table 8.2.

The first response listed in the table is the most interesting because it is similar to managers' main objection to the shirking model, that coercion fails to elicit good work.

> [Long laugh.] That sounds like prison. You can't do that. It is a clever idea though. People would probably work badly under such circumstances.
>
> —Director of a community service organization with 150 employees

TABLE 8.2   Why not have overqualified job applicants pledge performance bonds? (applies to 17 businesses)

Type of response	Number of businesses	Percentage of those responding
Employment bonds imply coercion, and this is not productive	5	29
Employment bonds are illegal or improper	5	29
Bonding would imply a guarantee of employment	3	18
Bonding would make it difficult to compete for labor	3	18
Workers would not have enough money to pledge	3	18

It would be a mistake to box people in like that, especially if you expect flexibility [in accepting new job assignments]. The feeling of being boxed in would hinder their creativity and their willingness to give extra effort. You want to reward rather than to penalize.

—One of four owners of a nonunion manufacturing company with 200 employees

It occurred to a few respondents that a bond would imply a reciprocal guarantee from the company.

Posting bond would be an administrative nightmare, for there would be an implication of guaranteed employment. We don't want that.

—Human resource official at the headquarters of a unionized manufacturing company with 8500 employees

In summary, performance bonds are not a practical alternative to antishirking wage premia and share with them the defect of antagonizing workers by implying coercion.

Various forms of deferred compensation exist that resemble performance bonds and bonds against quitting. Lazear (1979) has suggested that implicit performance bonds are created by paying workers less than their productivity for an initial period after hiring and increasing pay steadily thereafter. Some stockbrokers benefited from generous deferred compensation. This sort of incentive is not the same as a performance bond, however, for the bond is advanced by the employer, not the worker, and so is expensive, whereas performance bonds cost firms nothing. Deferred compensation is not necessarily cheaper than a wage premium as a means of achieving the incentives of the shirking model and is less likely to irritate and menace employees than a performance bond, for rewarding employees for loyalty has a psychological impact different from taking something away from them if they leave.

8.3 Salespeople

Superficially, the shirking theory seems to apply to salespeople, for many are made to understand they can keep their jobs only as long as they do well. A closer look, however, reveals that the theory does not describe their situation. They are paid commissions and are motivated primarily by these and other positive financial incentives rather than by the threat of firing. Most dismissals occur during the first year or two of work and are better described as part of a sorting rather than an incentive process. Salespeople who perform poorly are sometimes punished with reduced commission rates and may quit because they cannot make a living, contrary to the system envisioned in the shirking theory, where pay is high and poor performers are dismissed. Nevertheless, the management of sales forces smacks of coercion and seems to contradict employer claims that they abhor it. Why do salespeople respond well to rough treatment if other employees do not? The answer may be that salespeople are a special breed.

I learned about salespeople from managers in ten financial brokerage companies, in a car dealership, and in two large manufacturing companies. All said they had an interest in dismissing unproductive salespeople because of the fixed costs of keeping them.

> We want to increase both the size and the productivity of the sales force. One way to increase average productivity is to eliminate low producers. Brokers cost us fixed expenses, including office rent, phones, light, heat, air conditioning, secretaries, and other support services. The higher are the brokers' sales, the higher are our profits. We do computer models to calculate at what level of productivity we break even on a broker. We eliminate those who fall below the line.
>
> —Director of human resources for a financial brokerage and investment banking firm with 1,600 employees

> We want salesmen to produce or leave, since we have to pay them a salary, and there are the other overhead expenses of secretarial services, phones, and so on. Also, they have a territory or a portfolio of accounts or a combination of both that we could give to someone else.
>
> —Vice president of sales of a large manufacturing company with 4,000 salespeople

Selling involves approaching a great many people and being turned down by most. Most people cannot tolerate being rebuffed repeatedly. Only the tough and resilient are suited for the job.

> It is during the training program that we get lots of attrition. You get lots of rejection over the phone, and people get mad at you when their investments lose value. Also, your income fluctuates. You need a strong constitution to be a broker.
>
> —Director of human resources for a financial brokerage and investment banking firm with 1,600 employees

> The threat of being fired is a motivator for salesmen. These people are egotists. They want to be number one. They work for themselves, not for the company.
>
> —Head of the human resource department of a nonunion manufacturing company with 9,500 employees

Despite large training costs in many cases, companies permitted high turnover in their sales forces. The cost of training a stockbroker was said to be $50,000 in two companies and $35,000 in a third.

If someone hasn't produced after some years, he receives only a 25 percent commission on sales. This is a punitive level. People get the message usually and leave, so that they don't have to be fired per se.

—Senior sales manager of a branch office of a large financial brokerage company

After all that training and 18 months into the business, half of those trained [as stockbrokers] are no longer in the industry. The specific requirements are that 30 accounts be opened within six months after training is completed, and after the first year they should have brought in 90 accounts and have brought in at least $3 million in client assets. If they don't meet these requirements, it is cut and dry. . . . Brokers normally work 12-hour days and two Saturdays a month. It is like building any business. By the time they have been in the business five years, probably 80 percent of those who have been through training have been lost.

—Branch manager of a large financial brokerage firm

High turnover occurred despite great efforts to hire good salespeople.

Brokers go through a strenuous screening process before hiring. There is a preliminary interview to see if they understand what the job is and have the educational background and work ethic to be successful. Then an aptitude test is administered, which gives us an indication of whether they can pass the series 7 test. Then they go through a structured interview lasting one and a half hours. Then they come into the office and do a telephone simulation. They call a group of psychologists in New York, who role play with them and determine whether they have the skill to solicit individuals who are looking for alternative investments. Then there is a 45-minute phone interview with the regional sales manager. Finally, the branch manager checks at least three references.

—Branch manager of a large financial brokerage firm

Some salespeople were paid according to elaborate and lucrative incentive schemes, which created a possibility of winning that made negative incentives more tolerable.

In our compensation package, there is a scale for broker commissions. A broker earns 30 percent of the first $200,000 in commissions earned for the company, 32 percent retroactively of commissions earned between $250,000 and $300,000, and so on, until 40 percent is earned on all commissions if the total exceeds $1,000,000. This gives a big incentive to generate business. . . . The last leg of the incentive package is the system of recognition clubs or sales clubs. Brokers are given a certain amount of money for each $500,000 of sales, which may be used for country club memberships, expense accounts, and the like. Depending on the amount of sales, a broker belongs to a certain club. I belong to the [5] Club. Members of the club get taken on business trips with their wives to resort areas. The trips usually last five or six days. They go with a group of brokers [from the same company]. They have business meetings in the mornings where they learn about research, sales methods, and so on. In the afternoon, they play golf, tennis, do white-water rafting, and similar things. Every night, there is a present on your pillow, which would be jewelry for the ladies or a western belt for the men. Once you have been on a trip, you want to go again. Spouses feel the same way and put pressure on their husbands or wives. . . . The next level club after the [5] Club is the [4] Club. Members of this club go to nicer places and get nicer presents. A man might get cowboy boots rather than a western belt. You have to be five consecutive years in the [4] Club before being admitted to the [3] Club. The next level after that is the [2] Club, which is for $1 million in revenue. After that comes the [1] Club for those with over $2 million in revenue. This is a small group.

—Senior sales manager of a branch office of a large financial brokerage company

Some salespeople in effect post bonds against quitting, though the bond is financed by the company.

Recruiting brokers is like a free agency draft. We may give a new [experienced] broker a $500,000 loan up front, $100,000 of which would be forgiven each year he stayed with us.

—Director of human resources for a financial brokerage and investment banking firm with 1,600 employees

A manager of a financial company was one of the rare respondents who found the shirking theory accurate.

[The shirking] theory applies 100 percent. The company doesn't cut bonuses in bad times. This gives good people two types of motivation. They feel proud of [the company]. Also, it is a do or die place. If you don't get the bonus certificates, you feel you are doing badly and will be fired. In fact, you probably will be. If you don't do well, you are out of here. The bonus makes you value your job. It gets you to feel a part of [the company] and to want to get the business you are in out of a hole and find new ideas for doing it. If you are here, you are doing well.

—Human resource manager in a financial company with 24,000 employees

A manager of another brokerage firm disagreed.

The fear of dismissal does drive new brokers to work hard, but this is not why we have this system.

—Director of human resources of a financial brokerage firm with 14,000 employees

8.4 Discipline and Firing

Although in the theoretical framework of the shirking model no one is ever fired, since workers never shirk, as a practical matter some workers should be fired if the model is valid, for people are not always rational. With this thought in mind, I inquired about discipline and the frequency of discharge.

Companies and the law distinguish discharge for cause, for performance, and for lack of work. The first is brought on by repeated and willful misconduct, the second results from substandard work, and the third is a layoff. Reasons for firing people for cause include absenteeism, tardiness, insubordination, dishonesty, substance abuse, sabotage, theft, harassment, carrying a weapon to work, and fighting with customers or other employees. It is firing for performance that is relevant to the shirking theory. I did not obtain precise information on the frequency of performance discharge or on fear of it, but I discussed the subject in 27 interviews in companies. Performance dismissals were most common in professional and financial brokerage firms. Managers asserted that most firings are for cause, that most discharges for performance occur during the probationary period following hiring, and that after that period few are fired for any reason. It is not easy to fire workers after probation, for companies must be able to defend themselves in court against suits for discrimination or unreasonable discharge. Except in cases of serious wrongdoing, a pattern of poor performance or misconduct has to be established, and workers are not supposed to be fired without adequate warning and time to correct their behavior. For this reason, most companies follow progressive disciplinary procedures, with each step carefully documented. A typical procedure is verbal warning, followed by a written warning or reprimand, suspension, and termination. Performance reviews provide part of the documentation. These conclusions about disciplinary procedures are based on interviews with managers of 61 companies in a wide range of types of business.

I do not know to what degree workers normally feared dismissal for performance reasons. I did not ask workers for their views on the matter, though many managers said they did not want workers to fear dismissal and doubted that they did so (section 8.1). At the time of the study, many workers were probably worrying about layoff, and many companies laid off their poorest performers first. Some managers claimed that performance-based layoffs did stimulate effort (section 13.10), which is evidence that workers behave as the shirking theory assumes, though they might respond better to pressure from layoffs than firings, since layoffs are less provocative.

It should not be thought that workers never shirk, that discipline is not important, or that firing is not used to enforce it. On the contrary, I was told that discipline is very important both for productivity and for morale and that dismissals earned managers respect. The interesting questions are whether the threat of firing motivates many employees to work well or serves only to deter egregious behavior by a few and whether the threat is so important to productivity that employers are willing to pay more to increase the loss from being fired. Primary-sector managers told me they did not want most workers to sense any menace and that the need for one did not influence pay.

> Threats don't motivate people well. After a while, people get numb and say, "Go ahead and fire me." We don't sit around and say, "Let's raise pay in order to make the threat of firing more effective."
>
> —Human resource manager in an insurance company with 2,500 employees

8.5 The Effect of the Bad Labor Market on Work Effort

If the incentive mechanism of the shirking theory were correct, then recessions would push people to work harder by making job loss more dangerous. There is statistical evidence that higher unemployment is associated with greater work effort, and this evidence has been interpreted by some authors as supporting the shirking theory. The support is weak, however, for the evidence does not imply that employers adjust pay so as to optimize the trade-off between labor costs and productivity. A correlation between unemployment and effort has several possible explanations; recessions stimulate managers to pay more attention to productivity and performance, workers work hard to prevent their firms from failing, and layoffs frighten employees into working harder, so that they will look good and not be selected for dismissal. Evidence on these alternatives is given in this section and in sections 13.1, 13.2, and 13.10. Few statistical studies distinguish these effects from the impact of unemployment itself, though Brockner's studies, cited at the end of Appendix 13B (section 13.10), examine the effect on effort of layoff alone.[3] I attempted to make the distinctions when inquiring about the effect on performance of increased unemployment, and employer responses indicated that unemployment alone probably has little systematic effect on effort, additional evidence against the shirking theory.

OVERVIEW OF INTERVIEW EVIDENCE

As Table 8.3 indicates, no single opinion dominated regarding the impact of unemployment on job performance.

MANAGERS' EXPLANATIONS

When managers said that the bad labor market hurt productivity, they referred to the effects of depressed morale or to employees' stretching out work in order to avert layoff.

> Productivity goes down during a recession, because the men make the work last, not wanting to be laid off.
>
> —President of a unionized architectural woodwork firm with 125 employees

TABLE 8.3   Effect of the bad labor market on performance

Type of response	Number of businesses	Percentage of those responding
Performance somewhat improved	20	42
Little or no effect	20	42
Performance worsened	7	15
Total number of businesses responding	47	100

> When bonuses drop, morale is hurt. There is nothing you can do about this. People feel lousy. People in the industry are typically ambitious and aggressive and recognize that their incomes will fluctuate, but it is only human nature that they may slack off in bad times. Nevertheless, they know they will be unemployed if they don't produce.
>
> —Director of human resources of a financial brokerage firm with 14,000 employees

A few managers reported that employees worked harder during the recession in order to help the company and thereby save their jobs.

> Everyone knows the economy is terrible, so people work hard to keep the company going. Everyone knows their ass is on the line if we go under. They would have a tough time getting a new job and the new one wouldn't pay as well and wouldn't be as much fun.
>
> —Part-owner of a nonunion architectural woodwork company with 12 employees

Some managers claimed that high unemployment made employees value their jobs more and so work harder.

> There is more fear in a recession and you get more productivity from that. It is easier to be a supervisor. You don't have to tell people to work hard. The company couldn't have gotten away with asking as much of its employees in 1986 as it does now. You would have heard, "Why should I?" People don't argue now, because they want to keep their jobs.
>
> —Human resource manager of a unionized manufacturing company with 30,000 employees

There was other evidence that in extreme circumstances the fear of job loss induces workers to cooperate.

> I have had good luck with halfway houses. These people are easier to control, because if they do not have a job, they go back to prison.
>
> —Manager of a fast-food restaurant with 40 employees

The higher cost of job loss made workers more amenable to discipline.[4]

Sometimes, my waitresses have bad attitudes. They get discouraged and I have to pump them up. It is harder now to keep up morale. On the other hand, they tolerate more criticism or direction than in good times, for they have no place to go. In good times, I have to bend the rules more. Now, I can tell people to polish their shoes or that their uniforms are not well pressed. But they do their work just as well as in good times.

—Manager of a restaurant with 35 employees

The recession has made people a little more afraid of losing their job. As a result, attendance and punctuality have improved. This is even truer of newer employees. They have a better idea of what it's like out there.

—Personnel manager of a department store with 300 employees

Many believed the change in the cost of job loss had no effect on effort.

The recession doesn't make people work harder. It does make changes easier, such as the company's move from [a Connecticut city] to [another Connecticut city].

—Human resource manager of a nonunion manufacturing company with 80 employees

Discipline problems have not changed because of the recession. People look inward not outward. They don't work harder because of a recession.

—Human resource manager of a unionized manufacturing firm with 90 employees

The workers don't work harder now, but during a recession you have fewer complaints about pay and requests for increases. The men want the company to survive.

—Owner of a nonunion manufacturing company with 1,500 employees

8.6 Published Evidence Pertaining to the Theory

The shirking theory is not well supported by published empirical work. Authors have found that performance increases with unemployment, but the interpretation of this fact is ambiguous, as already noted. Surveys of businesspeople do not support the theory, nor does experimental evidence. Some puzzling facts about wages are consistent with efficiency wage theories in general, but are not more consistent with the shirking model than with a number of others.

THE BENEFITS OF PARTICIPATORY MANAGEMENT

The success of reforms involving a participatory management style are evidence against the shirking theory, since this style nearly precludes the use of threats. Participatory management increases responsibilities and cooperation at lower levels of the company hierarchy and requires trust and free communication (section 4.3). There is an impressive amount of evidence regarding the success of these reforms (Seashore, 1954; Likert, 1961; Guzzo Jette, and Katzell, 1985; Cutcher-Gershenfeld, 1991; Batt and Appelbaum, 1995; Huselid, 1995; Ichniowski and Shaw, 1995; Huselid and Becker, 1996; and Ichniowski et al., 1996). Hackman (1996) expresses a dissenting view about the success of work teams. Osterman (1994) shows that the reform efforts are widespread in the United States, affecting in 1992 about 35 percent of private firms with 50 or more employees.

THE RELATION AMONG WAGES, MONITORING, DISCIPLINE, AND PERFORMANCE

Underlying the shirking model is the idea that monitoring improves job performance. Support for this assertion may be found in Nagin et al. (1998), who report on a field experiment with telemarketers; as monitoring decreased, more workers cheated in order to increase their earnings, though many did not cheat. Telemarketers should probably be thought of as belonging to the secondary sector, and I know of no similar study applying to primary-sector workers, who might be more loyal to their firm and hence more conscientious.

The shirking theory predicts that workers need less supervision if their pay is high relative to other firms' pay for the same type of work. However, any negative relation between pay and supervision may be due to differences in worker quality, for better pay attracts better workers, who require less attention. The relation may also be due to reciprocity, for better-paid workers may offer more effort out of gratitude. Studies of the relation between pay and monitoring give mixed results. Contrary to the shirking theory, David Gordon (1990) and Neal (1993) find a positive relation. Leonard (1987a) finds no relation. Rebitzer (1995) finds a negative relation for temporary workers, as predicted by the theory. Groshen and Krueger (1990) obtain similar results for nurses, and Arai (1994a, b) finds a negative relation in data for Swedish industry. Krueger (1991) finds that company-owned fast-food restaurants pay slightly higher wages than franchise-owned ones and he interprets the difference as due to the greater difficulty of monitoring labor in company-owned restaurants. However, the effect could be due to the relative poverty of franchise owners, for they must pay franchise fees to the parent corporations.

Some studies show that there may be a positive relation between employee performance and pay relative to the market, though other studies obtain contradictory results. A positive relation is consistent with all efficiency wage models and so would not give particular support to the shirking model. Raff and Summers (1987) argue that Henry Ford doubled wages in 1914 in order to increase productivity and that this objective was achieved.[5] A positive relation between pay and measures of employee effort, discipline, and output have been found by Holzer (1990), Cappelli and Chauvin (1991), Wadhwani and Wall (1991), Drago and Heywood (1992), and Levine (1992, 1993b). On the other hand, Spitz (1993) and Agell (1994) find little or no relation. Gerhart and Milkovich (1990) and Leonard (1990) find that the financial success of companies is not positively related to the pay level of executives and managers, but is improved by giving managers greater financial incentives related to the success of the business. Hirsch and Hausman (1983) find that productivity in British coal mines was negatively related to wages in the late nineteenth and early twentieth centuries, evidence against the theory and in favor of a backward-bending supply curve of effort. Frey (1993) argues that monitoring and threats of discipline offend workers by showing distrust and so hurt motivation and work effort. He supports his reasoning with extensive references to sources in industrial psychology and management science. In reviewing management science and psychology research on pay and performance, both Vroom (1964, p. 252) and Lawler (1971, p. 133) declare that there are no data supporting the idea that higher pay levels increase motivation or productivity, though there is ample evidence that effort is increased by incentives that make pay depend on performance.

PERFORMANCE AND UNEMPLOYMENT

Consistent with the shirking theory, several authors have found evidence of a positive relation between unemployment and effort or productivity (Franke and Kaul, 1978; Stern and Friedman, 1980; Wadhwani and Wall, 1991; Drago and Heywood, 1992; and Agell, 1994). Drago and Heywood find that effort decreases with workers' perception of the probability of finding another job if dismissed. Agell finds a positive relation between effort and workers' perception of the likelihood of layoff, whereas Drago and Heywood find no significant relation. The findings of Drago and Heywood are among those most favorable to the idea that increased unemployment stimulates effort. In contrast, Spitz (1993) finds no relation between the productivity of food clerks and the unemployment rate, perhaps because the food clerks were not threatened with layoff.

Surveys find that most managers believe that increased unemployment has a positive impact on performance (Blinder and Choi, 1990; Agell and Lundborg, 1995; and John Hall, 1993), though Hall detected this belief only among managers of firms with recent layoffs, which may indicate that it was the layoffs that stimulated effort.

SURVEYS

Important evidence against the shirking theory is contained in surveys of managers that ask about factors influencing pay. Most respondents make no reference to shirking, in itself evidence against the theory (Lester, 1948; Myers and Shultz, 1951, chap. 8; Reynolds, 1951, chap. 6; Daniel, 1976; Foulkes, 1980, chap. 8; Daniel and Millward, 1983; Behrend, 1984, chap. 10; Gregory, Lobban, and Thomson, 1985, 1986; and Blanchflower and Oswald, 1988).

A few recent surveys have addressed the theory directly and, by and large, contradict it, obtaining results similar to my own (Blinder and Choi, 1990; Agell and Lundborg, 1995; John Hall, 1993; and Campbell and Kamlani, 1997). None of the authors reports that managers see a causal link between pay levels and discipline or job performance.

Interesting evidence about management methods was gathered by Burawoy (1979), who studied a single factory, working there as a machinist. He tried to explain why employees work as hard as they do rather than why they restrict output, the topic of earlier similar studies, such as Roy (1952). He found that workers have a great deal of independence; they consent to participate in a production game in which they see their own interests and those of management as to some extent compatible. Burawoy does not discuss the shirking theory, but his findings refute it indirectly.

Another important piece of survey evidence against the theory is Juster's (1985) finding that most people enjoy work more than activities associated with leisure. This conclusion contradicts the fundamental idea of the theory that people dislike effort so much that they must be pushed to provide it.

EXPERIMENTAL EVIDENCE

Fehr, Kirchsteiger, and Riedl (1996), Fehr, Gächter, and Kirchsteiger (1997), and Fehr and Gächter (1998) produce experimental evidence bearing out what managers said about the shirking model. In the experiments, subjects play the roles of workers and firms interacting in a labor market, and firms are able to punish workers for shirking. The results show that workers are more willing to reciprocate effort for generous wage payments when they are not threatened with punishment for underperformance—precisely what managers assert. Fehr and Schmidt (1997) emphasize that a minority of people are quite selfish and that institutions can create circumstances in which unselfish people influence the selfish to act cooperatively or vice versa. Discipline should perhaps be regarded as one way of preventing the selfish minority from controlling organizational outcomes.

SUGGESTIVE EVIDENCE

Some authors cite as evidence in favor of the shirking theory regularities in wage data not explained by the competitive model. However, other efficiency wage theories besides the shirking theory are consistent with these regularities.

One is the existence of large wage differentials between industries and between firms within an industry (Katz, 1986; Dickens and Katz, 1987a, b; Krueger and Summers, 1987 and 1988; Katz and Summers, 1989; and Groshen, 1991a–c). There has been controversy about whether these differentials are due to un-observed differences in worker ability (Krueger and Summers, 1988; Katz and Summers, 1989; Murphy and Topel, 1987a, 1990; Gibbons and Katz, 1992; and Keane, 1993). Another regularity is the negative relation between regional wage and unemployment rates within a country (Blanchflower and Oswald, 1994).

HISTORICAL CONDITIONS

It is possible that the shirking theory applied in earlier eras. Slichter (1920) pleaded for the importance of morale and described as current a harsh system of management that involved firing for slight offenses. This system no doubt persists in isolated companies. More recently, Goode and Fowler (1949) de-scribed an electroplating plant, where physical conditions were terrible, pay was low, management ruled by fear, turnover was high, and a core of stable employees stayed because they had various defects that made them almost un-marketable. These instances associate severe discipline with low pay, not with high pay as the theory implies. The association with low pay is consistent with the observation mentioned in section 8.1 that the theory may currently apply to some kinds of temporary labor. As mentioned above, Rebitzer (1995) pro-vides evidence in support of this assertion, finding a trade-off between pay and the amount of supervision for temporary workers hired to repair oil refineries. Indirect supporting evidence is contained in Rebitzer (1987), where he finds that labor productivity growth increases most with the unemployment rate in those industries with the highest labor turnover. The temporary labor industry has, of course, high turnover.

8.7 Summary

The shirking theory asserts that employers motivate workers in part by dis-missing them if their performance does not meet some standard. Furthermore, firms make the threat of dismissal more dangerous by paying workers more than is necessary to attract and retain them, and this excess payment has been interpreted as an explanation of downward wage rigidity. Most businesspeople denied that the theory described their behavior. They believed that having peo-ple work because of a threat of dismissal would be bad for morale. Dismissal is used mainly to remove poor workers and to protect firms from destructive people. It is not intended to create work motivation.

Appendix 8A Related Literature

SALESPEOPLE (SECTION 8.3)

An interesting question is whether salespeople really are a special breed or are simply treated differently than others because they face high financial risk. Ford, Walker, and Churchill (1981) have shown that salespeople are motivated primarily by financial incentives, but in this they may not differ from most people. I have found no work comparing salespeople with other types of workers.

DISCIPLINE AND FIRING (SECTION 8.4)

Brief descriptions of the legal background on firing may be found in Adams, Adell, and Wheeler (1990) and Wheeler, Klaas, and Rojot et al. (1994). In the United States employment-at-will is the norm, which means that firms may terminate employment without notice or reason. Nevertheless, wrongful dismissal suits grew rapidly during the 1980s. These are possible because employers have obligations of good faith and fair dealing.

There are little data on firing. The Bureau of Labor Statistics reports that from 1948 to 1954 the average monthly firing rate in manufacturing was 0.3 per 100 employees, which is about one-fifth the average monthly layoff rate for the same period.[6] This rate is neither large nor insignificant. Roughly similar dismissal rates are reported for Britain in workplace surveys (Daniel and Millward, 1983, p. 171, and Millward et al., 1992, pp. 199–200). Campbell (1994) finds that dismissal rates depend negatively on the unemployment rate, consistent with the spirit of the shirking model.

There is somewhat inconclusive work on the effects of threats and punishment contained in the literature on management styles. The conclusion is that harsh styles can increase output in the short run, but damage employee attitudes in ways that hurt productivity in the long run (Bass, 1990, chap. 21; Likert, 1961, chap. 5). Harsh supervision increases turnover (Mobley, 1982, p. 95; Telly, French, and Scott, 1971). Kleiner, Nickelsburg, and Pilarski (1995) report on a plant in which an authoritarian style increased productivity along with discipline-related grievances. Other tentative conclusions from the literature are that rewards have a stronger effect on employee performance than punishments (Sims, 1980), though punishment can be an effective instrument of control (Wheeler, 1976), and is appropriate for clearly unethical behavior (Bennett, 1998).

9

THE PAY OF NEW HIRES IN THE PRIMARY SECTOR

In this chapter I present evidence that in the primary sector the rigidity of hiring pay stems from the rigidity of the pay of existing employees, because internal structure links the pay of new and old employees. In addition, I discuss the related issue of why unemployed workers do not bid down wages by offering themselves as cheap replacements for existing employees. The answer is twofold; the need to preserve internal equity restrains firms from accepting offers to work for little money, and the ability of job applicants to bid for jobs is limited, for few know what positions are open within a firm and what these pay.

Some firms did cut hiring pay while leaving the pay of existing workers unchanged. The cuts were incorporated in the internal structure and two pay structures were created, one for workers hired before a certain date and a lower one applying to subsequent hires. These two-tier structures were in fashion in the 1980s, but were unusual and out of favor during the period of this study. In the primary sector, both managers and labor leaders complained of the stress caused by inequity between the tiers. The attitude toward the tiered structures was quite different in the secondary sector, where multiple-tier systems were common in some large retail businesses (Chapter 17).

If it is internal structure that prevents established companies from cutting their hiring pay during a recession, then new hires should have been paid less in new than in old companies, for there are no highly paid old employees in new firms. In order to check this implication, I interviewed in new companies, and managers of a few of these believed the recession had reduced their hiring costs. Managers of other small new firms believed that the effect of the recession on hiring pay was offset by their need for versatile employees, who were as scarce in hard as in good times, or even scarcer.

9.1 Internal Structure and Nonunion, Primary-Sector Hiring Pay

Companies generally fix the pay of new nonunion, primary-sector employees so that it is the same as that of existing employees with comparable skills and experience, and union contracts normally determine the pay of new hires so as to achieve the same end. The pay of new nonunion employees is usually in the bottom half or third of pay ranges and is near the bottom for inexperienced people, especially if they are factory workers. I found that, because of the difficulty of foreseeing ability, the pay of some new hires was set tentatively for an initial probationary period of a few days to several months, with adjustments up or down made at the end of it, a practice particularly applicable to skilled manual work. The policy of paying according to the internal structure prevailed in both small and large companies and those with informal as well as formal pay structures. Most managers did not want to give the impression they were taking unfair advantage of the recession by reducing hiring pay. They were also careful not to pay new employees more than existing ones, a possibility that was not often a concern during the recession. When labor market shortages force up the pay of new hires, that of existing employees is normally increased accordingly so as to maintain traditional differentials.

Despite the attention to fairness, hiring pay was somewhat flexible during the recession. For many jobs, employers took into account applicants' previous pay, their expectations and demands, and competing offers from other firms. Previous pay was relevant because employers did not want workers to be disappointed by too great a decrease. Flexibility in hiring pay seemed to be least for skilled and semi-skilled manual jobs and greatest for exempt employees. The extra factors mentioned probably changed pay by as much as 15 percent for exempt employees, though with my method of investigation, I could not measure precisely the range of discretion.

OVERVIEW OF INTERVIEW EVIDENCE

When discussing hiring pay, I usually asked managers how they decided what to pay individual new hires. I obtained ready answers, since these decisions were part of everyday life. Tables 9.1 and 9.2 describe the incidence of factors mentioned. The tables indicate managers' preoccupations, for I avoided raising specific issues.

MANAGERS' EXPLANATIONS

Respect for internal pay structure was paramount.

I maintain pay equity within the company. Pay is strictly proportional to capabilities

TABLE 9.1 Considerations in setting hiring pay for primary-sector workers in nonunion companies with informal pay structures (applies to 31 businesses)

Factors	Number of businesses	Percentage of businesses
Adjust pay of new hires to internal pay structure	20	65
Pay adjusted after a trial or probationary period	17	55
The boss's personal judgment is a strong factor	9	29
Entry-level pay is set at a flat rate for the job	4	13

TABLE 9.2 Considerations in setting hiring pay for primary-sector workers in nonunion companies with formal pay structures (applies to 54 businesses)

Factors	Number of businesses	Percentage of businesses
Adjust pay of new hires to internal pay structure	41	76
Pay adjusted after a trial or probationary period	16	30
The boss's personal judgment is a strong factor	0	0
Entry-level pay is set at a flat rate for the job	10	18

and willingness to work. New workers who are good get the same pay as others within the company.

—Owner of a nonunion mechanical contracting company with 30 employees

In setting entry-level pay, we look at what an experienced person is getting. A new person should earn somewhat less so that they would need two or three increases to get what an experienced person does. For instance, an experienced power press operator might earn $10 an hour. A new one might get $8 an hour and get an additional 50¢ after three months.

—Personnel officer of a nonunion manufacturing company with 80 employees

In setting the pay of new hires, we try to fit people in with their peers—people who have similar years of experience. We don't pay them more than comparable people at the same location. To pay them less would be a problem too. New hires learn quickly what other people are paid. If new hires catch on fast, we move them up.

Jealousy is a real management problem. People tend to think too well of their own work, especially if they are being buttered up by someone who wants to be mentioned in the paper.

—Newsroom editor of a major newspaper with 580 employees in the news department

In some jobs, entry level pay was the same for all recruits.

My starting pay rates are flat. They don't depend on experience, for new people have to be trained. If they are good, their pay catches up through the regular review process.

—Owner of a nonunion manufacturing company with 35 employees

New drivers are put on the dock for 30 days, even if they are experienced drivers. There, they are paid $11 an hour. This is done so that they learn how the company operates, how freight is loaded, etc. Once he is on the road, he receives $12. If he works out on the road, after 6 months he receives $13. Eventually, he gets $14. They go up faster if they are really good.

—Part-owner of a nonunion trucking company with 150 employees

Entry-level pay varies with the individual. The company has three offers. For typical undergraduates, there is a premium offer of $31,500 and a regular offer of $31,000. The choice depends on the school, not on the individual's grades. The third offer of $33,600 is for someone with an MBA.

—Human resource official of a very large accounting firm

For some types of work, pay was set tentatively during a short trial period. Some firms took advantage of the recession to reduce pay for this period, while leaving regular pay unchanged. This practice was acceptable because it did not upset the internal structure and caused only temporary resentment or none at all.

When I hire someone with experience, the initial pay is negotiated with him. There is an informal three-day probationary period. During this period, the foreman sees what the guy can do. At the end of three days, his pay is adjusted up or down accordingly.

—Owner of a nonunion roofing company employing 25 people

The entry-level pay of tool-and-die makers is determined by experience. We try to find out where someone worked before. We know the quality and precision of the type of work done by other companies. By doing reference checks, we can get a feel of what someone is worth, in spite of the law. Entry level pay is negotiated with individuals. There is a 90-day evaluation period. . . . After the 90-day period, the evaluation is discussed with the employee, who may receive a raise or pay cut, as a result.

—General manager of a nonunion machine shop with 60 employees

I am now paying a new guy an extra low wage because of the poor labor market, but his pay will be moved up in line with that of the other [nonunion] employees if he works out. I am just saving money during the probationary period.

—Human resource manager of a unionized manufacturing firm with 90 employees

Nevertheless, most employers made certain that they paid no new hires on a permanent basis noticeably less than corresponding existing employees, after allowing for experience and skill.

No one is ever hired below scale, even in a recession. An employee hired below scale might at first be glad to have a job, but would resent it when he learned of his low pay, and this would affect morale and performance.

—Human resource manager of a nonunion manufacturing company with 150 employees

Bringing in someone for less than the floor rate would cause pandemonium. Existing employees would feel insecure about their pay or positions. They would worry that they would be replaced by someone cheaper. Feelings of insecurity would lead to bad performance and low productivity. Any sort of inequity can cause problems with morale and productivity.

—Human resource manager of a new and rapidly expanding nonunion company in the service sector with 3,500 employees

If you go for rock bottom in hiring, you may get internal inequities. New employees would find out quickly that they were underpaid by internal standards. They [are the ones who] would resent it, not the existing ones. If they are disgruntled, they might leave or they might look for someone to represent them. The company is also concerned about ego satisfaction. Some people would function less well if they were offended. Morale and company culture are a very important part of any company.

—Human resource manager of a 3,500-employee research division of a large corporation.

It is not good to bring in people for less than comparable existing people. You want people to feel they are adequately compensated. There are considerations of fairness and ethics. If you treat people unfairly, it will come back to bite you in the ass. What goes around comes around. You reap what you sow. In business, as communications get better and the world gets smaller, you want a good reputation. It makes it easier to sell products and to recruit people. You don't want people hating you.

—Human resource manager in an expanding nonunion manufacturing company with 8,500 employees

Only one employer mentioned that new hires would resent earning less than what new hires had been paid at an earlier date. The usual comparison was with the pay of existing employees.

> The companies [in this industry] raise starting pay simply because other companies do. New recruits [for positions as research scientists] don't know what last year's starting salary was.
>
> —Human resource manager for a corporate research facility with 2,000 employees

Paying new employees a good deal more than existing ones was viewed as a serious mistake, perhaps even more serious than underpaying new workers.

> Morale is always an issue, especially with bitching women. Pay influences morale when someone is promoted or a new person is brought in. I just had a problem of jealousy when a girl was promoted from sales support to marketing. Others felt just as qualified but lacked the artistic talent. We had a similar problem when a new receptionist was hired recently. Her starting pay was higher than what other girls had received, but general wage levels have gone up since they were hired. [The receptionist was not currently making more than the others.] These problems were settled by meetings of the staff concerned and were not serious enough to affect job performance. Paying new employees more than existing ones would probably be so disruptive as to impair performance.
>
> —Vice president of a unionized manufacturing company with 90 employees

> If a new employee were brought in for more than existing employees, there would be a roar. Managers' time would be wasted explaining the matter to disgruntled employees. Unhappiness affects morale and all dimensions of performance—punctuality, attendance, and productivity.
>
> —Operations manager of a nonunion wholesale distribution company with 170 employees

> Paying new people more than existing employees can cause resentment. When secretaries were in short supply, we did have new people paid more than existing employees. This is happening now with nurses. We worry a little about this leading to unionization, for many nurses are from a union background and managed care is new to the industry. It is also important for the company's public image that it not bring in new people for too much less than existing employees. Since the company has over 50,000 employees, its relations with its employees has a big effect on its public image. I tell two friends, they tell two, etc. The company wants to have a caring, Mother [company nickname] image, even though it wants to be lean and mean. . . . Image is not useful in sales. It can be a deciding factor when competing for employees.
>
> —Human resource manager for a group of 1,700 employees in a large insurance company

Some employers said that increases in pay to new hires sometimes drove up their entire pay structure.

We are influenced to some extent in setting entry-level pay rates by the pay of non-entry-level employees. We can't give first-year people more than second-year people without creating a morale problem. So, when entry-level pay rates are rising, we make adjustments in everyone's pay. The overall impact on costs of entry level pay increases can be unacceptable. This happened six or seven years ago.

—Managing partner of a law firm with 70 employees

A few years ago, when unemployment was low in Connecticut and the labor market was tight, we hired someone for the dark room at so high a wage that we had to give raises to everyone else. The labor market was so tight that you couldn't get people.

—Vice president of a publishing company with 70 employees

Rapid growth of the company meant that pay was all over the map, because people within the company were sending out offers all over the country. Managers within the company were competing with each other for the same people. We let them pay more and more, because we were losing revenue by not having enough people. Everyone knows what other employees are making, so that offers to people outside the company ratcheted up the whole compensation system.

—Head of the human resource department of a nonunion manufacturing company with 9500 employees

Employers felt they had some latitude in setting pay for new hires, so that it was influenced by factors other than the internal structure.

There is no resentment if the new employee is paid within 80 percent of the pay of other existing employees on the same job. People are excited to come to a successful company and there is a belief that experience should bring more pay.

—Chief human resources official of an investment company with 1,000 employees.

If I offer unemployed applicants less than they earned before, I agonize over it, because the pay affects how they value themselves and their sense of self-worth. If we do offer them less than they earned before, we are very candid with them. We don't do it often. Offering someone $40,000 who had earned $60,000 would be problematic. We have done it only a few times, and when we did it was refused.

—Director of human resources for a financial brokerage and investment banking firm with 1,600 employees

Within a labor grade, the pay of a new hire is determined by his background, which means experience and education. If he is unemployed but has offers elsewhere, we might go up a little. Whether we did would depend on how badly the department manager wanted him.

—Human resource official of a unionized manufacturing company with 2,700 employees

If someone is being competed away from another job, their pay on the old job matters.

—Human resource official at a partially unionized manufacturing company with 12,000 employees

Some employers said they took advantage of the range of flexibility, setting hiring pay as low as possible by selecting the cheapest candidates. Rapidly expanding companies could not be as selective and so paid a little more.

To hire faster, you have to pay more because different people require different amounts of money to bring them in. They may have illusions about their worth or some people's lifestyle requires more pay. A family man requires more than a single man. People write on their application what they made on their previous job. This figure influences my offer.

—Nonunion, site-work contractor with 20 employees

When we hire secretaries, we try to get the best deal. That is, we take the cheaper secretaries among the candidates.

—Managing partner of a law firm with 70 employees

I have underpaid people. If I can do it, I do. I give what I can get away with for a job. If the range for a job is $25,000 to $31,000, and a recruit says $25,000, I give $25,000. If they say $23,000, I give $25,000 in order to give them a sense of worth.

—Director of a community service organization with 150 employees

Employers said they were careful not to appear to take unfair advantage of a candidate's being unemployed.

We do not pay new hires less because they have been unemployed. Doing so would screw up our internal equity and that would make the new person unhappy. People talk about what they are paid. Paying a person less because they were unemployed would be to take advantage of them.

—Human resource officer of a 400 employee division of a large nonunion manufacturing company

Whether [people] are unemployed or not does not affect their starting pay, though if they are unemployed their pay on the previous job does not matter so much. We do not use the fact that someone is unemployed against them. We are not going to hire someone at a low rate and then worry about losing him later on. It is not a good idea to wait for outside offers and then bring people up by matching. . . . This would encourage employees to look for outside offers and increase turnover.

—Human resource official of a unionized manufacturing company with 17,000 employees

For new hires, we look at the salary range for the position. The lower third is for new hires who need training. Theoretically, the unemployed are treated the same as if they were employed. We tend to base pay not on what people are currently earning, but on what the job is worth to us. However, the person with a job would be a more aggressive negotiator. If he doesn't want to leave his job, he will set a high price on his skills.

—High-level human resource manager in a unionized manufacturing company with 27,000 employees

In executive hiring, unemployment is less of a stigma now than it was three years ago. Recruiters are aware of it, in that they can pay a little less for someone who is unemployed. It is enough to match their former pay. Rarely do they offer much less than what they had before. To do so is not a good practice. If they were low-balled, in the short-term they would be glad to have a job, but in the long-term, they would feel they had been taken advantage of and there would be a retention risk.

—Director of compensation at a unionized manufacturing corporation with 180,000 employees

Nevertheless, it was not unusual for unemployed people to be paid somewhat less than they had been in their previous job.

Typically, when we hire unemployed people, we offer less than what they made previously. If you are employed for many years, you get raises, so that over a period of time your pay goes up and up and up, and you become overpaid. Many of the people I see who are unemployed have lots of experience and are paid a lot. They were worth more to their old employers than to us. They have nontransferable knowledge. They are in a desperate situation and are willing to take a cut. You don't need to offer more than what they were making. It is not uncommon to offer 20 to 25 percent less. They are not brought in for less than existing comparable people.

—Human resource manager in an expanding nonunion manufacturing company with 8,500 employees

9.2 The Effect of the Recession on Hiring Pay in the Primary Sector

Some managers volunteered numerical estimates of the impact of the recession on the pay of newly hired, nonunion, primary-sector workers. This information, summarized in Table 9.3, may not have been accurate, as it often consisted of estimates of changes in average hiring pay for various categories of workers.[1] Because I had promised not to request quantitative information, my investigative method was not appropriate for collecting precise data on pay.

Several influences bias these results toward decreases in hiring pay. I almost surely oversampled companies that were in difficulty or were cutting pay. In preparing Table 9.3, I counted a company as having reduced hiring pay if a manager said pay had decreased for a significant group of new hires during the

TABLE 9.3   Impact of the recession on the hiring pay of nonunion primary-sector
            workers (applies to 97 businesses)

Percentage change in hiring pay	Number of businesses	Percentage of businesses
−30 to −21	3	3
−20 to −16	5	5
−15 to −11	3	3
−10 to −1	7	7
No change	45	46
Increase	34	35

recession. In 5 of the 19 companies with decreases, these applied only to portions of the work force, such as secretaries or engineers. In another 6 of the 19
companies, the cuts in hiring pay resulted from general pay cuts. This leaves 8
companies in which pay cuts applied to most new hires and solely to them.[2]
Taking bias into account, I conclude that decreases in hiring pay were not
common in the primary sector, though they certainly occurred.

9.3 Undercutting

Solow (1990, p. 37) asked why the unemployed "do not at least try to compete
for existing jobs by offering to work at less than the going wage," and referred
to such offers as undercutting. Undercutting should not be confused with the
overqualification issue discussed in sections 15.2 and 18.6. People are overqualified if they apply for positions significantly lower than those for which
they are qualified. People undercut when they offer to take a position at pay
which is very low for the type of work involved or much lower than the pay
of people currently doing the work.

I inquired about whether workers attempted undercutting and how employers reacted to it and was told that workers do not directly offer themselves as
cheap substitutes for existing jobholders. Job applicants do occasionally offer
to work for very little, however, and employers considered it a bad idea to take
advantage of such proposals. To profit overtly from a job applicant's weak
bargaining position was thought likely to create resentment, to hurt general
morale, and to shake confidence in the fairness of the company and its pay
structure. Usually the reason for rejecting low offers was not that the offer

revealed that the applicant had defects. The majority of employers interpreted low offers as demonstrating a good spirit on the part of the job seeker.

OVERVIEW OF INTERVIEW EVIDENCE

It was difficult to ask about undercutting directly. Some employers found the possibility preposterous since job candidates do not normally know the going wage at a firm for a particular type of work and would seem odd if they said something like, "Give me the job of one of your men for two-thirds of his pay." Workers being laid off were in a position to undercut, but were not usually given the opportunity to do so (section 13.7). One approach was to ask if workers ever offered to work for less than the pay of the job they applied for. This question was awkward, however, because workers seldom apply for specific jobs and usually do not know pay rates precisely until they receive an offer. The best method proved to be to ask whether job candidates ever tried to secure jobs by offering to work for little pay, leaving vague the meaning of "little."

Table 9.4 summarizes what was said about the frequency of offers to work for little, and Table 9.5 summarizes reactions to such offers. Although no employer said that low offers were common, the first table shows that employers

TABLE 9.4   Offers to work for little (applies to 65 businesses)

Answers to inquiries about whether workers offer to work for little money	Number of businesses	Percentage of businesses
Low offers never happen	28	43
People sometimes offer to work for little	26	40
People sometimes offer to work for nothing during a trial period	11	17

TABLE 9.5   Employer reactions to low offers (applies to 38 businesses)

Reactions	Number of businesses	Percentage of businesses
The offers are refused	30	79
The offers are accepted	5	13
The offers make a good impression	13	34
The offers make a bad impression	6	16

did encounter them. The second table indicates that the majority of low offers were probably refused, but made a good rather than bad impression. Workers whose offers were refused might be hired, but at the regular pay rate for the job.

Most job applicants did not know enough to undercut in a literal sense.

> People will never tell you what they want, except for people in the higher classifications. If you ask applicants for production jobs, "What are you expecting?" they reply, "What the job pays."
>
> —Owner of a nonunion electronics manufacturing company with 15 employees

> People never [offer to work for less than I pay], because they don't know my pay scale.
>
> —Vice president of human resources of a nonunion manufacturing company with 260 employees

> Because of the recession, a lot of people come looking for jobs who are willing to work for little money, but they don't offer to work for less than the amount we offer, since we don't make an offer per se. We have certain skills we are looking for. The pay offer comes at the end of the hiring process. Up front, applicants know what the pay is within a broad range, and we know within a broad range what the applicant wants and whether it fits.
>
> —Human resource manager of a 3,500-employee research division of a large corporation

Nevertheless, job applicants did sometimes offer to work for little.

> An engineer from [a large corporation] came in. He would do anything. He would work for $3.00 an hour [much less than the minimum wage] under the table. He had three kids to support and was desperate. He hoped to put several low-paying jobs together.
>
> —Owner of a fast-food restaurant with 18 employees

When I asked what kind of impression job candidates made if they offered to accept low pay, employers usually said the offers were a sign of good character. Some understood that people could be desperate for work. A few reacted badly.

> I have had people offer to work for nothing. If they do that, something is wrong somewhere. Desperate people can do desperate things.
>
> —President and part-owner of a nonunion electrical contracting firm with 60 employees

> Sure, people offer to work for less than I pay. I don't accept, but it's a good sign if someone has the heart to do it.
>
> —Part-owner and operator of a nonunion construction company with 90 employees

One person did offer to work for nothing for a while. I looked on the offer favorably, thinking it showed enterprise.

—Personnel director of a nonunion manufacturing plant with 120 employees

Begging for a job wouldn't affect pay, and few do that. You shouldn't, because the interviewers would know that you don't have the personality for the job. Begging shows a lack of dignity.

—Human resource official of a unionized manufacturing company with 2,700 employees

People do occasionally offer to work for less than our floor pay rate. I tell them that this is what the job pays. I don't hold it against people when they do that. It is neither a negative nor a positive. I am just looking for qualifications.

—Human resource manager of a new and rapidly expanding nonunion company in the service sector with 3,500 employees

Some employers accepted low offers, paying low wages, at least until it was clear how good the new hires were.

I have people who come who are desperate for work and offer to work for little. I may pay them $1 or $2 less than what is right, but I don't offer $6. I give $10 and generate enthusiasm. I try to get him below market worth, but not by much. I bring the man up if I keep him and he turns out to be good.

—Nonunion, site-work contractor with 20 employees

Job applicants do offer themselves for less than I pay. The job may be for $25,000 and the person may have written $19,000 for expected pay on the application. I ask them about that and they say, "I'll take the job for $19,000. I know I can do it and I'll work my way up." Twice, I have taken people up on such offers. I don't think badly of them for it. I know they want to work. I bring them up after a while, because everyone knows everyone else's pay, and inequities hurt morale and productivity. Also, he might leave, though he wouldn't leave today because jobs are so hard to find.

—President of a nonunion electronics manufacturing firm with 25 employees

When I hire people, I tell them, "You're worth nothing until I see what you can do." If the job applicant asks for $30 an hour, I stop and send the man away. If the applicant asks for $6, my attitude is, "We'll see how he does." I like it if men offer to work for nothing at first. It shows trust. Because of that, I trust the man.

—Owner of a nonunion mechanical contracting company with 30 employees

The dominant theme was that offers to work for little money had little influence on hiring and compensation. Employers did not want to be seen as taking advantage of unemployment.

There could be many things driving an offer to work for little. It could be sheer desperation. It wouldn't mean they'd be happy doing the job. The employer-employee relationship should be on a basis of mutual fairness and on an equal footing and the two sides should be up front with each other. I have to worry about their cheating me. If I am fair with them, I expect the same from them. If I cheat them, they might cheat me. The relationship would be inferior, though the person would not necessarily be.

—Vice president of a publishing company with 70 employees

No driver offers himself for low pay. Dockers may put $6 or $7 under "pay desired" on the job application form, because they have no idea what to ask. I can't take advantage of that. They would work alongside other dockers and eventually find out that they are paid $11.50 to $12.50. I would have dissension and would not get the productivity and attitude I need. I might get errors. Twenty-five thousand cases [boxes of freight] are handled at the terminal every night. Dockers have to be attentive to details and to have a clear and quick mentality. Misloading costs the company money.

—Director of operations of a nonunion trucking company with 75 employees

We ask job applicants how much they would like to make. Sometimes, they say less than what our minimum is for the range [of the job they would take]. It is considered to be poor business practice to take advantage of such situations. Suppose you said you wanted $9 an hour and the minimum for the job was $11 and I hired you for $9. Then, as soon as you found out that you were paid $2 or more less than others on the job, you would realize that you had started off your relationship with us at an Italian flea market, and this would end up costing the company far more than the saving on your pay. You would leave as soon as you found a better job, because you would consider that I had behaved unethically. Also, you could become dysfunctional. You could do poor quality work intentionally or bad-mouth the company to customers. It would be like enlisted men in the service. People get revenge. Also, dissatisfaction can be infectious. One disgruntled employee can upset others.

—Vice president of human resources of an insurance company and HMO with 220 employees

9.4 Reactions to Two-Tier Systems

I asked employers why they did not cut hiring pay while leaving the pay of existing employees intact, creating a two-tier system. The typical reaction was similar to what was said earlier about taking advantage of the unemployed; new hires would resent being paid according to a lower scale than employees hired at an earlier date. Some employers had at one time introduced two-tier systems, however, and their experiences were not as bad as might be expected given the fears expressed by those who rejected the idea. Such cuts were tolerated when they were small and temporary or the company was in trouble financially.

I discussed two-tier systems for primary-sector workers with managers in 55 companies and with 4 leaders of unions with primary-sector membership. Fifteen of the companies had tried two-tier systems, in some cases 10 to 15 years earlier. In only 2 of these 15 companies were the experiments considered a failure. In one other, the system led to complaints ignored by the employer. Two-tier systems were disdained in 39 of the 40 companies that had not tried them, and the owners of the remaining company were considering a two-tier structure. In 24 of these 39, the primary reason given for rejection was worry about the morale of the lower-tier workers. Various arguments were given in the other 15 firms, including concern about unionization, discrimination suits, and company reputation. Only two employers mentioned that they feared they would have difficulty hiring at lower wages, and they were referring specifically to unskilled labor. The four labor leaders were all opposed to two-tier systems, claiming they disrupted the workplace and had proved a failure when in fashion during the 1980s.

INFORMANTS' EXPLANATIONS

Employers worried that a two-tier structure would damage morale.

> If I lowered entry-level pay, I would have pay discrepancies. These matter. Everyone knows everyone else's pay. I don't want a new person to feel different. A class system would be created. Cliques would form. It would not be good for unity or morale. I want a team—a family-like atmosphere. Productivity, product quality, and loyalty then all follow naturally.
> —General manager of a nonunion hotel with 45 employees

Primary-sector union leaders concurred, and also worried that the structure would divide the membership.

> Two-tier wage systems go against my beliefs as to what unionism is all about. It should be equal pay for equal work. Two-tier systems divide the shop up. It reminds me of what I heard about a company with employee stock ownership. The higher-seniority employees finally accumulated so much stock that they opposed wage increases for fear of what they would do to the value of their stock. What a ridiculous position for a union to be in! Two-tier pay systems raise these same issues. The upper tier workers could imagine that they could earn more if the lower tier people earned less. These issues should not be raised.

It is all right to have new employees earn less at first until they learn or prove their skills.

—Business agent for manufacturing workers in a union local with 3,400 active members

Two-tier wage systems are terrible. We had one at [two large corporations]. What it produced was a very demoralized work force. The company hired new people for less. Productivity went down. There were fist fights in the shop. The lower-paid people were mad. They felt it to be unfair. It took a bitter strike to get rid of it three and a half years ago at [one of the corporations], which now says it was a mistake, because productivity has since increased. We are totally opposed.

—Directing labor representative of an industrial union local with an active membership of 12,000

Some businesspeople thought a two-tier system might lead to unionization.

We thought about having a two-tier wage system at one nonunion location, but didn't do it for fear of union organization. We wanted to do it in order to cut costs. A two-tier wage system can raise such disparity that resentment builds.

—Vice president of human resources of a partially unionized manufacturing company with 5,500 employees

Two-tier systems were in vogue in the 1980s, but were less popular by the early 1990s.

Two-tier compensation systems were fairly common four or five years ago. There were lots of experiments with them. It was found that they worked for a year or two, but that after that you really got morale problems with the lower tier. They didn't like being paid less for the same work. So two-tier systems have evaporated. Nevertheless, there may be an unconscious or unacknowledged tendency toward a two-tier system during a recession. Companies don't want to be seen as having them and claim they are simply paying for performance.

—Consultant working for a large management consulting firm

Two-tier systems create dissension. The newer younger workers resent being paid less for doing the same thing as the older ones, and the older workers fear being replaced by the younger ones, which also creates dissension. As a result of experience with such conflict, two-tier systems are out of fashion. Nonunion places are fearful that two-tier systems will bring on unionization. Older workers don't want to have to strike to bring the younger ones back up.

—Director of an industrial union local with 65,000 members

Some businesses reported that two-tier systems had not worked.

In the factories and warehouses, most of the positions are full-time career positions. We have tried two-tier systems in the warehouses, and they haven't worked. They applied to benefits, and then to wages. Neither the upper- nor the lower-tier people liked it. It didn't seem right to them. They voted to sacrifice some of the gains they could have had in a new contract in order to eliminate the tiers. The employees saw each other day after day. They had the same jobs and the same productivity standards. There might have been a fear that the reductions would spread to everyone. In any case, both the upper- and the lower-tier workers voted to reject the system. [The same person asserted that two-tier and multiple-tier structures were readily accepted by store clerks, a fact discussed in Chapter 17.]

—Vice president of a supermarket chain with 30,000 employees

But most employers who had tried two-tier systems said they had caused few problems. Acceptance was easier if the second tier made it possible for the company to expand employment.

We have had two-tier wage systems four to six times and at various plants. . . . They were done in the late 1980s and were typically done to bring in new work with new products. . . . The two-tier system is not popular, but it goes down each time. We promise to protect the older people, and they believe us.

—Vice president of human resources of a partially unionized manufacturing company with 18,000 employees

Workers also accepted two-tier systems more easily if they knew that the company was in trouble.

In past recessions, I cut entry-level pay by 10 to 15 percent. I did this because the company was in difficulty. Margins were being eroded and the two-tier system was a way to contain costs. I have not done it during this recession because the company has not been adversely affected by it. . . . The cuts caused no resentment. People were glad to have their jobs. Now, it wouldn't be accepted, for the company is doing too well. Earlier, everyone knew the company was in difficulty.

—Owner of a nonunion manufacturing company with 35 employees

Lack of contact among workers also made it easier to reduce hiring pay. This factor was cited by secondary-sector employers to explain why starting pay was flexible in their businesses (Chapter 17).

I paid newly hired people about 10 percent less than people in the ranks with similar skills. The men don't exchange that much information, so that they didn't know. They are not all under one roof, but are spread all over, so that they have little interaction and little opportunity to discuss pay.

—President of a nonunion mechanical contracting firm with 200 employees

Similarly, it is easier to reduce hiring pay if the new workers are at a different location from the old ones.

We have been thinking of forming a separate company with lower pay, say $8 or $8.50 an hour for drivers to take over the import-export business, which is expanding rapidly. The company is losing that business to cheaper little guys. We would have no trouble recruiting drivers at that pay. We have too many highly paid drivers [at $14 an hour]. Bringing in new guys at $8 internally would create a real mess. But, if everyone in the new company were equal, there would be no problem.

—Part-owner of a nonunion trucking company with 150 employees

It was important for success that the decrease in hiring pay not be too large.

Lately, starting pay rates have come down for [some types of engineers]. . . . The company is doing a lot more cross-training and having groups of engineers manage a project, the design of something or the implementation of a new component, so that engineers are brought into contact with each other as near equals. This makes them more aware of pay differentials and makes these harder to accept. This makes the situation more complex. You have to watch out what you do in reducing pay. In fact, the pay of new hires has come down only a little bit. This decline hasn't been an issue yet, but it could become one.

—Director of human resources of a unionized manufacturing company with 30,000 employees

9.5 Pay in New Companies

Because the hiring pay of companies founded during the recession was determined solely by the labor market, these companies could take advantage of the recession to pay low wages. In small companies, this advantage was limited by the need to hire people willing and able to undertake diverse tasks. Such people were scarce during the recession, because established firms were reluctant to lay them off (section 13.5).

OVERVIEW OF INTERVIEW EVIDENCE

I succeeded in interviewing in 6 companies founded during the recession and in 6 other companies that had been founded since 1985, but had retained their start-up character. One of the first 6 companies had over 3,500 employees, and another was medium sized, having 140 employees. The other 4 were small, as were 5 of the 6 older companies, all having no more than 30 employees. The founders of the large new company and one small one believed the recession made it possible for them to pay significantly less than otherwise. (It was not possible to compare the firms' pay levels with that of their industry, since they had no regional competitors.) All 6 new companies were guided solely by the forces of supply and demand in setting pay. Managers in 8 of the 9 small young companies spoke of the need for versatility in new hires and the difficulty of finding it. Managers in 3 of the young companies said the high risk of company failure increased the amount they had to pay.

The recession may have decreased labor costs.

The fact that there is so much unemployment has helped to a certain degree in filling entry-level positions cheaply. We were able to hire almost everyone at the starting rate. If there had not been a recession, we would have had to pay a lot more to expand.

—Human resource manager of a new and rapidly expanding nonunion company in the service sector with 3,500 employees

Managers of new companies paid what they believed was required to obtain labor of the desired quality.

I could pay people $5 an hour or less [instead of $6]. People come in and offer their services for the minimum wage. These people are willing to do anything. They are laborers with no training. If I hired them, I wouldn't benefit, because I need skilled people. I need spray painters and buffers. I have to pay a little more for their skill. They could get jobs elsewhere, though it wouldn't be easy. If I paid too little, I would get turnover.

—Owner and founder of a new nonunion manufacturing company with 7 employees

We are at the mean as far as pay goes. . . . We don't pay less than we do because we want good employees. We experimented with pay levels until we found the right one.

—General manager of a two-year-old, nonunion manufacturing company with 140 employees

Small young companies required adaptable employees, who were expensive.

Start-up companies have to attract people with broad backgrounds who are versatile and willing to do anything. No one can say, "That's not my job." We can't afford that luxury. Managers should be ready to type their own letters or shovel snow off the driveway. You need people who are able to have the perspective of a one hundred million dollar company, but are willing to roll up their sleeves. . . . We can't afford to train people. They are expected to hit the ground running. They are told, "This is your responsibility. Figure out how to do it and do it." You can't teach people how to do things you don't know how to do yourself. . . . When companies are cutting back, they want people who can wear many hats. That explains why flexible people are scarce now. . . . The recession makes it easier to find semi-skilled, task-oriented people, because they are being let go by many companies. But these people are not critical to us now. The people we want are versatile, and they are harder to find because of the recession. Also, the recession makes employed people more reluctant to move to a start-up company, which might fail and leave them without a job. . . . We pay a little more than [a large nearby corporation in the same industry] for positions of equivalent responsibility, because we have to pay for versatility, the complexity of jobs in a start-up, and the risk it would fail.

—Founder and part-owner of a new nonunion manufacturing company with 10 employees

The risk associated with start-ups was a common concern.

I have to pay a little more as a start-up, because they [the workers] don't trust me, thinking I may go out of business.

—Founder and owner of a new apparel manufacturing company with 20 employees

REMARK

A question I have heard from a number of economists is why unemployed workers do not get together, form companies, and undercut other firms in the product market. I did not collect much information related to this question, but did learn that small new companies had a great deal of trouble raising capital. The two larger new companies in my sample had ample financing, but the small ones were funded by means of personal savings, credit cards, money from friends, and small government grants.

9.6 Summary

It is possible to reduce the pay offered to new hires while cutting the pay of no existing employees. In the primary sector, the need to respect internal pay equity was the main force restraining firms from reducing hiring pay alone. The same consideration inhibited employers from taking advantage of offers by unemployed job seekers to work for very little money. Internal pay structure was not completely rigid, for the pay of new hires was more downwardly flexible than that of existing employees.

Appendix 9A Related Literature

EFFECT OF THE RECESSION ON HIRING PAY (SECTION 9.2)

There is little statistical data on the pay of new hires, and the data that do exist show little downward flexibility, reinforcing the conclusion that my findings may have been biased in favor of cuts. The College Placement Council, the only organization I know of that collects such data, publishes average starting salary offers to college graduates in professional fields (Connell, 1991, and recent issues of the *Statistical Abstract of the United States*). The series show no evidence of downward flexibility. On the contrary, starting salaries rise continually, though the rate of increase slows somewhat during recessions. Starting salaries are not more cyclically sensitive than the usual indices of wages and salaries for existing employees. Another source of information is the study of one firm by Baker, Gibbs, and Holmstrom (1994b). They find that over 20 years, the average pay of newly hired managers declined in real terms as the result of inflation and recession, though the real pay of existing employees had an upward trend, with a slight dip during the recession of 1980, when there was high inflation. The nominal pay of new hires seems never to have declined. Additional evidence of the flexibility of hiring pay is contained in Beaudry and DiNardo (1991) and Bowlus (1993). Beaudry and DiNardo find that in the Michigan Panel Study of Income Dynamics longitudinal data for households, the unemployment rate at the time of hire had a negative influence on current wages, even years after hiring. Similarly, Bowlus finds that in National Longitudinal Survey of Youth data, pay on new jobs is more cyclically sensitive than pay on existing jobs. These results do not indicate whether hiring pay ever declined, however. Also, the findings could result from the effects of recession on the level of jobs accepted during recessions rather than from the effects on hiring pay for particular jobs.

UNDERCUTTING (SECTION 9.3)

Solow (1990, p. 39) suggests that a social norm "forbids undercutting the going wage as a strategy for unemployed workers." He says that the social norm could be modeled as rational behavior in a repeated game, and such models have been formulated by Weibull (1987) and Sabourian (1988, 1989). I doubt that Solow's explanation is valid, since employers report that workers do offer to work for little money. Agell and Lundborg (1995) find in a survey of Swedish firms that many job applicants offer to work for little. Their results are similar to those reported in Tables 9.4 and 9.5. They find more evidence than I did that employers interpret low offers as indicating that job seekers are of inferior quality.

The experimental work of Fehr and Falk (1996) supports an efficiency wage explanation of firms' rejection of undercutting, namely, that firms do not accept low wage offers because increased effort from better-paid workers more than pays for higher wages.

REACTIONS TO TWO-TIER SYSTEMS (SECTION 9.4)

Informants said that two-tier systems had only recently fallen out of fashion among primary-sector employers, and surveys of managers by Jacoby and Mitchell (1986) and Essick (1987) show that the systems were viewed favorably in the mid-1980s.

Managers believed two-tier systems would generate discontent mainly among lower tier workers. Mixed evidence bearing on this assertion has been collected by several authors. McFarlin and Frone (1990) find, in a study of a tool-and-die company, that lower-tier workers are more likely to feel the structure is unfair. Martin and Peterson (1987) report similar results from a study of a store. Martin (1990) and Heetderks and Martin (1991) find dissatisfaction among both tiers in studies of retail stores. Cappelli and Sherer (1990), however, find greater dissatisfaction among upper-tier workers in a study of an airline. There is little evidence that two-tier systems have an adverse effect on productivity, though the subject has not been studied extensively (Martin, 1990, pp. 48–49).

Kaufman (1984) reports findings similar to mine from 26 interviews with managers of British firms made during a recession. He raised the possibility of employing new workers at wages below those paid to current employees. Almost all employers dismissed this suggestion, believing it would cause "intolerable frictions."

Fehr and Kirchsteiger (1994) give a theoretical explanation for the infrequency of two-tier systems based on the idea that production inefficiencies caused by internal inequity would more than offset the cost advantages of the lower tier. This theory is consistent with management thinking.

PAY IN NEW COMPANIES (SECTION 9.5)

Kaufman (1984, p. 108) finds in a study made during a recession that newly opened firms in Great Britain were employing people at about half the pay they had earned before layoff. He does not say whether the new firms were paying less than established ones in the same industry.

10

RAISES

Most firms continued regular raises during the recession, and we may ask why they did so. Companies paid raises to union members in part because of contractual obligations or union pressure. What is hard to understand is why nonunion workers received raises. Employers said the main reasons were to provide motivation and to control turnover. It may seem surprising that quits should have been an issue during a recession, but employers worried that their best workers could still find other jobs. Excellent workers are the most likely to leave, for they are eagerly recruited by other firms. Companies also worried that if their pay fell behind that of labor market competitors, turnover would soar when the economy recovered. It might be thought that turnover could then be controlled by raising pay quickly, but employers rejected this idea as impractical and unseemly.

During the recession, raises continued to be driven by the same factors as in good times, namely, raises at other firms, profits, product market competition, the cost of living, and the competition for labor. High unemployment had almost no impact, except that it meant the absence of upward pressure on wages from competition for labor. Employer concern about the market level of raises tended to make them uniform across companies, the average level being determined by the other forces.

The impact of profits is of interest because financial problems were one influence capable of bringing pay cuts (section 5.2). The role of the cost of living bears on the validity of implicit contract theory and on the question of whether pay rigidity was nominal or real, matters discussed in sections 20.4 and 12.4, respectively.

10.1 Type and Size of Raises

In order to understand the function of raises, it is necessary to know some-thing about how they are administered. People in business distinguish between merit and general or uniform increases. A merit increase depends on an as-sessment of the talents and accomplishments of the recipient, and a general increase gives everyone the same raise, usually proportionately. Merit raises depend on the position of an employee's pay within the range for the job, the raise decreasing with position and becoming zero at the maximum for the range. Most management and professional employees receive merit increases, as do many nonunion clerical and production workers. Labor unions nor-mally abhor merit increases, asserting that they leave too much power in the hands of management, power which can be abused and used to turn workers against the union. Production workers in some nonunion companies receive general increases in deference to manual workers' distrust of the merit system. Piece-rate workers receive general increases as uniform percentage increases in piece rates. General increases do not entirely prevent reward of accomplish-ment, since the more productive may be promoted or advanced to higher pay steps within their job.

It is helpful to distinguish between advance through the pay structure and increase in the structure itself. Merit increases are usually the sum of both types of raises. The general portion of merit raises is roughly the same as the accompanying structural increase in pay ranges. Increases in ranges were usu-ally smaller than average merit raises, and some firms gave merit increases while leaving their ranges unchanged. Some uniform raises also combined both structural increases and increases within the structure. For instance, in professional partnerships that paid the same salary to all associates with the same years of job tenure, annual raises for associates were the sum of the increase resulting from an additional year of tenure and the increase in pay of the succeeding tenure class. Elsewhere, certain uniform raises served only to shift the entire structure upward, an example being proportional increases in all piece rates.

Uniform increases are easy to administer, whereas the determination of merit increases absorbs a considerable amount of time and energy. In most firms with more than 50 employees, the increases depend on supervisors' written evalua-tions. Connecticut labor law required that workers see these, and in some com-panies workers participated in their own evaluations. This documentation was expensive to create, though it was useful in determining whom to lay off and could be needed to defend the company against charges of discrimination or unjustified discharge.

In addition to wages and salaries, many companies paid bonuses and incen-

TABLE 10.1   Average size of raises (applies to 49 businesses)

The average size of raises was	Number of businesses
Positive and less than 2%	5
At least 2% and less than 4%	16
At least 4% and no more than 5%	24
More than 5%	4

tives based on individual or group achievements and on profits of the whole company or of subunits. Bonuses served nearly the same purposes as raises, but were normally an important part of pay only for executives and salespeople. (Bonus reductions are discussed in section 12.5.)

The average size of raises was decided in the budget process at the highest levels of management. The money allocated was often referred to as the "merit pool," and its size was measured as a percentage of budgeted total expenditures on wages and salaries.

Merit increases were prevalent in the firms I studied. Among the 171 where I collected the relevant information, only 35 paid uniform increases to production workers, merit increases being paid in the other firms. All paid merit increases to overtime exempt workers. Merit increases were as common in the secondary as in the primary sector. Labor union demands and piece rates were the most common reasons for uniform increases.

In my sample, the majority of companies gave raises during the recession. Among the 235 companies where I interviewed, 6 had cut pay, and 39 had frozen it within the previous year, and the rest had given raises. Pay cuts and freezes were probably overrepresented in the sample, since I looked for them. Because I did not request quantitative information, I obtained precise information on the average size of the most recent raises in only 49 of the 190 businesses that had raises, and their distribution is given in Table 10.1. The businesses covered by the table are diverse in both size and industry. The figures are consistent with wage and salary surveys made by business consulting organizations, which showed average raises of from 3 to 5 percent in Connecticut in 1992 and 1993.

10.2 Why Give Raises?

The dominant motives for paying raises were the provision of incentives and control of turnover, with the first motive being somewhat more important. Incentives applied mainly to merit increases. Other important motives were fostering good morale, protecting employees' standard of living, and meeting their expectations of income growth.

Table 10.2 summarizes managers' reasons for giving raises. Only one respondent mentioned fear of unionization. There was no relation between responses and the nature and size of the business.

I found the emphasis on turnover puzzling, because employers also emphasized that the recession brought a decline in voluntary turnover. I sometimes pointed out the inconsistency and asked why the companies did not delay raises until the recession ended. Aggressive questioning of this sort was risky, but I obtained useful responses in 17 cases, summarized in Table 10.3.

Bureaucratic problems were mentioned only in large corporations, where conflicting interest groups struggle for shares of the company budget. The argument was that if the company gave no raises during the recession, its pay level would be far behind that of competitors by the time the recession ended

TABLE 10.2   Why pay raises? (applies to 78 businesses)

Reason	Number of businesses	Percentage of businesses
To provide incentives	44	56
To control turnover	39	50
To foster good morale	23	29
Because employees expect raises	12	15
To protect employees' living standards	8	10

TABLE 10.3   Why not delay raises? (applies to 17 businesses)

Reason	Number of businesses	Percentage of businesses
The concern is about current turnover	8	47
Bureaucratic problems prevent catch-up increases	5	29
Delay would hurt morale	6	35

and funds might prove politically difficult to obtain for large catch-up increases.

Another seeming inconsistency was the contrast between the emphasis given to the merit element of increases and the fear that the best workers would leave if average raises were too small. In some interviews, I asked why the company did not simply give large raises to the best and none to everyone else. I obtained answers in 13 cases, all of which were similar—management does not wish to discourage or antagonize workers. For the same reason, performance reviews are often not as negative as they might be. In other words, the pressure for internal equity does not permit full recognition of productivity differences.

MANAGERS' EXPLANATIONS

Discussions of why raises are given were confusing, because employers had many interlocking reasons in mind. Some emphasized turnover alone.

> If I find someone who is willing to show up every day on time with work shoes on, it's a miracle. I try to hang on to such people. [Said in explanation of why he gave raises.]
>
> —Owner of a nonunion roofing company employing 25 people

> Raises are paid as a cost-of-living adjustment in order to keep the best employees. We have to pay competitively in order to keep them. Good employees can always find something. Raises are not given for motivation. Architects are not very interested in upward mobility. They get their enjoyment from their product.
>
> —Human resource executive of an architectural engineering firm with 60 employees

> We give raises and regularly review the pay structure in order to be able to recruit and retain employees. Now, after downsizing, we have retained only key players— the best performers. We want to keep them.
>
> —Personnel director of a nonunion manufacturing plant with 120 employees

> Increases have been given throughout the recession. They are given because people would quit, even during a recession. We try to keep our most knowledgeable, best trained employees. They could leave.
>
> —Vice president of human resources of a partially unionized manufacturing company with 18,000 employees

Others stressed morale.

> You have to give increases. People need to feel appreciated. They expect the reward, and it is good for morale. I will insist on some sort of increase every year. I don't want a rotten apple in the barrel who will start grumbling. Discontent is contagious. A lack of raises would start grumbling that could be conveyed to customers. People

need to be rewarded. If times are terrible, you just don't hire as many people, but maintain the pay of the ones you have and hope they stay.

—Manager in charge of telemarketing at a publishing company with 70 employees

There were no raises from June 1989 through 1990 and 1991. In the spring of 1992, I gave the hourly people a 4 to 5 percent raise, realizing that I had to motivate them to help 1992 profits. Having given a raise, I could ask for more productivity, harder work on the job, more efficiency, starting to clean up later.

—Part-owner and operator of a nonunion construction company with 90 employees

We try to give the cost-of-living increase. If they get only that they usually leave. People like to feel they are gaining ground in life. If their raises don't match the cost of living, they feel they are losing ground and they become discouraged. Unhappy employees don't perform well.

—Owner and founder of a nonunion manufacturing company with 500 employees

When a business is doing badly, you need to have good people on hand to get it out of trouble. The pay of the best people has to stay at a high level and you have to pay the mass of people enough to keep them motivated. . . . The recession is going to end someday, so that increases have to be given. . . . The idea is to get people fired up before the recession ends.

—Human resource manager in a financial company with 24,000 employees

The impact on morale was tied to expectations of raises.

Raises are given because they are traditional. People expect them. Raises don't motivate people. But not giving raises would be demotivating.

—Owner and founder of a nonunion manufacturing company with 40 employees

The average person doesn't understand why they get increases. If there is no inflation in the cost of living and no productivity increase, why should we give increases? But workers expect them anyway. They think, "I did a good job, so I should be rewarded." In this company, an average performer has his standard of living protected. . . . The employees perceive that they should get a little more than the increase in the cost of living every year. We are interested in their perceptions, for they affect morale, their sense of self-worth and self-value.

—Human resource manager of a nonunion manufacturing company with 6,000 employees

Merit raises also provided incentives.

[Raises used to be automatic at one plant.] People perform better under the new all-merit system, though pride drives people more than pay. Incentives help people drive themselves.

—Human resource manager servicing 360 headquarters personnel of a large nonunion manufacturing company

Raises are given to reward performance. This meets people's expectations and is part of the American philosophy of life.

—Personnel manager of a fast-food restaurant franchise with 36 restaurants

A few managers spoke of raises as motivated by a sense of fairness.

Increases are given because it is equitable to give them. People need them to live. It's expensive to live. You don't need to look at statistics to know that. Then, certain key people are rewarded for their outstanding contribution. This is done in the spirit of reciprocity, not in order to retain them.

—Operations manager of a nonunion manufacturing company with 100 employees

Employers did not want to postpone raises until the end of the recession.

Now, because of high unemployment, we would not have to give any raises in order to retain people. But if we don't, we will have more trouble recruiting later when times will be better, for we will have damaged our reputation. Our own employees are our best recruiters.

—Human resource officer of an 850-employee, nonunion division of a manufacturing company

Our intention is to make sure the company doesn't get too far behind in being competitive when the economy is out of the recession. Everybody believes we will be out of it and back into a boom situation. . . . We don't want there to be any drastic changes in pay when the labor market tightens. If pay were allowed to slip behind, we would worry about morale, especially at a time when salaried people have harder work loads and the exempt have to work longer hours.

—Human resource officer in a partly unionized manufacturing company with 1,400 employees

We want to keep those remaining [after layoffs] happy. . . . You don't want to be herky-jerky and to appear weak. You want people to believe you are doing well. Otherwise, you run the risk of losing people after the recession. You could do lots of things with them during a recession when they are captive. We don't want to treat people like that or the good ones would be gone after this is over.

—High-level human resource official in a 3,000-employee, largely nonunion division of a huge consumer products company

In large companies, the politics of the company budgetary process was partly responsible for this attitude.

If [the employees] are underpaid now, they will leave when good times return, unless pay is increased then. It is not easy to increase pay, for everyone in a company is competing for funds. If pay were cut now, the funds would be gone and hard to get back later.

—Director of human resources of a unionized manufacturing company with 30,000 employees

Confining raises to the most productive employees who were most likely to leave was difficult, though a few employers claimed they did just that.

It is difficult to restrict increases to a few people. Where do you draw the line? Such selective increases could damage morale and lead to litigation.

—Human resource officer of a bank with 16,000 employees

[The idea of confining increases to the best people] sounds great, but it is hard for managers to administer. They would give everyone 2 percent if only 2 percent were available. They tend to distribute whatever you give them uniformly. We can do a better job of distinguishing performance with our incentive program. Base pay tends to be administered with flat distinctions.

—High-level human resource manager in a unionized manufacturing company with 27,000 employees

A common complaint was that managers give excessively positive performance evaluations because they do not wish to offend subordinates.

Performance reviews affect morale too. That is why they are half lies.

—Human resource manager in a nonunion manufacturing company with 250 employees

It is hard for managers to give bad news. Managers really do believe that their people are above average. They want to be supportive and encouraging.

—Corporate director of human resources of a mostly nonunion manufacturing company with 5,000 employees

10.3 Factors Influencing Raises

The most important influence on raises was company prosperity. Company wealth and profits affected raises mainly because firms could not afford them when in financial difficulty. Some employers also mentioned that workers expected to share in company successes. Others believed that making pay depend on profits helped motivate employees. In many cases, raises depended on the success of the operating unit as well as that of the parent company, a procedure adopted to strengthen incentives. For instance, raises in fast-food restaurants depended more on the success of individual stores than on that of the company owning them.

Other important influences were raises at other firms competing in the same labor markets and change in the cost of living. Employers wished to protect employees' standard of living, both to maintain morale and out of a sense of moral responsibility. Many firms did not, however, fully offset increases in living costs in all circumstances. Some compensation managers said they let pay fall behind the cost of living during periods of rapid inflation, catching up later. The cost of living also served as an indicator of changes in general wage levels, just as did wage surveys.

OVERVIEW OF INTERVIEW EVIDENCE

Tables 10.4 and 10.5 summarize what employers said about influences on raises. There was little relation between company characteristics and responses, except that the emphasis on the market level of raises increased with company size. Some human resource managers in large companies insisted that they cared more about keeping up with the competition than protecting living standards, and managers in 26 businesses claimed that they paid no attention to the cost of living.

Connecticut extended its state income tax to wages and salaries in 1991, and I asked 22 Connecticut employers whether they had increased pay in order to offset the tax, hoping to learn whether they were committed to maintaining standards of living against all setbacks. Only one of the 22 offset the tax and one other claimed that the tax was part of the cost of living considered when

TABLE 10.4   Factors influencing raises (applies to 153 businesses)

Factors	Number of businesses	Percentage of businesses
Company prosperity	115	75
Cost of living	77	50
Raises at other firms	74	48
Competition in the product market	12	8

TABLE 10.5   Why do raises depend on the cost of living? (applies to 49 businesses)

Reasons	Number of businesses	Percentage of businesses
Management feels obliged to protect living standards	26	53
Management uses the consumer price index to predict wage increases at other firms	15	31
Management is concerned about the effect of declining living standards on morale	14	29

TABLE 10.6   Factors influencing labor union wage demands (applies to leaders of 15
             union organizations)

Factors	Number of organizations	Percentage of organizations
Cost of living	11	73
Pay at other firms	11	73
Competition in the product market	10	67
Company prosperity	9	60

setting raises. The 20 others said the tax had no effect on raises, though in 7 of these companies employees demanded unsuccessfully that the company pay the tax.

Managers in 14 companies discussed why raises depended on the profits of subunits of the company as well as on those of the whole company. Managers in 12 of these companies stressed incentives, and managers in the other 2 said that if subunits could not somehow arrange to be profitable they would be sold or closed, remarks that I interpret as referring to motivation.

Fifteen labor leaders expressed views on the factors shaping their wage demands during contract negotiations. As Table 10.6 shows, the factors they cited were similar to those named by employers. I interviewed leaders in industrial, construction, and retail unions, and leaders of all three kinds cited the cost of living. Officials of industrial unions stressed the importance of profits, and construction union leaders stressed product market competition, since their companies faced intense competition from nonunion companies.

MANAGERS' EXPLANATIONS

The majority of employers said that pay increases were a compromise between the influences of profitability, wage surveys, and growth in the cost of living. No fixed formula applied, the appropriate level of raises being a matter of judgment.

In Chapter 5, I discussed the dependence of raises on profits. This dependence existed in large part because of budgetary constraints or company risk aversion, but was also part of the provision of incentives (Table 5.2).

The overall level of raises depends on store sales and profits—on how much I have to play with. If sales are down, something is wrong and I have to find out what it is. The fact that raises depend on sales adds a sense of urgency to the need to satisfy customers. Eighty percent of sales are to repeat customers.

—Manager of a fast-food restaurant with 20 employees

Increases and bonuses depend more and more on the profits of the operating unit rather than inflation or the profits of the company. . . . Affordability is an issue, since payroll is a big expense, being 60 percent of operating expenses. . . . Affordability is offset by the idea that good times will be shared. This adds motivation. The company doesn't want raises ever to be viewed as an entitlement. You and your business earn what you get. We try to make that obvious.

—Human resource manager in a financial company with 24,000 employees

The suffering of the division is shared with employees in order to let them know that they need to work collectively to improve it. It is a signal, a strategic message, which people understand.

—Human resources official for a nonunion manufacturing company with 30,000 employees

The dependence of wages on division profits can lead to problems of inequity between divisions, and I found one particularly clear case of such tension.

The pay of the exempt employees is set by [the corporation] on a national basis in that it sets the ranges and the merit budget. [This division] objects, because it is not doing well. It is a different matter with the research area across the street, which is doing fine and gives the maximum it can. It uses any old weird argument to justify higher pay for its members. This creates problems, for people talk. . . .

Research wants to maximize compensation, since they are trying to get the best of every kind of employee. They claim their secretaries have to interact with scientists and type scientific documents. That is ridiculous. My people have to do more jobs, for we are more short-handed. At research, the secretaries just do word processing. The research group is on a treadmill [of self-feeding expectations of higher pay]. In research, they also want equity between exempt and nonexempt employees, regardless of the local market, paying the nonexempts extra well because scientists are paid a lot. Our division is more pragmatic, because it has to compete.

—Director of human resources of a nonunion manufacturing company with 1,000 employees

An effect closely related to pressure from low profits was the need to compete in the product market.

I have given no raises because of the competitive disadvantage the company suffers and because I can't afford it. We are not losing money, but if there is no work, there are no jobs. I would go out of business if I couldn't get work. I won't take jobs at a loss just to keep my employees going.

—Owner of a unionized architectural woodwork firm with 40 employees

What governs compensation is our own product market. Our products seem to be price sensitive, so that is a constraint.

—Owner of a nonunion manufacturing company with 1500 employees

The influence of the cost of living on raises was almost as important as that of company finances.

> We try to take account of the cost of living when giving annual increases. We try to give the highly paid at least the increase in the cost of living and to do much better than that for the lower end. If we gave less, employees would be unhappy, because their living standards would fall. Happy workers are much more productive.
>
> —General manager of a nonunion machine shop with 60 employees

> The rate of inflation is like a minimum for increases. The company doesn't want people to slip backward. Part of the happiness deriving from pay has to do with how well expectations are managed. It is not that the employees wouldn't work as well if they were underpaid, but the company doesn't want its employees to be struggling financially. What goes on at home emotionally affects the plant. Things like divorce, financial pressures, and bill collectors affect performance at work.
>
> —President of a nonunion manufacturing company and ESOP with 240 employees

Some employers were concerned about the cost of living simply because employees and unions took an interest it.

> The company worries about the cost of living when negotiating pay rates with unions, because the unions worry about it. Exempt employees worry about it too.
>
> —Human resource official in a unionized manufacturing company with 250,000 employees

Some employers believed that it was their responsibility to maintain living standards.

> When hiring someone, I pay them a salary equal to the value of their job. Inflation effectively reduces it, and fairness requires that I offset the reduction. I think that is the way it ought to be. If I hire people at a certain rate, I want to keep that level constant in terms of standard of living.
>
> —Former owner of a nonunion, 20 employee manufacturing company that closed in 1992

In addition, the cost of living served as an indicator of the market level of raises.

> The changes in the cost of living are an estimate of what other employers are going to do. We don't use the cost of living for benevolent reasons. We want to stay ahead of the next guy.
>
> —Vice president of human resources of an insurance company and HMO with 220 employees

> The inflation rate is a factor, especially in adjusting the ranges. The purchasing power of pay is irrelevant. Pay is based on performance and what the market is

paying. But the rate of inflation is an indicator of what others are doing. If other companies factor in inflation, it will influence their pay decisions.

—Human resource official in a nonunion manufacturing company with 460 employees

In deciding on the level of raises, we look at the rate of inflation in the cost of living. It is an indicator of what the competition is doing, though the best indicator is a call to your neighbor.

—Vice president of human resources of a partially unionized manufacturing company with 5,500 employees

Attitudes toward inflation varied widely, and some managers insisted that they ignored living standards and were interested only in the market level of raises. They argued that taking inflation into account implied an obligation to pay cost-of-living raises, which blunted incentives.

We ignore the cost of living when fixing the merit pool. Cost-of-living increases are demotivating. They result in automatic increases which mean nothing.

—Human resource manager of an insurance company subsidiary with 90 employees

In setting raises, we look at the market and what we can afford. . . . We don't look at the cost of living. We didn't, even during the energy crises. No attempt is made to protect living standards. If the labor market recognizes cost-of-living inflation, we will too. Doing otherwise would put us at a disadvantage. . . . We want increases to be for merit and to match the market.

—Human resource official of a nonunion manufacturing company with 9500 employees

You don't want to lock step with the rate of inflation, for you want to motivate through pay for performance. There is pressure from employees to compensate for change in the cost of living, but most companies don't use it much. If [cost-of-living] inflation were now 8 percent [instead of 3 percent], that might nudge up our pay a little bit, but business conditions probably wouldn't allow it. In setting increases, you also have to look at where you are relative to the market.

—Director of compensation at a unionized manufacturing corporation with 180,000 employees

Employers wished to be free to give less than the increase in the cost of living if it seemed correct to do so because of low profits, small increases at other firms, surges in inflation viewed as temporary, or because of a worker's poor performance. These sentiments were reflected in strongly negative comments about COLAs, which are automatic cost-of-living adjustments.

A COLA was considered and rejected. It would make costs too hard to predict. The company needs to plan ahead in order to set prices, make investments, and to decide on products, product designs, and production processes. Prices cannot be changed suddenly without shocking customers. Product designs and production methods have a lot to do with costs and can't be changed suddenly.

—Personnel director of a partially unionized manufacturing company with 250 employees

We do not look at the consumer price, though for a few years in the late 1970s and early 1980s we had COLAs because of rapid inflation. After a few years, it became clear that they were killing us, so we scrapped them.

—General manager of a nonunion cooperative food store chain with 250 employees

If our competitors for labor have COLAs, then we look at the rate of inflation. We compare what our employees are making with what others make. COLAs get away from the basic point that we are comparing our pay with that of other companies.

—Vice president of human resources for a largely nonunion manufacturing company with 125,000 employees

Managers in most companies attached great importance to wage surveys.

In deciding on raises, we look at the competition through surveys. They report intentions, but companies, including us, modify intentions in the light of surveys.

—Human resource manager in an insurance company with 2,500 employees

In deciding on raises, we look at survey data, if the business is doing well. We also call up people in other companies to find out what kind of raises they are going to give. This is informal and gives ballpark figures.

—Human resource official at the headquarters of a unionized manufacturing company with 8,500 employees

LABOR LEADERS' EXPLANATIONS

Pressure from union members made the cost of living an issue for labor leaders.

The cost of living plays some role in determining compensation, for your money doesn't go as far as it used to, and members have an idea of a standard.

—Business manager of a construction union local with 600 members

When times are good, we always use the cost of living as an argument. Now, we wouldn't be able to get increases even if there were high inflation.

—Business agent for manufacturing workers in a union local with 3,400 active members

The profitability of individual firms or industries was an important consideration, and conflicted with the tendency of unions to maintain industry wage standards, a tendency mentioned in section 7.5. Concern about profits was linked to concern about product market competition and fear of layoff. The unemployment rate was almost irrelevant.

> Pay is not uniform across companies, even for companies that are right next door to each other. This has to do in part with profit margins. . . . The only outside force making rates the same across companies is the union, because we try to negotiate uniform increases. In fact, we don't have much success in this. . . . Profits are key. If a company is profitable, we will go after more, simply because we can get it.
>
> —Regional manager of an industrial union with 6,500 active members

> Profits and the fear of layoffs are the biggest factors in setting pay objectives. . . . The unemployment rate has nothing to do with it, though it might be looked at if layoffs were a worry. . . . If a company is hurting, it might not be able to compete or [it might] go under and we would lose jobs. We can have different people in different companies in the same job earning different amounts due to the health of the companies. If a company says it can't do certain things, we might work with it, if it were in our interest to do so. We might even take a cut in pay. If the company is doing well, we want our share.
>
> —Director of an industrial union local with 65,000 members

Nevertheless, wage standards were important to unions.

> Sometimes, we tell companies they have to go out of business, because if we give them a break on pay, we have to give others a break too. We even tell owners they are destroying the industry by bidding work too low.
>
> —Business agent for manufacturing workers in a union local with 3,400 active members

> We will not allow pay to be lowered permanently. We allow layoffs and closings instead. We want pattern agreements.
>
> —President of the district organization of a service workers' union with 18,000 members

A major union concern was product market competition, especially from nonunion firms.

> Wage levels are driven largely by nonunion wages, which have been decreasing during the recession.
>
> —President and business agent for a construction local with 750 members

> Pay rates are now dominated by the nonunion sector. The union has to relate to the industry.
>
> —President of a construction union local with 3,400 active members

10.4 Summary

Firms typically continued to pay raises during the recession despite high un-employment, poor sales, and low profits. The raises were paid mainly to add to work incentives and to control labor turnover. There was concern that failure to pay adequate raises would lead to increased quitting after the recession ended, if not earlier. The main factors influencing the size of average raises were company financial well-being, changes in the cost of living, and the size of raises at other firms. The size of the unemployment rate received almost no attention.

Appendix 10A Related Literature

WHY GIVE RAISES? (SECTION 10.2)

Other studies have noted that managers give excessively positive performance evaluations. Meyer (1975) discusses the difficulty managers have giving negative reviews. Medoff and Abraham (1980) find in a study of two American companies that most evaluations are positive, and Murphy (1992) contains more information of the same kind.

A psychiatrist I interviewed said in passing that the need for "pay increases sounds like an addiction phenomenon. The next time you need a pellet and a half, like rats in a box performing tasks." This may be a correct intuition about raises. Loewenstein and Sicherman (1991) questioned members of the public about their preferences among various hypothetical time paths of earnings or expenses, and found that given the choice between two paths, people choose the one that increases over time, even when it has lower present value. Clark (1996) finds that workers' self-declared happiness is positively related to year-to-year change in their pay, though it is not related to its level.

Campbell and Kamlani (1997) report that managers believe that pay raises have a positive impact on work effort, though the effect is thought to be less strong than the negative impact of a pay cut of the same size. Gibbs (1995) explains how promotions and raises are used in a particular company to reward performance and provide incentives.

FACTORS INFLUENCING RAISES (SECTION 10.3)

The main results of this section are roughly confirmed by numerous studies of wage determination, most of which are surveyed in Carruth and Oswald (1989). In the third chapter of their book, they review published surveys of managers and union leaders on factors influencing wages. These surveys report that among the important factors are the cost of living, profits, product market competition, and pay rates at other firms, all factors stressed by my informants. Often mentioned is risk of layoff, which I have subsumed under product market competition as the two were always coupled. Carruth and Oswald give extensive documentation of the importance of the effect of profits on wages. Oswald (1996a) contains a more recent survey of the literature on the impact of profits on wages. Ichniowski and Delaney (1990) find a positive relationship between contract wages and profitability of unionized grocery stores just before contract bargaining. In a survey of 139 compensation executives, Levine (1993a) finds that ability to pay does not affect the executives' recommended increase budget, but does affect the budget decided on by their superiors. He also finds that unemployment rates and other measures of labor market tightness have almost no impact on the increase budget. In a recent survey of Swedish companies, Agell and Lundborg (1995) find that the ability to pay is the most important factor influencing wage settlements with unions, followed by wage levels at other firms. In a recent study of 16 U.S. manufacturing industries over 22 years, Blanchflower, Oswald, and Sanfey (1996) find a strong relation between profits and wages. In related work, Abowd and Lemieux (1993) find that increased international product market competition reduces Canadian union wage settlements.

11

RESISTANCE TO PAY REDUCTION

Why didn't firms routinely cut pay during the recession when faced with layoffs, high unemployment, and low profits? By a pay cut, I mean a reduction in total nominal compensation for an employee continuing in the same job with the same employer, when the reduction is not explained by changes in hours or working conditions. It is common, I believe, for the hourly pay of individual production workers to fall because of changes in job or task assignments, especially among workers paid on a piece rate basis. Wage rates may also change when workers change shifts or when, during layoffs, they "bump" workers from lower-paying jobs. (Bumping is explained in section 13.7.) Such pay changes do not reduce firms' unit production costs and are not thought of as changing the price of labor. By wage rigidity, I mean the failure of companies to cut pay.

An alternative definition of wage rigidity is the failure of company pay structures to decline in nominal terms during recessions, a definition that is sensible because company labor costs depend directly on pay structure. It is possible for pay structures to be somewhat flexible downward when pay is rigid in the sense I use. Firms normally give annual raises to workers continuing in one job, in recognition of increased skill, experience, and seniority. These raises are called for by the pay structure and are consistent with its constancy, for employees who quit or retire are normally paid more than those newly entering a job, resulting in turnover savings that offset the cost of raises. The raises cease when a firm freezes pay, yet the turnover savings may continue for a while after a freeze, reducing the average cost of employees within one job category, and this decline may continue still longer if new workers are brought into the job at lower pay than previous ones.

Other definitions of wage rigidity are current. By wage flexibility, some authors mean declines in the rate of growth of real or nominal wages (Robert

Gordon, 1982, or Hyclak and Johnes, 1992), declines in real wages paid to continuing employees (Wilson, 1996), or declines in the average real or nominal wages earned by a fixed panel of workers, who may change jobs (Bils, 1985). Pay rates are somewhat flexible according to all three of these definitions, though it may be that the real wages of continuing employees decline more during periods of rapid inflation rather than during recessions. The procyclic behavior of average wages of a panel is probably accounted for by the tendency of people to move from lower- to higher-paying jobs in booms and to do the contrary during recessions. Such movements could make the average pay of a panel move up and down in sympathy with the economy even if pay levels for particular jobs or skill levels did not change at all. I know of no studies of the cyclic behavior of pay structures, though Wilson (1996) studied the historical record of pay ranges and increase budgets in two companies and found that these were insensitive to general business conditions. Baker, Gibbs, and Holmstrom (1993, 1994a, b) and Wilson (1996) have followed through time the pay of individual employees of a few firms, but these studies do not reveal the behavior of structures themselves, for employees move up through a structure from year to year. Groshen and Schweitzer (1998) find many decreases among year-to-year changes in average nominal wages paid by given employers to people in fixed occupations, where the data are from a private wage and salary survey. Their evidence shows that parts of pay structures are allowed to drift downward, even in good times.

Reductions in total compensation can result from cuts in benefits and bonuses as well as in wages or salaries. During the period of this study, reductions in health benefits were common and were justified by rapid increases in the costs of medical insurance. It is not evident that these should be called pay cuts, for they did not necessarily reduce company compensation expenses, since increases in medical costs were shared between employers and workers. Bonuses often decreased with sales and profits, and employers did not consider this reduction to be as hazardous as cuts in base pay. However, cuts in bonuses did sometimes cause trouble, though they were known to be contingent (section 12.5). In contrast, employers were averse to cutting base pay, fearing impacts on morale, productivity, and turnover and especially turnover among the better employees.

11.1 The Extent of Downward Rigidity

I had difficulty finding companies that had cut pay. At the end of most interviews, I asked whether the respondent knew of any firm that had recently cut pay, and few had heard of any. All but a few accepted wage rigidity as a fact of life. Of the 235 firms where I interviewed, 6 had instituted general pay cuts of wages and salaries within the previous year and an additional 6 had cut the pay only of managers or executives or in one case salespeople during the same period. I found another 5 that had general pay cuts sometime during the recession, and 7 others had cut the pay of some employees during the recession, usually of managers or executives. Thus 12 firms had cut the base pay of some workers during the previous year, and overall 24 had done the same during the recession. I also found 26 firms that had reduced benefits during the recession, and of these, 3 had general pay cuts and 16 had general freezes at some point during the recession, leaving 7 that continued giving raises. I do not know whether total nominal compensation declined in the remaining 7 firms, but the other 19 clearly reduced it. These findings are summarized in Table 11.1. The percentages of cuts are almost surely biased upward, as I devoted a great deal of energy to locating firms that had cut pay. Of the 6 firms with general pay cuts during the previous year, I had interviews in 4 specifically because I heard they had cut pay. Similarly, of the 11 firms with general pay cuts during the recession, I arranged interviews in 7 after learning of the pay cut.

Pay cuts were concentrated in construction and related industries. For instance, among the 27 businesses in my study that had general cuts in total compensation during the recession, 16 were in industries strongly affected by the downturn in construction, including 7 construction companies, 2 architectural engineering companies, 2 banks suffering from bad loans made to real estate developers, and 5 manufacturing companies producing for the construction industry. The companies that had reduced pay were small or medium sized. Among the 11 companies that had general cuts in base pay during the recession, 5 had fewer than 100 employees, and all had fewer than 1,000. Among the 16 that at some time during the recession had general freezes and reductions in

TABLE 11.1   Incidence of nominal pay cuts (applies to 235 businesses)

Type of nominal pay reduction	Number of businesses	Percentage of businesses
General cut in base pay during the previous year	6	3
General cut in base pay during the recession	11	5
Cut in base pay for some or all employees during the previous year	12	5
Cut in base pay for some or all employees during the recession	24	10
General cut in total compensation during the recession	27	11

benefits, 11 had fewer than 100 employees, 13 had fewer than 1,000, and none had more than 5,500.

Some companies reduced wage costs through outsourcing, which meant subcontracting to other companies work previously done within the company itself. For instance, it was not uncommon for companies to save money by outsourcing guard and janitorial services, and the subcontractors typically paid less for this work than had the client companies. Workers whose jobs had been outsourced sometimes transferred to the subcontractor, receiving lower pay from it. I do not regard these changes as pay cuts, since the identity of the employer changed.

11.2 Reasons for Resistance to Pay Reduction

Employers explained why they were reluctant to cut pay. Surprisingly, labor leaders had similar views.

OVERVIEW OF INTERVIEW EVIDENCE

All employers thought cutting the pay of existing employees would cause problems. The main argument was that employee reactions would cost the firm more money than a pay cut would save, so that it would be profitable only if workers accepted it. Table 11.2 summarizes views on the anticipated employee reactions. (In interpreting the table, it is important to keep in mind that I did not suggest arguments to employers.) In this table, productivity refers to the activity of existing employees and not to the effects of turnover on output.

Most of those who did not stress morale mentioned turnover as an important consideration. Turnover meant primarily quitting when new job opportunities arose, which could mean not until economic recovery.

Several plausible arguments received little emphasis, including union resistance, fear of sabotage, of unionization, or of damage to company reputation, and the difficulty of convincing employees that a pay cut was needed. Another possible argument hardly mentioned was the desire of company leadership not to have its own pay cut. It was accepted that the pay of ordinary workers could not be cut without cutting the pay of managers proportionately by as much or more.

Since some employers said that a pay cut might drive away their best workers, an obvious question was why not cut the pay of all but the best. I asked this of managers in 11 companies, and the general thrust of all but 2 responses was that the resulting inequities would cause too many problems with morale, which was also the reason given for not confining raises to the best employees (section 10.2). The 2 said they lacked the courage to proceed in this way.

Employers' view of the impact of pay cuts contrasted sharply with their opin-

TABLE 11.2   Arguments against cutting base pay (applies to 151 businesses)

Arguments	Number of businesses	Percentage of businesses
Pay cuts hurt morale and demotivate workers	104	69
Because of lower living standards	38	25
Because they are insulting	26	17
Pay cuts hurt productivity	63	42
Pay cuts increase turnover	62	41
Employees would leave slowly or at the onset of the next boom	45	30
The best employees would leave	18	12
Employees would quit out of rage	5	3
It is hard to convince workers that a pay cut is needed to save their jobs	11	7
Pay cuts invite sabotage	8	5
Pay cuts invite unionization	7	5
Unions resist pay cuts	4	3
Managers do not want to cut their own pay	5	3

ion about the effect of the long-term level of pay. Recall that most employers saw the impact of pay levels on turnover and recruitment as more significant than any effect on morale and productivity (section 7.1).

Pay cutting was discussed in 13 of 18 interviews with labor leaders. They emphasized that pay cuts were discouraging and pointless, except when they gave more work to union members. This occurred only in construction and in manufacturing closely linked to it or when businesses were in danger of closing.

MANAGERS' AND LABOR LEADERS' EXPLANATIONS
There was a danger that pay cuts would appear arrogant.

I never cut anyone's wage. That would be too personal. It would be putting too much power into your own hands and would be resented.
—Owner of a nonunion machine shop with 30 employees

There was also fear that pay cuts would be interpreted as an insult, expressing dissatisfaction with individual employees and provoking hostility.

I have never cut wages. It is like penalizing employees and inviting them to start stealing. They would not look at the business aspect of things. They would think I was hurting them personally. They are just silly, self-centered kids.

—Owner of a fast-food franchise with 10 employees

It's a personal thing. People can't explain a pay cut at home, whereas if they are laid off they can draw unemployment benefits and look for new work. A pay cut is like a criticism or an insult. Pay is so closely associated with self-worth that a cut is taken personally.

—Owner of a nonunion electronics manufacturing company with 15 employees

I have never cut anyone's pay. I don't believe in it in principle. . . . A pay cut would be interpreted as a punishment, even if it were done across the board. It would be insulting and would lower people's standard of living and for both those reasons, it would hurt morale and get people working against rather than for the restaurant. In this business, that could happen in a couple of days.

—Manager of a restaurant with 30 employees

I know something real. Never cut wages. If you do, you make enemies. They don't understand economics. They will wonder what they did wrong. And enemies hire lawyers.

—President of a nonunion manufacturing company with 40 employees

Morale suffers from a pay cut for psychic reasons. It says, "I am doing badly," even if everyone gets a pay cut. It is part of American culture. Individual performance is identified with how well you are paid. If your pay was cut, your neighbors would view you as working for a bad company.

—High-level human resource official in an insurance company with 50,000 employees

Some labor leaders expressed similar sentiments.

There are lots of penalties to cutting pay. You lose the enthusiasm and loyalty of your work force. People measure success with pay. A cut in pay means you haven't been doing well.

—Business agent of a retail workers' union local with 16,000 members

Employers believed pay cuts would probably be viewed as disloyal, unfair, and as a capricious denial of earned rewards. Pay cuts are resented and regarded as unfair in part because they remind employees that they are much poorer than company owners, who are better able to bear business risk.

A wage cut would give rise to morale problems. The employees would have a chip on their shoulders and would lose the fire in their bellies. Pay increases are a reward for effort, and the reward would be denied.

—Owner of a manufacturing company employing 30 unskilled workers

[A pay cut] is out of the realm of consideration. . . . It has something to do with the idea that if you have a decent life and the company isn't doing well, your employees shouldn't have to bear the brunt of it. You are driving a fancy car, and they are not.

—Personnel officer of a nonunion manufacturing company with 80 employees

Pay has never been cut, for morale reasons. Such a thing is just not done. To cut pay would be to take unfair advantage of people.

—Human resource official of a unionized manufacturing company with 2,700 employees

People would resent a pay cut. They would say, "The company didn't stand by me. Why should I stay?"

—Human resource official of a unionized manufacturing company with 17,000 employees

The impact of pay cuts on employee living standards was managers' greatest concern. Adjustment to lower incomes distracts employees and leads them to blame the company for their distress.

Regardless of what you pay people, they spend all they earn and more. An entry-level person may come in at the minimum wage and work up to $8 to $9 in a short time. He will move from a room to an apartment of his own. That is the reason you can't cut pay. Everyone is two paychecks away from homelessness. . . . Layoffs drown them too, but they don't calculate that way.

—Owner of a nonunion electronics manufacturing company with 15 employees

I never froze or cut pay, and never will. The employees have to live. You have to take into consideration their needs. They don't have much flexibility. They are not paid as much as factory owners or college professors.

—President and half-owner of a nonunion candy company employing 200 people

The fact that merit increases are not as high as they used to be has had no effect on morale, but morale would be affected by a pay cut. Employees would be pre-occupied with trying to make ends meet. The women who work here are not just trying to get out of the house.

—Personnel manager of a department store with 300 employees

Pay cuts are extremely demoralizing. Everybody gets used to a standard of living. If you cut pay by 5 percent, everyone would feel they had worked last year for nothing. The president of the company might say he was taking it too, but that would be meaningless. He could lose that much in one night in Las Vegas.

—Vice president of human resources of a partially unionized manufacturing company with 5,500 employees

A pay cut would be unacceptable. . . . At the clerical level and at the level of some exempts, pay is so low that people couldn't afford a cut. It would be hard to adapt to one. . . . People would suffer and then blame the company.

—Human resource manager in a 21,500 employee subsidiary of a large insurance company

Labor leaders also emphasized the impact on living standards.

Pay cuts are demoralizing. No one likes to see their standard of living going backward. Sensing a decline in living standards causes panic. Even pay freezes are hard. Pay cuts and freezes tend to make people feel they are being taken advantage of. They think it is a plot to steal their money and put it in the pockets of the owners.

—Business representative for an industrial union local with 2,000 active members

Pay cuts for all but the best workers were regarded as too risky because they would violate internal equity as well as impose suffering, and therefore be especially harmful to morale.

Question: Why not cut the pay of only the worst employees? *Answer:* If you did, you would have a bad morale problem—a revolt within the ranks. They wouldn't cooperate. The people whose pay had not been cut would be despised.

—One of four owners of a nonunion manufacturing company with 200 employees

If you cut the pay of all but the superperformers, you have a big morale problem. Everyone thinks they are a superperformer.

—Head of human resources of a nonunion consumer products company with 1,500 employees

Bad morale following pay cuts would affect work effort, work ethics, and the need for supervision.

If I lowered pay . . . bad attitudes might come across with a customer. The drivers are the company's best sales representatives. A customer might give business to your company rather than another because he likes you or your drivers. Rates [i.e., sales prices] don't differ by much [among companies]. Drivers' attitudes or performance might be affected even if pay were cut only to $10.50 [from $11.25] an hour. The money saved by the pay cut would be lost through customers lost because of grumpy drivers. You want them to be happy-go-lucky.

—Part-owner of a nonunion trucking company with 14 drivers

If the men are paid too little, they will go out on jobs without any fire in their bellies. In order to have an impact on the business, pay would have to be cut by about 30 percent. This would be to pay a carpenter as if he were a helper. Their attitude would be affected as would their desire to do the work. Their relations with customers might also be affected. It is a question of pride. Our people have been here so long that it wouldn't be the thing to do. One carpenter has been here since 1948.

—General manager of a nonunion construction company with 15 employees

A pay cut would be difficult. . . . Our philosophy is that if you pay them right, they will perform. If you nickel and dime them to death, they will play games with you and won't work well. There are many things they have to do without specific instruction. For instance, we get in clean linen before a dinner. There may be some extra left over after setting the tables up. I tell them not to leave the clean stuff around, for if there is a spill, the first thing someone will grab to wipe it up is a clean napkin. It costs 35¢ to get one washed. So, they put the clean stuff in the cellar. They do that on their own, but wouldn't if they wanted to play games.

—Manager of a catering business with 60 employees

If pay were cut, the work force would be very unhappy. Morale would be low. People don't work without half-way decent morale. If morale is low, they get so that all they want to do is beat the system. In this case, they need lots of supervision. People would not recognize that the market for their services was down. There is nothing rational about the way people judge their own situation.

—Personnel director of a partially unionized manufacturing company with 250 employees

What goes around comes around. If we did cut pay, turnover would increase, even during a recession. People would be angry and upset and might do little disruptive things and engage in minor forms of sabotage. Absenteeism would increase. You would pay for the bad feeling in the future. . . . If you come through for them, they will for you. . . . Pay cuts would certainly affect productivity.

—Human resource officer of an 850-employee, nonunion division of a manufacturing company

A pay cut would be a short-term gain. The company would get a one-year growth in earnings, and the employees would be pissed off. They would find ways to take away from the company the 5 percent that it had taken from them. It's just human nature.

—Human resources official for a nonunion manufacturing company with 30,000 employees

Employers were concerned about the effects of pay cuts on turnover, which could occur quickly or gradually or not until the economy recovered. Looking for a new job would itself distract from work. The increase in turnover would occur because of anger and low morale, because of fear for the company's future, because the pay of competitors would be relatively more attractive, and because the cut attracted attention to the idea of leaving. High turnover was viewed as one facet of low morale. Managers fear turnover because it gives them little control over the choice of who leaves and "distills your employee population in a negative way." Layoffs give greater control (section 13.5).

If pay were cut, some employees would leave, even though jobs are scarce. Key employees would be difficult to replace. We have long-term customers who know the employees and are used to dealing with them. We service old jobs, and the key people know the buildings of the old customers.

—President of a nonunion mechanical contracting company with 13 employees

If I cut pay, people would leave out of rage, even though they have no place to go. They would feel they had to. They live close to the edge anyway, spending 110 percent of their income, no matter what it is. The body shop people would certainly leave. They are crazy. They smell too many fumes. The girls in the office could be cut, but they are low paid anyway.

—Owner of a car dealership with 30 employees

I haven't cut pay because I have a lot of money invested in my people. This recession won't last forever and when it is over I want to be as strong as possible. For that, I need capable, knowledgeable people. They would leave if I cut their pay. If they were mad enough, they would leave even now. It is an illusion to believe they wouldn't. My motto is "Don't test anyone."

—Owner of a furniture store chain with 200 employees

If the pay of hourly employees working in this city were cut, most would have nowhere to go. This would amount to exploitation. As soon as the economy revived, they would bail out. . . . A pay cut would hurt performance too, especially if people were looking for another job.

—Chief human resource official for a 4,500-employee, nonunion division of a large manufacturing company

The arguments against pay cuts are retention issues—even during a recession. There is still a lot of work out there. . . . The trouble with the attrition resulting from pay cuts is that you can't control who leaves. The best people get jobs first. The people who would leave could be in human resources, finance, engineering, anywhere. They would leave because they could get more money elsewhere. . . . A pay cut would be a signal that people should start looking

—High-level human resource official at a unionized manufacturing company with 19,000 employees

If we held up pay due to a recession, only the good employees would leave. The philosophy of top management is that freezing or taking away base pay is short-sighted. Problems caused by a recession are short-term. If you freeze or cut pay, you come out of the recession with problems, namely, that you have lost your best people and have a salary structure that doesn't allow you to recruit without internal compression.

—High-level human resource manager in a unionized manufacturing company with 27,000 employees

The concerns about turnover were echoed by a few labor leaders.

> Pay cuts demoralize the work force. When I have negotiated them, the best people
> left, even during recessions, and productivity dropped. People saw the end coming.
> They didn't see the pay cut as temporary. They didn't see a future. A pay cut is a
> signal that you should start looking for something else to do.
>
> —Regional manager of an industrial union with 6,500 active members

Management caution may contribute to wage rigidity. Some of what I heard indicated that managers worry, clinging to known and trusted policies.

> No pay cuts have been made because no one has the nerve to do it. The partners
> deemed it radical not to give raises. . . . I do not know why pay is not cut, for no
> one has really thought about it.
>
> —Managing partner of a law firm with 200 employees

> The American public would probably be willing to pay higher taxes to eliminate
> the federal deficit. In the same way, employees would probably be willing to un-
> dergo a 10 percent pay cut to save their company. But management is not willing
> to take the risk. Layoff is less risky. . . . Productivity would probably not drop if
> pay were cut 10 percent across the board and if the cut was viewed as necessary.
> But management fears a drop in productivity.
>
> —Human resource official in a bank with 800 employees

I did not obtain much information about where managers got their ideas about pay cutting. These were so universal that they must be part of business culture. Some claimed to have learned from their own experience or that of others.

> Pay cuts would be regarded as unfair and would affect morale for a long time.
> Employees would never forget it. I know someone in another company who says
> the worst thing he ever did was to cut pay. . . . A year ago, we considered a 10
> percent pay cut. The CEO said that it had been done once at another company
> where he worked. The employees never forgot it. They felt they had been mis-
> treated.
>
> —Human resource manager of a nonunion machine shop with 225 employees

No employer or union leader brought up the information issues that have been central to many economic theories of labor contracts, matters discussed in section 19.1.

11.3 Reasons for Laying Off Workers Rather than Cutting Pay

I was surprised to learn that most managers did not believe that pay cuts would prevent many layoffs. The low elasticity of demand for labor made pay cuts hard to sell to the work force. The choice between layoffs and pay cuts existed only for companies that faced a very competitive product market or were in danger of going out of business. In most firms, labor costs, especially the costs of direct labor, were a small part of costs and product demand was not very price elastic, so that pay cuts would have little impact on product prices, quantities sold, and employment, at least within the short time span relevant to layoffs. Managers thought of variable inputs as being used in nearly fixed proportions in the short run, so that a 10 percent cut in total compensation would reduce marginal costs by only 1.5 percent, if the cost of direct labor were 15 percent of variable costs (a typical figure). If demand were not very elastic in the short run, a 1.5 percent reduction in marginal costs would increase the quantity sold by only several times this amount, say, by 3 percent to 7.5 percent, so that the short-run elasticity of demand for labor would be from 0.3 to 0.75.

A low elasticity of demand for labor is consistent with the implicit or efficient contract models, for these imply that wage costs have no impact on the short-run demand for labor. However, none of the managers I interviewed used arguments related to these models. When asked why wage cuts would have little impact on labor demand, they cited labor's small fraction of variable costs and the short-run insensitivity of product demand to price.

The low elasticity of demand for labor was an important argument against pay cuts as an alternative to layoffs. Other arguments were that the impact of layoffs on morale is temporary, that layoffs increase productivity (whereas pay cuts may hurt it), and that layoffs give employers some control over the selection of the workers who leave (whereas pay cuts may cause quits predominantly among the best employees). The generally accepted policy was to remove unneeded workers and to encourage those who remained to be as productive as possible by making them believe they could stay and by giving them raises. A final advantage of layoffs is that they save a great deal of money. Pay cuts reduce only wage or salary costs, whereas layoffs eliminate fixed costs of employment as well, which were said to be 25 percent to more than 40 percent of total compensation. The fixed costs included benefits, insurance, and the materials, supplies, and space needed for employed workers.

OVERVIEW OF INTERVIEW EVIDENCE

Asking directly about the choice between layoffs and pay cuts risked alienating managers, for most did not think of the two as alternatives. As a result, I did not bring up this topic as often as many others. Nevertheless, I did ask managers in 32 firms in a variety of types of business why they had laid workers off rather than cut pay, and many more managers made comments related to the topic. A common reaction to the question was puzzlement. Pay cuts would create little or no extra work and so would barely reduce the number of excess workers.

Retention of unneeded employees would be bad for morale and would encourage bad work habits and attitudes. Table 11.3 summarizes responses. Fourteen of the 32 managers volunteered opinions about whether they thought their workers preferred pay cuts or layoffs, and 9 said they thought workers preferred layoffs.

A question related to the choice between layoffs and pay cuts is why firms did not cut pay in order to reduce product prices and thereby expand sales and avoid layoffs. This question met with a lively response, and I asked it of managers of 53 firms in a wide variety of businesses. As may be seen from Table 11.4, the majority said that price cuts following pay cuts would not have a significant impact on sales and employment, though 9 said the contrary. Of these 9, 2 had recently had across the board pay cuts and 3 were in businesses where sales were obtained by sealed bidding, so that they were very price competitive.

An obvious follow-up question was why sales would respond little to price

TABLE 11.3 Why not cut pay rather than lay off workers? (applies to 32 businesses)

Reason	Number of businesses	Percentage of businesses
Pay cuts would not save or create jobs	18	56
Pay cuts would hurt morale and productivity more than layoffs would	14	44
Layoffs give better control over who leaves	9	28
Layoffs save more money than do pay cuts	8	25

TABLE 11.4 Why not cut pay and prices, thereby avoiding layoffs by selling more? (applies to 50 businesses)

Reason	Number of businesses	Percentage of businesses
Price cuts made possible by pay cuts would have little impact on sales and employment, at least in the short run	39	78
Price cuts would increase sales and employment significantly	9	18
The cost advantage from pay cuts would be lost to reduced productivity	4	8

TABLE 11.5 Why would employment respond little to wage cuts? (applies to 26 businesses)

Reason	Number of businesses	Percentage of businesses
Product demand would respond little to price cuts	21	81
Because the business's product demand responds little to price	8	31
Because the business does not compete on the basis of price	7	27
Because product market competitors would also lower their prices	6	23
Direct labor is a small fraction of costs	7	27

TABLE 11.6 The ratio of direct labor costs to sales (applies to 41 businesses)

	Range for the ratio r				
	$0 < r \leq 0.10$	$0.10 < r \leq 0.20$	$0.20 < r \leq 0.30$	$0.30 < r \leq 0.40$	$r > 0.40$
Number of businesses	12	11	9	3	6

reductions made possible by pay cuts. I asked this question in 26 firms, and the answers, summarized in Table 11.5, were that product demand was not very responsive to price, at least not in the short run relevant for avoiding layoffs, that competitors would lower their prices too, and that pay cuts would have little impact on prices because direct labor costs were a small fraction of total costs.

In connection with the impact of pay cuts on price, I obtained information on the ratio of direct labor costs to total sales revenue in 41 companies from various types of business and was surprised at how low the ratio was. In many companies, the bulk of variable costs are materials and supplies. The results are summarized in Table 11.6.

MANAGERS' EXPLANATIONS

An important theme was that layoffs do less damage to morale and productivity than do pay cuts. Layoffs can even improve productivity (section 13.10) and are sometimes made to finance raises.

It is easier to lay people off than to cut pay. It's like soldiers. If the guy next to me is shot, I say, "Wasn't I lucky it wasn't me."

—Owner of a nonunion manufacturing firm with 40 employees

It is hard for low-paid people to give up pay, for that cuts into bone. . . . The attitude is "I would rather kill you." [That is, I would rather lay you off.]

—Vice president of human resources of an insurance company and HMO with 220 employees

We couldn't have avoided layoffs through pay cuts, except in the short term. Pay would grow and we would still have internal inefficiencies. . . . With layoffs, people take an "It'll never be me" attitude. Pay cuts affect everybody. Layoffs affect a small percentage of the employees.

—High-level human resource official in a 3,000-employee, largely nonunion division of a huge consumer products company

Layoffs do hurt morale. There is a trade-off between [the number of] positions and the size of increases. We try to balance the damage to morale from both sources. A pay cut would have a worse effect. The effect of a layoff on the morale of survivors is temporary, provided they are taken care of.

—Vice president of human resources of a nonunion manufacturing company employing 5,000 people

Some managers emphasized that layoffs saved much more money than pay cuts.

If you lay someone off, you save on his pay, his benefits, and the overhead expense of phone, lights, rent, and what not associated with keeping him. Hopefully, you will be able to rent less space. You would have to make big cuts in pay to equal the savings from layoffs. From an employee relations standpoint, you upset one person, who is walked to the door, as opposed to upsetting hundreds of people with a pay cut.

—The director of human resources for a financial brokerage and investment banking firm with 1,600 employees

The amount of money saved by cutting pay is probably small, for benefits are a big part of compensation costs. If you did cut pay enough to reach the dollar figure you had in mind, you would have disgruntled employees and the best ones would leave the company. For modest cost savings, you shouldn't cut pay. For big ones, you couldn't cut pay enough. If the employees did stay, they would be disgruntled. Letting people go is neat and clean. You have control over who leaves. Layoffs create better employee relations, though layoffs also have their downsides. But the damage doesn't linger.

—Human resource manager for a corporate research facility with 2,000 employees

Layoffs also had the advantages of removing the least good workers and pushing the remaining workers to work harder.

We consider cutting pay at monthly board meetings where there is lots of internal debate. The choice is between cutting pay and employees. I say, "Cut bodies." That is controlled surgery. If we cut pay, they will all leave, or the best will. . . . I say, "It is cheaper to retain than to obtain." Training and the learning curve are expensive. . . . [People will leave] because they are pissed off. They need the money. They consider it poor treatment. If someone is happy in a job, why would he read the want ads? If I cut pay, they would understand, but their kids need shoes too. I try to keep people. If you have someone who is a producer, it is stupid to let them go. Some people say that turnover brings fresh ideas, but I don't like it. Hiring and training take my time away from other things, such as developing new programs and raising money.

—Director of a community service organization with 150 employees

A pay cut was considered as an alternative to layoff. . . . It wouldn't force operating efficiencies in the way that a layoff would. Doing without people forces the rest to work more systematically. A pay cut could bring a backlash on morale, which could lay us open to a unionization attempt.

—Human resource official at a partially unionized manufacturing company with 12,000 employees

Some respondents made it clear they did not believe pay cuts created jobs.

If I cut pay instead of laying people off, I would have lots of people with nothing to do. They would get into bad habits and it would be hard to get them back to full productivity when business picked up.

—Owner of a nonunion manufacturing company with 35 employees

What do pay cuts have to do with layoffs? A layoff is used when you don't have sufficient work for certain skills. What would you do with the extra help? It would be unfair to them to keep them around. . . . How could you ask everyone to take a pay cut in order to keep some idle people around?

—Human resource manager of a unionized manufacturing firm with 1,800 employees

Wage cuts are not an alternative to layoffs. You can't have a lot of people standing around doing nothing. You couldn't cut pay enough to make a difference in sales without losing your work force. The wage cut wouldn't go down.

—Vice president of human resources of a partially unionized manufacturing company with 5,500 employees

What are the men here to do if their jobs are saved—sweep the floors? . . . . If you cut the pay of exempts by 20 percent, you might save 4 percent of their jobs. Benefits are a big fixed cost.

—Human resource manager of a unionized manufacturing company with 30,000 employees

The dominant view was that pay cuts were a bad alternative to layoffs. Unnecessary workers should be dismissed and the remaining ones should be made happy and productive, not discouraged by lower wages and salaries.

> To cut pay rather than laying people off would be a wrong solution to a wrong problem. The company doesn't need the people. . . . Those who are kept after lay-offs should be taken care of. . . . There are too many things that could be done before that, and everyone knows it. First and foremost is rightsizing. Exotic trees on the campus [i.e., corporate headquarters] and expensive paintings in the corridors are symbolic of extravagance. You can't cut pay when everyone sees that. Employees see others not working hard, though they themselves are. They know that management is ignoring this.
>
> —Human resource manager in an insurance company with 2,500 employees

> Layoffs are more permanent. We want costs cut out permanently. Pay cuts are not permanent, because if they were, we would be behind the market when the economy turned around. . . . If we lowered pay due to the recession, it would create a climate where people would feel they had been taken advantage of. The better people would leave once the economy turned around, either because of the low pay or because of a company culture where people are taken advantage of. We want a core of properly motivated and well-paid people. Layoff is not viewed as unfair, except by the unusual person. People understand.
>
> —Director of compensation at a unionized manufacturing corporation with 180,000 employees

It was hard to find employers who believed that pay cuts would allow price cuts large enough to have a significant impact on sales. Employers from many different types of business gave a variety of explanations for the small effect.

> I would have to cut prices by 25 percent to get a 50 percent increase in sales, and this would not be enough to help me. . . . The small manufacturers I deal with would not want me to discount and would probably refuse to sell to me. They don't like discounting, because that brings price wars, and prices go so low that retailers are threatened with insolvency, and to keep them in business the manufacturers have to cut prices too. They prefer that the discounting be done in their own stores.
>
> —Owner and manager of a women's clothing store with 8 employees

> A pay and price cut wouldn't bring in business. There are no calls coming in. People are still so scared of losing their jobs that they don't spend, in spite of low interest rates. The work is not there.
>
> —Owner of a nonunion construction company with 10 employees

> You lower price against competition, not in order to counteract a downturn in sales. Price cuts don't generate more business. One cent per item would mean a great deal to us and very little to a buyer. We could raise prices, but we don't. We leave well enough alone. There is lots of inertia in everything. We would have to

really screw up to lose business. We have long-term relationships with our buyers and a relationship of mutual trust with them.

—Owner of a nonunion manufacturing company with 20 employees

Cutting pay and price wouldn't help. I could get a little temporary business by lowering prices. But then my competitors would lower their prices and the profitability of the industry would decline.

—Owner of a nonunion manufacturing company with 35 employees

Cutting prices doesn't bring in work. Demand takes too long to react to price. It can take two or three months to inform customers of a price change and for them to react.

—General manager of a nonunion machine shop with 60 employees

Law firms charge by the hour, and cutting the hourly rate would not generate new business. Our only competitors are some New York and D.C. specialty law firms. There is too little competition to make price cuts effective. Referrals by other lawyers do not depend on price.

—Personnel director of a law firm with 60 employees

A pay cut combined with a price cut would not increase sales by much. In the first place, direct labor costs are only about 10 percent of revenue. Also, if we were to reduce prices, our competitors would do the same. We are a price leader in our market.

—Human resource manager of a unionized manufacturing company with 150 employees

Price cuts wouldn't create work. The company has lots of competition, but price cuts wouldn't bid business away from them. Performance and the ability to deliver are more important than price to the customer.

—Human resource officer of a nonunion manufacturing company with 350 employees

Wage cuts would not be made to save jobs. Most sales are to long-term customers, so that cutting prices would not increase business much.

—Human resource manager of a nonunion printing company with 400 employees

I was in favor of a freeze, but the argument was that if there was a freeze, the government would ask for lower prices, so that the company would lose money anyway. If you change the cost assumptions on which a contract with the government was made, it can ask for money back. It won't buy more as a result of lower prices.

—Human resource manager of a unionized manufacturing firm with 1,800 employees

We want to maintain margins. Any company that cuts price is an outlaw. Price cuts turn a specialty market into a commodity market. Companies don't want that. They want customers to think about value, not price. . . . Relationships [of a product's price with those of related products] have to be maintained to keep the image of the product.

—Corporate director of human resources of a mostly nonunion manufacturing company with 5,000 employees

In theory, you could cut pay and prices enough to avoid the need for layoffs of production employees. But in practice, you have to be predictable to your customers as well. It would be difficult to increase the prices later. If you did cut prices, it would be better to leave them there.

—Vice president of human resources for a largely nonunion manufacturing company with 125,000 employees

We do not sell the kind of products for which sales could be expanded by cutting price. Demand is pretty inelastic, at least in the short run.

—Human resource manager in a corporation in the service sector with 135,000 employees

LABOR LEADERS' EXPLANATIONS

I solicited labor leaders' views on whether pay cuts saved jobs. All said that members' pay was limited by competition from nonunion labor, an assertion that reflects a conviction that the long-run wage elasticity of demand for union members' labor was significant.

Employment does depend on pay. Higher pay could force a company out of markets, and jobs would be lost. Pay increases could affect the profitability of the company in the future, which could mean more layoffs.

—Director of an industrial union local with 65,000 members

The impact of wage cuts on current layoffs depends, however, on short-run rather than long-run elasticity, and opinions about this impact depended on the industry. Many construction unions had institutionalized pay cutting through work or market recovery programs, which allowed selective pay cuts for projects where union firms had to bid against nonunion competition (section 12.5).

A pay cut wouldn't generate more work, because the work recovery program already achieves what is needed.

—President and business agent for a construction local with 750 members

In the retail trade industry, pay cuts were not much of an issue since entry-level pay for salesclerks fell almost automatically when local labor markets weakened (sections 17.2 and 17.3). With one exception, leaders of industrial unions saw little connection between pay reduction and layoff prevention. The exception was the labor leader mentioned at the end of Chapter 7, who was encouraging pay cuts to forestall plant closures. His organization was the only industrial union in my sample facing a high short-run elasticity of demand for its labor.

> Pay cuts don't guarantee jobs. They just guarantee profits. Being creative sells more, not pay and price cuts. You need machinery, better processes, and creative marketing.
>
> —Organizing director for Connecticut of a large national union

> If the company is not threatened with going out of business, jobs are not determined by wages. Employment is determined by the product market. To some degree, lower prices increase sales, but they are not a big factor. Price is, however, a factor in some competitive industries.
>
> —General counsel for a regional union council with 6,000 union members

> The union doesn't want pay cut to save jobs because it doesn't view high wages as inducing layoffs. Not even the company claims that.
>
> —Head labor representative of an industrial union local with an active membership of 12,000

11.4 Reasons for Resistance to Worksharing

An alternative to pay cuts or layoffs is worksharing, or short-time, which is avoidance of layoffs through substantial reduction in the hours of all employees' work, with a proportionate reduction in the pay of salaried workers. Worksharing is normally accomplished either through cutting workweeks from five to four days or through furloughs, which are rotating temporary layoffs, during which workers usually retain benefits. Since worksharing preserves benefits, it increases hourly labor costs. For this reason worksharing is not attractive to employers, unless the downturn is thought to be temporary and they wish to retain highly skilled workers, who might leave if laid off and would be hard to replace. Few employers used worksharing, and the idea was usually treated so dismissively that I did not pursue it in many interviews.

OVERVIEW OF INTERVIEW EVIDENCE

Among the 235 companies interviewed, only 5 had undertaken worksharing during the year before the interview, and one other had done so earlier during the recession. Forty-four employers discussed the topic. In general they said that though worksharing is not as offensive as cutting pay, it does reduce living standards and therefore hurts morale if continued too long, bringing lower productivity or higher turnover. Some employers said that special factors made worksharing inefficient for their type of work. There was a division of opinion as to whether workers preferred worksharing to layoffs. Some said

TABLE 11.7   Employer comments on worksharing (applies to 44 businesses)

Comments	Number of businesses	Percentage of businesses
Worksharing damages morale	19	43
Worksharing should be temporary	13	30
Worksharing hurts productivity	8	18
Worksharing saves less money than layoffs	8	18
Worksharing is inefficient	7	16
Worksharing preserves a valued work force	7	16
High-seniority workers resist worksharing	7	16
Workers prefer worksharing to layoffs	7	16

worksharing was less threatening than layoffs, and others said workers with high seniority resented losing income to protect the income of newer workers. The latter sentiment existed only in companies where layoffs were made in inverse order of seniority, a rule used only in a minority of companies (section 13.5). Table 11.7 summarizes the results.

MANAGERS' EXPLANATIONS

From the perspective of employers, the main problem with worksharing was its expense.

> We have never considered short-time. . . . Because of fixed employment costs, short-time is not financially advantageous for the company. It is better to be short staffed and use overtime.
>
> —Founding partner of an architecture firm with 45 employees

> The [rotating] furloughs were. . . . very costly. The company's unemployment insurance rating went up to the maximum and employees retained their benefits while on furlough. Vacations and holidays still accumulated. I won't do it again, even though furloughs did keep the existing work force together. . . .
>   I prefer the risk of losing people through layoff to the cost of furloughing. Furloughing is more humane. People hate layoffs. . . . Everybody liked the furloughs. It was like an extra five weeks of vacation.
>
> —Personnel manager of a unionized manufacturing company and ESOP with 200 employees

One of the main arguments against pay cuts was also used against short-time; reduced living standards hurt morale and productivity and increased turnover.

The objective of worksharing would be to keep people employed. It is bad to do that, it turns out. Pay cuts of 20 percent associated with a four-day week would have been demoralizing. People would have had less reason to put out for the job.

—One of three partners owning an advertising agency with 9 employees

Unhappiness from reduced hours or pay cuts would cut productivity. Short-time would lead to people's dogging it. Employees should be very busy and enjoy performing well.

—General manager of a nonunion machine shop with 60 employees

A four-day week was considered as an alternative to layoffs. It was rejected because it would be bad for morale. It is better to have 10 unhappy people outside the company than 120 unhappy ones inside.

—Personnel director of a nonunion manufacturing plant with 120 employees

Short-time would hurt morale, just as a pay cut would. People need the level of income they have. Bad morale would hurt productivity and the quality of service. If the economy were right, short-time or a pay cut would lead to quits.

—Human resource manager specializing in downsizing and working for an insurance company with 33,000 employees

Worksharing preserved the work force for employers, but it had this advantage only if it was temporary, for reduced incomes could increase quitting.

Furloughs help you preserve the work force, if the drop in the need for labor is thought to be temporary. We try to go with furloughing as long as we can, until we see that no turnaround is in sight. Layoffs allow you to reduce furloughs. This improves morale and makes employees more optimistic about the future.

—Vice president of human resources of a nonunion manufacturing company with 260 employees

The choice between layoff and short-time depends on how bad the cutback in demand is. If short-time is too prolonged, you start losing your best people.

—Owner of a nonunion manufacturing company with 1,500 employees

Some employers claimed that short-time was inefficient because of the way their work was organized.

Short-time wouldn't work for us. The men have to be on the job every day and work with other trades. If jobs were shared with other men, working on alternative days, say, coordination would break down. One man wouldn't know where the other had left off. Every job is different. Each job requires intelligence and special, concentrated attention.

—President of a nonunion mechanical contracting company with 13 employees

Shorter hours are very inefficient. Because of coffee breaks and the time taken to get organized, I get only 6 of 8 hours a day out of my employees. The extra time is still lost if I cut hours.

—Owner of a nonunion electronics manufacturing company with 15 employees

Worksharing would be very difficult for most positions. The continuity would not be there. At corporate [headquarters], each person does a separate project, so that worksharing would be nearly infeasible.

—Vice president of personnel of a diversified company in the service sector with 2,000 employees

In some companies where layoff was by inverse seniority, senior workers would have objected to short-time.

Union employees don't want worksharing. Union men want 40 hours and don't care about the newer employees who will be laid off. They also like the simplicity of the layoff system.

—Human resource manager of a unionized manufacturing firm with 90 employees

Layoffs are used rather than some sort of general pay reduction or worksharing because the existing or remaining work force doesn't care about those laid off. The seniority system identifies those most vulnerable to layoff. . . . You want to affect as small a number of people as possible.

—Human resource manager of a nonunion machine shop with 225 employees

11.5 Summary

Few firms cut the pay of existing employees. Employers were reluctant to cut pay mainly because of the adverse impact on morale, productivity, and turnover. Morale is hurt because pay cutting reduces living standards and is interpreted as an insult and an expression of dissatisfaction with employees. Pay reduction is usually not viewed as a good alternative to layoff. Layoffs do less harm than pay cuts to the morale of employees who remain. As will be explained in Chapter 13, layoffs are made to save money or to remove unneeded workers. Because layoffs eliminate fixed employment costs along with wage or salary expense, a pay cut normally would have to be impossibly large to save as much money as a moderately large layoff. Most firms have such a low elasticity of demand for labor that a pay cut would not create jobs for unneeded workers. Worksharing, another alternative to layoffs, is usually rejected for a reason that also applies to pay cutting; reduced living standards hurt morale. Worksharing is used mainly when the employer wishes to preserve a highly skilled work force that might disperse to other jobs during layoff.

Appendix 11A Related Literature

THE EXTENT OF DOWNWARD RIGIDITY (SECTION 11.1)

The historical record shows that wage and salary reductions are unusual, though there are enough ambiguities in the evidence to allow room for controversy. In the postwar period, aggregate wage averages have never declined in the United States, and average wages in manufacturing have always increased by at least 1 percent annually.[1] There were periods of aggregate wage deflation before World War II, especially during the Great Depression and the recession following World War I.

Little evidence is available on wages and salaries paid for particular jobs. There have been recent studies of the cyclic behavior of the pay of individual workers within companies (Baker, Gibbs, and Holmstrom, 1994a, b; Baker and Holmstrom, 1995; Wilson, 1996; and Solon, Whatley, and Stevens, 1997), and these papers indicate that recent pay increases due to promotions have not been sensitive to the business cycle, though the contrary was true between the world wars.

Data on pay cutting is also scarce, and the evidence that exists is confusing. The Bureau of Labor Statistics reported data from 1959 to 1978 on the incidence of various sizes of general wage changes for both union and nonunion production workers in manufacturing firms (Bureau of Labor Statistics, *Current Wage Developments* and *Monthly Labor Review*). These data show a negligible number of wage decreases (Akerlof, Dickens, and Perry, 1996, p. 8). In most years, less than 0.05 percent of the workers suffered decreases and in no year did more than 0.4 percent have decreases. The corresponding percentage for my sample is 0.14 percent. That is, 0.14 percent of the employees of all the companies in my sample suffered a general cut in base pay in the year before the interview. The same Bureau of Labor Statistics data show that during periods of low wage inflation, the distribution of wage changes shifts to the left and accumulates at zero with almost no spilling over into the negative region (Mitchell, 1986, table I). Bureau of Labor Statistics surveys of union wage settlements show an increase in wage cutting in the early 1980s. Mitchell (1985a, table I) estimates from these data that 13 percent of all workers covered by major new contracts suffered wage cuts in 1983.[2] Perhaps the difference in the two data sources exists because there is more wage cutting in union than in nonunion firms or because the time periods covered by the two surveys do not overlap. Baker, Gibbs, and Holmstrom (1994b) find few instances of nominal declines for individual employees (less than 200 out of over 60,000 observations) in salary data for managers at a medium-sized firm in a service industry, and Wilson (1996) also found almost no cases of nominal pay reduction in a study of two firms, one being that studied by Baker, Gibbs, and Holmstrom. Harry Holzer finds, in his survey of starting pay for workers without college degrees, that 4.8 percent of new hires had a wage cut within one year after being hired.[3] This figure is much higher than the U.S. establishment data for general pay cuts, but is not surprising, since employers sometimes lower workers' pay after their probationary period if they prove less productive than expected. Fortin (1996, fig. 4) tabulates wage changes in 1,149 large non-COLA union wage settlements in Canada from 1992 to 1994, a period of high unemployment and almost no inflation, and finds that 47 percent of the contracts were wage freezes and 6 percent were wage cuts. The large number of freezes relative to cuts indicates resistance to nominal cuts. Chapple (1996) finds little pay cutting in a survey of New Zealand employers made from 1988 through 1995. The survey gives changes in base pay for employees staying in the same job. He finds that less than 1 percent of the annual pay changes during the period of the survey were reductions, and the percentage of reductions never exceeded 2 percent, despite the occurrence of a recession with high unemployment and low inflation. Furthermore, a large percentage of pay differences equaled zero, especially during the recession. Contrary evidence was collected by Blinder and Choi (1990), who report that 5 of the 19 firms they surveyed cut the nominal wages of at least some of their workers in the recent past, even though the interviews were made in 1988, when local labor markets were tight.

Investigators find more wage decreases in household than in establishment data (McLaughlin, 1994, 1998; S. Kahn, 1995; Lebow, Stockton, and Wascher, 1995; and Card and Hyslop, 1996). For instance, McLaughlin estimates that about 17 percent of households who stay with the same employer suffer nominal wage or salary cuts from one year to the next. Such estimates may be very inaccurate, however. Akerlof, Dickens, and Perry (1996, pp. 12–17) attribute the findings to measurement error, an explanation that is plausible, since the person interviewed in a household may not know precisely the income of the household's main income earner and answers are not checked by asking respondents to compare pay in the current year with that in the previous year. In a telephone survey of households in the Washington, D.C., area, Akerlof, Dickens, and Perry found few people whose pay had been cut. McLaughlin argues from validation studies and other evidence that a substantial fraction of the pay cuts are not due to measurement error. The evidence he gives indicates that many of the pay cuts may be due to changed job assignments.

Wages seem to have been more rigidly downward since World War II than before, though this change may be due to the relative mildness of postwar recessions. The historical record of wage stickiness has been examined by Sachs (1980), Mitchell (1985b), Bernanke and Powell (1986), DeLong and Summers (1986), Taylor (1986), Allen (1992), Hanes (1996a), and Dighe (1997). Sundstrom (1990) and Allen (1992) argue that the greater cyclic sensitivity of wages before World War II is in part an illusion created by the method of constructing prewar wage series. Although wages may have been less rigid in the prewar period, authors have found ample evidence of downward rigidity in the period (Shergold, 1975; O'Brien, 1989; Carter and Sutch, 1990; Hanes, 1996b; and Dighe, 1997). There was little wage cutting in the United States during the first two years of the Great Depression, despite price deflation and dramatically increasing unemployment, and Bernanke and Carey (1996) find evidence of wage stickiness throughout the Depression in macroeconomic data for 22 countries.

There is a huge literature that I do not cite on the sensitivity of wage increases to business conditions. This sensitivity does not imply wage cutting and so is not evidence of wage flexibility in the sense used in this book.

REASONS FOR RESISTANCE TO PAY REDUCTION (SECTION 11.2)

Four other surveys of employers have addressed the question of downward wage rigidity, Kaufman (1984), Blinder and Choi (1990), Agell and Lundborg (1995), and Campbell and Kamlani (1997), and all four report findings similar to those described in this section. Kaufman interviewed managers of 26 British firms, and Blinder and Choi interviewed managers of 19 American firms, and they all were told that pay cuts would hurt morale and productivity. Swedish employers reported to Agell and Lundborg that at least half of a firm's jobs would have to be threatened before workers would accept an across-the-board wage cut. Campbell and Kamlani asked managers of 186 American firms for reactions to various theories of downward wage rigidity, and the theory receiving the highest rating was fear that the best workers would leave. Other theories considered important were fear of reduced effort, fear of increased turnover in general, and workers' dislike of unpredictable income fluctuations.

Kahneman, Knetsch, and Thaler (1986a, b) have surveyed popular attitudes about price and wage setting and found that most people believe it would be unfair for a firm to lower wages in response to a weak labor market, a view shared by almost all the businesspeople and labor leaders I interviewed. Many authors have emphasized the importance of social norms in the determination of pay and worker motivation, including Akerlof (1979, 1980, 1982), Solow (1980), and Baron (1988).

Some businesspeople claimed that workers might quit in response to a pay cut even during a recession, when they were not likely to find a new job soon. Such behavior might seem impulsive and irrational, but is probably real, for ample evidence is accumulating in experimental economics that people will damage themselves in order to punish someone who has hurt them. The phenomenon is observed in experiments with ultimatum games (Güth, Schmittberger, and Schwarze, 1982; Ochs and Roth, 1989; Roth et al., 1991; Camerer and Thaler, 1995; and Abbink et al., 1996) and contract fulfillment (Fehr, Gächter, and Kirchsteiger, 1996, 1997). Particularly interesting are Cameron's (1995) experiments with ultimatum games in Indonesia and Fehr and Tougareva's (1995) experiments with contract fulfillment in Moscow. In both cases payments represented two or more months' income, so that the irrationality was not due to the insignificance of the sums given up.

The negative reaction of workers to pay cuts is related to loss aversion; people lose more utility when giving something up than they gain by acquiring it. Loss aversion has been well documented by psychologists (Kahneman, Knetsch, and Thaler, 1986a, 1991; Kahneman and Tversky, 1979). Loss aversion is probably related to the observation that threats of punishments often provide weaker incentives than rewards. Carmichael (1998) develops a theory based on biological evolution to explain people's reluctance to give things up.

Numerous economists have remarked that management resistance to pay cuts is probably due to fear of damaging morale and hence productivity. The earliest, perhaps, is Slichter (1929, p. 432), and another early writer on the subject is Dunlop (1938, p. 428). Bull (1987) and Newberry and Stiglitz (1987) have suggested that poor morale following pay cuts is the mechanism enforcing implicit contracts.

REASONS FOR LAYING OFF WORKERS RATHER THAN CUTTING PAY (SECTION 11.3)

Statistical evidence and surveys are consistent with the findings reported in this section. Students of management science and labor have noticed that in U.S. manufacturing direct labor absorbs a small share of costs, a share that has been decreasing (Drucker, 1990; Mitchell, 1989, p. 215). I have found no compilation of data on this share for individual firms. However, the U.S. Census provides statistics for manufacturing industries at the four-digit level on sales and total wage costs of direct labor. Table 11A.1 gives summary statistics derived from the data. The first two digits of the industry code appear in the first column. The second column provides the number of four-digit industries with the given first two digits. For each four-digit industry, I computed the percent ratio of direct labor wage costs to the value of shipments. The median of those percentages for each two-digit industry is in the third column. The fourth column gives the ratio of direct labor to sales for the whole two-digit industry, and the last two columns list minimum and maximum ratios, respectively, for the four-digit industries. The table shows that though the ratios vary, the majority are less than 15 percent and almost all are less than 33 percent.

I know of no estimates of individual firms' elasticities of demand for labor, though there have been numerous estimates of aggregate labor demand elasticities, a literature reviewed in Hamermesh (1976, 1986, 1991, and chap. 3 of 1993). The consensus estimate of the short-run elasticity of demand for labor is about 0.15, which is small. Evidence supporting a low elasticity of demand is given by Ross and Zimmermann (1993), who find from survey data for

TABLE 11A.1   Ratio to sales of cost of direct labor in U.S. manufacturing in 1986

Two-digit SIC code	Number of four-digit industries	Median ratio (%)	Average ratio (%)	Minimum ratio (%)	Maximum ratio (%)
20	47	6.3	5.8	1.4	16.4
21	4	4.6	4.8	3.6	15.1
22	30	15.0	14.3	6.7	29.4
23	33	16.0	15.4	8.3	23.9
24	17	13.8	14.0	7.2	21.7
25	13	15.9	16.8	10.4	20.9
26	17	12.2	11.5	7.5	19.9
27	17	17.4	11.9	1.8	32.2
28	28	5.7	6.0	3.7	18.2
29	5	4.8	2.1	1.7	6.3
30	6	15.5	13.8	13.1	18.7
31	11	16.1	15.5	11.4	18.9
32	32	16.4	14.6	8.4	36.4
33	26	10.3	12.8	4.3	24.7
34	36	15.7	15.8	8.8	23.0
35	44	12.7	12.2	4.6	28.0
36	39	13.4	11.9	6.3	19.9
37	17	12.0	10.7	6.6	24.3
38	13	12.8	10.8	6.6	17.6
39	20	10.5	12.9	4.9	18.9

managers of German manufacturing firms that the main influence on labor use is product demand rather than labor costs. According to Dunlop (1938, pp. 423–424), trade union leaders argue that wage reductions have little impact on employment.

I know of only one survey bearing on the choice between layoffs and pay cuts, that of Campbell and Kamlani (1997). As I have already mentioned, they asked managers to rate the relevance to their firm of various reasons for not cutting wages during recessions. The reason given the most importance was that a pay cut would cause the most productive workers to leave, whereas the least productive could be laid off. This theory was not often mentioned when I asked managers why they did not cut pay rather than lay off workers (Table 11.3), but the low frequency is probably due to my not suggesting answers. Given what managers said about pay and layoffs, a large fraction would probably have agreed that layoffs have the advantage of controlling who leaves.

REASONS FOR RESISTANCE TO WORKSHARING (SECTION 11.4)

Brody (1980, chap. 2) describes the results of worksharing in large American corporations during the Great Depression. The policy was the outcome of a benevolent philosophy of management, but caused discontent and revolt after workers incomes had been reduced for a long time.

   Meager and Buchan (1988) surveyed employer attitudes toward job-splitting, which is the sharing of a full-time job by two part-time workers. Employers did not like the idea of using job-splitting as an alternative to layoff, and some mentioned that such a scheme would deprive them of the right to choose who left, a right enjoyed with layoffs (Meager and Buchan, 1988, p. 74).

12

EXPERIENCES WITH PAY REDUCTION

Although actual pay cuts caused trouble, their consequences were not as bad as might be expected from employer arguments against them. It was perhaps natural for managers to exaggerate harmful effects when justifying pay maintenance and to minimize the problems after having reduced pay. There was no doubt a selection bias as well, for managers almost certainly cut pay only when they were fairly sure employees would accept the loss.

The effects of actual pay freezes and decreases in profit share income were similar to those of pay cuts. Scarcity of interview time prevented me from asking companies that had not frozen pay or shared profits why they had not done so. Thus, I cannot compare the actual with the imagined consequences of freezes and decreased profit sharing.

A question I answered indirectly was whether it was real or nominal wages that were downwardly rigid. Freezes cause gradual loss of real pay, so that reactions to them provide information about this question. Real wage decline did cause problems, though deterioration in real wages from slow inflation was resented less than abrupt nominal pay reduction.

12.1 The Reasons for Pay Cuts and Freezes

Pay cuts and freezes were usually responses to crises brought on by current or anticipated financial problems or by the need to improve a company's ability to compete. None of the cuts or freezes I heard about was in response to a weak labor market, though they might not have been possible had the labor market been tight. Some companies did cut or freeze the pay of groups of employees whose pay was felt to be excessive. However, it was past management policy, not the recession, that caused pay to be high. These cuts usually occurred in newly acquired companies or resulted from a tightening of control over local management, and they were triggered by financial problems or increased product market competition. Not many cuts or freezes were said to be motivated by a desire to save jobs, though employers told workers that jobs would be threatened if the company were forced to shrink or close because of financial constraints or because it could not compete.

OVERVIEW OF INTERVIEW EVIDENCE

This chapter is based on information about 39 nominal cuts in base pay, 24 of which occurred during the recession. The other 15 occurred before it. Of these, 11 occurred during the previous boom and 4 during earlier recessions. Table 12.1 summarizes the nature of the pay cuts.

Pay cuts were usually moderate in size, and the majority were a flat 10 percent. Among the 16 general pay cuts about which I have the information, 3 were less than 10 percent, 10 were exactly 10 percent, and 3 were more than 10 percent. The maximum was 50 percent for salaries in a small architectural engineering company, where employees also went from working 60 hours a week to working only part time. I use here the figure applying to the lowest-ranking employees affected, for in some firms the size of the pay cut increased with rank. The willingness of firms to cut pay increased with the status of the employees affected.

Pay cuts brought on by financial emergencies were usually temporary, lasting from 6 to 18 months. Those brought on by the need to compete in the product market lasted longer. Tables 12.2 and 12.3 summarize the reasons for pay cuts and freezes.

MANAGERS' EXPLANATIONS

Chapter 5 contains quotations expressing the connection between pay freezes and cuts and their principal cause, budgetary problems. In some cases, bud-

TABLE 12.1   Types of nominal cuts in base pay

Type	Number during the recession of 1990–1993	Number during the preceding boom	Number during an earlier recession
General cut in base pay	11	6	2
Pay cut for management personnel only	11	5	2
Pay cut for a selected group	2	0	0
Total	24	11	4

TABLE 12.2   Reasons for pay cuts (applies to 36 businesses)

Reasons	Number of businesses	Percentage of businesses
Financial distress	31	86
To prevent bankruptcy	9	25
To preserve employees' jobs	8	22
To lower costs so as to meet competition	5	18

TABLE 12.3   Reasons for pay freezes (applies to 60 businesses)

Reasons	Number of businesses	Percentage of businesses
Financial distress	60	100
To prevent bankruptcy	3	5
To preserve employees' jobs	1	2
To lower costs so as to meet competition	5	8

getary problems were mixed with the need to improve the ability to compete for business.

> Last year, the company had a pay cut of from 7 to 15 percent. The cut varied among individuals, for some had their jobs adjusted up or down as a result of the company's contraction. . . . Everything was explained in a company meeting. . . . The cut was presented as a question of survival. It was needed to stay competitive. It was not something we wanted to do. We had three years of losses. Rather than continue as is, it would have been better to get out of business. The cut is working. We are now able to bid more aggressively for work and have gotten more. We are breaking even or better.
> —Part-owner and operator of a nonunion construction company with 90 employees

Even when the parent company was doing well, freezes or cuts were sometimes imposed on divisions or units that were performing badly, especially if pay was above market. Several of the divisions that had pay cuts were new acquisitions.

> There was a three-month pay freeze in [a Massachusetts city], which is about to be lifted. That plant lost money in October, November, and December of 1992. The

employees were told that it seemed only right to freeze pay until the business was back on its feet. The company is trying to break a culture of entitlement to wage increases. You have to earn your keep. It is healthy for the employees to realize that the plant has to stand on its own feet.

—President of a nonunion manufacturing company and ESOP with 240 employees

A wage freeze was announced at one nonunion location yesterday. There were a lot of long faces. At that location, the unskilled population was $3 per hour out of line with the local area. The location was an acquisition, and its business was doing poorly relative to expectations, though it was making money. Productivity there had been bad. The freeze was a penalty. We were being honest with the employees and trying to explain. Some locations have been doing badly, some well. We want costs to go down in the businesses that are doing badly. They have to get costs down in order to get prices down so as to meet the competition.

—Vice president of human resources of a partially unionized manufacturing company with 5,500 employees

In large companies the jobs saved by pay freezes and cuts were more often those of managers and professionals than of production workers. The purpose of pay restriction was to relieve financial stress, and when layoffs were made because of financial problems, overhead staff was more likely to be let go than were production workers (section 13.1).

For 8 months, from August 1991 to April 1992, there was an across-the-board 10 percent cut in pay. The purpose was to cut costs without laying people off. Nevertheless, people were laid off because of lack of work and for cost cutting and reorganization. . . . No prices were cut in response to the pay cut. . . . It was above all the jobs of indirect labor people that were saved. The employment of direct labor depends on demand. . . . The hourly people didn't understand that it wasn't their jobs that were being saved, and I didn't either until you asked. . . . The pay cut helped keep the company afloat. We are now in Chapter 11.

—Vice president of administration of a unionized manufacturing company with 900 employees

12.2 Effects of Cuts in Base Pay

A pattern that stood out in stories of current and past pay cuts was that it was easier to cut pay during recessions than economic booms. Most cuts during recessions gave rise to only minor problems with morale and productivity and to no increase in turnover, in contrast to those occurring in good times.[1] In addition, pay cuts were more easily accepted when employees understood that company problems justified them, a matter taken up in section 19.1.

TABLE 12.4 Effects of pay cuts (applies to 33 businesses)

Effects	Number of businesses	Percentage of businesses
Morale was hurt	20	56
Morale was not hurt	7	19
Productivity was hurt	9	25
Productivity was not hurt	11	31
Turnover increased	5	14
Turnover did not increase	22	61

TABLE 12.5 Effects of pay cuts made during recessions (applies to 22 businesses)

Effects	Number of businesses	Percentage of businesses
Morale was hurt	11	44
Morale was not hurt	7	28
Productivity was hurt	3	12
Productivity was not hurt	9	36
Turnover increased	0	0
Turnover did not increase	19	76

OVERVIEW OF INTERVIEW EVIDENCE

The findings on the impact of pay cuts are summarized in Tables 12.4, 12.5, and 12.6. (Productivity refers to the work effort of the existing employees, not to the effects of turnover.)

MANAGERS' EXPLANATIONS

The state of the economy and of the business had a marked impact on turnover and on the tolerance of the work force for pay reduction. The usual reaction to pay cuts during recessions was submissiveness. Employees might be upset, but any damage to productivity was mild or only temporary, and there was little or no increase in turnover, there being few other jobs to turn to.

TABLE 12.6 Effects of pay cuts made during economic booms (applies to 11 businesses)

Effects	Number of businesses	Percentage of businesses
Morale was hurt	9	82
Morale was not hurt	0	0
Productivity was hurt	6	55
Productivity was not hurt	2	18
Turnover increased	5	45
Turnover did not increase	3	27

The pay cut has been demoralizing, for everybody was already working harder than ever because every department had been stripped of employees. . . . Job performance has not been affected, but people are much less generous in charity drives organized by the bank. They feel squeezed. . . . Low morale is seen more on the social level. There is less loyalty, less willingness to go to bank parties. We have had no problems with punctuality or attendance. We had no quits until the last two months. . . . People have no place to go. [This city] has been hard hit by the recession. Low morale has had a bad effect on customer service. The employees are less cheerful. [Pay for all employees was cut by 7 percent in 1991.]

—Human resource officer of a bank employing 150 people

A severance package was available for those who would lose 10 percent or more in income, based on past sales. What took the luster off this package was the recession itself. People from the [Connecticut Department of Labor] Job Center came out and told the assembled salesmen that, given their high incomes, it would take 9 to 12 months to find a job that would replace the former income. There were gasps throughout the room. As a result, few took advantage of the severance package. . . . The commission on sales is higher now than it was, so that salesmen can recoup to some extent. Another consequence of the higher commission is that even if salesmen are disgruntled, they are more attentive to customers. Morale has been good. [The reduction, made in 1992, was for salespeople, who were overpaid as the result of a badly designed incentive system that allowed them to build up base pay salary through sales volume.]

—The manager of a nonunion department store with 325 employees

Some people left in response to the pay cut, but very few, because they had nowhere to go. . . . The pay cut hurt morale, very definitely, but it bounced back. Employees didn't like it. They became preoccupied with its personal effects. It augmented the financial anxiety at home. This anxiety got transferred to the workplace. But as time went on, people started to see that the cut was for the good of the company and hence of themselves. . . . The drop in morale was seen through more absenteeism. Productivity declined at first. There was no increase in grievances or labor relations issues. The union was behind [supported] the cut. [Pay for all employees was cut by 10 percent for 8 months in 1991 and 1992.]

—Vice president of administration of a unionized manufacturing company with 900 employees

Most of the pay cuts during good economic times were clear failures.

The company did have a 5 percent pay cut in 1986. Those earning less than $10 an hour were not affected. Only engineers, professionals, and administrators were. People didn't like it. No one likes to make less. The good performers become disenchanted and unmotivated. Little by little, people put in less effort. They didn't put in the extra five minutes or complete their last task before going home. Turnover was high. In fact, all employers had high turnover at that time, since that was a boom year.

—Human resource manager of a nonunion manufacturing company and ESOP with 250 employees

The company later realized that the pay cut in 1985 had been a big mistake. The chairman now says he will never cut pay again. The pay cut caused no quitting, but it caused a lot of complaining and a drop in morale. The productivity loss couldn't be measured, but it was real. The chairman now says that from now on he will lay people off rather than cut pay. He says, if you want to hire someone, lay someone else off; if you want to give raises, lay people off. [There was a 10 percent cut for all salaried personnel, but none for production workers.]

—Compensation manager for a nonunion manufacturing company with 1,750 employees

The company had a 10 percent pay cut in 1986. It didn't work. Stock was given in lieu of the pay forgone, but the price of the stock went down. This took away the motivation for those who stayed. People were doing the same job for less pay. The pay cut came in the middle of a boom, and anybody who could get another job did so. . . . People got outside offers, and counteroffers were given to key people, undoing the cut. When people's pay is cut, they say, "What did I do to deserve this?" They see waste everywhere in the company. The cut didn't pull people together, though lots of people will do incredible things for nothing. The pay cut was demotivating and caused high attrition. We lost lots of marketable people, who were those we didn't want to lose. . . . The pay cut lasted two years. . . . The cut saved little because of increased attrition, the greater hiring and training costs, and counteroffers.

—Human resource official of a nonunion manufacturing company with 9,500 employees

It was important for the success of a pay cut that employees understand that the company was in a crisis (section 19.1). Only two of the pay cuts made during recessions were clearly unsuccessful, and these failed because employees were not convinced they were justified by the condition of the company.

> Last August, the pay of hourly employees was cut by 10 percent in order to avoid layoffs. The hourly employees then called in the union. . . . So the pay cut was restored to hourly employees, and the union lost the election. . . . The pay cut upset the hourly people. Their lifestyles were adapted to their pay level. They slowed down their work by 10 percent. . . . The cut came too suddenly. They didn't know how bad the situation was. One speech on the floor didn't cut it. My father [the owner] has been trying to retire and so has withdrawn from the company. His style was to go out and talk to the guys frequently. The new management doesn't do that. If he had been there, the cut might have gone over more easily. There was a lack of communication. . . . The pay cut was taken as effrontery. This aspect of it made people angry. . . . A few hourly people quit, but no one in management did. [Pay was cut in 1992. It is illegal to rescind a pay cut in response to a unionization drive, but the law was ignored.]
>
> —Human resource manager in a nonunion manufacturing company with 250 employees

A clear understanding of company financial problems was necessary for, but did not guarantee the success of, a pay cut, for several of the failed pay cuts made during a boom were the result of obvious and serious financial difficulties.

Good feelings toward management also made pay cuts easier.

> There were no problems of morale caused by the pay cut. This is because the employees are loyal to me. . . . Loyalty to [the company] played no role. They have worked with me a long time and they think they will eventually get it [their pay] back. [The pay of the five highest paid employees was cut by modest amounts in 1991.]
>
> —Manager of a fast-food restaurant with 28 employees

It was also important that higher-level employees share in sacrifices made by lower-level ones.

> The business was not doing well, so that the exempt employees had been without increases for 3 years. The exempts were given a profit-sharing plan, which paid off just when the pay of the hourlies was cut. Demoralization resulted. The attitude of the hourlies was "what you took away from us, we'll make up in overtime." They still wanted the same pay. There was no increase in quits after the pay cut. [The city containing the plant] was a very depressed area, so that people had no place to go. The result of the pay cut was a 15 percent drop in productivity. The plant is just recovering from it. . . . We learned a lesson from this. [There had been a 10 percent negotiated reduction in wages, made in 1988 at one plant.]
>
> —Human resource official in a unionized manufacturing company with 250,000 employees

12.3 Effects of Pay Freezes

The reactions of employees to pay freezes and pay cuts occurring during recessions were remarkably similar. If anything the impact of freezes was a little worse than that of pay cuts. The difference may stem from the greater length of the freezes, many of which lasted from 18 to 30 months, whereas pay cuts usually lasted only 6 to 12 months. Freezes were more common than pay cuts, indicating that management considered freezes to be less dangerous.[2]

OVERVIEW OF INTERVIEW EVIDENCE

The 60 pay freezes about which I gathered information all occurred from 1989 to 1993, and most occurred from 1990 to 1993, which were years of relatively high unemployment. Hence the effects of these freezes should be compared with those of pay cuts made during recessions, and the similarity of their impacts may be seen by comparing Tables 12.5 and 12.7.

MANAGERS' EXPLANATIONS

Most companies experienced few problems with freezes.

> The lack of raises last year had no bad effects. It was not resented, though there were some complaints. I had a meeting with a few girls and showed them the want ads in the paper—there are few and for low pay. I pointed out that I could get more qualified people for less and that our selling prices are now where they were in

TABLE 12.7 Reactions to actual pay freezes during the recession (applies to 55 businesses)

Reactions	Number of businesses	Percentage of businesses
Morale was hurt	28	51
Morale was not hurt	16	29
Productivity was hurt	10	18
Productivity was not hurt	9	16
Turnover increased	5	9
Turnover did not increase	35	64

1985. They know that is true and that the company is in trouble, for they are involved. But they don't like to hear it.

—Part-owner of a nonunion trucking company with 150 employees

Five freezes were failures, hurting morale, damaging productivity, or increasing turnover. Four of these lasted a long time (three lasted 30 and one 18 months) and the fifth was for the year 1989, when unemployment was still low.

> I will never suggest a pay freeze in any company I work for. I fought it on morale and productivity grounds. In fact, we lost lots of productivity. It was awful. People wasted time groaning and complaining to each other. Management was constantly reminded of the pay freeze. If people had time off coming, they took it all. People would try to refuse overtime. . . . People do not have the right to refuse a reasonable request for overtime. Reasonable is not defined by law. According to the company rules, reasonable means six hours. . . . Employees would resist overtime in order to try to get back at the company. A security clearance on a new employee would take eight months, so that I was not anxious to hire new people to replace those dismissed. The employees knew that. People want to see progress over their life in their pay. For this reason, the pay freeze made them go wild. People always spend more than their incomes. They are over their heads in debt, so that they panic when their pay is frozen. [The freeze was for 1989.]

—Human resource officer of a manufacturing plant that had 2,000 employees a year earlier but was closing

12.4 Were Real or Nominal Wages Downwardly Rigid?

Real wages are downwardly rigid if employers feel obliged to increase pay by at least the rate of inflation in the cost of living. Nominal wages are rigid if there is resistance to cutting nominal pay but not to increasing pay by less than the rate of inflation in the cost of living. I had difficulty determining whether real or nominal wages were rigid, in part because there was little inflation at the time and in part because of my method of interviewing.[3]

Judging from what I heard, both real and nominal wages are rigid in the sense that neither is allowed to fall. Of course, neither rigidity is absolute. Cost-of-living inflation was a major factor in the determination of raises, which shows real-wage rigidity (section 10.3). Some employers mentioned that they did not feel obliged to set wages and salaries at levels that kept up fully with rapid inflation, which indicates that real-wage rigidity is not complete. Similarly, the pay of low-performing workers was often allowed to fall behind inflation. Still another indication of the weakness of real-wage rigidity was the frequency of wage freezes, for freezes brought slow degradation of the real value of pay. Of the 235 businesses interviewed, 39 had general pay freezes during the year before the interview, and another 21 had freezes earlier during the recession, so that 60, or 26 percent, had a freeze at some time during the recession and before the interview. (The 60 freezes applied to 11 percent of all the employees in the companies interviewed.) Reluctance to cut nominal pay was evidence of both real and nominal wage rigidity. The main argument against cutting the nominal pay of existing employees was that to do so would damage morale, because of reduced living standards and because cuts would be interpreted as insults. The impact of lowered living standards is a real effect and the insult is a nominal effect to the extent that it stems from the symbolic import of withholding nominal raises.

Real pay cuts were described as less threatening than nominal ones in the six discussions I recorded on the subject, evidence that nominal wage rigidity was stronger than real.

Question: Would a pay cut of 10 percent with no inflation have more impact on employees than a pay freeze with 10 percent inflation? *Answer:* Both are wage cuts. The impact would depend on the information you gave them. The company would have to be in trouble. In both cases, people might leave, even in these times. The pay freeze is psychologically easier. People don't factor in inflation so easily. The pay cut is quicker.

—Human resource manager of a nonunion machine shop with 225 employees

Real pay cuts [through inflation] are easier than nominal ones. Inflation is gradual. Real cuts give people more time to adjust than a sudden 10 percent cut in pay. A significant event, like a tax increase, may wake people up and make them angry. Nominal pay cuts are an insult, even if everybody is cut.

—President of a 32,000-employee division of an insurance company

During the energy crises, the fact that the rate of inflation in the cost of living exceeded the rate of wage inflation did not bother us. We had no morale problem as long as we were paying competitively and predictably.

—Vice president of human resources for a largely nonunion manufacturing company with 125,000 employees

A period of rapid inflation would be suitable for a study intended to gauge the strength of real rigidity. Similarly, a period of rapid deflation, if one ever occurs, would be suitable for estimating the relative strength of real and nominal rigidities.

12.5 Effects of Other Forms of Income Reduction

It is somewhat mystifying that so many employers insisted on the negative effects of reducing workers' incomes through worksharing or cuts in base pay, since it is not uncommon for employee incomes to fall as a result of decreases in bonuses, in profit shares, or in hours worked or because of increases in employee contributions to medical benefits. Construction unions also have work recovery programs, which reduce wages paid by contractors who bid against nonunion contractors. I asked about the effects of these various forms of income reduction and learned that they did sometimes cause employee relations problems, though these were less severe than the effects of discretionary cuts in base pay, probably because the income reductions were easier to justify.

REDUCTIONS IN OVERTIME

Fluctuations in overtime are a normal part of life for many production workers in construction and manufacturing. Nevertheless, some managers told of problems arising from the sudden termination of overtime after employees had grown accustomed to the extra pay involved. Managers tried to give advance warning of overtime termination and to rotate overtime assignments so that workers did not grow to rely on the extra income.

> Workers like overtime, if it is not too much. Reducing it is a take-away. . . . You have to address and explain the issue. People have a tendency to regard overtime as a part of their income. . . . We give 48-hour warnings of the cessation of overtime work.
>
> —The general manager of a two-year-old, nonunion manufacturing company with 140 employees

> I always tell people how long their overtime is going to last. Otherwise, they assume it will last forever and spend it before it's earned. Then, when it is taken away, they are desperate, saying, "But I've already bought a new car that I have to pay for."
>
> —Human resource officer of a manufacturing plant that had 2,000 employees a year earlier but was closing

> You can have a major problem if you have lots of overtime and suddenly cut it, for that is a cut in spendable income. We try to manage overtime so that people don't come to depend on it. Income swings affect morale and productivity.
>
> —Vice president of human resources for a largely nonunion manufacturing company with 125,000 employees

REDUCTIONS IN BENEFITS

During the recession it was fairly common for firms to increase employees' share of the costs of medical insurance, which were growing rapidly. Of the 235 firms where I interviewed, 26 had reduced benefits in this way during the recession. Workers usually accepted such reductions as reasonable, probably because most people were aware of increases in medical insurance costs. Some employers said that benefits were easier to reduce than wages or salaries because the change was felt less quickly. Nevertheless, I did hear a few stories of trouble caused by benefit reduction.

> I have cut benefits, but not base pay. I was paying 100 percent of the health insurance. Now, I pay 50 percent. . . . Initially, the men were shocked, but as the economy soured, they understood better. Now they are glad to have their jobs. There is no problem of morale this year, though at first, I had one. For about six months, men skipped work and production dropped considerably.
>
> —Owner of a nonunion roofing company employing 25 people

> The company is on a treadmill of rising expectations. For instance, a cut in medical benefits was announced suddenly in 1985. The announcement came out of the blue. People were used to getting a little more every year, and now something was taken away. They were mad. They went nuts and could talk about nothing else. The corporation didn't care, but it should have. The change undermined people's trust in the company and in management. Clear, frank communication is important, and nothing had been communicated. This interfered with the perception of the company. There was a danger of unionization. In fact, people talked union.
>
> —Director of human resources of a nonunion manufacturing company with 1,000 employees

WORK RECOVERY PROGRAMS

At the time of the interviews, Connecticut construction unions were rapidly losing market share to nonunion labor. In order to meet the competition, they used various market recovery schemes, which were systems for granting reduced pay rates to union companies bidding against nonunion competitors. According to some of these schemes, workers earned less money on work recovery projects than on normal projects. Under other schemes, wages were the same on all projects, and a union fund subsidized wages on target projects. The funds were introduced because of worker dissatisfaction at earning lower wages on certain projects. I discussed work recovery with four construction union leaders who had long-term experience with the programs. One union had a fund and no trouble with morale. A second had had severe problems and solved them by creating a special work recovery local of young workers who did the lower-wage work. The other two unions had two pay rates within the same local, and these had a history of causing trouble.

> Nine years ago, the union instituted cheaper categories of labor. . . . This was done in the hope that contractors would use the rates to respond to pressures in the industry. But contractors resisted them for years, perhaps for reasons of morale and

the difficulties caused by having men doing similar tasks and being paid at different rates. . . . During the boom, contractors were preoccupied with getting the work done and didn't care about costs. In order to attract people, they would offer the higher rates in the contract. They wanted to keep the men, and the focus was on other things than cutting costs. Now, these provisions are being used with a vengeance and even abused, and union members raise questions about them. . . . The reasons the men react negatively are multifaceted. They don't like having different pay rates for similar work, their pride is hurt, and they need to provide income.

—President of a construction union local with 3,400 active members

Some programs gained acceptance during the recession.

We have a work recovery program, and all unions participate in it. We can bid lower on certain jobs because of pay breaks. . . . When the program was first introduced, it caused trouble. Now, the men realize they are losing work. In 1976, 70 percent of the construction labor force in Connecticut was union. In 1986, it was 51 percent. In 1991, it was 38 percent and today it is 22 percent. . . . No one wants to have their pay cut by the program. The men become disgruntled. A typical normal working person budgets money. If you give up money, the money will already have been spent. They come to their senses only when layoffs are coming. They see that those laid off are not getting jobs. Now, we have no problem.

—President of a unionized highway construction company employing 1,000 people

Nonunion construction firms experienced similar problems with prevailing rate work covered by the Davis-Bacon law, which requires that if any part of the costs of a construction project are paid for by the federal government, employees on the project must be paid prevailing wages, which in practice are union wages. Problems arose when employees on prevailing rate projects earned more than others in the company doing what was known as private work. I discussed this problem with eight employers. Some refused to bid on prevailing work, others rotated employees through it, one paid prevailing rate wages to all workers, and another put up with the complaints.

REDUCTIONS IN PROFIT SHARES AND BONUSES

Weitzman (1983, 1984, 1985, 1986, 1988) has proposed that economies would spontaneously stay at full employment if each company paid its work force a fixed share of company sales revenue net of nonlabor costs, rather than wages or salaries. Firms would then always want to hire more workers, since by doing so they would not increase total compensation costs, though they would reduce pay per employee. The size of a firm's work force would adjust automatically to its revenues, as workers moved from firms with relatively low revenues per worker to those with high revenues. With this well-known proposal in mind, I recorded 17 stories of the impact of fluctuations in bonuses and profit-sharing payments. Most of the stories were similar. Variable income benefited employers by adding to incentives and by reducing expenses when firms were most in need of money. The main disadvantage was that declines in variable income had some of the bad effects of pay cuts, hurting morale and productivity and possibly increasing turnover, especially among the better workers. Such quitting can be regarded as an advantage of Weitzman's scheme, for it automatically allocates workers to the most productive firms. Employers would dislike such turnover, however, since they wish to select those who leave. A few firms found that employees accepted automatic income declines. Other companies abandoned variable income schemes or paid variable income into retirement accounts that had little impact on current living standards. Switching payments to retirement accounts had the disadvantage of blunting the impact on incentives and on the perceived value of compensation.

In the hope of gaining more information about the effects of variable pay, I arranged interviews in five employee-owned companies known as ESOPs (employee stock ownership plans). These companies behaved almost like ordinary ones, laying off unneeded workers. Workers were paid wages and salaries, but accumulated shares in the company and earned dividends on them. Dividends and share accumulation were, however, a small part of total compensation, and share accumulation was viewed as a retirement plan. In ESOPs, employee compensation is not a fixed share of sales net of non-labor costs, so these companies did not give a fair test of Weitzman's proposed reform.

MANAGERS' EXPLANATIONS

Some employers lost interest in variable pay schemes as a result of bad experiences.

In the last two years, I have given no bonuses, for I have had no profits. This has resulted in lots of griping. I will never return to bonuses. I never got any thank yous for them, even though they were large. Superintendents got up to $5,000. The men say, "We're busy, why are there no profits?" When times are good again, I may give individual bonuses sporadically for good work, but not regularly at Christmas. The men get too used to them. If you don't give them, morale sinks for six months. They take an "I don't give a shit" attitude. They don't take care of the equipment, and productivity declines.

—A nonunion, site-work contractor with 20 employees

At . . ., where I used to work, we had profit sharing. In 1978 there were no profits, and the company was in an uproar. As a result, profit sharing was replaced by a 401k [retirement plan] with dollar-for-dollar matching and profit shares going into the 401k. This plan killed the incentive aspect of profit sharing.

—Human resource manager in a financial company with 24,000 employees

Five years ago in the . . . division, we tried to get everyone onto variable pay. The wage earners were not ready for it. When we had a bad year, they screamed bloody murder. "You are taking bread off my table." This is a problem, because an unhappy employee is not a productive one. We should have hung in there. We stopped too soon. The pay system was ahead of the culture. Pay systems should not drive culture, but follow it.

—Vice president of human resources for a largely nonunion manufacturing company with 125,000 employees

Of the 17 managers who talked about the effects of variable income, all but three said that income variability was hard on employees, and these three spoke of bonuses for managerial or professional employees, not wage earners. A few managers also said that decreases in bonuses were easier than pay cuts, and a few comments indicated that employees accepted variable pay more easily if they thought they could control the outcome.

When the bonuses evaporated, people were not pleased. There was bonus money in June and none in December. People had counted on the money and didn't get it. People had understood that the money wasn't guaranteed, and it was a lot easier than pulling away salary. It meant reducing annual incomes from $32,000 to $28,000. So the plan was successful in that regard. We will probably continue, but with more money in other bonus plans. People want more individually tailored plans, for themselves and for groups. They would rather have bonuses be tied to the sales growth and profitability of their part of the store. We will set goals for salaried staff, and they will receive bonuses for exceeding them. An example of a goal would be to raise sales by 5 percent. The new plan will have the disadvantage that it will not be as good a financial safety valve for the company. The profit-sharing plan was criticized as being too complicated and as not entering people's calculations of what they needed to make when they were considering whether to work for us. . . . It did not enter their calculations because the bonuses were contingent, so that people couldn't count on them. It was not effective enough in raising people's perceived compensation levels. Bonuses tied to targets seem more in people's control. People are more willing to believe they can actually achieve the goals and get the bonus.

—General manager of a nonunion cooperative food store chain with 250 employees

It is conceivable that part of the problem with profit sharing is that employees don't believe employers when they say that profits have declined, yet disbelief was not an important issue (section 19.1).

12.6 Summary

Most pay cuts and freezes were brought on by company financial distress, and none was made in response to a weak labor market. Their effects were not as adverse as one might expect from employers' reluctance to cut or freeze pay. Pay cuts made during economic booms had worse effects than those made during recessions. Morale may be hurt by any form of income reduction and, in particular, by reduced income from profit sharing.

Appendix 12A Related Literature

THE REASONS FOR PAY CUTS AND FREEZES (SECTION 12.1)

Empirical work on the causes of pay cuts support my observation that they occur mainly when firms have financial problems or have trouble competing. The earliest work I know of on the reasons for pay cuts is that of Dunlop (1944, pp. 130–148 and 1988, p. 66), who finds that wage cuts in many industries during the Great Depression occurred soon after product price declines. He argues from this pattern that wages were driven down by declines in product prices rather than by high unemployment. There have been numerous studies of the origins of postwar wage concessions, where a concession occurs when a union gives up something that was in the previous contract. They include pay cuts, but are most often pay freezes or replacement of the benefit package by a less valuable one. These studies conclude that concessions are usually brought on by financial crises within firms or plants, or by the threat of a plant shutdown (Juris, 1969; Henle, 1973; Cappelli, 1982, 1983, and 1985; Becker, 1987; Ichniowski and Delaney, 1990; Nay, 1991; and Bell, 1995).

EFFECTS OF CUTS IN BASE PAY (SECTION 12.2)

I have found only five studies of the effect of pay cuts, Valenzi and Andrews (1971), Pritchard, Dunette, and Jorgenson (1972) and Greenberg (1989, 1990, and 1993). The first two papers report on laboratory experiments. Valenzi and Andrews find that pay cuts cause quitting but no change in productivity, whereas Pritchard, Dunette, and Jorgenson find that pay cuts for hourly employees reduce productivity. Greenberg, in his 1989 and 1990 papers, describes surveys of worker reactions to pay cuts in actual companies. In the first paper, he finds that workers felt underpaid during a 6 percent pay cut lasting 14 months, but overall job satisfaction did not decrease and workers focused greater attention on the nonfinancial advantages of their jobs. In the second paper, Greenberg reports that theft increased during the 10 weeks of a 15 percent pay cut in two plants, and in the 1994 paper he describes laboratory experiments where similar increases in theft followed pay cuts or, more precisely, payment of less than had been promised.

Actual pay cuts probably caused so little trouble because employers were able to convince workers the cuts were needed to save jobs or the company. This explanation is supported by psychologists' findings that justifications can bring people to accept adverse decisions by authorities (Appendix 19A, section 19.1).

EFFECTS OF PAY FREEZES (SECTION 12.3)

I know of only one study of the effects of a freeze, Schaubroeck, May, and Brown (1994), who investigate worker reactions to a pay freeze that continued for over a year. Employees felt underpaid, the freeze hurt job satisfaction, and dissatisfaction was positively associated with economic hardship caused by the freeze. Explanations of the freeze were given to a subset of workers and helped mitigate the discontent, adding to evidence mentioned above of the importance of justifications.

WERE REAL OR NOMINAL WAGES DOWNWARDLY RIGID? (SECTION 12.4)

Baker, Gibbs, and Holmstrom (1994b) study the history of the pay of individual employees of a medium-sized corporation from 1970 to 1988 and find that though the nominal pay of individual management employees almost never fell, the real value for many employees fell during the rapid inflation from 1979 to 1981, and the average real pay of new hires drifted downward from 1974 to 1980. Wilson (1996) obtains similar results for existing employees in a study of employee pay histories for two companies, one of which is the company studied by Baker, Gibbs, and Holmstrom. This is evidence that real wages are not as rigid as nominal ones. My evidence suggests that their findings are probably typical of many companies.

In a survey of popular attitudes, Shafir, Diamond, and Tversky (1997) find strong evidence of money illusion, which supports the conclusion that wage rigidity is to some extent nominal. That is, people are more shocked by a nominal pay cut than by an equivalent real cut involving no decrease in nominal pay.

EFFECTS OF OTHER FORMS OF INCOME REDUCTION (SECTION 12.5)

Little has been written on employee reactions to automatic declines in pay resulting from profit sharing and bonus plans. There is a large literature on incentive plans that put some pay at risk, such as gainsharing and Scanlon plans. A good review is Lawler (1990, chap. 7). However, this literature contains little discussion of income declines. Brown and Huber (1992) document dissatisfaction among bank employees with a new earnings-at-risk incentive pay plan that brought a decline in earnings after its introduction. Gross and Bacher (1993) discuss briefly a variable pay plan introduced in 1988 at the Fibers Department of Dupont and discontinued in 1990, in part because of discontent at the prospect of lower payments.

There is a considerable literature, reviewed in Kruse (1993), on the effects of employee ownership and profit sharing on firms' reaction to decreases in product demand. In addition, Craig and Pencavel (1992) and Pencavel and Craig (1994) compare the responsiveness to fluctuations in product demand of wages, employment, and hours worked of employee owned and conventional plywood factories in the Pacific Northwest. The studies indicate that profit sharing and employee ownership increase the cyclic variability of hourly earnings and decrease the variability of hours worked and employment, though the effects may be small (Chelius and Smith, 1990). There is also evidence that profit sharing increases productivity and productivity growth (Weitzman and Kruse, 1990; Kruse, 1993; and Craig and Pencavel, 1995), though Conte and Svejnar (1990) give a contrary view.

It is well known that Japanese corporations make less use of layoffs than do American companies (Hashimoto and Raisian, 1985), and Freeman and Weitzman (1987) argue that employment stability in Japan may be due to informal profit sharing through annual bonuses.

13

LAYOFFS

In this chapter I present material on layoffs that elaborates explanations given in Chapter 11 of why employers prefer layoffs to pay cuts. I also give employers' answers to another key question, why firms almost never take advantage of recessions to replace workers with cheaper unemployed ones, thereby reducing labor costs without cutting any employee's pay.

Layoffs may be classified as follows: (1) those made in response to decreases in the need for labor that stem from technical improvements and from declines in product demand; (2) those removing organizational slack, which is excess or poor quality labor that has accumulated because of sloppy management; (3) those that relieve financial distress by exchanging future income for current savings from cancellation of projects with long-term returns; (4) those that remove employees in order to replace them with cheaper new hires; and (5) those resulting from plant closure. I do not discuss the last type.

A major finding was that many employers spoke of layoffs of the second type, and it is also interesting that some spoke of the third and few of the fourth type. Pay cuts are not an appealing alternative to layoffs of the second kind, since it is unlikely that workers would accept pay cuts made to preserve the jobs of unnecessary or second-rate colleagues. The occurrence of layoffs of the third type is consistent with the view that firms are risk averse. That few layoffs were of the fourth type shows that firms seldom use this means of reducing pay.

Another important finding is that in many firms layoffs were associated with increases in productivity, despite the negative impact of dismissals on morale. Layoffs that removed organizational slack were accompanied by efforts to rearrange activities and to induce workers, especially exempt ones, to work more intensely. In the many firms where the lowest-performing workers were laid off first, employees worked harder, so as not to be picked in the next round of layoffs.

The findings about productivity might seem to contradict the premise accepted in macroeconomics that labor productivity is stimulated by booms and curbed by recessions. Robert Hall (1987, p. 421) has written, "Hardly any fact about the United States economy is better established than the pro-cyclical behavior of productivity." A major body of thought in macroeconomics, real business cycle theory, presupposes that exogenous productivity declines cause recessions (Kydland and Prescott, 1982; King and Plosser, 1984; and Prescott, 1986). Although Keynesian economists trace recessions to the weakening of aggregate demand rather than of productivity, they too assert that productivity growth sags during recessions and attribute the decline to labor hoarding, which is the retention of essential personnel during a downturn because of concern that after a layoff they would take other jobs and not be available for recall (Fair, 1969).

It is possible to reconcile my findings with the statistical behavior of labor productivity and with theories of labor hoarding. I found that both hoarding and "dishoarding" existed, with hoarding applying to skilled production workers and dishoarding applying mainly to overhead workers. Businesspeople attached little importance to labor hoarding, emphasizing rather reduction in organizational slack, which is labor dishoarding. Many managers were preoccupied with reform and boasted of productivity improvement, and none complained about the burden of carrying reserve labor. It is therefore troubling that productivity is said to be statistically pro-cyclical. The discrepancy is only apparent, however, and has to do with the definition of the pro-cyclicality of productivity. The definition can refer either to the level of productivity or to its rate of change and to the co-movement of either of these with the level of economic activity or its rate of growth, so that four definitions are possible.[1] Hall establishes that growth of productivity and of output are positively correlated, but it is also true that the growth of productivity and the level of output are negatively correlated. That is, though productivity is pro-cyclical in Hall's sense, it is countercyclical in the second sense. It is this sense that should be compared with businesspeople's claims about productivity, for they spoke about its improvement, not its level, and most believed they were suffering from a severe recession, despite growth in the economy at the time.

I found evidence contradicting well-known explanations of wage rigidity and layoffs, namely, implicit contract theory, the seniority rights model, and McLaughlin's (1990, 1991) theory that quits and layoffs are nearly equivalent.

Implicit contract theory implies that labor market conditions affect layoff decisions (section 20.4). According to it, workers are laid off when the revenue they add to their firm is less than their cost minus a quantity that reflects the decrease in their welfare caused by layoff. It is natural to assume that the decrease in welfare is greater in a poor than in a good labor market, for it takes longer to find a new job in hard times. Therefore, other things being equal, firms should lay off fewer workers if the unemployment rate is high than if it is low. Yet most employers told me that labor market conditions either had no effect on layoff decisions or had an effect contrary to that predicted by the theory; high unemployment made it easier to dismiss workers since those let go would be less likely to find other jobs and thus more likely to be available when needed.

The seniority rights model assumes that a majority of high seniority workers know in advance that they are not likely to be laid off and so are not willing to accept pay cuts to save the jobs of others (section 20.2). This argument is usually based on the belief that junior workers are laid off first. I found that many layoffs, especially of overhead personnel, are made on the basis of performance, with the least productive workers leaving first. This finding is not in itself conclusive against this type of theory, because it is possible that a majority consisting of the better performers resists pay cuts. However, I doubt that performance-based layoffs leave many feeling safe, for some managers complained that a disadvantage of the performance system was that it created widespread insecurity.

McLaughlin (1990, 1991) treats layoffs as voluntary separations, by assuming that firms lay off workers only after they refuse to work for lower pay (Chapter 1). I found no evidence supporting this assumption. Often workers were ordered to leave and were walked to the door without any discussion. Sometimes, firms offered transfers to other jobs, which might have lower pay. Many such offers were accepted during the recession, and few workers were let go because they refused lower pay.

The popularity with employers of the performance-based layoff system is significant, for by giving employers control over who leaves it adds to their preference for layoffs over pay cuts. It also helps explain the prejudice against unemployed job seekers (sections 15.3 and 18.12) and why layoffs often stimulate the remaining employees to work harder (section 13.10).

That firms lay off workers rather than cut pay is made more puzzling by the suffering that layoffs and unemployment cause. Are employers unaware of the damage done? Do they not care? Neither alternative is correct, for many employers affirmed that permanent layoff is often devastating and expressed concern about its consequences, though they saw no alternative.

13.1 Why Layoffs?

Managers' discussions of the reasons for layoffs indicated that the dominant cause was decline in product demand, and an almost equally important cause was the need to save money and improve operations in response to financial difficulties or increased competition.

OVERVIEW OF INTERVIEW EVIDENCE

An ample majority of the 235 companies studied had experienced layoffs, and managers of 130 discussed why. The most common reasons or precipitating causes were reduced sales or financial distress, as may be seen from Table 13.1. In preparing this table, it was not always easy to distinguish financial difficulties from reduced sales, though many respondents had the distinction in mind and were able to explain it. In almost half the 69 cases labeled "financial distress," there was no ambiguity, for the companies had suffered financial reversals with no declines in the volume of business. For instance, banks and insurance companies lost capital because of bad loans and the decline in value of real estate investments, while the volume of their basic activities did not decrease. Nevertheless, many banks and insurance companies had heavy layoffs, which were described as efforts to cut costs in order to offset financial losses.

Table 13.2 classifies descriptions of permanent layoffs into the first four categories listed earlier, for those instances in which I have enough information to make a clear choice. The table gives the number of companies having layoffs

TABLE 13.1   Reasons for layoff in sample businesses (applies to 130 businesses)

Reason for layoff	Number of businesses	Percentage of businesses
Reduced sales	79	61
Financial distress	69	53
Technical change	25	19
Layoffs made in order to increase the work of the remaining overtime exempt employees	22	17
Reorganization of operations	19	15
Removal of poor performers	16	12
Competitive pressures for greater efficiency	12	9
Elimination of unprofitable operations	8	6
Removal of overpaid employees	8	6
Replacement of unsatisfactory employees by new hires[a]	8	6
Consolidation of operations following merger	3	2

a. All the companies in this category also appear in the category "removal of poor performers."

TABLE 13.2   Types of layoffs (applies to 113 businesses)

Type of Layoff	Number of businesses	Percentage of businesses
(1) Reduced demand for labor because of technical change or decline in product demand	72	64
(2) Elimination of organizational slack	75	66
(3) Trading future revenue for current savings	10	9
(4) Replacement	8	7

of the given type. The type of a layoff does not always correspond to the reason for it. For instance, reduced sales pushed some companies to eliminate labor that had not been needed before the drop in sales, so that the layoff was of type 2 rather than of type 1. Some of the layoffs were of just a few people, and others of thousands, so that the numbers are *not* proportional to the number of people dismissed.

Among the 72 companies in the first category in Table 13.2, in only 3 were layoffs caused by technical change, though technical change was mentioned in connection with 25 layoffs (Table 13.1). In most of these 25 cases, managers said that financial or competitive pressure had pushed their company to make better use of technology, and I label such layoffs as elimination of organizational slack. Most layoffs of type 2 were brought on by financial stress or competition. A few were the result of mergers, and some were part of company reform efforts that had no external cause, other than perhaps popularity of downsizing among executives at the time. Layoffs of type 3 were all the result of pressures to obtain money quickly.

The number of layoffs of the fourth type may seem large. In only two of these, however, were layoffs part of an effort immediately to exchange expensive employees for cheaper ones. In two other companies, the exchange took place over a fairly long horizon. These two were professional partnerships where high-seniority associates were laid off in response to the decline in voluntary turnover brought on by the recession. Professional partnerships try to maintain a proper mix or pyramid of employees at various stages of their careers, for there is work for all stages and younger people are cheaper. Turnover normally reduces numbers at the upper levels. The two firms dismissed some associates before review for partnership in order to make room in the following year for new professionals just leaving school. The remaining four layoffs of the fourth type could also be thought of as either of the first two types, for the companies needed to reduce their work forces. When doing so, they dismissed expensive employees and replaced some of them.

Layoffs that eliminated organizational slack affected overhead employees more than production workers, as Table 13.3 shows. The employment of production workers was said to be closely tied to output, whereas the need for overhead workers was vague and a matter of judgment.

MANAGERS' EXPLANATIONS

Quotations in Chapter 5 describe layoffs of the third type, in which future gain is traded for current savings, and describe layoffs caused by financial distress. The latter were usually of the second type, reducing organizational slack.

> The layoffs were brought on by financial stress and the need for cost containment. Asset quality declined due to bad loans, especially bad loans on commercial real estate, such as condo projects. . . . We are not lending as much as before, but there has been no significant decrease in the overall volume of work to be done. Employees are simply worked harder than before. Also, more technology is used to eliminate people, jobs are redesigned, accountabilities and performance measurements are set up, and organization is brought to bear on the work process.
>
> —Director of human resources of a bank with 380 employees

> By the end of the 1980s, we found we had a huge portfolio problem with real estate. . . . We needed to save expenses. People are 75 percent of them, so we decided on downsizing. . . . Downsizing involved reengineering of processes. A lot of productivity can be gotten out of technology—work stations that allow easy access

TABLE 13.3   Types of layoff by type of worker (numbers of businesses where layoffs of the given type were described) (applies to 113 businesses)

Type of layoff	Production workers	Overhead workers
(1) Reduced demand for labor because of technical change or decline in product demand	70	6
(2) Elimination of organizational slack	27	67
(3) Exchanging future revenue for current savings	4	7
(4) Replacement	5	4

Note: There is some ambiguity in the classification of workers as production or overhead. For instance, I count lawyers as production workers in law firms and overhead workers in other kinds of companies. Similarly, engineers are overhead in manufacturing firms but are production employees in companies specializing in research.

to customer records, for instance. Some business was outsourced to other companies that specialized in certain tasks.

—High-level human resource official in an insurance company with 50,000 employees

Competition stimulated some layoffs.

Greater competition is forcing cost cutting. Electronic improvements have made regional markets national. Legislative changes have made it possible for banks to compete with insurance companies. Losses in real estate require cost cutting. . . . The organization is being flattened to some extent. We are trying to organize so as to take advantage of economies of scale. Some noncore work is being outsourced.

—Human resource manager specializing in downsizing and working for an insurance company with 33,000 employees

Layoffs to eliminate organizational slack affected overhead workers more than production staff (Table 13.3).

At the time [of a financial crisis a year earlier], office staff was reduced from 16 to 9 people. The work of those laid off was assigned to the remaining employees, so that the salaried staff now has both longer hours and added responsibility. Among the men in the field, layoffs are due to lack of work.

—Part-owner and operator of a nonunion construction company with about 90 employees

If I have to save bigger bucks, I go for exempt positions. I have laid off more exempts than nonexempts. If you lack clerical support, your infrastructure falls apart. Exempt employees can figure out how to do things faster.

—Director of a community service organization with 150 employees

Layoffs that accompanied reductions in organizational slack were made possible by a variety of measures to improve productivity. For those overhead workers who received a salary and no overtime premium, the object was to increase productivity per employee, and one way of doing so was to have people work harder, smarter, and for longer hours.

We are reducing staff because the income is not there. Upper management wants expenditures to match income. When there are staff cutbacks, there are fewer internal services, but services to customers are not cut. The human resource and financial staffs are cut, for instance. Finance produces fewer reports for managers.

—Human resource official in a bank with 800 employees

All the 25 laid off were indirect labor or support staff, both exempt and nonexempt. . . . These were done to save money. The total amount of work stayed the same. We just redivided it. We stopped doing some things. Layoffs like this require you to take a stronger look inward after you have become accustomed to looking outward. You work more hours per day, say eight rather than six and a half. You learn to do things better. . . . Not all people are opposed to working harder. They do what they are asked to do. Employees will tell you they could be more effective.

—Head of human resources of a nonunion consumer products company with 1,500 employees

Thirty percent of the human resource department was laid off. . . . The same was done in finance and will be done in information systems. There was less work to do, but mainly there was less money. You can always make work for people to do. With staff jobs, you have to decide what you need to do. . . . You try to streamline processes. Paperwork may get handled two or three times, and it may be possible to eliminate one step of the process. For instance, in the processing of requests for housing expense reimbursements for those living abroad, the request used to be checked. Now it is automatically approved, if it is within guidelines.

—Director of compensation at a unionized manufacturing corporation with 180,000 employees

When reducing organizational slack, some companies got rid of staff so as to force those remaining to figure out how to get work done with fewer people.

We had to cut back on overhead expenses. Twenty-five percent of the management and clerical staff were cut. [The total overhead workload did not change.] . . . We are trying to take the waste out of processes. We forced one before the other. That is, we cut back on personnel in order to force managers to find a better way of doing things. We took a you-figure-it-out attitude. People don't want to work 10 hours a day and so will find a better way of doing things. Top management didn't want people resisting and protecting jobs.

—High-level human resource official in a 3,000-employee, largely nonunion division of a huge consumer products company

When staff is cut, the remaining people pick up the work, find they can't do it, and get creative about how to do it. They say, "If I don't write a report, no one asks for it, so I won't do it."

—Director of human resources of a unionized manufacturing company with 30,000 employees

As was said earlier, only two layoffs were clearly intended to eliminate expensive employees to be immediately replaced by cheaper ones.

I also cut eight people in manufacturing. The layoffs were a weeding out of people who couldn't cut it. I replaced $10 [an hour] people who were no good with $6.50 [an hour] entry-level people who were good. I squeezed every nickel out. I was in survival mode. . . . Mostly, I was firing people for nonperformance. I was being polite about it by calling it a layoff. It is easier on morale to lay people off. Also, it is hard emotionally on me, so that a crisis makes it easier. In good times, I might not be able to find good replacements for those laid off, or good employees might get scared and jump ship.

—President of a nonunion manufacturing company employing 45 people

Four of the layoffs of the replacement type might well have occurred even if those dismissed had not been well paid. Pay was used as a criterion in selecting those to be laid off.

If a store has fewer sales, we don't need so many people there. Also, we like to keep a certain mix of full- and part-time people and don't want to have too many high-priced full-timers around. We choose stores that are heavy in full-time people or have high average pay rates for full-timers. Then we reduce the full-time work force there.

—Vice president of human resources of a supermarket chain with 10,000 employees

Professional firms used layoffs to offset decreases in voluntary turnover.

There have been times when there was less turnover than expected. This occurred two years ago [in 1991]. There were few outside opportunities for people and they were afraid to leave. As a result, I have had to counsel people out who would normally have been allowed to stay. This extra counseling was not due to a drop in business. We need a certain pyramid because of the way the work is done. We also want an inflow of new blood, of people fresh out of school.

—Human resource official of a very large accounting firm

13.2 Organizational Slack

Why did firms find themselves at the onset of the recession with badly arranged work processes and overpaid workers, who were underperforming or doing unnecessary work? Managers claimed that such waste was a natural consequence of prosperity and of the sloppy management that it permits.

OVERVIEW OF INTERVIEW EVIDENCE

Table 13.4 gives the distribution of explanations offered for organizational slack. The third and sixth explanations are consistent with economic rationality. According to the third, workers tolerated heavy workloads during the recession only because they could not find better jobs. The sixth explanation is that organizational slack results from the need to economize management time, for in good times executives make more profitable use of their energies by concentrating on issues such as acquisitions and new product development rather than on cost control.

TABLE 13.4 Explanations of organizational slack (applies to 49 businesses)

Explanation	Number of businesses	Percentage of businesses
Management cares less about waste in good times	28	57
The recession is used as a pretext for firing poor performers	10	20
In good times workers would quit if they were asked to work as hard as they do currently	8	16
A soft company culture encourages protection of employees	6	12
Managers had over-hired in anticipation of growth	6	12
In good times, executives had better things to do with their time than cut costs	3	6
The wrong type of executive becomes influential in good times	2	4

MANAGERS' EXPLANATIONS

The main reason given for waste was that managers were careless when their companies were prospering.

When the tide runs out, rocks appear, which you should have done something about before.
—Owner of a nonunion manufacturing firm with 40 employees

You don't take a close look at [waste] when things are good. Now, we go through workloads with a fine-toothed comb. . . . We just didn't realize that we could do with less when we were in a boom. We are tougher in tough times. We are worried about survival.
—President of a unionized architectural woodwork firm with 125 employees

Competitive pressures are forcing change. . . . The company has allowed itself, through a soft culture, to become overstaffed. It hasn't automated and it hasn't controlled administrative costs. . . . It is like tough love within a family. Losing 300 jobs would preserve the jobs of 2,000 other people.
—Human resource manager in an insurance company with 2,500 employees

Five years ago, there were not the competitive pressures to cut costs. The company had grown, and you didn't have to lay people off to make the money you needed to make. It wasn't something other companies were doing. Companies benchmark. They look at each other. No one else was restructuring.

—Human resource manager specializing in downsizing and working for an insurance company with 33,000 employees

Unneeded employees accumulate almost inevitably if managers do not aggressively resist the process.

We promote from within. Inevitably, people get promoted beyond their ability. When this happens, the tendency is to hire an assistant who can do the job.

—Human resource manager of a nonunion manufacturing company with 250 employees

We create bureaucracies. People are hired, have little to do, and make up work so they look busy. They get creative. . . . In 1987 and '88, we had an activity-worker analysis. Human Resources went through the whole company to see what people were doing. At the end, we would have to cut people. Early on, people had great ideas for saving money. Then, they realized they might lose their jobs, and creativity stopped.

—Director of human resources of a unionized manufacturing company with 30,000 employees

If you make a lot of money, it is easy to overlook inefficiencies. There is no need to make someone unhappy by cutting out their job. It is like a cellar. You accumulate people. It takes energy and creativity to eliminate them.

—Human resource manager at the same company

Some executives said they had accumulated extra employees in anticipation of growth.

It is hard to say no to job growth when a company is doing well. If margins are good, you can't go wrong in hiring. You don't recognize your errors until the music stops. Growth covers a lot of inefficiencies. Our growth has stopped in the last year, and we are examining our operational efficiency. Growth is like pyramiding. When there are demands for hiring, you give in because it is not a significant point.

—Vice president of human resources of an insurance company and HMO with 220 employees

If you think growth will continue, you hire in anticipation of it. Even in a successful company, there are peaks and valleys of demand. You want enough people for the peaks. If you use temporaries or consultants, you have a training problem.

—Human resource manager in an expanding nonunion manufacturing company with 8,500 employees

Several respondents blamed excess employment on bad leadership, and two gave impassioned descriptions of typical bad executives.

Many executives got where they are because they have good upward skills and can push themselves. They are good politicians and are good at presenting reports, but this doesn't mean they can get stuff done. . . . The contraction of personnel could have started in 1986, but management didn't have the courage to do it. [The former chairman] had been there for years. . . . He was Phi Beta Kappa, an athlete, polished, handsome, and absolutely analytical. He was totally administratively oriented. He had no intuition and no vision. His power in life was looking good. What was important to him was form and how you say things. . . . He aggressively pursued short-term high returns on investments. He went for high return and low quality. Suddenly, the company had 5 billion dollars of real estate default. . . . One type of change is an improvement of focus—to get out of certain businesses because the company doesn't have the management talent to do it. The other type of change is to stop doing things within operations that shouldn't be done. Operations have to be reengineered. It requires guts to do that. It is not enough to tell people what to do. Each guy runs his department the way he wants to. If the chairman wants action, he has to follow through. He has to say to people, "What is your plan?" He has to force them to commit. He has to fire people if they don't cooperate. This takes energy and personality.

—President of a 32,000 employee division of an insurance company

Because it is hard to fire people, the recession was a convenient disguise for dismissals for poor performance, which otherwise would require complicated procedures (section 8.4).

I consciously used layoff to strengthen the quality of my work force. . . . Because I had difficulty finding people on the upside [in 1986–1989 during a period of company expansion], there was a wide variation in the quality of my people. I wanted to cut my total payroll and to correct some of the problems brought on by hiring any warm body that came down the driveway [during the previous boom when there was a labor shortage].

—Owner of a nonunion manufacturing firm with 40 employees

It can be difficult to discharge people for performance. If things are going well, you are more understanding [of poor performance]. We also tend to keep people around due to the laws on unjustified discharge. People can sue for this. In order to discharge someone, there has to be documentation and they have to be given adequate time to improve. Also, the documentation can't be too old. . . . Discharge can lead to charges of discrimination as well. People can't accept that they are not doing a good job, so they blame the company and file lawsuits or go to Human Rights and Opportunities and file charges of discrimination. The charges could be discharge for being over 40 or because of race or a disability. Suits are time consuming and can cost a lot of money. In order to win them, you have to have a clear case. In good times, managers prefer not to face all that.

—Human resource officer in a partly unionized manufacturing company with 1,400 employees

Another explanation was that cost cutting in good times would have wasted management effort.

> My own time is a scarce resource. There were so many growth opportunities available to which I should devote my attention that it would have been silly for me to look into efficiency questions [with a view to making layoffs]. The returns to efficiency gains would have been too small.
> —Executive director of a 550-employee department of an investment company

The bad labor market made it easier for businesses to demand more of employees. Similar views were expressed in connection with the effect of the bad labor market on work effort (sections 8.5 and 13.10).

> There is a general tendency for [salaried] staff to be expected to do more. They work harder, smarter, and prioritize. . . . If the economy were better, people would leave rather than work so hard. The lack of alternatives affects their willingness to accept the greater workload.
> —Director of human resources for a unionized department store chain with 20,000 employees

> If so much had been demanded of people before the recession, they would have left. . . . Where are they going to go now? . . . No one would say that, but these considerations enter our thinking.
> —Human resource manager in a 21,500-employee subsidiary of a large insurance company

There was an expectation that more could be asked of exempt workers in hard times in exchange for additional leisure in easier circumstances.

> All salaried people are working 10 hours a day, 7 days a week. People are doing the jobs of 2 or 3 people, because of the layoffs. This alone amounts to a decrease in their hourly pay. . . . People can't keep up this pace forever. It is a temporary emergency measure. The company wants people who will work hard when it needs them so that they can play hard at other times. It prefers people with families who need the money. People can slack off when they are not so needed. When people are hired for salaried positions, they are told that they may be expected to work 84 hours a week if need be.
> —Human resource manager in a nonunion manufacturing company with 250 employees

13.3 Do Labor Market Conditions Influence Layoff Decisions?

The implicit contract theory implies that increased unemployment makes firms less inclined to let workers go. In order to test this assertion, I asked a number of employers whether labor market conditions influenced their layoff decisions.

TABLE 13.5   Influence of labor market conditions on layoff decisions (applies to 51 businesses)

Type of response	Number of businesses	Percentage of businesses
Labor market conditions are irrelevant	38	75
Labor market weakness encourages layoffs	13	25
Labor market weakness makes managers more cautious about layoffs	5	10
Labor market weakness stimulates the company to increase severance enefits	5	10

Responses varied, but the most common one was that the state of labor market was irrelevant.

OVERVIEW OF INTERVIEW EVIDENCE

Table 13.5 summarizes answers to questions about the influence of labor market conditions on layoff decisions.

MANAGERS' EXPLANATIONS

Many managers quickly dismissed the suggestion that the state of the labor market influenced layoffs.

> Layoffs tend to be tied more to business prospects than to the state of the labor market. That has no influence.
> —President of a nonunion manufacturing company and ESOP with 240 employees

> No one would even think of the connection between layoffs and labor market conditions. They might make managers think of giving outplacement services or verbal notice to someone not on the job market for 20 years.
> —Human resource official in a bank with 800 employees

A surprisingly large number of businesspeople said that labor market slackness made layoffs easier.

> In good times, you might not lay off someone when the workload was low, for they might get another job. You avoid the ordeal of training new people by keeping employees around a few weeks until work picks up. Now, you don't think about it. You lay them off and recall them when you need them. . . . Should I worry about

the difficulty of getting a new job? No. I worry about staying in business. If I don't, there won't be jobs for anyone.

—President and owner of a unionized manufacturing company with 135 employees

The [layoff] decision would be influenced by the labor market if we felt we might have to go to the market in the near future to hire. For instance, the supply and demand situation of chemical engineers fluctuates a lot. You don't lay them off if you think you couldn't get them in the future and you might have to.

—Director of human resources of a nonunion manufacturing company with 1,000 employees

We let people go more easily during a recession, because it is easier to replace them since there are a lot of unemployed people out there. During a recession, we are more likely to replace a poor performer. In a good market, we would be more likely to keep someone while we looked for someone else.

—Human resource manager in an expanding nonunion manufacturing company with 8,500 employees

Some managers said that sympathy for those laid off influenced the layoff decision.

Sometimes we create temporary slots for laid-off people until a new job opens up for them. This would not be done in a tight labor market. It is done out of sympathy for the people and for the reputation of the bank as a good employer.

—Human resource officer of a bank with 400 employees

13.4 Replacement and the Lindbeck-Snower Model

I now turn to the question of why it was not common practice during the recession to replace employees with cheaper new hires. Lindbeck and Snower (1988a) have proposed several explanations as part of their insider-outsider model, one of which I discuss here. The main assumption of this explanation is that existing employees would boycott replacement workers, refusing to train and cooperate with them. As a result, replacement workers would be so unproductive that it would not be profitable to hire them. Employers explained that they do not replace an entire work force because of the need to retain skills and because doing so would expose the firm to discrimination suits, tarnish its reputation, and be unethical. An additional reason for not replacing part of a work force was the impact on the morale of the remaining employees. It is interesting that no one said that unemployed replacements would be of low quality, which is evidence against the notion that employers regarded them as inferior. No employers thought the Lindbeck-Snower theory described their reasons for not replacing workers, though about half of those questioned thought

TABLE 13.6   Reasons for not replacing workers with cheaper new hires (applies to 63 businesses)

Reason	Number of businesses	Percentage of businesses
The company would lose employees' skills	27	43
Replacement would demoralize employees	26	41
The company would lose employee loyalty	19	30
Feelings of loyalty to employees	12	19
Fear of discrimination suits and other legal problems	11	17
Replacement would damage the company's reputation as a good employer	9	14
Replacement would be unethical	8	13
Employees would feel insecure	6	10

the boycott assumed by the model might occur. A typical answer was, "I had never thought of the possibility of a boycott, though it probably would occur, now that you mention it. But that is not why we don't replace workers."

OVERVIEW OF INTERVIEW EVIDENCE

Replacement was discussed in interviews with officials of 71 companies, and the Lindbeck-Snower theory was discussed by officials from 33 of these 71. In 8 of the 71 companies, some workers had been laid off to be replaced with cheaper or better ones. Table 13.6 gives the distribution among the remaining 63 companies of the reasons offered for not replacing workers.

Among the 33 employers who discussed the Lindbeck-Snower model, 16 thought the boycott assumed in the model would probably occur if workers were replaced, and another 7 employers thought the boycott unlikely. No one thought the boycott was relevant to the replacement issue.

MANAGERS' EXPLANATIONS OF WHY THEY DON'T REPLACE

The subject of replacing workers with unemployed people provoked lectures about the value of reciprocal loyalty between firm and employee, the importance of having a good reputation as an employer, and the practical matters of avoiding training and hiring costs and discrimination suits.

We have never done that, even among the nonprofessional staff. We run on personal relationships. You can't ignore them. Replacement would have an adverse effect on morale. The employees would look on us as being without heart. This is a highly stressful way to make a living. We make big demands on the staff for long hours and hard work. You want them to be happy, so that you can work with them. They want to feel they have control of their destiny.

—Managing partner of a law firm with 70 employees

To do that would be totally inconsistent with our values. It would be viewed by everyone as out of character. We have core values that everyone looks at. These are morals, folk ways, and myths, the glue that holds a human system together. You don't fool around with that for short-term gains.

—Human resource manager in a nonunion manufacturing company with 250 employees

I have a manager who has been with me 19 years. I could replace him with someone else who would cost less and do a better job. That would be smart business. I might advise my son to do it. But I personally am too loyal to do that. I will go to the wall for people who have helped me. . . . The people who have been with me a year or two are quality people. . . . If I replace employees with cheaper help, the others would start to worry. They would think, "No matter what I do, my position is insecure." . . . Management is basic common sense. If you are good to people in good times, they will help you in hard times.

—Owner of a janitorial service company with 500 employees

We home grow our own skills. We wouldn't consider replacing our people with cheaper ones. We would lose too many skills. No one else in [this city] could operate our machines. You need experience and exposure to our product line.

—Head of human resources of a nonunion manufacturing company with 1,200 employees

We couldn't do that. . . . People are not components that you can unplug and plug in. They have to fit into teams, there are training costs, and there is the risk that new people won't work out.

—Human resource official of a nonunion firm specializing in research and development with 1,800 employees

Affirmative action reasons keep us from doing that. You have to have due cause for dismissing someone and the case has to be documented. If you went through the expense of doing all that, you would spend more than you would save, especially if there was litigation.

—Human resource official of a unionized manufacturing company with 2,700 employees

Replacement would work in the short term, but not over a long time span. We want well-educated, good people. For this, you need a good reputation as an employer. It is important to be known as a good employer.

—High-level human resource official in a 3,000-employee, largely nonunion division of a huge consumer products company

Less money suggests less productivity. How could you demand that the new employees live up to the same demands as the former employees? If you are giving business advice, you are asking people to trust you. If you make your staff replaceable, who will trust you? The reputation of the company would be affected. We could lose clients. Employee morale affects clients.

—Human resource official in a brokerage and investment banking company with 3,000 employees

Managers wouldn't like to do that. An element of management is that managers recognize reciprocal loyalty. If you don't have to destabilize people's lives, don't. You would have to train the new people, which is expensive. The incremental savings might not be that significant, for labor is a small percentage of total costs.

—Human resource manager of a unionized manufacturing company with 30,000 employees

That would be very short-sighted. . . . It would encourage an atmosphere that workers were commodities. You don't want that climate. If people feel that way, you get automatons and you don't get the extra level of effort, imagination, creativity, or the competitive advantage you would otherwise.

—Director of compensation at a unionized manufacturing company with 180,000 employees

MANAGERS' REACTIONS TO THE LINDBECK-SNOWER MODEL

Managers found that the possibility of internal conflict was of minor importance compared with the other arguments against replacement.

I have no experience, but there probably would be conflicts between the old and new employees. The old employees would resent the company, feel threatened, and wonder if they were next. But we would never entertain the thought, and the possibility of conflict is not the reason for not replacing people.

—Human resource manager of a nonunion manufacturing company and ESOP with 250 employees

I have never experienced such a thing and the whole idea boggles my mind. I don't think that way.

—Human resource officer of a 400-employee division of a large nonunion manufacturing company

13.5 How Do Companies Choose Whom to Lay Off?

When companies lay off workers, they usually eliminate a certain number of positions within specified job or skill categories, and within these choose people for layoff according to some clear criteria. These have the same advantages as does internal pay structure; they promote good morale by creating an atmosphere of fairness, reduce the risk of legal actions against the company, and

TABLE 13.7 Selection of hourly workers for layoff (number of businesses)

Criterion	Union	Nonunion	Total
Inverse seniority	25	25	50
Performance	2	51	53
Both performance and inverse seniority	2	13	15
Total	29	89	118

help prevent administrative abuse. According to managers, unionized workers were usually laid off according to inverse seniority, and a majority of nonunion workers were laid off according to performance. That is, among union workers, the most recently hired were let go first, and among nonunion workers the poorest performers went first. Exceptions were construction, where layoffs of unionized craftsmen were according to performance, and some nonunion manufacturing firms, where layoff was according to inverse seniority. These firms imitated union rules in order to avoid unionization and because inverse seniority was fair and easy to administer and to defend in court. The performance criterion requires documentation, which is time consuming and awkward for managers, since by law employees are allowed to see their performance evaluations. Construction unions allow layoff by performance, because they wish employers to view them as reliable sources of high-quality labor. No firm selected workers randomly for layoff, as they are chosen in many economic models.

OVERVIEW OF INTERVIEW EVIDENCE

The selection of workers to be laid off was discussed in interviews with officials of 129 companies. In every case, layoffs of office personnel were made according to performance. Table 13.7 summarizes discussions of layoff of hourly employees in 118 companies.

The performance criterion was complicated. Employers considered productivity relative to pay, and performance meant projected performance in the environment following layoffs. Versatility was important as well as performance on the current job, since after layoffs the remaining workers normally performed a greater variety of tasks.

MANAGERS' EXPLANATIONS

The performance criterion was part of a complicated bureaucratic process.

A position is eliminated when we cannot figure out a way to performance-out an individual. The holders of the positions are usually mediocre performers that we didn't have time to warn. . . . The people eliminated in this way cannot be replaced. To do so would be against the law. It would amount to unfair discharge. The position eliminated is gone forever, though it can be redesigned so that the former incumbent is not qualified for it. This is sometimes done, but it is awkward. The law is stretched, but we are sensitive about this issue.

—Director of human resources of a bank with 380 employees

For management employees, we first target a job. If there are multiple incumbents, we turn to the performance appraisals, which usually is not productive, for managers say only nice things. So, we have management rank people. The lowest ones are eliminated. There is a strong legal need to do that. Everything has to be clearly documented.

—High-level human resource official in a 3,000-employee, largely nonunion division of huge consumer products company

There has been a three-tiered approach to choosing whom to lay off within a group. First, you look at the skills and volume you need to go forward after the layoff. You ask managers to find this out by considering the post-layoff environment. Then, you look at the incumbents and at who has the ability to do the post-RIF [reduction in force] work. Those who don't have the ability must go. This could be due to skill or training. . . . You compare documented performance on the old job with what they are going to do. . . . Generally, there are no ties at this point, but if there are, the tie-breaking criterion is seniority.

—Human resource officer of a bank with 16,000 employees

Versatility was valued by managers when reducing staff.

Layoffs are done by skill. We lay off those who are the least versatile, for those left have to do more jobs.

—Human resource manager for a nonunion printing company with 80 employees

Some managers made it clear that performance meant revenue generated net of pay, so that often the more expensive employees in a category went first.

Four years ago, the department wasn't doing well and there were layoffs. These were strictly performance based. . . . An attempt was made to quantify each trader's and salesman's contribution. The department got rid of people on whom it was just barely breaking even. . . . Scarce talent is never laid off. Those with ideas stayed.

—Executive director of a 550-employee department of an investment company

We look at two issues, performance and pay relative to contribution. With annual percentage salary increases, jobs can be no longer worth the salaries of people filling them. Salaries are compared with the value of the jobs.

—Human resource officer in a partly unionized manufacturing company with 1,400 employees

Seniority privileges were imposed by unions or were part of union avoidance strategies.

In choosing whom to lay off, we go by skill groups, such as materials handlers, inspectors, machinists, toolmakers, electricians, machine repairmen, and so on. We lay off the least senior people first. . . . I consider myself to be the union steward. If I don't play that role, we will have a union. The only thing employees have in a recession is their seniority. Performance is not an objective criterion for layoff. We have other ways of getting rid of underperformers—performance reviews, discipline, and the like. Managers want to choose the people to be laid off, but I won't allow it.

—Head of human resources of a nonunion manufacturing company with 1,200 employees

Managers disagreed about the usefulness of the inverse seniority system of layoff.

The union protects worthless people and the elderly. There are some good people among the new ones I have hired lately. Due to seniority, I will be forced to lay them off. Most of my older employees are useless, but I am stuck with them.

—President and owner of a unionized manufacturing company with 135 employees

If the work in a job is reduced, layoffs within the job are by inverse seniority. Everyone is assumed to be competent. This procedure encourages teamwork and discourages competitiveness. We want people to help each other to build good performance.

—Chief human resource official for a 4,500-employee, nonunion division of a large manufacturing company

In some cases, the seniority system was manipulated to disguise layoffs according to performance.

In most parts of the company, we will say that we lay off hourly people by seniority, because we have some fear of unions. People might seek the protection of unions if layoffs were by performance. In fact, we do it by seniority, but we define the class of people we are looking at so that we get rid of the weaker people or the less necessary jobs.

—Corporate director of human resources of a mostly nonunion manufacturing company with 5,000 employees

REMARK

Despite the widespread use of the performance criterion, the population of unemployed was probably not of low quality, for many firms laid off whole departments or large portions of them. The performance criterion was used only when choosing among people holding similar jobs.

13.6 Labor Hoarding

Labor hoarding is retention of key workers during downturns by placing them temporarily in jobs other than their usual ones. Often these are odd jobs that add little to current output, so that hoarding depresses labor productivity. I heard stories of hoarding of skilled production workers, which must have reduced productivity. However, the recession also stimulated productivity by pushing firms to eliminate organizational slack. This productivity-increasing effect of economic slumps may often more than offset the effect of labor hoarding, for historically aggregate labor productivity grows fastest during recessions.

OVERVIEW OF INTERVIEW EVIDENCE

Labor hoarding was discussed in interviews with managers of 20 companies. In 2 of them, managers denied hoarding labor. In 2 of the remaining 18 firms, labor hoarding was attributed to the desire to protect employees from a bad labor market or to foster employee goodwill, and in the other 16, labor was hoarded to retain skills.

REMARK

I mention in passing that I found no support for real business cycle theory. During hundreds of hours of contact with businesspeople, I never heard one description of an exogenous productivity decline. Rather, I heard of decline in product demand and of successful efforts to increase productivity. However, I asked no questions focused directly on real business cycle theory.

MANAGERS' EXPLANATIONS

Labor hoarding consisted of efforts to find work for employees in order to keep them on the payroll.

> In slack times, we find overhead projects for the architects to do. For instance, in order to apply for awards [i.e., prizes], we have to submit drawings which show how buildings would look from the outside, with the trees and terrain around them, a sort of aerial view. These are called presentation drawings. They are not normally made for clients. [In slow times] we might have architects make the drawings. We might also have them decide which drawings are to be archived or have them do maintenance work on the building. Those things are done to keep the staff together.
> —Founding partner of an architecture firm with 45 employees

> We do not lay off someone in a skilled position, unless we are desperate. We find something for them to do, such as maintenance work or making prototypes for a new project which had been neglected. We also bring in-house work which had

been subcontracted. It is bad to lay off highly skilled people, for they carry with them the informal knowledge on which the company's production processes depend.

—Personnel director of a partially unionized manufacturing company with 250 employees

We do hoard labor when sales drop, subtly, I hope. If we laid off strictly by seniority, we would lose some of our best producers. So, we keep them by finding odd jobs for them, especially as indirect labor.

—Human resource officer of an 850-employee, nonunion division of a manufacturing company

AGGREGATE STATISTICAL EVIDENCE ON THE CYCLICAL BEHAVIOR OF LABOR PRODUCTIVITY

I attempt only a minimal analysis of aggregate productivity, just enough to sketch a possible reconciliation of aggregate statistics with businesspeople's claims that they improved productivity during the recession. As an indicator of economic activity, I use total output of the United States nonfarm business sector, which is close to being the whole economy. I define productivity to be total output per man-hour of all employees in the sector. Hall (1987) uses Solow's total factor productivity, rather than output per man-hour, which I believe corresponds more closely to what businesspeople mean by productivity. The choice is immaterial, for the results reported are hardly changed by substituting Hall's definition. As was mentioned in the introduction to the chapter, there are at least four definitions of pro-cyclicality of productivity. Table 13.8 labels the various definitions and summarizes results on the cyclical behavior of produc-

TABLE 13.8   The cyclical behavior of productivity under various definitions

	Dependent variable	
Independent variable	Rate of productivity growth	Level of productivity
Rate of output growth	Definition 1	Definition 2
	Pro-cyclical	No relation
	(Regression 1, Figure 13.1)	(Regression 2)
Level of output	Definition 3	Definition 4
	Countercyclical	Pro-cyclical
	(Regression 3, Figure 13.2)	(Regression 4, Figure 13.3)

tivity. Productivity is defined to be pro-cyclical if the dependent variable has a positive and statistically significant coefficient in a regression of the independent variable on the dependent variable (as well as on a trend, when the trend is significant). Similarly, productivity is countercyclical if the same coefficient is significant and negative, and there is no relation if the coefficient is not significantly different from zero. The regressions are presented in the appendix to the chapter along with graphs. The large t-statistics should not be taken seriously, for both left- and right-hand side variables are endogenous and errors are probably serially correlated. Any error in output also appears in productivity, since productivity is the quotient of output and labor hours. The correlation of errors could give a positive or pro-cyclical bias to regression coefficients, adding weight to the countercyclical result of definition 3. The regressions do not indicate causality, but give only an idea of the extent to which endogenous variables move together. As was explained above, definition 3 is the one that should be related to businesspeople's statements about the relation of productivity improvement to the business cycle. According to this definition, productivity is countercyclical, which is consistent with what businesspeople said. Each of the four definitions is probably appropriate in some context. Hall (1987) uses definition 1 and Hart and Malley (1996) use definition 4, and they all find productivity to be pro-cyclical.

The pattern in Table 13.8 supports the idea that changes in organizational slack play an important role in productivity fluctuations. If slack is important, productivity growth should decrease when output is high and increase when output is low until most of the slack has been eliminated. It is not hard to construct simple models of oscillating output and productivity series in which productivity is countercyclical according to definition 3 of table 13.8 and is pro-cyclical according to the other three.[2]

13.7 Can Workers Choose between Less Pay and Layoff?

I looked in vain for evidence of McLaughlin's (1990, 1991) assertion that employers offer workers a choice between layoff for lack of work and continued work at lower pay. Respondents indicated that workers who were laid off were told to leave, often with no warning.

Some business practices could be interpreted as offering a choice between lower pay and layoff, but they were not sufficiently widespread to have much impact. Firms occasionally threatened layoffs to obtain concessions during wage negotiations with unions. A few firms succeeded in persuading their employees that general pay cuts would save jobs (Chapters 12 and 19). Finally, some layoffs of particular workers were avoided by offering alternative jobs paying less than the old job. The offers came about either through specially arranged transfers or demotions or through institutionalized bumping, where bumping is the practice of allowing workers to avoid layoff by taking a lower-level job of a lower-seniority worker, who is laid off or bumps someone else. Bumping and demotion did not always result in reduced pay, though workers who bumped usually received the pay of the new job. Policies toward demotion varied, with only some firms cutting pay. Demotions were unusual, but could prevent layoff, since they placed workers in vacant jobs. Bumping was common among unionized manufacturing workers, but did not give employees as a group a choice between pay cuts and layoff. Bumping simply changed the identity of the person laid off, since the last person in a chain of bumping had no alternative but to leave. Managers said that opportunities for bumping were usually accepted and that demotions in the face of layoff were sometimes accepted. In summary, layoff seldom resulted from refusal of pay cuts, a view confirmed by counselors of the unemployed, who said that almost no one left jobs because of pay reduction (section 18.1). I conclude that in practice quits and layoffs are not at all equivalent.

The possibility remains that layoffs and quits are equivalent in the sense that both are economically efficient separations of workers from firms, as McLaughlin (1990, 1991) and Mortensen (1978) suggest. Separations are efficient if the expected present value of workers' earnings after leaving exceeds the expected present value of their marginal product if they remain with the firm. It is difficult to know whether managers' reported layoffs were efficient, for the definition of efficiency requires comparison of two quantities that are hard to measure. I imagine that layoffs were not efficient, for if they were, labor market conditions would influence layoff decisions and they appear not to have done so (section 13.3).

OVERVIEW OF INTERVIEW EVIDENCE

In interviews with officials of 62 companies, I asked managers whether workers were offered the choice between layoff and continued work on the same job at lower pay. None of the companies offered this choice. In 19 of the 62, officials said that sometimes lower-level jobs were offered, if any were open. In every case, officials said such offers were unusual. In two other companies, managers mentioned offering part-time work to full-time workers as an alternative to layoff. The owners of two small companies said they had cut the pay of individuals whose performance did not meet expectations at the time of hiring. However, these pay cuts had to do with reducing pay at the end of the probationary period, not as an alternative to layoff for lack of work. In 21 of the companies, there was bumping among production workers. In all but 2 of the firms with bumping, workers received the pay rate of the new job and so suffered a pay cut.

I asked managers in 43 companies about their policies on pay following demotion. In 21, pay was cut in order to keep it within the ranges for the new jobs. In 19, employees kept their old pay, but were given no raises until the range on the new job caught up with their pay. Three companies used either practice, depending on circumstances.

In 15 companies with bumping, I asked whether employees accepted the lower pay after bumping, or preferred layoff. In 13 companies, managers said the lower pay was accepted, in 2 others managers said that the new job was sometimes refused if the pay was too low. Among the 19 companies where managers discussed offers of lower-level jobs as an alternative to layoff, in 8 managers discussed whether employees accepted such offers, and I conclude from what they said that about half the offers were accepted.

MANAGERS' EXPLANATIONS

Most managers were astonished by the idea of offering as an alternative to layoff continued work on the same job at reduced pay. Some gave reasons and others went on to discuss offers of lesser jobs or curtailed hours. No one mentioned bumping in this context, probably because it involves little management discretion. Bumping came up in the context of layoff procedures.

> We never [offer continued work in the same job at lower pay as an alternative to layoff]. At [a company where I once worked] there was some sort of demotion system, but it usually didn't work out. It hurt morale and left people with the impression that the company felt they weren't good employees.
>
> —Owner of nonunion manufacturing company with 37 employees

> No. A cut in pay would not be enough of a saving if it applied to only the 6 or 7 people laid off. Also, those whose pay was cut wouldn't be happy.
>
> —Personnel director of a nonunion manufacturing plant with 120 employees

> No. No one wants to work for less pay, especially if he alone gets it.
>
> —Owner of a nonunion apparel manufacturing company with 550 employees

> That idea has been discussed, but we have never gone to it. It would be too easily subject to misinterpretation and abuse. The decisions would be too subjective. It would be all right, I think, if there were a change of job.
>
> —Vice president of human resources of a nonunion manufacturing company employing 5,000 people

> No. If the company doesn't need a person on a job, it doesn't need him, no matter what the pay.
>
> —Vice president of human resources of a partly unionized manufacturing company with 5,500 employees

Special offers of reduced time or demotion (as opposed to bumping) were uncommon and received a mixed response.

> If we have the opportunity, we do move people to lower-level jobs, with a downward adjustment in pay if their old pay does not fall in the range of the new job. Out of 40 slated for layoff, 6 to 10 were moved down in 1989–90. About half took advantage of the opportunity and stayed.
>
> —Director of human resources for a financial brokerage and investment banking firm with 1,600 employees

> We do have BPOs [best possible offers] for long-service people, whereby people are put into retraining programs if they are willing to take a downward pay adjustment during retraining and into their new jobs. This doesn't happen often. About half of those to whom such plans are offered take advantage of them.
>
> —Top human resource official of a 19,000-employee division of an insurance company

Lower-paying jobs obtained through bumping caused resentment, but were better accepted than those obtained by special arrangements.

> People who can bump are pissed, but they bump, because they have a job. They don't quit.
>
> —Head of human resources of a nonunion manufacturing company with 1,200 employees

> Being bumped from a full-time to a part-time position makes people angry, though they retain their hourly pay rate. They start asking why they can't have more hours. They have gotten used to a certain standard of living and don't like having it reduced. Disgruntlement gets reflected in lower productivity, more theft, and mistreatment of customers.
>
> —Vice president of human resources of a supermarket chain with 10,000 employees

Managers' discussion of the compensation of demoted employees reflected the tension between internal equity and the bad effects of pay cuts. Employees are upset when their pay is reduced, but preserving the pay of demoted employees creates inequities, for they are then paid more than others in similar jobs.

> Because of this [demotion] system, there are lots of pay inequities. Many are overpaid compared to others. Some have moved to lower-paying jobs and are still paid at higher rates.
>
> —Personnel officer of a nonunion manufacturing company with 80 employees

> In this company, salaries are never reduced, even in the case of demotion. The philosophy is that you don't want to affect the living standard of anyone. If your pay were reduced, you would work your way up anyway. The company keeps you

stagnant for two years until the system catches up with you. . . . The company doesn't want anyone's standard of living to decline, for it doesn't want anyone to have a chip on his shoulder. If he did, he might not work well.

—Chief human resource official for a 4,500-employee, nonunion division of a large manufacturing company

13.8 Advance Notice of Layoff

Firms give workers advance notice of layoff when they inform them of their termination date ahead of time and allow them to stay on the job until then. Firms are legally required to give advance notice only to the workers who qualify as victims of mass layoffs, in which case the Wagner Act requires 60 days' notice. Businesses can avoid this requirement by adding 60 days' pay to the normal severance benefit.

Policy on advance notice reinforces the point made in the previous section that layoff is a unilateral business decision, not an arrangement negotiated with individual workers. Many companies gave no advance notice, and none gave notice to workers in sensitive positions where they could take revenge by seriously damaging the business. Policies varied among companies and depended on how management's opinion was swayed by opposing arguments on the issue. Besides fear of sabotage, the arguments against advance notice were that after receiving notice workers slacken and complain, depressing morale. Arguments in favor were that notice improves a company's image with its work force and gives workers time to look for new jobs and to train successors.

OVERVIEW OF INTERVIEW EVIDENCE

The subject of advance notice was discussed with officials of 41 companies, and Table 13.9 displays the incidence of advance notice among them. The one unionized company which gave no advance notice gave 60 days of extra pay as a severance benefit.

TABLE 13.9   Advance notice of layoff (number of businesses)

	Advance notice to no one	Advance notice to some	Advance notice to all	Send out rumors only	Total
Nonunion	15	8	10	2	35
Union	1	0	5	0	6
Total	16	8	15	2	41

Managers had a variety of opinions on the subject of advance notice of layoff.

I usually give salaried people one month's notice of layoff. I do not fear sabotage. People in the field receive no advance notice. If it is decided that a field person is not needed, he is not needed right away. When professional people are looking for a job, it helps them if they already have a job, so they need notice.

—President of a nonunion mechanical contracting firm with 200 employees

People are given no notice when they are laid off. We are not afraid of sabotage, but of reduced productivity and morale. Having a person around who has received notice would hurt the morale of the entire organization. When people are laid off, they are walked to the door.

—Compensation manager for a nonunion manufacturing company with 1,750 employees

Usually, people are told to clean out their desks and leave. This is true even for hourly employees. We are concerned about sabotage, bad mouthing, and a bad atmosphere.

—Corporate director of human resources of a mostly nonunion manufacturing company with 5,000 employees

We allow people to close out their business and hand it over in good shape to their successor. This gives them pride. They do a class job, but you can't let it go on too long. In the systems area where employees could sabotage the system or take information, we don't allow people to stay, but send them into outplacement right away.

The top human resource official of a 19,000 employee division of an insurance company

Vulnerability to sabotage was reason enough for businesses not to give advance notice.

We gave no advance notice of the layoff. They left immediately. We gave two weeks of pay in lieu of notice, because we were afraid of sabotage. We are vulnerable to that. If someone doesn't tighten a bolt, we could have a suit [from a customer].

—President of a truck dealership and ESOP with 45 employees

Salespeople are usually told to leave immediately, so that the company can prevent them from taking customer records. Clients often remain loyal to sales representatives, who use the records to contact and serve customers for a new employer. After salespeople quit or are dismissed, they typically race the employer to reach customers.

A client's relationship is with his [stock]broker. If we lose a broker, we recoup about 10 percent of his clients through aggressive calling. If a broker is entertaining leaving, on Saturday he comes in, picks up his files, cleans out his desk, photocopies stuff, and leaves a note saying he has left. [Similar events occur when a broker is fired or laid off.]

—Director of human resources for a financial brokerage and investment banking firm with 1,600 employees

13.9 The Effects of Layoff on Those Leaving

Employers asserted that permanent layoffs of full-time employees were a severe blow to them, especially during a recession. Not only were layoffs an economic hardship, but they were humiliating, and cut people off from social contacts at work. Temporary layoffs, which have a definite return-to-work date, were taken less seriously.

OVERVIEW OF INTERVIEW EVIDENCE

Table 13.10 summarizes managers' impressions of the impact of layoff on those let go. It may be seen that employers believed that temporary layoff was less of a setback than permanent layoff. Managers' dim view of permanent layoff was probably realistic, judging from published evidence and statements of advisers of the unemployed (Chapter 18).

Managers knew that workers' financial vulnerability varied, and some companies called for volunteers for layoff or early retirement. I heard accounts of such programs in 11 companies. Companies encouraged participation by giving extra severance or retirement benefits to those volunteering, even if they immediately found new jobs. Voluntary layoffs were easier on morale and were perceived as fairer than involuntary ones, although sometimes the wrong people volunteered or too many left particular jobs or departments. By law, companies can specify eligible jobs and caps on the number who may leave but not who may volunteer.

TABLE 13.10   Effects of layoff on those leaving

	Number of businesses saying that layoff is				
	A terrible hardship	A moderate hardship	No hardship	Don't know	Total
Permanent layoff	83	16	2	2	103
Temporary layoff	0	4	4	0	8
Total	83	20	6	2	111

Temporary layoff was said to be only a minor problem, because workers were accustomed to it and knew they would soon be back at work.

> The work is intermittent due to the weather, so that the men are used to being laid off. It is part of the nature of the business. . . . They typically find day work on side jobs.
>
> —Owner of a nonunion roofing company employing 25 people

> All layoffs are temporary. . . . The employees can make a year's income in nine or ten months. They come in knowing the work is intermittent—at least, whoever hires them should explain that to them. . . . Layoffs are not a big hardship. They can sit on the veranda and drink beer for a few weeks.
>
> —President and half-owner of a nonunion candy company employing 200 people

The loss of part-time jobs was not viewed as a disaster either.

> The loss of part-time jobs is not that hard. They can find another job quickly. These are people who are always looking for work.
>
> —Owner of a janitorial service with 500 employees

A few managers explained that permanent layoffs were much more of a hardship than temporary ones.

> Layoffs are not liked, though some, especially women, may like temporary layoffs in the summer, say, if they know when they are going to be recalled. What they fear are long-term layoffs, especially now in this bad labor market.
>
> —Vice president of human resources of a partially unionized manufacturing company with 5,500 employees

Some viewed the hardship of permanent layoff as only moderate.

> Layoff is a blow to the employees, but all of my carpenters found some sort of work. Many had been doing extra jobs on the side anyway.
>
> —General manager of a nonunion construction company with 15 employees

> The hourly work force is 25 percent female. For many of them, their income is a second family income. So layoff for them is not so bad a blow as it would be for primary income earners. There is some volunteering for layoff, but they normally don't like it. . . . Management and clerical workers don't like layoff at all. It was not envisioned when they were hired. We used to have very few layoffs.
>
> —High-level human resource official in a 3,000-employee, largely nonunion division of a huge consumer products company

Most described permanent layoff as horrible.

> People take layoff very hard, despite severance pay. It is hard to get a new job. One person is still out of work after 15 months. He was a vice president. The devastation of layoff is equal if you are a vice president or an entry-level clerk. Those at a higher level have a greater reaction. They experience more self-doubt and bewilderment.
>
> —Director of human resources of a bank with 380 employees

> Layoff is a terrible blow to employees. Some break down and cry. Even men do. There have been no violent reactions. Some men become hysterical. Some are more prepared for it than others, having seen it coming. Some were blindsided by it. Outplacement reports that it spends a lot of time on grief issues.
>
> —Human resource official of a nonunion firm specializing in research and development with 1,800 employees

> Layoff is the toughest thing you ever do. It destroys lives, families, kids, self-image, self-worth. The best you can do is to build in a system for easing the transition, like severance and outplacement. You need a compassionate environment.
>
> —Director of human resources of a unionized manufacturing company with 30,000 employees

A common theme was that the recession increased the hardship of permanent layoff.

> Losing a job is close to a death in the family. . . . Everyone is afraid in this labor market that they won't get another job for a long time. Two years ago, they would have said, "I don't care. I can go down the street and get another job."
>
> —Human resource officer in a partly unionized manufacturing company with 1,400 employees

> Layoff is a serious blow to people, though it doesn't have the stigma it used to have. It is no longer a euphemism for poor performance. But there are no outside opportunities. Now layoffs are less insulting but more dangerous.
>
> —Vice president of human resources for a nonunion manufacturing company with 95,000 employees

13.10 The Effects of Layoff on Those Remaining

Layoffs had conflicting effects on remaining employees and on productivity. Many layoffs were part of efforts to improve productivity. Layoffs according to the performance criterion stimulated those remaining to work harder so as to avoid dismissal. Workers at all levels were asked to work more intensely, and exempt employees typically were asked to work many more hours, increasing productivity per employee, though not necessarily per man-hour. Layoffs also damaged productivity through their effect on morale. Workers were depressed and distracted by fear of layoff and by worry about friends who had left. Layoffs were disruptive when workers had to get used to new colleagues and supervisors and a new organizational system. Some managers in manufacturing companies suspected factory workers of slowing down in order to reduce layoffs by making the work last. The effects on work effort and productivity depended to a large extent on the skill of company leadership in convincing workers that they were wanted and that their jobs depended on the cooperation of everyone in helping the company. It was useful not to have layoffs recur frequently. In addition, severance benefits reassured the remaining employees. The majority of employers believed they could turn layoffs to their advantage. Few expressed this confidence about pay cuts.

REMARK

I mention as an aside that the recession had contrasting effects on the hours worked by exempt and hourly workers. Exempt employees often had unusually long workdays during the recession. Most production workers in factories and in construction, in contrast, worked fewer hours, though many employers tried to get them to work more intensely.

OVERVIEW OF INTERVIEW EVIDENCE

Managers of 97 companies commented on the effects of layoffs on employees who stayed. In addition, managers in 46 companies talked about the effects on the productivity of these workers. The distribution of types of statements is summarized in Tables 13.11 and 13.12.

In 65 of the 95 companies covered by Table 13.11, employees were said to work harder after layoffs, either because they had more to do or because of fear of layoff. Increased workloads were associated more with layoffs of exempt overhead workers than with layoffs of production workers. Among the 53 companies where workers had more to do, the increase in workload applied only to exempt overhead workers in 30 companies, only to production workers in 3, and to all workers in 20.[3]

MANAGERS' EXPLANATIONS

Many managers mentioned that workloads had grown.

> Compounding the problems caused by layoffs and the co-payment of benefits is the fact that people are being asked to do more. Even the hourlies are.
>
> —Vice president of human resources of a nonunion manufacturing company employing 5,000 people

> A chronic complaint of the last four years is that we eliminate people but not the work. The work simply gets reassigned. This is true for both nonexempt and exempt employees. Most of the complaining is at the exempt and executive levels.
>
> —Human resource manager in a 21,500-employee subsidiary of a large insurance company

TABLE 13.11   Effects of layoffs on those remaining (applies to 95 businesses)

Statement	Number of businesses	Percentage of businesses
Workers have more to do, for there are fewer to do the work	53	56
Layoffs result in no increase in workloads	2	2
Employees work harder to avoid being selected for layoff	15	16
Layoffs hurt morale for a long ime	39	41
Layoffs hurt morale temporarily	12	13
Layoffs damage loyalty to the company	7	7
Layoffs bring more respect for management	6	6
Layoffs are not esented	4	4

Note: If the percentages in Tables 13.11 and 13.12 seem small, this is due to my interviewing style. I avoided specific questions, which might suggest answers, such as "Did layoffs increase the workload of exempt workers?" Rather, I asked, "What were the effects of layoffs on the remaining workers and their productivity?" or I let the subject come up spontaneously.

TABLE 13.12   Effect of layoffs on the productivity of the remaining employees (applies to 43 businesses)

Statement	Number of businesses	Percentage of businesses
Layoffs increase productivity	26	60
Layoffs hurt productivity for a long time	11	26
Layoffs hurt productivity temporarily	4	9
Workers stretch the work to avert layoffs	6	14
Layoffs have no effect on productivity	2	5
Don't know	3	7

The increase in work intensity was said to be concentrated among overhead or exempt employees.

The workload of overhead employees certainly goes up after layoffs. The workload of hourly employees is governed by contract and so does not change. The company gets away with increasing the workload of salaried employees because they are not represented by a union. People would be told, "If you don't like it, there's the door, my friend."

—Human resource official of a unionized manufacturing company with 2,700 employees

When salaried people are laid off, their work is shared by others. . . . Above all, people work harder and more efficiently. They get to work on time, work longer hours, and are forced to be more efficient. . . . In the case of hourly people, layoffs do not bring an increase in the work load. The work simply disappears.

—Vice president of human resources of a partially unionized manufacturing company with 5,500 employees

In some factories, workers tried to forestall layoffs by slowing down.

You can feel morale, especially now that the company is downsizing. People are dogging it on the job to stretch jobs out and perhaps to get overtime on the weekends.

—Human resource official of a unionized manufacturing company with 2,700 employees

In settings where layoffs were according to performance, the possibility of future layoffs stimulated work effort.[4]

The layoffs were viewed as threatening by the other associates. They asked whether there would be other layoffs. The threat probably stimulates more than demoralizes them. They want to demonstrate that they are someone worth keeping and elevating.

—Managing partner of a law firm with 70 employees

Productivity has increased with the recession, for no one wants to be the bottom man who is laid off. The guy who is goofing off is the first to be let go.

—President of a unionized highway construction company employing 1,000 people

Those who remain after layoff work harder than they did before. They are happy to have a job. They think, "I could be next." Morale is hurt, but they still work harder. They think, "I better make sure I am a performer."

—Director of human resources of a financial brokerage firm with 14,000 employees

Although the possibility of layoff stimulated productivity, the fear of layoff also upset and distracted workers, diminishing performance to some extent.

The layoff itself is hard on the group that stays. Managers tend to spend more time with those who are leaving, neglecting those that stay. I urge managers to depend on outplacement and not to neglect continuing employees. Managers should make those who stay feel they are wanted. Stress-related things, such as arguments and fights, increase after layoffs. The stress in itself affects output. . . . Others sit at their desks, wondering if they are going to be called in as well. They see people crying and packing up their desks. People wonder how they should treat others in such distress. The huge building is depressing too, because it is too big and empty.

—Head of the human resource department of a nonunion manufacturing company with 9,500 employees

People are apprehensive and afraid. A lot of time has been spent reassuring them. Performance has been slackening because people can't concentrate on their work. They talk all the time about what is going to happen.

—Human resource official of a unionized manufacturing company with 17,000 employees

Workers also suffered guilt.

Layoffs eat up the people who stay. There is extra tension for them, because if they help the company recover, then their buddies can be recalled.

—Human resource manager of a nonunion manufacturing company with 250 employees

Layoffs hurt morale. There is survivors' guilt. It is like witnessing an accident and thinking it could happen to me. It affects your level of security.

—Human resource manager of a unionized manufacturing company with 30,000 employees

Increased workloads had a depressing effect on morale.

Those of us left have been given more responsibilities. We have more to do with the same deadlines. We are supposed to work smarter, but it seems to me that we just work harder. I often work more than 40 hours a week and over weekends. This depresses morale. Our jobs are not upgraded and we get no additional payment and no increases. We are supposed to say, "At least we have a job," but now even that won't be true.

—Human resource manager of a corporation in the service sector with 10,000 employees

A few managers claimed to have gained prestige with employees as the result of layoffs.

I get respect for eliminating people who don't deserve to be here. I have fired people more than I have laid them off. . . . After a firing or layoff, there is a little wave of respect for me, and productivity goes up.

—Director of a community service organization with 150 employees

Survivors' reactions to layoffs were multifaceted.

The reactions of survivors are complex. They have an enhanced respect for management. Also, they have a feeling of guilt, sadness, and grief because of the loss of colleagues. People are thankful it is not themselves.

—Human resource manager in an insurance company with 2,500 employees

The morale of existing employees is improved by layoffs if hangers-on are eliminated, these being people whose skills are no longer needed. Morale is improved because people feel they are no longer carrying these people. But layoffs can make people nervous. People say to themselves, "I've got to get out of here before it happens to me." A lot depends on how the people laid off are treated, on whether they are given adequate separation pay and outplacement counseling and adequate explanations of why it is being done.

—Human resource officer of a bank with 16,000 employees

Setbacks to morale and productivity caused by layoffs were said by some to last only a few months.

Layoffs do affect the performance of the remaining employees. It takes three to six months to recover. People are worried that maybe they are next. The emotional upset affects their work.

—Human resource official of a nonunion firm specializing in research and development with 1,800 employees

Managers felt that it was best that layoffs be infrequent.

Continued layoffs are demoralizing. It is better to take your hit all at once. If you keep coming back, people spend more time looking over their shoulders, trying to cover themselves than doing their jobs. [The company] is now demoralized, for it has had layoffs every month.

—Head of human resources of a nonunion consumer products company with 1,500 employees

Layoffs should be done quickly. You should pay those left more and say that you are done. You should go deep and do it fast and say that you are finished and then get people to help you renew the organization. But we keep doing it again and again, for business is worsening faster than we thought it would. The company is not realistic about when layoffs will end. The market is moving so fast that realism is difficult.

—Vice president of human resources for a nonunion manufacturing company with 95,000 employees

The effects of layoffs on productivity varied as a result of the contradictory effects.

The layoffs caused an increase in productivity. Fifty of the 75 people laid off were poor producers hired during a period of labor shortage.
—President of a nonunion mechanical contracting firm with 200 employees

Layoffs give rise to seniority layoffs and to bumping, and these give rise to low productivity for a while.
—Vice president of administration of a unionized manufacturing company with 900 employees

The morale of the remaining employees is affected by layoffs. Productivity is hurt both because of morale and because the people who know how to do things are gone.
—Vice president of human resources for a nonunion manufacturing company with 95,000 employees

There has been no drop in productivity after layoffs. In fact, productivity has increased, for we ask more of employees.
—Director of compensation at a unionized manufacturing corporation with 180,000 employees

13.11 Summary

Most layoffs were made either to alleviate financial distress by reducing expenses or to remove workers no longer needed because of technical change or reduced product demand. Layoffs made solely to reduce expenses often reduced wasteful use of labor that had been tolerated during better times. Overhead workers bore the brunt of layoffs that were intended to reduce waste and costs, whereas layoffs caused by technical change or reduced demand usually fell on production workers. Layoffs were thought to be a severe blow to those leaving and also hurt the morale of workers who remained. These employees often had to work harder after layoffs, especially if they were overtime exempt. Some worked harder to avoid being selected for layoff, since many firms laid off their least productive workers first. A large majority of layoffs were believed to be associated with increases in labor productivity. The positive association between layoffs and productivity does not contradict the well-known procyclical behavior of productivity, for productivity tends to increase fastest when unemployment and hence layoffs are high. Few firms laid off workers in order to replace them with cheaper new hires. Employers avoided taking such actions because of the cost of training new workers and because such layoffs would antagonize and demoralize the work force. Firms did not offer workers a choice between layoff and reduced pay, as suggested by McLaughlin (1990, 1991). According to implicit contract theory, firms should be less willing to lay off workers when the labor market is slack than when it is tight. I found, however, that the state of the labor market had little to do with the propensity to lay off. If any-thing, increased unemployment made employers more willing to let workers go.

Appendix 13A Cyclicality of Productivity—Regressions

DATA

The data were obtained from the productivity section of the Bureau of Labor Statistics and consist of quarterly indices of real output and total hours of all employees in the U.S. nonfarm business sector for the years 1947 through 1995.

VARIABLES

Labor productivity is the quotient of output and total labor hours. Rates of growth are percentage changes from year to year. When regressing the rate of productivity growth on the level of output, I match growth from the year t to $t + 1$ with average output for the year ending in June of year $t + 1$, so that growth is compared with the time span over which it occurred.

REGRESSIONS

In the three regressions using levels, I use a quadratic trend, for the output series is slightly U-shaped, and the productivity series has the opposite form. Consequently, output has a negative coefficient when productivity is regressed on output plus only a linear trend, the coefficient being dominated by the gross shape of the data. When a quadratic term is introduced, the coefficient of output changes sign, probably because the quadratic term captures the overall shape, leaving the coefficient on output to reflect cyclical fluctuations.

In the regressions listed below, the first figure below each coefficient is the standard error, the second is the t-statistic, and the third is the P-value or sig-nificance level. The variable "Year" is years elapsed since the beginning of the data series. The F-statistics for all the regressions are significant at the 5 percent level. Key coefficents are written in bold face. They are significantly different from zero at the 5 percent level in every regression but the second.

Regression 1:

Productivity Growth = 1.86 + **0.62** (Output Growth).
$$(0.12)$$
$$(4.96)$$
$$(10^{-5})$$

Regression 2:

Productivity Level $= 35.37 + 1.77$(Year) $- (0.008)$(Year)^2 $+ 0.17$(Output Growth).
$\qquad\qquad\qquad\quad$ (0.08) $\qquad\quad$ (0.0015) $\qquad\qquad$ (0.086)
$\qquad\qquad\qquad\quad$ (22.66) $\qquad\quad$ (-5.21) $\qquad\qquad$ (1.96)
$\qquad\qquad\qquad\quad$ (7×10^{-26}) $\quad$ (4.8×10^{-6}) $\quad$ (0.057)

Regression 3:

Productivity Growth $= 19.67 + 0.51$(Year) $+ (0.01)$(Year)^2 $- 0.64$(Output Level).
$\qquad\qquad\qquad\quad$ (0.22) $\qquad\qquad$ (0.0045) $\qquad\qquad$ (0.2)
$\qquad\qquad\qquad\quad$ (2.35) $\qquad\qquad$ (2.59) $\qquad\qquad$ (-3.19)
$\qquad\qquad\qquad\quad$ (0.02) $\qquad\qquad$ (0.01) $\qquad\qquad$ (0.003)

Regression 4:

Productivity Level $= 23.97 + 1.28$(Year) $- (0.02)$(Year)^2 $+ 0.56$(Output Level).
$\qquad\qquad\qquad\quad$ (0.11) $\qquad\qquad$ (0.002) $\qquad\qquad$ (0.11)
$\qquad\qquad\qquad\quad$ (11.13) $\qquad\qquad$ (-8.00) $\qquad\qquad$ (5.20)
$\qquad\qquad\qquad\quad$ (2×10^{-14}) $\quad$ (3×10^{-10}) $\quad$ (5×10^{-6})

FIGURES

The figures give a visual image of co-movement between key variables. Figure 13.1 shows that the rates of growth of productivity and output fluctuate together, in agreement with regression 1. Figure 13.2 shows productivity growth and the difference between a quadratic output trend and output. The trend is the regression of output on the year and the year squared. Because output has been subtracted from the trend, the positive association between the two series shows that productivity growth and output level move cyclically in opposite directions, confirming regression 3. Figure 13.3 shows differences between productivity and a productivity trend and between output and its trend, the trends being quadratic in each case. The close association of the two series shows that they fluctuate together, reinforcing regression 4.

Appendix 13B Related Literature

ORGANIZATIONAL SLACK (SECTION 13.2)

The term "organizational slack" was defined by Cyert and March (1963) to be the excess of payments to members of an organization over the amount needed to retain them. Since payments include leisure on the job, the term can be interpreted as meaning inefficiency. Leibenstein (1976, 1978) applies the term "X-efficiency" to the same form of waste, and distinguishes it from inefficiency in the allocation of resources. Selten (1986) includes organizational slack in a model of imperfect competition and interprets slack as part of employees' consumption. In the literature on organizational slack and X-efficiency, it is asserted that success increases waste and that adversity and closer ownership control mobilize management to combat it. There is some documentation of organizational slack in Cyert and March (1956, 1963) and Leibenstein (1976, pp. 42–44).

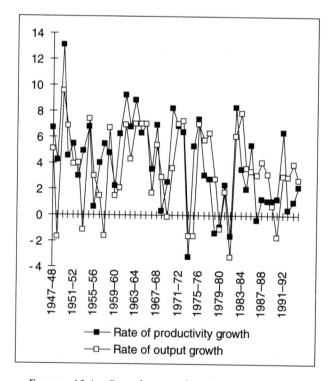

FIGURE 13.1   Growth rates of productivity and output

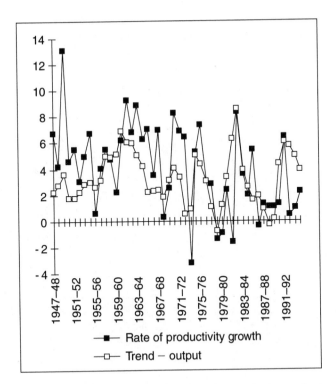

FIGURE 13.2   The rate of productivity growth and a quadratic trend minus output

DO LABOR MARKET CONDITIONS INFLUENCE LAYOFF DECISIONS? (SECTION 13.3)

I know of no statistical tests of implicit contract theory's implications regarding the propensity to lay off. Some authors test whether employment within firms depends on job opportunities outside them. Brown and Ashenfelter (1986) find little evidence of dependence, Card (1986) finds some evidence, and Bean and Turnbull (1988) find even more. Bean and Turnbull are the only ones to include the unemployment rate among the variables measuring alternative opportunities. The effect they detect may reflect labor hoarding (section 13.6).

REPLACEMENT AND THE LINDBECK-SNOWER MODEL (SECTION 13.4)

Campbell and Kamlani (1997) find that managers do not believe Lindbeck and Snower's explanation of why firms seldom replace workers, findings consistent with those reported here.

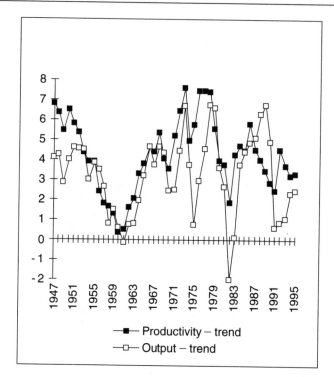

FIGURE 13.3   Productivity minus a quadratic trend and output minus a
quadratic trend

HOW DO COMPANIES CHOOSE WHOM TO LAYOFF? (SECTION 13.5)

A great many studies find that union contracts usually have provisions calling
for the layoff of the lowest-seniority workers first, whereas nonunion workers
are typically laid off according to performance (Aronson, 1950; Slichter, Healy,
and Livernash, 1960, chap. 6; 1960, Meyers, 1964; Tillery, 1971; Bureau of
Labor Statistics, 1972; Herding, 1972, chap. 2; Bureau of National Affairs,
1980; Abraham and Medoff, 1984; Oswald and Turnbull, 1985; McCune,
Beatty, and Montagno, 1988; and Oswald, 1993). Turnbull (1988) criticizes
the conclusion that union contracts protect high-seniority workers from layoff.
He cites evidence that workers do not know in advance which jobs will be
eliminated, that whole departments can be laid off at once, and that the rules
are sometimes manipulated to permit the layoff of high-seniority workers.
What I heard was consistent with these points.

LABOR HOARDING (SECTION 13.6)

Fair (1969, 1985), Scott Clark (1973), Sims (1974), Gordon (1979), and Hamermesh (1989) all show econometrically that labor input responds with a lag to output, which is consistent with labor hoarding. Fay and Medoff (1985) find direct evidence of labor hoarding in a survey of businesses, many of which reported assigning ancillary work to valuable workers during slow periods. These reports are similar to the stories I heard.

Some studies of individual plants show that productivity and workers' attitudes toward work improve during recessions (Katz, Kochan, and Gobeille, 1983, p. 7; Norsworthy and Zabala, 1985, p. 555). These studies are consistent with evidence cited in section 8.6 that high unemployment stimulates productivity.

CAN WORKERS CHOOSE BETWEEN LESS PAY AND LAYOFF? (SECTION 13.7)

Baker, Gibbs, and Holmstrom (1994a) and Baker and Holmstrom (1995) report that there were almost no demotions of managers over a period of 20 years in the company they studied, evidence that demotions are rare. Bumping procedures in union companies are described in Bloch and Platt (1957).

ADVANCE NOTICE OF LAYOFF (SECTION 13.8)

Surveys of union contracts find that they typically require advance notice of layoff (Theodore, 1957; Bureau of Labor Statistics, 1972). In a survey of workers, Brockner et al. (1994) find that advance notice diminishes hostility to firms among both victims and survivors of layoffs.

THE EFFECTS OF LAYOFF ON THOSE LEAVING (SECTION 13.9)

I have found nothing written on employers' beliefs about the impact of layoffs on the people let go, though there is a huge literature, cited in Chapter 18, on the actual effects of layoffs on the people dismissed.

THE EFFECTS OF LAYOFF ON THOSE REMAINING (SECTION 13.10)

The impact of layoffs on survivors has been studied extensively by a group of psychologists led by Joel Brockner, and their findings substantiate what my managers said. Brockner (1988) and Brockner et al. (1992) find an inverted-U relationship between fear of layoff and work effort among employees of a retail chain that was closing stores. The stimulus to effort apparently stemmed from efforts to counteract survivor guilt and to avoid layoff by being useful. If the fear of layoff was too great, workers gave up in despair. Brockner's group also found that layoffs were more likely to have a negative impact on job attitudes and productivity if survivors strongly identified with those laid off (Brockner et al., 1987; Brockner, 1988). This work as well as managers' assertions support the idea that layoffs can stimulate productive effort.

Brockner led numerous field and laboratory investigations that show the importance of fairness to survivors' reactions to layoffs, where fairness means good explanations given of the need for layoffs, just procedures for selecting those let go, and considerate treatment of them. Consideration includes politeness, advance notice of layoff, help in finding new employment, and severance benefits. Fairness is associated with better job attitudes and more work effort. The papers in question include Brockner (1990), and Brockner et al. (1987, 1990, 1993, and 1994). Brockner and Wiesenfeld (1993) survey work on the effects of layoffs on survivors.

14

SEVERANCE BENEFITS

Management views on severance benefits shed light on attitudes responsible for wage rigidity and are pertinent to implicit contract theory. This theory's fundamental assumption, that firms insure workers' income, implies that severance benefits would be so generous that a worker's marginal utility of wealth would be nearly the same after layoff as before. That is, workers would hardly be hurt financially by layoff. This implication could invalidate the theory, for few workers are so well protected. The inventors of implicit contract theory evaded this difficulty by assuming that moral hazard inhibits or prevents payment of severance benefits. One hazard is that workers might try to receive benefits by quitting or by shirking so as to be fired. Another is that workers might prolong benefits by making little effort to find a new job. However, I found no evidence of management concern about perverse incentives created by severance benefits. The unimportance of moral hazard leaves the puzzle of why many companies pay no severance benefits or only small ones. The puzzle becomes somewhat less baffling when it is realized that employers do not consider these benefits to be part of an insurance agreement permitting firms to collect premia in the form of lower pay. No such agreements are made, probably because few want to think about the possibility of layoff at the moment of hire. Firms do earn returns from severance benefits, but only when layoffs occur and in the form of intangibles, such as company reputation and good morale among the remaining employees. The importance of these advantages to a business depends on company or industry traditions regarding the protection owed to workers. In addition, severance benefits are a way of generating loyalty, and probably for this reason benefits often increase with employee tenure. The emphasis on morale, loyalty, and reputation adds to other evidence that these considerations dominate the relation between compensation and economic recession.

14.1 The Nature of Severance Benefits

Severance benefits varied widely among companies in my study. A legally mandated minimum was accrued vacation and holiday pay. The main benefit was usually a lump sum paid to workers who had been dismissed, sometimes a single payment, but normally a continuation of wage or salary and of health insurance for a specified period. The continuation time usually depended on the length of employment at the company, a typical figure being one week per year of service, and sometimes two or three. Often, a condition for receiving severance pay was that the recipient not sue the company, and in a few cases severance pay was larger if the recipient agreed not to sue. Some companies provided smaller benefits for temporary than for permanent layoff, and payments were often larger if layoff was voluntary or the result of a plant closing. Severance benefits at plants that closed were labeled as stay-on bonuses, for workers received them only if they remained on the job until dismissed. This arrangement encouraged employees to keep the plant operating and help with the closing. Some construction unions provided supplementary unemployment insurance, but none was paid by the companies where I asked about severance benefits. Many large companies included outplacement services in the severance package.

The most noticeable aspect of severance pay was how small it was for everyone except high executives. Someone employed five years might receive five weeks' pay, not much given the time it took unemployed people to find work and the small amount paid by unemployment insurance. It seemed that workers were poorly insured against layoff, as was confirmed by the view of both employers and advisers of the unemployed that layoff was a severe financial setback for most people (sections 13.9 and 18.2).

Although there was an obvious tendency for severance benefits to increase with job rank, I cannot document this extensively as I did not collect precise quantitative data on these benefits. Of 103 primary-sector companies that paid severance benefits to some employees, 23 paid them only to management, and every company that paid benefits to hourly workers also paid them to management. Of the 80 remaining companies, 14 paid more generous benefits to managers than to hourly workers in the sense that more weeks of pay per year of service were paid and additional benefits were provided, such as better outplacement services. The reverse situation never occurred. In sum, 37 of the 103 companies favored management, and none favored hourly workers.

There was some tendency to increase severance benefits because of the bad state of the labor market. Of 103 primary-sector companies paying severance benefits, managers in 6 mentioned that because it had become hard to find work, either severance benefits or outplacement efforts had been augmented.

14.2 The Incidence of Severance Pay

The prevalence of severance benefits varied sharply across industries, did not depend on the presence of a union, and increased with firm size. Table 14.1 displays the variation among industries.

Some but not all of this variation can be explained by commonsense arguments. It probably became a tradition not to have severance benefits in the construction industry because there both jobs and layoffs are thought of as temporary. Craftsmen are hired for a project and are let go as it is completed, when they look for work on a new project and very likely with a new employer. The loyalty of unionized craftsmen is often to their union, which finds them work, rather than to their employer. The absence of severance pay extended to manufacturing companies closely connected with construction, such as those making architectural woodwork. Within some companies producing equipment installed at construction sites, installers and repairmen received no severance benefits, whereas factory workers did. In the secondary sector, jobs of hourly employees are often part time and short term, and their loss is likely to be less harmful than the loss of permanent full-time jobs. I detected no relation within manufacturing between product type and severance benefits, apart from their absence in businesses associated with construction.

Table 14.2 supports the assertion that unionization had little influence on whether companies had severance benefits.

Table 14.3 provides evidence that severance benefits were more common among large than small firms. The increase in incidence with firm size probably reflects the increase in financial reserves and in the importance of reputation with company size, where financial strength is relevant because of company risk aversion (Chapter 5). Risk aversion was also revealed by severance

TABLE 14.1   Incidence of severance benefits paid to hourly employees by industry

Industry	Number of firms studied	Number asked about severance benefits	Number paying severance benefits to hourly workers	Percentage paying benefits to hourly workers
Financial[a]	30	22	22	100
Manufacturing	93	75	36	48
Construction	15	13	0	0
Secondary sector	63	19	5	26

a. By hourly employees in financial companies, I mean clerical workers, though they are sometimes paid a salary.

TABLE 14.2   Union presence and the incidence of severance benefits paid to hourly employees in manufacturing (applies to 73 businesses)

Union status	Number of firms	Number paying severance benefits to hourly workers	Percentage paying benefits to hourly workers
A significant union presence	20	9	45
No significant union resence	53	27	51

TABLE 14.3   Firm size and the incidence of severance benefits paid to hourly employees in manufacturing (applies to 73 businesses)

Size range	Number of firms	Number paying severance benefits to hourly workers	Percentage paying benefits to hourly workers
Fewer than 1,000 employees	46	16	35
At least 1,000 eployees	27	20	74

benefits reductions brought on by financial problems. Such reductions had recently occurred in 10 of 103 primary-sector companies paying severance benefits.

14.3 Do Severance Benefits Create Perverse Incentives for Workers?

Employers did not associate moral hazard with severance benefits. Since many companies pay the benefits and these are sometimes generous, perverse incentives clearly do not prevent payment, though they may curtail benefit size. There was no issue of workers' prolonging benefits by not finding work, for often salary continued even after recipients found new jobs. I asked managers of 14 primary-sector companies whether salary continued after a new job was found, and 12 replied that they did. The 2 who said benefits stopped also said the stipulation was nearly unenforceable. Few companies paid severance benefits to workers who quit or were fired. In the case of firing, a distinction was made between firing for cause and firing for poor performance, and fewer companies paid severance benefits in the former case. The motivation for paying benefits after firing was to reduce the likelihood of suits, payment being conditional on not suing.

Employees are also entitled to a separation allowance when they are fired, unless they are fired for a serious offense. This is less than the usual severance pay, but it helps keep down suits.

—Human resource manager for a group of 1,700 employees in a large insurance company

The evidence is summarized in Table 14.4, which applies to companies that paid severance benefits in cases of layoff.

Four managers mentioned that it was sometimes difficult to distinguish a firing from a layoff and that benefits were paid in ambiguous cases.

Employees who are fired for misconduct get nothing. They also get nothing if they are terminated for poor performance and the case is clear-cut and well documented, with warnings given, and so on. In the gray area, they get something if they sign a no-suit agreement, but what they get is never more generous than what they would get if they were laid off.

—Vice president of human resources for a nonunion manufacturing company with 95,000 employees

The possibility exists that because of the danger of suits for discrimination or unreasonable discharge, firms lay off workers rather than fire them, so that they receive severance pay even when they shirk. However, layoffs normally occur during contractions of the work force and are not part of regular disciplinary procedures. If workers shirk systematically, they are fired after documentation is gathered and proper procedures are followed.

No manager ever referred to perverse incentives associated with the payment of severance benefits, other than its being hard to enforce the stipulation that salary continuation cease upon starting a new job. But many mentioned that severance benefits give people the useful incentive not to sue after having been laid off. No manager mentioned that payment of the benefits might encourage poor work. Businesspeople would not have been likely to think in this way,

Table 14.4 Severance benefits in case of quits or firings

Type of separation	Number of businesses where question asked	Number of businesses paying no benefits	Percentage paying no benefits
Quit	57	57	100
Fired for cause	50	45	90
Fired for underperformance	22	9	41

since they believed job loss to be a serious setback, even for people receiving severance pay (section 13.9).

14.4 Why or Why Not Pay Severance Benefits?

Both businesspeople and labor leaders gave consistent explanations of why companies offered or did not offer severance benefits. The pressure for severance benefits came not from recruiting needs, but from the internal requirements of companies and the desire to foster a good public image. It was also widely recognized that severance benefits were needed primarily by long-term, full-time workers, while other workers were assumed to have lifestyles adapted to transient work.

OVERVIEW OF REASONS FOR NOT OFFERING SEVERANCE BENEFITS

The main reason given for not paying severance benefits was lack of interest on the part of employees, as Table 14.5 shows. The lack of interest could be because of optimism when taking a new job or unwillingness to consider future reverses. The table applies to companies that did not offer the benefits to hourly employees and where I asked why the benefits were not paid. Companies not paying severance benefits to hourly employees were usually small and in construction and related industries or in the secondary sector. When employers said benefits were too expensive, they meant they would have to be paid just when the company was short of money, evidence of company risk aversion.

MANAGERS' EXPLANATIONS

Managers of companies that did not pay severance stressed what they perceived to be workers' lack of interest in the benefits.

TABLE 14.5   Reasons for not paying severance benefits (applies to 30 businesses)

Reason	Number of businesses citing the reason	Percentage of businesses
Workers not interested	21	70
Not industry practice to do so	10	33
Too expensive	6	20

There is no severance pay. The union never raised the issue. Office people don't get it either. Severance is not common in the construction industry. Layoff was not common before the last two or three years, though there is a little seasonality.

—President of a unionized architectural woodwork company with 30 employees

We pay no severance. It would be throwing money away. You would get nothing for it. The employees have low aspirations. They all live from pay check to pay check.

—Part-owner of a dry cleaning company with 15 employees

Severance pay is never brought up. People know that there is none when they are hired. They are highly paid, and it is their responsibility to save. They get unemployment insurance or social security when they are laid off. Most get new jobs quickly. Roofers are used to not working a good part of the year. 1500 hours is a good year for a roofer.

—Owner of a unionized roofing company with 775 employees

Severance pay is not a big issue. I don't know why. There is little demand for it from the union. People prefer not to think about layoff. The thinking is very myopic.

—Vice president of human resources of a supermarket chain with 10,000 employees

UNION LEADERS' EXPLANATIONS

It would be a mistake to dismiss as self-serving businesspeople's view about workers' indifference to severance benefits, for labor leaders had the same opinion. Severance benefits were discussed in 12 of 18 interviews with labor leaders, and 6 of them said union members did not care about the benefits, whereas only 2 spoke of their interest. The 6 represented retail or construction workers or workers in small industrial companies. The 2 represented workers in large manufacturing companies. Another 6 of the 12 mentioned the difficulty companies had paying severance benefits during periods of financial distress. An obvious thought is that an advantage of the benefits from a union standpoint is that they discourage layoffs. Only one labor leader, however, mentioned this effect.

There is no severance pay. There never is in construction, for people have to spend half their time on unemployment insurance. No one expects to work steady, and lifestyles adjust to this. People work three months and then get laid off. This is part of their way of life. They have to save money and gauge their living standard according to the amount of time they can expect to work.

—Business agent for a construction union with 270 active members

There is no severance pay, at least not as a rule. In the last two years, there has been some demand for it. Companies of the size I deal with cannot afford it. If they are in trouble, they cannot pay it. If the company goes under, the boss is worse off than the men, for he has his house and everything in the business and loses it all.

—Business agent for manufacturing workers in a union local with 3,400 active members

Members don't usually think about severance at contract time. It is the ostrich phenomenon. The layoff will happen to the next guy.

—General counsel for a regional union council with 6,000 active union members

Severance pay is not a big issue. Members don't want to think about it. They do so only at the time of layoff. They wouldn't give up base pay for additional severance. Owners resist it, for they know they will have trouble paying it, and psychologically, they don't like thinking about it. Big companies with public reputations will pay it, sometimes even if it is not in the contract.

—Regional manager of an industrial union with 6,500 active members

INTEREST IN SEVERANCE BENEFITS AT THE TIME OF HIRING

There is other evidence of worker indifference to severance benefits. Managers claimed that job candidates showed little interest in severance benefits, as Table 14.6 indicates.

I was also told by 11 managers that questions about severance benefits would be taken as a bad sign during job interviews, and job applicants might have been aware of this. However, managers also thought job applicants did not think ahead or did not want to have gloomy thoughts at a moment calling for optimism.

No one asks about severance when they are being hired. Job applicants ask first about salary, then about health insurance, then holidays, then vacations, and then educational assistance.

—Personnel manager of a unionized manufacturing company and ESOP with 200 employees

TABLE 14.6 Do job candidates inquire about severance benefits? (applies to 47 businesses)

Answer	Number of businesses	Percentage of businesses
No one asks	41	87
Only candidates for high management positions ask	4	9
Candidates do ask	2	4

Note: In 14 of the 47 companies, no severance benefits were paid to hourly employees.

TABLE 14.7   Reasons for paying severance benefits (applies to 64 businesses)

Reason	Number of businesses citing the reason	Percentage of businesses citing the reason
They improve the morale of the remaining employees	22	34
They do not improve the morale of the remaining employees	2	3
They promote the reputation of the company	20	31
They soften the blow of layoff	19	30
It is the fair thing to do	17	27
They are given out of feelings of guilt	15	23
They reduce the number of suits	11	17
They reward loyalty to the company	8	12
They are needed to attract new employees	6	9
They give the company happy alumni	5	8

No job candidate ever asked about severance. If they did, it would be the kiss of death. It would reflect too negative an attitude.

—Newsroom editor of a major newspaper with 580 employees in the news department

People don't ask about severance when they are hired, for they don't think about layoff then. This is a timing issue. Also, the question may indicate that someone doesn't really want the job. Severance is highly valued at the time of layoff.

—Human resource manager of a unionized manufacturing firm with 1,800 employees

OVERVIEW OF REASONS FOR OFFERING SEVERANCE BENEFITS

The motives for paying severance were complicated, but the main emphasis was on issues other than having a good selling point when talking to prospective hires. Table 14.7 gives a sense of the distribution of reasons given by managers. Mention of company reputation was more common among managers of large than of small companies.

MANAGERS' EXPLANATIONS

It was obvious to many that a main advantage of severance benefits was their effect on the remaining employees.

Severance is paid because that is the [company name] way. Employees should feel that the company is fair and cares about its employees. That improves morale, makes people more willing and better able to use their heads to help the company, and it helps head off union sentiment.

—Director of human resources of a nonunion manufacturing company with 1,000 employees

We have found that treating those who leave well gives a better sense of comfort to those who stay. The treatment of those who leave gets back to those who stay. Outplacement is offered for that reason. We have gotten great feedback from those who remain.

—High-level human resource official in a 3,000-employee, largely nonunion division of a huge consumer products company

Company reputation affected employee mood, but was also important because of its impact on community relations and on potential future hires.

[We pay severance in part because the company] tries to be a good corporate citizen. There are heavy linkages with the community we live in due to the product we sell, so we want to project a good image.

—Top human resource official of a 19,000 employee division of an insurance company

The payment of severance doesn't make hiring easier. But the reputation for fairness is important for community relations and hiring. Good community relations are especially important with environmental issues in the air. We are usually the big player in a small community.

—High-level human resource manager in a unionized manufacturing company with 27,000 employees

One group of people with whom some companies want to have a good reputation are those laid off.

Severance pay is helpful in that it builds up the good will of employees who have been laid off repeatedly until they reach such seniority that it doesn't happen anymore.

—Human resource manager of a nonunion machine shop with 225 employees

Severance is paid because one, it is a way to get managers to make the tough decisions, two, you want people to have a bridge and be loyal alumni of the company—they may be customers or suppliers in the future, and three, it is becoming a norm.

—Vice president of human resources for a nonunion manufacturing company with 95,000 employees

Severance benefits were not sold to job candidates.

[Severance benefits] are part of the package I must offer to attract people with critical skills. It is not part of the package I sell hard. It is not needed to attract production workers.

—Owner of a nonunion manufacturing company with 35 employees

An executive argued that layoff benefits should be improved to make the company's compensation more competitive, and [the company chairman] retorted that nobody comes here for the layoff benefits. He argues that people come because they want to work here. He says that if people are worried about the future, we shouldn't want them. Business is risky. If someone asks about severance at a job interview, he shouldn't be hired.

—Human resource manager in a financial company with 24,000 employees

An important motive for paying severance benefits was fear that people would contest layoffs in court.

Severance is paid to give the company a good image and because of the increase in lawsuits by terminated employees, who accuse companies of unjustified dismissal. To reduce suits, the company lets people go as pleasantly and nicely as possible. A big company loses badly in court, for it is rich, so it is a good target for suits. Legal costs are huge too.

—Human resource manager for a group of 1,700 employees in a large insurance company

Managers' statements showed that the motives for helping victims of layoffs were above all complex.

Severance is bridge money. It is also guilt money. The leadership of the company feels guilty for not having planned better. It helps with the morale of the remaining employees. The payment of severance is not a competitive issue. It has to do with the internal functioning of the company. But the payment of severance is a common practice. I don't like it if job candidates ask about it, but I do like to tell them about it when I describe our benefits. If someone asks about it, I wonder why they are concerned about being let go. Do they have a performance problem? Candidates rarely ask. Maybe it has happened twice in the 30 years of my career.

—Director of human resources for a financial brokerage and investment banking firm with 1,600 employees

I tried to find out if there was a trade-off between pay rates and severance benefits by asking four managers whether their company's generous benefits made it possible to pay lower wages and salaries, and the answer was "no," though the question struck respondents as so naive that I soon stopped asking it. The trade-off may arise in labor negotiations, for it was well described by a labor leader who dealt with large corporations.

In my negotiations, there are trade-offs. Severance is traded off against pay. There is a pie. I see if I can expand the pie. Companies often don't care how the pie is split up, though some will resist supplementary unemployment benefits. . . . If you are skillful and a good leader, you can influence the agreement. You say, "We will get more severance for the younger workers and better vacations for the older ones."

—Director of an industrial union local with 65,000 members

14.5 Why Severance Benefits Increase with Job Tenure and Rank

I attempted to find out why the salary extension period after dismissal increased with job grade and years of service, for this practice is not easily explained by the role of severance pay as insurance. Statistical information indicates that the difficulty of replacing income lost through layoff increases with job tenure (Topel, 1990), but not with rank and income (Appendix 18A, section 18.13), so that insurance needs would have salary continuation lengthen only with tenure. Managers argued that severance benefits increased with tenure in order to foster loyalty and increased with rank because the difficulty of finding work also grew with rank. It is probably true that the increase in severance pay with tenure is meant to induce workers to stay with a company, for other benefits, such as pensions and vacations, also increase with tenure. The belief that the difficulty of job search increased with rank and income, though probably mistaken, was widespread among both businesspeople and advisers of the unemployed. Other reasons that benefits increase with rank and income may be that the importance of employees' morale to a company and their interest in severance benefits both increase with rank.

OVERVIEW OF INTERVIEW EVIDENCE

I asked managers in 24 companies for explanations of why severance pay increased with job rank and years of service. All 7 of those who talked about the increase with service said that this was a way of encouraging and rewarding loyalty. Eighteen of the 19 who talked about the increase with rank said that the difficulty of finding new jobs rose with rank and one said that hourly employees were looked upon as less important.

MANAGERS' EXPLANATIONS

Managers were quite uniform in their views about why severance benefits increased with rank and years of service.

Severance pay is in the benefits package—two weeks' pay for every year of service. This is paid because the employee has made a commitment to you. It is a reward for not having quit. . . . Those at the top of the pyramid have a harder time, even if they have been on the job only a short time. There are few managerial jobs available. A rule of thumb is that there is an extra month of job hunt for each $10,000 in annual pay. For this reason, severance is more generous at the top, even if the job has been short term.

—Human resource official in a 300-employee operations facility of an insurance company

Clerical employees get one week per year of service. Management gets from one and a half to three weeks per year of service, depending on their grade. The logic is that it takes higher-level employees longer to get reemployed. The hourly employees receive no severance pay. They can get a new job quickly. Also, cost enters into the reasons for not giving them severance. They ebb and flow all the time.

—High-level human resource official in a 3,000-employee, largely nonunion division of a huge consumer products company

14.6 Summary

Severance benefits were uneven in the sense that they were generous in some companies, modest in others, and nonexistent in many. The generosity of benefits and the likelihood of receiving them increased with employee rank and seniority. There was no evidence that perverse incentives discouraged payment of the benefits. The main reason for not paying benefits was lack of employee interest. The main reasons for paying benefits were the desire to promote the company's reputation as a good employer and the desire to sustain the morale of employees remaining after layoff.

Appendix 14A Related Literature

THE NATURE OF SEVERANCE BENEFITS (SECTION 14.1)

The theory of severance benefits is discussed in Rosen (1983), C. Kahn (1985), Arvan (1989), Booth and Chatterji (1989), and Chiang (1991).

THE INCIDENCE OF SEVERANCE PAY (SECTION 14.2)

Sources on the incidence of severance benefits are Lunden and Moore (1965), Miner (1978), H. Levine (1985), and Oswald (1986a). Their findings are roughly consistent with my own; many firms pay severance, many do not, and the benefits that are paid are not generous enough to insure workers fully.

DO SEVERANCE BENEFITS CREATE PERVERSE INCENTIVES FOR WORKERS? (SECTION 14.3)

Holmstrom (1983, p. 48) describes possible perverse incentives from severance benefits. I know of no one who has examined the question empirically.

Managers may well be correct in believing that severance benefits improve the morale and performance of layoff survivors, for Brockner et al. (1987, 1993) have gathered experimental and field evidence supporting this view. I know of no surveys of employers' reasons for paying the benefits.

15

HIRING

The criteria and methods employers used in hiring and their perceptions of the supply of labor during the recession bear on theories of unemployment and wage rigidity. According to one of the main theories of business fluctuations, the Lucas-Rapping theory, unemployment increases during downturns because unemployed people do not want to work at current wage rates (Chapter 1 and sections 20.1 and 20.3). Other theories attribute some of the increase in unemployment to employers' belief that job candidates who are unemployed are likely to be inferior (section 20.4). The hiring methods used may help explain the long duration of unemployment during recessions.

During the recession of 1990–1991 and during the period of this study, 1992–1993, hiring continued, though at a reduced level because of poor business conditions. Labor became more abundant in the sense that the number of job applicants increased and their quality improved as well. Almost no one indicated that the jobless were not willing to work at going pay rates. On the contrary, a common complaint was that job applicants were often willing to work for too little, making them overqualified. Only employers of menial labor claimed that applicants wanted too much money and preferred welfare and unemployment benefits to work. Employers had mixed reactions to unemployed job seekers. Some had negative views, but many felt the recession had diminished or removed the stigma of joblessness by making layoff and unemployment more understandable. The recession also weakened any stigma associated with holding low-level interim jobs. Employers emphasized that the best way to locate new hires was through employee referrals and personal contacts. People found in this way were thought to have been screened, and hiring employees' friends fostered a sense of community within a company. The prevalence of hiring through referrals meant that job hunters had to use personal contacts as well (section 18.4).

15.1 Labor Supply

Most employers claimed that labor was far more abundant than during the previous boom, though there were shortages of some skills. The recession may have caused a decrease in the supply of applicants in certain skill areas, because employed people were less willing to change jobs for fear new jobs would prove short-lived. The overall quality of applicants improved as well, despite an increase in the number of job candidates with inappropriate training and experience. The recession brought a large increase in the number of overqualified applicants.

OVERVIEW OF INTERVIEW EVIDENCE

The dominant theme in discussions of labor supply was labor abundance, as may be seen from Table 15.1. The quality of job applicants improved as well, as may be seen from Table 15.2. Of the 165 businesses reporting on labor supply, 53 were in the secondary sector, and the abundance of labor was about equal in the two sectors. In 28 companies, the previous boom was described as

TABLE 15.1   The effect of the recession on labor supply (applies to 165 business)

Response	Number of businesses	Percentage of businesses
Labor has been abundant during both boom and recession	6	4
Labor supply has increased	127	77
There are shortages of particular skills, despite the recession	26	16
Labor is in short supply, despite the recession	6	4

TABLE 15.2   Effect of recession on applicant quality (applies to 47 businesses)

Response	Number of businesses	Percentage of businesses
The recession has improved quality	32	68
Applicants are now less likely to fit the job	10	21
The recession has caused a decline in quality	5	11

a time of severe labor shortage. Five employers went so far as to say that the recession helped their businesses by making it easier to hire.

MANAGERS' EXPLANATIONS

Representatives of a wide variety of companies said that the number and quality of applicants had increased and that conditions contrasted sharply with the severe labor shortage during the previous boom.[1]

I get so many responses to ads that hiring is difficult. Five years ago, I had tumble-weeds coming in the door.
—Owner of a catering business with 15 employees

There are many more job applicants now because of the recession, and the quality is up. It is almost sad. In 1986–1989, you got the dregs. It is even possible to hire high school students. This used to be impossible because their parents were doing so well.
—Owner of a retail business with 30 employees

I put an ad in the paper and got 150 phone calls in three hours. I had eight people in the lobby at one time. . . . In the mid-1980s, I put ads in the paper for skilled cabinetmakers and often got no calls.
—Owner of a unionized architectural woodwork firm with 40 employees

There is lots of unemployment among architects. Good-quality people are looking for jobs. Four years ago, you couldn't find good employees.
—Human resource executive of an architectural engineering firm with 60 employees

Drivers were impossible to get in the 1980s. This started relaxing two years ago. Now, I can get anyone.
—Part-owner of a nonunion trucking company with 150 employees

We have better applicants and lots more of them than in the mid-1980s. We had 200 applications for a computer programming position. . . . Everyday, 15 to 25 people walk in. This was not true in the mid-1980s. One or two a week would walk in then.
—President of a unionized highway construction company employing 1,000 people

During the boom of the 1980s, it was just terrible to recruit people. It took longer than today. Positions were filled, though not with as good-quality people. Now positions are filled with the cream of the crop—top of the class engineers fresh out of school.
—Human resource officer in a partly unionized manufacturing company with 1,400 employees

All but 2 of the 14 temporary labor agents interviewed asserted that applicants wanted more work than the agency could provide. The situation had been quite different during the previous boom.

> I have a lot of applicants and no jobs. I can fill any order with the perfect person, but I have few orders. This is the situation throughout the industry. It is kind of scary.
> —Owner of a temporary employment agency specializing in clerical help

> We have lots of applicants who have been laid off and are willing to work at anything. There are lots who want to work but can't. People view temporary work as a way of making contacts or as something that could lead to a permanent position. It beats sitting at home.
> —Owner of a temporary labor service specializing in clerical and light industrial help

The recession helped some businesses by making it easier to hire.

> I started the company in 1982. . . . I couldn't get men. I put ads in the paper and got no response. There were few skilled people available. I did manage to train a few people myself, but I couldn't expand because of the lack of men. . . . I am delighted with the recession. It has allowed me to expand. There are lots of people in business who don't belong there, and during a recession they have to leave. This released some acceptable talent.
> —Owner of a nonunion mechanical contracting company with 30 employees

> We do better during recessions because it is easier to get drivers. We are killed at the cyclical peaks. No one wants to make a career of driving taxis, though some end up doing so. At the peaks, it is next to impossible to get anyone to drive for you.
> —Owner of a taxi company with 100 drivers

The recession brought an increase in the number of job seekers who were from other lines of work than the jobs for which they applied.

> During recessions, you receive many more applications for jobs, but not necessarily more qualified ones. Many will be from people from other occupations who are desperate for any kind of job.
> —Human resource manager in a financial company with 300 employees

Twelve employers remarked that hiring took more time during the recession because of the large number of applicants.

> It is tough to recruit during a recession because you are inundated with resumes that don't pertain to the job. Many are overqualified. But you can get good people.
> —Human resource official of a nonunion manufacturing company with 280 employees

Twenty employers asserted that in spite of the recession, it was hard to find qualified applicants with special skills.

> We put ads in the papers. . . . For hygienists, we get no response, but we have been overwhelmed in other categories. . . . AIDS has scared people off from going to hygienists' schools.
> —Dentist with 16 employees

> Although we never have trouble hiring assemblers, we cannot find a tool-and-die maker. Such people are always scarce.
> —Owner of a nonunion manufacturing company with 20 employees

> Since the whole [pharmaceutical] industry is expanding, the scientists are not feeling the recession. The group for which there is the most competition are Ph.D.-level synthetic organic chemists. There are 10 to 15 top-notch programs in this area in the country. Almost all the pharmaceutical companies recruit from them. Students go see them all.
> —Human resource manager for a corporate research facility with 2,000 employees

The recession brought a decrease in turnover (Chapter 16). For some specialized skills, the reduction in job applications from jobholders may have more than offset the increase from the unemployed, for 12 employers stated that this was the case.

> It is easier to hire now [1992] than in 1986–87. A specialized, technical opening might be harder to fill now because people are less willing to change jobs.
> —Personnel director of a nonunion manufacturing plant with 120 employees

15.2 Shunning of the Overqualified by Primary-Sector Employers

The rejection of overqualified workers stood out during the interviews, because it came up often and contradicted sharply the idea that excessive pay demands cause increases in unemployment during recessions. The label "overqualified" usually applied to unemployed job applicants who had made considerably more money on their previous job than they would on the new one. It is usually easy for firms to ascertain previous pay, for they routinely request pay information from former employers when doing a reference check. It is impossible to quantify precisely the size of pay decrease that made a candidate overqualified, but it seemed to be anything over 30 percent. The main reason for avoiding the overqualified was the belief that they would soon move on to higher-paying jobs, costing employers their investment in hiring and training costs. In addition, employers suspected that overqualified workers would be unhappy. There are similarities between the reluctance to hire the overqualified and the reluctance to cut pay. In both cases, employers worried about poor morale and high turnover among those suffering an income reduction.

Shunning the overqualified is one reason why firms do not collectively reduce pay by dismissing employees and replacing them with cheaper new ones let go by other firms, thereby decreasing hourly labor expense by paying low wages to workers from other companies, without cutting the pay of their own people. This exchange is doubly blocked, for not only do firms not like to replace employees (section 13.4), but they avoid hiring at severely reduced pay other firms' workers.[2] Although the overqualification phenomenon helps explain why unemployed job seekers could not find work easily by being sufficiently flexible about pay and working conditions, it does not explain why there was so much unemployment during the recession. The highly qualified probably had an easier time finding work than the less qualified, despite the overqualification problem. Furthermore, had the overqualified been favored rather than shunned, they would have taken the jobs of other applicants, who would in turn have had to wait for work because of the shortage of jobs.

OVERVIEW OF INTERVIEW EVIDENCE

Table 15.3 summarizes answers to the question whether any recent job applicants had been overqualified. Among the 7 companies where overqualified people did not apply, 5 offered low wages for unpleasant work and 1 was so huge that its spokesman claimed it had positions for people of any skill level. Of the 10 businesses where overqualification was irrelevant, 8 offered work requiring so much skill that overqualification was thought to be impossible.

Table 15.4 summarizes the reactions to overqualified job applicants in the 126 primary-sector companies that saw some of them. Among the 24 firms ready to hire them, attitudes may be categorized as follows. In 14 of the firms, the risks were recognized, but accepted in exchange for the chance to hire good

TABLE 15.3   Primary-sector businesses seeing overqualified applicants

Response	Number of businesses	Percentage of businesses
Some applicants are overqualified	126	88
Overqualification is irrelevant	10	7
Overqualified people do not apply	7	5
Total	143	100

Table 15.4 Reactions to overqualified job applicants

Response	Number of businesses	Percentage of businesses
Totally unwilling to hire them	88	70
Partially unwilling to hire them	13	10
Ready to hire them	24	19
Not hiring anyone	1	1
Total	126	100

Table 15.5 Reasons for shunning overqualified applicants (applies to 101 companies)

Reason	Number of businesses	Percentage of businesses
Concern that applicants would quit for better jobs as soon as possible	79	78
Concern that applicants would be unhappy with the job	50	50
Applicants' skills would be rusty	10	10

workers. Nine of the companies were growing so fast that overqualified new hires could be quickly promoted to appropriate positions. In the remaining one, the informant interpreted discrimination against the overqualified as age discrimination, which he was quick to disavow.

Table 15.5 summarizes the reasons given for shunning the overqualified in the 101 companies where officials admitted doing so. Employers who worried about quitting said that overqualified employees would find better jobs as soon as the economy improved, or even before. Those worried about dissatisfaction said they thought overqualified workers would resent reduced earnings, diminished responsibility, and boring work. These respondents explained that unhappiness interferes with performance and leads to quitting and that they wanted people who would view their work as a challenge. Several employers mentioned that overqualified workers would be disruptive because they would expect to be promoted faster than other employees. Three employers worried that overqualified workers would be a threat to their supervisors. Employers concerned about rusty skills noted that the overqualified would be doing tasks they had not performed in years.

Employers worried that overqualified employees would be unhappy and unreliable.

> I have had $80,000-a-year people applying for a $5-an-hour job. I tell them that it is not a job for them. They wouldn't stay. I want to bring people along. I prefer young people we can teach. . . . [A large unionized manufacturing company] is closing its woodwork shop. Their workers make $17 an hour. I wouldn't hire any of them. They would be irritated and upset at a $7 cut in pay, and would poison my people.
>
> —Owner of a unionized architectural woodwork firm with 40 employees

> A lot of overqualified people apply for work. They were making too much money for the position for which they apply. . . . I am afraid such people would continue to look for another job. Looking for another job is very distracting. Once you have decided to leave, it takes every ounce of your being to stay focused on your job. I know this from personal experience.
>
> —Director of human resources of a bank with 380 employees

> Overqualification is a problem, just as is underqualification. You cannot fulfill the needs of an overqualified person. They will be unhappy and will be a problem. They might leave or feel they know too much and not cooperate with other members of their team. We want people to work in self-managed teams.
>
> —Personnel manager of a manufacturing company with 430 employees

> We try not to hire people who are desperate for work. If I run an ad in the paper, I get a great many resumes from overqualified people if the positions are in general service and administration. I send such people a no-interest letter, for once the labor market opens up, they will leave the company. . . . Training costs are high. Agency fees, newspaper ads, and all the hours of interviews cost money. Adaptation to the company is a cost too. Someone has to guide new employees, and that costs money.
>
> —Compensation manager for a nonunion manufacturing company with 1,750 employees

> We do see overqualified job applicants, and we react negatively to that. They won't be happy with the job. It is read as a play to get their foot in the door. They will look for the first promotion opportunity. We want people to be promoted at a rate which provides incentives for them. I don't want them back in my office after a short time looking for more money. If there are no opportunities available, their pay can't be increased. We will lose them or they won't be interested in their position because they will have maxed out. With lower-level people, you can keep

adding pay and responsibilities to make jobs more interesting. We want jobs to be challenging. If people leave we lose the hiring and training costs.

—Human resource official in a brokerage and investment banking company with 3,000 employees

Some employers emphasized the drop in living standards that would be suffered by an overqualified employee, a consideration that also came up in discussions of pay cuts.

I never interview overqualified job applicants. . . . People don't give up what they had before, if they can help it. The cost of living is too high now to allow them to go down to less. . . . An overqualified employee would be frustrated and unhappy— all that life's training for nothing.

—President and owner of a unionized manufacturing company with 135 employees

Ten employers said the overqualified were not necessarily ready for the jobs for which they applied, since they would have lost some of the necessary skills and drive.

Sometimes, people come in who were contractors before. Typically, someone who was in business for himself before and failed does not make a good employee. He is not disciplined. He has bad habits, such as getting up late. He has lost some of his ambition and drive. It is better to have younger employees who are striving and full of hope.

—Owner of a nonunion mechanical contracting company with 30 employees

I advertised [for a management position] . . . and received over 2,300 resumes. . . . It was easy to screen these down to a short stack. I immediately eliminated overqualified candidates. . . . They would do a good job, but they wouldn't be first rate and up-to-date on things, because they would be doing what they had done 5 years ago. Their skills would be rusty.

—Human resource officer of a nonunion manufacturing company and ESOP with 300 employees

A few respondents said that overqualified employees would undermine authority.

I avoid overqualified people who used to have higher salaries than they would receive from us. Initially, they would be glad to have the job, but they would not fit in—their presence would be disruptive and create confusion in the job hierarchy.

—Human resource manager of an insurance company subsidiary with 90 employees

I don't want someone who would be threatening to their supervisor.

—Operations manager of a nonunion wholesale distribution company with 170 employees

It is hard to know whether the negative feelings about the overqualified were based on experience or prejudice, though I did hear some stories of bad experiences.

> During the shortage of hygienists [in the late 1980s], their hourly pay rates went from $10 to $12 an hour to $20 overnight. There was a surplus of dentists at the same time, so we hired dentists instead. But we got fooled, because dentists make shitty hygienists. This is a good example of overqualification. They did a bad job. They didn't have their heart in it and didn't clean teeth well or train the patients. We fired them.
>
> —Dentist with 16 employees

Some employers said that recruiting was complicated by the fact that they could not always tell who was overqualified.

> Hiring overqualified people is a crapshoot. They may leave if the economy improves too soon. . . . I hesitate to expand for that reason. I can't tell who is overqualified.
>
> —President of a nonunion manufacturing company employing 45 people

Six respondents mentioned that some applicants even downgraded their resumes to hide their qualifications.

Comments of six employers indicated that a pay loss of about 30 percent or more made job candidates overqualified.

> We would say "no" to a person who had been earning $50,000 and would now take $30,000.
>
> —Vice president of human resources of a nonunion manufacturing company employing 5,000 people

> A person hired at a 30 percent discount wouldn't be a good employee. Most people live on the edge of their capabilities and would have to retrench their lifestyles.
>
> —Head of a 40-employee computer consulting group within a large accounting firm

Although the stigma of overqualification may have been a problem mainly for professionals and managers, it thwarted people at all levels except the unskilled.

> I wouldn't hire a machinist to do unskilled work, because he would leave as soon as he found a better job.
>
> —Personnel director of a partially unionized manufacturing company with 250 employees

> We watch out for overqualified people at the clerical level. We keep them out, because hiring them worsens the turnover problem. There are no college graduates at the clerical level, because they get bored.
>
> —President of a 26,000 employee division of an insurance company

Employers of highly skilled people, especially in the manual trades, found overqualification irrelevant, since it was impossible to be too good at a trade.

> It would be tough to be overqualified as a carpenter.
>
> —General manager of a nonunion construction company with 15 employees

> Overqualification never comes up—it is impossible.
>
> —Human resource manager for a nonunion printing company with 80 employees

Some employers made a conscious decision to trade off the talents of the overqualified against increased turnover and possible morale problems.

> Overqualification is not an issue with lawyers. It is not an issue with staff either. They like them. The lawyers are smart and like to be around smart people, even if they don't stay long. We have a Ph.D. in medieval history on the word processor.
>
> —Personnel director of a law firm with 60 employees

> We don't avoid the overqualified. So what if we have more turnover? We get the best and the brightest.
>
> —Vice president of human resources of a partially unionized manufacturing company with 18,000 employees

Some employers were willing to hire overqualified people who said they wished to start a new way of life.

> Once in a while, people will be willing to work for very little pay. These people are desperate. There is usually something wrong with them [i.e., they are overqualified]. On the other hand, sometimes there is nothing wrong, for they want to switch gears and start in a new area, where they have to work for less pay. For instance, someone in operations might want to switch to lending and have to accept a drop in pay from $60,000 to $45,000 a year.
>
> —Director of human resources of a bank with 380 employees

Employers were sometimes willing to hire overqualified people if there was a strong possibility they could soon be promoted to positions for which they were exactly qualified. Employers in rapidly growing companies took this stance.

> I have no trouble with overqualified people. We have welders come in who are willing to work as helpers, for they can't find anything else and we have no openings for welders. I will be able to bump them up later. I take the risk that they will leave. Because we are growing, we will be able to make use of their skills later.
>
> —General manager of a two-year-old, nonunion manufacturing company with 140 employees

We see people who are willing to accept less than they earned on their previous job because there is hope that this company will grow. . . . You have to look at the person and see if they have made the mental transition. . . . We need experienced people and ones who know where the booby traps are.

—Vice president of human resources of an insurance company and HMO with 220 employees

Some employers were willing to hire overqualified people for positions where there was normally so much turnover that the overqualified would not increase it significantly. Many employers in the secondary labor market tolerated overqualification for the same reason (section 17.6).

All my employees are looking for something else, but they can't find anything because of the bad economy. One is a freelance writer. They are all overqualified. If boom times return, I will be in trouble.

—Manager in charge of telemarketing at a publishing company with 70 employees (the company's telemarketers worked part time, usually did not stay more than a year, and perhaps should be thought of as belonging to the secondary sector)

Overqualified people come in all the time. Bankers apply for laborers' jobs, as do truck drivers and equipment operators. I don't mind. If he wants to work, let him work. Nothing is forever. Once he leaves, neither side owes the other anything. [In construction, workers are often hired for specific projects.]

—Part-owner and operator of a nonunion construction company with 90 employees

I don't care about overqualification. I would even hire a professor. In the 1960s or '70s, when there was a surplus of schoolteachers, I had 25 of them in the plant. I encouraged them to leave as they found jobs, but let them stay as long as they wanted to. [The work was seasonal and required little skill.]

—President and half-owner of a nonunion candy company employing 200 people

Employers were willing to hire overqualified people who for some reason could hardly hope to find work in their specialty.

We do have engineers from India working as messengers. This breaks my heart, but they have experience in this country only as messengers. They make about $200 a week. They stay with the company because they can't get better jobs.

—Human resource official in a brokerage and investment banking company with 3,000 employees

A few employers said concerns about overqualification were diminishing, for it appeared that the economic slump would last so long that there was little chance of finding other jobs soon.

Two or three years ago, I would never have hired overqualified people, for they would keep on looking for better jobs after they were hired. Now perhaps things are different. The labor market is so bad that they may accept less and want job stability.

—Human resource official of a nonunion wholesale distribution company with 170 employees

Overqualification of job applicants is common only during recessions or among people whose skills are obsolete. A few respondents spoke of having dealt with this issue during previous recessions.

The problem of overqualification is not as bad as it was in the early 1970s, when unemployment was 12 or 13 percent.[3] The job market was a nightmare then. We had hundreds of people outside yelling and screaming for a job, even a poorly paid one. We had lots of overqualified applicants then. We had Ph.D.s looking for jobs microfilming at $4 an hour.

—Vice president of a publishing company with about 70 employees

Overqualification was a problem in 1983–84. Lots of people with college degrees were coming to [our plant] for jobs, because there was no other work available for them. It wasn't hard to motivate them to work, but they didn't stick around.

—High-level human resource official at a unionized manufacturing company with 19,000 employees

15.3 Is Unemployment a Stigma?

An important finding is that the recession diminished the stigma of unemployment, though it did not eliminate it. Employers suspicious of the jobless assumed that companies laid off their weakest workers first, and long-term unemployment was thought to be a sign of lack of energy and interest in work. Nevertheless, many believed that because of the recession good people were being laid off and having trouble finding work. Some recruiters no longer paid much attention to whether applicants were unemployed, though they had done so during the preceding boom. Unemployment did not disqualify job candidates; it simply raised questions. The stigma increased with job level. At the bottom end of the job ladder in the secondary sector, unemployment was considered to be almost normal, whereas it was a drawback for executives.

OVERVIEW OF INTERVIEW EVIDENCE

Tables 15.6 and 15.7 summarize employers' views on the stigma of unemployment. In 38 of the 99 primary-sector businesses, the recession was described as having weakened or eliminated the stigma. The exceptional secondary-sector company in Table 15.7 was a small chain of high-class stores, whose owner

TABLE 15.6   Reactions of primary-sector businesses to unemployed job applicants

Response	Number of businesses	Percentage of businesses
Do not care if candidates are unemployed	69	70
Unemployment is a negative factor	30	30
Total	99	100

TABLE 15.7   Reactions of noncontract labor, secondary-sector businesses to unemployed job applicants

Response	Number of businesses	Percentage of businesses
Do not care if candidates are unemployed	17	94
Unemployment is a negative factor	1	6
Total	18	100

TABLE 15.8   Reasons given for the stigma of unemployment by primary-sector managers (applies to 30 businesses)

Reason	Number of businesses	Percentage of businesses
Companies lay off their weakest employees	19	63
Prolonged unemployment indicates problems	15	50

wanted long-term, good-quality employees who would know clients by name. For this reason, the stores' jobs might be thought of as belonging to the primary sector.

In contract labor firms, which I classify as belonging to the secondary sector, the jobless were a normal part of the labor pool, the other part being people who wanted second jobs or whose lifestyle required part-time or intermittent work. Contract labor firms included temporary labor services, some consulting companies, and security or janitorial services.

Table 15.8 summarizes explanations given in the 30 primary-sector companies where the reaction to the unemployed was negative. In 7 of these companies, managers asserted that the stigma increased with job level.

MANAGERS' EXPLANATIONS

For many, unemployment was a bad sign.

> Those who are laid off and stay unemployed tend not to be good people. Good people find jobs. I still try to hire the employed. If someone was laid off, I try to find out why.
>
> —Human resource officer in a partly unionized manufacturing company with 1,400 employees

> Unemployment is a negative, but it won't kill a candidate. The reason why someone is unemployed is important. It is okay if you are redundant through no fault of your own. When I was hired, I was grilled about whether I was laid off, even though I was still working. I saw layoffs coming and started looking for another job.
>
> —Human resource manager in a financial company with 24,000 employees

Employers assumed that other employers laid off their least valuable employees first, a belief that was probably often correct (section 13.5).

> I usually hire inexperienced people and train them. There are few sources of good machinists. When I have hired experienced machinists, I have usually had a bad experience. Companies lay off their poorest men first. The only time you get a good man is when a company has gone under.
>
> —Owner of a nonunion machine shop with 31 employees

> I wouldn't want to hire anyone who was unemployed. Who wants someone else's rejects? [This was the only employer in the secondary sector to express such negative views.]
>
> —Owner of a retail business with 30 employees

> Layoffs raise a lot of questions. Why were they laid off? If they went to work for a shaky company that went under, you wonder about their decision-making abilities.
>
> —Human resource officer of a bank with 400 employees

Some employers asserted that job applicants who had been unemployed for a long time might lack drive. Only one employer, quoted below, mentioned loss of skills during unemployment, and none mentioned that long-term joblessness might indicate that other potential employers had found something wrong.

> Being unemployed is not a negative consideration. . . . It is normal to be unemployed. I don't care, unless the applicant has been out of work for a year or two. Driving trucks is a dangerous job. I don't want someone who is out of practice.
>
> —Part-owner of a nonunion trucking company with 14 drivers

If someone is unemployed, I ask them what they were doing last year. Did they have a part-time job? What did they do to get a job? If they were doing nothing, I wonder about their drive. In good times, I really wonder why someone is unemployed, unless they are new on the market.

—Head of human resources of a nonunion manufacturing company with 1,200 employees

The stigma of unemployment increased with position because the higher the level, the more likely it was that performance had been used as a criterion in making layoffs. Employers also demand a great deal of high-level employees and so are cautious when hiring them.

I am not hiring white-collar people. I am scared to. Manufacturing people are often victims of circumstance. In the white-collar area, good people are kept by companies. In the factory, there is only a five-day training period, and I don't care about churning [high turnover]. I don't want to do that in the office. These people have to learn the product lines and customers.

—President of a nonunion manufacturing company employing 45 people

Unemployment is not a stigma, generally. The longer a person is out of work, the more it begs the question of why. This is less true of clerical and hourly people. It is more true of management people. You have to be more careful with management people, for they have more discretion.

—High-level human resource official in a 3,000-employee, largely nonunion division of a huge consumer products company

Common sense indicates that the bad state of the economy should make unemployed job seekers more acceptable.

Unemployment is a stigma if someone has been unemployed too long. But one year is common in this area now. Under normal conditions, one year would raise eyebrows, but now professionals are often out 18 months or more.

—Human resource manager of a nonunion manufacturing company and ESOP with 250 employees

In some cases, there is a stigma attached to being unemployed, but not in most cases. A lot of the unemployed I see are good. There have been lots of mergers over the last decade. The new owners find duplication within the two organizations and consolidate operations. Mid-level managers get laid off. Others are laid off from companies that are not doing well, especially in Connecticut, where banking, insurance, and defense are all downsizing. In these circumstances, it is not necessarily the worst performers who get the ax. For many, it will be hard to find similar-level employment, for the jobs are just not there.

—Human resource manager in an expanding nonunion manufacturing company with 8,500 employees

The fact of being unemployed or having been unemployed is a stigma in good times. The worst are laid off. But when lots of companies are downsizing, as now, or when individual companies have huge layoffs, such as [a computer manufacturer], then there is less of a stigma. There is not much of one now.

—Human resource officer of a bank with 16,000 employees

The dominant view among employers was that unemployment was not a negative consideration. Most managers dismissed the idea of a stigma with little explanation, but nevertheless believed that unemployment raised issues to be examined.

I don't care if an applicant is unemployed. A couple of bells may go off, but I just ask a few questions. If they are here, they need a job and they are interested.

—Manager in charge of telemarketing at a publishing company with 70 employees

The fact that a job candidate was unemployed was not a problem for me. I myself have been unemployed twice, each time for seven months.

—Production manager of a nonunion manufacturing company with 500 employees

Unemployment is not a negative in hiring. During job interviews, it is clear that unemployed people are under a great strain, but the interviewers allow for this.

—Human resource manager of a new and rapidly expanding nonunion company in the service sector with 3,500 employees

At the bottom end of the job ladder, the stigma of unemployment was nearly irrelevant.

We don't view unemployment as a negative. It's almost normal.

—Part-owner and manager of a janitorial service with about 80 employees

We don't worry about people being unemployed. We would rather have someone who was unemployed for a long time, for they know what it is like out there. If someone has been unemployed only a short time, they may not have extended their job search long enough and discovered their opportunities, and might soon leave. Retention is important to us.

—District manager for a chain of department stores

15.4 Is Holding a Low-Paying Job a Stigma?

McCormick (1990) and Ma and Weiss (1993) propose that holding a low-paying stopgap job is a stigma that adds to the difficulty of getting a good permanent position. Their central assumption is that employers believe that

good workers find it more worthwhile to spend their time looking for good
jobs than working at bad ones.

The theory does not take account of employers' recognition that during recessions unemployed people suffer financially and have difficulty finding good
jobs. From the little I heard, low-paying stopgap jobs did not stigmatize job
seekers. Six employers said they were aware of no stigma, and one reacted
ambivalently. Three of the 6 who saw no stigma spoke of low-paying jobs as
showing enterprise. Employers might well react negatively, however, to a pattern of interim jobs as a sign of instability.

> I don't mind people having had very low paying jobs just to get by. Maybe I'd have
> a different answer if these were good times. The employee might then just be a
> hacker. [This was the ambivalent comment.]
>
> —Human resource officer of an 850-employee, nonunion division of a manufacturing company

> Low-paying jobs take time from the job search. Also, they look bad on the re-
> sume. . . . Is [the name of a large fast-food chain] a stigma? As a recruiter, I would
> say that it showed initiative. If you don't tell me and I check and find out, you are
> lost. A credit check will tell me.
>
> —Vice president of human resources for a nonunion manufacturing company with 95,000
> employees

15.5 Competition from Government Income Support Programs

Some employers said that unemployment insurance and welfare benefits reduced the supply of low-paid labor. No one said this of well-paid labor. I did
not often ask about this subject, it being only tangentially related to the central
issue of downward wage rigidity.

OVERVIEW OF INTERVIEW EVIDENCE

Of 24 employers who discussed competition for labor from income support
programs, 19 complained that low-paid laborers preferred collecting benefits
to working. A few said they felt no competition from income support systems
for better-paid workers. As a check on their statement, I asked 5 high-paying
employers whether they felt the competition, and they all denied it existed.

MANAGERS' EXPLANATIONS

The complaints about low-paid labor were spontaneous.

> When unemployment insurance was extended, the supply of people coming to look
> for work dried up.
>
> —General manager of a livery and taxi company with 90 drivers

The caliber of my employees didn't improve until lately. They don't come to me after being laid off until they run out of unemployment benefits. They make more on unemployment than with me, because I cannot guarantee a full week of work.

—Owner of a temporary labor service specializing in light industrial help

Unemployment insurance benefits set a floor on pay rates for the lower skills. About one third of the people who come in looking for work say their benefits have just run out, so they need something.

—Owner of a franchise for a large national temporary help firm, specializing in clerical, light industrial, and technical help

Employers of well-paid labor were less concerned about competition from income support programs, as is shown by the contrast between statements by low- and high-paying employers in the same business. For instance, all 6 temporary labor agents of low-wage labor said they felt the influence of income support programs, whereas the opposite was reported by the branch manager of a large temporary employment service specializing in well-paid accountants and bookkeepers. The plant manager of a laundry, which paid a little more than $5 an hour, said, "Lots of people are out of work, but welfare spoils people. They leave here to go on welfare. The welfare system has ruined menial labor for industry." The part-owner of a dry cleaning company, who paid about $7.50 an hour, said, "I pay well enough so as not to be in competition with the welfare system." I interviewed the owners of two janitorial service companies. One, who paid little more than the minimum wage of $4.27 an hour, complained of competition from the welfare and unemployment insurance systems, whereas the owner of the second, who paid $10 to $12 an hour, explained that he paid enough to avoid the problem. Income support programs did not seem to be a concern when jobs paid more than roughly $25,000 a year or $12.50 an hour.

I do see people come around who don't really want jobs, because they prefer unemployment benefits. This can be true for people who normally make up to $25,000 a year.

—Owner and founder of a nonunion manufacturing company with 40 employees

Unemployment insurance is in competition with temporary jobs for people earning from $10 to $15 an hour or less.

—Owner of a temporary labor service specializing in light industrial, clerical, and technical help

15.6 Hiring Methods

Many employers said they used networks of personal contacts to find job candidates, and advisers of the unemployed confirmed the value of personal con-

Table 15.9 Incidence of hiring methods (applies to 161 businesses, of which 118 were in the primary sector)

Method	Number of businesses	Percentage of businesses
Personal connections	96	60
Advertising	88	55
Direct application	38	24
Agencies	26	16
Schools	24	15
Unemployment office	14	9
Temporary help	5	3

nections (section 18.4). Reliance on networks in hiring makes it easier to understand why it often took a long time for people to find work, since a job hunter's personal contacts can be exhausted quickly.

OVERVIEW OF INTERVIEW EVIDENCE

Hiring methods may be categorized as personal connections, unemployment office referral, agencies, direct application, temporary help, hiring from schools and colleges, and advertising. Personal connections include referrals from employees or from friends and acquaintances of managers and owners. Agencies are professional recruiting companies paid by companies to find people with specialized skills. Private employment agencies paid by job seekers had all but ceased to function during the recession. Direct or unsolicited applications by job hunters were used mostly to fill low-level jobs. Some employers employed temporary workers and kept them permanently if they proved to be good.

Table 15.9 gives the number of businesses in which the methods listed were described as important. In most cases, personal connections meant employee referrals. Seventeen companies encouraged referrals by means of financial rewards. These rewards would probably have been more common during a period of labor shortage, for several employers mentioned that rewards had been discontinued because of the recession. In addition to the methods listed in the table, there was the union hiring hall. Among the firms where I interviewed, there were four unionized construction firms that depended on craft unions to provide labor for new projects.

Employers saw a variety of advantages in hiring through references.

I locate people through networking. I want people who have the best heads, hearts, and hands. Maybe there are five like that in the East. I talk to everyone I know who has those qualities, owners of other shops, builders who are good.

—Part-owner of a nonunion architectural woodwork company with 12 employees

We generally hire through personal connections. We prefer this, for we take fewer chances that way. This eliminates the possibility of hiring a crook or a drug addict. It's a way of screening people.

—Manager of a nonunion manufacturing company with 65 employees

A lot of hiring at upper levels comes from referrals from our own employees. No rewards are given, but an employee owns the guy he brings in. We like to hire relatives of employees with a good work ethic, even for production jobs. We have husband and wife teams.

—Vice president of a unionized manufacturing company with 90 employees

Referrals are good. People like working with people who are like themselves. There are many families in the company. You do have to avoid having subordinates and supervisors from the same family.

—Vice president of human resources of a nonunion manufacturing company with 260 employees

The majority of new hires are referrals. In a referral, employees receive between $1,000 and $2,000 if they bring in someone they know who is hired and does well. Those who bring people in know that their own reputation is at stake. The success or failure of the referral will be remembered.

—Human resource officer of a bank with 450 employees

Newspaper ads give rise to too many applications. We would advertise only if we wanted 50 employees. We get better people through referrals.

—Chief human resources official of an investment company with 1,000 employees

Some managers said referrals caused problems, chiefly the formation of cliques.

I don't prefer referrals. I feel an obligation to employees to hire their relatives, but if something goes wrong, there can be trouble with the whole family.

—Personnel manager of a partly unionized manufacturing company with 365 employees

We use newspaper ads for all positions. . . . We stay away from employee referrals. We would rather go through our procedures. This controls cronyism. Otherwise, the company becomes cliquey, and the men become hard to control.

—President of a unionized highway construction company employing 1,000 people

Hiring through referrals leads to better relations among the staff, though having too many relatives is bad. For instance, the consequences of a divorce are bad if both husband and wife work for you.

—Human resource officer of a bank with 16,000 employees

15.7 Reference Checking

When I undertook this project, I believed that theories involving stigmas could not be valid because recruiters can learn all they need to know about job candidates from their former employers, just as academics learn about potential candidates for faculty positions by reputation and references. The analogy with academic life, however, proved false. Managers claimed that former employers gave little information, because it was illegal and dangerous to say anything negative. It was possible to obtain information through networks of craftsmen or professionals, but similar channels did not exist for many categories of applicants.

OVERVIEW OF INTERVIEW EVIDENCE

Table 15.10 summarizes discussions about reference checking.

MANAGERS' EXPLANATIONS

Managers were reluctant to say negative things about former employees for fear of being sued for libel or defamation of character.

I do reference checks, but those are difficult. People are afraid to say something negative, in part out of fear of being sued. I behave in the same way. People give information on pay and the period of employment. It is also dangerous to say something good, for next time they might say, "You were more enthusiastic about some other person last time."

—Human resource official of a nonunion wholesale distribution company with 170 employees

TABLE 15.10   Reflections on the ease of reference checking

Response	Number of businesses	Percentage of businesses
It is difficult to get information from former employers	31	65
You can get some information by informal means	11	23
Former employers speak freely	6	13
Total	48	100

I obtain no information from reference checks. Employment law prevents that. By law, you can't destroy a person's ability to make a living. That way, people can start all over again.

—Human resource official in a 300-employee operations facility of an insurance company

Former employers won't tell you if someone was a good employee. People normally won't even give hints. You have to be very careful of defamation of character and libelous statements.

—Director of human resources for a financial brokerage and investment banking firm with 1,600 employees

Reference checks did yield some information.

I call up previous employers. They will give a hint. Some are evasive, but the tone of voice reveals a lot.

—Director of operations of a nonunion trucking company with 75 employees

Sometimes we can find supervisors who will talk. Human resource types never do. Sometimes company rules forbid supervisors to say anything.

—Personnel director of a partially unionized manufacturing company with 250 employees

I don't give out information on the performance of past employees, and others behave likewise. However, I try to get around this by knowing someone in the company where an applicant worked.

—Vice president of personnel of a diversified company in the service sector with 2,000 employees

Headhunters or professional recruiting agents provided an expensive way to obtain information on potential new hires.

People in some industries or professions formed communities through which information about individuals flowed easily.

We have a good idea how good people are, for we know who they worked for and what they did there and how long they worked there. We work in a small community of highly skilled craftsmen. It is very technical. We don't need to call up former employers to find out how good people are. We wouldn't do that, for we tend to steal people from other companies and so don't dare advertise ourselves. . . . We find out about people by word of mouth. We have people here who used to work at [competing companies] and they say who was good there.

—General manager of a two-year-old, nonunion manufacturing company with 140 employees

Routine reference checks are made. Former employers give little information about their employees when reference checks are made, but members of the industry meet each other at the annual [industry] fair in New York and know each other well.

—Human resource official at a partially unionized manufacturing company with 12,000 employees

15.8 Summary

Most employers found labor to be extremely abundant during the recession. Many unemployed job applicants were overqualified for the jobs they sought. Most primary-sector employers were reluctant to hire such people, out of concern that they would be unhappy and would quit soon after being hired. Unemployment stigmatized job applicants to some extent, though the recession weakened this stigma. The most frequently used method of hiring was through personal connections, and its importance may have contributed to the difficulty many unemployed people had finding work.

Appendix 15A Related Literature

LABOR SUPPLY (SECTION 15.1)

Though common sense indicates that the number of applicants per job opening increases sharply during recessions, I have found only one publication on this topic, Holzer, Katz, and Krueger (1991). Using data from a 1982 sample of U.S. firms, the authors regress the number of job applications per latest job opening on the local unemployment rate and find that the relation is positive and statistically significant.

There exists indirect statistical evidence on the tightness of the job market during recessions. It is well known that there is a negative relation, the Beveridge curve, between the unemployment rate and the vacancy rate, which is the number of job vacancies per member of the labor force (Abraham, 1987; Blanchard and Diamond, 1989; and Jackman, Layard, and Pissarides, 1989). More pertinent evidence of the cyclical behavior of the availability of applicants is the relation of the average duration of vacancies to the unemployment rate. Jackman, Layard, and Pissarides (1989), using British data, and Ours and Ridder (1991), using Dutch data, find that vacancy durations decrease as the unemployment rate increases, which is consistent with a positive association between the number of qualified applicants per job opening and the unemployment rate.

SHUNNING OF THE OVERQUALIFIED BY PRIMARY-SECTOR EMPLOYERS (SECTION 15.2)

I know of only a few references describing evidence of the stigma of overqualification, Lester (1954, pp. 55–56), Wood (1985, pp. 108–110),[4] and Bryson and Jacobs (1992, p. 190). The theoretical possibility of overqualification is discussed in Akerlof, Rose, and Yellen (1990, p. 7), who point out that efficiency wage models imply that employers should reject the overskilled. Studies by Hersch (1995) and Johnson and Johnson (1996) support employers' perceptions of the behavior of overqualified workers. Hersch finds, in a questionnaire study of workers at one firm, that workers who described themselves as overqualified require less training and have higher quit intentions than workers who describe themselves as exactly qualified. The reverse is true of workers who are underqualified. In a psychological study of postal workers, Johnson and Johnson find that overqualification is positively related to stress and depression. Sicherman (1991) and Robst (1995) find in data from the Michigan Panel Study of Income Dynamics that workers who have more education than required for their jobs are more likely to quit, which supports employers' prejudices. Robst, however, finds that among workers holding jobs requiring a certain level of education, the overeducated are not more likely than others to quit. A number of other studies have found that underemployed workers are more likely to intend to quit or to look for new jobs, where "underemployed" has nearly the same meaning as overqualified. This literature is surveyed in Feldman (1996). Kandel (1991) describes the legal risk resulting from the association of shunning of the overqualified with age discrimination.[5]

IS UNEMPLOYMENT A STIGMA? (SECTION 15.3)

I know of only three surveys on employers' bias against unemployed job seekers, Bakke (1933, p. 50), Wood (1985, pp. 109–110), and Meager and Metcalf (1987). Wood's study was made during a recession, and what he reports is similar to what I heard. Meager and Metcalf survey British firms in high unemployment areas, and find a bias against the long-term unemployed, which increases with the skill level of the job to be filled. Lazear (1986, p. 160) suggests that unemployment may be more of a stigma during booms than during recessions, since employers would find it understandable that a person would have difficulty finding work during an economic slump. Blanchard and Diamond (1994) base a theory of unemployment on employers' prejudice against unemployed job seekers.

COMPETITION FROM GOVERNMENT INCOME SUPPORT PROGRAMS (SECTION 15.5)

There is a large econometric literature, cited in section 18.11, that indicates that higher unemployment benefits are associated with longer job search. The little evidence presented in section 15.5 points to the conclusion that this association diminishes as the expected pay of a new job increases.

HIRING METHODS (SECTION 15.6)

A huge literature, cited in section 18.4, on the search methods of job hunters confirms the importance of personal contacts. The search activities of employers have been less investigated, though what has been written shows an employer preference for informal methods (Ullman, 1966; Rees and Shultz, 1970, p. 200; Jenkins et al., 1983; Wood, 1985; and Elias and White, 1991). Wood finds that one of the consequences of recession (in England and Germany) is to intensify the use of employee referrals, because they reduce recruiting expenses. I also heard comments of this sort, but did not focus on the effect of the recession on recruiting methods. Wanous (1992, pp. 34–39) documents the assertion that people hired through employee referrals tend to last longer on the job, in part because they know better what to expect. Kugler (1997) finds a positive statistical association between the pay level of an industry and the extent to which it uses employee referrals in recruiting, a correlation that I did not notice in my observations. A general source on hiring methods is Rynes (1991).

16

Voluntary Turnover

It is well known that voluntary turnover normally decreases during recessions, and a common explanation for this pattern is that there are fewer jobs in bad times than good, so that people are less likely to quit their job for a better one and are more reluctant to quit into unemployment. The interviews support a further explanation that in a poor job market employees hesitate to take a new job because it might prove to be insecure. Many workers recognized that the newly hired are often laid off first, so that it was risky to quit in favor of a new job when layoffs were common and jobs scarce.

The effect of a recession on turnover is important to the overall assessment of competing theories of downward wage rigidity and unemployment, for the Lucas-Rapping theory implies that during recessions turnover increases as workers quit to look for new jobs.

16.1 Overview of Interview Evidence

Table 16.1 summarizes the discussion of voluntary turnover by managers in 79 businesses, 69 of which were in the primary sector. In addition, 14 advisers of the unemployed spoke of the reluctance to quit during the recession. The two cases in the table of increases in turnover were a reaction to layoffs. Responses of primary- and secondary-sector employers were similar. Managers discussed the reason for the decline in turnover in 24 of the 79 businesses. Six of the 24 mentioned that workers had nowhere else to go because of the lack of jobs, and 18 said that workers were reluctant to switch jobs because of the fear that a new job would not last. The 14 advisers of the unemployed who spoke about turnover were 7 counselors and 7 headhunters. All 7 counselors said that the recession had made employed people less willing to quit into unemployment.

TABLE 16.1 Comments by managers on the effect of the recession on voluntary turnover

Comment on turnover	Number of businesses	Percentage of businesses
A dramatic decrease	12	15
A decrease	56	71
No change	9	11
Increase	2	3
Total	79	100

The 7 headhunters complained that the recession made employed people reluctant to change jobs, an annoyance for headhunters because they made money by arranging job switches.

Additional evidence was contained in employers' descriptions of the effects of pay cuts, for pay cuts made during recessions had less impact on turnover than did cuts made during booms (section 12.2).

16.2 Managers' and Headhunters' Explanations

The reluctance to switch jobs posed problems for recruiters of some types of specialized labor (section 15.1) and was often attributed to the fear that new jobs would prove unstable.

> The company seeks senior engineers. That market is very competitive and becomes even more so in bad times. . . . Now, people are not moving. They have lower expectations. Most companies have LIFO [last in, first out] systems of layoff, so that no one is moving.
>
> —Owner and founder of a 10-employee producer of specialized computers

> Highly qualified workers are likely to be protected by their employers and won't change jobs, for fear that the new job won't work out and they will be unemployed at a time when it is difficult to find a job. It is better to look for new employees in good times, for then qualified employees are more likely to have the confidence to quit their jobs.
>
> —Human resource manager of a nonunion machine shop with 225 employees

> A lot of people aren't in the labor market who would be there in better times, for they fear that in a new job they would be more vulnerable to layoff or would get low severance, if they were laid off.
>
> —Human resource officer of a bank with 16,000 employees

An alternative explanation for the fall in turnover was the lack of jobs.

The bank has no turnover problem. It is now 5 to 6 percent [per year]. It is higher in boom times. Now there is no place for people to go.

—Human resource officer of a bank with 400 employees

There has been low turnover because of the recession. Only the young leave, since they have nothing to lose. Unless you are highly skilled, you don't find opportunities outside.

—Human resource manager of a corporation in the service sector with 10,000 employees

Headhunters spoke of the reluctance to change jobs in the same terms as did businesspeople.

Lots of people who have jobs don't want to move. Moving disrupts lives and is tough on spouses, especially if they are working. Also, people are scared to move during a recession, since they don't want to be the last one in who will be the first one out.

—Headhunter specializing in market researchers

People are reluctant to quit their jobs in a recession, because they are more valuable on their current job. It is a mental attitude. The recession makes people more cautious about changing jobs. A new job is risky. You are on probation for the first six months. You understand your old company. You know how you fit in. On a new job, you put yourself under the spotlight again.

—Headhunter dealing in diverse professionals

Firms that have cut pay are good targets for raids. A firm is a sinking ship if it has frozen pay or even if its increases are not as much as expected. I call up people in such firms. But their lawyers are reluctant to move for fear that the situation is bad everywhere. . . . I have to convince them that the other firm is doing well.

—Headhunter specializing in lawyers

Job service counselors also noticed that few were willing to quit their jobs without having found other work. As one said,

In a booming economy, people might quit and look for a job, but today no one would unless they had a new job lined up. Everybody reads the paper.

To some extent, the dampening effect of the recession was offset by the disruptive effects of layoffs. These can increase quits, because people take other jobs before being laid off or because layoffs sour the atmosphere at work. Employees normally undertake a job search as soon as they believe they will be laid off, as it is considered a disadvantage to wait until the moment of an inevitable layoff to look for another job. This is one reason companies closing plants pay stay-on bonuses.

The effects of layoffs on quitting were mentioned by 9 employers. In 3 instances, layoffs increased quitting. In the other 6 cases, the effect of layoffs on quits was offset by the effect of the recession.

> Turnover is under 10 percent. It has been as high as 15 percent, but the recession has reduced it. Layoffs didn't push it up, for there was nowhere to run. Everyone is in the same sinking boat.
>
> —Human resource manager of a unionized manufacturing firm with 1,800 employees

> The quit rate picks up when there are rumors of losses or layoffs. It stops just before actual layoffs, as people wait to see who will be laid off. After a wave of layoffs, the quit rate is high again, for the organization is unsettled. People may not like their new bosses or jobs. [This company had repeated waves of layoffs and shrank from 31,000 employees in 1988 to 9,500 in 1992.]
>
> —Human resource official of a nonunion manufacturing company with 9,500 employees

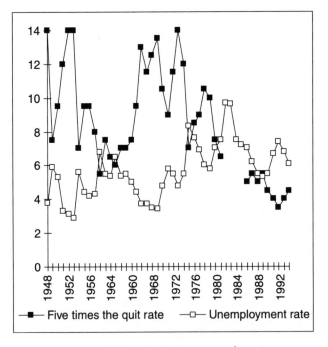

FIGURE 16.1   Quit rate in manufacturing

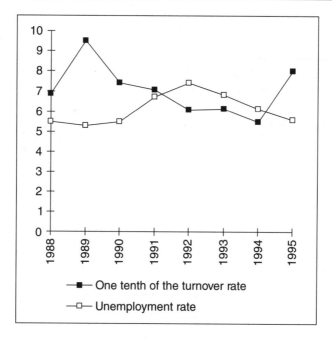

FIGURE 16.2 Total turnover in specialty stores

16.3 Summary

The recession reduced quitting sharply. Jobholders were reluctant to change employers for fear that a new job would prove unstable and leave them unemployed at a time when jobs were scarce.

Appendix 16A Related Literature

That recessions reduce voluntary turnover is revealed in Figures 16.1 and 16.2. The first figure shows the history of the U.S. unemployment rate and the number of quits per month per 500 employees in U.S. manufacturing for the years for which data are available.[1] The same pattern is visible in the second figure, which shows total turnover in U.S. specialty stores and the national unemployment rate for the years 1988–1995.[2]

Reynolds (1951, p. 216) finds as I do that people cling to their jobs during a recession because a new position might prove risky. He bases his conclusion on interviews with workers as well as with businesspeople. Akerlof, Ros

Yellen (1988) develop a theory expressing the idea that the disappearance of alternative jobs during recessions decreases turnover, a view reinforced by the findings of Mattila (1974) and Black (1980). Mattila finds that the majority of quitters locate new jobs before leaving their old ones, and Black finds that job changes bring bigger pay increases in good times than bad. The negative correlation between unemployment and quit rates is well documented (Pencavel, 1970, chap. 4; Armknecht and Early, 1972; Akerlof, Rose, and Yellen, 1988, fig. 1; and Campbell, 1993, 1995a).

17

THE SECONDARY SECTOR

Contrasts between the primary and the secondary sectors throw light on labor market mechanisms relevant to wage rigidity. Recall that the secondary sector is characterized by short-term or part-time employment, features that weaken the need for internal equity. The greater flexibility of hiring pay in the secondary sector adds to the evidence supporting the explanation of the downward rigidity of hiring pay in the primary sector; the need for internal equity ties the pay of new hires to that of existing employees, whose pay is downwardly rigid for other reasons. The more relaxed attitude in the secondary sector toward overqualification strengthens the argument that turnover was the main concern that discouraged primary-sector employers from hiring overqualified people.

Downward wage flexibility in the secondary sector was confined to starting pay in retail firms and to pay on new contracts for interim labor. In many retail firms, starting pay for salesclerks and some other hourly positions was quite flexible, but the pay of existing employees was seldom cut. Although pay on new contracts was flexible, pay cuts at contract renewal met resistance. In the temporary help industry, downward flexibility did not extend to engineers and to managers hired for long-term assignments (typically lasting six months to two years). Temporary labor agents insisted that these specialists be paid at least as much in total compensation as the permanently employed equivalents with whom they worked. Agents made these demands in order to avoid offending the professional pride of their workers. Since the pay of permanently employed engineers and managers seldom fell, it blocked a decline in the pay of temporary ones.

In the categories of pay that were downwardly flexible, actual reductions were not dramatic. What is important is not the size of the reductions but the fact that market forces rather than worker dissatisfaction prevented further declines.

Pay flexibility in the secondary sector was due largely to the absence of reference wages. For instance, retail companies were able to reduce starting pay, because new hires had no clear idea of what pay to expect. Few workers have a precise notion of market wages or wages that are fair in some absolute sense. Rather, they make comparisons with their own past pay and with the pay of co-workers. The latter standard is imprecise in retail companies, for new employees are often isolated by high turnover, by erratic part-time schedules, and by the nature of retail work itself, and they often do not know their co-workers well enough to learn their pay.

The absence of reference wages also explains the flexibility of contract wages. Flexibility occurred when contract workers did not compare their pay with that of permanent employees at the work site. Pay reductions after contract renewal met resistance because workers could use their former pay as a reference, while the absence of this standard made possible wage reduction on new contracts.

Other factors contributed to flexibility in the secondary sector. For instance, interim and part-time workers seldom view their jobs as careers and so do not feel as menaced by pay cuts or inequities as do workers who hope to keep their positions. Another factor is the competitiveness of the contract labor market, which makes it easy for agents to argue that workers cannot hope to obtain more pay than is offered. This observation adds to the evidence that workers accept pay cuts when these seem unavoidable (sections 12.2 and 19.1).

In retail companies, there was an interesting asymmetry between increases and decreases in starting pay. Although decreases caused few problems, some retail managers mentioned that it would be unwise in times of labor shortage to raise starting pay above that of existing employees. No informant gave a clear explanation of the asymmetry, which I believe was due to the concentration of turnover among new employees. In most stores and restaurants, there exists a core of old-timers, who would be aware of starting pay increases, and managers do not want trouble with them.

Management attitudes toward core employees were confusing, for certain practices made it clear that loyalty to them was limited. Regular raises can make long-term employees expensive, especially if they were hired during a tight labor market, and employers counted on normal attrition to eliminate them. If not enough high-priced workers left, some managers restricted their hours, cut their pay, or laid them off.

17.1 The Amount of Turnover and Part-Time Employment

Scraps of statistical material and evidence from interviews indicate that the industries I label as belonging to the secondary sector have relatively high voluntary turnover and large numbers of part-time employees, as required by the definition of that sector.

PART-TIME EMPLOYMENT

Few primary-sector managers mentioned part-time workers. Banks employed part-time tellers, but only two manufacturers said that an important fraction of their employees worked part time. In contrast, managers of secondary-sector companies were preoccupied with issues related to part-time employment. I obtained numerical data, summarized in Table 17.1, on the proportion of part-time employees in 27 of 48 secondary-sector firms that were not temporary employment agencies.

Available statistics confirm the high incidence of part-time employment in the secondary sector. Table 17.2 gives summary statistics obtained from a federal survey of households. Although the government collects no data from firms

TABLE 17.1   Percentage of part-time hourly employees in businesses studied

Range of percentages	Number of secondary-sector firms
1–10	1
11–40	4
41–80	9
81–100	13
Total	27

TABLE 17.2   Percentage of all employees who normally worked part-time in 1995: BLS data

Industry	Percentage
Eating and drinking places	89
Retail trade other than eating and drinking places	58
Finance, insurance, and real estate	22
Construction	15
Manufacturing	9

Source: Bureau of Labor Statistics.

TABLE 17.3   Percentage of all employees who worked part-time in 1995: trade
association data

Industry	Percentage
Specialty store retailers[a]	83
Fast-food restaurants[a]	65
Chain supermarkets[b]	63
Independent supermarkets[b]	58
Janitorial services[c]	56
Full-service restaurants with average check $10 and over[d]	55

a. I am grateful to Wilfred Roy of Management Service Associates for this information.

b. *Progressive Grocer* (April 1995), p. 26.

c. From the *1995 Compensation and Benefits Survey* of the Building Service Contractors Association International, whose help I gratefully acknowledge.

d. National Restaurant Association and Deloitte and Touche LLP, *Restaurant Operations Report, 1995.*

TABLE 17.4   Annual voluntary turnover data from the businesses studied

Range of percentages	Number of primary-sector firms	Number of secondary-sector firms
0–10	43	3
11–30	15	9
31–60	3	2
61–	0	6
Total	61	20

on part-time employment, private organizations do so and some of their findings appear in Table 17.3.

VOLUNTARY TURNOVER

The interviews yielded some turnover data, summarized in Table 17.4, which shows that turnover was higher in secondary-sector companies. Some individual secondary-sector companies reported extremely high turnover. For instance, a janitorial service with 500 employees and a department store chain with 20,000 employees both reported turnover of over 200 percent.

Table 17.5 gives turnover statistics derived from private sources and confirms that turnover is much higher in the secondary than in the primary sector.

Several respondents in the secondary sector reported that turnover was much higher among part-time than full-time workers. For instance, the vice president of human resources of a supermarket chain said that annual turnover in his company was 9 percent among full-time workers and was usually from 70 to 100 percent among part-time workers. Reports by three trade associations contain additional evidence of high turnover among part-time help. According to

TABLE 17.5 Annual voluntary turnover data for employees: trade association data

Type of company	Percentage annual average turnover	Year
Fast-food restaurants (hourly workers)[a]	140	1994
Security guard services[b]	121	1991
Specialty store retailers (part-time salesclerks)[c]	109	1994
Full-service restaurants with average check $10 and over[d] (hourly workers)	92	1994
Janitorial services (part-time workers)[e]	77	1995
Supermarkets (all employees)[f]	50	1994
Banking (part-time tellers, total turnover)[g]	19	1993
Banking (full-time tellers, total turnover)[g]	14	1993
Manufacturing[h]	10	1994

a. National Restaurant Association and Deloitte and Touche LLP, *Restaurant Operations Report, 1995.*

b. Cunningham, Strauchs, and Van Meter (1990), p. 142.

c. W. Roy (1995).

d. National Restaurant Association and Deloitte and Touche LLP, *Restaurant Operations Report, 1995.* The percentage given is the median response in the sample.

e. I am grateful to Wilfred Roy of Management Service Associates for this information.

f. Food Marketing Institute (1994). This number is the median response in the sample and is for the number of separations, regardless of cause, per full-time equivalent.

g. This number was provided by the Bank Administration Institute, Chicago.

h. Bureau of National Affairs (1995), "The BNA Policy and Practice Series, Bulletin to Management" (August): 87.

the trade association for janitorial companies, median turnover in the industry in 1995 was 38 percent among full-time and 77 percent among part-time employees.[1] According to the Food Marketing Institute, median turnover among full-time employees in supermarkets in 1994 was 12 percent, whereas it was 59 percent among part-time workers.[2] The National Retail Association reports that in 1994 average annual turnover among salesclerks in specialty retail stores was 55 percent for full-timers and 109 percent for part-timers.[3]

17.2 The Size of Pay Reductions

Although the interviews revealed flexibility of hiring pay in the secondary sector, no relevant statistical data are available to confirm this finding.

PAY REDUCTIONS FOR CONTRACT LABOR

Respondents in each of the 22 contract labor firms where I interviewed discussed the impact of the recession on pay. Seventeen claimed that average pay had declined in their companies, 4 said it had not changed, and a consulting firm manager said there had been increases for some kinds of programmers and decreases for others. Declines in janitorial and security companies were due mostly to lower rates on new contracts. Few individuals suffered pay cuts. The magnitude of the declines were small, from 5 to 20 percent, and were biggest and most prevalent in the temporary labor industry.

PAY REDUCTIONS IN RETAIL BUSINESSES

I was told that it was customary in both union and nonunion retail companies for starting pay to fluctuate with labor market conditions. Some union contracts in the industry specified only a minimum for the starting wage and a schedule of raises taking effect at specified time intervals, the floating progression system described in section 6.1. The minimum was often the legal minimum wage. Some union stores could reduce starting pay freely, and others had first to consult labor representatives.

Of the 33 retail businesses where pay changes were discussed, one had increased starting pay, 17 had left it unchanged, and 15 had reduced it. None reported a general pay cut, though a few had cut the pay of specific groups of existing employees. Decreases in starting pay ranged from 5 to 30 percent or more, with the biggest decreases reported by fast-food restaurants. Central management of store chains was poorly informed on the matter, as local management fixed starting pay.

> I have seen no statistics on it. Starting pay is set by the people in the field. Cuts are made only for people we haven't hired yet—for new hires. All I know is that we

do it and consider it to be successful. . . . The decreases are in 40¢ intervals, because people have to fall somewhere on the table of steps [specified by union contracts].

—Vice president of a supermarket chain with 30,000 employees

This person claimed that there were probably 30 tiers of pay in the company's stores as a result of frequent starting pay adjustments and differences in raises given to people hired before and after new union contracts took effect.

The three retail union leaders I interviewed acknowledged that entry-level pay had fallen with the onset of the recession.

In 1988–89, when you couldn't get help, stores were hiring at $6 to $6.50, though the union starting wage was $4.27 an hour [the Connecticut minimum wage], with 25¢ more after 30 days. . . . Since then, the new hire rate has gone back down to the [union] contract rate.

—Business agent of a retail workers' union local with 16,000 members

STATISTICAL INFORMATION

I have found no statistical confirmation of respondents' assertions about starting wage declines. The Bureau of Labor Statistics publishes no statistics on starting pay, and data published on it by trade associations are not comparable from year to year because of changes in the sample of companies. The bureau does publish data on average wages for help supply services, building maintenance services, and various categories of retail establishments, but nothing specifically on security guard services. Help supply and building maintenance services include the temporary labor and janitorial industries, respectively.[4] According to the bureau's statistics, average national wages in these industries continued to grow during the recession. It is nevertheless possible that average starting pay declined, since existing employees received raises and turnover declined. Also, starting wages may have declined only in particular regions, such as the Northeast.

The bureau's data show that secondary-sector wages react more to unemployment than do manufacturing wages. The greater cyclic sensitivity of secondary-sector wages may reflect some downward flexibility, though other explanations are possible. In order to compare the cyclical behavior of secondary sector with manufacturing wages, I computed for a few secondary-sector industries an elasticity with respect to the unemployment rate of the ratio of industry wages to manufacturing wages. These elasticities, appearing in Table 17.6, indicate the percentage increase in the wage ratio associated with a one percentage point increase in the unemployment rate. It may be seen that all but one are negative.

TABLE 17.6   Elasticity of wage ratios with respect to the unemployment rate

Industry	SIC code	Elasticity[a]
Department stores[b]	531	−0.09*
Grocery stores[c]	541	0.21*
Women's clothing stores[d]	562	−0.13*
Eating and drinking places[e]	58	−0.01
Building and maintenance services[f]	7349	−0.02*
Temporary help services[g]	7363	−0.06*

a. The elasticity is the coefficient c in the regression $\log(w_t/W_t) = a + bt + c\log(U_t)$, where t is time, measured in months or years, where w_t and W_t are the wage in the industry and the average manufacturing wage, respectively, and where U_t is U.S. unemployment rate. All data are from the Bureau of Labor Statistics and are published in its *Earnings and Employment*. An asterisk indicates statistical significance at the 5% level.

b. Annual data, 1958–1995.

c. Annual data, 1972–1995.

d. Annual data, 1958–1995.

e. Annual data, 1964–1995.

f. Monthly data from January 1988 to December 1995.

g. Monthly data from January 1982 to December 1995.

17.3 Reasons for Downward Flexibility

The extent of pay flexibility in secondary-sector companies depended almost entirely on the importance of pay comparisons between new and existing employees.

INTERNAL EQUITY IN CONTRACT WORK

Temporary labor agents said that when they dicker with customers over price, they talk about the trade-off between employee quality and pay, not equity with the customer's permanent workers. Nine agents discussed comparisons between the pay of semi-skilled temporary and permanent employees at one work site, and all said that the comparisons normally did not influence what they paid. There was a link between the pay of permanent and contract workers if the work was highly technical, especially when assignments were long term. Five agents mentioned that temporary engineers and other technical specialists earned roughly 30 percent more than equivalent permanent employees at the same site. The differential compensated for the absence of benefits for contract workers and was needed to avoid wounding the egos of the contract workers.[5]

In addition, setting pay too high relative to that of permanent workers could cause problems for the client company. All categories of temporary workers except technical professionals received less pay than permanent workers at the same site, after allowance for benefits. Agency mark-ups, however, usually made temporary workers more expensive than permanent ones for the client company.

> I try to find out from clients what they pay permanent employees doing the work of the position they are trying to fill with a temporary. This gives me an idea of what the position entails. . . . If there is a gap between what permanent and temporary workers would receive, I explain that the temporaries probably won't be as competent as the permanent employees they work with. You get what you pay for. . . . Resentment over the pay differential would not be a problem.
> —Owner of a temporary labor service specializing in clerical help and manual laborers

> My employees are paid a little more than in-house employees. If the client pays $10 an hour plus $3 in benefits, I may pay $13 or $14. This is company policy. I wouldn't deal with a client who wouldn't go along with it. . . . I would not pay my employees too much more than the client's employees, for fear of putting him in a bad spot.
> —Regional manager for a national temporary labor service specializing in engineers

When temporary labor agents spoke of pay comparisons with other temporary workers at the same site, it was taken to be obvious that all temporaries from one agency received the same pay for the same job at a given location. Problems sometimes arose from inequities among temporary workers from different agencies at one place.

> Clients don't care about what temporaries are paid. They care only about the cost to themselves. They don't worry about pay equity between temporaries and permanent employees. Nevertheless, I tell my employees not to talk about pay while on the job, for comparisons between temporaries from different agencies can cause problems.
> —Owner of a temporary employment agency specializing in clerical help

> If I tried to achieve pay equity with permanents for my employees, I would price myself out of the market. . . . If several agencies have men on a job, I want all the men to be paid the same. I tell the client to do that. Otherwise, there could be trouble and men could walk off the job.
> —Owner of a temporary labor service specializing in light industrial help

Similar things were said by managers of security guard and janitorial services. Pay equity was discussed in six of the seven interviews with them, and each made it clear that workers on one contract were treated equally and pay differences were dictated by duties and longevity. Pay differences between sites could be large. Trouble could be caused by pay disparities between workers from different employers at one site, but these problems were not taken seriously. As a manager in a security company said, "There is nothing anyone can do. The pay can't be changed. . . . Some effort may be made to transfer the malcontents."

PAY FLEXIBILITY IN CONTRACT WORK

The market for temporary labor is close to being a true auction market for labor. Agents propose rates on the basis of the job or the skills to be employed. They may ask for a little more money if an applicant is particularly good, where "applicant" is the industry term for worker. Because of competitive pressures, agents often cannot obtain the price asked, but haggle with clients and applicants, who sometimes refuse jobs because of low pay.[6]

Pay setting in janitorial and guard companies is done much as in temporary labor agencies, with the difference that the haggling is over the price for a crew of workers and the companies sometimes cut pay when contracts are renewed at reduced prices. No temporary labor agent mentioned having cut the pay of workers on a job. Janitorial and guard service companies complained that clients in financial difficulty sometimes demanded concessions when renewing contracts, and such demands were said to be typical of recessions. Pay cuts sometimes occurred when one company took over a job from another, for in such situations the new company used some or all of the workers who had been doing the job for the old employer. Pay cuts could cause problems with morale and turnover, but the attitude was that workers had to adapt or leave.

> If a client newly out-sources its security operation, we would like to use the supervisors and other good people from the client's old operation. We would like to keep their pay the same. But if the contract says the pay has to be less, the officers take it or leave it. Nevertheless, we try to maintain the pay of people we want to retain. Even in these times, some could leave. They may think they can get their old pay elsewhere, even if they cannot. We worry about the effect of pay cuts on morale too.
>
> —District manager supervising 230 guards for a large security service

> Pay can go down for employees when contracts are renewed. I make employees an offer—I ask them if they are willing to accept the new pay level. If someone refuses who is good, I transfer them to another job at the old pay or better. If they are not good, they leave.
>
> —Owner of a janitorial service with 500 employees

PAY FLEXIBILITY IN THE RETAIL INDUSTRY

Little other than supply and demand constrained starting pay for hourly retail workers. My information on this matter came from managers and labor leaders in the retail business. Respondents in the restaurant industry had no clear idea of why they could reduce hiring pay. Cuts were simply part of the normal way of doing business.

Among the 16 retail store managers interviewed, 7 commented on the ease of reducing starting pay for hourly employees, as did all 3 of the caterers and the 3 retail union leaders interviewed. They said that newly hired employees are usually too disoriented to discover they are underpaid and if they do they hardly care.

> A few years ago, [starting pay for hourly employees] was $7 an hour. Now, it is $6 an hour. This occurred because labor market conditions permitted it. I would have done it even if the company had been doing well. It should make existing employees happy to be paid more than new ones. But no one really noticed the decrease in starting pay, because no hourly employees work here for very long.
>
> —Owner of a catering business with 15 employees

> The retail setting is different from the industrial one, because about 80 percent of the work force is part-time. This makes decreases in starting pay easier. Part-timers often treat their pay as a supplement to family income, so that things like benefits are not as important. Turnover levels are higher for part-timers. They do notice each other's pay, but I just don't think that part-timers are as concerned about it as full-timers.
>
> —Vice president of human resources of a supermarket chain with 10,000 employees

> The reduction [in starting pay] at the onset of the recession caused no trouble, for people in stores don't work side by side, except at the registers. There are a lot of people milling around, and the customers get between the employees. There is also a lot of turnover. There is not a lot of pay jealousy. Part-timers are not there for a career. In the stores, it is only important that the senior people make more than the junior ones. The differences in pay between junior and senior people are not great. Also, the compensation is collectively bargained, so that employees theoretically had some input.
>
> —Vice president of a supermarket chain with 30,000 employees

Retail union leaders had similar opinions.

> There was never any resentment from new people because they were paid less. . . . It is hard for people to discover that entry-level pay rates have come down. To calculate this, someone would have to know the annual increments by which pay goes up and calculate backwards to find out what other employees were paid at their dates of hire. There are also lots of part-timers. [A well-known supermarket chain] is only 20 percent full-time. The people are not together that much.
>
> —Chief attorney for a retail workers' union local with 11,000 members

No tension was caused when the higher hiring rates were reduced with the onset of the recession. . . . There are all kinds of job classifications—cashiers, checking clerks, bag boys, meat cutters, etc. These are confusing and make comparison difficult. Everyone is very busy and has little time to sit around worrying about pay.

—President of a retail workers' union local with 16,000 members

The remarks of these retail union leaders differ sharply from those of the leaders of industrial unions quoted in section 9.4.

The ease of reducing starting pay in the secondary sector contrasted with the difficulty of increasing it above the pay of existing employees, though I heard little about increases. Nevertheless, three businesspeople and two labor leaders said retrospectively that increasing starting pay without adjustments for older employees caused dissension. These informants noticed the asymmetry between the consequences of increases and decreases and found the difference normal. One explained that existing employees can compare their own pay with that of newcomers, whereas new ones have trouble determining the starting pay of others.

17.4 Advantages of Turnover

Managers believe there is a trade-off between pay and turnover (section 7.1). Retail employers count on it to keep wage costs down, as do security guard and janitorial companies, and several respondents mentioned that the fall in turnover during the recession had increased labor costs by increasing the proportion of well-paid employees who had accumulated increases on high initial pay. These employers gave regular increases to encourage effort, but nevertheless hoped that enough of the more expensive people would leave. A few fast-food restaurants went so far as to cut the hours or pay of high-priced employees or lay them off. Such strong measures were not, however, common practice in the retail industry.

We don't expect people to stay long, unless they go into management. After three months, people are at peak performance. After three years, performance dips—the job gets boring and has no future. The job is for students or people with a temporary need to work. Crew positions are not career positions.

—Personnel manager of a fast-food restaurant franchise with 36 restaurants

In the determination of overall labor costs, there are two forces at work. One is the labor market. The other is what you can do with hours and hiring. Within limits, the hours of the more expensive employees can be restricted. Turnover also helps keep costs down. There are no rules in the [union] contract about assigning hours, but the stores do have to respect seniority. There is no policy about reducing hours until people quit, but I cannot guarantee that some managers don't do that. Turnover does go down during recessions. The main effect of this is that more people start accruing benefits, this effect being more expensive than the increase in wages. Benefits are 40 percent of total labor costs. Labor costs increase during recessions as a result of the lower turnover. All we can do is to work with the hours and hope for more turnover. But the company wants happy, motivated employees as well, because they give higher productivity.

—Vice president of a supermarket chain with 30,000 employees

I have several long-term employees who are paid at top rates. . . . I almost hope they will leave. I can't pay them more. As a result of the lack of raises, they will become disgruntled. I am playing a waiting game with them. . . . I won't dismiss them out of compassion for their circumstances. As long as they are reasonably productive for the wage, I will do nothing. Replacing them with cheaper men might hurt morale. I have never seen that done. Usually, such problems are solved through attrition—they move on or become supervisors. The recession has blocked that solution.

—Part-owner and manager of a janitorial service with 80 employees

It is interesting that one of two manufacturers in my sample with a large proportion of part-time help also wanted more turnover.

Menial labor gets stale after three years and gets too expensive. I have found a way to get rid of them. I put them on part-time until they leave.

—President of a nonunion manufacturing company with 40 employees

17.5 What Prevented Contract and Starting Pay from Falling Further?

The interviews lead to the unsurprising conclusion that where pay was downwardly flexible, it was sustained by market forces and the minimum wage.

OVERVIEW OF INTERVIEW EVIDENCE

Table 17.7 summarizes the comments of managers of secondary-sector companies on the forces supporting pay. Four of the five who spoke of the minimum wage were in the fast-food industry, and the fifth was a temporary labor agent. Concern about the trade-off between pay and employee quality was widespread. Talk of fairness, performance, and morale was nearly absent from discussions of contract and starting pay.

Table 17.7   Factors putting a floor under pay (applies to 51 businesses)

Factors	Number of businesses	Percentage of businesses
The need to pay enough to recruit labor of appropriate quality	33	65
The impact of pay on turnover	15	29
The minimum wage	5	10

REMARKS FROM INTERVIEWS

A variety of comments revealed the forces creating a wage floor in the secondary sector.

I have been hiring [counter help] at $5.50 to $7 an hour in order to attract the right sort. I wanted people from the neighborhood who wouldn't need to have me stand over their shoulders. It is worth it in this industry to pay a little more rather than have someone who will steal from you. Other restaurant owners who prefer to pay less have lots of turnover, figuring the help will steal anyway. . . . Because of all the layoffs, good people come in. This affects what I pay. I hired someone last week for $5 an hour. I might have paid $5.50 if I hadn't had four other people I could have hired.

—Owner of franchise restaurant with 12 employees

For kitchen help, I pay as little as I can for each individual at the entry level. I look at the job application and see how long someone has been out of work and how badly they need it. Only one girl ever refused an offer. A lot of people are out of work, so that I can negotiate strongly.

—Manager of a restaurant with 30 employees

Since there are so many people looking for work, the company asked me to reduce starting pay back to $4.27 [the minimum wage]. I tried it for two weeks, but people refused to work for that little, so I gave it up.

—Manager of a unionized department store with 125 employees

The base rate for sitting in a building is $6 an hour. This is the lowest I will go. If you pay less, you get bad people and there is more turnover. Reducing turnover is beneficial, especially if a place is complex. Training costs are expensive.

—District manager supervising 500 guards for a large security service

At the bottom end, the minimum wage [$4.27 an hour] provides the floor. For such people, pay rates have been $5.50 to $6 an hour. There is no reluctance to work at the lower pay.

—Owner of a temporary labor service specializing in light industrial help

Our mark-up has declined. We are trying to maintain a living wage for the temporaries, so we absorb the decrease. They have to dress themselves, drive a car to work, and live.

—Branch manager for a large temporary employment service specializing in accountants and bookkeepers

The rates that companies are willing to pay are still falling. Why they don't fall more is for an economist to answer. There is no straight answer. The demand is always for people with certain specific attributes, with specific skills and technology. Not everyone is equally qualified. Eighty percent of the positions are specific. Companies want someone who has worked with a certain technology. It is not often that I have two people with the desired attributes, so they don't compete each other down on price.

—General manager of a temporary labor service specializing in engineers and technicians

You can't get decent people to work for less than $5.50. If they take the job, they don't take it seriously and may not show up regularly. Some make more money not working because of unemployment insurance. Some highly skilled people stay home rather than take $10 an hour. This can be because of a second income in the family or because of blind pride. At the lower levels, particularly, we find resistance to lower pay. Those who are up against it and have no alternative will come to work. They'll take anything. How people react to adversity is a very individual thing. Some would rather search for permanent work. Some take what they can to survive, and with enthusiasm.

—Regional manager of a large temporary help firm specializing in clerical and light industrial workers

EFFECT OF THE MINIMUM WAGE

Interviews with fast-food restaurant managers provided interesting evidence that they kept wages as low as they could. Those paying more than the minimum wage had more difficulty hiring than those paying exactly that amount, which indicates that firms offering the minimum wage would probably have offered less had it been legal to do so. Three managers were paying the minimum wage (to inexperienced new crew members on the cheapest shifts), and none of these three said they had trouble obtaining help. Of the 8 offering more, 4 said they had trouble hiring, and the 4 others said that a significant reduction in starting pay would cause an undesirable increase in turnover or fall in the quality of applicants. Fast-food restaurants usually hire from the immediate neighborhood, and local labor market conditions vary considerably over a distance of just a few miles. The pattern is consistent with the findings of Holzer, Katz, and Krueger (1991) in their investigation of the relation between wages and the number of job applicants.[7] They found a spike in the application rate distribution at the minimum wage. That is, jobs offering the minimum wage received more applications per job than did jobs paying slightly more.

17.6 Attitudes toward Overqualification

Among secondary-sector employers, the greater the need for employee stability, the greater the hostility to overqualified applicants.

OVERVIEW OF INTERVIEW EVIDENCE

Managers of 53 of 63 secondary-sector companies discussed overqualification. In only 6 of the 53, no overqualified people or few of them ever applied for work. Table 17.8 summarizes the comments of managers in the remaining 47. The corresponding percentages for the primary sector were 70, 10, and 19, respectively, in descending order in the right-hand column (Table 15.4). All three taxi company managers interviewed said they welcomed overqualified drivers, and overqualification was hardly an issue among employers of contract labor. Among the 13 employers of contract labor who discussed the issue, only one said he would not hire overqualified people, and one other expressed some reluctance. Taxi and contract labor companies have high turnover. Retailers were more likely than other secondary-sector employers to have negative attitudes. Among the 30 retail managers who expressed views and said they saw many overqualified applicants for jobs as salesclerks, 9 expressed no resistance to hiring them, 10 expressed some resistance, and 11 refused to hire them. The

TABLE 17.8   Reactions to overqualified job applicants (applies to 47 businesses)

Reactions	Number of businesses	Percentage of businesses
Totally unwilling to hire them	14	30
Partially unwilling to hire them	11	23
Ready to hire them	22	47
Total	47	100

more exclusive a store's clientele, the more negative were its managers' attitudes, probably because exclusive stores need well-trained personnel who know the customers. Fast-food restaurant managers expressed a surprising amount of hostility to overqualification. Among the 6 fast-food restaurant managers who saw significant numbers of overqualified applicants, only 2 expressed no reservations about hiring them for crew positions and one refused to hire them at all.

REMARKS FROM INTERVIEWS

Brokers of contract labor showed no concern about overqualification.

> Overqualification is not a problem in the market for temporaries. It is even an advantage when selling a person as a temp, though it would be a disadvantage in selling the person for a permanent job. . . . We do not worry about turnover.
>
> —Branch manager for a large temporary employment service specializing in accountants and bookkeepers

A little more concern was expressed by temporary labor agents dealing in technical specialists, for their assignments could last up to two years.

> There are lots of overqualified applicants today. Companies have been reluctant to hire them as temporaries, for fear they would leave. But in the last three months, companies have been changing their stance, for they realize that the overqualified have no place to go and that they are very good people.
>
> —General manager of a temporary labor service specializing in engineers and technicians

Some positive reactions to overqualified people were expressed by managers running security guard and janitorial services.

> We get all kinds of applicants. There are engineers, executives, kids, and retirees. Lots are unemployed. . . . I don't like overqualified applicants particularly. I like being able to help them, but I don't like it when they quit. Occasionally, they try to tell their supervisors what to do. But they also tend to be more responsible than other employees, such as giving two weeks' notice before quitting. They are better employees. . . . I expect turnover in any case.
>
> —District manager supervising 230 guards for a large security service

The managers of taxi companies had good things to say about overqualified drivers.

> Overqualified people do come in, such as a computer programmer and a disbarred attorney. I don't care. I would like to have more of them. They are more reliable. They quit soon after being hired, but so does everyone else, except a few.
>
> —General manager of a livery and taxi company with 90 drivers

Attitudes varied widely among retail managers. Managers of inexpensive stores were usually tolerant.

> [Overqualified employees] want something to hold them over until something better comes along. This is all right with us. It is not a bad thing. It doesn't take long to train someone to work in our stores. I wouldn't want them in our management training program, but it is all right to have them as clerks.
>
> —Vice president of human resources of a supermarket chain with 10,000 employees

The opposite view was expressed by managers of expensive stores.

> I do not hire the overqualified. As soon as times are better, they will leave. They would be frustrated on the job. This would be bad for morale. One bad apple spoils the barrel. It takes three to six months to integrate a new employee. I don't want turnover in the sales force either, for customers are more loyal if salespeople recognize them and address them by name. [The store sold medium- to high-priced furniture and household furnishings.]
>
> —Owner of a retail business with 30 employees

17.7 Cyclic Sensitivity of Employment in the Secondary Sector

The secondary sector should be able to absorb excess labor during recessions, for it is large and accepts the overqualified and its hiring wages are somewhat flexible. The sector is indeed enormous; employment in the retail trade alone is nearly equal to that in manufacturing. Nevertheless, the sector does not act as a buffer, though many who are out of work probably do take stopgap secondary-sector jobs. During recessions, employment shrinks in the secondary just as it does in the primary sector, as may be seen from Table 17.9. This gives elasticities with respect to the unemployment rate of the proportion of the labor force employed in various U.S. industries. Although the table may seem to conflict with the observation that people move to better-paying industries during booms (Okun, 1973; Bils and McLaughlin, 1992), there is no contradiction and there would be none even if the elasticities were the same in all industries, because the employed work force grows during economic expansions. That is, as people move to higher-level industries during booms, unemployed people may take jobs in lower-level industries in just the right numbers so as to keep constant relative employment in all industries.

17.8 Summary

Because of high turnover and heavy use of part-time labor, workers in the secondary sector do not get to know one another well enough to make internal

TABLE 17.9 Elasticity of employment share with respect to the unemployment rate

Industry	SIC code	Elasticity[a]
Manufacturing[b]	20–39	−0.138*
Retail[c]	52–59	−0.062*
Department stores[d]	531	−0.171*
Grocery stores[e]	541	−0.044
Women's clothing stores[f]	562	−0.002
Eating and drinking places[g]	58	−0.040
Building maintenance services[h]	7349	−0.103*
Temporary help services[i]	7363	−0.545*

a. The elasticity is the coefficient c in the regression $\log(E_t/L_t) = a + bt + c \log(U_t)$, where t is time, measured in months or years, E_t is employment in the industry, L_t is the civilian labor force, and U_t is the unemployment rate in the U.S. All data are from the Bureau of Labor Statistics and are published in its *Earnings and Employment*. An asterisk indicates statistical significance at the 5% level.

b. Annual data, 1947–1995.

c. Annual data, 1947–1995.

d. Annual data, 1958–1995.

e. Annual data, 1972–1995.

f. Annual data, 1958–1995.

g. Annual data, 1958–1995.

h. Monthly data from January 1988 to December 1995.

i. Monthly data from January 1982 to December 1995.

equity as important as it is in the primary sector. For this reason, hiring pay is more flexible downward in the secondary than in the primary sector. Low training and hiring costs make secondary-sector employers less concerned about labor turnover and hence more willing to hire the overqualified than are primary-sector employers.

Appendix 17A Related Literature

THE AMOUNT OF TURNOVER AND PART-TIME EMPLOYMENT (SECTION 17.1)

I know of no literature on whether two-tier systems are more common in the secondary than the primary sector, nor on whether the systems are accepted more easily in the secondary sector. Martin and Peterson (1987), Martin (1990), and Heetderks and Martin (1991) study employee attitudes toward two-tier systems in retail stores and find general dissatisfaction with them. Okun (1973, p. 239; 1981, p. 106) mentions that the wages of casual labor are likely to be more flexible than those for career jobs, and his distinction between casual and career labor jobs is similar to that between the secondary and the primary sectors. He bases his assertion on theoretical arguments.

WHAT PREVENTED CONTRACT AND STARTING PAY FROM FALLING FURTHER? (SECTION 17.5)

The observation about the effect of the minimum wage is consistent with published evidence that increases in the minimum wage increase employment (Katz and Krueger, 1992; Card and Krueger, 1994, 1995; and Dickens, Machin, and Manning, 1994). There is controversy about the validity of these findings (Neumark and Wascher, 1992, 1993; Card, Katz, and Krueger, 1993; and Kennan, 1995). Firms paying a little more than the minimum wage may be paying so little that they do not have an adequate flow of job applicants. Forcing them to pay more increases the number of applicants and hence induces them to hire more, as Card and Krueger explain.

18

THE UNEMPLOYED

This chapter is based on 41 interviews with what I call observers of the unemployed. Fifteen of these were headhunters and 26 were advisers of the unemployed, who were job service counselors, outplacement counselors, and support group leaders. I arranged these interviews because I wished to understand the point of view of unemployed job seekers and did not have the resources to interview a random sample of unemployed workers. Advisers of the unemployed were probably good informants, for they saw hundreds and in some cases thousands of jobless people every year, wished to help them, and were trained to do so. Headhunters understood the functioning of the labor market, though they had only limited dealings with the unemployed.

The impressions of these informants were vivid. Most of the unemployed they saw were out of work because of layoffs, plant closures, or business failures. Job loss was usually a terrible blow, especially for people supporting families, and living standards declined during unemployment. During a period of shock following the loss, some people were unrealistic and lethargic in their job search. Later, most became realistic and energetic, especially as they began to suffer from low income and realized how bad the job market was. The biggest problem facing job hunters was lack of job opportunities. Advisers counseled flexibility and energy in job searches. All methods of searching were worthwhile, though the most effective was making inquiries through acquaintances, friends, and relatives. Flexibility was important for success in a job search, especially since many had to take a cut in pay to obtain work. However, looking for work at too low a level was a waste of time, for the applicant was usually rejected as overqualified. Nevertheless, desperation drove many to go too low. Though energy and flexibility helped, they did not guarantee quick success because of the shortage of jobs and the overqualification problem. It was not true that any person could immediately find some job, even a stopgap, and counselors advised against taking interim jobs, for they distracted from the search for good ones. Although many people found work quickly because of luck or good connections, an important proportion took many months or more than a year. The experience of being rejected as overqualified was itself a source of exasperation for job hunters. One counselor in a state job service quoted as typical the words of a client, who said that he felt he had been thrown into a deep well with a ladder on one side, the ladder turning out to have no rungs when he reached out for it while falling.

The above description is largely confirmed by what employers said about overqualification and the flood of job applications. The description is also supported by statistical information and published surveys, though there is little work on overqualification and on whether anybody can find work immediately (appendix to this chapter).

18.1 How People Became Unemployed

Advisers of the unemployed said that most of the increase in the flow into unemployment during the recession was due to involuntary layoffs and almost none came from quits, as is to be expected since the recession made people less willing to give up their jobs (Chapter 16).

Some job service counselors remarked that an unusually large proportion of clients were on permanent rather than temporary layoff. The preponderance of permanent layoffs may have been due to conditions obtaining only in the Northeast, for national statistics do not confirm the trend (appendix to this chapter). Historically, between a fifth and a tenth of unemployed workers in the United States have been on temporary layoff, and this low proportion is not consistent with the idea advanced by Feldstein (1976) that cyclical unemployment is produced primarily by temporary layoffs.

INTERVIEW EVIDENCE

Seventeen advisers of the unemployed discussed how clients became unemployed, and all said that most of the unemployed had lost their jobs through involuntary layoffs or plant closings. Four outplacement counselors mentioned that some clients lost their jobs because they did not get along with their bosses. I asked 18 advisers whether many clients had quit because of a pay cut, and all 18 said that few or no clients were in this position. One of them said that some clients had been offered the choice of leaving or accepting a lower-level job. Seven of the 18 went on to say that few were willing to quit their jobs before finding other work.

18.2 Reactions to Job Loss

Permanent layoff was a terrible blow. It brought not only loss of income but fear of never being able to replace it, the humiliation of no longer earning money and of no longer being wanted, and the isolation resulting from loss of social contacts at work. The initial psychological impact of job loss often impeded job search. Temporary layoff, in contrast, was not a major setback.

INTERVIEW EVIDENCE

Seventeen advisers of the unemployed discussed reactions to layoff and all said it was usually an immobilizing shock that lasted a few weeks or months and was often associated with denial of loss and lack of realism about job prospects.

> At first after layoff, people doubt their self-worth. They need a week just to get used to the idea of looking for work. A few are more practical and are immediately on the ball and disciplined.
>
> —Job service counselor

> For some people, layoff is a bad blow, especially if it is permanent with no recall. . . . For most people, even their identity is wrapped up in their job. They lose self-esteem. Their social circles too were at their place of work. They ask, "Now what do I do?" There is grieving, denial, and anger, as after a death. . . . We tell them about these reactions, but they still have to be worked through, because they get in the way of job hunting. . . . They have a chip on their shoulder that offends employers.
>
> —Job service counselor

> Most take layoffs very hard. They have responsibilities. Unemployment is not a vacation. . . . How hard it is depends on whether there are a mortgage, a wife, and children, and whether the wife is working. No one says, "I'll take time off."
>
> —Job service counselor

> A lot don't realize at first how bad the job market is. Some fix up their homes for a month or so before they start looking seriously for work. Others start right away. Others try to find another position in their old company, though this usually turns out to be hopeless. For many, this is the first time they've lost their job, after having worked for 30 years or so.
>
> —Support group leader

> Initially, people go through a period of shock and denial in which they won't settle for anything less than they've had. After that, most search hard for work. Few do nothing. A few are so depressed they can't get out of bed. The period of shock can last a few months.
>
> —Support group leader

One of the very important phenomena in my group is the psychological effect of no longer being the breadwinner. . . . New group members are devastated. They don't want to admit they don't have a job. It is difficult for them to come [to support group meetings] the first time. . . . If they thought, "I can fix the roof or paint the garage," that doesn't last long.

—Support group leader

One obstacle [to reemployment] is the emotional roller coaster of job search. It is difficult to sell yourself and rejection is hard to take. . . . Our purpose is to give a person control of his situation. Job loss is traumatic precisely because of the loss of control.

—Outplacement counselor

Job loss is one of the worst events in life. Other problems in life, marital, financial and parental, can be worsened by it. Kids can be shaken. These other issues are serious in about one out of ten cases and arise in one out of four.

—Outplacement counselor

18.3 Changes in Living Standards When Unemployed

Living standards declined during unemployment, especially those of people who did not have sufficient financial resources to cushion the blow.

INTERVIEW EVIDENCE

The 15 job service counselors and support group leaders who talked about living standards spoke of decline and even destitution among the people they advised.

Job loss is a financial disaster. People can't sell their homes and use up their savings trying to meet mortgage payments. . . . CEOs can wind up at the poverty level, for they are too ashamed to apply for unemployment insurance and they exhaust their savings. If they put off applying, it is too late, for the benefits depend on earnings in the previous four quarters. We see lots of clients who lose their telephones, which makes getting a job very difficult. They allow car insurance to lapse and drive anyway. Cars get repossessed. Homes are lost. Marriages break up, especially if the wife is working. Substance and spouse abuse are increasing.

—Job service counselor

Clients tell us that their living standards are declining, that the husband or wife is threatening to leave, that the bill collector is at the door. Some threaten suicide. Mental health problems result.

—Job service counselor

Many people live from paycheck to paycheck, so that they suffer a lot from unemployment. Lots have trouble paying the rent or mortgage. Many have no health insurance, even on their new job. [This was said during a discussion of blue-collar workers.]

—Support group leader

The majority have a spouse earning money. The kids are put to work earning money for the car. People take care of near-term issues and don't worry about long-term ones, such as retirement. They live on IRAs in order to maintain living standards and protect their homes. [This was said during a discussion of professional and managerial people.]

—Support group leader

Outplacement counselors saw less suffering, probably because their clients were better protected.

No client has lost his house or dropped out. I know of few stories of dire financial stress. People do cut back on luxury items—dinners out, fancy cars. They live on severance, employed spouses, and the unemployment insurance system.

—Outplacement counselor

18.4 Job Search Methods

The best way to find a job was through networking, which means asking acquaintances, friends, relatives, and business contacts whether they know of job openings or know someone who might know of one, making the same inquiries of the people named, and continuing sequentially. It was important to be realistic and to concentrate energetically on a narrow segment of the job market. Some advisers of the unemployed said it was unwise to rely on newspaper advertisements, for so many people answered that there was little chance that one individual would find work by doing so. These observations were supported by employers' complaints, described in section 15.1, of being overwhelmed by job applications.

INTERVIEW EVIDENCE

Seventeen advisers of the unemployed discussed job search methods, and 15 of these mentioned networking as a useful method or the most useful one. Three respondents advocated approaching companies directly, and seven mentioned that job searchers usually got no response when they answered newspaper advertisements.

You have to knock on doors. You never know, but you might know someone who knows someone, and so on. Newspapers are another resource. Some people must be getting jobs that way. Many feel that newspaper ads aren't worth answering, because companies don't respond at all. It is difficult to follow up on newspaper ads, for often they give just a post office box number. . . . It is important to get to the business section of newspapers to find out which companies have new contracts. You should read obituaries to see if the deceased worked, for their job might be open. We get very creative around here.

—Job service counselor

If someone sees an ad, he sends his resume and waits for a phone call, which never comes. Companies are overwhelmed with resumes.

—Support group leader

Most clients have worked for one company for their whole life, so that they lack contacts. They have to build these [by networking].

—Outplacement counselor

[Clients] often have no experience in job search. They want to answer ads and write letters to companies. Doing these things is a waste of time [since companies don't answer]. . . . Jobs get created through networking. Companies create jobs for people they like. . . . Networking tends to lead to a better fit and is an inexpensive way for companies to recruit.

—Outplacement counselor

18.5 Pay Negotiations

A job search involves not only finding openings, but sorting through them and agreeing on pay. These processes were discussed in 23 interviews with observers of the unemployed, and the story they told was as follows. Both firms and job seekers use pay information during the initial screening process. Firms screen on the basis of pay at the previous job. Job hunters either ask employers directly or make discreet inquiries among friends or other contacts about pay levels. If both sides wish to proceed, the firm's selection is based almost entirely on qualifications. Firms do not usually look for the cheapest person to fill a job and normally discuss pay only after offering a job. Firms are restricted in setting the pay of new hires by their internal pay structure, and the restrictions are greater the lower the level of the job. Pay negotiations almost never fail, especially when the job hunter is unemployed.

Counselors tell people to talk about pay only after the employer says he'll hire them. This is the only appropriate time. You are not supposed to be concerned about the money. You don't want pay to get in the way, though a good employer should bring it up early in the interview. Pay should be discussed only after a good relationship has been established with the interviewer. . . . For most jobs, there is a range for negotiation. If a job requires little experience, the pay tends to be fixed. If a job requires more experience, more negotiation is possible. Employers will pay for more experience.

—Job service counselor

Inflated pay expectations do not play a role in pay negotiations, but [in choosing] the types of jobs considered. People learn about pay by calling the personnel department or talking to people. Once someone has a job interview, pay negotiations rarely get in the way.

—Job service counselor

Companies don't look for cheap people to buy. They are interested in whether people can do the job and whether they will grow. They are ready to pay what they have to to get the person they need. Salary is not even a tie breaker between candidates. In order to break ties, they go to great lengths to put people in unusual situations in order to test their problem-solving abilities. . . . It is very uncommon for people to price themselves out of a job. If someone asks for too much money, he never gets to first base with a company and doesn't know why. Pay is not much discussed until the last stages of the hiring process. Pay on the previous job is used by employers as a criterion for making an initial selection among candidates. Normally, pay is negotiable only within limits, especially in a large corporation.

—Outplacement counselor

Pay negotiations do not often fail if we do our job properly. We have to screen the client [i.e., company] and the applicant beforehand. If the offer is a surprise to either side, we haven't done our job.

—Headhunter specializing in accountants

18.6 How Much Flexibility Was Advisable?

Flexibility about all aspects of jobs reduces the time needed to find work. Observers of the unemployed cautioned, however, that flexibility could be carried too far, for employers rejected applicants judged to be overqualified, a view consistent with what employers told me (sections 15.2 and 17.6). Flexibility was a delicate issue, and many jobless people did suffer pay cuts in taking new jobs. A job hunter was overqualified only for jobs involving too big a cut. The problem frustrated and confused both job hunters and their advisers.

INTERVIEW EVIDENCE

Flexibility in one's job search was discussed in all 41 interviews with observers of the unemployed. Sixteen of these informants said that some flexibility about all aspects of a job was important for success in a job search. No one said that unlimited flexibility was useful, and all but one said that excessive flexibility risked making the job hunter overqualified. The exception was a headhunter (for lawyers), who claimed that overqualification was irrelevant in her business. Two others minimized its importance. The obvious advantage of flexibility was that it enlarged the set of choices. The arguments against excessive flexibility were that it led to rejection, for it made employers suspect that an applicant would be bored, dislike reduced pay, and take another job as quickly as possible, exactly the concerns expressed by employers (section 15.2). No respondent could define precisely the boundary between useful and excessive flexibility.

The emphasis given here to flexibility should not distract from the need for energy and imagination in job search. Fifteen of 20 job service and outplacement counselors stressed that the unemployed should treat job search as a demanding full-time job.

It is a job to get a job. It is lots of work. It takes 8 hours a day.
—Job service counselor

We try to convince [clients] that job search takes 40 hours a week. You have to scope out your area and mount a major campaign.
—Job service counselor

Flexibility was clearly useful.

A willingness to accept less helps them to get a job. . . . People have to expand their job search too. Good machinists have to consider operators' jobs. This is a big step backward, but you have to tell people to be realistic and look at their own needs.
—Job service counselor

The earlier a person loses his reluctance to accept lower pay, the quicker he finds work.
—Job service counselor

People must accept lower pay, at least for a while until their pay is increased. It helps to look at transferable skills. If someone was an underwriter, he can use his analytical skills elsewhere.
—Job service counselor

Excessive flexibility also had its dangers.

People have to be willing to go low enough, but not so low as to be viewed as unserious by the employer. . . . If they go too far down, ... he considers them to be in a desperation mode and assumes they will leave as soon as something better comes along. He doesn't want to lose a new employee 18 months later when the recession ends.

—Job service counselor

As people drop their sights, they run into the overqualification problem. Then, they drop their sights even further as they get rejected. We try to keep people at the same level and to direct their attention to transferable skills.

—Job service counselor

Lots of job applicants are told they are overqualified. This could mean you used to be paid too much, you are too old, or you'll jump ship. . . . In job search, it is always better to go higher. No one likes someone who lowballs themselves. You have to be in the right ball park. . . . The overqualification problem is severe and not understood by job seekers. When unemployment insurance benefits run out, people are willing to take anything. They are looking for the wrong thing or willing to take jobs for the wrong reasons. Employers fear they will quit. This is very common.

—Job service counselor

Flexibility in general helps—a willingness to move and a willingness to accept a cut in pay. It is hard to generalize about pay flexibility. Having been paid well in the past can be a strike against you. Many clients are ready and willing to step down in both position and pay, but this doesn't help much. Most employers are uncomfortable with that. They are suspicious you'll treat the job as a stopgap. Yet people often do take a slight cut in pay. . . . Not all employers are trying to take advantage of the buyers' market. They want to start off the relationship with a happy employee. . . . There is also the fear that the employee will be bored. . . . There are many other job applicants who are not overqualified. . . . Flexibility on pay doesn't help much. It is a slippery slope. One should be flexible in pay negotiations, but this flexibility won't help dramatically.

—Outplacement counselor

Companies do not want people to be flexible about pay. . . . The companies don't worry about boredom. They worry that the person will continue to look for another job. They want the person to be challenged by the job and happy doing it. They don't want any malcontents, for a malcontent is not a good employee. This is true for all relationships. Discontent doesn't make for loyalty. People who take a job out of desperation become resentful of the person they are working for.

—Headhunter specializing in engineers

A person who is unemployed and overqualified is in a catch 22 situation. In his previous job, he was overpaid relative to his contribution and so he was laid off. Now, he can't get a job because he was paid too much before. If he says he will accept less, people ask, "Why is he doing that?". . . . If you are willing to work for less than you got on your previous job, employers wonder if you are not just parking your hat there until you get a better job. They probably don't think there is anything wrong with you.

—Headhunter specializing in physical therapists, engineers, and information system specialists

Three informants reported that the overqualification problem angered job hunters.

I have had someone who was told he was overqualified to manage a [fast-food restaurant]. This makes [support group members] very angry. When unemployment benefits are about to run out, they are ready to do anything, but they are told they won't be hired because they'll leave as soon as times get better.

—Support group leader

Eight respondents went so far as to advise clients to write their resumes so as to hide qualifications.

People have to downgrade their resumes. I advise people to do that. Businessmen aren't very good at detecting it.

—Job service counselor

Downgrading may have been common, for some businesspeople complained about it (section 15.2).

Some employers said they would hire overqualified people who could convince them that the new job would fulfill a desire to change careers or start a new way of life (section 15.2). Five advisers of the unemployed made remarks to the same effect.

Applicants have to have a logical and candid explanation for why they are stepping down. This works. You can't say you'll do anything until something better comes along. You can say you have a health problem and need to slow down, that you have changed your life style and have a different set of objectives now.

—Outplacement counselor

Overqualification may have sometimes been used as a pretext for age discrimination, for eight advisers of the unemployed claimed it was, and two others said that older people were more likely to face the problem. However, overqualification was not a problem solely for older employees. Six of the eight just mentioned said that overqualification could be a problem for anyone.

Overqualification is used as an excuse for age discrimination. It is becoming a problem even for the young. When they apply for a job below what they are trained for, they are sometimes told they are overqualified.

—Support group leader

It is natural that older people would be more likely to face the problem, since pay and skill often increase with age, at least until middle age.

Overqualification affected everyone but the unskilled, though the problem increased with skill level. Four advisers of the unemployed claimed the problem affected people other than professionals and executives, and no one contradicted this view.

> The overqualification problem exists throughout the labor spectrum, right down to the bottom.
>
> —Job service counselor

> Even blue-collar workers face the overqualification issue. . . . Machinists face it too. Someone with 20 years of experience is overqualified for a job requiring 7 to 10 years of experience.
>
> —Job service counselor

Advisers of the unemployed did not perceive that overqualification was less of a problem in the secondary than in the primary sector, though employers in the secondary sector were more relaxed about the question. The advisers did not make a distinction between primary and secondary sectors, and only two mentioned that overqualification was less of a problem for low-level jobs.

> [Unemployed people] arrive at the bottom, where overqualification is not a problem. Fast-food restaurants, building maintenance companies, and security services will take anyone.
>
> —Job service counselor

(This statement should not be interpreted as meaning that jobs of this kind were always available, though it was easier to find such jobs (section 18.8).)

In section 15.2, I present evidence from employer interviews that overqualification arises when the drop in pay from the previous job is more than 30 percent. Similar evidence is contained in interviews with advisers of the unemployed.

> Someone going from $30,000 to $25,000 with good benefits might stay. Someone going from $30,000 to $20,000 would probably leave.
>
> —Job service counselor

> People become seriously overqualified if they are willing to accept 30 percent less than what they used to work for. We don't want clients to do that. It discourages employers and is a negative presentation.
>
> —Job service counselor

Most employers are leery of offering an unemployed person too much less than he earned previously. They might be reluctant to offer someone who had made $100,000 only $60,000 or $70,000.

—Headhunter specializing in computer programmers

18.7 Stopgap Jobs

Stopgap jobs are interim jobs taken until a better permanent one is found. Some, such as consulting, are explicitly temporary, but others are ostensibly permanent. Advisers of the unemployed believed that stopgap jobs were a bad idea, unless they might lead to a good permanent job, for they interfered with searching for a job. A little concern was also expressed that potential employers might look askance at a record of low-paying employment.

INTERVIEW EVIDENCE

Nineteen advisers of the unemployed discussed stopgap jobs. The dominant view, expressed by 13 of these informants, was that such jobs were a distraction from job hunting and should be avoided if possible. Four respondents spoke more favorably, arguing that interim jobs could lead to permanent ones. Two respondents expressed both points of view, disparaging only low-paying interim jobs. Few knew whether it was common for unemployed people to take stopgap jobs.

It is not advisable to take a stopgap job unless you are at the poverty level and the alternative is becoming homeless. People don't want to work for $6 an hour with no benefits. . . . They take [such jobs] only when their unemployment insurance benefits run out.

—Job service counselor

Consulting is a distraction from job search. . . . Job search is a demanding, full-time job.

—Outplacement counselor

Clients do offer to work part-time or temporarily. This is a compromise. It allows both sides to test one another and it fills in a resume. Sometimes, clients are well liked and stay on. They get to do something too. Some people make a career of it and love it. It does distract from job search. If you work, you can't spend ten hours a day networking.

—Outplacement counselor

Six advisers of the unemployed thought low-paying jobs would be interpreted negatively by potential employers, and two had the opposite view.

Holding a low-paying job would indeed be a stigma.

—Outplacement counselor

Potential employers may question stopgap jobs. But they question unemployment too.

—Job service counselor

If you worked at [a well-known fast-food chain] for survival, [potential employers] would understand. They might even look on it favorably.

—Outplacement counselor

This evidence is in conflict with that from employers denying a stigma in stopgap jobs (section 15.4). I believe that counselors' views may have been influenced by the desire to find arguments to dissuade clients from taking stopgap jobs.

Counselors' warnings may seem to contradict the evidence mentioned in sections 15.3 and 18.12 that being unemployed is a disadvantage in a job search. However, stopgap jobs probably do not remove the stigma of having been laid off and do not provide the business contacts and prestige that may give an advantage in a job search to people holding permanent jobs.

18.8 Could Sufficiently Energetic and Flexible Job Hunters Find Work Quickly?

I asked whether people could find work quickly if they were sufficiently flexible and energetic in their job search. The answer was usually an emphatic "no." Respondents claimed that the general shortage of jobs and the overqualification problem made finding a job of any type a long, difficult process, though some job hunters were lucky. The shortage of jobs relative to the number of job seekers preoccupied advisers of the unemployed. They said that only in certain fields, such as nursing and physical therapy, was it possible to find work easily.

INTERVIEW EVIDENCE

The question of whether work could be found quickly was answered by 15 advisers of the unemployed and 3 headhunters. All but one of these 18 said it normally took a long time to find work, even if job searchers were energetic and completely flexible. The exception spoke of graduates from a training program she ran. The other 17 respondents mentioned overqualification and the general shortage of jobs as the chief barriers to finding work. Because of the job shortage, it took time to find even unskilled positions, such as cleaning buildings or hotel rooms, clerking in a store, or unskilled contract labor. Ten informants made it clear, however, that such jobs were easier to find than better ones.

> Even if people are flexible about pay, they don't get work immediately. There are too many job applicants, and their skills are often too specialized. A person who is flexible may take two to three months to find work. Someone who is inflexible may take six months or more. [This counselor worked almost exclusively with blue-collar workers.]
>
> —Job service counselor

> Flexibility does not guarantee you will get a job right away. If you are laid off, the chances are that your skills have been affected by the economy, so that there is no demand for them. Tool-and-die makers are in demand and are not laid off either. . . . Once people are realistic, it still takes time to get a job. Many people are unemployed for over a year through no fault of their own.
>
> —Job service counselor

> Being able to work for $5 to $8 an hour wouldn't guarantee anything, for so many are looking for similar jobs.
>
> —Job service counselor

> If you are willing to take $7 an hour, you can't necessarily get a job right away. A former middle manager wouldn't have much chance. He'd be asked, "Why are you willing to do that?" They would be afraid he'd leave if something came up. There is lots of competition for jobs. Eight hundred showed up when [a large retailer] was hiring for a new store.
>
> —Support group leader

> No, [people cannot find work right away if they search energetically and are willing to accept low enough pay]. There is the problem of overqualification, and the jobs aren't there. Even [a large fast-food chain] doesn't want you, for they want kids.
>
> —Outplacement counselor

The job shortage was a concern in every interview with advisers of the unemployed.

> The biggest obstacle [to finding work] is the dearth of jobs in comparison with the number of people looking for them. There are more applicants for fewer positions.
>
> —Outplacement counselor

> The obstacles to job hunting are that there are so many alternate ways for employers to meet their needs. They can use temporaries, even as executives. . . . An employer can also simply make existing employees work harder, for where can they go?
>
> —Outplacement counselor

The weakness of the labor market came out clearly in interviews with head-hunters.

> We used to do a brisk business in office service people. But now if you put an ad in the paper, you get 200 secretaries, so companies have no use for a service for getting them.
> —Headhunter specializing in physical therapists, engineers, and information system specialists

> Since 1987, a lot of companies in my business have dropped out. There is a lot of free meat out there, and employers don't need agents. In 1986, they got no resumes for openings for which they get 60 or 70 now. I survive because companies come to me for specific skills.
> —Headhunter specializing in computer programmers

> The job market is now perceived as a buyers' market, so that it is not necessary to do any risky hiring. If you show a client four people, they say "show me four more," and then four more again.
> —Headhunter specializing in human resource officers

> We are seeing more unemployed people than three or four years ago. . . . When we run an ad in the paper for a management or a sales job, we get 300 or 400 responses as opposed to 20 or 30 four years ago.
> —Headhunter specializing in international placement

18.9 How Flexible Were the Unemployed?

Job hunters varied greatly in flexibility. Some were realistic from the moment they became unemployed, whereas others insisted on jobs as good as their old ones. Although a lack of realism was common just after layoff, most people became very flexible after prolonged unemployment. Estimates varied widely as to how long it took for attitudes to change. Some respondents said almost immediately and others spoke of a year. Though some unemployed people were not realistic, inflexibility was not responsible for unemployment. As was said in the previous section, advisers of the unemployed insisted that many job hunters could not find work quickly no matter how flexible and energetic they were.

A related question is the willingness of the unemployed to relocate. The little information I obtained on this matter indicates that few jobless, other than professional and managerial workers, moved to take new jobs.

INTERVIEW EVIDENCE

Thirty-one observers of the unemployed discussed the degree to which unemployed job seekers were flexible about their demands for pay and type of work.

Eighteen said that most unemployed people were quite inflexible initially after layoff, but became more so as they learned about the poor state of the job market and ran out of money. Another 13, including all 7 outplacement counselors, claimed that job hunters were as flexible as they should be, and the outplacement counselors asserted that the training they gave clients made them realistic.

> Often a lack of realism gets in the way of getting a job. But people become more realistic very quickly. It used to be that no one would take less than what they'd earned before. Now people tend to say, "I'll take anything I can get," especially if the job is a supplementary income. There are others who still want their old pay. They think at first that you are putting them down if you say they should accept less.
>
> —Job service counselor

> Most people tend to stay in their general occupational area. People look for what they know. When they see what they must do to change vocations, they lose interest. Going to school just increases their bills.
>
> —Job service counselor

> There is sometimes an immediate reluctance to accept lower wages. Others say, "I'll do what I have to do." This second group is now bigger than the first and bigger than it used to be. The newly unemployed are now more open because they are being dumped on the labor market after lots of other people have been. They know lots of jobs have been taken. Also, they have been getting feedback from others who have been laid off that the labor market is difficult and that new jobs pay less than their old ones did. Blue-collar people are pretty sophisticated.
>
> —Job service counselor

> Members [of the support group] are willing to take a pay cut just to go to work. Nevertheless, there is some stubbornness about pay. They do not look at jobs they feel are beneath them—as in fast-food restaurants. Usually, they cannot afford to, for the pay is less than [unemployment] benefits. Underlying all excuses is the idea "I'm an X. I won't work at that." Men identify with their jobs so closely that it is hard for them to imagine not doing the same thing again. How flexible can you be about pay when you have a mortgage and car payments?
>
> —Support group leader

Outplacement counselors had more optimistic views about the realism of their clients.

> Unrealistic pay expectations are not an obstacle to finding a job. We have reality checks. Candidates are told what it is realistic to expect.
>
> —Outplacement counselor

I do not need to make a big effort to get people to have realistic pay expectations. Rather, people often imagine they can get a job by going for lower positions and pay. That strategy does not work—or helps little [because of the overqualification problem].

—Outplacement counselor

There were some tales of stubbornness, most referring to people who had been overpaid on previous jobs.

[Two unionized manufacturing companies] closed in 1988–89. Each worker got about $20,000 in severance pay. They thought someone would come and hire them back at their old pay. They tended to do handyman work and off the record, underground stuff. As a result, it took them a long time to get back into the labor market. After a training program, they wouldn't take a job, for the pay was too low compared with the $20 an hour they had before.

—Job service counselor

It is tough to devalue yourself by considering lower-paying jobs. You see the rest of the world going on. Others are getting higher pay. The moment when you come out of school is the only time in your life that you are really in a job market situation. Job offers come simultaneously. Later in life, the leads you get never come in synch. You have one unsatisfactory offer in hand and a better one is only a possibility. Your hope for a better job keeps you going and looking for better opportunities. You don't want to devalue yourself. It is hard to give up the career-building mode. Maybe you are just on a temporary plateau. Stepping off that plateau can be an ego hit.

—Support group member who had been the director of marketing of a medium-sized corporation

Sometimes people were overpaid in their jobs because automatic annual increases had boosted their pay over a long period of service. It is hard for them to face that they were overpaid. Usually, they don't believe their counselor and have to learn it for themselves.

—Outplacement counselor

Since the recession was worse in the Northeast than in some other parts of the country, people might have been able to improve their chances of finding work by moving to another state. It was hard to get information about this matter. The subject was discussed in 19 of the 41 interviews with observers of the unemployed. They spoke of immobility, except among professionals. Outplacement counselors saw mostly upper-income clients and gave high estimates of the numbers finding work out of state, the estimates being one third in one case and one tenth in two others. The other respondents said they knew of little emigration, probably because they dealt with middle- to low-income workers.

> My clients are average middle-class people. They are not like professionals. It is hard for them to go out of state. They have family responsibilities or grown-up children in the area with grandchildren. A few do pick up and leave without a job, but that is scary.
>
> —Support group leader

These reports almost surely give a biased view of the of the amount of migration, since it is unlikely that someone who wanted to move would go to a local job service or support group. Outplacement counselors, however, saw even those who wished to move, since clients were sent to them by former employers.

It makes sense that professionals should be mobile, since their business contacts probably reach farther than those of other people. The geographic scope of labor markets increases with job level (section 7.2).

18.10 How Hard Did the Unemployed Search?

Most unemployed people wanted work badly and hunted hard for it, though not as hard as job search counselors would have liked. Search efforts were sometimes impaired, at first by shock and inexperience and later by discouragement.

INTERVIEW EVIDENCE

The energy with which the jobless looked for work was discussed in 21 of 26 interviews with advisers of the unemployed. All 11 of the support group leaders and outplacement counselors who commented on the subject asserted that their clients hunted industriously, though one spoke also of the difficulty of maintaining effort after repeated disappointments. This latter problem was more on the minds of job service counselors. Five of them spoke of discouraged job seekers, while 4 asserted that the unemployed searched hard, and 2 said laxness was common.

> The lack of search effort can be a problem. After a while, people suffer from rejection shock. More secure people can take it. Others become afraid to go out and search for fear they will be rejected. They rationalize by saying, "Nothing is there, they're not going to hire me." This reinforces their negative self-image.
>
> —Job service counselor

> People look hard for work, after an initial period during which they are shocked. As living standards go down, people become more highly motivated. . . . After a year out of work, people have to go on general assistance or go back to mom and

dad. A lot of people don't like to do either of these things. Some give up. It is hard to motivate yourself on and on and on. At the end, some accept nothingness.

—Job service counselor

People generally look hard for work. But blue-collar people tend to concentrate on the published job market. I urge them to network—to approach anyone they know. But writing up a resume and asking around are new to them. They are used to getting in a car and driving around looking for signs. Now, companies aren't advertising jobs. . . . [Blue-collar workers] are ashamed of networking, because that involves admitting they're out of work.

—Job service counselor

Ninety-five percent of the clients are dying to work. They are not malingering. . . . Some will be energetic about it for five weeks, get no interviews and give up.

—Job service counselor

[The group members] looked hard for work. They were highly motivated. They spent 40 hours a week job hunting.

—Support group leader

One obstacle [to success in job hunting] is the emotional roller coaster of job search. It is hard to sell yourself and rejection is hard to take. . . . Clients do seek work actively, unless they have an illness or personal problems, such as marital ones. . . . Job search is exhausting. It requires an effort all day every day.

—Outplacement counselor

18.11 The Effect of Financial Resources on Job Search

The search effort and flexibility of some of the jobless diminished as financial security increased. They relaxed when protected by unemployment benefits and severance benefits and became energized as poverty threatened. However, nothing was said that indicated a general tendency to become interested in work only when financial resources dwindled.

INTERVIEW EVIDENCE

I do not believe I ever asked about the effects of financial security on job search, for I judged the topic to be only tangentially related to the central issue of downward wage rigidity. Financial protection does cause some people to withhold labor, and 13 advisers of the unemployed brought this matter up on their own. Some said that financial well-being discouraged job hunting, that job searchers refused to take jobs earning less than their unemployment benefits and panicked and searched harder as benefits ran out.

When the job market was better, people tended more to wait for the end of their [unemployment] benefits. Now, the care-free ones who live on benefits are the young living with their parents. Few are discouraged from job search by benefits. Some are ashamed to take them. . . . Some panic after 19 weeks of unemployment, because there is a 26-week limit. They don't know about the extension [of benefits]. The panic from 19 to 26 weeks makes people more effective. They are spurred on by fear.

—Job service counselor

Clients do seek work actively. The exceptions tend to be those who have received extensive severance packages and simply take a vacation for a year.

—Outplacement counselor

A few thought unemployment benefits had no effect on job search.

No one views unemployment as a vacation. They know benefits will end.

—Job service counselor

18.12 Was Being Unemployed a Disadvantage in Job Search?

Comments of advisers of the unemployed confirmed what employers said about the stigma of unemployment; it existed but was weakened by the recession (section 15.3).

INTERVIEW EVIDENCE

Twenty-seven observers of the unemployed discussed the effect of unemployment on job search, and 18 of these said that unemployment was a disadvantage and 9 said it was not. There was a division of opinion between headhunters and the others. All but 1 of the 15 headhunters interviewed said that unemployment was a disadvantage, and most expressed this view in strong terms. Among the 12 other informants who dealt with the subject, only 4 said that unemployment was a hindrance in job search. This divergence of views is probably due to the fact that headhunters perform a service different from that of counselors and support group leaders. Headhunters make money as brokers and find the unemployed a nuisance.

Most of the people I place are employed. I don't like working with the unemployed. The perception is that there is something wrong with someone who has been laid off. If a guy is laid off, I compete with him and other agencies to find him a job. I don't want the competition. I find people for companies, not companies for people. I'd go broke quickly doing that.

—Headhunter specializing in computer programmers

Advisers of the unemployed wish to persuade clients to see their situation in a positive way.

> Long-term unemployment is not a stigma, but this stigma is on the client's mind. This is especially true of white-collar people. We try to reassure them that their situation is not unusual and is not a problem for finding work.
>
> —Job service counselor

The views of observers of the unemployed on the stigma of unemployment were similar to those of employers; unemployment carries a stigma because of the belief that companies lay off their least useful employees first, long-term unemployment looks especially bad, and yet the recession was erasing the stigma.

> There is a stigma to being unemployed. The consequence of that depends on the way people interview. People want to get back as quickly as possible. After a while, they begin to slip and to blame themselves. . . . When they slip, some of their self-worth declines. This limits their interviewing skills. They look like victims.
>
> —Job service counselor

> It is easier to place an employed person because of the stigma of being unemployed. It is easier if the unemployed person can say that his whole department was shut down or that the company left town. But if companies let go just a part of a department, they don't let their best people go, and everyone knows that.
>
> —Headhunter specializing in computer programmers

> Being unemployed is too common to be a stigma these days. Many managers doing the hiring were themselves out of work or know someone who was.
>
> —Outplacement counselor

18.13 The Job-Hunting Experience of the Unemployed

Advisers of the unemployed asserted that a substantial fraction of the jobless suffered long spells of unemployment, even if they searched hard and intelligently for work. Although the impressions of advisers were surely biased, it was probably true that many people were unemployed for a long time. Statistical studies confirm that a significant proportion of unemployment durations are long and that their average length increases during recessions, though many people find work quickly (appendix to this chapter).

Statements by some advisers of the unemployed indicated that it may have been easier to find work in the secondary than the primary sector, for respondents who listed expected search times by type of job gave the shortest times for secondary-sector jobs.

Some advisers of the unemployed asserted that unemployment duration increased with income on the previous job, though others disagreed. An oft-cited rule of thumb was one month of search per $10,000 in annual income. Those who mentioned this rule, which is probably not correct, seemed to have in mind professionals. Studies of unemployment durations do not confirm the rule, though none uses data applying exclusively to middle- and upper-income people (appendix to this chapter).

INTERVIEW EVIDENCE

I asked 27 observers of the unemployed how long it would take an energetic and flexible unemployed person to find work. The times were long, varying from months to more than a year. Outplacement counselors gave especially long estimates, these being in the neighborhood of seven months to a year, and their estimates were not based on whim, for the counselors' companies calculated statistics on the unemployment durations of clients. Informants believed that durations increased with skill and income level,[1] nine asserting that it took much less time to find work in types of business belonging to what I call the secondary sector. Seven respondents mentioned that unemployment durations had increased sharply with the recession.

> People can always get a job in the food industry or in retail, but it might take time. Someone with experience in the women's department of a store could get a job within a month or two. People with experience in the health care industry can get jobs there right away. . . . It is much harder to get higher-paying jobs. There are lots of vice presidents, trust officers, and insurance executives who have been out of work for six months or more.
>
> —Job service counselor

> College graduates take six to seven months to find work. . . . It can take a few days to find a job in retail trade, though employers now want sales experience. . . . There are few jobs for assemblers in factories. . . . Factory work is obtained by word of mouth. It takes forever for such people to get work, but the time depends on your connections. There are not many jobs for machinists around here. It can take a long time to find such a job—months—if you are qualified. . . . It takes ages for someone in middle management to find work. . . . Now, you can get a job right away as a nurse. There are no nurses on unemployment.
>
> —Job service counselor

Estimates of durations by advisers of the unemployed were surely exaggerated, for they were probably not in contact with people who found work quickly, a bias discussed in the economics literature.[2] An additional bias is that the advisers did not count taking a stopgap job as reemployment, while unemployment surveys do so. Despite these biases, the interviews do indicate that an important population took a long time to find work.

18.14 Summary

This chapter contains the impressions of those whom I call observers of the unemployed. Most of the jobless seen by these people had been laid off. Permanent layoff was usually a terrible financial and emotional blow. Until people recovered from this shock, they were apt to entertain unrealistically optimistic expectations about their job prospects. Most got over this denial stage after a few weeks or months, however, and undertook an energetic and realistic job search, which often took many months or even one or two years. Declining living standards added to the pressure to find work. The main barrier to success was the lack of jobs, not job seekers' inflexibility. In fact, negotiations over pay rarely failed. Job seekers could not expect to find work right away by being sufficiently flexible. Excessive flexibility was ill advised, as low-level temporary jobs distracted from the search for good positions, and job seekers who applied for work at too low a level were often rejected as overqualified. The best method of job search was to use personal contacts.

Appendix 18A   Related Literature and Statistical Information

HOW PEOPLE BECAME UNEMPLOYED (SECTION 18.1)

The U.S. Bureau of Labor Statistics has various classifications for the jobless. Those not looking for work are "out of the labor force," whereas those seeking work are "unemployed." Those looking for work for the first time are "new entrants," and "reentrants" are those who have been out of the labor force after having worked and have started looking for work again. Those who quit are "job leavers," and those who were laid off or fired are "job losers." Layoff is "temporary" if the worker is given an approximate date of recall, and "permanent" otherwise.

Advisers of the unemployed may not have seen a representative sample of jobless people, for according to the Bureau of Labor Statistics only about half the unemployed are job losers. In 1993, 55 percent of the unemployed in the United States were job losers, 11 percent were job leavers, 25 percent were reentrants into the labor force, and 10 percent were new entrants.[3] These figures may be misleading, for the distinction between being unemployed and out of the labor force is ambiguous, so that many reentrants may be people classified as out of the labor force in one period and unemployed in the next, though their actual state has not changed.[4] Nevertheless, the statistics do not reflect the clear dominance of layoff victims seen by my informants, though they confirm that job leavers are a small proportion of the jobless.

Statistical data indicate that during recessions, the number of people who quit decreases relative to the number of those laid off. Historically, the total number of layoffs has been strongly positively correlated with the unemployment rate and negatively correlated with quit rates. The positive correlation between layoffs and unemployment can be seen strikingly in Akerlof, Rose, and Yellen (1988, p. 534, fig. 2) and is evident in Figure 18A.1, which shows the national unemployment rate and the number of layoffs in U.S. manufacturing. Similarly, the proportion of U.S. unemployed who quit their previous jobs is negatively correlated with the unemployment rate, and the proportion of U.S. unemployed who are job losers is positively correlated with the unemployment rate. These correlations have been noted by Gilroy (1973), and can be seen in Figures 18A.2 and 18A.3, which show the history of annual averages for the

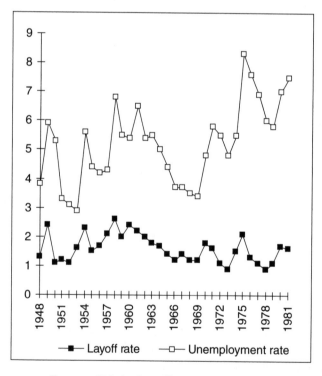

FIGURE 18A.1   Layoff rate in manufacturing

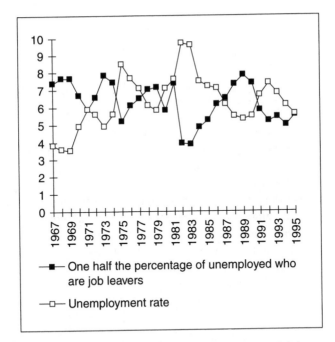

FIGURE 18A.2   Percentage of unemployed who are job leavers

national unemployment rate and, respectively, the proportions of unemployed who are job leavers and job losers.[5] The total number of jobless who are job leavers is not correlated with the unemployment rate, whereas the total number of job losers moves in tandem with it, as may be seen in Figures 18A.4 and 18A.5, respectively. The proportions of the unemployed who are reentrants and new entrants into the labor force are negatively correlated with the unemployment rate, as may be seen in Figures 18A.6 and 18A.7, respectively.[6] All these correlations indicate that layoff is one of the primary forces driving up unemployment during recessions. I have found no information on the number of people who quit because of pay cuts.

It would be interesting to have data on the number of people who quit and become unemployed rather than immediately taking a new job. The Lucas-Rapping theory implies that this number increases during recessions. Though no U.S. data exist on this variable, other data indicate that quits into unemployment probably decline during recessions. The total number of unemployed job leavers is hardly influenced by the unemployment rate (Figure 18A.4) and average unemployment durations increase sharply during recessions (Figure

18A.18). Since the number of unemployed job leavers is roughly equal to the average duration of unemployment for these people times the inflow of newly unemployed people who quit, it is likely that recessions decrease the inflow of newly unemployed quitters.

There is no statistical support in U.S. national data for statements that an unusually large fraction of unemployed were laid off permanently during the recession. Figure 18A.8 shows the history for the United States of the fraction of unemployed on temporary layoff together with the unemployment rate. It may be seen that this fraction was not unusually low during the recession of the early 1990s, nor was it declining sharply.

Nor is there statistical support for the idea that this was the first middle-class recession. Appropriate data do not exist. Figure 18A.9 shows the history of the unemployment rate among managerial and professional workers together with the U.S. unemployment rate, with the first rate multiplied by three so as to show how closely the two rates move together. It may be seen that during the recession of the early 1990s, unemployment among managers and professionals only slightly exceeded its normal relation with the national rate. The proportion

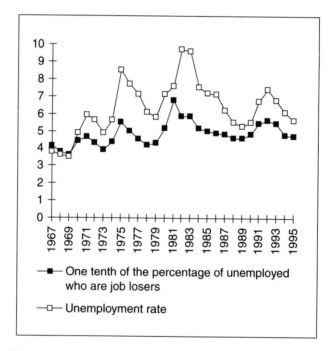

FIGURE 18A.3   Percentage of unemployed who are job losers

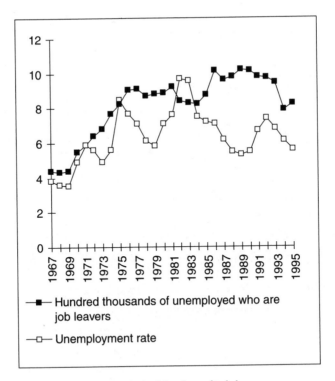

FIGURE 18A.4   Number of job leavers

of the unemployed who had been managers and professionals has increased steadily in the decade ending in the recession, from 7.4 percent in 1983 to 11.2 percent in 1992. However, about one third of this growth was accounted for by the increase in the fraction of working people who were managers and professionals, this fraction growing from 23.4 percent in 1983 to 27 percent in 1993. The history of these fractions may be compared in Figure 18A.10. Farber (1997a) has found that the rates of job loss among the well-educated have increased in recent years, though this rate remains less than that of less-educated workers.

REACTIONS TO JOB LOSS (SECTION 18.2)

I have found little published material on the initial psychological impact of job loss. Hamermesh (1987) finds indirect evidence that layoff comes as a surprise. The reactions described by advisers of the unemployment are consistent with Harrison's (1976) "wave model," according to which the unemployed experi-

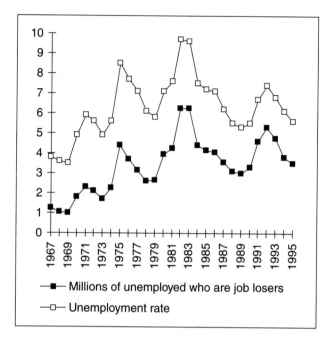

FIGURE 18A.5   Number of job losers

ence paralyzing shock immediately after layoff, followed by increasing optimism and more energetic job search, followed in turn by increasing pessimism
if the search is unsuccessful.[7] This model summarizes the findings of psychologists and sociologists.

A great deal has been written on the impact of long-term unemployment,
and these works give a dismal picture, worse than that gathered from my interviews. Some detailed studies were done during the Great Depression (Bakke,
1933, 1940a, 1940b; Jahoda, Lazarsfeld, and Zeisel, 1971). Since World War II,
a number of surveys of the unemployed were made by sociologists and economists, particularly in Britain. Many of these are reviewed in Sinfield (1981) and
White (1991). Particularly thorough surveys are Daniel (1974, 1990), and Daniel and Stilgoe (1977). Recent U.S. surveys are Leana and Feldman (1990, 1992,
1995). The findings of the latter are close to what I found.

There is a large medical literature on the effects of unemployment on health.
O'Brien (1986) reviews the literature on psychological effects and concludes
that unemployment causes mental distress, but provokes mental illness only in
people already vulnerable. Wilson and Walker (1993) review the literature on

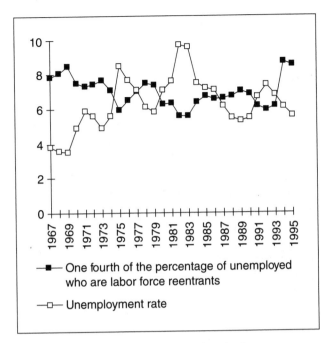

FIGURE 18A.6   Percentage of unemployed who are reentrants

the consequences for physical health and conclude that the effects are adverse. Recent surveys of mental states also indicate that unemployment causes mental distress and unhappiness (Clark and Oswald, 1994; Blanchflower, Oswald, and Warr, 1993; Blanchflower, 1995; and Winkelmann and Winkelmann, 1995). Juster (1985) found in a survey of ordinary people that they prefer work to the activities associated with leisure.

STATISTICAL EVIDENCE

The Lucas-Rapping theory of unemployment and wage rigidity supposes that those who become unemployed choose to do so because their pay falls or is below expectations. It has been established that most of the increase in unemployment during a recession is a consequence of layoffs (section 18.1 of this appendix). Therefore, the Lucas-Rapping theory describes recessions only if those who are laid off would choose to quit even if they were not laid off. Because employers seldom cut pay or offer workers a choice between a pay cut and layoff (section 13.7), it follows that if the theory applies, unemployed workers prefer being jobless to working at the pay they were receiving on their job.

It is conceivable that this theory might apply to people who are marginally attached to the labor force, such as some housewives, teenagers, or people near retirement age. However, even if the theory does apply to these people, fluctuations in their unemployment do not explain cyclical variation in the aggregate unemployment rate. On the contrary, a crude look at government statistics shows that the unemployment of these groups is less sensitive to business fluctuations than that of average workers. Figures 18A.11–18A.13 show the histories of the U.S. unemployment rate and the percentage of U.S. unemployed who are, respectively, teenagers, married women, or at least 65 years old.[8] It may be seen that, if anything, these percentages move in the direction opposite to that of the unemployment rate, so that fluctuations in unemployment could hardly be driven by job loss for people in these categories. The appearance of a negative relation between the percentages and the unemployment rate is confirmed by regression analysis. An opposite impression is obtained from the plot in Figure 18A.14 of the unemployment rate and the percentage of unemployed who are married men. This proportion moves in the same direction as the unemployment rate, showing that employment of these people, many of whom

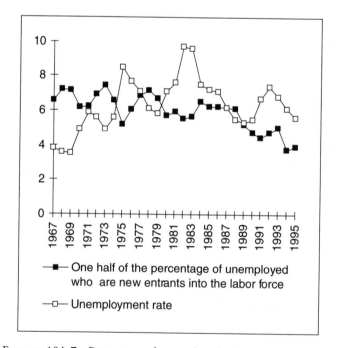

FIGURE 18A.7   Percentage of unemployed who are new entrants

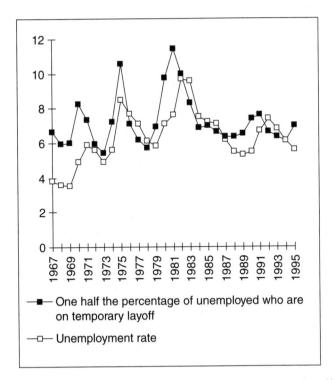

FIGURE 18A.8   Percentage of unemployed on temporary layoff

probably badly need their jobs, is more sensitive than average to business fluc-tuations, a pattern again confirmed by regression analysis. For all categories of people, total employment moves in sympathy with the unemployment rate, so that business fluctuations affect all groups. This point is illustrated by Figures 18A.15 and 18A.16 for teenagers and married men, respectively. It is the un-employment of married men, however, that fluctuates most.

CHANGES IN LIVING STANDARDS WHEN UNEMPLOYED (SECTION 18.3)

Published work on living standards during unemployment shows that they de-cline, especially if unemployment lasts more than a few months (Burgess and Kingston, 1981; Dynarski and Sheffrin, 1987a; Heady and Smyth, 1989; Coch-rane, 1991; Hajivassiliou and Ioannides, 1995; and Gruber, 1997). There is also evidence that the greater the financial resources of a household, the smaller is the decline in living standards (Burgess and Kingston, 1981; Heady and Smyth, 1989, table 8.7; and Gruber, 1994). Various studies note that the jobless reduce expenditures on leisure activities, such as traveling, restaurant meals, theater tickets, and having friends over for meals (Wilcock and Franke, 1963, fig. 10; Daniel, 1974, table V9; Marjory Clark, 1978; Burgess and Kingston, 1981; and Heady and Smith, 1989, table 8.3). These observations are evidence against the intertemporal substitution theory of unemployment of Lucas and Rapping (1969), which asserts that people choose to become unemployed in order to enjoy the consumption of leisure. Heady and Smyth (1989) find that living standards rebound after reemployment, which indicates that the decline in living standards during unemployment is due not just to the expectation that future jobs will be lower paying, but to the loss of income during unemployment. Studies of the long-term unemployed emphasize their poverty (Jahoda, Lazarsfeld, and Zeisel, 1971, chaps. 3 and 4; Bakke, 1933, 1940a, b; and Daniel, 1974). Sinfield (1981) and White (1991) review British studies made since 1945. Daniel (1990, fig. 5.4) presents evidence that the unemployed are dissatisfied with their incomes. In summary, the published information supports

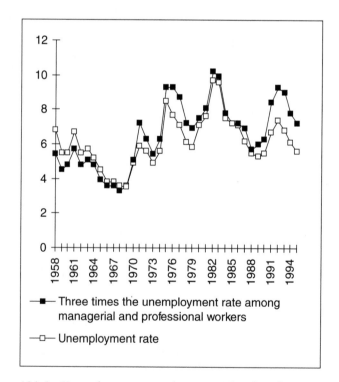

FIGURE 18A.9 Unemployment rate of managerial and professional workers

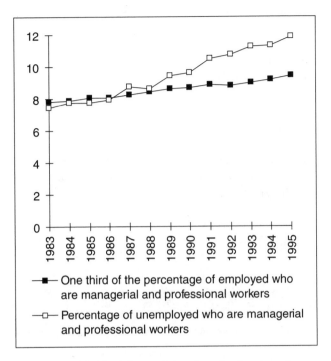

FIGURE 18A.10   Managerial and professional workers

the conclusion that unemployment is a financial setback, which many or most people would be unlikely to choose voluntarily, as it leaves them dissatisfied and interferes with the enjoyment of life.

JOB SEARCH METHODS (SECTION 18.4)

A great deal has been published about job search methods. The U.S. Bureau of Labor Statistics publishes in *Employment and Earnings* survey data on job search methods used by job hunters. Of more interest are data on the relative numbers of jobs found by different methods. Many researchers have collected such data, which show that the main methods by which people learn about the jobs they actually take are asking friends and relatives and approaching firms directly, without prior knowledge of a job opening. People learn about relatively few jobs from newspapers and other forms of advertising. This information supports the importance attached to networking by advisers of the unemployed. Table 18A.1 lists the results of relevant statistical studies. When authors give percentages for various samples, I give the range of the percentages.

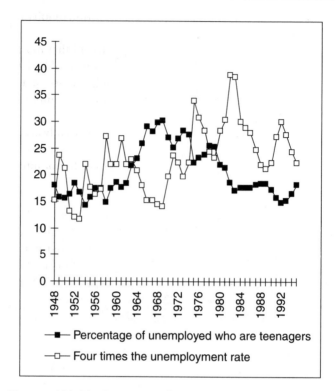

FIGURE 18A.11   Percentage of unemployed who are teenagers

The published studies on the relative efficiency of job search methods supports the conclusion that networking and direct application are somewhat more effective than answering advertisements (Bakke, 1933, pp. 127–140; Corcoran, Datcher, and Duncan, 1980b; Rees, 1966; Rees and Shultz, 1970, table 8; Reid, 1972, table 8; Daniel, 1974, p. 73; Granovetter, 1974, tables 1 and 3; Rosenfeld, 1975, table 1; Stevens, 1978, tables 2 and 3; Blau and Robins, 1990; and Wial, 1991). Informal methods also give a better match between worker and employer, for people are less likely to quit jobs found in this way (Datcher, 1983).

PAY NEGOTIATIONS (SECTION 18.5)

I found no statistics on the success rate of pay negotiations. However, scattered in various labor market studies is evidence that the unemployed accept a large majority of job offers, which is indirect evidence that pay negotiations usually do not fail. Table 18A.2 gives statistics on the proportion of job offers accepted by various samples of jobless workers.

In an interview survey of workers, Wial (1991) found that most workers accepted the first primary-sector job offer received, and Reynolds (1951, pp. 108–109) found that unemployed workers typically took the first suitable job they found. Table 18A.3 gives statistics on the proportion of unemployed in various samples who had rejected jobs during job search.

Although these tables show that unemployed people usually accept job offers, it would not be correct to conclude that they take the first job they find, for job hunters may simply not pursue leads on jobs that do not interest them.

HOW MUCH FLEXIBILITY WAS ADVISABLE? (SECTION 18.6)

Statistical studies use reservation wages as an indicator of pay flexibility, these being the minimum wages that job hunters say they would accept. Surveys usually show that lower reservation wages are associated with shorter job search time, though the relation is weak, and some authors find no relation at all (Sheppard and Belitsky, 1966, pp. 71–73; Kaspar, 1967; Sandell, 1980b;

FIGURE 18A.12   Percentage of unemployed who are married women

Warner, Poindexter, and Fearn, 1980; Moylan, Millar and Davies, 1984; Lancaster, 1985; Holzer, 1986; Jones, 1988; and White and McRae, 1989). I know of nothing published on the overqualification problem from the job searcher's point of view, though there are a few references, cited in Appendix 15A, section 15.2, on the issue as seen by employers.

It might be thought that because the overqualification problem applies more to managerial and professional people than to others, unemployment among professionals should exceed that among the general population or should fluctuate more. This argument is not valid, for overqualification does not hinder reemployment at pay rates that are not too far below previous pay. Unemployment rates are lower among professionals than among the general population, though the duration of their unemployment is longer. Table 18A.4 makes the comparisons for the United States. Figure 18A.9 shows that the unemployment rate among managerial and professional workers remains roughly one third the

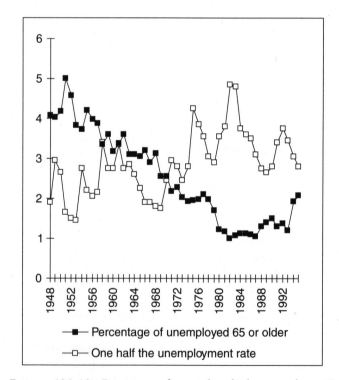

FIGURE 18A.13   Percentage of unemployed who are at least 65

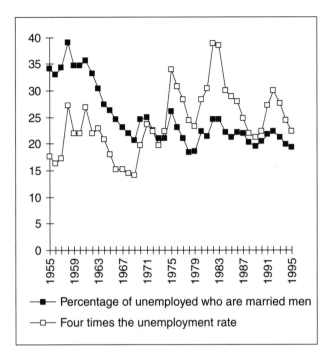

FIGURE 18A.14   Percentage of unemployed who are married men

national rate over the course of the business cycle, so that cyclic unemployment affects them about as much as it does the general population.

STOPGAP JOBS (SECTION 18.7)

It is hard to know how common stopgap work is. I have found no data or studies on the subject pertaining to the United States, though there are several British studies. These suggest that many unemployed people do take stopgap work. Businesspeople's fears about overqualification may reflect the fact that it is common for people to take unsatisfactory jobs with the intention of quitting as soon as something better is found.

British studies show that a significant proportion (from 20 to 70 percent) of unemployed workers take short-term jobs with the intention of looking for more permanent ones while employed. Compared with people who look for permanent jobs, such "job snatchers"[9] find work faster and receive less pay on their first job after unemployment (H. Kahn, 1964; MacKay, 1972; MacKay

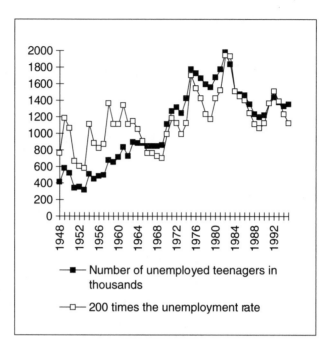

FIGURE 18A.15   Number of unemployed teenagers

and Reid, 1972; and Daniel, 1990). Farber (1997b) has found in data from household surveys that U.S. job losers are significantly more likely than other working people to hold temporary jobs, and that this tendency increases during recessions.

COULD SUFFICIENTLY ENERGETIC AND FLEXIBLE JOB HUNTERS FIND WORK QUICKLY?
(SECTION 18.8)

Data on hiring rates, job vacancy rates, and vacancy durations provide evidence of a shortage of jobs during recessions. Increases in unemployment during recessions are usually accompanied by decreases in vacancies and vacancy durations (Appendix 15A, section 15.1). Rates of hiring decline during recessions, as is illustrated in Figure 18A.17, which plots the history of the U.S. unemployment rate and the number of hires per 100 employees in U.S. manufacturing from 1952 to 1981. Hiring rates in Britain behave in a similar way (Burgess and Nickell, 1990).

I know of no statistics on the relative ease of finding jobs in the primary and secondary sectors. However, Wial (1991) found in interviewing workers that they believed that secondary-sector positions were much easier to obtain.

Published studies of pay flexibility are analyses of data on reservation wages and job acceptance behavior. These works show that reservation wages equal, on the average, what was earned on previous jobs and approximately equal what people can expect to earn on jobs for which they qualified. There is a considerable amount of dispersion about the averages, with many people asking for more pay than they earned previously, a demand that would be sensible if the former jobs were low-paying stopgap jobs (Sheppard and Belitsky, 1966; Kaspar, 1967; Perella, 1971; Barnes, 1975; Stephenson, 1976; Warner, Poindexter, and Fearn, 1980; Moylan, Millar, and Davies, 1984; White and McRae, 1989; Feldstein and Poterba, 1984; Jones, 1989a; Daniel, 1990; and Bryson

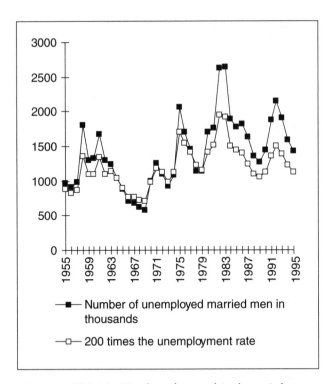

FIGURE 18A.16   Number of unemployed married men

TABLE 18A.1   Percentage of jobs or job offers obtained using method listed

Source	Friends/ relatives	Direct application	Newspaper
De Schweinitz (1932), table 15	58	22	3
Bakke, Clague, and Cooper (1934), table 29	36	45	3
Kerr (1942), table 15	35–50	—	19–37
Myers and MacLaurin (1943), table 7	39	33	2
Reynolds (1951), table 16	28	30	9
Myers and Shultz (1951), pp. 21–22 and table 9	36–41	14–21	0–11
Wilcock and Franke (1963), figure 14	30–50	20–40	—
Hilda Kahn (1964), table 26	19	32	12
Wedderburn (1965), table 5.15	46	24	13
Lurie and Rayack (1966), table III	34	50	3
Sheppard and Belitsky (1966), table 4-11	56	14	4
Rees and Shultz (1970), table 13.1	24–40	2–8	1–20
MacKay et al. (1971), p. 357	20–46	28–41	5–17
Reid (1972), table 9	32–35	—	18–25
Daniel (1974), table VII.5	25	21	14
Granovetter (1974), p. 11	56	19	10
Rosenfeld (1975), table 1	26	53	13
Stevens (1978), table 2	37	15	15
Corcoran, Datcher, and Duncan (1980a)	18–78	—	—
White (1983, table VII.6	41	9	12
Moylan, Millar, and Davies (1984), table 4.4	31	20	30
Holzer (1987b), table 1	38	32	6
White and McRae (1989), table 6.5	50	18	12
Daniel (1990), table A4.5	27	26	11

and Jacobs, 1992). There is also evidence that job hunters become more flexible as the urgency or difficulty of obtaining work increases. Reservation wages decline slowly during the course of unemployment and increase with the probability of receiving a job offer (Bakke, 1940a; Reynolds, 1951, pp. 109–10; Kaspar, 1967; Barnes, 1975; Stephenson, 1976; Crosslin and Stevens, 1977; Sant, 1977; Sandell, 1980a; Lynch, 1983; Feldstein and Poterba, 1984; Jones, 1989c; Lancaster and Cheshire, 1983; and Devine and Kiefer, 1991, chap. 4). Also, the proportion of job offers which are accepted increases with the unemployment rate (Blau and Robins, 1990, table 4; Jones, 1989a, table 8).

TABLE 18A.2   Acceptance rates for job offers

Source	Percentage of job offers accepted
Stephenson (1976), p. 110	90
Stevens (1978), table 3	79
Yoon (1981), p. 607[a]	91
Holzer (1987a), table 2	40
Blau and Robins (1990), table 3	66
Berg (1990), table 3	97

a. Yoon's figure is an estimate obtained by indirect econometric methods.

TABLE 18A.3   Proportion of workers who had rejected job offers

Source	Percentage of workers
Wilcock and Franke (1963), p. 115	14
Sheppard and Belitsky (1966), p. 73	14
Daniel (1974), pp. 125–126	50
Rosenfeld (1977a), p. 41	10
Lynch (1983), p. 280	15
White (1983), table IX.5	12
Jones (1989a), p. 289	15
Daniel (1990)	10

TABLE 18A.4   U.S. unemployed rates and durations among professionals and all workers

Year	Percentage unemployed		Average weeks unemployed	
	Professional and managerial workers	Entire labor force	Professional and managerial workers	Entire labor force
1988	1.9	5.5	14.4	13.5
1989	2.0	5.3	13.5	11.9
1990	2.1	5.5	14.1	12.1
1991	2.8	6.7	16.3	13.8
1992	3.1	7.4	22.4	17.9
1993	3.0	6.8	22.4	18.1

Source: Bureau of Labor Statistics.

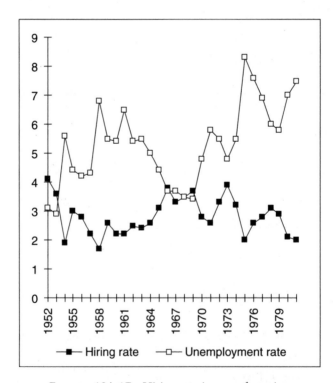

FIGURE 18A.17   Hiring rate in manufacturing

Finally, many people who are laid off accept lower pay on new jobs than they earned before, especially if they were employed a long time on the previous job or if they switch industries (Reynolds, 1951, p. 215; Cooke, 1979; Blau and Kahn, 1981; Bartel and Borjas, 1981; Chowdhury and Nickell, 1985; Mincer, 1986; Podgursky and Swaim, 1987b; Ruhm, 1987 and 1991; Topel, 1990; Daniel, 1990; Kletzer, 1991; Ong and Mar, 1992; Jacobson, LaLonde, and Sullivan, 1993; Neal, 1995; and Farber, 1997a, b). Two explanations of the impact of tenure on the old job are that people who stay a long time at one firm lack social contacts outside their firm useful for finding a job (Granovetter, 1988) or acquire specific human capital that boosts their pay (Topel, 1990). Feldman (1996) and Farber (1997b) review other recent literature on the subject. Recognizing the cost of switching, workers try to stay within the same industry (Fallick, 1993). The drop in income following layoff contrasts with the increase in income typically enjoyed by people who change jobs voluntarily, even when they are unemployed before finding a new position (Antel, 1991).

Reservation wages reported to surveyors may mean little, for people may adapt quickly as they learn about the realities of the job market. Moylan, Millar, and Davies (1984, chap. 9) discuss the reservation wages of over 2,000 workers in the British survey they analyze. Two thirds of the workers gave as a reservation wage an amount which turned out to be less than the amount they received when reemployed. For a third, the reservation wage was no more than 74 percent of what they received. For a third, the reservation wage was more than what they received, and for half of these people, the reservation wage was 25 percent more than what they finally earned. White and McRae (1989, pp. 220–221), in their analysis of a British survey of unemployed youth, also find that many people accept jobs paying much less than their reported reservation wage.

Murphy and Topel (1987b) find that unemployed people in the United States seldom migrate. Some information on emigration from Connecticut is contained in Lawson et al. (1993), who report on a survey of people who had exhausted their unemployment insurance benefits between December 1990 and February 1992. The authors find that one eighth of the exhaustees had left the state, and an additional three eighths were considering doing so. The interest in moving increased with income and education.

There has been a great deal of controversy about the response of migration to regional or international differences in unemployment rates. Some early institutional economists found evidence that mobility reacts too slowly to equilibrate labor markets effectively (Myers and MacLaurin, 1943; Dunlop, 1944, 1957; Lester, 1946a; Palmer, 1954; Parnes, 1954; and Reynolds, 1951). Other studies have found that unemployment influenced migration within the United States (Bunting, 1961–62; Raimon, 1962) and into it (Jerome, 1926; Easterlin,

1961; and Fleischer, 1963). Rosenfeld (1975, table 3) and Daniel (1990, table A6.2) document the reluctance to move of many job hunters, especially low-income workers. Two British studies, Robinson (1951) and Pissarides and McMaster (1990), have found that migration responds slowly to interregional differences in wages and unemployment rates. Two American studies, Topel (1986) and Blanchard and Katz (1992) associate a significant fraction of the change in employment in particular states to interstate migration. However, these studies do not use data on migration, as do the two British studies just referred to, but infer it from labor force data. Oswald (1996b) attributes high unemployment in industrialized countries to the immobilizing effects of home ownership.

HOW HARD DID THE UNEMPLOYED SEARCH? (SECTION 18.10)

Surveys confirm the impressions of informants, though typical unemployed job searchers spend much less time on their job search than the 40 hours a week recommended by counselors. Surveys of hours spent on job search show that it varies widely among individuals and averages from 5 to 8 hours a week (Bakke, 1933, p. 128; Jahoda, Lazarsfeld, and Zeisel, 1971, p. 24; Rosenfeld, 1975, table 3; Bureau of Labor Statistics, 1975, table H-2; Stephenson, 1976, p. 107; Rosenfeld, 1977a, table 3; Young, 1979, table 4; Clark and Summers, 1979, table 9; Holzer, 1987a, table 1; and Jones, 1989a, table 1). Some surveys show that many people give up after prolonged unemployment (Hughes and McCormick, 1989; Jones, 1989a, table 3; and Wadsworth, 1991, table 3a). Daniel (1974, pp. 24–30) is the only survey I know of with estimates of the number of unemployed who seriously want work. Only 12 percent of his sample said they really did not intend to find work; the majority said that finding work was important. Surveys show that the magnitude of search effort may have little impact on its success (MacKay and Reid, 1972, table III; Dyer, 1973, table 1; Barron and Mellow, 1981, tables 1 and 2; Holzer, 1987a; and Jones, 1989a, table 7). This work is hard to evaluate, however, because of the difficulty of interpreting correlations between the two endogenous variables, effort and success, in job search. Indirect evidence that search effort declines with the duration of unemployment is contained in regressions showing that upward pressure on wages for a given level of total unemployment decreases with the proportion of unemployed who have been jobless for a long time (Franz, 1987; Jackman and Layard, 1991).

THE EFFECT OF FINANCIAL RESOURCES ON JOB SEARCH (SECTION 18.11)

A great deal has been written about the effects of financial security, and especially of unemployment insurance benefits, on job search and unemployment duration. This literature provides fairly clear evidence that increased financial security is associated with higher job aspirations and more prolonged unemployment (Bryson and Jacobs, 1992; MacKay and Reid, 1972; Dyer, 1973; Kingston and Burgess, 1975; Marston, 1975; Burgess and Kingston, 1976; Ehrenberg and Oaxaca, 1976; Classen, 1977 and 1979; Feinberg, 1977; Hamermesh, 1977; Nickell, 1979a, b; Lancaster, 1979; Newton and Rosen, 1979; Warner, Poindexter, and Fearn, 1980; Barron and Mellow, 1981; Moffitt and Nicholson, 1982; Clark and Summers, 1982; Lancaster and Cheshire, 1983; Moffitt, 1985; Narendranathan and Nickell, 1985; Katz and Meyer, 1990b; Meyer, 1990; and Groot, 1990). Marston (1975), Ham and Rea (1987), Katz and Meyer (1990a and 1990b), and Meyer (1990) find that the probability of finding work increases near the expiration date of unemployment insurance benefits. Some studies measure the effect of unemployment insurance benefits on reservation wages, and find a small but positive effect (Daniel, 1974; Sandell, 1980a; Lancaster and Cheshire, 1983; Feldstein and Poterba, 1984; Narendranathan and Nickell, 1985; and Berg, 1990). Studies by Daniel (1974), Young (1979), Jones (1989a), and Wadsworth (1991) indicate that unemployment insurance and generous severance benefits may discourage job search effort. Evidence that financial incentives speed job search comes from an experiment in Illinois in which a random sample of unemployment insurance claimants received a $500 bonus for finding work within 11 weeks of filing claims (Woodbury and Spiegelman, 1987).

WAS BEING UNEMPLOYED A DISADVANTAGE IN JOB SEARCH? (SECTION 18.12)

Statistical evidence shows that the unemployed are by no means the only job hunters in the labor market. The unemployed must compete with employed job seekers for work. Rosenfeld (1977b, pp. 59–60), calculates from U.S. survey data collected in the recession year 1976 that in some occupations there were more employed than unemployed job seekers.

Podgursky and Swaim (1987a, table 6) and Gibbons and Katz (1991) produce convincing evidence that layoff is a hindrance to job search. They find that victims of plant closures are unemployed for less time than victims of partial layoffs, for the latter are likely to be suspected of having been among a firm's weakest employees.

There is contradictory evidence as to whether being unemployed is a disadvantage in job search. Kahn and Low (1982) have estimated that the unemployed search for jobs more effectively than the employed. Blau and Robins (1990, tables 2 and 4) calculate from U.S. survey data that employed job seekers make more contacts with employers than do unemployed ones and that the probability of each of their contacts leading to an offer is somewhat higher. Antel (1991) finds that among voluntary job changers, those who suffer a period of unemployment enjoy greater pay increases in going from their old to new jobs. Holzer (1987a, table 4) estimates from a survey of American youth that being unemployed had no effect on the chance of receiving a job offer.

Also contradictory is evidence on the stigma of long-term unemployment. If long-term unemployment is a disadvantage in job search, then the rate at which people find work should decline during unemployment. Several authors have estimated whether reemployed rates do decline, reaching conflicting conclusions (Kiefer and Neumann, 1979; Heckman and Borjas, 1980; Narendranathan, Nickell, and Stern, 1985; Budd, Levine, and Smith, 1988; Groot, 1990; and Jackman and Layard, 1991). The interpretation of exit rates from unemployment is ambiguous, for they could be influenced by the stigma, by slackening search effort, and by flexibility brought on by desperation.

No author has, as far as I know, studied the question of whether the stigmas of layoff or unemployment are stronger in booms than in recessions.

THE JOB-HUNTING EXPERIENCE OF THE UNEMPLOYED (SECTION 18.13)

Many studies show that a substantial fraction of unemployed people take a long time to find work during recessions, while another substantial fraction finds work quickly. The most informative works on the subject are studies of displaced workers, and these inquiries show that during recessions typically at least 40 percent of the workers took more than six months to find work, and more than 10 percent took more than a year (Wilcock and Franke, 1963, fig. 5; Moylan, Millar and Davies, 1984; Podgursky and Swaim, 1987a, table 1; Jones, 1989b, p. 274; and Daniel, 1990, table A8.5).

There is ample evidence that unemployment durations increase with the unemployment rate. One bit is Table 18A.5, showing exhaustion rates for Connecticut, where this rate is the ratio for one month of the number of people whose six-month unemployment benefits expire to the number of first payments

TABLE 18A.5   Connecticut unemployment benefit exhaustion rates

Year	December exhaustion rate
1988	16.7%
1989	21.5%
1990	30.2%
1991	39.9%
1992	38.1%
1993	38.9%

Source: Connecticut Department of Labor.

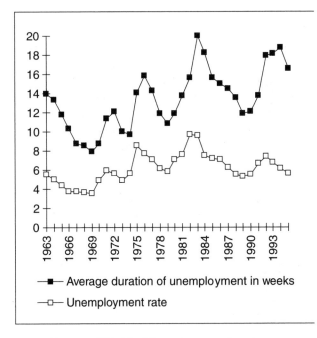

FIGURE 18A.18   Unemployment durations

on initial claims made six months earlier. The table shows that unemployment durations lengthened with the onset of the recession and that during it almost 40 percent of claimants had durations of at least six months. Average unemployment durations are highly correlated with the unemployment rate, as may be seen in Figure 18A.18, which shows the history of the U.S. unemployment rate and the average amount of time that unemployed people were out of work.[10] Various studies show that the unemployment rate and average unemployment durations move together (Moffitt and Nicholson, 1982; Leighton and Mincer, 1982, p. 239; Kooreman and Ridder, 1983, table 2; Narendranathan, Nickell, and Stern, 1985, table 1; Podgursky and Swaim, 1987a, table 2; Dynarski and Sheffrin, 1987b, table 7.7; and Ham and Rea, 1987).

I could find no direct statistical evidence that it is easier to find jobs in the secondary than the primary sector, as some job service counselors asserted. Indirect evidence is contained in studies, cited in section 18.7 of this appendix, showing that people who take stopgap jobs find work faster.

I mentioned earlier that some job counselors and businesspeople believed that the duration of job search increased with income, a belief that applied only to the primary sector. I know of no supporting statistical data. On the contrary, studies of unemployment durations usually show that they are negatively related to income on the previous job (Ehrenberg and Oaxaca, 1976; Holen, 1977, p. 48; Classen, 1977, tables 2 and 3 and 1979, table 10.3; Moffitt, 1985, table 3; Addison and Portugal, 1987, table 3; Podgursky and Swaim, 1987a, table 2; Ham and Rea, 1987, table 3; Katz and Meyer, 1990b, table 2; Meyer, 1990, table VI; Groot, 1990, table 4.1; Gibbons and Katz, 1991, table 6; and Swaim and Podgursky, 1991, table 4). A key problem in the study of the effect of income on unemployment durations is controlling for age, which is positively correlated with both income and duration. Perhaps informants mistook the effect of age for that of income.

19

INFORMATION, WAGE RIGIDITY, AND LABOR NEGOTIATIONS

Economists commonly ascribe inefficiencies to difficulties in conveying or obtaining information, usually about factual matters, such as productivity or profits. It is assumed that people possessing information have an interest in lying, and so are not believed if they do nothing more than communicate verbally or in writing. Instead, they must prove their honesty by taking actions that are in their interest only if what they say is true. It is these actions that create inefficiency. It is argued that information problems must be the source of inefficiencies because people who have the same information find it in their common interest to agree to avoid waste. This argument leads to the conclusion that strikes and wage rigidity are caused by information differences, termed information asymmetries. Both strikes and wage rigidity cause waste, the loss from wage inflexibility being unnecessary layoffs and unemployment.

The interviews made it clear that information asymmetries have little to do with wage rigidity, though they are germane to strikes. Businesspeople said that financial distress is an acceptable justification for a pay cut and that they often do not have great difficulty convincing workers that company financial problems are real. Because most businesspeople had experienced few labor disputes, I discussed these mainly with labor leaders and labor lawyers. According to them the information asymmetries relevant to strikes have to do with subjective matters rather than with the objective financial data assumed to be important in many game-theoretic models of strikes.

19.1 Information and Downward Wage Rigidity

Although low-level workers sometimes refuse to believe that financial setbacks justify low raises or pay cuts, this resistance results more from stubborn rejec-

TABLE 19.1   Employers' statements relating downward pay rigidity to information
(applies to 49 businesses)

Statements	Number of businesses	Percentage of businesses
Employees accept pay restraint if they know the business is in trouble[a]	32	65
Employees do not accept pay restraint if they know the business is in trouble	0	0
Employees understand when the business is in trouble, or can be convinced	28	57
Employees refuse to believe that financial problems justify pay restraint	14	29

a. By "pay restraint," I mean pay cuts or freezes, worksharing, two-tier systems, or reduced raises.

tion of the obvious than from lack of information. The dominant message in what I heard was that a company can reduce raises or even cut pay if it has serious problems.

OVERVIEW OF INTERVIEW EVIDENCE

Three labor leaders and 49 employers discussed information in the context of low raises, pay freezes and cuts, worksharing, and two-tier pay systems. Almost a third of the 49 employers spoke of worker suspicion, but usually the distrust was described in terms that are not consistent with the assumptions of asymmetric information models. Workers, especially unsophisticated ones, refused to face bad news, even when they had adequate information. Distrust could be lessened by developing a reputation for candor. Table 19.1 categorizes employer views about the role of information.

All three labor leaders who discussed the topic said that employees accept pay cuts if necessary and all anticipated no difficulties in convincing members that problems were real.

Bumping provides additional evidence that workers accept pay cuts that save their jobs. Bumping places workers in new jobs paying less than the jobs from which they were laid off, and I was told that most people who bump accept their new assignments (section 13.7).

INFORMANTS' EXPLANATIONS

Nine of the 14 employers who spoke of worker disbelief attributed it to backwardness or recalcitrance mixed with distrust.

Question: Would pay cuts be accepted as a way of getting more business? *Answer:* My men don't want to be burdened with my problems. They don't want to hear about them or think about them.

—Owner of a nonunion electrical contracting business with 6 electricians

Question: Why not cut wages and prices and bid for more business? *Answer:* That would be too hard to explain. It is difficult to communicate with my men. They always think they are being screwed, no matter what. It is like dealing with children, even on safety issues. The foreman is just like the men in this regard.

—Owner of a nonunion roofing company employing 25 people

Sometimes, in order to keep a job, I have to lower the labor rate on it. Since each job tends to be done by only one person, this means a pay cut for that person. I usually lose them when this happens. I ask them if they want to run the job for less money. They don't understand or refuse to understand the fact that the company has to survive. If the part's price goes down, the pay rate has to go down. I have never been able to get a satisfactory reading of what they are thinking. They get angry and say they can't afford it. . . . I tell the employees that if I don't lower the price, I will lose the job anyway. They say, "Raise the price." I can't, because it can't be sold for more money. Some understand. You can't tell who will understand. The less educated and intelligent sometimes see it better. There is a lack of trust of the employer. Laborers don't want to hear about the possibility that the employer could lose money.

—Owner of a nonunion manufacturing company with 25 employees

A pay cut also represents a lack of recognition. This is true of anybody. People never understand and don't want to understand. They don't want to believe that the company is in that much trouble. They live in their own world and make very subjective judgements. Even if the owner and upper management cut their own pay, a cut isn't possible, for the help sees that upper management lives better than they do.

—Owner of a retail business with 30 employees

The men didn't want to hear about a pay cut. . . . The guys on the shop floor have a low mental attitude. It is hard for them to comprehend. They flop in front of the TV and open a beer. All they know is that the company is making millions on their sweat and blood. They don't believe it is not making money.

—Owner of a unionized architectural woodwork firm with 40 employees

Three employers blamed disbelief on the difficulty of understanding a new situation, especially after abrupt business reversals.

For the past few weeks, the company has gone from a five- to a four-day week. . . . The cutbacks have been difficult, because the employees don't understand why it's being done. Since they don't go out and sell, they don't understand the effort involved in selling, though they do see that business is slow. They don't speak up for fear of being let go. They feel insecure and helpless. Upper management tries to talk to them and explain that the reason they have gone to 32-hour weeks is that the company wants to keep all its employees.

—Human resource executive of an architectural engineering firm with 60 employees

Two others blamed information problems in part on management policy.

The union doesn't look at the books. We don't say we can't afford the men. A privately owned company is reluctant to reveal its finances. They are the owners' private concern. If the union did an audit, they would use it. We have had lawsuits from the union due to a disagreement over the pension plan.

—President of a unionized architectural woodwork firm with 125 employees

A prominent theme in the interviews was that employees accept pay cuts or reduced raises if their company is in financial difficulty and especially if these measures would save jobs or decrease the chance that their company would go out of business.

The overall level of raises depends on profitability. We pay what we can afford. If we can't afford raises, this must be explained to employees. At the beginning after [we bought the company], raises were delayed because the company was struggling. There were no Christmas bonuses, though the company had always had them. Now bonuses and raises have been restored, as management had promised they would be if the company recovered. People don't mind being part of a tightening up if they feel everyone is doing it—if it is a group effort that will lead somewhere.

—One of four owners of a nonunion manufacturing company with 200 employees

Pay could be cut if the alternative were layoffs. . . . People would have to be educated about the finances of the company. This could be too alarmist. Anxieties about a possible shut-down could be too distracting. There is a fine margin between being galvanizing and distracting. It would depend on the leadership's convincing people that it was committed to keeping the plant open.

—President of a nonunion manufacturing company and ESOP with 240 employees

If a pay cut would mean keeping the gate open, and we could prove that to people, we would do it. *Question:* How would you prove it? *Answer:* That is a good question. We have been open with employees, but there are limits, for we do not want to give away information to our competitors.

—High-level human resource official at a unionized manufacturing company with 19,000 employees

If it is a choice between closing a plant and a pay cut, the members would probably give in. Employees understand that choice to a degree. Their reaction would depend on their trust in the president and the human resource guy—on whether they had been lied to before.

—Business representative for an industrial union local with 2,000 active members

Serious financial problems were often obvious to employees from their experiences at work.

Employees get disgruntled with the freeze. They have been grumbling. We say that it is better than a layoff. They look at the boss, who is rich. I say, I live off my salary. I don't rape the business. We don't handle the books. They handle the books. That's important. The office manager writes the checks, so she knows that no illegitimate expenditures are made.

—Dentist with 16 employees

I felt that the people at the core of the business understood. They also understood that pay would be restored to its old level if we recovered. . . . I didn't think I had any trouble getting them to believe we were in trouble. People who are building products know they are building fewer than before. Those involved in buying or the financial end knew how hard it was to pay bills. There are no secrets in a small business. I still deal with many of the same people and I know of no hard feelings.

—Former owner of a nonunion, 20-employee manufacturing company that closed in 1992

No one left as a result of the [pay] cuts. There were not many places to go. The company has no quits at all—maybe one in the last two months. Productivity and work effort don't change with pay. Pay and hours cuts brought grumbling. Some were forced to take second, part-time jobs and as a result were tired. . . . We did a lot of communicating to explain the pay cuts. There were plant meetings, but the communicating was done mostly through correspondence posted in the plant and sent home and through verbal explanations given within departments. We gave sales and financial figures, and these were believed. The employees could see the drop in activity. Many have been here for years and have seen slowdowns before.

—Human resource officer of a nonunion manufacturing company with 400 employees

We are extremely resistant to pay cuts. We don't want to step backwards. It could start an unending process. Our reaction is tied to the reason cuts are thought to be necessary. A lot depends on the degree of trust between the company and the union and on the financial state of the company. We must believe that their position is not just a ploy to get wages down. If we are convinced a pay cut would save the company, we go along with it and try to convince the employees to accept it. But the employees would probably know better than I did how well the company was doing, for they would know how busy they were.

—Business representative for an industrial union local with 2,000 active members

Cutbacks of any kind could cause problems, even when clearly necessary. Problems were mitigated, however, by understanding and by good explanations of the situation.

If I said, "If I don't cut pay, I'll close my doors," the men would go along with me, but they'd be out looking for new work and they'd be an unproductive labor force.

—Nonunion, site-work contractor with 20 employees

I could have kept stores open by cutting pay, but I would have lost lots of staff. I proposed such cuts, but my managers did not want them, and without their support, I would not have been able to get that of my staff. If I had gone ahead anyway, my whole company would have fallen apart. Bad morale would have cut into sales, for customers won't buy if they sense a glum atmosphere when they go into a store. Now, a pay cut would work, because people see how bad things are. They didn't believe it in 1989.

—Owner of a retail business with 30 employees

When I cut pay, I called in the employees by groups to meetings where I explained the financial situation. They believed me and recognized the need. Enough people came so that word got around. . . . The pay cut caused no perceptible decrease in productivity, and the layoffs brought an increase in productivity, for 50 of the 75 people laid off were poor producers hired during a period of labor shortage. . . . A pay cut leads to groaning, but people's self-respect makes them keep performing. . . . No one left because of the cut.

—President of a nonunion mechanical contracting firm with 200 employees

If you can talk realistically about survival and the employees believe that what the company says is true, then you have a shot at having a pay cut accepted. If the cut is an edict from above that the employees don't understand, then you are lost.

—Human resource official in a unionized manufacturing company with 250,000 employees

If you make pay cuts which members think are unjustified, morale sags. If members believe concessions are necessary and will keep the company in business and that they can get their benefits back when business picks up, then they accept the cuts. People will be angry anyway. The difference between a union and a nonunion shop is that union shops have labor representatives who say the same things as the bosses. The representatives tell the men that the same things are happening throughout the industry. This helps, though the members still suffer and are angry and have a difficult time. Hopefully, they continue to produce. I tell the men that union people have to get the stuff out the door faster than nonunion people in order to compete. I give them the facts.

—Business agent for manufacturing workers in a union local with 3,400 active members

We have had wage cuts, but pay freezes have been more common. . . . We try to make cuts temporary, so that members get them back plus an increase within a year. Pay cuts come only after a company demonstrates that it is in trouble and is likely to go under. Then, people are not happy, but they will understand and try to go along with the cut to preserve their jobs. . . . If after a pay cut, the managers give themselves raises, there can be wildcat slowdowns and strikes.

—General counsel for a regional union council with 6,000 union members, most of whom were factory workers

It would be especially bad to cut pay simply to take advantage of high unemployment.

[If pay were cut solely because of high unemployment,] they would be pissed and demoralized as well. Morale is definitely related to productivity. There could also be sabotage if people were angry. If we can afford to pay them, we should. I would say we have a moral obligation to maintain pay. Of course, if we were in desperate straits, they would understand and we could do it.

—Owner of a nonunion manufacturing company with 20 employees

If I cut pay just because of high unemployment, I would create bad will. The animosity and anger wouldn't go away later when I needed them. I don't know if they'd work less hard, but they would try to leave as soon as they could and go where they would be treated fairly. . . . If a pay cut were necessary for the survival of the company, it would be accepted and should be done.

—Owner of a nonunion manufacturing company with 35 employees

Each person is an investment for us. If we had to cut pay in order to survive, the employees would go along with it. If we took advantage of the recession to cut pay, they would feel we were being unfair. If we did that, there would be a whole change in our relationship. They would feel we were taking advantage of them when they were down, and that could trigger unionization. Workers and management have to be together, or the company won't succeed. Morale is tremendously important.

—Personnel manager of a nonunion manufacturing company with 430 employees

19.2 Strikes

The best-known information-based theories of strikes are the screening, signaling, and attrition models. In the attrition model, each side is ignorant of the cost of the strike to the other, and work stoppage continues until one side yields because it finds that the cost to itself of a continued strike exceeds the expected gain from waiting to see if the other will give in. The side that yields first loses in that it must accept terms that leave it just as well off as if it broke off the relationship by closing the business or leaving.

The screening and signaling models formalize the idea that strikes communicate profitability. In the screening model, the union presents the firm with a schedule of wage rates and strike lengths; the firm can have any wage rate on the schedule after a strike of the specified length. Strike duration increases as the wage decreases, and the company picks the most profitable wage-duration pair. This choice reveals how much the firm earns from labor, since the more profitable the firm the more it loses from the strike. That is, more profitable companies choose higher wages and shorter strikes. In the signaling model, the firm and the union alternate making offers, and the firm delays making a serious offer, until a time that reveals its profitability in the same way that delay does in the screening model. A wage is then agreed on immediately.

In screening and signaling models, it is assumed either that the firm refuses to reveal its profitability directly or that the union does not believe the firm's statements. Another assumption is that rich firms settle sooner than poor ones. Interviews indicated that these assumptions are often invalid. Firms that suffer financially are sometimes willing to reveal their accounts to union leaders, who in any case often find other ways to inform themselves of company resources. Nor is it true that more profitable firms usually yield more quickly, for profitability brings wealth, which increases the capacity to resist strikes. The screening and signaling models assume correctly that greater profitability increases the monetary loss from strikes. The theories err in not taking account of a firm's budget constraint (Chapter 5). The effects of long strikes on the budget often outweigh forgone profits.

I did not pursue the investigation far enough to be convinced that I understood fully why strikes occur, though I am persuaded that they have little to do with asymmetries of information about company finances. My evidence indicated that strikes are caused by anger, by the need to protect a reputation for toughness, by negotiating errors, and by gambles on being able to defeat the other side. Union leaders sometimes call strikes to vent worker rage over an accumulation of past conflicts with management. Unions and firms both invest in reputation, and unions sometimes go so far as to put companies out of business as a show of strength. Typical errors occur when union leaders misjudge their members and negotiate a contract they reject or when either side grossly underestimates the opponent's determination. Mistakes of estimation are nearly inevitable since the will to resist depends on psychological imponderables. For instance, the consequences of a wage increase to a firm is a question of judgment, and union leaders cannot know exactly how the employer sees the matter. These errors are a form of asymmetric information, but about subjective concerns. Gambles are like errors of judgment, except that the possibility of error is recognized. Strikes that are gambles on victory are usually initiated by the owners, who wish to weaken or destroy the union's influence. It may be appropriate to model such strikes as wars of attrition. However, in that model each side knows the cost of the strike to itself, whereas in reality each side is uncertain of its own strength as well as that of the opponent. Labor leaders do not know how long members will man and respect picket lines, and employers do not know whether managers will remain loyal, whether replacement workers can be hired, and how customers will react. In negotiations and strikes, complex psychological interactions are paramount, and it is probably a mistake to imagine that insight can be gained from simple game-theoretic models of bargaining.

OVERVIEW OF INTERVIEW EVIDENCE

The abstract question of why strikes occur was discussed in all 18 interviews with labor leaders, with explanations as tabulated in Table 19.2.

Labor leaders and lawyers believed that the main asymmetries of information leading to errors in judgment were the union's misjudging management's willingness to resist and management's underestimating union members' willingness to strike. Asymmetries of information about company finances had little importance. Table 19.3 summarizes the views of 16 labor leaders regarding the relation between strikes and information about a company's ability to pay. Union leaders' sources of company financial information are shown as in Table 19.4. The views of the four labor lawyers interviewed hardly differed from those of labor leaders. Comments by employers bore out the same opinions.

My contacts were with leaders of small- to medium-sized labor organizations

TABLE 19.2   Labor leaders' explanations of why strikes occur (applies to 18 labor leaders)

Explanation	Number of labor leaders	Percentage of labor leaders
Management wants to rid itself of the union	9	50
Errors of judgment	7	39
Compromise is impossible	5	28
Building union reputation	4	22
Venting union members' anger	2	11

TABLE 19.3 Strikes and company financial information, according to union leaders (applies to 16 labor leaders)

Statement	Number of labor leaders	Percentage of labor leaders
Unions never go on strike to obtain financial information	11	69
Unions sometimes go on strike to obtain financial information	0	0
Before a strike, the union has adequate information about company profitability	7	44
Before a strike, the union has little information about company profitability	2	13
Strike length is not influenced by profitability	9	56
The worse the financial condition of a company, the sooner a strike is over	6	38
The more orders a company has, the sooner a strike is over	3	19

TABLE 19.4 Union sources of company financial information, according to union leaders (applies to 10 labor leaders)

Source	Number of labor leaders	Percentage of labor leaders
Stockholder reports	7	70
Spying by union members and sympathizers	5	50
Union research	3	30
Casual observation by union members	3	30
Documents provided by employer	1	10

and lawyers working for companies of a similar size, so that my conclusions may not apply to dealings between large organizations.

INFORMANTS' EXPLANATIONS

No respondent reacted favorably to the signaling or screening models of strikes.

Economists are trying to reduce things to objective, quantifiable analysis. In my view, we are dealing with events which are to a large extent the result of passion and emotion. [The screening theory] of strikes seems remote from reality. Generally, unions don't learn about firms from a strike.

—Labor lawyer who for 25 years has represented companies in over 100 contract negotiations

Unions don't strike to learn anything. They strike to hurt the company and force compliance.

—Organizing director for Connecticut of a large national union

If companies are making lots of money, they are not going to want to be shut down. But strikes are not a way of learning anything. The strike threat is simply a mechanism for holding out for more than is offered.

—Business representative of a construction local with 3,000 members

The strike itself does not give information [about company finances]. It might in a small company, but it certainly does not in big companies, for they put all their resources into resisting. Sometimes we agree on total confidentiality [and the company lets us see its books], though we may have to tell union members when a company is in trouble. This situation is usually awkward. The report to members would be verbal and not very specific.

—-Director of an industrial union local with 65,000 members

I was told I was naive to imagine that unions cannot learn about company resources before negotiations begin. The larger unions manage pension funds, which are stockholders and provide business contacts through which a great deal of information flows informally. Union members have a good idea of the level of activity at the places they work, and middle managers sometimes leak information to unions. If companies claim they are financially unable to pay what a union demands, they are legally obliged to let union representatives examine their accounts. For this reason, companies usually do not plead poverty.

Financial information is one of those ritualistic minuets. Employers never want to open their books. They say, "It would be crazy to let them see them." A company won't claim an inability to pay. It will say that it is its own judgment that this is what it should pay. But, in half a dozen situations, companies have offered to let the union look at the books and the union hasn't accepted, for it didn't question the company's word. This is a phony issue. Most companies don't keep phony books. If they say they lost $9 million last year, nobody doubts it. The real issue is that if the union looks at the books, it can argue indefinitely about what they mean or question decisions, the accounting for future pension liability, or why did you pay the president so much. There are a million details to quarrel over. This is not a real issue in collective bargaining. Unions tend to believe that companies that are making money behave differently every day than ones that are losing money. They have friends and relations in the accounting office. There are no secrets. The question is how the company's discretionary income is going to be allocated. That is what it boils down to. Will it be spent on stockholders, executives, union members, investment in equipment, research and development, or sales and marketing?

—Labor lawyer who for 25 years has represented companies in over 100 contract negotiations

We never go on strike to learn about the financial state of the employers. This is known in advance. What is not known is their willingness to give in. We do a lot of analyzing. Everything is discussed in meetings. . . . We already understand the financial well-being of the contractors before a strike. The Dodge Reports [a construction industry publication], for instance, tell us how much work they have.

—Business agent for a construction union with 270 active members

Question: Do you learn about the finances of the company from the length of the strike? *Answer:* No. We know that ahead of time, for the most part. If they ask for concessions, we will ask for proof. If they refuse to show us the books, we take that as an indication that they are lying. Some owners object on principle to showing their books. 10K forms don't tell you that much. Stockholder reports don't either, unless they mention the plant or company division you are dealing with. We spy on companies. We do what is necessary [said sheepishly]. Some of our greatest allies are managers, especially lower-level supervisors. They know they benefit from any gains we make, for if our pay goes up, theirs does too. Some are former union members. Their livelihood is tied to ours.

—Business representative for an industrial union local with 2,000 active members

[I explained the screening theory of strikes.] You are making the wrong calculation. Information is not the issue. The members know the place. I go to each place once a week, at least, for grievances or just to check in. You can keep your finger on the heartbeat of a place. I know their suppliers. I get a good idea of their bottom line without looking at their books.

—President and business representative for a union local with a diversified industrial membership of 4,000

Our union has a large research department. It knows about the finances of companies. The companies are mostly publicly held. The workers know how the companies are doing, for they handle the cash. Most of the time, companies don't say they can't pay.

—Business agent of a retail workers' union local with 16,000 members

You don't learn anything about the employer's finances during a strike. You have to do your homework beforehand, and even before you enter into discussion with your members. You use 10K reports, the AFL-CIO research staff, you snoop. You need to know the employer's plan of action, his agenda, his direction, and capacity to pay. You need to know the company's capacity to resist a strike, as well as that of the membership. You need to know what is key to beating the company and you need a plan of action in case of a strike.

—Official in an umbrella organization of labor union locals, together representing 30,000 workers

Not all union leaders expressed complete confidence in their financial knowledge.

We try to find out about the company's finances, even spying on them. Through accounting, companies can do a lot of smoke-and-mirror tricks. You never know exactly how much they are making. [He then flaunted the success of his espionage by pulling out of a desk drawer a stack of papers, which he claimed were surreptitiously photocopied financial records from a company he was trying to organize.]

—Organizing director for Connecticut of a large national union

When negotiating, we get financial information on companies only if they say they will go out of business if they meet our demands. Then we look at the books. Sometimes, we don't know how well the company is doing. The men know how much work is on the floor, but they cannot tell if the owner underbid to get it. We have to look at the books to find that out.

—Business agent for manufacturing workers in a union local with 3,400 active members

We have a research department that evaluates the financial reports of companies. They don't report on individual subunits, and we can't tell how a particular plant is doing. In this case, the person across the table becomes important. He might not know either. . . . We use information from members too, even rumors, just anything.

—Director of an industrial union local with 65,000 members

Many labor leaders saw little or no relation between a firm's profitability and its willingness to resist a strike.

I don't know if more profitable companies hold out longer during strikes. If they were very profitable, we probably wouldn't be there, for they could afford to pay and the strike would hurt them more. I don't know. I have seen examples both ways.

—Business representative for an industrial union local with 2,000 active members

I see no link between company financial strength and strike length. Strike lengths depend on personalities and the reasons for the strike. Strikes are seldom a matter just of economics. There is lots of emotionalism. There is pride. Both sides tend to feel betrayed. The capability of the negotiators is important.

—Regional manager of an industrial union with 6,500 active members

Some observers believed that in many cases firms' ability to resist strikes increased with financial strength, contrary to the screening and signaling models.

> It is not clear that more profitable companies give in more quickly to strikes, for if they are more profitable, they are richer and can afford to hire replacements and lawyers and hang on.
>
> —Head of an association of unionized construction companies who handled labor negotiations for member companies

> Management thinks of costs in the long term. In a sense, the more profitable a company is, the easier it is for it to give in and pay. But also, the stronger it is, the bigger its reserves, the better its ability to subcontract, and the greater are its inventories. Those who settle first are those who depend on the payment from next week's shipments.
>
> —Chairman in a large law firm of the department representing firms in labor disputes

> The financially weaker companies don't want a strike. The stronger ones think they can fight. If an owner maintains a strike, you have to assume he has money and is spending a lot on scabs and damaged goods.
>
> —Organizing director for Connecticut of a large national union

> Unions do learn about the financial condition of a company through a strike. If a company is hurting, a strike is over quickly. If a company comes back quickly, it is in a financial crunch or has orders it must fill right away to avoid one, [and we might reduce our demands to help the company]. . . . If a company has lots of money, it doesn't mind enduring a long strike to cut things away. The weaker the company, the quicker it gives in.
>
> —Directing labor representative of an industrial union local with an active membership of 12,000

Companies in financial difficulty might endure long strikes to try to rid themselves of the union.

> In manufacturing, if the company has inventory and reserves of cash, it can last longer. These things come from profitability. . . . Many different scenarios are possible. Business could take a very long-term view of strikes. For instance, someone may want to buy the company but wants the union busted first. Others could be so poor that they are desperate and they could ruin themselves trying to bust the union. Ego gets involved.
>
> —Official in an umbrella organization of labor union locals, together representing 30,000 workers

> A strong company is in a better position to resist a strike. But there are also weak companies that try to beat the union back so they can prosper. This is a difficult

decision problem for unions. Do we build up companies so that they can take us on, or do we keep them weak? Some companies grow and become strong and continue to work with the union, being willing to share the gains with it, understanding that the union allowed them to happen. Usually, stronger companies are better able to resist strikes, though this is not always true. [A large company] was on the verge of bankruptcy, but was willing to take on the union. It figured that was the way to survive. It is in the in-between range that resistance increases with the strength of the company. . . . In this range, stronger companies are in a better position to hold out longer. . . . While the strike is on, circumstances can change. A company can be put in poor financial shape by a strike, so that the union is willing to settle quickly.

—Director of an industrial union local with 65,000 members

Companies with contractual obligations to fill orders give in more quickly.

A week after striking, the pressure on contractors is greater to settle, because they have contracts to complete on schedule. They have deadlines and penalty clauses. . . . Those contractors who have more work want to settle earlier, and we use this fact to put pressure on them, taking them aside to talk to them.

—Business agent for a construction union with 270 active members

A company can't resist a strike if it has back orders, because it doesn't want to lose customers—at least if the customers can go elsewhere. Profitability has little to do with the resistance to strikes. Resistance depends on greed.

—General counsel for a regional union council with 6,000 union members, most of whom were factory workers

Strikes have diverse causes, and several respondents reacted to descriptions of information-theoretic models by saying that many strikes were not about pay, but were over relationship issues, such as the right to bargain collectively or the need to express worker discontent.

In the majority of strikes, the longer and more bitter ones are not about money. They are about what people regard as principles, which people can feel strongly about. . . . They are about union representation, jurisdiction, subcontracting, or job security.

—Labor lawyer who for 25 years has represented companies in over 100 contract negotiations

Another category of strikes are those that are meant to break the union. The company takes a legal and extreme stand and forces the union to back down or go on strike, and then replaces the strikers.

—Prominent Connecticut labor lawyer

Once a strike starts, the goals become nothing to do with money. They are about whether the union will be there. They [employers] usually try replacing the work force, and if that doesn't work, they come back.

—President of the district organization of a service workers' union with 18,000 members

Passion and resentment caused and sustained strikes.

There are different kinds of situations. The short-term strike is typically a situation where some anger has built up over time and has to be let off. Some union leaders orchestrate this to let off steam and it has nothing to do with the contract. Maybe the employees don't like a new plant manager or the company has done something it has the right to do but that they didn't like, such as eliminating departments. . . . There are strikes that have nothing to do with negotiations.

—Prominent Connecticut labor lawyer

If both sides were fully informed, some strikes could probably be avoided, but some occur because companies want them to. Sometimes, members are hostile and want to hurt the company. Some companies will do enormous damage to themselves through a strike, losing markets, with no gain in sight.

—Regional manager of an industrial union with 6,500 active members

Negotiations are also about the whole relationship—how people are treated and how the work is done. Sometimes, things get away from you, for the work force needs a strike to vent its anger or the boss may be afraid of losing his supervisors' support if he is not tough at the table. . . . It helps the union to have a pattern to show what it wants and that justifies the demands. The union needs an argument to save face. The willingness to pay has to do both with psychology and finances. The union has to organize the labor force to strike, in order to be credible and to find out what it is willing to do. On the second day of the strike, you had better believe what you said before the strike. Sometimes, there are not enough people on the picket lines to sustain it.

—President of the district organization of a service workers' union with 18,000 members

Some large unions use strikes to promote their reputation.

At each strike, you think about the next one. If we had given in to [a company's] demands, the other companies [in the local industry] would have asked the same.

—President of a retail workers union local with 16,000 members

When a strike starts, it is not about that one, but the next one. The union is an institution, and the members buy into it. The members understand the need to pressure employers to pay more. They understand that their own job is to push the edge. Once a strike starts, it is as much about the next employer as this one, for we show that a strike is costly. Sometimes, we close the place, and that is a victory.

—President of the district organization of a service workers union with 18,000 members

Information asymmetries were important causes of strikes, but the ignorance was of intangibles, such as the other side's psychological will to resist or even one's own strength.

A more typical category is the strike that occurs over a distinct, maybe a single issue, where at the outset the members believe they cannot or will not back down, such as sharing in the cost of medical insurance. The employers look to see if they can continue to operate using supervisory or nonunion personnel, moving work to another site, hiring temporary or permanent replacements. The employer is looking to see if the workers can hold out and whether they will cross the picket line. Someone eventually backs down.

—Prominent Connecticut labor lawyer

The origin of strikes is mistakes in judging the other side's resistance. The resistance of the owner has to do with his judgment of what he should pay and of where he wants his pay to be relative to that of the competition—what quantile of pay in the surveys he needs to be in to attract the quality of employees wanted.

—Chairman in a large law firm of the department representing firms in labor disputes

Strikes can result from mistakes or a misunderstanding of the issues. The contractors often underestimate the resolve of the employees and the length of time they are willing to stay on strike.

—Business manager of a construction union local with 600 members

In [a certain strike], both management and the union leadership miscalculated the strength of feelings of the membership. . . . [T]he agreement was voted down by two votes. Usually strikes after a vote like that won't last. In this case, most of the members were Italian, Turkish, or from the Dominican Republic. They were all from tight-knit families and communities and were reluctant to break ranks. They received community and neighborhood support and held together despite the company's attempt to hire replacements. Because of community support, it was difficult to find people willing to work as replacements.

—Regional manager of an industrial union with 6,500 active members

You never really know if you got enough money—whether there was more money there or not. When you push really hard, you get the best information about what they can afford. A strike is a way of knowing how much they can afford. . . . It is not a matter of not being able to read their books. It is how they see the future that you don't know.

—President of the district organization of a service workers' union with 18,000 members

Strikes also tested organizational resolve.

Strikes often change people's sensibilities about how much power they have. This is true on both sides. It is sobering for managers to be locked up in their plant. I went through one long strike [at another company] in which after twelve months, some strikers lost their homes.

—Human resource official of a nonunion firm with 1,800 employees specializing in research and development

Question: Does the notion of what you can live with change during the strike? *Answer:* Yes. Both sides rethink their positions. I think this is more true on the company side than on the union side.

—Business representative for an industrial union local with 2,000 active members

The work force learns from a strike. The workers at [a certain company] were enlightened by the company's advertising for replacement workers. Having an unexpected strike can also enlighten the company. After a strike, things often change. The company takes complaints, grievances, and bad supervisors more seriously.

—General counsel for a regional union council with 6,000 union members, most of whom were factory workers

A lot is learned during a strike. People come forward giving information about the company, even financial information. Lower-level supervisors may do that. They may turn against the company in a private way. In this way, the union learns about how the company is responding to the crisis. In [one] strike, the company tried to convince our people that the factory was running. It ran vans through the picket lines with cardboard over their windows and allegedly full of replacement workers. In fact, the vans were empty. Supervisors revealed this over drinks at bars. People who worked at the owners' homes described the houses, the paintings they had recently bought. This kind of information spread spontaneously.

—Regional manager of an industrial union with 6,500 active members

You learn a lot during a strike. You are building your union and you find leaders out there. If you are well organized, you send a clear message to the employer about your strength.

—Official in an umbrella organization of labor union locals, together representing 30,000 workers

Interviews touched on other matters relevant to the theory of strikes, though not pertaining directly to asymmetries of information. Three of the four labor lawyers claimed that labor leaders sometimes encouraged strikes in order to persuade union members to reduce their demands, a finding that supports a theory of Ashenfelter and Johnson (1969). Seven of the 18 labor leaders said that high unemployment discouraged strikes because it made it easier for firms to hire replacement workers, and no labor leader said that high unemployment had the opposite effect or had no impact on the willingness to strike. The fear of replacements may explain the greater frequency of strikes during booms than recessions (Rees, 1952; Vroman, 1989). My respondents described something of the process of negotiation, particularly the need to have arguments as much for the sake of ritual as persuasion, for arguments allow the other side to save face when yielding. I was told that compromise comes through skill in communication and by encouraging a problem-solving atmosphere in which both sides seek common advantage. These are among the themes of the psychological literature on bargaining.

19.3 Summary

Information asymmetries do not explain wage rigidity. Workers view a company financial crisis as a legitimate reason for cutting pay, particularly if the cut would save jobs or the company. Employers believe they would have little difficulty convincing employees that a financial crisis was real. Some workers might be hard to convince, but their resistance often has more to do with a psychological refusal to face adverse circumstances than with distrust of the employer. Asymmetries of information do help explain strikes, but the asymmetries are about subjective estimates of the other side's objectives and will to resist and not about financial information. Unions find ways to learn about company finances before negotiations begin.

Appendix 19A Related Literature

INFORMATION AND DOWNWARD WAGE RIGIDITY (SECTION 19.1)

I know of no empirical literature on the extent of employee distrust of company statements about profits and productivity.

Managers believed that workers tolerate a pay cut or freeze more easily when it is made clear it would save jobs or keep the company in operation. This conviction is amply supported by evidence collected by psychologists who have studied the impact of justifications. People harmed by an authority's decision react more favorably to it if given a good explanation, citing necessity, the long-term interest of those affected, or universal principles of justice. Numerous experiments and surveys have confirmed this effect, and it has several competing interpretations. One resembles an economic theory in that it appeals to self-interest; people prefer to be part of a just organization, because in the long run they can count on benefiting from its rewards. As Brockner and Wiesenfeld (1996, p. 203) point out, this theory does not explain the favorable reactions to fairness of people only temporarily attached to organizations. The evidence indicates that the value people attach to fairness is to some extent independent of self-interest (Folger, 1993). Psychologists at first analyzed explanations as part of procedural justice, which Thibaut and Walker (1975) distinguished from distributive justice. Recently, psychologists have noted the importance of other aspects of explanations, such as politeness and respect (Tyler and Bies, 1990). Bies (1987), Sitkin and Bies (1993), and Brockner and Wiesenfeld (1996) review the subject. Brockner et al. (1993, 1994) have studied the impact of explanations on reactions to layoffs of both the victims and the survivors, and Greenberg (1990, 1993) and Schaubroeck, May, and Brown (1994) have surveyed the effect of justifications on reactions to pay cuts and pay freezes, respectively.

Kahneman, Knetsch, and Thaler (1986a) find that pay cuts are thought by the public to be more acceptable if made in response to losses than if made to take advantage of high unemployment. The public's views reflect practice, for most pay cuts are made in response to losses (section 12.1).

More evidence on the tolerance of justified pay cuts is contained in union voting for a General Motors contract involving wage concessions. The plants most menaced by layoffs gave the most support to the agreement (Capelli and Sterling, 1988; Kaufman and Martinez-Vazquez, 1988).

A final bit of evidence is contained in Campbell and Kamlani (1997). According to them, managers affirm that the impact of a pay cut on work effort would be less severe if workers thought the company was losing money than if they believed it was highly profitable.

STRIKES (SECTION 19.2)

According to economic and game-theoretic reasoning, strikes must be the result of information asymmetries, if people are rational. Hicks (1932, chap. 7) pointed out that if a union and firm are collectively rational and have the same information, then they will reach an agreement without a strike. In Rubinstein's (1982) model, symmetric information implies that agreement is reached without a strike, even if the two sides are only individually rational. There is an extensive literature developing theoretically the view that strikes or bargaining delays stem from asymmetric information. Important papers include Fudenberg and Tirole (1983), Hayes (1984), Admati and Perry (1987), Hart (1989), Cramton (1992), Cramton and Tracy (1992, 1994), and Leach (1992), and the literature is surveyed in Kennan (1986) and Kennan and Wilson (1993).

Tests of asymmetric information theories of strikes have been quite indirect and do not provide strong support for the theories. The signaling and screening models and Hicks' asymmetric information model all imply that strike frequency should increase with uncertainty about a firm's prosperity and prospects, and this implication has been confirmed by Cousineau and Lacroix (1986), Tracy (1986, 1987, 1988), Gramm, Hendricks, and Kahn (1988), and Fisher (1991). However, the relation tested does not necessarily reflect the impact of asymmetries of objective information, but may occur because greater uncertainty increases the complexity of the issues to be discussed or is associated with greater subjective differences in interpretation of factual information known to both sides. Hirsch and Addison (1986, chap. 4) review this literature. The screening model implies that settlement wages decrease with strike length, and estimates of this relationship have varied. McConnell (1989) finds that wages decrease, whereas Card's (1990a, c) results are more ambiguous. Kennan and Wilson (1989) examine the dependence of the rate of strike termination on strike duration, and find that the data are consistent with the attrition and screening models, but not the signaling model. I know of no inquiries regarding whether labor leaders use strikes to infer profitability. Pillsbury (1958) surveys the views of labor union research directors on corporate financial reports and finds, as I do, that they seldom doubt financial statements.

It is not necessary to appeal to asymmetries of objective information to explain strikes, for extensive experimental studies have shown that bargainers frequently suffer losses from disagreement, even when they have the same objective information. Roth (1995) surveys this interesting literature. It is not clear whether the disagreements result from irrationality or asymmetries of information about subjective matters. Other evidence contradicts game-theoretic models in which bargaining with symmetric information is concluded without delay. For instance, the Rubinstein solution is contradicted by experimental evidence that negotiators violate subgame perfection, the key assumption of that model. In ultimatum games, the person with the right to make an offer often does not have a great advantage. Low offers are often rejected out of indignation or desire for revenge (Güth, Schmittberger, and Schwarze, 1982; Ochs and Roth, 1989; Roth et al., 1991; Camerer and Thaler, 1995; and Abbink et al., 1996), even when the stakes are large compared with subjects' annual income (Cameron, 1995). The Nash (1950) bargaining solution is rejected by field and experimental data (Hamermesh, 1973; Svejnar, 1986; and Roth, 1987).

Social psychologists and sociologists, when writing about strikes, emphasize social context, the passions aroused by the issues, the role of the public stance taken by negotiators in mobilizing support from their constituents, and the importance of subtle communications between negotiators through word, tone, and gesture. The importance of these exchanges is supported by experimental work, for there is less disagreement when negotiators meet face to face than when they interact anonymously through a computer (Roth, 1995, pp. 294–295). An excellent source on the process of labor negotiations is Friedman (1994). Other sources on noneconomic theories of strikes are Walton and McKersie (1965), Morley and Stephenson (1977), Wheeler (1985), Stagner (1987), Kochan and Katz (1988, chap. 8), Godard (1992), Kaufman (1992), and Walton and Cutcher-Gershenfeld (1994). Gallagher and Gramm (1997) review the entire literature on strikes and collective bargaining.

20

EXISTING THEORIES

It is now possible to assess the various theories of wage rigidity in the light of my own findings and other evidence. I organize the theories according to the source of wage rigidity.

20.1 Labor Supply Theories

In the theories of this section, wages are downwardly rigid because people withdraw their labor when wages fall.

THE INTERTEMPORAL SUBSTITUTION THEORY

Lucas and Rapping (1969) claim that cyclical increases in unemployment occur when workers quit their jobs because wages or salaries fall below expectations. The authors claim that such people are counted in government statistics as unemployed because unemployment surveys ask people whether they are looking for work and do not establish whether they are insisting on jobs with unrealistically high pay. In the theory, job hunters can always find some position quickly, though it may pay little. Lucas and Rapping give two reasons why people withdraw labor, one discussed below in section 20.3 and the other being the intertemporal substitution theory discussed here. According to this explanation, when wages are unusually low, people become unemployed in order to enjoy free time, substituting leisure for income at a time when they lose the least income.

This theory does not accurately describe labor market behavior during a recession. According to the theory, quits into unemployment increase during recessions, whereas historically quits decrease sharply and roughly half of unemployed workers become jobless because they are laid off (Chapter 16 and

Appendix 18A, section 18.1). During the recession I studied, people were even afraid to change jobs because new ones might prove unstable and lead to unemployment. Although the theory asserts that workers quit because wages fall below reservation levels, wage cuts were unusual during the recession, and counselors of the unemployed knew of almost no one who had quit because of a pay cut (sections 11.1 and 18.1). If pay was disappointing, it must have been that raises were smaller than anticipated, not that wages and salaries fell. Other evidence against the theory is the observation that actual pay cuts made during the recession caused little extra turnover, probably because new jobs were hard to find (section 12.2). Similarly, the lowering of hiring pay in the secondary sector created difficulties in recruiting only when carried too far (section 17.5). If the unemployed were holding out for higher pay, it would have been difficult for firms to recruit, whereas many were overwhelmed by unemployed job applicants of good quality (section 15.1). Far from finding the unemployed fussy about working conditions and pay, many recruiters were afraid of accidentally hiring overqualified job applicants, and there were many of these (sections 15.2 and 17.6). Only employers of low-paid labor complained that applicants wanted too much money and preferred living on unemployment insurance benefits or welfare payments to working (section 15.5). Advisers of the unemployed asserted that many job seekers were quite flexible, especially after recovering from the shock of layoff (section 18.9). One of the advisers' tasks was to discourage clients from taking stopgap jobs or from applying for positions for which they were overqualified (sections 18.6 and 18.7). Job acceptance rates increase rather than decline during recessions (Appendix 18A, section 18.9).

If wages and salaries hardly ever fall, the intertemporal substitution theory is widely applicable only if the unemployed prefer jobless leisure to continued employment at their old pay. However, the attitudes and circumstances of the unemployed are not consistent with their having made this choice. Indeed, their condition makes the notion that they consume or enjoy leisure incongruous. Most find joblessness extremely disagreeable. Living standards typically decline during unemployment, and decreases in spending on activities associated with leisure are especially pronounced (sections 18.2 and 18.3 and their appendices). Heckman (1974) and Ghez (1975) suggest that consumption declines during unemployment because leisure is a substitute for goods and services, not because the jobless run out of money. This defense of the Lucas-Rapping theory is weakened by evidence that possession of liquid financial assets diminishes the drop in consumption during unemployment (section 18.3 and its appendix). During the recession, many unemployed had little leisure, for they spent a great deal of time looking for work (section 18.10). It was not true that anyone could find some job quickly, and the lack of openings prolonged job search (section 18.8 and 18.13).

Even if it were true that wages declined during recessions, it is not clear that workers would respond by withdrawing labor. On the contrary, they might take second jobs to maintain their income, and Camerer et al. (1997) provide evidence favoring this possibility. They find that New York City cabdrivers work more rather than less on slower days, when hourly earnings are low. The drivers often quit for the day once they reach a target daily income level.

The Equivalence of Layoffs and Quits   McLaughlin (1990 and 1991) buttresses the Lucas-Rapping theory by asserting that layoffs are quits induced by pay cuts (Chapter 1). I found no evidence to support McLaughlin's theory. No employer I asked about the subject ever offered a worker a pay cut on his or her current job as an alternative to dismissal for lack of work (section 13.7). Doing so would call into question the moral and legal basis for layoff and might demoralize the work force. There existed arrangements by which workers could avoid layoff by taking new lower-paying jobs within the same company. Firms sometimes transferred workers to open positions rather than let them go, and a bumping system applied to some production workers. Transfers and bumping, however, were often accepted. Furthermore, bumping does not prevent layoffs, but merely shifts the identity of the person laid off. Few could avoid layoff by accepting a pay cut.

REAL BUSINESS CYCLE THEORIES

In real business cycle theory, unemployment is interpreted as leisure optimally selected by workers, as in the Lucas-Rapping model. It has proved difficult to construct business cycle models consistent with this assumption and with real wage fluctuations as small as they are in reality, relative to fluctuations in employment. Hansen (1985) and Rogerson (1988) have proposed that this difficulty be avoided by assuming that workers are indifferent between working and not working, so that changes in the demand for labor affect the number employed with no impact on real wages.

This suggestion is unrealistic, since a common complaint of advisers of the unemployed was that their clients were desperate for work and miserable being jobless, and it is hard to believe that many employed workers would have failed to anticipate the difficult situation they would find themselves in after losing their jobs. Many surveys have established that unemployment causes great unhappiness. Certain workers in certain categories, such as housewives, the elderly, and high school students, may be nearly indifferent between working and not working. However, these groups do not drive increases in unemployment, for their joblessness fluctuates less than does average unemployment (Appendix 18A, section 18.2). Furthermore, advisers of the unemployed were preoccupied with layoffs of numerous primary-income earners for whom job loss was a crisis.

Hansen and Wright (1992) and Benhabib, Rogerson, and Wright (1991) have suggested that workers have access to household production processes by which they can transform their own labor into income and to which they turn when the productivity of outside employment declines, as during recessions. These authors assume that people working in the household sector are counted statistically as unemployed.

This theory is not reasonable either, for advisers of the unemployed asserted that few of the jobless had access to any important means of support other than unemployment insurance benefits, severance pay, savings, and help from relatives (section 18.3). Some secondary-sector jobs, such as consulting or handyman work, might be thought of as household production, but these usually are not reliable sources of income, and people doing such work are most likely counted statistically as employed.

20.2 Worker Bargaining Theories

I now turn to theories in which workers' collective or individual bargaining power causes downward wage rigidity.

THE MONOPOLY UNION MODEL

Monopoly union models attribute unemployment and downward wage rigidity to the bargaining power of labor unions. It is assumed that these do not care about the unemployed, can prevent them from bidding down the wage, and do not find wage cutting to be in their interest. Formalization of the model requires specification of a union objective function. A simple idea often used is that of Dunlop (1944, pp. 32–44), who argues that unions maximize total wage payments to all union members. This assumption can be justified by assuming that union leadership wishes to maximizes total membership dues and that these are proportional to wages. Firms set employment so as to maximize profits, given the wages specified by union contracts. Under these assumptions, it is easy to calculate that at the union's optimal wage, the elasticity of the firm's demand for labor must be one. Although the theory offers an explanation of wage inflexibility in the face of high unemployment, special assumptions are required to explain why wages do not fall when a firm's demand for labor declines. One assumption is that a firm's elasticity of demand for labor is not affected by changes in product demand, and another assumption is that unions do not care that recessions raise the cost of layoffs to union members, a consideration that could induce unions to reduce layoffs by cutting pay.

The theory is vaguely consistent with my findings, for unions resisted pay cuts, unless they believed these would save a large number of jobs (sections 7.5, 11.2, and 19.1). It is, however, probably a mistake to assume, as is done in the theory, that unions can set wages freely within limits determined by firms' demand for labor, for union leaders feel constrained by employer bargaining power (section 19.2). These leaders usually want higher pay than they are able to obtain and are willing to consider pay cuts only under extreme conditions. The main problem with the theory is that it currently applies to few U.S. firms, since only a small percentage of them are unionized (section 3.2). Another problem is the implicit assumption that opposition to pay cuts comes principally from union leaders or the work force, as if owners wanted to cut pay and were prevented from doing so by employees. This assumption did not apply to most of the firms I studied. In only a few was management thwarted from cutting pay by union opposition. In a like number, union leaders suggested pay cuts that management did not want because of possible damage to morale and productivity. The first line of resistance to pay reduction was almost always management.

THE SENIORITY RIGHTS MODEL

The seniority rights model of Shister (1943), Oswald (1986a), and others helps solve a logical difficulty in the monopoly union model. If the union wanted to maximize the total earnings of its members, then it would be willing to exchange a lower wage for a sufficiently large increase in employment. Since the firm chooses employment so as to maximize profits at the given wage, the rate of change of profits with respect to employment must be zero at the chosen point and the firm should be willing to employ a few more workers in exchange for a wage reduction small in proportion to the number of additional workers hired. Hence the union and firm should be able to find a mutually advantageous reduction in wages and increase in employment. This observation is puzzling, since most actual labor contracts do not specify total employment, but allow the employer to choose it. Contracts sometimes do specify work rules, but these increase employment only by decreasing the efficiency of labor, not an optimal arrangement from the point of view of the joint interests of union and firm.

The seniority rights model solves this inconsistency between theory and practice by assuming that unions are controlled by a majority of members with the highest seniority, whose jobs are so well protected by seniority privileges that they do not care about layoffs, except when these are large enough to reach workers in the controlling majority. Hence the union permits the firm to choose the employment level and has little incentive to cut pay so as to prevent layoffs. The model thus explains why union wages do not fall when layoffs threaten, something the monopoly union model cannot do without special assumptions, such as constancy of the elasticity of demand for labor.

This model found some support in my interviews, for a few union leaders mentioned that older members were unwilling to accept pay reductions to protect younger members. There are many reasons for skepticism, however, about any version of the seniority rights model. Labor leaders said that pay cuts would be accepted if they were seen to be necessary to save jobs (section 19.1). Seniority rights did not always protect workers against layoff (section 13.5), and managers said that layoffs sent a wave of fear throughout the remaining work force. No employer remarked on a sharp division of opinion among workers over pay cuts. Leaders of industrial unions believed that pay cuts do not significantly reduce layoffs (section 11.3), and this belief may be the main explanation for unions' reluctance to cut pay.

THE INSIDER-OUTSIDER MODEL

Lindbeck and Snower address the question of how existing employees, termed "insiders," prevent unemployed workers, called "outsiders," from taking their jobs or bidding down wages and salaries during a recession (Chapter 1). Lindbeck and Snower (1988a, b) propose a number of answers, all based on the assumption that unorganized workers bargain individually with employers. Their most striking suggestion is that existing workers would refuse to train or cooperate with replacement workers and so would reduce their productivity and make the jobs less attractive to them.[1]

The term "insider-outsider" is applied to models other than that of Lindbeck and Snower. Some authors use the terms "insider" and "outsider" when discussing models of collective bargaining in contexts where competition from unemployed workers might depress wages (for example, Layard, Nickell, and Jackman, 1991, chap. 4, sect. 2). Economists have used the insider-outsider idea to conclude that pay rates are an increasing function of a firm's profits and a decreasing function of the unemployment rate, since wages determined by bargaining probably would behave in this way. Some economists assume that company employment fluctuates around a normal level. Under this assumption, the insiders feel less vulnerable to layoff after a contraction of a company's work force and hence apply extra upward pressure on wages at such times. Similarly, after an expansion, the recently hired who have become insiders feel vulnerable to layoff and hence oppose pressuring the firm for more pay. These lagged impacts are termed hysteresis effects.

Insider-outsider theories do not correspond to what I observed. Few nonunion employees bargain with their employers, collectively or individually, even implicitly. Normally, only top executives and people with unusual skills can bargain effectively as individuals. It is unusual for nonunion companies in the United States to encourage any collective action by workers, and company unions are illegal. Pay rates are set by management, and the major factors it takes into account have to do with competition and incentives. Although employee reactions and morale play some role, these are not the same as employee pressure or participation in bargaining (sections 7.1 and 10.3). I heard nothing in nonunion firms indicating a division in attitudes toward pay cuts between new and old employees, high and low performers, the highly skilled and less skilled, or any other groups that might be interpreted as insiders and outsiders. I also heard nothing about hysteresis effects, and informants would almost surely have mentioned them, if they were real. Although Lindbeck and Snower (1988a, 1990) list a number of quite sensible reasons for not replacing workers with cheaper new hires, their idea that there might be conflict between new and old workers did not occur to businesspeople (section 13.4).

The main problem with the theories is that they assume conflict where there is none. There is usually no conflict between insiders and outsiders over pay cutting, because pay reduction is not thought of as saving jobs. There is no conflict between the employed and the unemployed over jobs, because firms do not normally replace employees with unemployed workers, for reasons that have nothing to do with dissension between new and old workers. Nor does hiring depress the pay of existing employees, for the considerations determining average pay levels within a company are independent of the size of its labor force. These considerations are hiring, turnover, and past pay levels.

A SOCIAL CONVENTION AGAINST UNDERCUTTING

Several authors, including Sabourian (1988) and Solow (1990), have proposed that the reason firms almost never replace workers with cheaper unemployed ones is that the latter refuse to offer themselves as replacements due to a social convention among unemployed workers against bidding jobs away from employed people. I found that no such convention exists, and that unemployed job applicants often lack the information needed to bid for jobs. Bids of this sort are probably discouraged by social mores, but the people offended would be employers, not other workers. That is, an offer to replace an existing job-holder would seem so bizarre, self-seeking, and antisocial as to make a bad impression on an employer. When unemployed workers offer to work for pay that is very low for the type of work, firms usually do not take advantage of the offers, for they do not want to violate their pay schedules or appear to be unfair (section 9.3). Employers normally treat undercutters like other job applicants and pay those they hire at rates consistent with internal structure.

20.3 Theories Based on Market Interactions

I now turn to theories that explain wage rigidity as the outcome of the functioning of markets.

SEARCH THEORIES

I discuss two kinds of search models, the market misperceptions type and the transactions type. In addition, I discuss "hold-up" models, which are related to search models with fully flexible pay.

THE MARKET MISPERCEPTION APPROACH

The market misperception models of Lucas and Rapping (1969), Mortensen (1970a), and others formalizes the following story. Workers' knowledge of market wage rates is limited to their own workplace. They learn about wages elsewhere through looking for a job, which is easier when unemployed than when employed. When the demand for labor diminishes, wages either decline or fail to increase as fast as expected, and workers imagine that only their own wages are disappointing and that wages elsewhere in the labor market are at the expected level. They therefore quit or allow themselves to be laid off, in the hopes that they can use their time while unemployed to find better-paying work, and this behavior causes unemployment to increase. Gradually, unemployed workers realize that wages are disappointing everywhere and take work at lower rates of pay than they would have accepted previously, causing unemployment to decline.

Most of what was said above about the intertemporal substitution theory also applies to the misperception theory (section 20.1). In addition, the misperception theory exaggerates the importance of worker ignorance. Advisers of the unemployed asserted that most job hunters were realistic about job and pay opportunities after getting over the shock of job loss. Many had trouble finding work even when they were realistic about their prospects, so that it was not misperceptions that kept them from finding work. Statistical data support these observations (Appendix 18A, sections 18.2 and 18.9). The misperception theory is probably correct in its assumption that job search is easier when unemployed than when employed, for this was the view of counselors who discouraged people from taking stopgap jobs, asserting that these distract from hunting for permanent ones (section 18.7). To the extent that this advice was followed, the theory is accurate in predicting that some people withhold labor in order to search for jobs better than those easiest to obtain.

THE TRANSACTIONS APPROACH

In the transactions models of Diamond (1981), Pissarides (1985), and others, unemployment rises during recessions, because structural economic change obliges workers to change jobs. The models describe in detail the determination of job vacancy and unemployment rates, but do not address the question of downward wage rigidity. Rather, wages are assumed to be completely flexible.

In transactions as well as misperception theories, workers accept only jobs that pay more than their reservation wage, and unemployment occurs because this wage is excessive. The focus on this wage is probably mistaken in the context of a recession. In the one I studied, the reservation wage of most unemployed people was probably below the range in which they could expect offers for regular permanent jobs. Job hunters had two ranges of jobs available to them, jobs for which they were nearly exactly qualified and stopgap jobs.

The reservation wage was relevant only for those people considering low-paying stopgap jobs or for the lucky few in demand. Even during the recession, employers competed vigorously for skills in short supply, and people with such skills held out for the highest bid, so that their reservation wage affected their decisions. Workers in demand, however, were usually either already employed or fresh out of college or professional school, not typical unemployed job seekers. When considering whether to take stopgap jobs, people had to weigh the advantage of having some pay against the disadvantage of having less time to search for better-paying work. This choice is of the type analyzed in job search theory, which does apply to some extent to the world of interim work. For example, temporary or contract workers dickered over wages and refused jobs (section 17.3).

The world of regular permanent jobs was quite different. Most job offers to unemployed people were accepted, and when there was bargaining over pay rates, it usually had little impact (sections 9.1 and 18.5). People could expect to get regular jobs only of a sort and at pay rates closely matching their qualifications, because of the overqualification problem and because employers were not likely to hire the underqualified during a recession (sections 15.2 and 18.6). Because people had to look in a fairly narrow range for regular jobs, the pay they could expect was similarly confined. A rough guess is that most pay offers for regular jobs to a given person were within 30 percent of one another. Given the difficulty unemployed people usually had finding regular jobs, it seldom made sense for them to refuse a regular job offer because of pay. Internal considerations normally prevented firms from taking advantage of high job acceptance rates to reduce hiring pay (Chapter 9).

THE HOLD-UP PROBLEM

Economists have proposed models where wages are the outcome of bargaining between individual workers and firms and in which wage flexibility is the central problem. In these "hold-up" models of Grout (1984), Williamson (1985), Caballero and Hammour (1996a), Malcomson (1997), and others, firms or workers must invest in their relationship for it to be productive, and the firm may reduce the returns on the worker's investment by reducing pay, or the worker may diminish the firm's returns by insisting on too much pay. Anticipating these problems, neither side invests enough. Although these models do not directly bear on wage rigidity, I comment on them, both because they appear in the literature discussing business cycles and unemployment and because I collected information that is relevant.

The hold-up problem appears naturally in search models that use the Nash bargaining solution and make the wage a weighted average of the worker's reservation wage and the revenue the firm earns from the worker's labor. It follows that the wage grows if the revenue generated by the worker increases, and the wage falls if a poor labor market depresses the reservation wage. The logic of this model can lead far. For instance, Stole and Zwiebel (1996) and Rotemberg (1997) conclude that firms overhire in order to depress the marginal product of labor and drive wages down.

I found that the hold-up problem hardly exists; though holding-up may be important in commercial relations (I have no information as to whether it is), it is not a consideration in labor relations. Firms do not hold up workers by cutting pay, and ordinary unorganized workers do not hold up firms for more pay. Only high-ranking executives and specialized professionals have enough bargaining power to do that. Although employers use raises to reward training and increase productivity, these increases are specified by overall policy and are usually not the outcome of individual bargaining. Nonunion firms often increase raises when profits rise, but this sharing of success is not forced on management by bargaining. Rather, it is a way of eliciting effort and loyalty. Wages rise quickly and sometimes dramatically in response to increases in the market demand for certain types of labor, but these increases are a reaction to competition from other firms, not to internal pressure from employees. Furthermore, most workers have little idea of the marginal revenue generated by their labor. Profit maximization implies that firms hire until this marginal product equals the wage plus an amount needed to offset the cost of hiring and training (section 6.6). Hence the only surplus to be divided between the firm and a single worker is this set-up cost, and I doubt they often squabble over it. I never heard employers complain about pressure from unorganized workers for excessive pay, though I heard bitter complaints about union wage demands. Individual demands for raises are often frowned upon, and individual workers are treated as traitors if they try to blackmail their employers by threatening to leave. Workers can get away with such behavior only if they have scarce talents (section 7.4). In short, the hold-up idea seems fanciful.

MULTIPLE EQUILIBRIA IN SEARCH MODELS

Diamond (1982b) and others have pointed out that in search models multiple equilibria can result from interaction between the search efforts of buyers and sellers. If buyers increase their efforts, sellers are likely to do so as well and may also offer more for sale. Similarly, selling efforts can stimulate demand and buyers' efforts to locate sellers. Because of these interactions, markets theoretically can have many equilibria, with different levels of trade. In a low-volume equilibrium, demand is low and buyers make little effort to find sellers, who in turn make little effort to find buyers and offer little for sale. Each side is discouraged by the other's inactivity. These ideas have been applied both to models with a single labor market and to ones with both goods and labor markets. High-activity equilibria are interpreted as booms and low-volume ones as recessions.

These models do not describe business fluctuations accurately. What occurs in labor markets during the transition from boom to recession is a shift in the ease of trading from sellers to buyers and a shift in search activity in the opposite direction. The diminution of buying effort accompanying the onset of a recession does not discourage the job hunting efforts of most unemployed people, though some who are marginally committed to the labor force withdraw from it and the employed have less interest in changing jobs (Chapter 16). Fear of prolonged unemployment probably stimulates the search efforts of most jobless people, and most firms experienced an abundance of qualified applicants during the recession (section 1.4). Product markets probably followed the same pattern. Multiple equilibrium models do not give a convincing explanation of downward wage rigidity, because they do not describe labor as in excess supply during recessions and so do not include the paradoxical granting of raises in the face of labor surplus.

KEYNES'S RELATIVE WAGE THEORY

Keynes (1936, pp. 14–15) attributes nominal downward wage rigidity to workers' preoccupation with relative pay rates among firms (section 1.4). This specific theory does not reflect the circumstances of wage determination, though Keynes was accurate in portraying wages as downwardly rigid and much unemployment as involuntary. Nonunion companies are like islands, with most workers having little systematic knowledge of pay rates outside their own company (Chapter 7). Pay rates in different nonunion companies are connected by the forces of supply and demand, but these allow a good deal of latitude in setting pay. Although concern about worker reaction and morale curbed pay cutting, employers said the reaction arises because pay cuts reduce pay relative to its former level. The fall relative to levels at other firms was believed to have little impact on morale, though it might increase turnover. Keynes's theory implies that a firm's workers would react to small raises as they do to pay cuts, if the raises were smaller than those given by other firms. However, no one in my study made this comparison, and managers did not expect small raises to provoke outrage, which was the anticipated consequence of pay cuts.

The situation differed somewhat in unionized companies, for labor unions foster awareness of pay rates in the labor market in order to stimulate member interest in wage gains. But no labor leader used wage differentials as an argument against pay cuts. Union leaders' main concern was whether pay reduction would save jobs. Labor unions would like to organize all the labor in a particular industry and have all its firms pay similar wage rates, in order to avoid giving low-paying firms an advantage that would allow them to expand at the expense of the others. This union strategy creates strong links between pay in different firms, but does not necessarily imply wage rigidity, for unions strong enough to control interfirm pay differentials may be able to coordinate pay cuts within an industry. I observed an example of just such coordination (section 7.5). Keynes's theory might apply to industries organized by competing unions, but too small a fraction of the American labor force is organized for the theory to apply widely (section 3.2).

20.4 Theories Attributing Wage Rigidity to Firms' Behavior

In an important body of theories, company policies are responsible for downward wage rigidity, which is sensible since nonunion firms have considerable freedom in setting pay.

IMPLICIT CONTRACTS
Some theories attribute wage rigidity to implicit contracts, which are informal agreements between employers and workers about the terms of employment.

THE IMPLICIT INSURANCE CONTRACT MODEL
In the implicit contract theory of Baily (1974), Gordon (1974), and Azariadis (1975), downward wage rigidity is a consequence of an agreement by employers to insure employees against income decline (section 1.4). Workers exchange lower long-run average wages for stability of real income.

The theory is attractive, for it explains wage rigidity using a commonsense argument and has a rigorous formulation with precise implications. If firms are risk averse, then real wages move in sympathy with a firm's financial state, though they do not fall in response to increased unemployment. The rigidity is only downward, for wages may rise freely in response to an excess demand for labor. The theory implies that real, not nominal wages, are rigid, so that nominal wages keep pace with the cost of living. An assumption of the model is that workers' hiring wages are determined by competition for their services, so that these wages are negatively related to the unemployment rate and may even decline when unemployment is high. Another implication of the theory is that unless problems of moral hazard make severance benefits impractical, laid-off workers receive enough severance pay to leave them as well off at the time of layoff as they would be had they kept their jobs.

Implicit contract theory implies that during recessions firms retain workers longer before laying them off than they do during booms. The theory asserts that when workers can find equivalent jobs easily firms lay off workers as soon as their marginal contribution to revenue is less than their pay. When jobs are hard to find, however, firms do not lay off workers until their marginal contribution is somewhat less than pay, even if the firm provides severance benefits. This policy is a low-cost way of increasing the expected future utility of workers at the time of hire, thereby decreasing the amount of pay needed to attract them. This aspect of implicit contracts is thought of as enforced by reputation; companies must pay higher wages if it is known that they lay off workers too soon during recessions.

The theory's implications regarding layoffs are far-reaching. If a firm offers optimal severance benefits, then it lays off workers only when their marginal contribution falls below their expected earnings from the new job they would find after leaving, where these earnings are adjusted to take into account the lack of earnings during job search. It follows that layoff decisions are independent of the wage level, so that the implicit contract disconnects layoff decisions from pay levels. This reasoning implies that a firm's employment during periods with layoffs is as high as or higher than it would be if there were no implicit contracts and workers earned only just enough to keep them indifferent between retaining their jobs and quitting into unemployment. It follows that employment could be as high as or higher than it would be if the firm's wages were perfectly flexible, so that the implicit contract model does not explain increases in unemployment during recessions. This "overemployment" result is one of the motivations for implicit contract models with asymmetric information (below in this section).

Many of the empirical implications of implicit contract theory are valid. Actual hiring wages are depressed to a limited extent by high unemployment (section 9.2). Pay does increase when profits increase (section 10.3), a phenomenon consistent with the theory if firms are risk averse, as they are (Chapter 5). In addition, firms protect the purchasing power of wages and salaries (section 10.3).

Nevertheless, the theory appears less realistic on closer examination. One difficulty is that severance pay is not as generous as it should be according to the theory. Many firms pay no severance benefits, and even when benefits are generous, they fall far short of full insurance (sections 14.1 and 14.2). Nearly all employers view permanent layoff as a financial disaster for those let go, even when severance benefits are generous by industry standards (section 13.9). The inadequacy of severance pay is not explained by moral hazard, for employers expressed no concerns about the hazard in this connection (section 14.3). Severance pay is not thought of as the benefit part of an insurance contract with a premium collected as lower pay, so that payment of severance benefits is not evidence in favor of implicit contract theory (section 14.4). Other evidence against implicit contract theory is the fact that firms seldom take account of labor market conditions when laying off workers. If increased unemployment has any effect, it is to encourage rather than to discourage layoffs (section 13.3).

Still another bit of evidence against the theory is that firms were not willing to compensate workers for the increase in the Connecticut state income tax in 1991 (section 10.3), as they would have done if the theory were correct.

The major problem with the theory is that managers do not think in a way consistent with it. I tried asking about the model, but respondents found it so strange that I desisted.[2] Employers do not usually imagine that they would have to pay more in the future if they cut pay now, for long-run pay levels are thought of as determined by competitive conditions. Employers acknowledged that pay cuts might make future hiring more difficult, but they associated the increased difficulty with greater managerial recruiting efforts, not with the need to pay more. Although pay stability and severance benefits obviously insure income, no employer recognized these as part of an insurance contact. Other considerations, such as morale, dominated business thinking, so that insurance economics probably does not apply. My attempts to have managers acknowledge implicit insurance contracts provoked impatience. Respondents did not articulate why they reacted this way, but the explanation was self-evident. Insurance contracts imply a precise exchange of premia for benefits. What are the premia paid for income protection? According to the theory, they are lower pay, but lower than what and by how much? The agreements of implicit contract theory struck employers as too vague. More concrete was bad morale caused by pay cuts and layoffs. Managers might offer explicit income insurance, if there were money to be made in it, but the protection provided by wage stability and severance pay is too nebulous to sell well. Employers focus on workers' state of mind, which might be worsened by talk of mutual insurance agreements, for such discussions would raise the difficult issue of how large the premia should be and would draw attention to the possibilities that the economy might worsen or the firm might need to lay off workers.

A possible way to reconcile the implicit contract model with what employers say is to assume that bad morale enforces implicit contracts, a proposal of Bull (1987) and Newberry and Stiglitz (1987).[3] This approach is incorrect, however, since business people do not believe the contracts exist.

THE MORAL OBLIGATION IMPLICIT CONTRACT MODEL

The subject of implicit contracts is confusing, for though employers do not recognize even an informal contract by which they insure workers' income, they do think of wage stability and severance benefits as part of a general implicit arrangement, and some even use the words "implicit contract" to express a company's obligation to absorb most business risk and to treat workers fairly. This contract arises from an idea of reciprocation and from an obligation stemming from the owner's being much richer than employees.

This notion of implicit contract appears in a theory proposed by Wachter and Williamson (1978), Hashimoto and Yu (1980), and Okun (1981), and defended by Malcomson (1997). They assume that jobs require an investment by the worker and employer of time, energy, and money in job search, hiring costs, and training. The firm must promise workers enough compensation to make their investment worthwhile, and workers have to promise the firm not to make its investment unprofitable by insisting on too much pay. After the investments are made, both sides have an incentive to renege on the agreement and change the rate of pay in their favor—that is, there is a hold-up problem (section 20.3). In order to counteract this temptation, they agree to a plan for future pay rates. The commitment is an implicit contract that is enforced in part by the expense of negotiating changes in the plan. (These fixed costs of wage adjustment are a form of menu costs (below in this section).) Okun proposes that firms comply with the contract because pay cuts provoke decreases in productivity and increases in future turnover and hiring difficulties. Although he does not use the word "morale," he clearly has it in mind.

There is some truth in this theory and especially in Okun's version of it. Firms avoid cutting pay because they anticipate problems with productivity, turnover, and recruiting, and one of the reasons that morale is hurt by pay cuts is the feeling that the firm has reneged on a promise. Breach of promise itself, however, is not a central issue in the reaction to pay cuts. If it were, firms could achieve pay flexibility by indexing wages to variables such as the unemployment rate, the firm's profits, or indicators of product demand. That is, wages could be a function of these things and fall when profits or demand fell or when unemployment rose. Such wage changes would incur no additional bargaining costs once the functional relationship was agreed upon. Prospective workers could evaluate the expected future income from indexed wages and compare it with the cost of investing in a job. Pays cuts would involve no violation of commitment as long as they were agreed upon in advance, and such agreements could be advantageous to both sides. Indexing wages to profits or sales would enable firms and workers to share risk. If wages were indexed to the unemployment rate, firms would be better able to compete for labor during booms, since they would not be restrained from raising wages by the inability to lower them later. Nevertheless, little use is made of such indexing, and automatic pay cuts resulting from profit sharing cause personnel problems similar to those brought on by discretionary pay cuts (section 12.5). Thus something more than the need for a commitment to a clear wage policy stands in the way of pay cutting. Another problem with the theory is that though it attributes wage rigidity to the firm's desire to induce workers to invest in their jobs, no employer I talked to ever linked pay cuts to workers' willingness to undergo training, though they did mention promotions in this connection.

An argument supporting the theory is that the possibility of hold-ups gives rise to internal pay structure, which in turn adds to wage rigidity. It is true that structure is an obstacle to hold-ups by individual workers, but no employer mentioned this effect as a reason for having structure. Although structure prevents hold-ups directed against individual workers, it does not prevent the firm from cutting the pay of all employees simultaneously.

EFFICIENCY WAGE THEORIES

Efficiency wage theories are descriptions of mechanisms by which increases in wages increase productivity. The positive association between pay and efficiency creates upward pressure on wages that puts them above the market-clearing level, so that the theories imply the existence of unemployment in equilibrium. Only some of the theories explain wage rigidity. Perhaps the best known efficiency wage theory is the shirking model, already discussed and rejected in Chapter 8.

THE TURNOVER AND FLAT LABOR SUPPLY CURVE MODELS

The turnover model of Stiglitz (1974), Schlicht (1978), and Salop (1979) is inspired by the empirically accurate observation that voluntary turnover in a firm decreases with its wage (section 7.1) and increases with labor market tightness (Chapter 16). In the model, firms weigh turnover costs against wage costs when setting pay and raise wages during periods of low unemployment in order to reduce quitting. It follows that low unemployment brings rapid wage inflation and that there must be some unemployment in an equilibrium with constant wages. The model does not explain wage rigidity, since wages fall when unemployment rises above the equilibrium level and turnover diminishes.

The flat labor supply curve model of Weiss (1990, sections 6.1 and 6.2) attributes nominal downward wage rigidity to extreme responsiveness of turnover to wages. Weiss assumes that individual companies cannot lower pay at all without soon losing a large proportion of their employees to other firms, so that each firm's labor supply curve is nearly horizontal at the existing wage. This model is not convincing. Although many employers did fear that pay cuts would stimulate turnover, the quitting anticipated was more a response to bad morale than a result of market forces (section 11.2). Moreover, actual pay cuts made during the recession had little impact on turnover, at least in the short run (section 12.2).

THE DUAL LABOR MARKET MODEL

This model, developed by Bulow and Summers (1986), combines the shirking model with the notion of dual labor markets to obtain a model of wage rigidity and unemployment. The dual labor markets are a primary one for well-paid career jobs and a secondary one for low-paid menial jobs, a distinction borrowed from Doeringer and Piore (1971) and close to the one I make. There are constant returns to labor in both sectors, so that the marginal product of labor does not decrease with output. Since workers are paid the value of their marginal product, the product real wage is constant in both sectors, where the product real wage is the nominal wage divided by the price of the commodity produced. People can find work immediately in the secondary sector, but may have to wait before finding primary-sector jobs. Primary-sector employers never hire anyone working in the secondary sector, because secondary-sector workers are believed to be of inferior quality. It follows that a worker must become unemployed to shift from the secondary to the primary sector. In an economic equilibrium, workers are indifferent between working in the secondary sector and being unemployed while looking for a job in the primary sector. It follows that there is an increasing relation between the waiting time for a job in the primary sector and the difference in pay between the two sectors. Since the waiting time increases with the ratio of total unemployment to primary-sector employment, there is an increasing relation between the pay difference and this ratio. In the primary sector, and only in this sector, pay is used as a means of strengthening discipline, as in the shirking model. Since an immediate job in the secondary sector is an alternative to work in the primary sector, pay in the primary sector is a mark-up over that in the secondary sector. It follows that two conditions, the no-shirking condition and indifference between unemployment and work in the secondary sector, uniquely determine two variables, the difference in pay between the two sectors and the ratio of total unemployment to primary-sector employment. These variables are also independent of total employment in the secondary sector and hence of total employment. Therefore, real pay rates and the relative prices of output in the two sectors are independent of demand for output, so that real wages are rigid with respect to aggregate demand. Demand determines employment in both sectors, but does not affect the ratio of unemployment to primary-sector employment. A decrease in the demand for primary-sector output causes no change in real wages and causes a decrease in unemployment and an increase in employment in the secondary sector. The model, therefore, does not describe accurately the events occurring during recessions, when employment in almost all industries declines and joblessness increases.[4]

The assumptions underlying this model are unrealistic. The shirking theory does not describe business behavior in the primary sector (Chapter 8). In the model, wage rigidity in the primary sector stems from that in the secondary sector, whereas in reality hiring pay rates in the secondary sector are fairly flexible. It is hiring pay rates that are relevant to the model, since workers laid off from the primary sector are paid as new hires if they take work in the secondary sector. Another assumption that may be unrealistic is that the shirking model does not apply in the secondary sector. When interviewing, I had the contrary impression that the shirking model may apply to low-paid, short-term jobs, though it does not apply to the primary sector.

THE MORALE MODEL

The fundamental assumption of the Solow (1979) and Akerlof (1982) morale model is that pay rates have a positive effect on productivity through their impact on morale (Chapter 1). The theory is correct in emphasizing morale, but errs to the extent that it attaches importance to wage levels rather than to the negative impact of wage cuts. Employers doubted that pay levels themselves have much effect on morale and work effort, though they certainly believed that pay levels affect productivity through the quality of workers that can be recruited (section 7.1). Pay cuts were thought likely to damage morale and productivity (section 11.2).

THE FAIR WAGE MODEL

The fair wage model of Akerlof (1982) is an elaboration of the morale model and is also a version of Keynes's relative wage theory (section 20.3). The fundamental assumption of the model is that work effort increases as wages increase relative to what workers believe to be a fair pay rate. This fair rate is imprecisely defined, but depends on the pay of other workers at the same and at other firms, as well as on past pay and on labor market conditions. Given the fair wage, firms choose their own wage so as to maximize profits. Dependence of the fair wage on past wages creates nominal downward wage rigidity, as does dependence on wages at other firms, as in Keynes's theory. Dependence of the fair wage on labor market conditions introduces the possibility of downward flexibility.

The theory is correct insofar as the fair wage depends on past wages and wages of other employees at the same work site (sections 6.4, 6.5, and 11.2). The theory is inaccurate to the extent that the fair wage depends on wages at other firms and on labor market conditions (chapter 7 and section 11.2).

MODELS ASSUMING ASYMMETRIC INFORMATION

Theories based on asymmetric information attribute wage rigidity and layoffs to the difficulty of conveying information. Basic assumptions are that workers cannot directly give firms information about their abilities and firms cannot directly give workers the information required to convince them that pay cuts are necessary.

THE IMPLICIT INSURANCE CONTRACT MODEL WITH ASYMMETRIC INFORMATION

In models developed by Grossman and Hart (1981) and others, layoffs serve to demonstrate to workers that profits or productivity are low enough to justify

pay cuts, the cuts being made in accord with an implicit agreement between
the firm and its employees to diminish costs when profits fall. The authors
assume that the employer is risk averse, so that it is worthwhile for workers to
share in the employer's risk. Workers cannot observe profits or productivity,
and in order to prove that profits are low, the firm lays off labor that it would
want to use if profits and productivity were higher. Because layoffs are used in
this way, they can be so extensive that the marginal product of labor after
layoffs is higher than the wage and is therefore certainly higher than the minimum wage needed to retain workers. Thus the model does not have the overemployment property of implicit insurance contracts with symmetric information (above in this section), a property the model is designed to avoid. The
theory implies that unemployment increases during recessions and that wages
do not fall in response to high unemployment. The theory does not imply wage
rigidity in the face of layoffs and company financial distress, since pay cuts
accompany layoffs.

The theory does not describe reality, for most layoffs occur without pay cuts
(sections 11.1 and 13.1). After layoffs companies typically continue to give
regular pay increases, and some layoffs are made precisely to finance pay increases. A few employers did say that layoffs created a crisis atmosphere that
made workers more willing to consider a pay cut. It is also true that many
companies in financial difficulty simultaneously lay off workers and reduce or
eliminate raises. A few even cut pay. However, no employer told me that layoffs
were used to demonstrate distress. Normally no such signal is needed, for when
a company is in a crisis, almost everyone working there knows it. When companies are in serious trouble, workers are likely to accept pay cuts, especially
if they prevent layoffs (sections 12.1 and 19.1).

THE ADVERSE SELECTION MODEL

Andrew Weiss (1980 and 1990), in his adverse selection model, makes the trade-
off between pay and work force quality responsible for wage rigidity, even when
there is no shortage of skilled labor. Weiss assumes that employers are uncertain
about the quality of job applicants, even after taking into account interviews,
references, and other sources of information. He also assumes that employers
use the wage or salary acceptable to candidates as an important indicator of
their quality. For each set of observable job candidate characteristics, there is
an optimal hiring wage that maximizes the expected revenue generated by each
worker per dollar of compensation. This wage would be downwardly flexible,
if recessions raised the relation between quality and acceptable pay rates, as
would occur if workers' wage expectations fell. In the theory, the relation between quality and pay is kept constant through interaction with the secondary
labor market. The model applies to industrial jobs, which may be identified

with the primary sector, as defined in this book. Weiss assumes that workers can find alternative work in either home production or nonindustrial jobs, which can be thought of as the secondary sector. He further assumes that pay in these alternative jobs is closely tied to ability, so that the secondary sector fixes the relationship between pay and worker quality. Finally, he assumes that real wages in the secondary sector are downwardly rigid because of constant returns to labor in production there. It follows that the relation between worker quality and real wages in both sectors is not affected by labor market conditions. Notice that the rigidity of primary-sector hiring pay is a consequence of wage rigidity in the secondary sector.

Weiss uses similar arguments to explain the downward rigidity of the pay of existing primary sector workers. He assumes that employers cannot determine workers' quality precisely and hence lay them off rather than reduce pay because the best workers would quit if pay were cut.

It is certainly true, as the theory assumes, that higher pay attracts better-quality workers. For employers, this was a self-evident fact of life. Though the trade-off between pay and worker quality puts a floor under pay in the secondary sector, informants seldom cited this trade-off as a cause of wage rigidity in the primary sector and they did so only when particular skills were in short supply (sections 9.1, 9.4, 11.2, and 17.5). Weiss's theory focuses on rigidity in the pay of new hires, whereas the pay of new hires was more flexible than that of existing employees (section 9.2).

I had little luck asking employers about the adverse selection theory, for it is hard to describe quickly and convincingly. No employer said anything showing that pay demands indicated quality. Employers always discussed the relation between pay and quality as if the latter was observable and could be determined from interviews, personal appearance, and obvious credentials.

The theory shares with the dual labor market theory the weakness that it derives downward rigidity of primary-sector wages from downward rigidity of alternative wages in the secondary and household sectors. In reality, the household sector is seldom an important source of income, and hiring wages are more flexible in the secondary than the primary sector (sections 9.2, 17.2, and 17.3).

The theory is correct in its assumption that employers fear that their best workers will quit if pay is cut. However, this fear does not stem from an inability to determine worker quality, but from an inability to reward it sufficiently because of constraints imposed by internal equity (sections 6.6 and 10.2).

THE STIGMA OF UNEMPLOYMENT

Numerous authors propose that one reason high unemployment persists and does not cause wage rates to fall is that the unemployed carry a stigma that makes them ineffective competitors for jobs (Greenwald, 1986; Layard and Bean, 1989; and Gibbons and Katz, 1991). According to the theory, employers suspect that people who have been laid off are of low quality, because firms lay off their worst workers first. Similarly, people unemployed for a long time are suspected of not wanting to work, of being incapable of making an effective job search, of having personal problems, or of having lost skills and motivation while out of work.

The unemployed did suffer from a stigma for the reasons just described, though loss of skills was hardly ever mentioned, and the stigma was considerably diminished by the recession (sections 15.3 and 18.12). The stigma may prolong unemployment, but I doubt it has much to do with wage rigidity, for employers enjoyed an abundance of qualified and desirable job applicants (section 15.1).

THE MENU COST AND RELATED THEORIES

The menu cost model attributes downward wage rigidity to the expense of changing wages. The name of the theory was suggested by the cost of printing restaurant menus. Menu costs are usually used to explain price rigidity (Mankiw, 1985; Akerlof and Yellen, 1985a), but have been applied to the labor market (Blanchard and Kiyotaki, 1987; Akerlof and Yellen, 1985b). Although the costs of wage adjustment might seem minor, Akerlof and Yellen argue that the resulting wage rigidity can be large. Suppose that wages are set so as to maximize profits, as in the turnover and shirking models. If profits are a smooth function of wages, then small deviations of wages from their optimal level would have little impact on profits, so that small fixed costs of wage adjustment could discourage any change until a large one was needed.[5]

A theory related to menu costs is the overlapping contract theory proposed by Fischer (1977) and Taylor (1979, 1980). The starting point of the theory is the observation that both union and nonunion pay rates are usually fixed administratively for a period of at least a year. The times at which wages and salaries are changed differ among firms, and this staggering of contracts implies that economywide average wages and salaries adjust slowly to changes in economic conditions, even if each firm is willing to cut pay when it renews contracts. The theory does not address the heart of the wage rigidity question, for it fails to explain why pay rates are not reduced when they are reset or renegotiated.

Although the overlapping contracts model is realistic, the menu cost theory is not. It is true that most union contracts specify wages for fixed periods and that nonunion companies typically fix wages at one-year intervals as long as inflation is moderate. No manager, however, ever said that administrative or negotiation costs interfered with pay cutting. These costs could hardly explain why pay was increased rather than cut.

20.5 Theories of Recessions as Reallocators of Labor

Although labor reallocation theories do not explain downward wage rigidity, I discuss them here because they offer an explanation of unemployment popular among economists and one roughly in the spirit of the Lucas-Rapping model. In these theories, recessions are both inevitable and useful, and the unemployment accompanying them is merely a cost of adjustment to structural economic change, as in search models using the transactions approach. Recessions are said to be caused by waves of shocks to individual businesses or industrial sectors, and these sudden changes create a need for labor reallocation. The shocks destroy jobs, forcing people to find new ones. Recessions bring high unemployment, because job switching is a slow process and new jobs may not be available for some time. The shocks can be decreases in demand for particular products or localized declines in productivity. Recessions can also result from a temporary decrease in the value attached by society to current consumption, creating a low-cost opportunity for labor reallocation.

In discussing these models, I focus on their explanation of the causes of recessions and relate this to what I observed. I do not discuss the idea that recessions are useful, though I find it dubious. The literature describing recessions as labor reallocations began with David Lilien (1982), who pointed out that U.S. unemployment is positively correlated with the variance across industrial sectors of employment growth rates. He went on to infer that increases in unemployment during recessions are in part caused by increases in the need to move labor from declining to expanding sectors. Davis and Haltiwanger (1990) and Davis, Haltiwanger, and Schuh (1996) have found in U.S. data for manufacturing a tremendous amount of fluctuation in employment from period to period in individual productive establishments. They label as "job creation" employment at a new establishment or an increase in employment at an existing one and they define "job destruction" to be loss of employment from the closure of an establishment or a decrease in its employment. Using quarterly and annual data, they sum all job creation and all job destruction and divide the totals by manufacturing employment in the United States to express the sums as rates. The rate of job creation fluctuates little and shows a slight tendency to decline during recessions, whereas the job destruction rate varies much more and increases sharply during economic downturns. The authors define the sum of the job creation and job destruction rates as the "job reallocation rate," which is dominated by and shows the same cyclical pattern as the job destruction rate (Davis and Haltiwanger, 1990, p. 132, and Davis, Haltiwanger, and Schuh,

1996, p. 33). From the cyclical behavior of the job reallocation rate, they conclude that job reallocation is a major cause of unemployment growth during recessions. They assume that labor reallocation occurs because idiosyncratic shocks to individual businesses cause them to change employment. Their definition of shocks is more all-embracing than that used in reallocation theories, where shocks are usually local changes in demand or productivity. In addition to these, they include as shocks changes in the supply of inputs and in the financial condition of a company and even changes brought about by fluctuations in aggregate demand.

Davis and Haltiwanger (1990, pp. 145–155) express their point of view using a formal theoretical model in which there are high and low productivity work sites and an unlimited supply of each. In every period, some high productivity sites become low-productivity ones. A worker can move from a low to a high productivity site, but loses one period of labor while doing so, so that the shift is an investment of lost current output that brings greater output in the future. The average utility from consumption fluctuates, and, from the point of view of social welfare, it is better to have more workers switch from low to high productivity sites during periods when the utility of consumption is low than when it is high, for the drop in utility diminishes the social cost of the reduction in output during the switch. Periods of low utility for consumption are interpreted as recessions, for then work time is lost to unemployment as workers move. Similarly booms are periods of high consumption utility and little labor reallocation, during which the need for reallocation accumulates. In the model, recessions are analogous to summer vacation shutdowns during which automobile assembly plants retool. The model includes nothing about wage behavior, but can be combined with a Lucas-Rapping model of wage formation. For instance, elaborations of the model have people choose among work, leisure, and time unemployed spent moving to a new work site. Caballero and Hammour (1996b) have constructed a model similar to that of Davis and Haltiwanger with job search and endogenous wages.

It may seem strange that job destruction and creation models are labeled as models of labor reallocation when so much more destruction than creation occurs during recessions. Caballero and Hammour (1996c) propose that this discrepancy may be resolved by assuming that it costs more to create than to destroy jobs. Similar ideas are contained in Palley (1992) and Hosios (1994).

Hamilton (1988) formalizes Lilien's point of view in a general equilibrium model in which shocks, such as oil price increases, reduce demand for the output of certain sectors, such as the automobile industry. These sectoral shocks increase unemployment either because it takes time to find jobs in other sectors or because unemployed workers prefer to consume leisure and wait for the revival of the industry in which they used to work.

The arguments of Davis, Haltiwanger, and Schuh rest in part on terminology.

The term "total job reallocation" is probably misleading, for the sum of job destruction and creation could fluctuate as it does even if all business establishments expanded and contracted simultaneously at the same rate, with no idiosyncratic shocks affecting different job sites. In this case, the shocks causing unemployment would be entirely aggregate. A more appropriate measure of job reallocation would be the cross-sectional variance of employment growth rates in various establishments, and indeed Davis and Haltiwanger show that such a measure moves in sympathy with their measure of reallocation. However, cross-sectional variance might still be misnamed as "reallocation," for many people who lose their jobs may not find new ones for a long time, so that they would be reallocated to long-term idleness.

In evaluating work on reallocation models, the key issue is the interpretation of the factual findings, not these findings themselves, which seem correct and correspond to my interviewing experience. The important question is whether idiosyncratic shocks to industrial sectors and productive establishments cause recessions or whether the shocks and economic contractions are both the result of aggregate demand fluctuations and financial crises. If the idiosyncratic shocks cause recessions, then these probably cannot be avoided by adjusting aggregate demand and preventing financial disturbances, whereas macroeconomic policy could avert contractions if the causation were in the reverse direction (provided policy could affect aggregate demand and financial conditions). It is difficult to determine the direction of causation from aggregate data, for all the relevant variables move together. Even in the case of oil price shocks, there is ambiguity, though these are often cited as clear examples of sectoral shocks. Oil price increases reduce aggregate demand if they depress demand in some sectors more than they stimulate it in others. They reduce the nominal value of aggregate demand by increasing the value of imports, and they diminish the real value of aggregate demand by increasing prices. The most important effect of oil shocks may be their impact on monetary policy, which becomes restrictive in an effort to fight inflation. Another awkwardness for resource allocation theories is that the same sectors, namely, defense and durable goods, especially the construction and automobile industries, contract in almost all recessions and expand in almost all booms. Durable goods expenditures are cyclically sensitive because they are discretionary and depend on the availability of credit. Contractions in defense expenditure and in the demand for durable goods are sectoral fluctuations in a mechanical or statistical sense. Demand for these goods, however, is closely linked to macroeconomic policy, and it is not appropriate to label as "reallocation" movement of labor into and out of the same sectors. (This argument is similar to that of Abraham and Katz, 1986.) Perhaps more could be learned about the direction of causation by detailed microeconomic studies of what happens to companies during recessions.

Although my field research was not oriented toward reallocation theories, I did learn that many of the companies in the greatest difficulty were in the typical cyclical industries, namely, construction, consumer durables, and defense, and it was clear that their problems resulted from tight credit and demand contraction. I never heard an employer complain of a decline in productivity, so that there was no evidence of negative productivity shocks. Nor were oil prices rising noticeably at the time, though the increase in oil prices after Iraq's invasion of Kuwait may have initiated the recession. Just as Davis, Haltiwanger, and Schuh (1996) assert, there was enormous variation among companies within the contracting sectors. For instance, companies specializing in the design of new weapons were expanding, despite the reduction in defense spending, and construction and architectural firms specializing in institutional buildings for governments, schools, and universities were doing well, despite the slump in construction. Major manufacturers sometimes reduced the number of their providers rather than uniformly cutting back orders from all, so that the impact on these suppliers was unequal. General hardware stores did well, whereas some suppliers of expensive household furnishings were hard hit. The biggest cause of variation in the success of companies seemed to be their financial condition. Lack of money made it impossible for some to stock retail outlets or to fill orders and it even forced a few to cease operations. Financial problems were contagious, for companies were hurt when major customers that were in difficulty did not pay their bills or canceled orders or when troubled banks recalled loans. These diverse company fates qualify as idiosyncratic shocks according to the definition of Davis and Haltiwanger, but the high incidence of the shocks seemed to be the consequence rather than the cause of obvious aggregate events. It should not be surprising that tight credit or sharp declines in industry demand do not affect all its firms in the same way, just as it is not surprising that epidemics do not make all people a little sick, but make some very sick and leave others unharmed.

My observations were hard to reconcile with Hamilton's (1988) idea that unemployment is the consequence of shifting labor from declining to expanding sectors and of people's choosing to consume leisure while waiting for jobs to reopen in their own sector. Indeed, what I saw was not consistent with any model of recessions as reallocators of labor. There are two variants of such models. According to one, aggregate demand does not decline during recessions, but demand or output declines in some sectors or firms and grows in others. Growth is slower than decline, however, because high expansion costs or the difficulty of reallocating labor prevent the growing firms or sectors from meeting demand (Palley, 1992; Hosios, 1994; and Caballero and Hammour, 1996c). According to the other variant, aggregate demand declines because of a decrease in utility for current consumption, creating a convenient time for labor reallocation (Davis and Haltiwanger, 1990; Caballero and Hammour,

1996b). For either story to be distinct from the Keynesian one, there must be enough job creation during recessions for more labor reallocation to occur then than during booms. Otherwise, reallocation models would have the same implications as Keynesian models of fluctuating aggregate demand, there being nothing in the latter that precludes the transfer of labor and jobs among sectors or firms over the course of a business cycle. In reality, more reallocation may occur during booms. For instance, Murphy and Topel (1987b) find that the flow of labor between sectors is greatest during booms, which is consistent with the fact that these are the times with the highest voluntary turnover. During the period of the interviews, there seemed to be little job creation to offset job destruction. Job counselors were discouraged about local job prospects. Jobs were said to be available in the Midwest and South, but among the jobless in the Northeast only the well-to-do could afford to move that far. Most unemployed had leisure forced on them and many had to search long and hard to find work. Only a few firms were growing rapidly, and I heard of no large sectors that were expanding or even getting ready to do so. Nor did I learn of companies that were desperately trying to expand to meet demand, but were prevented from doing so by the difficulty of obtaining qualified labor, by the expense of installing new equipment, by construction delays, or by difficulties in securing materials and supplies. If expansion costs were what inhibited job creation, such companies should have been common, and I should have found at least one, for expanding companies were one of the categories on which I concentrated my search. The firms that were expanding had no trouble doing so.

20.6 Summary

The only one of the many theories of wage rigidity that seems reasonable is the morale theory of Solow and Akerlof. The others fail because of the lack of realism of their basic assumptions.

Appendix 20A Related Literature

LABOR SUPPLY THEORIES (SECTION 20.1)
Researchers, beginning with Lucas and Rapping, have performed numerous econometric tests of the intertemporal substitution theory. Many of the tests involve estimation of labor supply responses to wages and expected wages, for the theory predicts that employment responds positively to the difference between actual and expected wage rates. Papers using macro data include Lucas and Rapping (1969), Sargent (1973), Altonji and Ashenfelter (1980), Altonji (1982), Andrews and Nickell (1982), Ashenfelter and Card (1982), and Alogoskoufis (1987).

Mankiw, Rotemberg, and Summers (1985) find that because consumers normally reduce or increase all forms of consumption together, it is impossible to reconcile rationality with the fact that people consume more leisure but fewer goods and services during recessions than booms. The choice during recessions of more leisure and less of other things is consistent with rational behavior only if people have peculiar utility functions or if real wages fall during recessions. The authors point out that there is little or no systematic relation between real wages and business fluctuations. Abraham and Haltiwanger (1995) and Brandolini (1995) review the literature on the cyclical behavior of real wages.

Some studies use survey data on individuals to estimate labor supply elasticities. These data show an additional form of correlation between wages and labor supply, for when wages and average hours worked are plotted against workers' age both graphs have upside down U-shapes (Smith, 1977, fig. 1; Browning, Deaton, and Irish, 1985, figs. 1 and 2). This correlation may be a response of labor supply to wage rates, or may result from other factors. For instance, Browning, Deaton and Irish (1985) find that for manual workers, the number of children in a household explains labor supply better than wage rates. The micro studies contain many estimates of labor supply elasticities. A typical estimate for adult men is 0.15, that of MaCurdy (1981). A typical estimate for women is around 2, which is that of Heckman and MaCurdy (1980, 1982). The large literature on this subject has been reviewed by Killingworth and Heckman (1986) and Pencavel (1986).

Low estimates of labor supply elasticities would be evidence against the Lucas Rapping model, but high estimates would not confirm it since the studies of labor supply elasticities do not distinguish between unemployment and being out of the labor force and so cannot determine whether unemployment is a voluntary or forced withdrawal of labor. Some studies have attempted to determine whether unemployment is voluntary. Browning, Deaton, and Irish (1985) find that dummy variables for each year are highly significant in their micro data regressions for labor supply and they believe these year dummies express cyclical effects on hours worked. Similarly, Ashenfelter and Ham (1979) and Ham (1986) find that inclusion of independent variables indicating whether a person is unemployed are significant in labor supply functions estimated from micro data, and Ashenfelter (1980) applies a similar idea to a labor supply function estimated from aggregate data. Card (1990b) interprets unpublished work of Ham as showing that variables reflecting the demand for an individual's labor are significant in labor supply equations estimated from micro data. All these results indicate that people are not always able to sell as much labor as they would like at "market" wages. From the point of view of a strict interpretation of the intertemporal substitution theory, however, it is to be expected that variables reflecting labor demand conditions are statistically significant in labor supply functions, for labor supply responds to wage rates that apply only to single individuals, and these wages are not observed and are probably correlated with variables reflecting labor demand conditions. This point is acknowledged by Ham (1986) and stressed by Heckman and MaCurdy (1988).

THE MONOPOLY UNION MODEL (SECTION 20.2)

Dunlop's (1944) monopoly union model has been used to model wage rigidity (M. Reynolds, 1981; Hart, 1982; McDonald and Solow, 1985; and Layard, Nickell, and Jackman, 1991, pp. 100–104). The idea that labor's collective monopoly power causes unemployment has been developed in theoretical economics, key papers being Hahn (1978) and Negishi (1979). Mitchell (1972) and many others have pointed out that union demands are limited by employer resistance. Surveys of union bargaining theory may be found in Oswald (1982, 1985), Pencavel (1985), Farber (1986), Nickell (1990), Ulph and Ulph (1990), Creedy and McDonald (1991), and McDonald (1995).

The Seniority Rights Model   Leontief (1946) was the first to point out the inefficiency of fixed wage contracts. The seniority theory has occurred to many people; it was hinted at by Shister (1943) and McDonald and Solow (1981, 1984), brought up by Chapman and Fisher (1984), and formalized by Oswald (1986a), Carruth and Oswald (1987), and McDonald (1989). Similar ideas may be found in many recent papers on unemployment, especially ones using the insider-outsider idea (Solow, 1985; Blanchard and Summers, 1986 and 1988; Gottfries and Horn, 1987; Lindbeck and Snower, 1987; Layard and Bean, 1989; and Holden, 1990). Oswald (1986b) takes a skeptical view of the model as an explanation of wage rigidity, on the grounds that senior workers should be willing to exchange wage cuts in bad times for higher wages in good times.

The Insider-Outsider Model   Lindbeck and Snower (1988b) have been the chief architects of the insider-outsider theory. Hysteresis effects in the insider-outsider model are discussed by Blanchard and Summers (1986) and Gottfries and Horn (1987). Fehr (1990, 1991) makes a theoretical argument against Lindbeck and Snower's theory, to which they reply in their paper of (1990).

A Social Convention against Undercutting   The idea of a social convention against undercutting has been advanced by Weibull (1987), Sabourian (1988, 1989), Solow (1990), and Lindbeck (1992, p. 210). The convention is usually modeled as the outcome of a repeated game among workers and firms in which any breach of the convention is punished by reversion to a low-wage equilibrium.

THE MARKET MISPERCEPTION APPROACH (SECTION 20.3)

The market misperceptions theory was suggested in intuitive terms by Friedman (1968) and was elaborated by Lucas and Rapping (1969) and Lucas (1972).

The theory has since been extended by many authors (Mortensen, 1970a, 1970b, 1970c; Phelps, 1970b; and Wright, 1986). Job search theory is reviewed in Mortensen (1986). Okun (1980; 1981, pp. 42–43) criticized the market misperceptions theory, especially for its incorrect predictions regarding the cyclical behavior of quits.

The Transactions Approach   One of the earliest works using the transactions approach is that of Lucas and Prescott (1974). In their model, people move among separate labor markets, within each of which the wage rate is determined by supply and demand. In many other models, wages are determined by bargaining between individual employers and prospective employees. It is assumed that there is a surplus to be split between prospective workers and a company, in the sense that the company would be willing to pay workers more than the amount required to recruit them. It is usually assumed that the wage is set according to some rule, such as a Nash bargaining solution, that splits the surplus (Diamond, 1981, 1982a; Pissarides, 1985, 1990; Blanchard and Diamond, 1989; and Mortensen and Pissarides, 1993, 1994). In other papers, it is assumed that companies unilaterally fix pay rates, adjusting them so as to achieve the optimal balance between labor costs and availability (Hosios, 1985; Burdett and Mortensen, 1989; Mortensen, 1990; Lang, 1991; and Montgomery, 1991). In almost all search models using the transactions approach, increased labor market slackness causes pay rates to decline, and in most of the models the decline is accompanied by increased unemployment and a reduction in the stock of job vacancies.[6]

The Hold-Up Problem   The hold-up notion appears in Caballero and Hammour (1996a, b) in the context of job reallocation models and also appears in Stole and Zwiebel (1996) and Rotemberg (1997). Ramey and Watson (1997) have constructed a model similar in spirit to that of Caballero and Hammour (1996b) in which not only wages but worker or firm effort may be changed opportunistically.

Multiple Equilibria in Search Models   Perhaps the simplest multiple equilibria model is that of Howitt (1985). In his model, firms buy labor and sell output, and workers buy output and sell labor, and both types of sellers incur selling costs. Low- and high-volume equilibria are possible. Prices can be the same in both equilibria. Diamond (1982b, 1984a, b) formulates similar models.

A somewhat different model appears in Howitt and McAfee (1987). The model is of a single labor market, not of a whole economy. In this market, both buyers and sellers incur search costs and both must decide how much effort to devote to searching for jobs or employees. The decisions interact, so that for a given wage rate there can be high- and low-volume equilibria, there being more search by both sides and more employment in high-volume equilibria.

Mortensen (1989, p. 366) proposed quite a different mechanism for the generation of multiple equilibria in the labor market. According to his model, increases in labor market activity make it easier to transact, and there is more activity when there are more sellers, that is, when the unemployment rate is higher. Therefore, the smaller the unemployment rate, the harder it is for unemployed people to find jobs and hence the lower are wages. The drop in wages in turn stimulates firms to hire more workers, further reducing unemployment. The interaction between unemployment and wages can give rise to both a low-employment, high-wage equilibrium and a high-employment, low-wage equilibrium.

Keynes's Relative Wage Theory Keynes (1936) did not describe the precise mechanism he had in mind by which relative wages affect a firm's ability to cut pay. Trevorithick (1976) formalizes Keynes's theory, by assuming that the labor supply to each firm depends on its wage relative to wages paid at other firms, a theory close to Weiss's (1990) flat labor supply curve model (section 20.4). Another possibility is that a drop in relative wages hurts morale and productivity, and Summers (1988) gives rigorous expression to this version of the theory. Bhaskar (1990) proposes yet another version using the monopoly union model. In this model, unions maximize the average utility of employed and unemployed members, so that a union's objective function depends on the wage of its own members and on the average level of wages elsewhere in the labor market. The union utility function depends on these variables in such a way that the utility for the members' wage has a kink at the wage norm established by the labor market. That is, the union's utility increases faster with respect to its own members' wage when this wage is less than the norm than when it exceeds it. As a result, the union finds it optimal to set its wage equal to the norm for a wide range of values of the norm. When the norm is thought of as determined by interacting unions, the model implies that the market norm is indeterminate within a certain range. The model implies downward wage rigidity if it is assumed that the norm does not move when labor market conditions change.

THE IMPLICIT INSURANCE CONTRACT MODEL (SECTION 20.4)

The implicit contract model was introduced by Baily (1974), Gordon (1974), and Azeriadis (1975) and was further developed by Harris and Holmstrom (1982) and Holmstrom (1983). The relation to the propensity to lay off is discussed by Barro (1977), Akerlof and Miyazaki (1980), Holmstrom (1983), and Stiglitz (1986). A key paper on the enforcement of implicit contracts through reputation is Thomas and Worrall (1988). Beaudry and DiNardo (1991) found important empirical evidence supporting the model, which is that workers' wages are negatively related to the unemployment rate at the time they were hired, even if it was years earlier. However, this finding is not conclusive, for it may be explained by the manner in which raises are administered and by the influence on hiring pay of current labor market conditions.

The Morale Model   The morale model is due to Solow (1979) and has been advocated and extended by Akerlof (1982) and Akerlof and Yellen (1988, 1990). Akerlof suggested that pay and productivity are linked because workers offer extra effort out of gratitude for generous pay. Akerlof (1982) and Akerlof and Yellen (1990) support their theory with numerous references to empirical literature in sociology and management science. Nevertheless, the model has received little attention in labor economics and has been criticized as smacking of irrationality (Weiss, 1990, pp. 12–13), as leaving too short a distance between assumptions and conclusions, and as not lending itself to mathematical development (Carmichael, 1990, pp. 275–277, 291).

The Fair Wage Model   The fair wage theory was proposed by Akerlof (1982) and is discussed further in Akerlof and Yellen (1988, 1990) and Summers (1988).

The Implicit Insurance Contract Model with Asymmetric Information   There is a large literature on implicit contracts with asymmetric information. A central conclusion is that asymmetric information overcomes the overemployment problem only if employers are sufficiently risk averse in comparison with workers. Key papers are Grossman and Hart (1981, 1983), Green and Kahn (1983), and Cooper (1983). Surveys of the subject are Hart (1983), Rosen (1985), and Cooper (1987).

The Adverse Selection Model   Blinder and Choi (1990) report that none of the businesspeople they interviewed believed that high wage demands indicated superior worker quality, evidence against the adverse selection theory. However, Agell and Lundborg (1995) report that a majority of the Swedish managers they interviewed gave varying degrees of support to the idea that wage demands indicate quality. None of their questions connects this idea to wage rigidity. In Campbell and Kamlani's (1997) survey, employers support the assertion that an important reason for not cutting pay is that the best workers would leave, a finding in agreement with my own (section 11.2). Though this finding is consistent the adverse selection theory, as Campbell and Kamlani point out, it is also consistent with the idea that the need for internal equity prevents firms from retaining their best workers by not cutting their pay.

The Stigma of Unemployment   Authors have proposed a variety of reasons for the stigma of unemployment. Greenwald (1986) and Gibbons and Katz (1991) suggested the connection with the belief that employers lay off their best workers first. Montgomery (1993) went so far as to propose that business cycles may be caused by fluctuations in the quality of the pool of unemployed workers. Flinn (1993) has proposed that employers have a collective strategy of shunning the unemployed in order to punish malingerers laid off for inadequate performance. Pissarides (1992) and Layard and Bean (1989, p. 379) suggested that unemployment erodes skills and reduces motivation and morale, making people less desirable as employees.

THEORIES OF RECESSIONS AS REALLOCATIONS OF LABOR (SECTION 20.5)

Leonard (1987b) wrote the earliest paper on employment fluctuations at the establishment level. He found in data for Wisconsin that there was greater variance in employment growth rates across establishments than across industrial sectors. Other evidence of job formation and disappearance is contained in Blanchard and Diamond's (1990) study of Bureau of Labor Statistics data on hiring and layoffs in manufacturing from 1951 to 1981. Their time series on job creation and destruction are similar to those of Davis and Haltiwanger (1990).

Reallocation theories have inspired controversy. Abraham and Katz (1986) pointed out that Lilien's results could be explained by negative correlation between sectors' trend growth rates and their sensitivity to cyclical fluctuations. The authors also argued that the well-known negative correlation between the job vacancy and unemployment rates indicates that unemployment fluctuations are due to changes in aggregate demand rather than to sectoral shifts. Palley (1992) and Hosios (1994) replied that this result on vacancies does not contradict the sectoral shifts hypothesis, if expansion costs cause growing firms to hire more slowly than contracting ones lay off, even if aggregate demand does not contract. Hamilton (1983, 1985, 1996) argued that oil price increases caused a number of post–World War II recessions. Hooker (1996a, b) claimed that the importance of oil price shocks has weakened or disappeared since 1973.

Other papers on reallocation models of business cycles are Davis (1987a, b), Oi (1987), Loungani and Rogerson (1989), Altonji and Ham (1990), Loungani, Rush, and Tave (1990), Brainard and Cutler (1993), Mills, Pelloni, and Zervoyianni (1995), Kwanho Shin (1997). Robert Hall (1991, 1995, 1997) developed a theory of recessions in the spirit of that of Davis and Haltiwanger (1990).

21

REMARKS ON THEORY

The views of businesspeople and labor leaders suggest a morale theory of wage rigidity. Key questions are whether the theory is consistent with rationality and whether it can be developed formally. Crucial aspects of the theory are that productivity depends on employees' mood, that workers with good morale internalize their firm's goals, and that pay cuts impair both mood and identification with the employer. None of these aspects is closely connected with rationality, which, in economists' usage, has to do with striving to achieve given objectives rather than with the selection of objectives or with the psychological capacity to accomplish them, matters central to morale. Nor does there seem to be a useful way to discuss formally the choice of objectives. I propose below a choice theoretic theory of mood that does not glaringly conflict with rationality. When state of mind and the degree of identification with the firm are given, the theory is completely consistent with rationality.

Another domain for rigorous theory is the impact of wage and price rigidity on the behavior of the macroeconomy. Although such an inquiry is beyond the scope of this project, my findings do suggest a model of the impact of cost of living increases on the average costs of primary-sector labor.

21.1 The Morale Theory

I summarize informally the theory of wage rigidity inspired by the interviews. Resistance to pay reduction comes primarily from employers, not from workers or their representatives, though it is anticipation of negative employee reactions that makes employers oppose pay cutting. The claim that wage rigidity gives rise to unexploited gains from trade is invalid, because a firm would lose more money from the adverse effects of cutting pay than it would gain from lower wages and salaries.

In economics, it is normally assumed that people, being self-interested, must be either coerced or bribed into performing tasks. However, the main causes of downward wage rigidity have to do with employers' belief that other motivators are useful as well, which are best thought of as having to do with generosity. Employers want their workers to accept organizational objectives and to cooperate in good spirit with their co-workers and supervisors. Good management practice uses punishment and dismissal largely to deter and weed out bad characters and incompetents and to protect the company from malefactors. Managers stress that punishment should seldom be used to obtain cooperation. Although good practice offers financial rewards, when possible, for good performance, the complexity of work tasks and the difficulties of measuring a worker's contribution to output make it difficult to use financial incentives in all but certain types of work, such as sales and some kinds of manufacturing. Inappropriate financial incentives can be harmful if they cause workers to increase their own income at the expense of the firm's. Even when effective financial incentives exist, they and employee goodwill are thought of as mutually reinforcing. Workers have so many opportunities to take advantage of employers that it is not wise to depend on coercion and financial incentives alone as motivators. Employers want workers to operate autonomously, show initiative, use their imagination, and take on extra tasks not required by management; workers who are scared or dejected do not do these things. All these matters of the spirit are referred to as morale. Good morale motivates workers to perform well even when no supervisor can check on them. It reflects reciprocation; people benefit those who help them and hurt those who harm them. Satisfaction is another significant aspect of morale, for cheerfulness makes people more constructive and work better. Managers do not expect employees to enjoy boring or unpleasant work. Employers merely hope that good morale makes workers more willing to tolerate disagreeable tasks as a sacrifice for the good of the organization as well as for personal gain. Nevertheless, it is thought to be highly desirable that workers be happy in some broad sense, happiness being especially desirable in people who have to make imaginative and creative mental efforts or who have contact with the public, such as bank tellers, receptionists, and salespeople. Another effect of good morale is that it engenders spontaneous cooperation among employees and sharing of information among them and with supervisors. Since low-level employees deal with customers and with the production process, they are often the only source of important information. Cooperation and information sharing are particularly difficult to monitor.

Managers can promote good morale by giving attention to individual employees, by showing appreciation for their work, and by idealism, that is, by making them conscious of the company's contribution to society and of their role in achieving company goals. Employees are thus made to feel part of something important outside of themselves. Morale is also improved by fairness, which includes internal equity, reciprocity, honesty, and honoring promises. Although unjust punishment hurts morale, so does excessive leniency, for workers lose enthusiasm for their jobs when they see colleagues allowed to shirk, and some will shirk if given the opportunity to do so.

What restrains employers from cutting pay is the belief that doing so hurts morale and increases labor turnover. The increase in turnover occurs both because pay falls relative to competitors and because of bad morale; people try to leave a job they dislike and may quit to retaliate against their firm. They do so even when the job market is bad and they will probably have difficulty finding work. Turnover among the better workers is especially feared, because they are more valuable and can find new jobs more easily. Good morale is valued not only because it brings high productivity and low turnover, but because it gives companies a good reputation that makes them more attractive to good quality job applicants.

Pay cuts damage morale, because of an insult effect and a standard of living effect. The latter occurs because a sudden decline in living standards distracts, depresses, and aggravates workers, and causes them to blame the company for their difficult adaptation to a lower income. Declines in living standards disrupt people's lives and cause much more damage to well-being than increases of an equal size improve it. The insult effect occurs because workers associate pay with self-worth and recognition of their value to the company. Many workers receive increases regularly, grow used to them, and interpret them as recognition of loyalty and good performance. Hence a pay cut is interpreted as a signal of dissatisfaction with employees, even if everyone's pay is reduced. Furthermore, employees feel that employers owe them their regular pay and even raises. Although morale is hurt by automatic pay cuts due to contractual arrangements, such as profit sharing, these do not have the insult effect of deliberate pay cuts resulting from a management decision, and so have a less negative impact.

The level of pay itself has little impact on morale, unless pay is so low as to be perceived as grossly unfair. Nonunion workers usually lack the information needed to compare their pay accurately with that at other companies, though they would be conscious of blatant underpayment. Workers soon get used to pay that is high relative to the market and grow to believe they have a right to it. Only pay cuts or inadequate raises affect morale, and do so negatively.

Many macroeconomists distinguish between real and nominal wage rigidity, asserting that if real wages alone are rigid, then changes in aggregate demand cannot affect employment and excessive real wages cause unemployment that can be eliminated only by real wage reduction.[1] I found that actual wage policies contained elements of both real and nominal rigidity, though low inflation at the time of the interviews made it difficult to distinguish real from nominal effects. Gradual reductions in real wages were acceptable, for the slow decline in living standards caused by pay freezes was less noticeable and more tolerable than abrupt nominal cuts.

Employers might be able to reduce labor costs during a recession by replacing workers with cheaper unemployed people. Few firms do so, however, because they need to retain the skills of the existing employees and they fear damage to morale and to their reputation as good employers. Firms continue to hire during recessions, though seldom using new recruits to replace existing workers; typically new hires replace workers lost through attrition. Although hiring and layoffs often occur simultaneously when firms reorganize operations, new hires usually have skills different from those of the people laid off.

Downward rigidity of the pay of new hires derives from that of existing employees because of links between the pay rates of all of a firm's employees. Reduced hiring pay increases differentials between existing and new employees, unless the pay of existing employees is cut as well. The higher differentials violate established standards of equity incorporated in a company's internal pay structure, angering new employees when they discover they are underpaid.

Managers regarded anything that upsets internal equity as potentially disruptive. Lack of equity spawns jealousies, resentments, and perceptions of unjust treatment. Fairness is complicated and difficult to achieve, because of conflict between the goals of equality and of rewarding productivity. In addition, an employee's contribution can be hard to estimate. Internal equity does not necessarily conflict with financial incentives, but to some extent requires them, for employees consider it fair to be rewarded for loyalty and good work. At the same time, equity may restrain management from paying the best performers the full value of their contribution.

The need for internal equity limits management's ability to cut pay, since it requires that pay cuts apply to everyone in a company. It is almost unthinkable to cut the pay of only the least able workers in the hope of retaining the best. Similarly, managers did not offer workers a choice between layoff and a pay cut applying only to those selected for layoff. Partial pay cuts did occur, but these applied only to management or to groups that were clearly overpaid.

In considering the impact of pay, it is important to specify the frame of reference, which may be pay at other firms, pay of other workers at the same firm, job performance, or past wages and salaries. The relation of a firm's pay to that at other companies usually has little effect on morale or work effort, because most workers know little about pay levels outside their own organization. This relation has a big impact, however, on a firm's supply of labor, which in practical terms means turnover and the number and quality of workers the business can attract and retain. Work force quality does, of course, affect productivity. The relation of employees' pay to that of others at the same work site has a major impact on morale and effort, as does the relation of pay to performance. The relation of current to past pay has asymmetric effects, for pay cuts can hurt morale and productivity, whereas pay increases normally give only a small and temporary lift to morale.

Most employers do not view pay cuts as a feasible alternative to layoffs, mainly because the cuts would have little impact on their need for labor, particularly in the short run. Nearly the same number of workers would be let go whether or not pay was cut. If pay were cut in exchange for no layoffs and no reductions in work time, then workers might be standing around with little to do, and idleness itself hurts morale. The elasticity of demand for labor is low because labor costs are a small fraction of marginal variable costs and because companies have market power, so that price elasticities of product demand are not high. Even small companies usually have market power. Many have market niches, sometimes at a national or an international level. Others selling products locally have only a few competitors. I had difficulty finding companies that faced stiff price competition, except those in construction and related manufacturing, and these were precisely the lines of business where wage cutting was most common. Pay cuts have a less negative impact on morale if they are viewed as justified, which means that they would prevent a large number of layoffs. For this reason, pay cuts typically occur in companies that are in danger of going out of business or that could increase sales significantly by reducing prices. Curiously, pay cuts were successful in many of the companies that had them, and I believe this was so because employers reduced pay only when they believed cuts would be accepted. Pay cuts are unusual, because not many companies have a highly elastic product demand or are severely distressed, except during disastrous depressions.

Businesspeople and labor leaders are confident they can usually convince employees, with some effort, that pay cuts are justified, if they indeed are. Barriers to the flow of information from management to workers have little to do with the explanation of wage rigidities. Normally information flows freely enough within businesses that most employees know when their company is in trouble. In some small- and medium-sized companies, the workers may know this before management does, because it is low-level employees who take orders and keep accounts, and gossip spreads quickly.

However, barriers to the flow of information from workers to management do underlie the explanation of wage rigidity. Morale is important in large part because management finds it prohibitively expensive to monitor employees closely. Management cannot hope to follow workers so carefully as to learn all the information received by workers that is relevant to the production process. For this reason, companies rely on workers to do what they are supposed to do and to use their information to help the firm without being told what to do, even when supervisors are unlikely to check up on them or will never do so. Workers are likely to be so cooperative only if they have good morale.

A common argument in favor of layoffs as opposed to pay cuts was that they save much more money than do pay cuts, since the latter apply only to wages, salaries, and a few benefits, whereas there are important fixed costs of employment, such as most benefits and the expense of work space, materials, and supplies. In an office environment, layoffs save on telephone, lighting, paper, and administrative costs and on heating and rent, if offices are given up. In manufacturing, work areas are often shut down or vacated after layoffs. A pay cut would have to be unacceptably large to save as much money as is saved by a typical important layoff. Fixed employment costs are so important that for many employers hourly labor costs are minimized when everyone works overtime, for the overtime premium is small compared with the fixed costs, which in this calculation include all benefits.

Although layoffs may damage morale, their effects are less serious than those of pay cuts. The impact of layoffs on morale is slight and brief. Those laid off may suffer terribly, but once they are gone they cannot disrupt the workplace. Those who remain may fear further layoffs or worry about friends who were dismissed, but skilled management can relieve the tensions quickly, by convincing those in a work group that they are valued and will experience no more layoffs for six months or more. Pay cuts, in contrast, hurt everyone, push those with debt into financial difficulty, and cause resentment that may fester for a long time, unless management can persuade employees that the cuts avert heavy layoffs or a shutdown. Many layoffs were made in part to improve productivity and were even thought of as rejuvenating company operations, whereas pay cuts were viewed as dragging down company spirit. Firms often used layoffs to rid themselves of their least competent workers, whereas a pay cut might cause the best producers to leave.

A pertinent, though gruesome, analogy involves people adrift on an overloaded life raft. A few are pushed over the side or even eaten to save the rest, who may be horrified at first, but cheer up once they think they are going to survive. All might be willing to reduce rations and keep everyone on board, if doing so increased the total food supply (corresponding to a high elasticity of demand for labor), but since the supply is fixed some are forced off the raft. Despite or even because of the inequity of sacrificing a few for the good of the whole, it is vital to be fair when distributing food, though this might mean giving more to the strongest who can do the most to save the rest. Equity and a sense of justice help maintain commitment to the group, though the situation may become unbearable as more and more people are lost.

Similar arguments apply against worksharing or short-time. During the recession, it was common to reduce the amount of overtime for wage earners and even to reduce their regular weekly hours somewhat, though the hours of salaried employees often increased. Worksharing involves much larger reductions. There is a trade-off between retention of valued employees and damage to morale from reduced incomes. Firms use worksharing when a slowdown is thought to be temporary and when they employ highly skilled workers, who might go to other companies if laid off.

It might seem that employees would prefer worksharing because it spreads risk. If workers do not know who is likely to be laid off, then everyone should prefer to sacrifice a little to having a few suffer severely. This mutual insurance argument may apply to workers before layoffs occur and may explain why there are few stories of cannibalism among shipwrecked sailors. However, this calculation has little relevance to the business context, since management is in charge and is concerned chiefly about the state of mind of the continuing work force. Returning to the raft analogy, management prefers all those on board to be strong paddlers, even if few in number. A full load of feeble survivors is of little use.

A theme recurring frequently in interviews was that businesspeople and labor leaders were preoccupied with the defense of civilized values, which they depended on to hold their organizations together. Although there were obvious scoundrels among business and labor leaders, as among all groups of people, the majority believed that success required decency and trust, a belief that contrasts sharply with the standard model of man in economics, according to which people are so self-interested as to be ready to lie, cheat, or steal for their own advantage. The standard economic model is a product of neoclassical economics in which firms pursue profits, consumers and workers maximize their own welfare, and market interaction coordinates all their activities for the common good, while firms obtain work effort and loyalty through financial incentives. Much of this vision is accurate. Companies do use financial incentives and try to maximize profits, and workers want as much money as possible. Workers do cheat, and discipline is vital to organizational effectiveness. What is missing is an appropriate theory of the firm as a community, because more than financial incentives and discipline are needed to make companies function well. It is expensive to police people, there may be no punishments available severe enough to deter some forms of misconduct, and rewards and punishments alone may bring only the appearance of cooperation. Leaders strive to inspire enthusiasm and trust, so that subordinates do the right thing of their own volition. Trust is vital for the free flow of information within an organization. Many businesspeople believe that moral commitment is all that stands between them and chaos. The society within a firm is brittle and constantly threatened by waves of suspicion, many caused by individual managers' abuse of authority. This fragility is one reason employers are sensitive to morale, and the main drawback of pay cuts is that they fill the air with disappointment and an impression of breached promise, which dissolves the glue holding the organization together.

21.2 Some Distinctive Implications of the Theory

The morale theory has certain implications that distinguish it from competing theories. One has been discussed; pay cuts are most likely to occur in firms with a high elasticity of demand for labor, namely, in those selling products with high price elasticities of demand and in those that are in danger of shutting down. None of the other theories has this implication.

Another implication is that the factors that make the Shapiro-Stiglitz efficiency wage model likely to apply also diminish the importance of morale and make pay cuts likely. These factors are ease of monitoring worker effort, little need for spontaneous cooperation among employees or for workers to share information, little need for creativity or for workers to be cheerful, and short-term employment that gives little time for employees to develop an emotional attachment to the firm. Because these factors weaken the importance of morale, they encourage management to threaten to punish or fire workers who do not provide full effort and also to cut pay when the labor market is slack. There is some evidence confirming this implication, for the Shapiro-Stiglitz model applies best to temporary workers performing simple manual tasks, and the pay of such workers was also fairly flexible. There is no contradiction here, for the shirking model implies downward wage rigidity only if the relationship between the efficient wage and labor market slackness is flat, and it probably is not flat.

Still another implication is that the pay of new hires is most flexible relative to that of continuing employees when internal pay equity is least important for morale. Equity is likely to be unimportant when workers have little chance to get to know one another and when they do not take their jobs seriously as careers. This implication is not shared by other theories, but is not necessarily inconsistent with them. The theories simply do not address the relation between the pay of new and continuing employees. The implication is confirmed by the observation that hiring pay is more flexible in the secondary than in the primary sector.

The morale theory implies a trade-off between coercion and morale. If morale is bad, employers can obtain a certain level of productivity through coercion, and if pay is low it may be impossible for morale to be good. Therefore an implication of the morale theory is that employers are more likely to coerce low-paid than well-paid labor. Other theories of wage rigidity do not bear on the choice between coercion and morale.

21.3 Further Discussion of Morale

Motivation may be thought of as occurring at three levels, direct exchange, indefinite exchange, and internalization of employer objectives. Under direct exchange, rewards and punishments for various actions are specified in advance. These include the usual financial incentives. Under indefinite exchange, rewards and punishments are not specified in advance, though workers may have imprecise expectations about them. This type of exchange is what Akerlof (1982) called "gift exchange." When workers internalize their firm's objectives, they may expect no reward, but help the company simply because doing so gives them pleasure or is felt to be a duty, though this motivation may be a subliminal form of exchange.

The second and third types of motivation, indefinite exchange and internalization, are most affected by morale, though workers may not respond to direct incentives if they are furious with their employer. Both indefinite exchange and internalization depend on trust. Indefinite exchange cannot take place if workers believe the firm will not reward their efforts. Nor would workers be likely to internalize the objectives of a firm that they did not expect to look out for their interests.

Wages would probably not be downwardly rigid if only the first type of motivation mattered and if it were unaffected by morale, for wages, salaries, and incentive payments could be made contingent on factors other than effort and output without affecting the inducement to work hard. For instance, piece rates or wages can be made flexible by making them conditional on the unemployment rate, and this arrangement need not diminish the financial incentive to produce, which depends only on how rapidly pay increases with productive effort.

It is the third form of motivation that may seem hardest to reconcile with neoclassical economics, for why should a rational person act in the interests of someone else with no expectation of reward? Though tempting, this line of thinking is mistaken, as was explained earlier. Rationality has to do with acting so as to achieve given goals, so that there is nothing irrational about adopting and furthering someone else's objectives.

Though perhaps puzzling, internalization should not be dismissed, for it is important in the workplace. It is probably a more important source of motivation than gift exchange, for if the latter were important workers would offer increased effort in return for large raises or high pay, which I was told they do not do. Unselfish or generous actions play an important role. To what else can we attribute the huge amount of charitable giving and volunteer work in modern societies? Many people work hard with few financial incentives. There are no statistics on how many people in the United States work for fixed wages and salaries, but Carlson (1982) finds that the proportion of manufacturing workers on incentive pay declined from around 30 percent in 1947 to 20 percent in 1968–1970 and had decreased still further by 1980. People working for wages or salaries do receive incentives in the form of raises, promotions, and sometimes bonuses, but these are usually weak inducements compared with piece rates or sales commissions. The motivation of workers on wages and salaries has perplexed economists, and two solutions have been proposed. Brown (1990) assumes that there is some minimal, easily monitored level of effort and that workers are fired when effort falls short of it, as in the shirking model. Holmstrom and Milgrom (1991) assume that employees voluntarily offer a certain amount of labor simply because they like working.

One possibility is that workers' unselfishness is illusory, because, as Brown (1990) suggests, the shirking model applies and people work well only out of fear of punishment. This explanation is not convincing, however, because in reality much work is done with little or no monitoring and workers are not often punished, though supervisors may warn them and try to talk them into greater efforts. Furthermore, good morale increases productivity in part because it brings workers to perform tasks on their own initiative that do not belong to their normal duties, and failure to do such things is not likely to invite retribution.

There is no doubt that people have the capacity to identify with groups and to internalize collective goals, though, of course, some people are utterly selfish. Internalization is familiar in psychology and the concept is very old. For instance, Adam Smith (1759) proposed that morality stems from the ability of people to feel or sympathize with the emotions of others. Experiments have shown that people can easily be induced to categorize themselves as belonging to a particular group (Turner, 1987). Merely telling experimental subjects that they have been randomly assigned to one of two groups is enough to induce them to act so as to further its interests and to hurt those of the other group, even though the subjects do not know each other's identities or have any contact with each other (Tajfel, 1970).[2] Eric Hoffer (1951) interprets the success of political and religious mass movements as a reversion to a primitive tribal identification with a group or cause. Students of the military recognize the tremendous amount of energy generated by group enterprise (Janowitz and Shils, 1948; Stouffer et al., 1949; and Baynes, 1967) and collective ideology (Bartov, 1991).[3]

Although it may be obvious that people identify with organizations, it is not clear exactly why they do so. Morale may be the product of the age-old conflict between the needs for cooperation and selfishness. Most human accomplishments and even survival require the close collaboration of groups, which can be families, clubs, schools, labor unions, businesses, armies, or nations. It would not be surprising if an ancient need for unity had created in us an ability to identify with collective achievements and to feel a duty and even pleasure in contributing to them. Frank (1988) argues that seemingly irrational emotions, such as love or the desire for revenge, evolved because they made it easier for people credibly to commit to enforcing or fulfilling agreements to cooperate. A difficulty with arguments based on natural selection is that we lack precise knowledge of people's circumstances when human emotional capacities evolved. Perhaps there was little place for kindness in the lives of early humans, and the propensity to join may even have diminished the chances of survival by making groups so aggressive that they fought with their neighbors.

Several ways come to mind of making sense of identification with a firm, and I momentarily experiment with two, one assuming an instinct for group action and the other emphasizing conscious decision making. The first, labeled the self-interest theory, is like that of Frank; humanity evolved a capacity to identify with groups because of the advantages of collective action to individual members. Because selfish advantage is the ultimate goal, individuals instinctively identify with those groups that seem likely to benefit them. The other theory, the conceptual theory, is that imagination is so generally useful that it has evolved so that it is keen enough to grasp that individual participation is necessary for the success of joint enterprises and so that it is powerful enough to stimulate emotional drives to further collective goals. Identification with a firm is, in this interpretation, part of a sense of justice. Another plausible theory is that people confuse participation in group activities with the exchange of favors occurring in ordinary life and believe unconsciously that their contributions to the group will be rewarded, even if unnoticed. Still another possibility is that through training a sense of duty becomes a reflex that is hard to resist. It is not possible to choose among the theories on the basis of current knowledge. What I hope to make clear is that there are plausible and coherent theories of motivation consistent with management views on morale.

According to the self-interest theory, good morale and identification with the company are promoted by anything that creates the impression that the firm will protect and promote employee interests. For this reason, morale is improved by fairness and idealism as well as by praise. Praise is important because people feel that they will be safe and treated well if they are liked. Threats of punishment hurt morale, because they imply suspicion and hence that the worker is not valued and is even disliked, making the organization a dangerous place from which little will be gained. Similar remarks apply to measures to extract effort by force, where contributions to a firm are said to be obtained forcibly if workers give more than they would offer freely if they had good morale. Coercion and threats may be consistent with good morale in dangerous military situations where no one wants to do his duty, but everyone must do so for the good of all. Force is normally not acceptable in business, probably because it is not necessary. Unjustified pay cuts are certainly not consistent with good morale in the self-interest theory, because they represent capricious and arbitrary injury to employees and may be interpreted as a betrayal of promises. The self-interest theory is hard to reconcile with the enormous sacrifices made by soldiers, for it requires that all calculation of immediate private advantage be overwhelmed by dedication to a group judged compatible with overall self-interest. It is possible, of course, that the brain is constructed so as to allow just such commitments.

In the conceptual theory, individuals are capable of formulating through reason a sense of justice according to which people reciprocate benefits and in which the common welfare requires that individuals sacrifice their own interests for those of groups. An organization appeals to the imagination if is compatible with this view of justice, that is, if it is fair, creates benefits for its members or for other people, and makes effective use of individual contributions. For the same reasons, idealistic company behavior sustains good morale, and praise boosts it by reassuring people that they make a worthwhile contribution to common goals. Threats and coercion hurt morale by drawing attention to conflict between the worker and firm and by making the firm's goals seem evil. Because an unjustified pay cut hurts employees for no good reason or is thought of as treacherous, it clashes with the image of justice that underlies the view of duty as a rational necessity. This theory may be too intellectual, but perhaps ordinary employees should not be underestimated.

The self-interest and the conceptual theories do not explain morale's fragility. The function of this brittleness may be to protect individual self-interest. Although commitment to a group helps overcome prisoner's dilemma or free-rider problems arising in cooperative activity, the same sense of responsibility exposes individuals to exploitation. It is useful to have a system that balances private and group advantage, and conventional standards of fairness offer an orderly way of doing so. These establish rules of reciprocation among group members and between them and the organization, and the duties specified by these rules are accepted by members when they agree emotionally to join. Perhaps the fragility of morale is a self-protective reflex provoked by unfairness. A reading of a psychology textbook, such as that by Gleitman (1995), makes it clear that many parts of the nervous system operate through offsetting pairs of activating and inhibiting signals. The teetering between group commitment and indignant rebellion may reflect just such a pairing built into the psyche.

Another theoretical issue is why tolerance of some employees' malingering hurts the morale of others. One answer is that the acceptance of shirking creates an impression of an inequitable distribution of the burden of work, and so damages morale according to either of the proposed theories. Another possibility is that breakdowns of morale caused by lax discipline are analogous to those occurring on the battlefield when the flight of some soldiers prompts others to run. However, the analogy is, I believe, false. In battle, soldiers who stay in line are in greater danger and are probably less effective after their comrades have run away. In contrast, workers run few risks and the contribution of each worker probably becomes more important when colleagues shirk, because of diminishing marginal returns to collective effort.

21.4 Mood and Work Effort

Mood is an important component of morale and affects the disutility of labor. Disutility is probably the wrong term, for managers and labor leaders did not usually speak of jobs as disagreeable, but assumed that employees liked to work. It is nearly universally recognized that one of the bad effects of layoff is the loss of the pleasure of working and of social contacts on the job. Juster (1985) has found in a survey that people prefer work to typical leisure activities. However, in the standard model of work effort and incentives, it is necessary to assume that effort is unpleasant, for if effort brings pleasure rather than displeasure, then people should work hard, even if they have no financial incentive to do so, an implication that contradicts common sense. I attempt to make sense of mood and the utility of work by using a speculative model of work motivation that places ideas from psychology in the maximizing framework typical of economics.

In order to grasp the ideas I present, it may be helpful to consider the analogy of a lion hunting an antelope. In chasing an antelope, the lion expends energy, loses time, and risks injury. These costs must be weighed against the probability of catching the prey and the pleasure of eating it. Imagine that the lion unconsciously or half-consciously weighs the costs against the benefits before deciding whether to give chase and before choosing the level of physical effort to expend on the pursuit. Once the decision is made, the lion's mind automatically adjusts his mood and level of nervous and physical arousal to handle the effort required. If the lion decides not to go after the antelope, he will not be aroused, will feel lazy, and may find running uncomfortable. If he decides to try for a kill, he will be mobilized and excited and will probably be exhilarated by the effort. Given this decision, he will consciously decide how much effort to put into the hunt and how to go about it. We may imagine that the lion's mind and body unconsciously choose the mood and level of arousal so that he consciously chooses an effort level that optimizes an unconscious utility depending on his probability of success, energy expenditure, and risk of injury. The lion's unconscious choice of mood may be constrained by his preexisting state of mind.

If he just lost his wives to a rival, he may be discouraged and not feel like hunting, whereas if he is a hopeful young bachelor, he may feel vigorous.

Another illuminating analogy may be that of a virtuoso pianist. For an appreciative and sensitive audience, she will probably play at her best and love doing so. If she hears snores and catcalls, she will no doubt feel her fingers stiffen, stumble, and will hate playing.

It is important, in my opinion, to recognize that mood adjusts automatically to fit the perceived net benefits of tasks. I believe it is general human experience that capacities to act and perceptions of pain or pleasure adapt to circumstances. Danger stimulates us to fight or flee. Anger makes us ignore danger and pain. A decline in our material well-being causes discomfort and unhappiness, probably so that we will react by doing something to rectify our situation. However, we get used to prolonged hardship, perhaps so that we can cope with unavoidable misery. Soldiers and prisoners living in frightful conditions eventually cheer up and joke about their state, though, of course, they are not happy. It is a mistake to separate the disutility of labor from the utility of its reward or to imagine that labor is normally perceived as disagreeable. The utilities of labor itself and of its reward interact.

21.5 A Formal Model of Mood and Effort

I now represent these ideas in a formal model that preserves the utility maximizing principle used in economics. Focus on an action (or program of actions), e, to be taken by a person over a fixed period of time. Although e may be thought of as effort, it is better to interpret it as productive activity. The action has an unconsciously felt mental and physical cost, measured as the number, $C(e)$, and earns income $w(e)$.[4] The unconsciously felt benefit to the worker of the wage is the number $B(w(e))$, and the net unconscious gain is

$$B(w(e)) - C(e).[5]$$

Unconscious goals could include the basic psychological drives as well as fidelity to family, firm, or country. Assume that the function B is increasing and strictly concave.

I propose that people unconsciously adjust their mood and general state of mobilization so that conscious choices maximize $B(w(e)) - C(e)$. The conscious person does not choose e but makes a decision (or program of decisions), d. The actual action taken is $e = E(d, m)$, where m is the person's mood and state of mental and physical arousal. The decision d might correspond to the pace of work desired by the person, in which case $E(d, m)$ would be the realized pace of work; the person might actually work faster or slower than he or she intended. The person's consciously experienced utility is

$$U(w(E(d, m)), m) + V(E(d, m), m),$$

where the first term is the utility of the earnings and the second is the utility from the action itself. The person chooses the decision, $d = D(m, w)$, so as to solve the problem

$$\max_{d \in D}[B(w(E(d, m)), m) + V(E(d, m), m)],$$

where D is the set of possible decisions. The unconscious mind chooses the mood, m, so as maximize the unconscious utility, that is, to solve the problem

$$\max_{m \in M}[B(w(E(D(m, w), m))) - C(E(D(m, w), m)))],$$

where M is the set of possible moods.

If the person has a preexisting state of mind or mood, then his or her unconscious self may not be able to choose m freely, but must chose from a subset, SM, of M. The subset SM may be thought of as representing restrictions imposed by solution of a larger unconscious utility maximization problem that determines the context of the one under consideration. For instance, the person may be angry with his or her firm and wish to take revenge on it, and the actions under consideration may contribute to that goal.

Standard results in the theory of incentives are that increasing the function $w(e)$ by adding a positive constant decreases effort, whereas the worker's optimal level of effort increases when the slope of $w(e)$ at the optimum is increased without increasing the function's level there. These conclusions, when interpreted properly, apply to this model. Imagine a two-dimensional plot with $-C(E(D(m, w), m))$ on the abscissa and $B(w(E(D(m, w), m)))$ on the ordinate, as in Figure 21.1. The unconscious chooses m so as to maximize the sum of the two components, so that the northeast frontier of the plot is the relevant set of points. I compare two earnings functions, w and w', and assume that

$$\{E(D(m, w), m): m \in SM\} = \{E(D(m, w'), m): m \in SM\} = E,$$

so that the set of possible actions achievable by manipulation of mood does not depend on the earnings function. Then the two-dimensional plots are of the sets

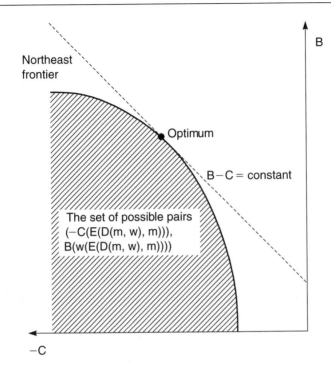

Northeast
frontier

• Optimum

B − C = constant

The set of possible pairs
(−C(E(D(m, w), m))),
B(w(E(D(m, w), m))))

B

−C

FIGURE 21.1   Cost and benefits of effort

$\{(-C(e), B(w(e))): e \in E\}$ and $\{(-C(e), B(w'(e))): e \in E\}$.

If w' is w plus a positive constant, then, because of the strict concavity of the function B, the northeast frontier of $\{(-C(e), B(w'(e))): e \in E\}$ is no steeper than that of $\{(-C(e), B(w(e))): e \in E\}$, so that at the optimum the disutility of effort, $C(e)$, is no higher with the earnings function w' than with the function w.

In devising an analogue of the second standard result mentioned earlier, it is not possible to speak of the slope of w because the action variable, e, may not be a number. However, by an analogous definition, w' is "at least as steep" as w at $\underline{e}$ if $w'(\underline{e}) = w(\underline{e})$, where $\underline{e}$ is the optimum for w, and if $w'(e) \geq w(e)$, whenever $w(e) \geq w(\underline{e})$, and $w'(e) \leq w(e)$, whenever $w(e) \leq w(\underline{e})$. Given this definition, it is obvious that if w' is at least as steep as w at $\underline{e}$, then $-C(\underline{e}') \leq -C(\underline{e})$ and $w'(\underline{e}') \geq w(e)$, where $\underline{e}'$ is the optimum with earnings function w'. That is, steepening the earnings function does not decrease the unconscious disutility of effort at the optimum.

The utility $V(E(d, m), m)$ may be positive if mood favors effort, though V

may decrease with effort when it is increased beyond a point appropriate for the mood. What I have in mind may perhaps best be explained by returning to the usual model in which the effort variable is a number corresponding to the pace of work. In this spirit, assume for the moment that d and m are non-negative numbers, where larger values of m correspond to a better mood. Assume also that $E(d, m) = d$, and that $w(e) = e$, so that e and w can be suppressed. Finally, assume that U and V are twice differentiable functions satisfying the following conditions:

$$\frac{\partial U(d, m)}{\partial d} > 0, \quad \frac{\partial^2 U(d, m)}{\partial d^2} < 0, \quad \frac{\partial^2 U(d, m)}{\partial m\, \partial d} > 0, \quad \frac{\partial V(0, m)}{\partial d} > 0,$$

$$\frac{\partial^2 V(d, m)}{\partial d^2} < 0, \quad \text{and} \quad \frac{\partial^2 V(d, m)}{\partial m\, \partial d} > 0,$$

for all d and m. Let $d = D(m)$ solve the problem

$$\max_{d \geq 0} [U(d, m) + V(d, m)].$$

Under the given conditions, it is easy to see that D is a nondecreasing function of m and is increasing at values of m for which $D(m) > 0$. That is, improved mood increases effort. Notice also that at the optimum,

$$\frac{\partial V(d, m)}{\partial d} < 0,$$

so that the worker finds increased effort unpleasant. From now on, I drop the assumption that d and m are numbers.

Rationality   Strictly speaking, people behaving as in the above model are rational in the economists' sense that they reason correctly and use all available information in order to maximize their utility. However, people's rationality is unusual in that utility maximization occurs at two levels, the conscious and the unconscious. The effect of mood on realized actions and on conscious objectives does not contradict rationality. However, in a loose sense the model is inconsistent with rationality. Realistic models of conventional rationality take account of limits on the ability of the conscious mind to reason and use information. No doubt sentiment influences imperfect logic, so that a more realistic version of the above model should take account of the effect of mood on reasoning.

Reward and Punishment   I now assume that the unconscious mind forms a notion of what is normal in terms of unconscious living standards. The normal or expected path of welfare may grow, shrink, or fluctuate over time. The notion of normality may be thought of as useful for two reasons; it tells the mind what to store as habits or mental subroutines and it serves as a trigger level for alarm. The mind adapts habits to the way of life that is expected to be normal. Decline of living standards below normal signals the unconscious that something is wrong, provoking anger, unhappiness, or distress. These moods, in turn, stimulate the conscious mind to make efforts to find solutions to the problems that have arisen. It is not efficient for the conscious mind always to be stimulated and on the look-out for new solutions, for bad moods and the efforts they incite are exhausting. Bad moods should therefore be called upon only when needed. For instance, salespeople expect their income to fluctuate sharply and probably react badly only to prolonged patterns of low income. A fall in welfare below the expected level may not trigger alarm if the conscious mind can persuade the unconscious one that there is no reason to worry, that the bad situation will soon be rectified, or that there is nothing to be done about it. The unconscious probably adapts gradually to lower welfare, as do the soldiers mentioned earlier.

Rewards may be defined to be payments that provide welfare in excess of the normal level, whereas punishments bring welfare below the normal level. Punishments have a greater impact than rewards because they provoke a powerful negative emotional reaction and rewards trigger no corresponding positive reaction. Rewards or punishments that are too frequent become normal and so lose their impact, a matter of concern to managers.

The standard of living effect of a pay cut causes anxiety and discontent because the fall in workers' welfare below the normal level both triggers bad moods and requires the effort of adopting new habits appropriate to the new standard of living. Pay cuts that are perceived as justified are thought of as inevitable, and so do not provoke a strongly negative mood.

It is easy to incorporate a normal welfare level in an intertemporal version of the formal model. The external conditions of the person's decision problem at one time, t, are defined by the earnings function, $w_t(e)$, and by the set of possible decisions, D_t. Let the function $D_t(m, w_t)$ be the solution to the problem

$$\max_{d \in D_t}[U(w_t(E(d, m)), m) + V(E(d, m), m)].$$

The unconscious welfare in period t is

$$W_t = \max_{m \in SM}[B(w_t(E(D_t(m, w_t), m))) - C(E(D_t(m, w_t), m))],$$

The expected or normal welfare level may be assumed to be a constant, $\underline{W}$, so that the person reacts with anger and discontent when W_t falls below $\underline{W}$.

Coercion and Freedom   Managers and labor leaders stressed that workers are energized by the feeling that they control their lives and are antagonized and made passive by compulsion and excessive control. These matters are beyond the scope of the model presented here and are not easy to think about carefully. For instance, it is difficult to define coercion precisely. Presumably it implies a lack of freedom, but a person who is coerced into doing something, strictly speaking, also chooses to do it, for he or she could refuse to comply and suffer the consequences. Also, everyone works under some degree of compulsion. For instance, stealing from the company or punching the boss usually lead automatically to firing, so that people are in a sense forced not to do these things. Similarly, blatant insubordination can bring firing, so that workers may be said to be compelled to take orders. When managers spoke of coercion, they did not refer to cases such as these. A rough definition of what they had in mind might be that a worker is compelled to do something if not doing it results in punishment and if the worker would do something else if there were no threat of punishment and he or she had good morale. The key aspects of coercion that managers and labor leaders found demotivating were that they hurt morale, frighten people, and diminish self-confidence. Although fear is understood by all to be a powerful and useful motivator, managers typically use threats only to discourage extreme behavior. They do not want workers to be preoccupied with fear, for it distracts and undermines self-confidence. The latter is important, because it frees the mind and body to act smoothly and efficiently. Apprehensive employees consciously think through every step of what they do lest they make a mistake, and conscious thought overrides the mental subroutines that guide much of what people do. In relation to the formal model, lack of self-confidence limits the set of moods to a disadvantageous subset.

Extreme forms of coercion may lead to what psychologists call learned helplessness, which involves not just loss of self-confidence but reduction in mental activity as well, perhaps with the unconscious goal of desensitizing the brain to pain.

21.6 Extension to Morale

Recall that morale has two key aspects, mood and internalization of organizational objectives. Internalization may be expressed by including the firm's objectives among those of the worker. This procedure is appropriate, since utility functions are inferred from behavior and workers who internalize their firm's objectives act as if these were their own. Formally, let $R(e)$ be the revenue the firm earns from a worker's output, so that the firm's profit is $R(e) - w(e)$. Internalization may be expressed formally by adding multiples of the firm's profit to the worker's conscious and unconscious utility functions, so that these become

$$B(w(e)) + \mu_1[R(e) - w(e)] - C(e) \quad \text{and}$$

$$U(w(e), m) + \mu_2[R(e) - w(e)] + V(e, m),$$

respectively, where μ_1 and μ_2 are constants that are positive if morale is good. The impact of morale on mood may be expressed by varying the subset SM of possible moods available to the unconscious side of the person. Improvements in morale increase the size of the set SM, thereby giving the unconscious a larger selection of possible states of mind. Improvements in mood resulting from improved morale do not decrease and may increase the maximized value of the unconscious objective function $B(w(e)) + \mu_1[R(e) - w(e)] - C(e)$, because it is maximized over a larger set of moods. That is, if $d = D(m, w)$ solves the problem

$$\max_{d}[U(w(E(d, m), m) + \mu_2[R(E(d, m)) - w(e)] + V(E(d, m), m)],$$

then the value of

$$\max_{m \in SM}\{B(w(E(D(m, w), m))$$
$$+ \mu_1[R(E(D(m, w), m) - w(E(D(m, w), m)] - (E(D(m, w), m)\}$$

does not decrease as the size of the set SM increases.

Without more assumptions, it is not possible to say whether the effect of improved morale on mood increases profits. A plausible set of assumptions is that the wage function, w, is constant and that improvements in morale enlarge SM in such a way as to make available actions or effort levels, e, that increase $R(e)$ for each level of $C(e)$ and furthermore increase $R(e)$ more, the greater is $C(e)$. Imagine a two-dimensional diagram, such as Figure 21.2, with $-C(e)$ on the abscissa and $B(w) + \mu_1(R(e) - w)$ on the ordinate. Then improvement in morale causes the northeast frontier of the set of possible points $(-C(e), B(w) + \mu_1(R(e) - w))$ to rise vertically in such a way that the vertical increase is greater the larger is $C(e)$ (that is, the smaller is $-C(e)$). Because w is constant, it follows that the new optimum yields a higher value of $R(e)$ and a lower value of $-C(e)$. In other words, improved morale affects mood in such a way as to increase profits.

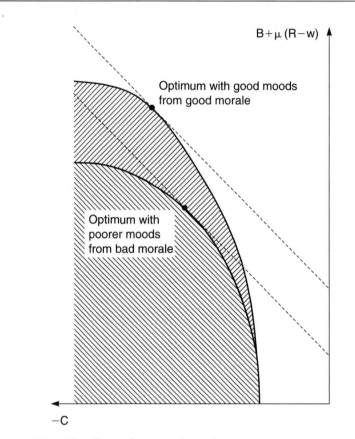

FIGURE 21.2   The effects of improved morale

Assume that the utility functions B and U are differentiable with respect to income, w, so that the unconscious and conscious marginal utilities of income,

$$\frac{dB}{dw} \quad \text{and} \quad \frac{\partial U}{\partial w},$$

respectively, are well defined. It must be that

$$\mu_1 < \frac{dB(w(e))}{dw} \quad \text{and} \tag{21.1}$$

$$\mu_2 < \frac{\partial U(w(e), m)}{\partial w}, \tag{21.2}$$

for levels of e and m that are actually realized. If these inequalities did not hold, the worker would be indifferent to having his or her wage increased, or would prefer to have it reduced, contrary to common sense.

The inclusion of profit in the worker's utility function does not portray the sort of good morale that inhibits theft, for according to inequalities (21.1) and (21.2), workers could improve their welfare by stealing from the employer. In order to give a utilitarian interpretation to moral values, it is necessary either to include punishment, to introduce a sense of guilt, or to have people take into account the consequences of having other people break moral codes they break themselves.[6]

Although the model cannot explain the impact of morale on morality, it does capture important consequences of good morale. It is easy to see that the inclusion of the terms

$$\mu_1[R(e) - w(e)] \quad \text{and}$$

$$\mu_2[R(e) - w(e)]$$

does not decrease and may increase profits. More precisely, profits do not decrease, provided μ_1 is positive and provided the inclusion of these terms does not change the set of actions, e, achievable by varying mood, m. In order to see why, let $\underline{e}$ be the choice of e that maximizes $B(w(e)) - C(e)$ and let $\underline{e}'$ be the choice of e that maximizes $B(w(e)) + \mu_1[R(e) - w(e)] - C(e)$. Then

$$B(w(\underline{e}')) + \mu_1[R(\underline{e}') - w(\underline{e}')] - C(\underline{e}') \ge B(w(\underline{e}))$$
$$+ \mu_1[R(\underline{e}) - w(\underline{e})] - C(\underline{e}) \ge B(w(\underline{e}')) + \mu_1[R(\underline{e}) - w(\underline{e})] - C(\underline{e}'),$$

which implies that $R(\underline{e}') - w(\underline{e}') \ge R(\underline{e}) - w(\underline{e})$, as is to be shown.

Financial Incentives and Morale   I next show that financial incentives and morale complement each other. An argument similar to the one just made shows that increasing μ_1 does not decrease and may increase profits, for any wage function w, including ones offering financial incentives. In order to see how to make the argument, assume that $\mu_1' > \mu_1$, notice that

$$B(w(e)) + \mu_1'[R(e) - w(e)] - C(e) = B(w(e)) + \mu_1[R(e) - w(e)] - C(e)$$
$$+ (\mu_1' - \mu_1)[R(e) - w(e)],$$

and assume that increasing μ_1 to μ_1' does not change the set of actions achievable by varying mood.

I next show that if μ_1 is positive, then increasing financial incentives increases profits, provided the function B is not too concave and provided the change in μ_1 does not change the set of actions attainable by choice of mood. Introduce explicit incentives by assuming that $w(e) = w_0 + w_1R(e)$, where $w_1 > 0$. Assume that the firm varies w_0 and w_1 so that $w_0 + w_1R(e)$ remains constant, where e is the worker's choice of action. Now hold w_0, w_0', w_1, and w_1' fixed, where $w_1' > w_1$. Assume that B is linear, that is, $B(w) = bw$, where b is a positive number. By inequality (21.1), we must assume that $b > \mu_1$. I show that increasing w_1 to w_1' increases profits. Let $\underline{e}$ and $\underline{e}'$ be the worker's optimal choices of e when the wage is $w_0 + w_1R(e)$ and $w_0' + w_1'R(e)$, respectively. By the optimality of $\underline{e}$ and $\underline{e}'$, it follows that

$$b[w_0 + w_1R(\underline{e})] + \mu_1[R(\underline{e}) - w_0 - w_1R(\underline{e})] - C(\underline{e}) \geq \tag{21.3}$$
$$b[w_0 + w_1R(\underline{e}')] + \mu_1[R(\underline{e}') - w_0 - w_1R(\underline{e}')] - C(\underline{e}')$$

and

$$b[w_0' + w_1'R(\underline{e}')] + \mu_1[R(\underline{e}') - w_0' - w_1'R(\underline{e}')] - C(\underline{e}') \tag{21.4}$$
$$\geq b[w_0' + w_1'R(\underline{e})] + \mu_1[R(\underline{e}) - w_0' - w_1'R(\underline{e})] - C(\underline{e}).$$

These inequalities imply that

$$(b - \mu_1)w_1[R(\underline{e}) - R(\underline{e}')] \geq C(\underline{e}) - C(\underline{e}')$$
$$+ \mu_1[R(\underline{e}') - R(\underline{e})] \geq (b - \mu_1)w_1'[R(\underline{e}) - R(\underline{e}')].$$

Because $b - \mu_1 > 0$ and $w_1' > w_1$, the last inequalities imply that

$$R(\underline{e}') \geq R(\underline{e}).$$

Since by assumption $w_0 + w_1R(\underline{e}) = w_0' + w_1'R(\underline{e}')$, it follows that profits are not decreased by increasing incentives. Profits would be strictly increased if there were strict inequality in either of inequalities (21.3) or (21.4). In this case, profits would still increase if the function $B(w)$ were a slightly concave approximation to the linear function bw. It is easy to make an example in which B is very concave and increased incentives decrease profits. This completes the argument that increased incentives may increase profits, even when morale is good, just as improved morale increases profits even when workers receive financial incentives. It is in this sense that incentives and morale are complementary.

Cooperation   The model can be used to demonstrate one reason good morale fosters cooperation among workers; it gives them a common objective. Let there be N workers and let the subscript n indicate variables and functions applying to the nth worker. The employer observes worker n's output to be

$$y_n(e_n) = y_n(E_n(d_n, m_n))$$

and pays him or her

$$w_n(y_n(e_n)) = w_n(y_n(E_n(d_n, m_n))).$$

The actual output of all N workers is

$$y(e_1, \ldots, e_N) = y(E_1(d_1, m_1), \ldots, E_N(d_N\ m_N)).$$

Worker n's unconscious utility is

$$B_n(w_n(y_n(e_n))) + \mu_{n1}[R(y(e_1, \ldots, e_N)) - w_1(y_1(e_1))$$
$$- \ldots - w_N(y_N(e_N))] - C(e_n),$$

and his or her conscious utility is

$$U_n(w_n(y_n(E_n(d_n, m_n))), m_n) + \mu_{n2}[R(y(E_1(d_1, m_1), \ldots, E_N(d_N, m_N)))$$
$$- w_1(y_1(E_1(d_1, m_1))) - \ldots - w_N(y_N(E_N(d_N, m_N)))] + V(E_n(d_n, m_n), m_n).$$

Interaction among the N workers suggests a coordination game, for they all derive utility from profits. In order to see the connection more clearly, assume that workers' moods adjust so that the utility of labor, $V(E_n(d_n, m_n), m_n)$, is the same for all decisions d_n actually adopted by the workers, so that this term may be ignored. In addition, suppress mood and the distinction between the conscious choice, d_n, and the realized action, e_n, and focus on conscious utility, since cooperation is arranged deliberately. Suppose that the choice of action has two components, selection of a method of production and the selection of effort, thought of as the pace of work. Since effort is influenced by mood, which is governed unconsciously and almost automatically, it makes sense to ignore the effort part of actions and to think of these solely as production methods. Under these assumptions, the relevant utility functions are

$$U_n(w_n(y_n(e_n))) + \mu_{n2}[R(y(e_1, \ldots, e_N)) - w_1(y_1(e_1))] \tag{21.5}$$
$$- \ldots - w_N(y_N(e_N))],$$

for $n = 1, \ldots, N$. If the parameters μ_{n2} are positive and the functions w_n are constant, as would be the case for truly fixed wages, then the workers in effect play a coordination game with payoff $R(y(e_1, \ldots, e_N))$ for all players, and the obvious solution is to maximize this payoff jointly. However, management normally gives workers at least some financial incentives linked to individual performance, such as production targets, performance evaluations, promotion criteria, and piece rates. I was told that it is difficult to design incentives so that workers' financial interests are entirely consistent with those of the firm. An important function of good morale is to motivate workers to act in the firm's interest, even when it conflicts with their own financial advantage. I show that the above model includes this function. More precisely, I argue that cooperation induced by internalization of the firm's goals increases profits.

Suppose that morale is neutral. That is, suppose that $\mu_{n2} = 0$, for all n. In addition, suppose that the wage functions, w_n, include financial incentives. For each n, let $\underline{e}_n$ be that value of e_n that maximizes $U_n(w_n(y_n(e_n)))$. With these choices of effort, the firm's profit is

$$R(y(\underline{e}_1, \ldots, \underline{e}_N)) - w_1(y_1(\underline{e}_1)) - \ldots - w_N(y_N(\underline{e}_N)).$$

In contrast, suppose now that morale is good, so that the μ_{n2} are all positive. Though it is hard to say how the workers would behave, it would be to their mutual advantage to choose actions $(\bar{e}_1, \ldots, \bar{e}_N)$ that (1) were a Nash equilibrium for the game with payoffs as in (21.5) and (2) gave each worker, n, a payoff exceeding $U_n(w_n(y_n(\underline{e}_n))) + \mu_2[R(y(\underline{e}1, \ldots, \underline{e}_N)) - w_1(y_1(\underline{e}_1)) - \ldots - w_N(y_N(\underline{e}_N))]$. Suppose that such an equilibrium exists. Because of the form of utility (21.5) and because μ_{n2} is positive and $\underline{e}_n$ maximizes $U_n(w_n(y_n(e_n)))$, for all n, it follows that

$$R(\bar{e}_1, \ldots, \bar{e}_N) - w_1(\bar{e}_1) - \ldots - w_N(\bar{e}_N) > R(y(\underline{e}_1, \ldots, \underline{e}_N))$$
$$- w_1(y_1(\underline{e}_1)) - \ldots - w_N(y_N(\underline{e}_N)).$$

That is, internalization of the firm's objectives increases profits.

Information Sharing   One of the reasons it is difficult to give workers incentives consistent with the firm's objectives is that the conditions workers face change frequently, so that the actions that are correct from the employer's point of view also change. If management knew conditions precisely, it could order workers to do exactly what was needed or it could include the conditions in the specification of incentives. However, often only the workers observe the relevant changes in circumstances. Managers said that one of the benefits of good morale is that it induces workers to share information with one another and with superiors. This advantage can be introduced into the above model by having company revenues depend on random variables observed by the workers alone. For instance, assume that worker n observes the random variable θ_n and that company revenue depends on all the θ_n so that utility function (21.5) becomes

$$U_n(w_n(y_n(e_n))) + \mu_{n2}[R(y(e_1, \ldots, e_N); \theta_n, \ldots, \theta_n))$$
$$- w_1(y_1(e_1)) - \ldots - w_N(y_N(e_N))],$$

If all workers reveal the values they observe of the θ_n, they can cooperate more effectively and expected profits and hence expected individual utilities earned from cooperation may incrsease and will not decrease, provided the parameters μ_{n2} are all positive. Hence workers have a positive incentive to share their observations with one another and with management.

Morale versus Coercion Managers explained that the chief disadvantage of using threats to obtain cooperation is the loss of worker initiative. Although force may succeed in making people work with great intensity, people working under such pressure may only make a show of cooperation and may not use their heads to help the firm. I was told that coercion works well for tasks that are easily monitored and when management knows what employees should do; managers said that compulsion is inefficient when workers know best what they ought to do because of information they alone receive. I express these ideas formally using an example in which I suppress mood, the unconscious, and the distinction between decisions and realized effort, since these are irrelevant here. Suppose a worker may do one of two types of tasks, A and B, and that these are performed with intensities I_A and I_B, respectively, where I_A and I_B are non-negative numbers. The action $e = (i, I)$ is task i done with intensity I, where $i = A$ or B. Let the disutility of doing either task, i, with intensity I be $- V(i, I) = I^2$ and let the utility of wage, w, be simply $U(w) = w$. Suppose that one and only one of the tasks is profitable, that management does not know which task is profitable, and that the worker can learn which is profitable at a small cost in utility. Suppose further that task A is profitable with probability p, where $\frac{1}{2} < p < 1$, that management observes the intensity level, and that a task done with intensity I earns revenues $R(i, I) = \sqrt{I}$, when it is profitable, and earns no revenue otherwise. Finally, suppose that to retain the worker, management has to offer a reservation utility level of at least $\frac{1}{16}$. If the firm obtains cooperation through threats, morale is zero and the worker cannot be counted on to do the task that is profitable. In this case, optimal management strategy is to set the wage, w, equal to $[1 + (2p)^{4/3}]/16$, to fix the task to be A, and to require work intensity,

I, to be $(2p)^{2/3}/4$, for these values solve the profit maximization problem

$$\max_{w,\ I}[pR(A,\ I)\ -\ w]$$

$$\text{s.t.}\ \ U(w)\ +\ V(I)\ \geq\ \tfrac{1}{16}$$

or $$\max_{w,\ I}[p\sqrt{I}\ -\ w]$$

$$\text{s.t.}\ \ w\ -\ I^2\ \geq\ \tfrac{1}{16}.$$

The firm fires the worker if work intensity is less than $(2p)^{2/3}/4$, in which case the worker earns his or her reservation utility level of 1/16. The firm's expected profits are the positive number $[3p(2p)^{2/3}/8] - \tfrac{1}{16}$ and expected revenues are $[p(2p)^{1/3}]/2$.

Suppose management does not threaten, but depends on positive morale. Assume that in this case the morale parameter, μ_2, equals $\tfrac{1}{2}$. Then the worker's total utility function is

$$U(w)\ +\ V(I)\ +\ \mu_2[R(i,\ I)\ -\ w]\ =\ w\ -\ I^2\ +\ 0.5[R(i,\ I)\ -\ w],$$

minus a small quantity if the worker verifies which task is profitable. Assuming the worker knows which task is profitable, he or she solves the problem

$$\max_I[-I^2\ +\ 0.5\sqrt{I}],$$

so that work intensity is $I = \tfrac{1}{4}$, which is less than the intensity in the previous case with compulsion and no morale. However, because the worker chooses the profitable task, the firm's expected revenues are $\sqrt{I} = \tfrac{1}{2}$, which exceeds the level with no morale. If the firm continues to pay wage $w = [1 + (2p)^{4/3}]/16$, then total expected worker utility, $U(w) + V(I) + \mu_2[R(i,\ I) - w]$, is at least 1/16, and expected profits are higher with positive morale than with no morale, unless $[p(2p)^{1/3}]/2 > 1/2$, that is, unless $p > 0.5^{1/4} \cong 0.84$. That is, coercion is more profitable than dependence on morale alone only if management knows with high probability which task is profitable, a result that corresponds to the intuition I wish to express.

21.7 Macroeconomic Policy

An understanding of wage stickiness does not resolve the important policy questions hinging on the interaction between unemployment and inflation. This topic is controversial, and the many cross-currents in its discussion make the debate confusing and difficult to organize along ideological lines. Most of the disagreement concerns how the economy functions. In the context of the Great Depression, Keynes gave little heed to the danger of inflation, concentrating on the need to expand the economy in order to reduce unemployment. In the prosperous postwar environment, interest in price change increased, and the Phillips curve (section 1.5) attracted attention and was interpreted as a trade-off between inflation and unemployment. The task of policy was believed to be to keep unemployment low, but not so low as to cause excessive inflation. Later it was observed that the Phillips curve seemed to shift upward during periods of inflation, and this observation led to the idea that the trade-off between inflation and unemployment exists only in the short run, because expectations eventually adapt to the inflation experienced, shifting the Phillips curve. The long-run Phillips curve was said to be vertical at an unemployment rate labeled as the natural rate, where this rate is understood by some to be optimal. A related term is the non-accelerating inflation rate of unemployment, or NAIRU, which is not thought of as optimal but has a pragmatic interpretation as the unemployment rate at which the inflationary pressures in the many diverse labor markets are zero on average. Proponents of NAIRU models assert that the rate of inflation increases as long as unemployment is less than the NAIRU and decreases when unemployment exceeds it. An extreme stance is that policy, especially monetary policy, affects only the price level and cannot affect aggregate real income or employment, even in the short run. Proponents of these ideas usually believe that the actual rate of unemployment always equals the natural rate, so that the natural rate fluctuates, a point of view at variance with the findings of this study.

Underlying some of the policy discussions are divisions over the mechanisms connecting economic activity to inflation. One view is that excess demand or supply causes changes in wages and prices, so that changes in unemployment cause changes in inflation. A point of view based on the Lucas-Rapping model is that the unemployment rate is a decreasing function of the difference between the actual and expected rates of wage inflation and that changes in inflation cause unemployment. According to this view, the natural rate of unemployment is the one realized when the actual rate of inflation equals the expected one. This model implies that macroeconomic policy should be unchanging, because policy fluctuations risk increasing inflation or unemployment, by surprising the public. There is even less room for policy when this model is combined with the hypothesis of rational expectations, which postulates that people make the best possible predictions about future values of economic variables, given the information available. Under these assumptions, systematic policy cannot influence employment, but serves only to determine the price level. Policy affects real income and employment only when it surprises people, which would be hard to do repeatedly if expectations were rational.

Still another area of disagreement concerns the amount of momentum in the inflation process. Some believe that if the rate of unemployment stays at the natural or NAIRU level, then a given rate of inflation will continue indefinitely until checked by higher unemployment; others believe it will gradually abate.

Participants in the policy debate have appealed to empirical work using aggregate data. Because aggregates change in response to many conflicting influences that are hard to distinguish, much might be learned from microeconomic studies. A good approach could be to develop models for particular sectors by using econometric studies of wage and price data along with survey and field studies of the mechanisms controlling change in wages, prices, and expectations. Such sectoral models could later be joined into a grand model of the whole economy.

Key matters which need closer study are how wages and labor costs change in response to fluctuations in labor demand and to actual and projected changes in the cost of living. Although my study did not address these issues, it did provide some useful clues and suggested that much more could be discovered by means of interviews, for businesspeople and labor leaders were ready and able to explain what they did and how they thought about their problems. I now describe tentative conclusions about the impact of price inflation on average labor costs in the primary sector.

Inflation and Average Labor Costs   In the primary sector, turnover and workers' progression through the internal pay structure diminish the impact on average labor expenses of cost-of-living pay increases. Even if no worker's pay falls in real terms, a firm's average real wages or salaries per employee may decline during a recession. Recall that the internal pay structure determines the pay of employees at every stage in their career (section 6.1). As employees progress, their pay rises in the manner specified by the structure, even if the structure itself does not increase. On the basis of what I heard, I conclude that most employers and especially nonunion ones did not maintain the real value of the raises associated with career advance during the recessionary period of my study. However, they did protect the purchasing power of the pay of those workers whose performance was adequate according to accepted standards. If the raises implied by the structure were at least as great as the rate of inflation, there was no need to increase the structure. Average labor costs normally increase by less than the average pay of individual workers because of turnover savings, which are the difference between the pay of workers who leave as a result of attrition and the pay of new hires who replace them. Because of turnover savings, average real labor costs decline if the average raises received by employees only just suffice to maintain the purchasing power of an average employee. Turnover savings occur only when firms continue to hire new workers to replace those who leave and may be negative when companies lay off workers who are less well paid than the average employee. Turnover savings may be small for low-level employees, for many of them have few opportunities for promotion and are paid at the maximum rate for their job.[7]

In order to clarify the main points, assume that a business's internal structure has N levels and that workers advance one level per year. Suppose the internal wage structure specifies a wage, w_{tn} for each level n in year t, where $n = 1, \ldots, N$. For simplicity, assume that

$$w_{t,n+1} = b w_{tn}, \tag{21.6}$$

for all n and t, where $b > 1$. (In reality, internal structures are not so mechanical.) Assume that the nominal wages of individual workers are downwardly rigid, so that

$$w_{t+1,n+1} \geq w_{tn}, \tag{21.7}$$

for all t and n. Suppose also that w_{tn} is set at the beginning of period t, before the consumer price level for the period is known. Finally, suppose that the firm protects the expected real pay of individual workers, so that

$$w_{t+1,n+1}/p_{t,t+1} \geq w_{tn}/p_t, \tag{21.8}$$

where p_t is the actual consumer price level in year t and $p_{t,t+1}$ is the consumer price level for year $t + 1$ expected in year t. (Actual adjustment of pay to changes in living costs is often much more complicated, since firms may correct previous mistakes in adjusting to price-level changes and may react only partially to sudden changes.) It follows from equation (21.6) and inequality (21.8) that $b w_{t+1,n} = w_{t+1,n+1} \geq w_{tn}(p_{t,t+1}/p_t)$, as long as $p_{t,t+1} \geq p_t$, or

$$w_{t+1,n} \geq b^{-1} w_{tn}(p_{t,t+1}/p_t),$$

for all n. Similarly, (21.6) and (21.7) imply that

$$w_{t+1,n} \geq b^{-1} w_{tn},$$

for all n. Labor market conditions also affect the price of labor, and these may be expressed by the inequality

$$w_{t+1,n} \geq \gamma w_{tn}(p_{t,t+1}/p_t),$$

where γ is a positive parameter. A labor shortage corresponds to $\gamma > 1$, a neutral or full-employment labor market corresponds to $\gamma = 1$, and $\gamma < 1$ when the labor market is slack. The previous three inequalities may be expressed as

$$w_{t+1,n} = (w_{tn})\max(b^{-1}, \ b^{-1}(p_{t,t+1}/pt), \ \gamma(p_{t,t+1}/p_t)). \tag{21.9}$$

In order to relate equation (21.9) to inflation, define the average labor costs of the business in year t to be

$$W_t = (L_{t1} + L_{t2} + \ldots + L_{tN})^{-1}(w_{t1}L_{t1} + w_{t2}L_{t2} \tag{21.10}$$
$$+ \ldots + w_{tN}L_{tN}),$$

where L_{tn} is the number of workers in the firm at the nth level in year t. Assuming that the ratios L_{tn}/L_{t1} do not change from year to year, equation (21.10) implies that

$$W_{t+1} = (W_t)\max(b^{-1}, \ b^{-1}(p_{t,t+1}/p_t), \ \gamma(p_{t,t+1}/p_t)) \tag{21.11}$$

This equation implies that real average labor costs may decline during a recession if there is inflation. For instance, suppose that $\gamma \leq b^{-1}$ and that people have perfect foresight or rational expectations, so that $p_{t,t+1} = p_{t+1}$. Then equation (21.11) implies that if inflation is positive, then

$$W_{t+1}/p_{t+1} = b^{-1}W_t/p_t. \tag{21.12}$$

The employers I interviewed behaved as if the most recently announced inflation rate would continue unchanged, so that

$$p_{t,t+1} = p_t(p_t/p_{t-1}).$$

In this case, equation (21.12) becomes

$$W_{t+1}/p_t = b^{-1}W_t/p_{t-1} \tag{21.13}$$

Since the constant b is probably close to 1, the effect just described is likely to be small, which is consistent with macroeconomic empirical studies. Since b is constant, the effect does not increase with the unemployment rate, an assertion consistent with Keynesian views. However, high unemployment is associated with other negative influences on pay, such as low profits, company financial crises, and the decline of starting pay in the secondary sector. The aggregate impact of these effects probably increases with unemployment and may outweigh the effects I have described.

Equations 21.12 and 21.13 do not reflect the impact on wages of expectations of wage inflation, as opposed to price inflation. The effect of wage expectations may be important, for many employers I talked to were preoccupied with keeping up with increases at other firms, even though unemployment was high. It would require a detailed study to determine to what extent expectations of wage inflation add to inflation's momentum, for employers exchange information about wages and so may automatically coordinate changes in wage inflation, weakening the momentum derived from wage expectations.

The Impact of Turnover Savings on Inflation   The effect of turnover savings on average wage costs may imply that inflationary shocks have only a temporary effect on inflation when labor is not too scarce. The shocks could come from increases in the prices of primary inputs or from other sources. The following example illustrates the point.

Suppose there is only one kind of output in the economy, produced from labor and from one other primary input according to the production function

$$y_{t+1} = \min(\alpha^t L_t, a^{-1} M_t),$$

where $\alpha > 1$ and represents the rate of technical progress, a is a positive constant, y_t is the amount of output in period t, L_t is labor input, and M_t is the quantity of the other primary input. Suppose that all firms are identical and that each uses an equal quantity of labor at each level in its internal hierarchy. Let L_t be the total quantity of labor used at one level, so that W_t, as defined by formula (21.10), is the average price of one unit of labor. Let p_t and q_t be, respectively, the price of output and the price of the nonlabor input in period t and suppose, for simplicity, that q_t is linked to the price of output according to the formula

$$q_t = cp_t,$$

where c is a positive constant satisfying $ac < 1$. It follows that

$$p_{t+1} = \alpha^{-t} W_t + acp_t$$

or

$$p_{t+1}/p_t = \alpha^{-t} W_t/p_t + ac. \tag{21.14}$$

Next suppose that people have perfect foresight, so that

$$p_{t,t+1} = p_{t+1}.$$

Then according to (21.11),

$$W_{t+1}/W_t = \max(b^{-1}, \ b^{-1}(p_{t+1}/p_t), \ \gamma(p_{t+1}/p_t)).$$

If inflation is positive so that $p_{t+1}/p_t > 1$, then

$$W_{t+1}/p_{t+1} = (W_t/p_t)\max(b^{-1}, \ \gamma).$$

If $\alpha^{-1}\max(b^{-1}, \gamma) < 1$, then $\alpha^{-t} W_t/p_t$ converges to zero as t increases, as long as inflation remains positive. Hence, by equation (21.14) and because $ac < 1$,

$$p_{t+1}/p_t < 1,$$

for large enough t, and inflation then ceases. The condition $\alpha^{-1}\max(b^{-1}, \gamma) < 1$ implies that $\gamma < \alpha$, which means that the rate of inflationary pressure in the labor market does not exceed the rate of technical progress. Because $\alpha > 1$, inflation in the product price may subside even when $\gamma > 1$, that is, even in the presence of some inflationary pressure in the labor market.

Appendix 21A Related Literature

EXTENSION TO MORALE (SECTION 21.6)

Akerlof and Kranton (1998) model psychological identity as a set of rules restricting a person's utility function. They describe several economic contexts in which identity is important. The model of section 21.6 is similar to those of Akerlof (1982) and Rabin (1993) in that it expresses reciprocity. Reciprocity is exchange and is distinguished from altruism, which is unconditional giving. Fehr and Gächter (1998a, b) describe the impressive amount of experimental evidence that many people are willing voluntarily to suffer losses either to punish harmful acts or to compensate others for benefits previously received from them. I differ from these authors only in emphasis, in presenting reciprocation by an organization as a means of reinforcing attachment to it, and in stressing that people are able to identify with a group and are willing to sacrifice for it with no quid pro quo, as long as they feel appreciated or valued. Annable (1988) and Campbell (1997) propose models somewhat similar to that of this section. In their models, morale appears as an argument of the production function and depends on wages, on changes in them, or on the ratio of wages to a wage norm. Rotemberg (1994) develops a mathematical model describing a link between morale and cooperation among workers. In his model, it is selfishly rational for workers to be unselfish toward one another. Workers choose to internalize the welfare of other workers if the compensation system is such that cooperation is beneficial to all. That is, workers help each other to earn higher pay, whereas in the model presented here, people have a common interest in helping the firm. In a model of Fehr and Schmidt (1997) of inequality aversion, people internalize the utility of others in judging distributional equity.

MACROECONOMIC POLICY (SECTION 21.7)

Okun (1981, p. 93) is the only author I have found who discusses turnover savings.

There is a huge literature on the trade-off between inflation and unemployment. Some of the papers presenting Keynesian points of view are Samuelson and Solow (1960), Tobin (1972, 1975). Akerlof, Dickens, and Perry (1996) describe beneficial effects of inflation, neoclassical positions are presented in Friedman (1968), Phelps (1968), Lucas (1976, 1978), and Sargent (1996), and the debate is reviewed by Gordon (1981). A few of many empirical contributions are Gordon (1972, 1977, 1997), Blanchard (1986, 1987), King and Watson (1994), and Staiger, Stock, and Watson (1997). Fair (1993, 1997a, 1997b) performs econometric tests of the impact of inflation expectations on prices and finds that though expectations do have an impact, they are not strong enough to justify the conclusion of the NAIRU model that too little unemployment brings ever-increasing inflation.

The literature just cited discusses policy in terms of macroeconomic models and data. Related issues have also been addressed using general equilibrium models of various sorts, including temporary equilibrium and overlapping generations models. For instance, several authors have proved that there can be unemployment in general equilibrium models with downwardly rigid wages. Papers with proofs of this assertion include Barro and Grossman (1971), Drèze (1975), Benassy (1975, 1976), Malinvaud (1977), Hahn (1978), Grandmont, Laroque, and Younès (1978), and Hart (1982).

22

WHERETO FROM HERE?

While I was engaged in this project, ideas for more narrowly focused data collection occurred to me, a few of which I sketch here. If studies are sufficiently narrow, it should be possible to sample randomly and to use statistical techniques (sections 1.10 and 1.11).

22.1 Statistical Background

Little is known about the incidence and magnitude of pay cuts in the general population of companies in good and bad times. Even less is known about downward flexibility of the pay of new hires. Given sufficient resources, it would be simple to collect data on these matters from a fixed panel of companies over a period of years. Such data would make possible a careful comparison of hiring pay flexibility in the primary and secondary sectors. In order to pinpoint the causes of pay cuts, it would be essential to know the condition of companies at the time they cut pay, that is, whether they were suffering financially, had recently had layoffs, or had recently been taken over by new owners. In measuring hiring pay, it would be important to measure the pay of new hires for specific jobs and with specific qualifications and experience. Otherwise, the data might be contaminated by changes in the quality of the new hires relative to the types of positions filled. The quality of new hires for given positions probably increases during recessions.

As has been noted, household income surveys show a large number of year-to-year pay reductions (Appendix 11A, section 11.1). It is hard to evaluate these findings because the data may be inaccurate and because they do not reveal the reason for pay decreases; they may result from new job assignments, demotions, loss of overtime, or cuts in base pay. More reliable conclusions might be reached by following a sample of, say, 500 households for several years, and asking precise questions about income, its sources, and changes in it. These responses should be checked with employers for accuracy.

There is almost no information available on the frequency with which firms use various types of punishment. Firms would probably be reluctant to share such data, unless they were collected in a way making it impossible to trace the source, for firms would worry about their possible use in employee suits. The data would help in assessing the shirking model.

Although some authors assume that the unemployed seldom take low-level stopgap jobs (for example, McCormick, 1990), I believe many do so, and other surveys support this conclusion. Evidence could be gathered by following a fixed panel of unemployed workers. The issue is important as it bears on the flexibility of the unemployed.

22.2 Tests of Hypotheses

According to the standard scientific method, the best strategy for testing a theory is to attack it from its weakest side, using the data most likely to contradict its implications. In economics, it is often difficult to perform powerful tests of theories, for typically little or no data are available bearing on key assumptions and implications. Investigators could make better tests if they collected their own data, and some ideas for such tests follow.

THE SHIRKING MODEL

One test of the shirking theory would be to conduct a questionnaire survey of workers in a few firms, asking them if they believed they would be fired for poor performance and if fear of firing motivated them. It would be important to learn the views of supervisors and managers as well on these matters. The theory would be contradicted if the fear of firing were not an important motivator. It would be interesting to see if the theory applies to unskilled labor filling short-term jobs; I believe it may.

Another test would be to find a few prosperous nonunion businesses, located in an area that had recently changed from a situation of labor shortage to one of extreme labor surplus and where laid-off employees had little hope of finding new work at wages close to those earned previously. Such situations arise when large plants using specific skills shut down in isolated areas. If the shirking model were valid, wage rates within the prosperous firms would decline.

KEYNES'S RELATIVE WAGE THEORY

Keynes's relative wage theory could be tested by finding a group of neighboring firms where workers knew a great deal about pay levels at all the firms. This knowledge could be tested by means of questionnaires filled out by employees and from information provided by the firms about actual pay levels. Keynes's theory predicts that pay should remain downwardly rigid even during a severe downturn. I conducted a limited test of this sort, and found that pay was somewhat flexible in businesses where mutual knowledge of pay was great, contrary to the theory (section 7.5). Contrasting data could be provided by an isolated group of neighboring firms where workers knew almost nothing about pay outside their own workplace. The theory predicts that pay would fall at these firms during a recession.

THE LUCAS-RAPPING MODELS

The Lucas-Rapping theories could be tested by following a panel of unemployed workers during a recession, establishing how and why they lost their jobs, whether they preferred home production or nonmarket opportunities to jobs paying current wages, and whether they rejected or failed to investigate job opportunities because they paid too little. The study might be similar to that of Daniel (1990), while focusing more on the questions just listed. Daniel found that the jobless had few nonmarket opportunities and a great deal of difficulty finding work.

As was mentioned earlier, the Lucas-Rapping models predict that the number of quits into unemployment increase during recessions (section 20.1). No U.S. government data exist on such quits, as far as I know. The Bureau of Labor Statistics estimates the stock of currently unemployed who had quit their jobs, not the flow of quitters into unemployment. The cyclical behavior of this flow could be measured by following a representative panel of workers. Appropriate data have been collected since 1968 by the Michigan Panel Study of Income Dynamics, but it seems that no one has totaled up the number of quits into unemployment for every year of the survey.[1]

THE IMPLICIT CONTRACT MODEL

An obvious test of the implicit contract model is to compare the pay of firms that have cut pay in the past with that of similar firms that never cut pay. According to the theory, the pay cutters would be obliged to pay more, and enough more to discourage pay cutting. Another test would be to see if companies give raises to offset increases in wage taxes. The theory predicts that firms do so, if they are risk neutral. My study took place shortly after the introduction of a new state wage income tax in Connecticut, and I found that firms were unwilling to make up for the tax increase (section 10.3).

THE ELASTICITY OF DEMAND FOR LABOR, AND THE SAVINGS GENERATED BY LAYOFFS

Reasons employers gave for preferring layoffs to pay cuts were that pay cuts save few jobs and layoffs save a great deal of money. A questionnaire survey could determine whether these beliefs are widely held. It might be possible to estimate firms' actual elasticity of demand for labor by comparing labor use before and after pay cuts. More insight could be gained by investigating in detail the actual cost structure of a few firms, in order to calculate the impact of a hypothetical pay cut on marginal variable costs. The effect of a change in marginal costs on sales and employment would depend on the firm's pricing policy and on the elasticity of demand for its products, topics that are probably harder to study than wage rigidity. Knowledge of a firm's cost structure would also make possible accurate estimation of savings from layoffs.

22.3 Search for New Hypotheses

Explorations in search of hypotheses would most likely entail extensive inter-action with economic decision makers and with observers of economic life.

WHY DO PAY CUTS HURT MORALE?

My conclusions about why pay cuts damage morale require elaboration, for my information comes from managers, who may not fully understand subor-dinates' feelings. It might be revealing to question workers about their reactions to hypothetical and actual pay cuts. I am aware of only two field studies of actual pay cuts, those of Greenberg (1989, 1990).

WHAT HAPPENS WHEN MORALE CRUMBLES?

Although many managers told vivid stories of having dealt with collapsing morale, such incidents have never been studied, as far as I know. It might be difficult to gain access to firms suffering from poor morale, for companies do not want to make their problems public. If cooperation could be obtained, both managers and workers should be questioned about their feelings and their un-derstanding of the situation. Information should also be gathered on changes in productivity, turnover, and the ease of recruitment, since managers said these were strongly affected by morale. Such a study would be useful for management science as well as for understanding wage rigidity.

WHY ARE FIRMS RISK AVERSE?

Although theoretical speculations abound, little is known about why firms are reluctant to borrow money to cover losses and why they so dislike having temporary declines in profits. More information could be obtained by inter-viewing financial officers of firms as well as people who provide capital, such as lending officers of banks and insurance companies, and rich investors. Stock and bond brokers should be able to provide useful insights about the willingness of investors to advance money to companies in difficulty. The crucial issue is why companies reduce investment expenditures in response to financial pressure.

ORGANIZATIONAL SLACK
It is not clear how organizational slack can be recognized and measured and why it exists when it does. These questions could be clarified by careful study of the use of labor in one or a few firms over the course of a business cycle. Key objectives would be the identification of waste and establishing the reasons for it.

WHY DO STRIKES OCCUR?
Despite many studies of labor negotiations and strikes, the causes of strikes remain unclear. A great deal might be learned by following actual negotiations and interviewing participants on both sides. Previous studies have not concentrated on the main issues of interest to economists, namely, the role of asymmetries of information and why the two sides do not avoid strikes.

22.4 Conclusion

The subject of economics has an enormous impact on everyone's life, and yet the discipline lacks the status of a real science, follows rather than leads ideological trends, and sometimes indulges in fanciful theoretical representations of reality. Many branches of economics are not anchored in empirical knowledge, probably because the subject originated as part of moral philosophy and is still regarded as having to do more with thinking than with observation. This attitude is compatible with the field's dependence on easily accessible statistical data, which, though essential, are also inadequate. Often it is not clear what they measure, and without this knowledge they can be used to support almost any contention. How can the unemployment rate be interpreted without knowledge of what it means to be unemployed? What sense can be made of wage data without knowing the impact on workers of pay raises and cuts? Empirical knowledge means systematic experience with the object of study, and this can be had only by taking responsibility for data collection. Unfortunately, the gathering of economic data is considered to be hardly within the scope of academic inquiry. This attitude is in conflict with the view expressed in texts on economic history that great progress in science and technology occurred only when thinking people came in contact with the practical realities of production and when pragmatic attitudes took precedence over religious and ideological ones. I do not claim to have made great discoveries or that my observations are unimpeachable, but I believe I have shown that much can learned by confronting economic reality.

NOTES / REFERENCES / INDEX

NOTES

1. Introduction

1. The Keynesian point of view is articulated in Tobin (1972).
2. Lucas and Sargent (1979, pp. 11–12, or 1981, pp. 310–312) argue forcefully that labor markets always clear, though they define market clearance so broadly that their statement is difficult to contradict. They assert that markets clear if "all observed prices and quantities are viewed as outcomes of decisions taken by individual firms and households." Market clearance according to this definition was not contradicted by anything I observed, though there was abundant evidence that labor markets did not clear according to the usual definition that supply equals demand.
3. The belief that workers can always find some job at once is stated by Robert Lucas (1978, p. 354).
4. The neoclassical point of view is explained in Friedman (1968).
5. Blinder (1990) makes this argument and others I use in defense of the interview method. These arguments appear also in chapter 1 of Blinder et al. (1998).
6. The term "transactions" is borrowed from Mortensen (1989, p. 350).
7. Recent examples of the transactions type may be found in Mortensen and Pissarides (1994) and Pissarides (1994).
8. Hausman (1989, p. 121) makes related comments on Friedman's methodology.
9. This discussion of circularity and the example are an imitation of Popper (1957). In his example, rough seas are attributed to Neptune's anger. I owe knowledge of the argument and the reference to Werner Hildenbrand.
10. The emphasis on such prediction is illustrated by the following quotation from Lucas and Sargent (1979, p. 11, or 1981, p. 311): "The facts we actually have, however, are simply the available time series on employment and wage rates plus the responses to our unemployment surveys. Cleared markets is simply a principle, not verifiable by direct observation, which may or may not be useful in constructing successful hypotheses about the behavior of these series." One of the by-products of this project is direct evidence against the hypothesis that labor markets clear.

11. Important field research has recently been done in development economics (Townsend, 1995, and Udry, 1994, 1995).

12. "It very rarely happens that the nominal price of labour universally falls, but we well know that it frequently remains the same while the nominal price of provisions has been gradually rising," from Thomas Malthus, "An Essay on the Principle of Population," reprinted as selection 14 in Kapp and Kapp (1949), where the quotation appears on page 126. I owe knowledge of this passage to Morton Kamien.

13. I owe this quip to my colleague William Nordhaus.

14. I owe this analogy to my colleague William Brainard.

15. Although Heckman and MaCurdy speak of these variables as unobserved, data exist on them, as in the surveys of British unemployed organized by Daniel (1974, 1990).

16. The Blinder study of price rigidity has a fixed list of unprovocative questions and achieved a high response rate of 61 percent in a random sample (Blinder, 1990, 1991, and Blinder et al., 1998).

17. This distinction differs slightly from that of Peter Doeringer and Michael Piore (1971), who emphasize differences between the two sectors in pay, status, and possibilities for promotion. Piore (1973) contains more discussion of the secondary sector. Dickens and Lang (1993) review empirical work on the validity of the distinction between secondary and primary labor markets.

2. Methods

1. These I probably could not have discovered in any case (Nisbett and Wilson, 1977).

2. One company, where I interviewed by telephone, had its headquarters in California.

3. Time and Location

1. See U.S. Department of Commerce, *Statistical Abstract of the United States, 1995,* tables 695 and 697.

2. The low rate of collection of unemployment insurance benefits is widespread and is discussed in Burtless (1983).

4. Morale

1. This argument has been questioned by Mawhinney (1990).

2. Osterman (1994) estimates that in 1992 management reforms of this sort had been undertaken by 35 percent of U.S. firms.

3. This list is given in table 1 of Podsakoff, MacKenzie, and Hui (1993).

4. Viteles (1953), Likert (1961), and Seashore (1954) do stress values, however.

5. The econometric methodology of Norsworthy and Zabala (1985) has been criticized by Straka (1993).

6. I am grateful to Major Guy A. Lofaro of West Point for guidance on the literature on military morale.

5. Company Risk Aversion

1. In technical terms, risk aversion is equivalent to concavity of the utility function for money.

6. Internal Pay Structure

1. Such people are said to be "red circled."
2. Some companies appearing in Table 6.1 do not appear in Table 6.2, because part of the structure was formal and part was informal or because I lacked sufficient information.

7. External Pay Structure

1. I have borrowed the term "external structure" from institutional labor economists, such as Livernash (1957).
2. The surveys list, for each job, the number of firms reporting salary or wage data together with the average number of workers doing the job in those firms. Table 7.8 applies to jobs for which the ratio of the number of workers to number of firms is no more than 1.3, so that most firms must have had only one person doing the jobs.
3. Examples of jobs with narrow gaps were computer programmer, engineer, bank teller, clerk-typist, secretary, janitor, guard, and toolmaker. Examples of jobs with wide gaps are personnel manager, regional sales manager, national sales manager, environmental affairs director, telemarketing representative, and electronics technician.
4. These figures are for hourly wages and do not include benefits and other burdens, which probably increased with pay. The drivers' duties and the kinds of trucks and customers varied somewhat among the companies, and these differences probably explained some of the pay differences.

8. The Shirking Theory

1. The prohibition is contained in section 31–51r of the Connecticut General Statutes, which prohibits an employer from requiring as a condition of employment that an employee or prospective employee execute what it defines as an "employment promissory note." I owe this information to George E. O.Brien, Jr., of Tyler, Cooper, and Alcorn in New Haven.
2. I owe this inquiry to the advice of my colleague William Nordhaus. I found I could not ask about bonding in the context of the shirking model because employers did not agree that they paid more than needed to hire and retain the quality of labor desired, except perhaps in the temporary conditions of the recession.
3. Another exception is Drago and Heywood (1992).
4. The comments of these managers were classified as "performance somewhat improved."
5. In a later paper, Raff (1988) argues that Ford increased wages in order to head off unionization rather than to increase productivity.
6. See various issues of *Earnings and Employment*.

9. The Pay of New Hires in the Primary Sector

1. The pay of new hires is not the same as starting pay, which is usually what is offered to inexperienced new workers, beginning at the lowest level of their job category. New workers may be hired at all levels of experience.
2. These companies were all small. They ranged in size from 8 to 100 employees, with

an average number of 42. The companies included 5 in manufacturing, one bank, one medical laboratory, and one accounting firm. The other 90 companies represented a full range of sizes and types of business.

11. Resistance to Pay Reduction

1. Bureau of Labor Statistics, *Earnings and Employment*, annual issues.
2. See also Bell (1995, table I) and Mitchell (1994).
3. This number was communicated by Holzer to Akerlof, Dickens, and Perry and is cited on page 17 of their paper of 1996.

12. Experiences with Pay Reduction

1. Perhaps managers tried to see the good side of current pay cuts, whereas the bad aspects stood out when they looked back at previous ones. Because of this possibility, it would be useful to study pay cuts made during booms at the time they occurred.
2. I did not collect stories about freezes occurring before the recession, so that I cannot compare freezes during recessions with freezes during economic booms.
3. In order to explore the matter vigorously, I would have had to ask about policy during past periods of rapid inflation and about the comparative impact of real and nominal wage cuts. However, I considered retrospective and hypothetical questions perilous and tried to confine discussion to the concrete and immediate (section 2.2). I now believe I should have taken more risks regarding the issue, for when I did ask some employers about these matters, I obtained sensible answers.

13. Layoffs

1. Okun (1973, p. 213) notes the distinction between the impact on productivity of the level of economic activity and the change in it.
2. An example is output $= 5 + \sin(2\pi t/32)$ and productivity $= 5 + \sin(2\pi t/32 + \pi/4)$, in each period t.
3. In making this tabulation, I have counted clerical workers as production workers. I also counted professional workers in professional firms as part of the production staff, though they are overtime exempt.
4. Theoretically, an increased probability of layoff could discourage work effort. Since permanent layoff would preclude future rewards, workers might feel little need to impress their bosses if they expected to be let go. This argument is made in Drago and Heywood (1992).

15. Hiring

1. It was not always clear whether quality improvement meant increase in average quality or in the number of high-quality applicants. The distinction was hard to explain during an interview.
2. I am grateful to Morton Kamien for pointing out the parallel between the reluctance to cut pay and to hire the overqualified.

3. Unemployment was not this high.
4. I owe this reference to Peter Gahan of the Department of Management and Industrial Relations at the University of Melbourne.
5. I owe the last two references to Vicki Fung.

16. Voluntary Turnover

1. The data on unemployment are from the Bureau of Labor Statistics, as are the data on quits from 1948 to 1981. The data on quits from 1986 to 1994 are from the Bureau of National Affairs, "Bulletin to Management" in "The BNA Policy and Practice Series." Figure 16.1 shows the quit rate multiplied by five in order to aid visual comparison with the unemployment rate.
2. I am grateful to Winthrop Roy of Management Service Associates for providing me with the turnover data for Figure 16.2. Total turnover includes layoffs and firings as well as quits. Layoffs increase during recessions, and the figure shows that during the last recession the decrease in quits more than offset the increase in layoffs. Figure 16.2 shows one tenth the turnover rate to aid comparison with the unemployment rate.

17. The Secondary Sector

1. 1995 Compensation and Benefits Survey of the Building Service Contractors Association International. The data are the median responses in the samples.
2. Roy (1995).
3. 1995 Annual Specialty Store and Human Resource Director's Wage and Benefit Survey of the National Retail Federation.
4. The definitions of industrial classifications are contained in Office of Management and Budget (1987).
5. Contract engineers are called "job shoppers" in the trade.
6. In dealings with large clients, the prices or agent's mark-ups are sometimes fixed by an overall agreement.
7. Larry Katz informed me of the relevance of this reference.

18. The Unemployed

1. Exceptions were skills that happened to be in short supply, such as nursing and physical therapy.
2. Kaitz (1970), Akerlof and Main (1981), Carlson and Horrigan (1983), and Horrigan (1987).
3. U.S. Bureau of Labor Statistics, Employment and Earnings.
4. This point has been emphasized by Clark and Summers (1979, 1982).
5. These figures show, respectively, one half and one tenth of the percentage of unemployed who are job leavers or job losers. Such fractions are used to aid comparison with the unemployment rate.
6. The data for 1970–1993 are from the January issues of U.S. Bureau of Labor Statistics, Employment and Earnings. The data for 1967–1969 are from Gilroy (1973).

7. I owe this reference to Leslie Moore.
8. The data are from the Bureau of Labor Statistics.
9. This term is borrowed from MacKay and Reid (1972).
10. The data for Figure 18A.18 come from Bureau of Labor Statistics, *Earnings and Employment.*

20. Existing Theories

1. Akerlof (1980, p. 752) proposes the same idea.
2. The failure of the implicit contract theory was a disappointment, as it was one of my favorite theories.
3. Annable (1988) and MacLeod and Malcomson (1993) have a similar idea that poor morale is used deliberately by workers to punish employers for breach of contract, though the contracts are not insurance agreements.
4. The theoretical conclusions I have drawn differ slightly from those of the authors of the model, Bulow and Summers (1986), though I have, I believe, been faithful to their assumptions.
5. Caplin and Spulber (1987) argue that menu costs might not cause aggregate prices or wages to be sticky, though they cause individual prices to be changed only infrequently.
6. An exception is the model of Jovanovic (1987), in which real wages are fixed by construction, for each worker earns the value of his or her output, which, at each work site, is a constant independent of the number of workers engaged.

21. Remarks on Theory

1. Grandmont (1989) states the first argument.
2. I am grateful to Mahzarin Banaji of the Yale Department of Psychology for the previous two references.
3. I am grateful to Major Guy A. Lofaro for these references.
4. The earnings, $w(e)$, could be a vector including pay, praise, promotion, and other rewards.
5. Here and elsewhere, I choose the additively separable functional form for convenience of exposition, not out of conviction.
6. Akerlof and Kranton (1998) model the moral aspects of identity as internalized rules restricting the utility function.
7. William Brainard explained turnover savings to me on our way to our first interview. His explanation was reinforced many times by informants in later interviews.

22. Whereto from Here?

1. I am grateful to Michael Boozer, Ann Huff Stevens, and Greg Duncan for information about the Michigan survey.

REFERENCES

Abbink, Klaus, Gary E. Bolton, Abdolkarim Sadrieh, and Fang-Fang Tang. 1996. "Adaptive Learning versus Punishment in Ultimatum Bargaining." Discussion Paper no. B-381, Sonderforschungsbereich 313, University of Bonn, Germany.

Abowd, John A., and Thomas Lemieux. 1993. "The Effects of Product Market Competition on Collective Bargaining Agreements: The Case of Foreign Competition in Canada." *Quarterly Journal of Economics,* 108, 983–1014.

Abraham, Katharine G. 1987. "Help-Wanted Advertising, Job Vacancies, and Unemployment." *Brookings Papers on Economic Activity,* 207–243.

Abraham, Katharine G., and John C. Haltiwanger. 1995. "Real Wages and the Business Cycle." *Journal of Economic Literature,* 33, 1215–64.

Abraham, Katharine G., and Lawrence F. Katz. 1986. "Cyclical Unemployment: Sectoral Shifts or Aggregate Disturbances?" *Journal of Political Economy,* 94, 507–522.

Abraham, Katharine G., and James L. Medoff. 1984. "Length of Service and Layoffs in Union and Nonunion Work Groups." *Industrial and Labor Relations Review,* 38, 87–97.

Adams, James D. 1985. "Permanent Difference in Unemployment and Permanent Wage Differentials." *Quarterly Journal of Economics,* 100, 29–56.

Adams, J. Stacy. 1965. "Inequity in Social Exchange." In Leonard Berkowitz, ed., *Advances in Experimental Social Psychology,* 2:267–299. New York: Acadmic Press.

Adams, Roy J., Bernard Adell, and Hoyt N. Wheeler. 1990. "Discipline and Discharge in Canada and the United States." *Labor Law Journal,* 41, 596–601.

Addison, John T., and Pedro Portugal. 1987. "The Effect of Advance Notification of Plant Closings on Unemployment." *Industrial and Labor Relations Review,* 41, 3–16.

Admati, Anat, and Motty Perry. 1987. "Strategic Delay in Bargaining." *Review of Economic Studies,* 54, 345–364.

Agell, Jonas, and Per Lundborg. 1995. "Theories of Pay and Unemployment: Survey Evidence from Swedish Manufacturing Firms." *Scandinavian Journal of Economics,* 97, 295–307.

Agell, Susanne A. 1994. "Swedish Evidence on the Efficiency Wage Hypothesis." *Labour Economics*, 1, 129–150.

Akerlof, George A. 1979. "The Case against Conservative Macroeconomics: An Inaugural Lecture." *Economica*, 46, 219–237.

—— 1980. "A Theory of Social Custom, of Which Unemployment May Be One Consequence." *Quarterly Journal of Economics*, 94, 749–775.

—— 1982. "Labor Contracts as Partial Gift Exchange." *Quarterly Journal of Economics*, 97, 543–569.

Akerlof, George A., William T. Dickens, and George Perry. 1996. "The Macroeconomics of Low Inflation." *Brookings Papers on Economic Activity*, 1–76.

Akerlof, George A., and Lawrence F. Katz. 1989. "Workers' Trust Funds and the Logic of Wage Profiles." *Quarterly Journal of Economics*, 104, 525–536.

Akerlof, George A., and Rachel E. Kranton. 1998. "Economics and Identity." Russel Sage Foundation Working Paper no. 136. August.

Akerlof, George A., and Brian G. M. Main. 1981. "An Experience-Weighted Measure of Employment and Unemployment Durations." *American Economic Review*, 71, 1003–1011.

Akerlof, George A., and Hajime Miyazaki. 1980. "The Implicit Contract Theory of Unemployment Meets the Wage Bill Argument." *Review of Economic Studies*, 47, 321–338.

Akerlof, George A., Andrew K. Rose, and Janet L. Yellen. 1988. "Job Switching and Job Satisfaction in the U.S. Labor Market." *Brookings Papers on Economic Activity*, 495–582.

—— 1990. "Waiting for Work." National Bureau of Economic Research Working Paper no. 3385. Cambridge, Mass.

Akerlof, George A., and Janet Yellen. 1985a. "Can Small Deviations from Rationality Make Significant Differences to Economic Equilibria?" *American Economic Review*, 75, 708–720.

—— 1985b. "A Near-Rational Model of the Business Cycle, with Wage and Price Inertia." *Quarterly Journal of Economics*, 100 (suppl.), 823–838.

—— 1988. "Fairness and Unemployment." *American Economic Association, Papers and Proceedings*, 78, 44–49.

—— 1990. "The Fair Wage-Effort Hypothesis and Unemployment." *Quarterly Journal of Economics*, 105, 255–283.

Allen, Steven G. 1992. "Changes in the Cyclical Sensitivity of Wages in the United States, 1891–1987." *American Economic Review*, 82, 122–140.

Alogoskoufis, George S. 1987. "On Intertemporal Substitution and Aggregate Labor Supply." *Journal of Political Economy*, 95, 938–960.

Altonji, Joseph. 1982. "The Intertemporal Substitution Model of Labour Market Fluctuations: An Empirical Analysis." *Review of Economic Studies*, 49, 783–824.

Altonji, Joseph, and Orley Ashenfelter. 1980. "Wage Movements and the Labour Market Equilibrium Hypothesis." *Economica*, 47, 217–245.

Altonji, Joseph G., and John C. Ham. 1990. "Variations in Employment Growth in Canada: The Role of External, National, Regional, and Industrial Factors." *Journal of Labor Economics*, 8, S198–S236.

Amihud, Yakov, and Baruch Lev. 1981. "Risk Reduction as a Managerial Motive for Conglomerate Mergers." *Bell Journal of Economics*, 12, 605–617.

Andreoni, James. 1988. "Privately Provided Public Goods in a Large Economy: The Limits of Altruism." *Journal of Public Economics,* 35, 57–73.

Andrews, I. R., and Mildred M. Henry. 1963. "Management Attitudes toward Pay." *Industrial Relations,* 3, 29–39.

Andrews, Martyn, and Stephen Nickell. 1982. "Unemployment in the United Kingdom since the War." *Review of Economic Studies,* 49, 731–759.

Angle, Harold L., and James L. Perry. 1981. "Empirical Assessment of Organizational Commitment and Organizational Effectiveness." *Administrative Science Quarterly,* 26, 1–13.

Annable, James. 1988. "Another Auctioneer Is Missing." *Journal of Macroeconomics,* 10, 1–26.

Antel, John J. 1991. "The Wage Effects of Voluntary Labor Mobility with and without Intervening Unemployment." *Industrial and Labor Relations Review,* 44, 299–306.

Arai, Mahmood. 1994a. "An Empirical Analysis of Wage Dispersion and Efficiency Wages." *Scandinavian Journal of Economics,* 96, 31–50.

——— 1994b. "Compensation Wage Differentials versus Efficiency Wages: An Empirical Study of Job Autonomy and Wages." *Industrial Relations,* 33, 249–61.

Armknecht, Paul A., and John F. Early. 1972. "Quits in Manufacturing: A Study of Their Causes." *Monthly Labor Review,* 95, 31–37.

Aronson, Robert L. 1950. *Layoff Policies and Practices.* Princeton, N.J.: Industrial Relations Section, Department of Economics, Princeton University.

Arvan, Lanny. 1989. "Optimal Labor Contracts with On-the-Job Search: Are Involuntary Layoffs Used as an Incentive Device to Make Workers Search Harder?" *Journal of Labor Economics,* 7, 147–169.

Ashenfelter, Orley. 1980. "Unemployment as Disequilibrium in a Model of Aggregate Labor Supply." *Econometrica,* 48, 547–564.

Ashenfelter, Orley, and David Card. 1982. "Time Series Representations of Economic Variables and Alternative Models of the Labor Market." *Review of Economic Studies,* 49, 731–760.

Ashenfelter, Orley, and John Ham. 1979. "Education, Unemployment, and Earnings." *Journal of Political Economy,* 87, S99–S116.

Ashenfelter, Orley, and George E. Johnson. 1969. "Bargaining Theory, Trade Unions, and Industrial Strike Activity." *American Economic Review,* 59, 35–49.

Ashenfelter, Orley, and Richard Layard. 1986. Handbook of Labor Economics. Amsterdam: North Holland.

Azariadis, Costas. 1975. "Implicit Contracts and Underemployment Equilibria." *Journal of Political Economy,* 83, 1183–1202.

Babbie, Earl. 1990. *Survey Research Methods,* 2nd ed. Belmont, Calif.: Wadsworth.

Bagwell, Laurie Simon. 1991. "Shareholder Heterogeneity: Evidence and Implications." *American Economic Review,* 81, 218–221.

——— 1992. "Dutch Auction Repurchases: An Analysis of Shareholder Heterogeneity." *Journal of Finance,* 47 (March), 71–105.

Baily, Martin Neil. 1974. "Wages and Employment under Uncertain Demand." *Review of Economic Studies,* 41, 37–50.

Baker, George, Michael Gibbs, and Bengt Holmstrom. 1993. "Hierarchies and Compensation: A Case Study." *European Economic Review: Papers and Proceedings,* 37, 366–378.

—— 1994a. "The Internal Economics of the Firm: Evidence from Personnel Data." *Quarterly Journal of Economics,* 109, 881–919.

—— 1994b. "The Wage Policy of the Firm." *Quarterly Journal of Economics,* 109, 921–55.

Baker, George, and Bengt Holmstrom. 1995. "Internal Labor Markets: Too Many Theories and Too Few Facts." *American Economic Review, Papers and Proceedings,* 85 (May), 255–259.

Bakke, E. Wight. 1933. *The Unemployed Man.* London: Nisbet and Co.

—— 1940a. *The Unemployed Worker.* New Haven: Yale University Press.

—— 1940b. *Citizens without Work.* New Haven: Yale University Press.

Bakke, E. Wight, Ewan Clague, and Walter Cooper. 1934. *After the Shutdown.* New Haven: Institute of Human Relations, Yale University.

Barbach, R. H. 1964. *The Pricing of Manufactures.* London: Macmillan.

Barclay, Michael J., Clifford W. Smith, and Ross L. Watts. 1995. "The Determinants of Corporate Leverage and Dividend Policies." *Journal of Applied Corporate Finance,* 7 (Winter), 4–19.

Barnes, William F. 1975. "Job Search Models, the Duration of Unemployment, and the Asking Wage: Some Empirical Evidence." *Journal of Human Resources,* 10, 230–240.

Baron, James N. 1988. "The Employment Relation as a Social Relation." *Journal of Japanese and International Economies,* 2, 492–525.

Barro, Robert J. 1977. "Long-Term Contracting, Sticky Prices, and Monetary Policy." *Journal of Monetary Economics,* 3, 305–316.

Barro, Robert J., and Herschel I. Grossman. 1971. "A General Disequilibrium Model of Income and Employment." *American Economic Review,* 61, 82–93.

Barron, John M., and Wesley Mellow. 1981. "Changes in Labor Force Status among the Unemployed." *Journal of Human Resources,* 16, 427–441.

Barsky, Carl B., and Martin E. Personick. 1981. "Measuring Wage Dispersion: Pay Ranges Reflect Industry Traits." *Monthly Labor Review,* 104, 35–41.

Bartel, Ann P., and George J. Borjas. 1981. "Wage Growth and Job Turnover: An Empirical Analysis." In Sherwin Rosen, ed., *Studies in Labor Markets,* 65–84 Chicago: University of Chicago Press.

Bartov, Omer. 1991. *Hitler's Army: Soldiers, Nazis, and War in the Third Reich.* New York: Oxford University Press.

Bass, Bernard M. 1990. *Bass and Stogdill's Handbook of Leadership.* New York: Free Press.

Batt, Rosemary and Eileen Appelbaum. 1995. "Worker Participation in Diverse Settings: Does the Form Affect the Outcome, and If So, Who Benefits?" *British Journal of Industrial Relations,* 33, 353–374.

Baynes, John. 1967. *Morale.* New York: Praeger.

Bean, C. R., and P. J. Turnbull. 1988. "Employment in the British Coal Industry: A Test of the Labour Demand Model." *Economic Journal,* 98, 1092–1104.

Beaudry, Paul, and John DiNardo. 1991. "The Effect of Implicit Contracts on the Movement of Wages over the Business Cycle: Evidence from Micro Data." *Journal of Political Economy,* 99, 665–668.

Becker, Brian E. 1987. "Concession Bargaining: The Impact on Shareholders' Equity." *Industrial and Labor Relations Review,* 40, 268–279.

Becker, Gary S., and George J. Stigler. 1974. "Law Enforcement, Malfeasance, and Compensation of Enforcers." *Journal of Legal Studies*, 3, 1–18.

Behrend, Hilde. 1984. *Problems of Labour and Inflation*. London: Croom Helm.

Bell, Linda A. 1995. "Union Wage Concessions in the 1980s: The Importance of Firm-Specific Factors." *Industrial and Labor Relations Review*, 48, 258–275.

Benassy, Jean-Pascal. 1975. "Neo-Keynesian Disequilibrium Theory in a Monetary Economy." *Review of Economic Studies*, 42, 503–523.

—— 1976. "The Disequilibrium Approach to Monopolistic Price Setting and General Monopolistic Equilibrium." *Review of Economic Studies*, 43, 69–82.

Benhabib, Jess, Richard Rogerson, and Randall Wright. 1991. "Homework in Macroeconomics: Household Production and Aggregate Fluctuations." *Journal of Political Economy*, 99, 1166–87.

Bennett, Rebecca J. 1998. "Taking the Sting out of the Whip: Reactions to Fair Punishment for Unethical Behavior." *Journal of Experimental Psychology: Applied*, 4, 248–262.

Berg, Gerard J. van den. 1990. "Search Behaviour, Transitions to Non-Participation, and the Duration of Unemployment." *Economic Journal*, 100, 842–865.

Bernanke, Ben S., and Keven Carey. 1996. "Nominal Wage Stickiness and Aggregate Supply in the Great Depression." *Quarterly Journal of Economics*, 111, 853–883.

Bernanke, Ben S., and James L. Powell. 1986. "The Cyclical Behavior of Industrial Labor Markets: A Comparison of the Prewar and Postwar Eras." Chapter 10 in Robert J. Gordon, ed., *The American Business Cycle*. Chicago: University of Chicago Press.

Bernard, H. Russell. 1994. *Research Methods in Anthropology*. Thousand Oaks, Calif.: Sage.

Bhaskar, V. 1990. "Wage Relativities and the Natural Range of Unemployment." *Economic Journal*, 100 (conference), 60–66.

Bies, Robert J. 1987. "The Predicament of Injustice: The Management of Moral Outrage." In L. L. Cummings and Barry M. Staw, eds., *Research in Organizational Behavior*, 9, 289–319.

Bils, Mark. 1985. "Real Wages over the Business Cycle: Evidence from Panel Data." *Journal of Political Economy*, 93, 666–689.

Bils, Mark, and Kenneth J. McLaughlin. 1992. "Inter-Industry Mobility and the Cyclical Upgrading of Labor." National Bureau of Working Paper no. 4130. Cambridge, Mass.

Bishop, John. 1987. "The Recognition and Reward of Employee Performance." *Journal of Labor Economics*, 5, 536–556.

Black, M. 1980. "Pecuniary Implication of On-the-Job Search and Quit Activity." *Review of Economics and Statistics*, 62, 222–229.

Blanchard, Olivier. 1986. "The Wage Price Spiral." *Quarterly Journal of Economics*, 101, 543–565.

—— 1987. "Aggregate and Individual Price Adjustment." *Brookings Papers on Economic Activity*, 57–109.

Blanchard, Olivier, and Peter Diamond. 1989. "The Beveridge Curve." *Brookings Papers on Economic Activity*, 1–60.

—— 1990. "The Cyclical Behavior of the Gross Flows of U.S. Workers." *Brookings Papers on Economic Activity*, 85–155.

—— 1994. "Ranking, Unemployment Duration, and Wages." *Review of Economic Studies*, 61, 417–434.

Blanchard, Olivier, and Michael Katz. 1992. "Regional Evolutions." *Brookings Papers on Economic Activity*, 1–61.

Blanchard, Olivier, and Nobuhiro Kiyotaki. 1987. "Monopolistic Competition and the Effects of Aggregate Demand." *American Economic Review*, 77, 647–666.

Blanchard, Olivier, and Lawrence H. Summers. 1986. "Hysteresis and the European Unemployment Problem." *NBER Macroeconomics Annual, 1986*, 16–78.

——— 1988. "Beyond the Natural Rate Hypothesis." *American Economic Review*, 78, 182–187.

Blanchflower, David G. 1995. "Youth Labor Markets in Twenty-Three Countries: A Comparison Using Micro Data." Discussion Paper, Department of Economics, Dartmouth College.

Blanchflower, David G., and Andrew J. Oswald. 1988. "Internal and External Influences upon Pay Settlements." *British Journal of Industrial Relations*, 26, 363–370.

——— 1994. *The Wage Curve*. Cambridge: MIT Press.

Blanchflower, David G., Andrew J. Oswald, and Mario D. Garrett. 1990. "Insider Power in Wage Determination." *Economica*, 57, 143–170.

Blanchflower, David G., Andrew J. Oswald, and Peter Sanfey. 1996. "Wages, Profits, and Rent Sharing." *Quarterly Journal of Economics*, 111, 227–251.

Blanchflower, David G., Andrew J. Oswald, and Peter B. Warr. 1993. "Well-Being over Time in Britain and the USA." Discussion Paper presented at the CEP Conference on the Economics and Psychology of Happiness and Fairness, November 1993.

Blau, David M., and Philip K. Robins. 1990. "Job Search Outcomes for the Employed and Unemployed." *Journal of Political Economy*, 98, 637–655.

Blau, Francine D., and Lawrence M. Kahn. 1981. "Causes and Consequences of Lay-offs." *Economic Inquiry*, 19, 270–296.

Blinder, Alan S. 1990. "Learning by Asking Those Who Are Doing." *Eastern Economic Journal*, 16, 297–306.

——— 1991. "Why Are Prices Sticky? Preliminary Results from an Interview Study." *American Economic Review, Papers and Proceedings*, 81, 89–96.

Blinder, Alan S., Elie R. D. Canetti, David E. Lebow, and Jeremy B. Rudd. 1998. *Asking about Prices: A New Approach to Understanding Price Stickiness*. New York: Russell Sage Foundation.

Blinder, Alan S., and Don H. Choi. 1990. "A Shred of Evidence on Theories of Wage Stickiness." *Quarterly Journal of Economics*, 105, 1003–1015.

Bloch, Joseph W., and Robert Platt. 1957. "Layoff, Recall, and Work-Sharing Procedures, III–Seniority and Bumping Practices." *Monthly Labor Review*, 80, 177–185.

Blum, Milton L. 1956. *Industrial Psychology and Its Social Foundations*. New York: Harper and Row.

Bodnar, Gordon M., Gregory S. Hayt, Richard C. Marston, and Charles W. Smithson. 1995. "Wharton Survey of Derivates Usage by U.S. Non-Financial Firms." *Financial Management*, 24 (Summer), 104–114.

Boland, Lawrence A. 1979. "A Critique of Friedman's Critics." *Journal of Economic Literature*, 17, 503–522.

Booth, Alison, and Monojit Chatterji. 1989. "Redundancy Payments and Firm-Specific Training." *Economica*, 56, 505–521.

Bowlus, Audra J. 1993. "Job Match Quality over the Business Cycle." In Henning Bunzel, Peter Jensen, and Niels Westergoerd-Nielsen, eds., *Panel Data and Labour Market Dynamics*, 21–41. Amsterdam: North-Holland.

Brainard, W. Lael, and David M. Cutler. 1993. "Sectoral Shifts and Cyclical Unemployment Reconsidered." *Quarterly Journal of Economics,* 108, 219–243.

Brandolini, Andrea. 1995. "In Search of a Stylized Fact: Do Real Wages Exhibit a Consistent Pattern of Cyclical Variability?" *Journal of Economic Surveys,* 9, 103–163.

Brayfield, A. H., and W. H. Crockett. 1955. "Employee Attitudes and Employee Performance." *Psychological Bulletin,* 52, 396–424.

Brockner, Joel. 1988. "The Effects of Work Layoffs on Survivors: Research Theory, and Practice." In Barry M. Staw and L. L. Cummings, eds., *Research in Organizational Behavior,* 10, 213–255.

—— 1990. "Scope of Justice in the Workplace: How Survivors React to Co-Worker Layoffs." *Journal of Social Issues,* 46, 95–106.

Brockner, Joel, Rocki Lee DeWitt, Steven Grover, and Thomas Reed. 1990. "When It Is Especially Important to Explain Why: Factors Affecting the Relationship between Managers' Explanations of a Layoff and Survivors' Reactions to the Layoff." *Journal of Experimental Social Psychology,* 26, 389–407.

Brockner, Joel, Steven L. Grover, Thomas Reed, and Rocki DeWitt. 1992. "Layoffs, Job Insecurity, and Survivors' Work Effort: Evidence of an Inverted-U Relationship." *Academy of Management Review,* 35, 413–425.

Brockner, Joel, Steven L. Grover, Thomas Reed, Rocki DeWitt, and Michael O'Malley. 1987. "Survivors' Reactions to Layoffs: We Get by with a Little Help for Our Friends." *Administrative Science Quarterly,* 32, 526–541.

Brockner, Joel, Mary Konovsky, Rochelle Cooper-Schneider, Robert Folger, Christopher Martin, and Robert J. Bies. 1994. "Interactive Effects of Procedural Justice and Outcome Negativity on Victims and Survivors of Job Loss." *Academy of Management Journal,* 37, 397–409.

Brockner, Joel, and Batia M. Wiesenfeld. 1993. "Living on the Edge (of Social and Organizational Psychology): The Effects of Job Layoffs on Those Who Remain." Chapter 6 in J. Keith Murnighan, ed., *Social Psychology in Organizations: Advances in Theory and Research.* Englewood Cliffs, N.J.: Prentice Hall.

—— 1996. "An Integrative Framework for Explaining Reactions to Decisions: Interactive Effects of Outcomes and Procedures." *Psychological Bulletin,* 120, 189–208.

Brockner, Joel, Batia M. Wiesenfeld, Thomas Reed, Steven Grover, and Christopher Martin. 1993. "Interactive Effect of Job Content and Context on the Reactions of Layoff Survivors." *Journal of Personality and Social Psychology,* 64, 187–197.

Brody, David. 1980. *Workers in Industrial America.* New York: Oxford University Press.

Brown, Charles. 1990. "Firms' Choice of Method of Pay." *Industrial and Labor Relations Review,* 43 (special issue), 165S–182S.

Brown, James N., and Orley Ashenfelter. 1986. "Testing the Efficiency of Employment Contracts." *Journal of Political Economy,* 94, S40–S87.

Brown, Karen A., and Vandra L. Huber. 1992. "Lowering Floors and Raising Ceilings: A Longitudinal Assessment of the Effects of An Earnings-at-Risk Plan on Pay Satisfaction." *Personnel Psychology,* 45, 279–311.

Brown, William, and Keith Sisson. 1975. "The Use of Comparisons in Workplace Wage Determination." *British Journal of Industrial Relations,* 13, 23–53.

Browning, Martin, Angus Deaton, and Margaret Irish. 1985. "A Profitable Approach to Labor Supply and Commodity Demands over the Life-Cycle." *Econometrica*, 53, 503–543.

Bryson, Alex, and John Jacobs. 1992. *Policing the Workshy: Benefit Controls, the Labour Market and the Unemployed.* Aldershot: Ashgate Publishing.

Budd, Alan, Paul Levine, and Peter Smith. 1988. "Unemployment, Vacancies, and the Long-Term Unemployed." *Economic Journal*, 98, 1071–91.

Bull, Clive. 1987. "The Existence of Self-Enforcing Implicit Contracts." *Quarterly Journal of Economics*, 102, 147–159.

Bulow, Jeremy I., and Lawrence H. Summers. 1986. "A Theory of Dual Labor Markets with Applications to Industrial Policy, Discrimination, and Keynesian Unemployment." *Journal of Labor Economics*, 4, 376–414.

Bunting, Robert L. 1961–62. "A Test of the Theory of Geographic Mobility." *Industrial and Labor Relations REview*, 15, 75–82.

Burawoy, Michael. 1979. *Manufacturing Consent.* Chicago: University of Chicago Press.

Burdett, Kenneth, and Dale T. Mortensen. 1989. "Equilibrium Wage Differentials and Employer Size." Department of Economics, Northwestern University, Discussion Paper no. 860.

Bureau of the Census. 1990. *County Business Patterns 1988,* document CBP-88-01. Washington, D.C.: U.S. Department of Commerce.

Bureau of Labor Statistics. 1972. "Layoff Provisions." Chapter 3 of *Bulletin no. 1425-13.* Washington, D.C.: U.S. Department of Labor.

——— 1975. *Jobseeking Methods Used by American Workers,* Bulletin no. 1886. Washington, D.C.: U.S. Department of Labor.

Bureau of National Affairs. 1980. *Layoff and Unemployment Compensation Policies, Personnel and Policies Forum Survey no. 128.* Washington, D.C.: Bureau of National Affairs.

Burgess, Paul L., and Jerry L. Kingston. 1976. "The Impact of Unemployment Insurance Benefits on Reemployment Success." *Industrial and Labor Relations Review*, 30, 25–31.

——— 1981. "Changes in Spending Patterns Following Unemployment." Washington, D.C.: U.S. Department of Labor Occasional Paper 81-3.

Burgess, Simon M., and Stephen Nickell. 1990. "Labour Turnover in UK Manufacturing." *Economica*, 57, 295–317.

Burtless, Gary. 1983. "Why Is Insured Unemployment so Low?" *Brookings Papers on Economic Activity,* 225–249.

Burton, John F., and John E. Parker. 1969. "Interindustry Variations in Voluntary Labor Mobility." *Industrial and Labor Relations Review*, 22, 199–216.

Caballero, Ricardo J., and Mohamad L. Hammour. 1996a. "The 'Fundamental Transformation' in Macroeconomics." *American Economic Review, Papers and Proceedings*, 86, 181–186.

——— 1996b. "On the Timing and Efficiency of Creative Destruction." *Quarterly Journal of Economics*, 111, 805–852.

——— 1996c. "The Cleansing Effect of Recessions." *American Economic Review*, 86, 1350–68.

Caldwell, Bruce. 1982. *Beyond Positivism: Economic Methodology in the Twentieth Century.* London: George Allen and Unwin.

—— 1991. "Clarifying Popper." *Journal of Economic Literature*, 29, 1–33.

Callahan, Charlene, and Catherine S. Elliott. 1996. "Listening: A Narrative Approach to Everyday Understandings and Behavior." *Journal of Economic Psychology*, 17, 79–114.

Calomiris, Charles W., and R. Glenn Hubbard. 1995. "Internal Finance and Investment: Evidence from the Undistributed Profits Tax of 1936–7." *Journal of Business*, 68, 443–482.

Camerer, Colin, Linda Babcock, George Loewenstein, and Richard Thaler. 1997. "Labor Supply of New York City Cabdrivers: One Day at a Time." *Quarterly Economic Review*, 112, 407–441.

Camerer, Colin, and Richard H. Thaler. 1995. "Anomalies: Ultimatums, Dictators, and Manners." *Journal of Economic Perspectives*, 9, 209–219.

Cameron, Lisa. 1995. "Raising the Stakes in the Ultimatum Game: Experimental Evidence from Indonesia." Working Paper no. 345, Industrial Relations Section, Princeton University, Princeton, N.J.

Campbell, Carl M. 1993. "Do Firms Pay Efficiency Wages? Evidence with Data at the Firm Level." *Journal of Labor Economics*, 11, 442–470.

—— 1994. "The Determinants of Dismissals: Tests of the Shirking Model with Individual Data." *Economics Letters*, 46, 89–95.

—— 1995a. "A Cross-Industry Time Series Analysis of Quits." *Quarterly Review of Economics and Finance*, 35, 53–72.

—— 1995b. "The Relative Impacts of the Level and Change in Wages on Quits." *International Journal of Manpower*, 16, 31–41.

—— 1997. "An Efficiency Wage Model of the Wage Curve, the Phillips Curve, and the Natural Rate of Unemployment." Working Paper, Dartmouth College.

Campbell, Carl, and Kunal Kamlani. 1997. "The Reasons for Wage Rigidity: Evidence from a Survey of Firms." *Quarterly Journal of Economics*, 112, 759–789.

Campbell, Tim S., and William Kracaw. 1987. "Optimal Managerial Incentive Contracts and the Value of Corporate Insurance." *Journal of Financial and Quantitative Analysis*, 22, 315–328.

Cantor, Richard. 1990. "Effects of Leverage on Corporate Investment and Hiring Decisions." *Federal Reserve Bank of New York Quarterly Review*, 15 (Summer), 31–41.

Caplin, Andrew S., and Daniel F. Spulber. 1987. "Menu Costs and the Neutrality of Money." *Quarterly Journal of Economics*, 102, 703–725.

Cappelli, Peter. 1982. "Concession Bargaining and the National Economy." In *Proceedings of the Thirty-Fifth Annual Meeting*, 362–371. Madison, Wis.: Industrial Relations Research Association.

—— 1983. "Union Gains under Concession Bargaining." In *Proceedings of the Thirty-Sixth Annual Meeting*, 297–305. Madison, Wis.: Industrial Relations Research Association.

—— 1985. "Plant-Level Concession Bargaining." *Industrial and Labor Relations Review*, 39, 90–104.

Cappelli, Peter, and Keith Chauvin. 1991. "An Interplant Test of the Efficiency Wage Hypothesis." *Quarterly Journal of Economics*, 106, 769–787.

Cappelli, Peter, and Peter Sherer. 1990. "Assessing Worker Attitudes under a Two-Tier Wage Plan." *Industrial and Labor Relations Review*, 43, 225–244.

Cappelli, Peter, and W. P. Sterling. 1988. "Union Bargaining Decisions and Contract Ratifications: The 1982 and 1984 Auto Agreements." *Industrial and Labor Relations Review,* 41, 195–214.

Card, David. 1986. "Efficient Contracts with Costly Adjustment: Short-Run Employment Determination for Airline Mechanics." *American Economic Review,* 76, 1045–71.

——— 1990a. "Strikes and Wages: A Test of an Asymmetric Information Model." *Quarterly Journal of Economics,* 105, 625–659.

——— 1990b. "Intertemporal Labor Supply: An Assessment." Working paper no. 269, Industrial Relations Section, Princeton University, Princeton, N.J.

——— 1990c. "Strikes and Bargaining: A Survey of the Recent Empirical Literature." *American Economic Review,* 80, 410–415.

Card, David, and Dean Hyslop. 1996. "Does Inflation 'Grease the Wheels of the Labor Market'?" National Bureau of Economic Research Discussion Paper no. 5538. Cambridge, Mass.

Card, David, Lawrence F. Katz, and Alan B. Krueger. 1993. "Comment on David Neumark and William Wascher, 'Employment Effects of Minimum and Subminimum Wages: Panel Data on State Minimum Wage Laws.' " Working Paper no. 316, Industrial Relations Section, Princeton University, Princeton, N.J.

Card, David, and Alan B. Krueger. 1994. "Minimum Wages and Employment: A Case Study of the Fast Food Industry in New Jersey and Pennsylvania." *American Economic Review,* 84, 772–793.

——— 1995. *Myth and Measurement: The New Economics of the Minimum Wage.* Princeton, N.J.: Princeton University Press.

Carlson, John A., and Michael W. Horrigan. 1983. "Measures of Unemployment Duration as Guides to Research and Policy: Comment." *American Economic Review,* 73, 1143–52.

Carlson, Norma W. 1982. "Time Rates Tighten Their Grip on Manufacturing Industries." *Monthly Labor Review,* 105 (May), 15–22.

Carmichael, Lorne. 1985. "Can Unemployment Be Involuntary?: Comment." *American Economic Review,* 75, 1213–17.

——— 1990. "Efficiency Wage Models of Unemployment—One View." *Economic Inquiry,* 28, 269–295.

——— 1998. "Fighting for Turf in an Internal Labour Market." Chapter 4 in Isao Ohasi and Toshiaki Tachibanaki, eds., *Internal Labour Markets, Incentives, and Employment.* London: Macmillan Press.

Carpenter, Robert E., Steven M. Fazzari, and Bruce C. Petersen. 1994. "Inventory Investment, Internal-Finance Fluctuations, and the Business Cycle." *Brookings Papers on Economic Activity,* 75–122.

Carruth, Alan A., and Andrew J. Oswald. 1987. "On Union Preference and Labour Market Models : Insiders and Outsiders." *Economic Journal,* 97, 431–445.

——— 1989. *Pay Determination and Industrial Prosperity.* Oxford: Clarendon Press.

Carter, Susan, and Richard Sutch. 1990. "The Labour Market in the 1890s: Evidence from Connecticut Manufacturing." In Erik Aerts and Barry Eichengreen, eds., *Unemployment and Underemployment in Historical Perspective.* Leuven: Leuven University Press.

Chapman, Paul G., and Malcolm R. Fisher. 1984. "Union Wage Policies: Comment." *American Economic Review,* 74, 755–758.

Chapple, Simon. 1996. "Money Wage Rigidity in New Zealand." *Labour Market Bulletin: A Journal of New Zealand Labour Market Research,* 2(1), 23–50.

Chelius, James, and Robert S. Smith. 1990. "Profit Sharing and Employment Stability." *Industrial and Labor Relations Review,* 43, 256S–273S.

Chiang, Sin-Hwan. 1991. "Redundancy Payments and Firm-Specific Training: A Comment." *Economica,* 58, 257–259.

Chowdhury, Gopa, and Stephen Nickell. 1985. "Hourly Earnings in the United States: Another Look at Unionization, Schooling, Sickness, and Unemployment Using PSID Data." *Journal of Labor Economics,* 3, 38–69.

Clark, Andrew E. 1996. "Are Wages Habit-Forming? Evidence from Micro Data." Discussion Paper, DEELSA, OECD, Paris.

Clark, Andrew E., and Andrew J. Oswald. 1994. "Unhappiness and Unemployment." *Economic Journal,* 104, 648–659.

———— 1996. "Satisfaction and Comparison Income." *Journal of Public Economics,* 61, 359–381.

Clark, C. Scott. 1973. "Labor Hoarding in Durable Goods Industries." *American Economic Review,* 63, 811–824.

Clark, Kim B., and Lawrence H. Summers. 1979. "Labor Market Dynamics and Unemployment: A Reconsideration." *Brookings Papers on Economic Activity,* 13–72.

———— 1982. "Unemployment Insurance and Labor Market Transitions." In Martin N. Baily, ed., *Workers, Jobs, and Inflation,* 279–318. Washington, D.C.: Brookings Institution.

Clark, Marjory. 1978. "The Unemployed on Supplementary Benefit: Living Standards and Making Ends Meet on a Low Income." *Journal of Social Policy,* 7, 385–410.

Classen, Kathleen P. 1977. "The Effect of Unemployment Insurance on the Duration of Unemployment and Subsequent Earnings." *Industrial and Labor Relations Review,* 30, 438–444.

———— 1979. "Unemployment Insurance and Job Search." Chapter 10 in S. A. Lippman and J. J. McCall, eds., *Studies in the Economics of Search.* Amsterdam: North Holland.

Cochrane, John H. 1991. "A Simple Test of Consumption Insurance." *Journal of Political Economy,* 99, 957–976.

Coleman, James S. 1990. *Foundations of Social Theory.* Cambridge: Harvard University Press.

Connell, Michael L. 1991. *Starting Salary Offers: An Historical Perspective.* Bethlehem, Pa.: College Placement Council.

Conte, Michael A., and Jan Svejnar. 1990. "The Performance Effects of Employee Ownership Plans." In Alan S. Blinder, ed., *Paying for Productivity,* 95–140. Washington, D.C.: Brookings Institution.

Cooke, William N. 1979. "Turnover and Earnings: Some Empirical Evidence." *Industrial Relations,* 18 (Winter), 220–226.

Cooper, Russell W. 1983. "A Note on Overemployment/Underemployment in Labor Contracts under Asymmetric Information." *Economics Letters,* 12, 81–87.

—— 1987. *Wage and Employment Patterns in Labor Contracts: Microfoundations and Macroeconomic Implications*. London: Harwood Academic Publishers.

Corcoran, Mary, Linda Datcher, and Greg Duncan. 1980a. "Most Workers Find Jobs through Word of Mouth." *Monthly Labor Review*, 103 (August), 33–35.

—— 1980b. "Information and Influence Networks in Labor Markets." Chapter 1 in Greg J. Duncan and James N. Morgan, eds., *Five Thousand American Families— Patterns of Economic Progress*, vol. VIII. Ann Arbor: Institute for Social Research, University of Michigan.

Cousineau, Jean-Michel, and Robert Lacroix. 1986. "Imperfect Information and Strikes: An Analysis of Canadian Experience, 1967–82." *Industrial and Labor Relations Review*, 39, 377–387.

Cowherd, Douglas M., and David I. Levine. 1992. "Product Quality and Pay Equity between Lower-level Employees and Top Management: An Investigation of Distributive Justice Theory." *Administrative Science Quarterly*, 37, 302–320.

Cragg, John G., and Burton G. Malkiel. 1982. *Expectations and the Structure of Share Prices*. Chicago: University of Chicago Press.

Craig, Ben, and John Pencavel. 1992. "The Behavior of Worker Cooperatives: The Plywood Companies of the Pacific Northwest." *American Economic Review*, 82, 1083–1105.

—— 1995. "Participation and Productivity: A Comparison of Worker Cooperatives and Conventional Firms in the Plywood Industry." *Brookings Papers on Economic Activity, Microeconomics*, 131–160.

Cramton, Peter C. 1992. "Strategic Delay in Bargaining with Two-Sided Uncertainty," *Review of Economic Studies*, 59, 205–225.

Cramton, Peter C., and Joseph S. Tracy. 1992. "Strikes and Holdouts in Wage Bargaining: Theory and Data." *American Economic Review*, 82, 100–121.

—— 1994. "Wage Bargaining with Time-Varying Threats." *Journal of Labor Economics*, 12, 594–617.

Creedy, John, and Ian M. McDonald. 1991. "Models of Trade Union Behaviour: A Synthesis." *Economic Record*, 67, 346–359.

Crosslin, Robert L., and David W. Stevens. 1977. "The Asking Wage-Duration of Unemployment Relation Revisited." *Southern Economic Journal*, 43, 1298–1302.

Cunningham, William C., John J. Strauchs, and Clifford W. Van Meter. 1990. *Private Security Trends 1970 to 2000, the Hallcrest Report II*. Boston: Butterworth-Heinemann.

Cutcher-Gershenfeld, Joel E. 1991. "The Impact on Economic Performance of a Transformation in Workplace Relations." *Industrial and Labor Relations Review*, 44, 241–260.

Cyert, Richard M., and James G. March. 1956. "Organizational Factors in the Theory of Oligopoly." *Quarterly Journal of Economics*, 70, 44–64.

—— 1963. *A Behavioral Theory of the Firm*. Englewood Cliffs, N.J.: Prentice-Hall.

Daniel, W. W. 1974. *A National Survey of the Unemployed*. London: Political and Economic Planning.

—— 1976. *Wage Determination in Industry*. London: Political and Economic Planning.

—— 1990. *The Unemployed Flow*. London: Policy Studies Institute.

Daniel, W. W., and Neil Millward. 1983. *Workplace Industrial Relations in Britain.* London: Heinemann Educational Books.

Daniel, W. W., and Elizabeth Stilgoe. 1977. *Where Are They Now? A Follow-Up Study of the Unemployed.* London: Political and Economic Planning.

Datcher, Linda. 1983. "The Impact of Informal Networks on Quit Behavior." *Review of Economics and Statistics,* 65, 491–495.

Davis, Steven J. 1987a. "Fluctuations in the Pace of Labor Reallocation." *Carnegie-Rochester Conference Series on Public Policy,* 27, 335–402.

———— 1987b. "Allocative Disturbances and Specific Capital in Real Business Cycle Theories." *American Economic Review, Papers and Proceedings,* 77, 326–332.

Davis, Steven J., and John Haltiwanger. 1990. "Job Creation and Destruction: Microeconomic Evidence and Macroeconomic Implications," *NBER Macroeconomics Annual,* 1990, 123–168.

Davis, Steven J., John Haltiwanger, and Scott Schuh. 1996. *Job Creation and Destruction.* Cambridge: MIT Press.

Deci, Edward L., and Richard M. Ryan. 1985. *Intrinsic Motivation and Self-Determination in Human Behavior.* New York: Plenum Press.

DeLong, J. Bradford, and Lawrence H. Summers. 1986. "The Changing Cyclical Variability of Economic Activity in the United States." Chapter 12 in Robert J. Gordon, ed., *The American Business Cycle.* Chicago: University of Chicago Press.

DeMarzo, Peter M., and Darrell Duffie. 1995. "Corporate Incentives for Hedging and Hedge Accounting." *Review of Financial Studies,* 8, 743–771.

De Schweinitz, Dorothea. 1932. *How Workers Find Jobs.* Philadelphia: University of Pennsylvania Press.

Deutsch, Morton. 1985. *Distributive Justice: A Social-Psychological Perspective.* New Haven: Yale University Press.

———— 1986. "Cooperation, Conflict, and Justice." Chapter 1 in Hans Werner Bierhoff, Ronald L. Cohen, and Jerald Greenberg, eds., *Justice in Social Relations.* New York: Plenum Press.

Devereux, Michael, and Fabio Schiantarelli. 1990. "Investment, Financial Factors, and Cash Flow: Evidence from U.K. Panel Data." Chapter 11 in R. Glenn Hubbard, ed., *Asymmetric Information, Corporate Finance, and Investment.* Chicago: University of Chicago Press.

Devine, Theresa J., and Nicholas M. Kiefer. 1991. *Empirical Labor Economics.* Oxford: Oxford University Press.

Diamond, Peter. 1981. "Mobility Costs, Frictional Unemployment, and Efficiency." *Journal of Political Economy,* 89, 798–812.

———— 1982a. "Wage Determination and Efficiency in Search Equilibrium." *Review of Economic Studies,* 49, 217–227.

———— 1982b. "Aggregate Demand Management in Search Equilibrium." *Journal of Political Economy,* 90, 881–894.

———— 1984a. "Money in Search Equilibrium." *Econometrica,* 52, 1–20.

———— 1984b. *A Search-Equilibrium Approach to the Micro Foundations of Macroeconomics.* Cambridge: MIT Press.

Dickens, Richard, Stephen Machin, and Alan Manning. 1994. "The Effects of Minimum Wages on Employment: Theory and Evidence from the United Kingdom." National Bureau of Economic Research Working Paper no. 4742. Cambridge, Mass.

Dickens, William T., and Lawrence F. Katz. 1987a. "Inter-Industry Wage Differences and Theories of Wage Determination." National Bureau of Economic Research Working Paper no. 2271. Cambridge, Mass.

―――― 1987b. "Inter-Industry Wage Differences and Industry Characteristics." Chapter 3 in Lang and Leonard, 1987.

Dickens, William T., Lawrence F. Katz, Kevin Lang, and Lawrence H. Summers. 1989. "Employee Crime and the Monitoring Puzzle." *Journal of Labor Economics,* 7, 331–347.

Dickens, William T., and Kevin Lang. 1993. "Labor Market Segmentation Theory: Reconsidering the Evidence." In William Danty, ed., *Labor Economics Problems in Analyzing Labor Markets,* 141–180. Norwell, Mass.: Dordrecht Kluwer Academic.

Dighe, Ranjit. 1997. "America's High-Wage Economy in the 1930s." Ph.D. dissertation, Department of Economics, Yale University.

Doeringer, Peter, and Michael Piore. 1971. *Internal Labor Markets and Manpower Analysis.* Lexington, Mass.: Heath Lexington Books.

Dolde, Walter. 1985. "Hedging, Leverage, and Primitive Risk." *Journal of Financial Engineering,* 4, 187–216.

―――― 1993a. "Use of Foreign Exchange and Interest Rate Risk Management in Large Firms." Working Paper 93-042, School of Business, University of Connecticut.

―――― 1993b. "The Trajectory of Corporate Financial Risk Management." *Journal of Applied Corporate Finance,* 6, 33–41.

Donaldson, Gordon. 1961. *Corporate Debt Capacity.* Boston: Harvard Graduate School of Business Administration.

Drago, Robert, and John S. Heywood. 1992. "Is Worker Behaviour Consistent with Efficiency Wages?" *Scottish Journal of Political Science,* 39, 141–53.

Drèze, Jacques H. 1975. "Existence of an Exchange Equilibrium under Price Rigidities." *International Economic Review,* 16, 301–320.

Drucker, Peter E. 1990. "The Emerging Theory of Manufacturing." *Harvard Business Review,* 68, 94–102.

Dunlop, John T. 1938. "The Movement of Real and Money Wages." *Economic Journal,* 48, 413–434.

――――. 1944. *Wage Determination under Trade Unions.* New York: Macmillan Company.

―――― 1957. "The Task of Contemporary Wage Determination." In George W. Taylor and Frank C. Pierson, eds., *New Concepts in Wage Determination.* New York: McGraw-Hill.

―――― 1988. "Labor Markets and Wage Determination: Then and Now." In Bruce E. Kaufman, ed., *How Labor Markets Work.* Lexington, Mass.: Lexington Books.

Dyer, Lee D. 1973. "Job Search Success of Middle-Aged Managers and Engineers." *Industrial and Labor Relations Review,* 26, 969–979.

Dynarski, Mark, and Steven M. Sheffrin. 1987a. "Consumption and Unemployment." *Quarterly Journal of Economics,* 102, 411–428.

―――― 1987b. "New Evidence on the Cyclical Behavior of Unemployment Durations." In Lang and Leonard, 1987.

Easterlin, Richard A. 1961. "Influences in European Overseas Emigration before World War I." *Economic Development and Cultural Change,* 9, 331–351.

Eaton, Curtis, and William D. White. 1983. "The Economy of High Wages: An Agency Problem." *Economica,* 50, 175–181.

Ehrenberg, Ronald G., and Ronald L. Oaxaca. 1976. "Unemployment Insurance, Duration of Unemployment, and Subsequent Wage Gain." *American Economic Review,* 66, 754–766.

Elias, Peter, and Michael White. 1991. "Recruitment in Local Labour Markets: Employer and Employee Perspectives." Institute for Employment Research, University of Warwick, Research Paper 86.

Essick, Charles E. 1987. "A Survey of Two-Tier Wage Systems." *Compensation and Benefits Management,* 3, 229–332.

Fair, Ray C. 1969. *The Short-Run Demand for Workers and Hours.* Amsterdam: North Holland.

––––––– 1985. "Excess Labor and the Business Cycle." *American Economic Review,* 75, 239–245.

––––––– 1993. "Inflationary Expectations and Price Setting Behavior." *Review of Economics and Statistics,* 75, 8–18.

––––––– 1997a. "Testing the NAIRU Model for the United States." Discussion Paper, Department of Economics, Yale University.

––––––– 1997b. "Testing the NAIRU Model for 27 Countries." Discussion Paper, Department of Economics, Yale University.

Fallick, Bruce Chelimsky. 1993. "The Industrial Mobility of Displaced Workers." *Journal of Labor Economics,* 11, 302–323.

Farber, Henry. 1986. "The Analysis of Union Behavior." Chapter 18 in Ashenfelter and Layard (1986).

––––––– 1997a. "The Changing Face of Job Loss in the United States: 1981–1995." *Brookings Papers on Economic Activity* (Microeconomics), 55–128.

––––––– 1997b. "Alternative Employment Arrangements as a Response to Job Loss." Working Paper no. 391, Industrial Relations Section, Princeton University, Princeton, N.J.

Fay, Jon A., and James L. Medoff. 1985. "Labor and Output over the Business Cycle: Some Direct Evidence." *American Economic Review,* 75, 638–655.

Fazzari, Steven M., R. Glenn Hubbard, and Bruce C. Petersen. 1988. "Financing Constraints and Corporate Investment." *Brookings Papers on Economic Activity,* 141–206.

––––––– 1996. "Financing Constraints and Corporate Investment: Response to Kaplan and Zingales." National Bureau of Economic Research Working Paper no. 5462. Cambridge, Mass.

Fehr, Ernst. 1990. "Cooperation, Harassment, and Involuntary Unemployment: Comment." *American Economic Review,* 80, 624–630.

––––––– 1991. "Erratum: Cooperation, Harassment, and Involuntary Unemployment: Comment." *American Economic Review,* 81, 384.

Fehr, Ernst, and Armin Falk. 1996. "Wage Rigidity in a Competitive Incomplete Contract Market." Discussion Paper, University of Zurich.

Fehr, Ernst, and Simon Gächter. 1998a. "Reciprocity and Economics: The Economic Implications of *Homo Reciprocans.*" *European Economic Review,* 42, 845–859.

––––––– 1998b. "How Effective Are Trust- and Reciprocity-Based Incentives?" Chapter

13 in A. Ben-Ner and L. Putterman, eds., *Economics, Values, and Organizations.* Cambridge: Cambridge University Press.

Fehr, Ernst, Simon Gächter, and Georg Kirchsteiger. 1996. "Reciprocal Fairness and Noncompensating Wage Differentials." *Journal of Institutional and Theoretical Economics,* 152, 608–640.

———— 1997. "Reciprocity as a Contract Enforcement Device—Experimental Evidence." *Econometrica,* 65, 833–860.

Fehr, Ernst, Erich Kirchler, Andreas Weichbold, and Simon Gächter. 1998. "When Social Norms Overpower Competition—Gift Exchange in Experimental Labor Markets." *Journal of Labor Economics,* 16, 324–51.

Fehr, Ernst, and Georg Kirchsteiger. 1994. "Insider Power, Wage Discrimination, and Fairness." *Economic Journal,* 104, 571–583.

Fehr, Ernst, Georg Kirchsteiger, and Arno Riedl. 1993. "Does Fairness Prevent Market Clearing? An Experimental Investigation." *Quarterly Journal of Economics,* 108, 437–459.

———— 1996. "Involuntary Unemployment and Non-Compensating Wage Differentials in an Experimental Labour Market." *Economic Journal,* 106, 106–121.

Fehr, Ernst, and Klaus M. Schmidt. 1997. "A Theory of Fairness, Competition, and Cooperation." Working paper, University of Zurich.

Fehr, Ernst, and Elena Tougareva. 1995. "Do Competitive Markets with High Stakes Remove Reciprocal Fairness? A Note." Discussion Paper, University of Zurich.

Feinberg, Robert M. 1977. "Risk Aversion, Risk, and the Duration of Unemployment." *Review of Economics and Statistics,* 59, 264–271.

Feldman, Daniel C. 1996. "The Nature, Antecedents, and Consequences of Underemployment." *Journal of Management,* 22, 385–407.

Feldstein, Martin. 1976. "Temporary Layoffs in the Theory of Unemployment." *Journal of Political Economy,* 84, 937–957.

Feldstein, Martin, and James Poterba. 1984. "Unemployment Insurance and Reservation Wages." *Journal of Public Economics,* 23, 141–167.

Fenn, George W., Mitch Post, and Steven A. Sharpe. 1996. "Debt Maturity and the Use of Interest Rate Derivatives by Nonfinancial Firms." Finance and Economics Discussion Series, Division of Research and Statistics, Division of Monetary Affairs, Federal Reserve Board, Washington, D.C., no. 96-36.

Fischer, Stanley. 1977. "Long-Term Contracts, Rational Expectations, and the Optimal Money Supply Rule." *Journal of Political Economy,* 85, 191–205.

Fisher, Timothy C. G. 1991. "An Empirical Study of the Adverse Selection Model of Strikes." *Canadian Journal of Economics,* 24, 499–516.

Fite, David, and Paul Pfleiderer. 1995. "Should Firms Use Derivatives to Manage Risk?" In William H. Beaver and George Parker, eds., *Risk Management: Problems and Solutions,* 139–169. New York: McGraw-Hill.

Fleischer, Belton M. 1963. "Some Economic Aspects of Puerto Rican Migration to the United States." *Review of Economics and Statistics,* 45, 245–253.

Flinn, Christopher J. 1993. "Equilibrium Dismissal without Stigma." Sect. III, chap. 3 in Jan C. van Ours, Gerard A. Pfann, and Geert Ridder, eds., *Labor Demand and Equilibrium Wage Formation.* Amsterdam: North Holland.

Folger, Robert. 1993. "Reactions to Mistreatment at Work." In J. Keith Murninghan, ed., *Social Psychology in Organizations.* Englewood Cliffs, N.J.: Prentice Hall.

Food Marketing Institute. 1994. *The Food Marketing Industry Speaks: Detailed Tabulations.*

Ford, Neil M., Orville C. Walker, Jr., and Gilbert A. Churchill, Jr. 1981. "Differences in the Attractiveness of Alternative Rewards among Industrial Salespeople: Additional Evidence." Report no. 81-107, Marketing Science Institute, Cambridge, Mass.

Fortin, Pierre. 1996. "The Great Canadian Slump." *Canadian Journal of Economics.* 29, 761–787.

Foster, Kenneth E. 1985. "An Anatomy of Company Pay Practices." *Personnel,* 62 (September), 67–71.

Foulkes, Fred K. 1980. *Personnel Policies in Large Nonunion Companies.* Englewood Cliffs, N.J.: Prentice-Hall.

Frank, Robert H. 1984. "Are Workers Paid Their Marginal Products?" *American Economic Review,* 74, 549–571.

——— 1985. *Choosing the Right Pond.* New York: Oxford University Press.

——— 1988. *Passions within Reason.* New York: W. W. Norton and Co.

Franke, Richard H., and James D. Kaul. 1978. "The Hawthorne Experiments: First Statistical Interpretation." *American Sociological Review,* 43, 623–643.

Franz, Wolfgang. 1987. "Hysteresis, Persistence, and the NAIRU: An Empirical Analysis for the Federal Republic of Germany." In Richard Layard and Lars Calmfors, eds., *The Fight against Unemployment,* 91–122. Cambridge: MIT Press.

Freeman, Richard B. 1971. *The Labor Market for College-Trained Manpower.* Cambridge: Harvard University Press.

——— 1988. "Does the New Generation of Labor Economists Know More than the Old?" In Bruce E. Kaufman, ed., *How Labor Markets Work.* Lexington, Mass.: Lexington Books.

Freeman, Richard B., and Martin L. Weitzman. 1987. "Bonuses and Employment in Japan." *Journal of Japanese and International Economies,* 1, 168–194.

Frey, Bruno S. 1993. "Shirking or Work Morale? The Impact of Regulating." *European Economic Review,* 37, 1523–32.

Friedman, Milton. 1953. "The Methodology of Positive Economics." Part I in *Essays in Positive Economics.* Chicago: Chicago University Press.

——— 1968. "The Role of Monetary Policy." *American Economic Review,* 58, 1–17.

Friedman, Raymond A. 1994. *Front Stage, Backstage: The Dramatic Structure of Labor Negotiations.* Cambridge: MIT Press.

Froot, Kenneth A., David S. Scharfstein, and Jeremy C. Stein. 1993. "Risk Management: Coordinating Corporate Investment and Financing Policies." *Journal of Finance,* 48, 1629–58.

Fudenberg, Drew, and Jean Tirole. 1983. "Sequential Bargaining with Incomplete Information." *Review of Economic Studies,* 50, 221–247.

Fukuyama, Francis. 1995. *Trust: The Social Virtues and the Creation of Prosperity.* New York: Free Press.

Gallagher, Daniel G., and Cynthia L. Gramm. 1997. "Collective Bargaining and Strike Activity." In David Lewin, Daniel J. B. Mitchell, and Mahmood A. Zaidi, eds., *The Human Resource Management Handbook, Part II,* 65–93. London: JAI Press.

Gartrell, C. David. 1982. "On the Visibility of Wage Referents." *Canadian Journal of Sociology,* 7, 117–143.

—— 1985. "Relational and Distributional Models of Collective Justice Sentiments." *Social Forces,* 64, 64–83.

George, Jennifer M., and Arthur P. Brief. 1992. "Feeling Good–Doing Good: A Conceptual Analysis of the Mood at Work—Organizational Spontaneity Relationship." *Psychological Bulletin,* 112, 310–329.

Gerhart, Barry, and George T. Milkovich. 1990. "Organizational Differences in Managerial Compensation and Financial Performance." *Academy of Management Journal,* 33, 663–691.

Ghez, Gilbert R. 1975. "Education, the Price of Time, and Life-Cycle Consumption." In F. Thomas Juster, ed., *Education, Income, and Human Behavior,* 295–312. New York: McGraw-Hill.

Gibbons, Robert, and Lawrence F. Katz. 1991. "Layoffs and Lemons." *Journal of Labor Economics,* 9, 351–380.

—— 1992. "Does Unmeasured Ability Explain Inter-Industry Wage Differentials?" *Review of Economic Studies,* 59, 515–535.

Gibbs, Michael. 1995. "Incentive Compensation in a Corporate Hierarchy." *Journal of Accounting and Economics,* 19, 247–277.

Giese, William James, and H. W. Ruter. 1949. "An Objective Analysis of Morale." *Journal of Applied Psychology,* 33, 421–427.

Gilroy, Curtis L. 1973. "Job Losers, Leavers, and Entrants: Traits and Trends." *Monthly Labor Review,* 96 (August), 3–15.

Gleitman, Henry. 1995. *Psychology.* New York: W. W. Norton.

Godard, John. 1992. "Strikes as Collective Voice: Towards an Integrative Theory of Strike Activity." In John F. Burton, Jr., ed., *Proceedings of the Forty-Fourth Annual Meeting,* 512–521. Madison, Wis.: Industrial Relations Research Association.

Goode, William J., and Irving Fowler. 1949. "Incentive Factors in a Low Morale Plant." *American Sociological Review,* 14, 618–624.

Goranson, Richard E., and Leonard Berkowitz. 1966. "Reciprocity and Responsibility Reactions to Prior Help." *Journal of Personality and Social Psychology,* 3, 227–232.

Gordon, David M. 1990. "Who Bosses Whom? The Intensity of Supervision and the Discipline of Labor." *American Economic Review, Papers and Proceedings,* 80, 28–32.

Gordon, Donald F. 1974. "A Neo-Classical Theory of Keynesian Unemployment." *Economic Inquiry,* 12, 431–459.

Gordon, Robert J. 1972. "Wage-Price Controls and the Shifting Phillips Curve." *Brookings Papers on Economic Activity,* no. 2, 385–421.

—— 1977. "Can the Inflation of the 1970s Be Explained?" *Brookings Papers on Economic Activity,* 8:1, 253–277.

—— 1979. "The 'End-of-Expansion' Phenomenon in Short-Run Productivity Behavior." *Brookings Papers on Economic Activity,* 447–461.

—— 1981. "Output Fluctuations and Gradual Price Adjustment." *Journal of Economic Literature,* 19, 493–530.

—— 1982. "Why U.S. Wage and Employment Behaviour Differs from That in Britain and Japan." *Economic Journal,* 92, 13–44.

—— 1997. "The Time-Varying NAIRU and Its Implications for Economic Policy." *Journal of Economic Perspectives,* 11 (Winter), 11–32.

Gottfries, Nils, and Henrik Horn. 1987. "Wage Formation and the Persistence of Unemployment." *Economic Journal,* 97, 877–884.

Gramm, Cynthia L., Wallace E. Hendricks, and Lawrence M. Kahn. 1988. "Inflation Uncertainty and Strike Activity." *Industrial Relations,* 27, 114–129.

Grandmont, Jean-Michel. 1989. "Keynesian Issues and Economic Theory." *Scandinavian Journal of Economics,* 91, 265–293.

Grandmont, Jean-Michel, Guy Laroque, and Yves Younès. 1978. "Equilibrium with Quantity Rationing and Recontracting." *Journal of Economic Theory,* 19, 84–102.

Granovetter, Mark S. 1974. *Getting a Job: A Study of Contacts and Careers.* Cambridge: Harvard University Press.

———— 1988. "Sociological and Economic Approaches to Labor Market Analysis: A Social Structural View." Chapter 9 in George Farkas and Paula England, eds., *Industries, Firms, and Jobs.* New York: Plenum Press.

Green, Jerry, and Charles M. Kahn. 1983. "Wage-Employment Contracts." *Quarterly Journal of Economics,* 98, 173–187.

Greenberg, Jerald. 1978. "Effects of Reward Value and Relative Power on Allocation Decisions: Justice, Generosity, or Greed?" *Journal of Personality and Social Psychology,* 36, 367–379.

———— 1982. "Approaching Equity and Avoiding Inequity in Groups and Organizations." Chapter 11 in Jerald Greenberg and Ronald L. Cohen, eds., *Equity and Justice in Social Behavior.* New York: Academic Press.

———— 1988. "Equity and Workplace Status." *Journal of Applied Psychology,* 73, 608–613, and Chapter 15 in Greenberg (1996).

———— 1989. "Injustice and Cognitive Reevaluation of the Work Environment." *Academy of Management Journal,* 32, 174–184, and Chapter 16 in Greenberg (1996).

———— 1990. "Employee Theft as a Reaction to Underpayment Inequity: The Hidden Cost of Pay Cuts." *Journal of Applied Psychology,* 75, 561–568, and Chapter 10 in Greenberg (1996).

———— 1993. "Stealing in the Name of Justice: Informational and Interpersonal Moderators of Theft Reactions to Underpayment Inequity." *Organizational Behavior and Human Decision Processes,* 54, 81–103.

———— 1996. *The Quest for Justice on the Job: Essays and Experiments.* Thousand Oaks, Calif.: Sage Publications.

Greene, Charles N., and Robert E. Craft, Jr. 1979. "The Satisfaction-Performance Controversy—Revisited." In Richard M. Steers and Lyman W. Porter, eds., *Motivation and Work Behavior,* 270–287. New York: McGraw-Hill.

Greenwald, Bruce C. 1986. "Adverse Selection in the Labour Market." *Review of Economic Studies,* 53, 325–347.

Greenwald, Bruce C., and Joseph E. Stiglitz. 1990. "Asymmetric Information and the New Theory of the Firm: Financial Constraints and Risk Behavior." *American Economic Review,* 80, 160–165.

Gregory, Mary, Peter Lobban, and Andrew Thomson. 1985. "Wage Settlements in Manufacturing, 1979–84: Evidence from the CBI Pay Databank." *British Journal of Industrial Relations,* 23, 339–357.

———— 1986. "Bargaining Structure, Pay Settlements, and Perceived Pressures in Manufacturing, 1979–84: Further Analysis from the CBI Databank." *British Journal of Industrial Relations,* 24, 215–232.

Groot, Wim. 1990. "Heterogeneous Jobs and Re-employment Probabilities." *Oxford Bulletin of Economics and Statistics,* 52, 253–267.

Groshen, Erica L. 1991a. "Sources of Intra-Industry Wage Dispersion: How Much Do Employers Matter?" *Quarterly Journal of Economics,* 106, 869–884.

——— 1991b. "Five Reasons Why Wages Vary among Employers." *Industrial Relations,* 30, 350–381.

——— 1991c. "Do Wage Differences among Employers Last?" Discussion Paper, Federal Reserve Bank of Cleveland.

Groshen, Erica L., and Alan B. Krueger. 1990. "The Structure of Supervision and Pay in Hospitals." *Industrial and Labor Relations Review,* 43, 143S–146S.

Groshen, Erica L., and Mark E. Schweitzer. 1998. "Firms' Wage Adjustments: A Break from the Past?" Discussion Paper, Federal Reserve Bank of New York.

Gross, Steven E., and Jeffrey P. Bacher. 1993. "The New Variable Pay Programs: How Some Succeed, Why Some Don't." *Compensation and Benefits Review,* 5, 51–56.

Grossman, Sanford J., and Oliver D. Hart. 1981. "Implicit Contracts, Moral Hazard, and Unemployment under Models of Labor Market Equilibrium." *American Economic Review, Papers and Proceedings,* 71, 301–307.

——— 1983. "Implicit Contracts under Asymmetric Information." *Quarterly Journal of Economics,* 98, 123–156.

Grout, Paul A. 1984. "Investment and Wages in the Absence of Binding Contracts: A Nash Bargaining Approach." *Econometrica,* 52, 449–460.

Gruber, Jonathan. 1997. "The Consumption Smoothing Benefits of Unemployment Insurance." *American Economic Review,* 87, 192–205.

Güth, Werner, Rolf Schmittberger, and Bernd Schwarze. 1982. "An Experimental Analysis of Ultimatum Bargaining." *Journal of Economic Behavior and Organizations,* 3, 367–388.

Guzzo, Richard A., Richard D. Jette, and Raymond A. Katzell. 1985. "The Effects of Psychologically Based Intervention Programs on Worker Productivity: A Meta-Analysis." *Personnel Psychology,* 38, 275–291.

Hackman, J. Richard. 1996. "Why Teams Don't Work." In R. S. Tindale, J. Edwards, and E. J. Posavac, eds., *Applications of Theory and Research on Groups to Social Issues.* New York: Plenum.

Hahn, Frank. 1978. "On Non-Walrasian Equilibria." *Review of Economic Studies,* 45, 1–18.

Hajivassiliou, Vassilis, and Yannis Ioannides. 1995. "Unemployment and Liquidity Constraints." Cowles Foundation Discussion Paper no. 1090.

Hall, Bronwyn H. 1992. "Investment and Research and Development at the Firm Level: Does the Source of Financing Matter?" National Bureau of Economic Research Working Paper no. 4096. Cambridge, Mass.

Hall, John David. 1993. "The Wage Setters' Guide to Wage Rigidity." M.Sc. (Economics) dissertation, University of Southampton.

Hall, Robert E. 1987. "Productivity and the Business Cycle." *Carnegie-Rochester Conference Series on Public Policy,* 27, 421–444.

——— 1991. "Labor Demand, Labor Supply, and Employment Volatility." *NBER Macroeconomics Annual, 1991,* 19–47.

——— 1995. "Lost Jobs." *Brookings Papers on Economic Activity,* no. 1, 221–256.

—— 1997. "The Temporal Concentration of Job Destruction and Inventory Liquidation: A Theory of Recessions." Discussion Paper, Hoover Institution, Stanford, Calif.

Ham, John C. 1986. "Testing Whether Unemployment Represents Intertemporal Labour Supply Behaviour." *Review of Economic Studies*, 53, 559–578.

Ham, John C., and Samuel A. Rea. 1987. "Unemployment Insurance and Male Unemployment Duration in Canada." *Journal of Labor Economics*, 5, 325–353.

Hamermesh, Daniel S. 1973. "Who 'Wins' in Wage Bargaining." *Industrial and Labor Relations Review*, 26, 1146–49.

—— 1976. "Econometric Studies of Labor Demand and Their Applications to Policy Analysis." *Journal of Human Resources*, 11, 507–525.

—— 1977. *Jobless Pay and the Economy*. Baltimore: Johns Hopkins University Press.

—— 1987. "The Costs of Worker Displacement." *Quarterly Journal of Economics*, 102, 51–75.

—— 1986. "The Demand for Labor in the Long Run." Chapter 8 in Ashenfelter and Layard (1986).

—— 1989. "Labor Demand and the Structure of Adjustment Costs." *American Economic Review*, 79, 674–689.

—— 1991. "Wage Concessions, Plant Shutdowns, and the Demand for Labor." Chapter 3 in John T. Addison, ed., *Job Displacement*. Detroit: Wayne State University Press.

Hamilton, James D. 1983. "Oil and the Macroeconomy since World War II." *Journal of Political Economy*, 91, 228–248.

—— 1985. "Historical Causes of Postwar Oil Shocks and Recession." *Energy Journal*, 6, 97–116.

—— 1988. "A Neoclassical Model of Unemployment and the Business Cycle." *Journal of Political Economy*, 96, 593–617.

—— 1996. "This Is What Happened to the Oil Price-Macroeconomy Relationship." *Journal of Monetary Economics*, 38, 215–220.

Hanes, Christopher. 1996a. "Changes in the Cyclical Behavior of Real Wage Rates, 1870–1990." *Journal of Economic History*, 56, 837–861.

—— 1996b. "Nominal Wage Rigidity and Industry Characteristics in the Downturns of 1893, 1929, and 1981." Discussion Paper, Federal Reserve Board, Washington, D.C.

Hansen, Gary D. 1985. "Indivisible Labor and the Business Cycle." *Journal of Monetary Economics*, 16, 309–327.

Hansen, Gary D., and Randall Wright. 1992. "The Labor Market in Real Business Cycle Theory." *Quarterly Review, Federal Reserve Bank of Minneapolis* (Spring), 2–12.

Harris, Milton, and Bengt Holmstrom. 1982. "A Theory of Wage Dynamics." *Review of Economic Studies*, 49, 315–333.

Harrison, Richard. 1976. "The Demoralising Experience of Prolonged Unemployment." *Department of Employment Gazette*, 84, 339–348.

Hart, Oliver. 1982. "A Model of Imperfect Competition with Keynesian Features." *Quarterly Journal of Economics*, 97, 109–138.

—— 1983. "Optimal Labour Contracts under Asymmetric Information: An Introduction." *Review of Economic Studies*, 50, 3–35.

—— 1989. "Bargaining and Strikes." *Quarterly Journal of Economics*, 104, 25–44.

Hart, Robert A., and James R. Malley. 1996. "Labor Productivity and the Cycle." Working Paper, University of Glasgow.

Hashimoto, Masanori, and John Raisian. 1985. "Employment Tenure and Earnings Profiles in Japan and the United States." *American Economic Review,* 75, 721–735.

Hashimoto, Masanori, and Ben T. Yu. 1980. "Specific Capital, Employment Contracts, and Wage Rigidity." *Bell Journal of Economics,* 11, 536–549.

Hausman, Daniel M. 1989. "Economic Methodology in a Nutshell." *Journal of Economic Perspectives,* 3, 115–127.

Hayes, Beth. 1984. "Unions and Strikes with Asymmetric Information." *Journal of Labor Economics,* 2, 57–83.

Heady, Patrick, and Malcolm Smyth. 1989. *Living Standards during Unemployment,* vols. 1 and 2. London: HMSO.

Heckman, James J. 1974. "Life Cycle Consumption and Labor Supply: An Explanation of the Relationship between Income and Consumption over the Life Cycle." *American Economic Review,* 64, 188–194.

Heckman, James J., and George J. Borjas. 1980. "Does Unemployment Cause Future Unemployment? Definitions, Questions, and Answers from a Continuous Time Model of Heterogeneity and State Dependence." *Economica,* 47, 247–283.

Heckman, James J., and Thomas E. MaCurdy. 1980, 1982. "A Life Cycle Model of Female Labour Supply." *Review of Economic Studies,* 47, 47–74, and *Corrigendum,* 49, 659–660.

——— 1988. "Empirical Tests of Labor-Market Equilibrium: An Evaluation." *Carnegie-Rochester Conference Series on Public Policy,* 28, 231–258.

Heckscher, Charles. 1995. *White-Collar Blues.* New York: Basic Books.

Heetderks, Thomas D., and James E. Martin. 1991. "Employee Perceptions of the Effects of a Two-Tier Wage Structure." *Journal of Labor Research,* 12, 279–295.

Henle, Peter. 1973. "Reverse Collective Bargaining? A Look at Some Union Concession Situations." *Industrial and Labor Relations Review,* 26, 956–968.

Herding, Richard. 1972. *Job Control and Union Structure.* Rotterdam: Rotterdam University Press.

Hersch, Joni. 1995. "Optimal 'Mismatch' and Promotions." *Economic Inquiry,* 33, 611–624.

Herzberg, Frederick, Bernard Mausner, Richard O. Peterson, and Dora Capwell. 1957. *Job Attitudes: Review of Research and Opinion.* Pittsburgh: Psychological Service of Pittsburgh.

Hicks, John R. 1932. *The Theory of Wages.* London: Macmillan.

Hills, Frederick. 1987. *Compensation Decision Making.* Chicago: Dryden.

Himmelberg, Charles P., and Bruce C. Petersen. 1994. "R & D and Internal Finance: A Panel Study of Small Firms in High-Tech Industries." *Review of Economics and Statistics,* 76 (February), 38–51.

Hirsch, Barry T., and John T. Addison. 1986. *The Economic Analysis of Unions: New Approaches and Evidence.* Boston: Allen and Unwin.

Hirsch, Barry T., and William J. Hausman. 1983. "Labour Productivity in the British and South Wales Coal Industry, 1874–1914." *Economica,* 50, 154–157.

Hoffer, Eric. 1951. *The True Believer.* New York: Harper and Row.

Holden, Steinar. 1990. "Insiders and Outsiders in Labour Market Models." *Journal of Economics*, 52, 43–54.

Holen, Arlene. 1977. "Effects of Unemployment Insurance Entitlement on Duration and Job Search Outcome." *Industrial and Labor Relations Review*, 30, 45–50.

Holmstrom, Bengt. 1983. "Equilibrium Long-Term Labor Contracts." *Quarterly Journal of Economics*, 98, 23–54.

Holmstrom, Bengt, and Paul Milgrom. 1991. "Multitask Principle-Agent Analyses: Incentive Contracts, Asset Ownership, and Job Design." *Journal of Law, Economics, and Organization*, 7 (special issue), 24–52.

Holzer, Harry J. 1986. "Reservation Wages and Their Labor Market Effects for Black and White Youth." *Journal of Human Resources*, 21, 157–177.

—— 1987a. "Job Search by Employed and Unemployed Youth." *Industrial and Labor Relations Review*, 40, 601–611.

—— 1987b. "Informal Job Search and Black Youth Unemployment." *American Economic Review*, 77, 446–452.

—— 1990. "Wages, Employer Costs, and Employee Performance in the Firm." *Industrial and Labor Relations Review*, 43, 147S—164S.

Holzer, Harry J., Lawrence F. Katz, and Alan B. Krueger. 1991. "Job Queues and Wages." *Quarterly Journal of Economics*, 106, 739–768.

Hooker, Mark A. 1996a. "What Happened to the Oil Price-Macroeconomy Relationship?" *Journal of Monetary Economics*, 38, 195–213.

—— 1996b. "This Is What Happened to the Oil Price-Macroeconomy Relationship: Reply." *Journal of Monetary Economics*, 38, 221–222.

Horrigan, Michael W. 1987. "Time Spent Unemployed: A New Look at Data from the CPS." *Monthly Labor Review*, 110 (July), 3–15.

Hoshi, Takeo, Anil Kashyap, and David Scharfstein. 1990. "Bank Monitoring and Investment: Evidence from the Changing Structure of Japanese Corporate Banking Relationships." Chapter 4 in R. Glenn Hubbard, ed., *Asymmetric Information, Corporate Finance, and Investment*. Chicago: University of Chicago Press.

—— 1991. "Corporate Structure, Liquidity, and Investment: Evidence from Japanese Industrial Groups." *Quarterly Journal of Economics*, 106, 33–60.

Hosios, Arthur J. 1985. "Unemployment and Recruitment with Heterogeneous Labor." *Journal of Labor Economics*, 3, 175–187.

—— 1994. "Unemployment and Vacancies with Sectoral Shifts." *American Economic Review*, 84, 124–144.

Howitt, Peter. 1985. "Transactions Costs in the Theory of Unemployment." *American Economic Review*, 75, 88–100.

Howitt, Peter, and R. Preston McAfee. 1987. "Costly Search and Recruiting." *International Economic Review*, 28, 89–107.

Hubbard, R. Glenn. 1998. "Capital-Market Imperfections and Investment." *Journal of Economic Literature*, 36, 193–225.

Hubbard, R. Glenn, Anil K. Kashyap, and Toni M. Whited. 1995. "Internal Finance and Firm Investment." *Journal of Money Credit and Banking*, 27, 683–701.

Hughes, Gordon and Barry McCormick. 1989. "Hidden Unemployment and Suppressed Labour Mobility in the British Labour Market." Working Paper, University of Southampton.

Huselid, Mark A. 1995. "The Impact of Human Resource Management Practices on Turnover, Productivity, and Corporate Financial Performance." *Academy of Management Journal*, 38, 635–772.

Huselid, Mark A., and Brian E. Becker. 1996. "Methodological Issues in Cross-Sectional and Panel Estimates of the Human Resource–Firm Performance Link." *Industrial Relations*, 35, 400–422.

Hyclak, Thomas, and Geraint Johnes. 1992. *Wage Flexibility and Unemployment Dynamics in Regional Labor Markets*. Kalamazoo, Mich.: Upjohn Institute.

Iaffaldano, Michelle T., and Paul M. Muchinsky. 1985. "Job Satisfaction and Job Performance: A Meta-Analysis." *Psychological Bulletin*, 97, 251–273.

Ichniowski, Casey. 1986. "The Effects of Grievance Activity on Productivity." *Industrial and Labor Relations Review*, 40, 75–89.

Ichniowski, Casey, and John Thomas Delaney. 1990. "Profitability and Compensation Adjustments in the Retail Food Industry." *Industrial and Labor Relations Review*, 43 (suppl.), 183–202.

Ichniowski, Casey, Thomas A. Kochan, David Levine, Craig Olson, and George Strauss. 1996. "What Works at Work: Overview and Assessment." *Industrial Relations*, 35, 299–333.

Ichniowski, Casey, and Kathryn Shaw. 1995. "Old Dogs and New Tricks: Determinants of the Adoption of Productivity-Enhancing Work Practices." *Brookings Papers on Economic Activity: Microeconomics*, 1–65.

Isaac, R. Mark, and James M. Walker. 1988a. "Group Size Effects in Public Goods Provision: The Voluntary Contributions Mechanism." *Quarterly Journal of Economics*, 103, 179–199.

———— 1988b. "Communication and Free-Riding Behavior: The Voluntary Contribution Mechanism." *Economic Inquiry*, 26, 585–608.

Isen, Alice M., and Robert A. Baron. 1991. "Positive Affect as a Factor in Organizational Behavior." *Research in Organizational Behavior*, 13, 1–53.

Jackman, Richard, and Richard Layard. 1991. "Does Long-Term Unemployment Reduce a Person's Chance of a Job? A Time-Series Test." *Economica*, 58, 93–106.

Jackman, Richard, Richard Layard, and Christopher Pissarides. 1989. "On Vacancies." *Oxford Bulletin of Economics and Statistics*, 51, no. 4, 377–394.

Jacobson, Louis S., Robert J. LaLonde, and Daniel G. Sullivan. 1993. "Earnings Losses of Displaced Workers." *American Economic Review*, 83, 685–709.

Jacoby, Sanford M. 1984. "The Development of Internal Labor Markets in American Manufacturing Firms." Chapter 2 in Paul Osterman, ed., *Internal Labor Markets*. Cambridge: MIT Press.

———— 1985. *Employing Bureaucracy*. New York: Columbia University Press.

Jacoby, Sanford M., and Daniel J. B. Mitchell. 1986. "Management Attitudes toward Two-Tier Pay Plans." *Journal of Labor Research*, 7, 221–237.

Jahoda, Marie, Paul F. Lazarsfeld, and Hans Zeisel. 1971. *Marienthal*. Chicago: Aldine, Atherton. (First published in German in 1933 as *Die Arbeitslosen von Marienthal*.)

Janowitz, Morris, and Edward A. Shils. 1948. "Cohesion and Disintegration in the Wehrmacht in World War II." *Public Opinion Quarterly*, 12, 280–315. Reprinted in Morris Janowitz, ed., *Military Conflict*. Beverly Hills, Calif.: Sage Publications.

Jarrell, A. N. 1959. "Job Pay Levels, Differentials, and Trends in Twenty Labor Markets." *Monthly Labor Review*, 82, 1120–27.

Jenkins, Richard, Alan Bryman, Janet Ford, Teresa Keil and Alan Beardsworth. 1983. "Information in the Labour Market: The Impact of Recession." *Sociology,* 17, 260–267.

Jerome, Harry. 1926. *Migration and Business Cycles.* New York: National Bureau of Economic Research.

Johnson, Gloria Jones, and W. Roy Johnson. 1996. "Perceived Overqualification and Psychological Well-Being." *Journal of Social Psychology,* 136, 435–445.

Johnson, Jeffrey C. 1990. *Selecting Ethnographic Informants.* Newbury Park, Calif.: Sage.

Jones, Stephen R. G. 1988. "The Relationship between Unemployment Spells and Reservation Wages as a Test of Search Theory." *Quarterly Journal of Economics,* 103, 741–765.

——— 1989a. "Job Search Methods, Intensity, and Effect." *Oxford Bulletin of Economics and Statistics,* 51, no. 3, 277–296.

——— 1989b. "After Redundancy—Labour Market Adjustment and Hysteresis Effects: Evidence from the Steel Industry." *Oxford Bulletin of Economics and Statistics,* 51, 259–275.

——— 1989c. "Reservation Wages and the Cost of Unemployment." *Economica,* 56, 225–246.

Jovanovic, Boyan. 1987. "Work, Rest, and Search: Unemployment, Turnover, and the Cycle." *Journal of Labor Economics,* 5, 131–148.

Juris, Hervey A. 1969. "Union Wage Decisions." *Industrial Relations,* 8, 247–258.

Juster, F. Thomas. 1985. "Preferences for Work and Leisure." Chapter 13 in F. Thomas Juster and Frank P. Stafford, eds., *Time, Goods, and Well-Being.* Ann Arbor: Institute for Social Research, University of Michigan.

Kahn, Charles. 1985. "Optimal Severance Pay with Incomplete Information." *Journal of Political Economy,* 93, 435–451.

Kahn, Hilda R. 1964. *Repercussions of Redundancy.* London: George Allen and Unwin.

Kahn, Lawrence, and Stuart Low. 1980. "The Relative Effects of Employed and Unemployed Job Search." *Review of Economics and Statistics,* 234–241.

Kahn, Shulamit. 1997. "Evidence of Nominal Wage Stickiness from Microdata." *American Economic Review,* 87, 993–1008.

Kahneman, Daniel, Jack L. Knetsch, and Richard Thaler. 1986a. "Fairness as a Constraint on Profit Seeking: Entitlements in the Market." *American Economic Review,* 76, 728–741.

——— 1986b. "Fairness and the Assumptions of Economics." *Journal of Business,* 59, S285–S300.

——— 1991. "The Endowment Effect, Loss Aversion, and Status Quo Bias." *Journal of Economic Perspectives,* 5, 193–206.

Kahneman, Daniel, and Amos Tversky. 1979. "Prospect Theory: An Analysis of Decision under Risk." *Econometrica,* 47, 263–291.

Kaitz, Hyman B. 1970. "Analyzing the Length of Spells of Unemployment." *Monthly Labor Review,* 93 (November), 11–20.

Kandel, William L. 1991. " 'Overqualified' or 'Appropriately Qualified': New ADEA Risks." *Employee Relations Law Journal,* 17, 287–306.

Kaplan, Steven M., and Liugi Zingales. 1997. "Do Investment-Cash Flow Sensitivities

Provide Useful Measures of Financing Constraint?" *Quarterly Journal of Economics*, 112, 169–215.

Kapp, K. William, and Lore L. Kapp, eds. 1949. *Readings in Economics*. New York: Barnes and Noble.

Karambayya, Rekha. 1990. "Good Organizational Citizens *Do* Make a Difference." In *Proceedings of the Administrative Sciences Association of Canada*, 110–119. Whistler, British Columbia.

Kaspar, Hirschel. 1967. "The Asking Price of Labor and the Duration of Unemployment." *Review of Economics and Statistics*, 49, 165–172.

Katz, Daniel, and Robert L. Kahn. 1966. *The Social Psychology of Organizations*. New York: John Wiley.

Katz, Harry C., Thomas A. Kochan, and Kenneth R. Gobeille. 1983. "Industrial Relations Performance, Economic Performance, and QWL Programs: An Interplant Analysis." *Industrial and Labor Relations Review*, 37, 3–17.

Katz, Harry C., Thomas A. Kochan, and Mark R. Weber. 1985. "Assessing the Effects of Industrial Relations Systems and Efforts to Improve the Quality of Working Life on Organizational Effectiveness." *Academy of Management Journal*, 28, 509–526.

Katz, Lawrence F. 1986. "Efficiency Wage Theories: A Partial Evaluation." *NBER Macroeconomics Annual, 1986*, 235–276.

Katz, Lawrence F., and Alan B. Krueger. 1992. "The Effect of the Minimum Wage on the Fast Food Industry." *Industrial and Labor Relations Review*, 46, 6–21.

Katz, Lawrence F., and Bruce D. Meyer. 1990a. "Unemployment Insurance, Recall Expectations, and Unemployment Outcomes." *Quarterly Journal of Economics*, 105, 973–1002.

——— 1990b. "The Impact of the Potential Duration of Unemployment Benefits on the Duration of Unemployment." *Journal of Public Economics*, 41, 45–72.

Katz, Lawrence F., and Lawrence H. Summers. 1989. "Industry Rents: Evidence and Implications." *Brookings Paper on Economic Activity*, 208–275.

Katzell, Raymond A., and Daniel Yankelovich. 1975. *Work, Productivity, and Job Satisfaction*. New York: Harcourt, Brace, and Jovanovich.

Kaufman, Bruce E. 1992. "Research on Strike Models and Outcomes in the 1980s: Accomplishments and Shortcomings." Chapter 3 in David Lewin, ed., *Research Frontiers in Industrial Relations and Human Resources*. Madison, Wis.: Industrial Relations Research Association.

Kaufman, Bruce E., and Jorge Martinez-Vazquez. 1988. "Voting for Wage Concessions: The Case of the 1982 GM-UAW Negotiations." *Industrial and Labor Relations Review*, 41, 183–194.

Kaufman, Roger. 1984. "On Wage Stickiness in Britain's Competitive Sector." *British Journal of Industrial Relations*, 22, 101–112.

Keane, Michael P. 1993. "Individual Heterogeneity, Interindustry Wage Differentials." *Journal of Human Resources*, 28, 134–161.

Kennan, John. 1986. "The Economics of Strikes." Chapter 19 of Ashenfelter and Layard (1986).

——— 1995. "The Elusive Effects of Minimum Wages." *Journal of Economic Literature*, 33, 1950–65.

Kennan, John, and Robert Wilson. 1989. "Strategic Bargaining Models and Interpretation of Strike Data." *Journal of Applied Econometrics*, 4 (suppl.), S87–S130.

—— 1993. "Bargaining with Private Information." *Journal of Economic Literature*, 31, 45–104.

Kerr, Clark. 1942. *Migration to the Seattle Labor Market Area, 1940–42.* Seattle: University of Washington Press.

—— 1988. "The Neoclassical Revisionists in Labor Economics (1940–1960)—R.I.P." In Bruce E. Kaufman, ed., *How Labor Markets Work.* Lexington, Mass.: Lexington Books.

Keynes, John Maynard. 1936. *The General Theory of Employment, Interest, and Money.* London: Macmillan.

Kiefer, Nicholas M., and George R. Neumann. 1979. "An Empirical Job-Search Model, with a Test of the Constant Reservation-Wage Hypothesis." *Journal of Political Economy*, 87, 89–107.

Killingworth, Mark, and James J. Heckman. 1986. "Female Labor Supply: A Survey." Chapter 2 in Ashenfelter and Layard (1986).

Kim, Oliver, and Mark Walker. 1984. "The Free Rider Problem: Experimental Evidence." *Public Choice*, 43, 3–24.

King, Robert G., and Charles I. Plosser. 1984. "Money, Credit, and Prices in a Real Business Cycle." *American Economic Review*, 74, 363–380.

King, Robert G., and Mark W. Watson. 1994. "The Postwar U.S. Phillips Curve: A Revisioninst Econometric History." *Carnegie-Rochester Conference Series on Public Policy*, 41, 157–219.

Kingston, Jerry L., and Paul L. Burgess. 1975. "Unemployment Insurance and Unemployment Duration." *Quarterly Review of Economics and Business*, 15, 65–79.

Kirk, Jerome, and Marc L. Miller. 1986. *Reliability and Validity in Qualitative Research.* Beverly Hills, Calif.: Sage.

Kleiner, Morris M., Gerald Nickelsburg, and Adam Pilarski. 1995. "Monitoring, Grievances, and Plant Performance." *Industrial Relations*, 34, 169–189.

Kletzer, Lori Gladstein. 1991. "Earnings after Job Displacement: Job Tenure, Industry, and Occupation." Chapter 4 in John T. Addison, ed., *Job Displacement, Consequences and Implications for Policy*, 107–135. Detroit: Wayne State University Press.

Kochan, Thomas A., and Thomas A. Barocci. 1985. *Human Resource Management and Industrial Relations.* Boston: Little, Brown, and Co.

Kochan, Thomas A., and Harry C. Katz. 1988. *Collective Bargaining and Industrial Relations.* Homewood, Ill.: Irwin.

Koopmans, Tjalling C. 1957. "The Construction of Economic Knowledge." Chapter 2 in *Three Essays on the State of Economic Science.* New York: McGraw-Hill.

Kooreman, Peter, and Geert Ridder. 1983. "The Effect of Age and Unemployment Percentage on the Duration of Unemployment: Evidence from Aggregate Data." *European Economic Review*, 20, 41–57.

Kragt, Alphons J. C. van de, John M. Orbell, and Robyn M. Dawes. 1983. "The Minimal Contributing Set as a Solution to Public Goods Problems." *American Political Science Review*, 77, 112–122.

Krueger, Alan B. 1991. "Ownership, Agency, and Wages: An Examination of Franchising in the Fast Food Industry." *Quarterly Journal of Economics*, 100, 75–101.

Krueger, Alan B., and Lawrence H. Summers. 1987. "Reflections on the Inter-Industry Wage Structure." Chapter 2 in Lang and Leonard, 1987.

—— 1988. "Efficiency Wages and Inter-Industry Wage Structure." *Econometrica, 56,* 259–293.

Kruse, Douglas L. 1993. *Profit Sharing, Does It Make a Difference?* Kalamazoo, Mich.: W. E. Upjohn Institute.

Kugler, Adriana. 1997. "Employee Referrals and the Inter-Industry Wage Structure." Working Paper, Department of Economics, Universitat Pompeu Fabra, Barcelona.

Kydland, Finn E., and Edward C. Prescott. 1982. "Time to Build and Aggregate Fluctuations." *Econometrica, 50,* 1345–70.

Lamont, Owen. 1997. "Cash Flow and Investment: Evidence from Internal Capital Markets." *Journal of Finance, 52,* 83–109.

Lancaster, Tony. 1979. "Econometric Methods for the Duration of Unemployment." *Econometrica, 47,* 939–956.

—— 1985. "Simultaneous Equations Models in Applied Search Theory." *Journal of Econometrics, 28,* 113–126.

Lancaster, Tony, and Andrew Cheshire. 1983. "An Econometric Analysis of Reservation Wages." *Econometrica, 51,* 1661–76.

Lang, Kevin. 1991. "Persistent Wage Dispersion and Involuntary Unemployment." *Quarterly Journal of Economics, 106,* 181–202.

Lang, Kevin, and Jonathan Leonard, eds. 1987. *Unemployment and the Structure of Labor Markets.* New York: Basil and Blackwell.

Lawler, Edward E. III. 1971. *Pay and Organizational Effectiveness: A Psychological View.* New York: McGraw-Hill.

—— 1990. *Strategic Pay: Aligning Organizational Strategies and Pay Systems.* San Francisco: Jossey-Bass.

Lawler, Edward E. III, and Lyman W. Porter. 1967. "The Effect of Performance on Job Satisfaction." *Industrial Relations, 7,* 20–28.

Lawson, Catharine, Marc Goldstein, Antonia Moran, and Sharon Reilly. 1993. "A Survey of Unemployment Benefit Exhaustees." Center for Social Research, Central Connecticut State University, Research Paper.

Layard, Richard and Charles Bean. 1989. "Why Does Unemployment Persist?" *Scandinavian Journal of Economics, 91,* 371–396.

Layard, Richard, Stephen Nickell, and Richard Jackman. 1991. *Unemployment, Macroeconomic Performance, and the Labour Market.* Oxford: Oxford University Press.

Lazear, Edward P. 1979. "Why Is There Mandatory Retirement?" *Journal of Political Economy, 87,* 1261–84.

—— 1986. "Raids and Offer Matching." In Ronald Ehrenberg, ed., *Research in Labor Economics,* vol. 8, part A, 141–165.

—— 1989. "Pay Equality and Industrial Politics." *Journal of Political Economy, 97,* 561–80.

—— 1992. "The Job as a Concept." In William J. Bruns, ed., *Performance Measurement, Evaluation, and Incentives.* Boston: Harvard Business School Press.

—— 1995. *Personnel Economics.* Cambridge: MIT Press.

Leach, John. 1992. "Strikes as the Random Enforcement of Asymmetric Information Contracts." *Journal of Labor Economics, 10,* 202–210.

Leana, Carrie R., and Daniel C. Feldman. 1990. "Individual Responses to Job Loss: Empirical Findings from Two Field Studies." *Human Relations, 43,* 1155–81.

———— 1992. *Coping with Job Loss.* New York: Lexington Books.

———— 1995. "Finding New Jobs after a Plant Closing: Antecedents and Outcomes of the Occurrence and Quality of Reemployment." *Human Relations,* 48, 1381–1401.

Lebow, David E., David J. Stockton, and William L. Wascher. 1995. "Inflation, Nominal Wage Rigidity, and the Efficiency of Labor Markets." Board of Governors of the Federal Reserve System, Finance and Economic Discussion Series 94-45.

Leibenstein, Harvey. 1976. *Beyond Economic Man.* Cambridge: Harvard University Press.

———— 1978. *General X-Efficiency Theory and Economic Development.* New York: Oxford University Press.

Leighton, Linda, and Jacob Mincer. 1982. "Labor Turnover and Youth Unemployment." Chapter 8 in Richard Freeman and David Wise, eds., *The Youth Labor Market Problem: Its Nature, Causes, and Consequences.* Chicago: Chicago University Press.

Leonard, Jonathan S. 1987a. "Carrots and Sticks: Pay, Supervision, and Turnover." *Journal of Labor Economics,* 5, S136–S152.

———— 1987b. "In the Wrong Place at the Wrong Time: The Extent of Frictional and Structural Unemployment." In Lang and Leonard (1987).

———— 1989. "Wage Structure and Dynamics in the Electronics Industry." *Industrial Relations,* 28, 251–275.

———— 1990. "Executive Pay and Firm Performance." *Industrial and Labor Relations Review,* 43, 13S—29S.

Leontief, Wassily. 1946. "The Pure Theory of the Guaranteed Annual Wage Contract." *Journal of Political Economy,* 54, 76–79.

Lester, Richard A. 1946. "Wage Diversity and Its Theoretical Implications." *Review of Economic Statistics,* 28, 152–159.

———— 1948. *Company Wage Policies.* Princeton, N.J.: Industrial Relations Section, Princeton University.

———— 1954. *Hiring Practices and Labor Competition.* Princeton, N.J.: Industrial Relations Section, Princeton University.

Levine, David I. 1991. "You Get What You Pay For: Tests of Efficiency Wage Theories in the United States and Japan." Working Paper no. 26, Institute of Industrial Relations, University of California at Berkeley.

———— 1992. "Can Wage Increases Pay for Themselves? Tests with a Production Function." *Economic Journal,* 102, 1102–1115.

———— 1993a. "Fairness, Markets, and Ability to Pay: Evidence from Compensation Executives." *American Economic Review,* 83, 1241–59.

———— 1993b. "What Do Wages Buy?" *Proceedings of the Forty-Fifth Annual Meeting,* Industrial Relations Research Association, 133–141.

Levine, Hermine Z. 1985. "Outplacement and Severance Pay Practices." *Personnel,* 62 (September).

Likert, Rensis. 1961. *New Patterns of Management.* New York: McGraw-Hill.

Lilien, David M. 1982. "Sectoral Shifts and Cyclical Unemployment." *Journal of Political Economy,* 90, 777–793.

Lincoln, James F. 1946. *Lincoln's Incentive System.* New York: McGraw-Hill.

———— 1951. *Incentive Management.* Cleveland: Lincoln Electric Co.

Lindbeck, Assar. 1992. "Macroeconomic Theory and the Labor Market." *European Economic Review*, 36, 209–235.

Lindbeck, Assar, and Dennis J. Snower. 1987. "Union Activity, Unemployment Persistence, and Wage-Employment Ratchets." *European Economic Review*, 31, 157–167.

——— 1988a. "Cooperation, Harassment, and Involuntary Unemployment: An Insider-Outsider Approach." *American Economic Review*, 78, 167–188. Also appears as chapter 5 in Lindbeck and Snower (1988b).

——— 1988b. *The Insider-Outsider Theory of Employment and Unemployment*. Cambridge: MIT Press.

——— 1990. "Cooperation, Harassment, and Involuntary Unemployment: Reply." *American Economic Review*, 80, 631–636.

Livernash, Robert E. 1957. "The Internal Wage Structure." In George W. Taylor and Frank C. Pierson, eds., *New Concepts in Wage Determination*. New York: McGraw-Hill.

Locke, Edwin A. 1970. "Job Satisfaction and Job Performance: A Theoretical Analysis." *Organizational Behavior and Human Performance*, 5, 484–500.

——— 1976. "The Nature and Causes of Job Satisfaction." In M. D. Dunnette, ed., *Handbook of Industrial and Organizational Psychology*, 1297–1356. Chicago: Rand McNally.

Loewenstein, George, and Nachum Sicherman. 1991. "Do Workers Prefer Increasing Wage Profiles?" *Journal of Labor Economics*, 9, 67–84.

Loungani, Prakash, and Richard Rogerson. 1989. "Cyclical Fluctuations and Sectoral Reallocation: Evidence from PSID." *Journal of Monetary Economics*, 23, 259–273.

Loungani, Prakash, Mark Rush, and William Tave. 1990. "Stock Market Dispersion and Unemployment." *Journal of Monetary Economics*, 256, 367–388.

Loury, Glenn C. 1987. "Why Should We Care about Group Inequality." *Social Philosophy and Policy*, 5, 249–271.

Lucas, Robert E. 1972. "Expectations and the Neutrality of Money." *Journal of Economic Theory*, 4, 103–124.

——— 1976. "Econometric Policy Evaluation: A Critique." *Carnegie-Rochester Conferences on Public Policy*, 1, 19–46.

——— 1978. "Unemployment Policy." *American Economic Review, Papers and Proceedings*, 68, 353–357.

Lucas, Robert E., and Edward C. Prescott. 1974. "Equilibrium Search and Unemployment." *Journal of Economic Theory*, 7, 188–209.

Lucas, Robert E., and Leonard A. Rapping. 1969. "Real Wages, Employment, and Inflation." *Journal of Political Economy*, 77, 721–754.

Lucas, Robert E., and Thomas J. Sargent. 1979. "After Keynesian Macroeconomics." *Federal Reserve Bank of Minneapolis Quarterly Review*, 3 (Spring), 1–16. Reprinted in Lucas and Sargent (1981), 295–319.

——— 1981. *Rational Expectations and Econometric Practice*, Minneapolis: University of Minnesota Press.

Lunden, Leon E., and Ernestine M. Moore. 1965. "Severance Pay and Layoff Benefit Plans." *Monthly Labor Review*, 88, 27–34.

Lurie, Melvin, and Elton Rayack. 1966. "Racial Differences in Migration and Job Search." *Southern Economic Journal*, 33, 81–95.

Lynch, Lisa M. 1983. "Job Search and Youth Unemployment." *Oxford Economic Papers*, 35 (suppl.), 271–282.

Ma, Ching-to Albert, and Andrew M. Weiss. 1993. "A Signaling Theory of Unemployment." *European Economic Review*, 37, 135–157.

MacCrimmon, Kenneth R., and Donald A. Wehrung. 1986. *Taking Risks: The Management of Uncertainty.* New York: Free Press.

Machlup, Fritz. 1946. "Marginal Analysis and Empirical Research." *American Economic Review*, 36, 519–554.

MacKay, D. I. 1972. "After the 'Shake-Out,' " *Oxford Economic Papers*, 24, 89–110.

MacKay, D. I., D. Boddy, J. Brack, J. A. Diack, and N. Jones. 1971. *Labour Markets under Different Employment Conditions.* London: George Allen and Unwin.

MacKay, D. I., and G. L. Reid. 1972. "Redundancy, Unemployment and Manpower Policy." *Economic Journal*, 82, 1256–72.

MacKenzie, Scott B., Philip M. Podsakoff, and Richard Fetter. 1991. "Organizational Citizenship Behavior and Objective Productivity as Determinants of Managerial Evaluations of Salespersons' Performance." *Organizational Behavior and Human Decision Processes*, 50, 123–150.

——— 1993. "The Impact of Organizational Citizenship Behavior on Evaluations of Salesperson Performance." *Journal of Marketing*, 57, 70–80.

MacLaurin, W. Rupert, and Charles A. Myers. 1943. "Wages and the Movement of Factory Labor." *Quarterly Journal of Economics*, 57, 241–264.

MacLeod, W. Bentley, and James M. Malcomson. 1989. "Implicit Contracts, Incentive Compatibility, and Involuntary Unemployment." *Econometrica*, 57, 447–480.

——— 1993. "Motivation, Market Contracts, and Dual Economies." University of Southampton, Department of Economics Discussion Paper no. 9319.

MaCurdy, Thomas E. 1981. "An Empirical Model of Labor Supply in a Life-Cycle Setting." *Journal of Political Economy*, 89, 1059–85.

Malcomson, James M. 1997. "Contracts, Hold-Up, and Labor Markets." *Journal of Economic Literature*, 35, 1916–57.

Malinvaud, Edmond. 1977. *The Theory of Unemployment Reconsidered.* Oxford: Basil Blackwell.

Mankiw, N. Gregory. 1985. "Small Menu Costs and Large Business Cycles: A Macroeconomic Model of Monopoly." *Quarterly Journal of Economics*, 100, 529–537.

Mankiw, N. Gregory, Julio J. Rotemberg, and Lawrence H. Summers. 1985. "Intertemporal Substitution in Macroeconomics." *Quarterly Journal of Economics*, 100, 225–251.

Marston, Stephen T. 1975. "The Impact of Unemployment Insurance on Job Search." *Brookings Papers on Economic Activity*, 13–48.

Martin, James E. 1990. *Two-Tier Compensation Structures.* Kalamazoo, Mich.: W. E. Upjohn Institute.

Martin, James E., and Melanie M. Peterson. 1987. "Two-Tier Wage Structures: Implications for Equity Theory." *Academy of Management Journal*, 30, 297–315.

Martin, Joanne. 1981. "Relative Deprivation: A Theory of Distributive Injustice for an Era of Shrinking Resources." In L. L. Cummings and Barry M. Shaw, eds., *Research in Organizational Behavior*, 3:53–107. Greenwich, Conn.: Aijai Press.

Mathewson, Stanley B. 1931. *Restriction of Output among Unorganized Workers.* New York: Viking.

Mathieu, John E., and Dennis M. Zajac. 1990. "A Review and Meta-Analysis of the Antecedents, Correlates, and Consequences of Organizational Commitment." *Psychological Bulletin,* 108, 171–194.

Mattila, J. Peter. 1974. "Job Quitting and Frictional Unemployment." *American Economic Review,* 64, 235–239.

Mawhinney, T. C. 1990. "Decreasing Intrinsic 'Motivation' with Extrinsic Rewards: Easier Said than Done." *Journal of Organizational Behavior Management,* 11, 175–190.

Mayers, David, and Clifford W. Smith, Jr. 1982. "On the Corporate Demand for Insurance." *Journal of Business,* 55, 281–296.

———— 1987. "Corporate Insurance and the Underinvestment Problem." *Journal of Risk and Insurance,* 54, 45–54.

———— 1990. "On the Corporate Demand for Insurance: Evidence from the Reinsurance Market." *Journal of Business,* 63, 19–40.

McConnell, Sheena. 1989. "Strikes, Wages, and Private Information." *American Economic Review,* 79, 801–815.

McCormick, Barry. 1990. "A Theory of Signalling during Job Search, Employment Efficiency, and 'Stigmatized' Jobs." *Review of Economic Studies,* 57, 299–313.

McCune, Joseph T., Richard W. Beatty, and Raymond V. Montagno. 1988. "Downsizing: Practices in Manufacturing Firms." *Human Resource Management,* 27, 145–161.

McDonald, Ian M. 1989. "The Wage Demands of a Selfish, Plant-Specific Trade Union." *Oxford Economic Papers,* 41, 506–527.

———— 1995. "Models of the Range of Equilibria." In Rod Cross, ed., *The Natural Rate Hypothesis: Reflections on Twenty-five Years of the Hypothesis.* Cambridge: Cambridge University Press.

McDonald, Ian M., and Robert M. Solow. 1981. "Wage Bargaining and Employment." *American Economic Review,* 71, 896–908.

———— 1984. "Union Wage Policies: Reply." *American Economic Review,* 74, 759–761.

———— 1985. "Wages and Employment in a Segmented Labor Market." *Quarterly Journal of Economics,* 100, 1115–41.

McFarlin, Dean B., and Michael R. Frone. 1990. "A Two-Tier Wage Structure in a Nonunion Firm." *Industrial Relations,* 29, 145–154.

McGregor, Douglas. 1960. *The Human Side of Enterprise.* New York: McGraw-Hill.

McLaughlin, Kenneth J. 1990. "General Productivity Growth in a Theory of Quits and Layoffs." *Journal of Labor Economics,* 8, 75–98.

———— 1991. "A Theory of Quits and Layoffs with Efficient Turnover." *Journal of Political Economy,* 99, 1–29.

———— 1994. "Rigid Wages?" *Journal of Monetary Economics,* 34, 383–414.

———— 1998. "Are Nominal Wage Changes Skewed away from Wage Cuts?" Discussion Paper, Hunter College, City University of New York.

Meager, Nigel, and James Buchan. 1988. *Job-Sharing and Job-Splitting, Employer Attitudes.* Brighton: Institute of Manpower Studies, University of Sussex.

Meager, Nigel, and Hilary Metcalf. 1987. "Recruitment of the Long Term Unemployed." Institute of Manpower Studies Report no. 138. University of Sussex.

Medoff, James L., and Katharine G. Abraham. 1980. "Experience, Performance, and Earnings." *Quarterly Journal of Economics*, 95, 703–736.

Meij, J. L., ed. 1963. *Internal Wage Structure*. Amsterdam: North Holland.

Meyer, Bruce D. 1990. "Unemployment Insurance and Unemployment Spells." *Econometrica*, 58, 757–782.

Meyer, Herbert. 1975. "The Pay for Performance Dilemma." *Organizational Dynamics*, 3, 39–50.

Meyer, John R., and Edwin Kuh. 1959. *The Investment Decision*. Cambridge: Harvard University Press.

Meyers, Frederic. 1964. *Ownership of Jobs*. Los Angeles: Institute of Industrial Relations, University of California, Los Angeles.

Mian, Shehzad L. 1996. "Evidence on Corporate Hedging Policy." *Journal of Financial and Quantitative Analysis*, 31, 419–439.

Milgrom, Paul, and John Roberts. 1988. "An Economic Approach to Influence Activities and Organizational Responses." *American Journal of Sociology*, 94 (suppl.), S154–S179.

Milkovich, George T., and Jerry M. Newman. 1990. *Compensation*. Homewood, Ill.: Richard D. Irwin.

Mills, Terence C., Gianluigi Pelloni, and Athina Zervoyianni. 1995. "Unemployment Fluctuations in the United States: Further Tests of the Sectoral-Shifts Hypoethesis." *Review of Economics and Statistics*, 77, 294–304.

Millward, Neil, Mark Stevens, David Smart, and W. R. Hawes. 1992. *Workplace Industrial Relations in Transition*. Aldershot: Dartmouth.

Mincer, Jacob. 1986. "Wage Changes in Job Changes." In Ronald Ehrenberg, ed., *Research in Labor Economics*, 8, Part A, 171–187.

Miner, Mary Green. 1978. *Separation Procedures and Severance Benefits*. Personnel Policies Forum Survey no. 121. Washington, D.C.: Bureau of National Affairs.

Mitchell, Daniel J. B. 1972. "Union Wage Policies: The Ross-Dunlop Debate Reopened." *Industrial Relations*, 11, 46–61.

——— 1985a. "Shifting Norms in Wage Determination." *Brookings Papers on Economic Activity*, 575–599.

——— 1985b. "Wage Flexibility: Then and Now." *Industrial Relations*, 24, 266–279.

——— 1986. "Explanations of Wage Institutions and Incentives." Chapter 3 in Wilfred Beckerman, ed., *Wage Rigidity and Unemployment*. Baltimore: Johns Hopkins University Press.

——— 1989. *Human Resource Management: An Economic Approach*. Boston: PWS-Kent.

——— 1994. "A Decade of Concession Bargaining." Chapter 17 in Clark Kerr and Paul D. Staudahar, eds., *Labor Economics and Industrial Relations: Markets and Institutions*. Cambridge: Harvard University Press.

Mobley, William H. 1982. *Employee Turnover: Causes, Consequences, and Control*. Reading, Mass.: Addison-Wesley.

Moffitt, Robert. 1985. "Unemployment Insurance and the Distribution of Unemployment Spells." *Journal of Econometrics*, 28, 85–101.

Moffitt, Robert, and Walter Nicholson. 1982. "The Effect of Unemployment Insurance on Unemployment: The Case of Federal Supplemental Benefits." *Review of Economics and Statistics*, 44, 1–11.

Montgomery, James D. 1991. "Equilibrium Wage Dispersion and Interindustry Wage Differentials." *Quarterly Journal of Economics*, 106, 163–179.

——— 1993. "Adverse Selection and Employment Cycles." Department of Economics, Northwestern University, Discussion Paper.

Moorman, Robert H. 1993. "The Influence of Cognitive and Affective Based Job Satisfaction Measures on the Relationship between Satisfaction and Organizational Citizenship Behavior." *Human Resources*, 46, 759–776.

Morley, Ian, and Geoffrey Stephenson. 1977. *The Social Psychology of Bargaining*. London: George Allen and Unwin.

Mortensen, Dale T. 1970a. "Job Search, the Duration of Unemployment, and the Phillips Curve." *American Economic Review*, 60, 847–862.

——— 1970b. "A Theory of Wage and Employment Dynamics." In Edmund S. Phelps (1970a), 167–211.

——— 1970c. "Job Search, the Duration of Unemployment, and the Phillips Curve." *American Economic Review*, 60, 847–862.

——— 1978. "Specific Capital and Labor Turnover." *Bell Journal of Economics*, 9, 572–576.

——— 1986. "Job Search and Labor Market Analysis." Chapter 15 in Ashenfelter and Layard (1986).

——— 1989. "The Persistence and Indeterminacy of Unemployment in Search Equilibrium." *Scandinavian Journal of Economics*, 91, 347–370.

——— 1990. "Equilibrium Wage Distributions: A Synthesis." In J. Hartog, G. Ridder, and J. Theeuwes, eds., *Panel Data and Labor Market Studies*, 279–296. Amsterdam: North Holland.

Mortensen, Dale T., and Christopher A. Pissarides. 1993. "The Cyclical Behavior of Job Creation and Job Destruction." Section III.1 in Jan C. van Ours, Gerard A. Pfann, and Geert Ridder, eds., *Labor Demand and Equilibrium Wage Formation*. Amsterdam: North Holland.

——— 1994. "Job Creation and Job Destruction in the Theory of Unemployment." *Review of Economic Studies*, 61, 397–415.

Moylan, S., J. Millar, and R. Davies. 1984. *For Richer, for Poorer? DHSS Cohort Study of Unemployed Men*. Department of Health and Social Security, Social Research Branch Research Report no. 11. London: HMSO.

Murphy, Kevin J. 1992. "Performance Measurement and Appraisal: Motivating Managers to Identify and Reward Performance." Chapter 2 in William J. Bruns, ed., *Performance Measurement, Evaluation, and Incentives*. Boston: Harvard Business School Press.

Murphy, Kevin M., and Robert H. Topel. 1987a. "Unemployment, Risk, and Earnings: Testing for Equalizing Wage Differences in the Labor Market." Chapter 5 in Lang and Leonard (1987).

——— 1987b. "The Evolution of Unemployment in the United States: 1968–85." *NBER Macroeconomics Annual*, 1987, 11–58.

——— 1990. "Efficiency Wages Reconsidered: Theory and Evidence." Chapter 8 in

Yoram Weiss and Gideon Fishelson, eds., *Advances in the Theory and Measurement of Unemployment.* London: Macmillan, 1990.

Myers, Charles A., and W. Rupert MacLaurin. 1943. *The Movement of Factory Workers: A Study of a New England Industrial Community.* New York: John Wiley and Sons.

Myers, Charles A., and George P. Shultz. 1951. *The Dynamics of a Labor Market.* New York: Prentice-Hall.

Myers, Stewart C., and Nicholas S. Majluf. 1984. "Corporate Financing and Investment Decisions When Firms Have Information That Investors Do Not Have." *Journal of Financial Economics,* 13, 187–221.

Nagin, Daniel, James Rebitzer, Seth Sanders, and Lowell Taylor. 1998. "Monitoring and Motivation in an Employment Relationship: An Analysis of a Field Experiment." Discussion Paper, Carnegie Mellon University.

Narendranathan, Wiji, and Stephen Nickell. 1985. "Modelling the Process of Job Search." *Journal of Econometrics,* 28, 29–49.

Narendranathan, Wiji, Stephen Nickell, and J. Stern. 1985. "Unemployment Benefits Revisited." *Economic Journal,* 95, 307–329.

Nash, John. 1950. "The Bargaining Problem." *Econometrica,* 18, 155–162.

Nay, Leslie A. 1991. "The Determinants of Concession Bargaining in the Airline Industry." *Industrial and Labor Relations Review,* 44, 307–323.

Neal, Derek. 1993. "Supervision and Wages across Industries." *Review of Economics and Statistics,* 75, 409–417.

———— 1995. "Industry-Specific Human Capital: Evidence from Displaced Workers." *Journal of Labor Economics,* 13, 653–77.

Negishi, Takashi. 1979. *Microeconomic Foundations of Keynesian Macroeconomics.* Amsterdam: North Holland.

Neumark, David, and William Wascher. 1992. "Employment Effects of Minimum and Subminimum Wages: Panel Data on State Minimum Wages." *Industrial and Labor Relations Review,* 46, 55–81.

———— 1993. "Employment Effects of Minimum and Subminimum Wages: Reply to Card, Katz, and Krueger." National Bureau of Economic Research Working Paper no. 4570. Cambridge, Mass.

Newbery, David M., and Joseph E. Stiglitz. 1987. "Wage Rigidity, Implicit Contracts, Unemployment and Economic Efficiency." *Economic Journal,* 97, 416–430.

Newton, Floyd C., and Harvey S. Rosen. 1979. "Unemployment Insurance, Income Taxation, and Duration of Unemployment: Evidence from Georgia." *Southern Economic Journal,* 45, 773–784.

Nickell, Stephen. 1979a. "The Effect of Unemployment and Related Benefits on the Duration of Unemployment." *Economic Journal,* 89, 34–49.

———— 1979b. "Estimating the Probability of Leaving Unemployment." *Econometrica,* 47, 1249–66.

———— 1990. "Unemployment: A Survey." *Economic Journal,* 100, 391–439.

Nickell, Stephen, and Sushil Wadhwani. 1991. "Employment Determination in British Industry: Investigations Using Micro-Data." *Review of Economic Studies,* 58, 955–969.

Nisbett, Richard E., and Timothy DeCamp Wilson. 1977. "Telling More than We Can Know: Verbal Reports on Mental Processes." *Psychological Review,* 84, 231–259.

Nolan, Peter, and William Brown. 1983. "Competition and Workplace Wage Determination." *Oxford Bulletin of Economics and Statistics*, 45, 269–287.

Norsworthy, J. R., and Craig A. Zabala. 1985. "Worker Attitudes, Worker Behavior, and Productivity in the U.S. Automobile Industry, 1959–1976." *Industrial and Labor Relations Review*, 38, 544–557.

Notz, William W. 1975. "Work Motivation and the Negative Effects of Extrinsic Rewards: A Review with Implications for Theory and Practice." *American Psychologist*, 30, 884–891.

O'Brien, Anthony Patrick. 1989. "A Behavioral Explanation for Nominal Wage Rigidity during the Great Depression." *Quarterly Journal of Economics*, 104, 719–735.

O'Brien, Gordon E. 1986. *Psychology of Work and Unemployment*. New York: John Wiley and Sons.

Ochs, Jack, and Alvin E. Roth. 1989. "An Experimental Study of Sequential Bargaining." *American Economic Review*, 79, 355–384.

Office of Management and Budget, Executive Office of the President of the United States. 1987. *Standard Industrial Classification Manual*. Springfield, Va.: National Technical Information Service.

Oi, Walter. 1987. "Comment on the Relation between Unemployment and Sectoral Shifts." *Carnegie-Rochester Conference Series on Public Policy*, 27, 403–420.

Okun, Arthur M. 1973. "Upward Mobility in a High-Pressure Economy." *Brookings Papers on Economic Activity*, 207–252.

——— 1980. "Rational-Expectations-with-Misperceptions as a Theory of the Business Cycle." *Journal of Money, Credit and Banking*, 12, 817–825.

——— 1981. *Prices and Quantities: A Macroeconomic Analysis*. Washington, D.C.: Brookings Institution.

Ong, Paul M., and Don Mar. 1992. "Post-Layoff Earnings among Semiconductor Workers." *Industrial and Labor Relations Review*, 45, 366–379.

Orbell, John M., Robyn M. Dawes, and Alphons J. C. van de Kragt. 1988. "Explaining Discussion-Induced Cooperation." *Journal of Personality and Social Psychology*, 54, 811–819.

O'Reilly, Charles III, and Jennifer Chatman. 1986. "Organizational Commitment and Psychological Attachment: The Effects of Compliance, Identification, and Internalization on Prosocial Behavior." *Journal of Applied Psychology*, 71, 492–499.

Organ, Dennis W. 1988. *Organizational Citizenship Behavior*, Lexington, Mass.: Lexington Books.

Organ, Dennis W., and Mary Konovsky. 1989. "Cognitive versus Affective Determinants of Organizational Citizenship Behavior." *Journal of Applied Psychology*, 74, 157–164.

Organ, Dennis W., and Andreas Lingl. 1995. "Personality, Satisfaction, and Organizational Citizenship Behavior." *Journal of Social Psychology*, 135, 339–350.

Organ, Dennis W., and Katherine Ryan. 1995. "A Meta-Analytic Review of Attitudinal and Dispositional Predictors of Organizational Citizenship Behavior." *Personnel Psychology*, 48, 775–802.

Organization for Economic Co-operation and Development. 1965. *Wages and Labour Mobility*. Paris: OECD.

Osterman, Paul. 1984a. "Introduction: The Nature and Importance of Internal Labor

Markets." Chapter 1 in Paul Osterman, ed., *Internal Labor Markets.* Cambridge: MIT Press.

———— 1984b. "White-Collar Internal Labor Markets." Chapter 6 in Paul Osterman, ed., *Internal Labor Markets.* Cambridge: MIT Press.

———— 1994. "How Common Is Workplace Transformation and Who Adopts It?" *Industrial and Labor Relations Review,* 47, 173–188.

Ostroff, Cheri. 1992. "The Relationship between Satisfaction, Attitudes, and Performance: An Organizational Level Analysis." *Journal of Applied Psychology,* 77, 963–974.

Oswald, Andrew J. 1982. "The Microeconomic Theory of the Trade Union." *Economic Journal,* 92, 576–595.

———— 1985. "The Economic Theory of Trade Unions: An Introductory Survey." *Scandinavian Journal of Economics,* 87, 160–193.

———— 1986a. "Unemployment Insurance and Labor Contracts under Asymmetric Information: Theory and Facts." *American Economic Review,* 76, 365–377.

———— 1986b. "Is Wage Rigidity Caused by 'Lay-offs by Seniority?'" In Wilfred Beckerman, ed., *Wage Rigidity and Unemployment.* Baltimore: Johns Hopkins University Press.

———— 1993. "Efficient Contracts Are on the Labor Demand Curve : Theory and Facts." *Labour Economics,* 1, 85–113.

———— 1996a. "Rent-Sharing in the Labour Market." Warwick Economic Research Paper no. 474, Department of Economics, University of Warwick.

———— 1996b. "A Conjecture on the Explanation for High Unemployment in the Industrialised Nations: Part I." Warwick Economic Research Paper no. 475, Department of Economics, University of Warwick.

Oswald, Andrew J., and Peter J. Turnbull. 1985. "Pay and Employment Determination in Britain: What Are Labour 'Contracts' Really Like." *Oxford Review of Economic Policy,* 1, 80–97.

Ours, Jan C. van, and Geert Ridder. 1991. "Cyclical Variation in Vacancy Durations and Vacancy Flow: An Empirical Analysis." *European Economic Review,* 35, 1143–55.

Palley, Thomas I. 1992. "Sectoral Shifts and Cyclical Unemployment: A Reconsideration." *Economic Inquiry,* 30, 117–133.

Palmer, Gladys. 1954. *Labor Mobility in Six Cities.* New York: Social Science Research Council.

Parnes, Herbert S. 1954. *Research on Labor Mobility.* New York: Social Science Research Council.

Patchen, Martin. 1961. *The Choice of Wage Comparisons.* Englewood Cliffs, N.J.: Prentice-Hall.

Pencavel, John H. 1970. *An Analysis of the Quit Rate in American Manufacturing Industry.* Princeton, N.J.: Princeton University Press.

———— 1972. "Wages, Specific Training, and Labor Turnover in U.S. Manufacturing Industries." *International Economic Review,* 13, 53–64.

———— 1974. "Analysis of an Index of Industrial Morale." *British Journal of Industrial Relations,* 12, 48–55.

———— 1977. "Industrial Morale." In Orley C. Ashenfelter and W. E. Oates, eds., *Essays in Labor Market Analysis.* New York: John Wiley.

—— 1985. "Wages and Employment under Trade Unionism: Microeconomic Models and Macroeconomic Applications." *Scandinavian Journal of Economics,* 87, 197–225.

—— 1986. "Labor Supply of Men: A Survey." Chapter 1 in Ashenfelter and Layard, (1986).

Pencavel, John, and Ben Craig. 1994. "The Empirical Performance of Orthodox Models of the Firm: Conventional Firms and Worker Cooperatives." *Journal of Political Economy,* 102, 718–744.

Perella, Vera C. 1971. "Young Workers and Their Earnings." *Monthly Labor Review,* 94 (July), 3–11.

Perry, George. 1966. *Unemployment, Money Wage Rates, and Inflation.* Cambridge: MIT Press.

Pfeffer, Jeffrey, and Nancy Langton. 1993. "The Effect of Wage Dispersion on Satisfaction, Productivity, and Working Collaboratively: Evidence from College and University Faculty." *Administrative Science Quarterly,* 38, 382–407.

Phelps, Edmund S. 1968. "Money-Wage Dynamics and Labor-Market Equilibrium." *Journal of Political Economy,* 76, 678–711.

——, ed. 1970a. *Microeconomic Foundation of Employment and Inflation Theory.* New York: W. W. Norton.

—— 1970b. "Introduction: The New Microeconomics in Employment and Inflation Theory." Chapter 1 in Phelps (1970a).

Phillips, Aaron L. 1995. "1995 Derivatives Practices and Instruments Survey." *Financial Management,* 24 (Summer), 115–125.

Phillips, A. W. 1958. "The Relation between Unemployment and the Rate of Change of Money Wage Rates in the United Kingdom, 1862–1957." *Economica,* 25, 283–299.

Pillsbury, Wilbur F. 1958. "Organized Labor's Views of Corporate Financial Information." *Journal of Accounting,* 105, 46–56.

Piore, Michael J. (1973). "Notes for a Theory of Labor Market Stratification." In Richard C. Edwards, Michael Reich, and David M. Gordon, eds., *Labor Market Segmentation,* 125–150. Lexington, Mass.: D. C. Heath and Co.

Pissarides, Christopher A. 1985. "Short-Run Equilibrium Dynamics of Unemployment, Vacancies, and Real Wages." *American Economic Review,* 75, 676–690.

—— 1990. *Equilibrium Unemployment Theory.* Oxford: Basil Blackwell.

—— 1992. "Loss of Skill during Unemployment and the Persistence of Employment Shocks." *Quarterly Journal of Economics,* 107, 1371–91.

—— 1994. "Search Unemployment with On-the-Job Search." *Review of Economic Studies,* 61, 457–475.

Pissarides, Christopher A., and Ian McMaster. 1990. "Regional Migration, Wages, and Unemployment: Empirical Evidence and Implications for Policy." *Oxford Economic Papers,* 42, 812–831.

Podgursky, Michael, and Paul Swaim. 1987a. "Duration of Joblessness Following Displacement." *Industrial Relations,* 26, 213–226.

—— 1987b. "Job Displacement and Earnings Loss: Evidence from the Displaced Worker Survey." *Industrial and Labor Relations Review,* 41, 17–29.

Podsakoff, Philip M., Michael Ahearne, and Scott B. MacKenzie. 1997. "Organizational

Citizenship Behavior and the Quantity and Quality of Work Group Performance." *Journal of Applied Psychology*, 82, 262–270.

Podsakoff, Philip M., and Scott B. MacKenzie. 1994. "Organizational Citizenship Behaviors and Sales Unit Effectiveness." *Journal of Marketing Research*, 31, 351–363.

————— 1997. "The Impact of Organizational Citizenship Behavior on Organizational Performance: A Review and Suggestions for Future Research." *Human Performance*, 20, 133–151.

Podsakoff, Philip M., Scott B. MacKenzie, and Chun Hui. 1993. "Organizational Citizenship Behaviors and Managerial Evaluations of Employee Performance: A Review and Suggestions for Future Research." *Research in Personnel and Human Resources Management*, 11, 1–40.

Podsakoff, Philip M., Scott B. MacKenzie, Robert H. Moorman, and Richard Fetter. 1990. "Transformational Leader Behaviors and Their Effects on Followers' Trust in Leader, Satisfaction, and Organizational Citizenship Behaviors." *Leadership Quarterly*, 1, 107–142.

Popper, Karl. 1957. "The Aim of Science." *Ratio*, 1, 24–35.

Prescott, Edward C. 1986. "Theory Ahead of Business Cycle Measurement." *Quarterly Review, Federal Reserve Bank of Minneapolis* (Fall), 9–22.

Price, James L. 1977. *The Study of Turnover*. Ames: Iowa State University Press.

Pritchard, Robert D., Marvin D. Dunnette, and Dale O. Jorgenson. 1972. "Effects of Perceptions of Equity and Inequity on Worker Performance and Satisfaction." *Journal of Applied Psychology*, 56, 75–94.

Putnam, Robert D. 1993. *Making Democracy Work: Civic Traditions in Modern Italy*. Princeton, N.J.: Princeton University Press.

Rabin, Matthew. 1993. "Incorporating Fairness into Game Theory and Economics." *American Economic Review*, 83, 1281–1302.

Raff, Daniel M. G. 1988. "Wage Determination Theory and the Five-Dollar Day at Ford." *Journal of Economic History*, 48, 387–399.

Raff, Daniel M. G., and Lawrence H. Summers. 1987. "Did Henry Ford Pay Efficiency Wages?" *Journal of Labor Economics*, 5, S57–S86.

Raimon, Robert L. 1962. "Interstate Migration and Wage Theory." *Review of Economics and Statistics*, 44, 428–438.

Ramey, Garey, and Joel Watson. 1997. "Contractual Fragility, Job Destruction, and Business Cycles." *Quarterly Journal of Economics*, 112, 873–911.

Rebitzer, James B. 1987. "Unemployment, Long-Term Employment Relations, and Productivity Growth." *Review of Economics and Statistics*, 69, 627–635.

————— 1995. "Is There a Trade-Off between Supervision and Wages? An Empirical Test of Efficiency Wage Theory." *Journal of Economic Behavior and Organization*, 28, 107–129.

Rees, Albert. 1952. "Industrial Conflict and Business Fluctuations." *Journal of Political Economy*, 60, 371–382.

—————. 1966. "Information Networks in Labor Markets." *American Economic Review, Papers and Proceedings*, 56, 559–566.

————— 1993. "The Role of Fairness in Wage Determination." *Journal of Labor Economics*, 11, 243–252.

Rees, Albert, and George P. Shultz. 1970. *Workers and Wages in an Urban Labor Market*. Chicago: University of Chicago Press.

Reid, Graham L. 1972. "Job Search and the Effectiveness of Job-Finding Methods." *Industrial and Labor Relations Review, 25,* 479–495.

Reiss, Peter C. 1990. "Economic and Financial Determinants of Oil and Gas Exploration Activity." Chapter 7 in R. Glenn Hubbard, ed., *Asymmetric Information, Corporate Finance, and Investment.* Chicago: University of Chicago Press.

Reynolds, Lloyd. 1951. *The Structure of Labor Markets.* New York: Harper Brothers.

Reynolds, Lloyd, and Cynthia Taft. 1956. *The Evolution of Wage Structure.* New Haven: Yale University Press.

Reynolds, Morgan O. 1981. "Whatever Happened to the Monopoly Theory of Labor Unions?" *Journal of Labor Research, 2,* 163–173.

Ritter, Joseph A., and Lowell J. Taylor. 1994. "Workers as Creditors: Performance Bonds and Efficiency Wages." *American Economic Review, 84,* 694–703.

Robinson, Herbert W. 1951. "The Response of Labour to Economic Incentives." Chapter 6 in T. Wilson and P. W. S. Andrews (eds.), *Oxford Studies in the Price Mechanism.* Oxford: Clarendon Press.

Robinson, Sandra L. 1996. "Trust and Breach of Psychological Contract." *Administrative Science Quarterly, 41,* 574–599.

Robinson, Sandra L., and Elizabeth Wolfe Morrison. 1995. "Psychological Contracts and OCB: The Effect of Unfulfilled Obligations on Civic Virtue Behavior." *Journal of Organizational Behavior, 16,* 289–298.

Robst, John. 1995. "Career Mobility, Job Match, and Overeducation." *Eastern Economic Journal, 21,* 539–550.

Rock, Milton L., ed. 1972. *Handbook of Wage and Salary Administration.* New York: McGraw-Hill.

Rogerson, Richard. 1988. "Indivisible Labor, Lotteries and Equilibrium." *Journal of Monetary Economics, 21,* 3–16.

Romer, David. 1992. "Why Do Firms Prefer More Able Workers?" Department of Economics, University of California, Berkeley.

Rosen, Sherwin. 1983. "Unemployment and Insurance." *Carnegie-Rochester Conference Series on Public Policy, 19,* 5–49.

———— 1985. "Implicit Contracts: A Survey." *Journal of Economic Literature, 23,* 1144–75.

Rosenfeld, Carl. 1975. "Jobseeking Methods Used by American Workers." *Monthly Labor Review, 98* (August), 39–42.

———— 1977a. "Job Search of the Unemployed, May 1976." *Monthly Labor Review, 100* (November), 39–43.

———— 1977b. "The Extent of Job Search by Employed Workers." *Monthly Labor Review, 100* (March), 58–62.

Ross, Arthur M. 1948. *Trade Union Policy.* Berkeley: University of California Press.

———— 1957. "The External Wage Structure." In George W. Taylor and Frank C. Pierson, eds., *New Concepts in Wage Determination.* New York: McGraw-Hill.

Ross, David R., and Klaus F. Zimmermann. 1993. "Evaluating Reported Determinants of Labor Demand." *Labour Economics, 1,* 71–84.

Rotemberg, Julio J. 1994. "Human Relations in the Workplace." *Journal of Political Economy, 102,* 684–717.

—— 1997. "Cyclical Movements in Wages and Consumption in a Bargaining Model of Unemployment." Discussion Paper, Harvard Business School.

Roth, Alvin E. 1987. "Bargaining Phenomena and Bargaining Theory." Chapter 2 in Alvin E. Roth, ed., *Laboratory Experimentation in Economics, Six Points of View.* Cambridge: Cambridge University Press.

—— 1995. "Bargaining Experiments." Chapter 4 in John H. Kagel and Alvin E. Roth, eds., *The Handbook of Experimental Economics.* Princeton, N.J.: Princeton University Press.

Roth, Alvin E., Vesna Prasnikar, Masahiro Okuno-Fujiwara, and Shmuel Zamir. 1991. "Bargaining and Market Behavior in Jerusalem, Ljubljana, Pittsburgh, and Tokyo: An Experimental Study." *American Economic Review,* 81, 1068–95.

Roy, Donald. 1952. "Quota Restriction and Goldbricking in a Machine Shop." *American Journal of Sociology,* 57, 427–442.

Roy, Wilfred A. 1995. *1995 Annual Specialty Store and Human Resource Directors' Wage and Benefit Survey.* Washington, D.C.: National Retail Federation.

Rubinstein, Ariel. 1982. "Perfect Equilibrium in a Bargaining Model." *Econometrica,* 50, 97–109.

Ruhm, Christopher J. 1987. "The Economic Consequences of Labor Mobility." *Industrial and Labor Relations Review,* 41, 30–42.

—— 1991. "Are Workers Permanently Scarred by Job Displacements?" *American Economic Review,* 81, 319–324.

Ryan, Ann Marie, Mark J. Schmit, and Raymond Johnson. 1996. "Attitudes and Effectiveness: Examining Relations at an Organizational Level." *Personnel Psychology,* 49, 853–882.

Rynes, Sara L. 1991. "Recruitment, Job Choice, and Post-Hire Consequences: A Call for New Research Directions." Chapter 7 in Marvin D. Dunette and Leaetta M. Hough, eds., *Handbook of Industrial and Organizational Psychology,* 2nd ed., vol. 2. Palo Alto, Calif.: Consulting Psychologists Press.

Rynes, Sara L., and George T. Milkovich. 1986. "Wage Surveys: Dispelling Some Myths about the 'Market Wage.'" *Personnel Psychology,* 39, 71–90.

Sabourian, Hamid. 1988. "Wage Norms and Involuntary Unemployment." *Economic Journal,* 98, 177–188.

—— 1989. "Repeated Games—Some Applications to Under-Cutting and Harassment in the Labour Market." *European Economic Review,* 33, 625–634.

Sachs, Jeffrey. 1980. "The Changing Cyclical Behavior of Wages and Prices: 1890–1976." *American Economic Review,* 70, 78–90.

Salop, J., and S. Salop. 1976. "Self-Selection and Turnover in the Labor Market." *Quarterly Journal of Economics,* 90, 630–649.

Salop, Steven C. 1979. "A Model of the Natural Rate of Unemployment." *American Economic Review,* 69, 117–125.

Samuelson, Paul A., and Robert M. Solow. 1960. "Analytical Aspects of Anti-Inflation Policy." *American Economic Review,* 50, 177–194.

Sandell, Steven H. 1980a. "Job Search by Unemployed Women: Determinants of the Asking Wage." *Industrial and Labor Relations Review,* 33 (April), 368–378.

—— 1980b. "Is the Unemployment Rate of Women Too Low? A Direct Test of the Economic Theory of Job Search." *Review of Economics and Statistics,* 62, 491–501.

Sant, Donald T. 1977. "Reservation Wage Rules and Learning Behavior." *Review of Economics and Statistics,* 59 (February), 43–49.

Sargent, Thomas J. 1973. "Rational Expectations, the Real Rate of Interest, and the Natural Rate of Unemployment." *Brookings Papers on Economic Activity,* 4, 429–472.

———— 1996. "The Conquest of American Inflation." Marshall Lecture, delivered at Cambridge University. Discussion Paper, Hoover Institution, Stanford University.

Schatzman, Leonard, and Anselm Strauss. 1973. *Field Research.* Englewood Cliffs, N.J.: Prentice-Hall.

Schaubroeck, John, Douglas R. May, and R. William Brown. 1994. "Procedural Justice Explanations and Employee Reactions to Economic Hardship: A Field Experiment." *Journal of Applied Psychology,* 79, 455–460.

Schlicht, Ekkehart. 1978. "Labour Turnover, Wage Structure, and Natural Unemployment." *Zeitschrift für die gesamte Staatswissenschaft,* 134, 337–46.

Schmit, Mark J., and Steven P. Allscheid. 1995. "Employee Attitudes and Customer Satisfaction: Making Theoretical and Empirical Connections." *Personnel Psychology,* 48, 521–536.

Schnake, Mel. 1991. "Organizational Citizenship: A Review, Proposed Model, and Research Agenda." *Human Relations,* 44, 735–759.

Seashore, Stanley. 1954. *Group Cohesiveness in the Industrial Work Group.* Ann Arbor, Mich.: University of Michigan Press.

Selten, Reinhard. 1986. "Elementary Theory of Slack-Ridden Imperfect Competition." Chapter 4 in Joseph E. Stiglitz and G. Frank Mathewson, eds., *New Developments in the Analysis of Market Structure.* Cambridge: MIT Press.

Shafir, Eldar, Peter Diamond, and Amos Tversky. 1997. "Money Illusion." *Quarterly Journal of Economics,* 112, 341–374.

Shapiro, Alan C., and Sheridan Titman. 1986. "An Integrated Approach to Corporate Risk Management." In Joel Stern and Donald Chew, eds., *The Revolution in Corporate Finance.* Oxford: Basil Blackwell.

Shapiro, Carl, and Joseph E. Stiglitz. 1984. "Equilibrium Unemployment as a Worker Discipline Device." *American Economic Review,* 74, 433–444.

Sharpe, Steven A. 1994. "Financial Market Imperfections, Firm Leverage, and the Cyclicality of Employment." *American Economic Review,* 84, 1061–74.

Sheppard, Harold L., and A. Harvey Belitsky. 1966. *The Job Hunt.* Baltimore: Johns Hopkins Press.

Shergold, Peter R. 1975. "Wage Rates in Pittsburgh during the Depression of 1908." *American Studies,* 9, 163–188.

Shin, Hyun-Han, and René M. Stulz. 1998. "Are Internal Capital Markets Efficient?" *Quarterly Journal of Economics,* 113, 531–552.

Shin, Kwanho. 1997. "Intra- and Intersectoral Shocks: Effects on the Unemployment Rate." *Journal of Labor Economics,* 15, 376–401.

Shister, Joseph. 1943. "The Theory of Union Wage Rigidity." *Quarterly Journal of Economics,* 57, 533–542.

Sicherman, Nachum. 1991. " 'Overeducation' in the Labor Market." *Journal of Labor Economics,* 9, 101–122.

Silberston, Aubrey. 1970. "Surveys of Applied Economics: Price Behavior of Firms." *Economic Journal,* 80, 511–582.

Sims, Christopher A. 1974. "Output and Labor Input in Manufacturing." *Brookings Papers on Economic Activity*, 695–728.

Sims, Henry P. 1980. "Further Thoughts on Punishment in Organizations." *Academy of Management Review*, 5, 133–138.

Sinfield, Adrian. 1981. *What Unemployment Means*. Oxford: Martin Robertson.

Sitkin, Sim B., and Robert J. Bies. 1993. "Social Accounts in Conflict Situations: Using Explanations to Manage Conflict." *Human Relations*, 46, 349–370.

Slichter, Sumner H. 1920. "Industrial Morale." *Quarterly Journal of Economics*, 35, 36–60.

——— 1929. "The Current Labor Policies of American Industries." *Quarterly Journal of Economics*, 43, 393–435.

——— 1950. "Notes on the Structure of Wages." *Review of Economics and Statistics*, 32, 80–91.

Slichter, Sumner H., James J. Healy, and E. Robert Livernash. 1960. *The Impact of Collective Bargaining on Management*. Washington, D.C.: Brookings Institution.

Smith, Adam. 1759. *The Theory of Moral Sentiments*. Indianapolis: Liberty Fund, 1969.

Smith, Clifford W., and René M. Stulz. 1985. "The Determinants of Firms' Hedging Policies." *Journal of Financial and Quantitative Analysis*, 20, 391–405.

Solon, Gary, Warren Whatley, and Ann Huff Stevens. 1997. "Wage Changes and Intra-firm Job Mobility over the Business Cycle: Two Case Studies." *Industrial and Labor Relations Review*, 50, 402–415.

Solow, Robert M. 1956. "A Contribution to the Theory of Economic Growth." *Quarterly Journal of Economics*, 70, 65–94.

——— 1979. "Another Possible Source of Wage Stickiness." *Journal of Macroeconomics*, 1, 79–82.

——— 1980. "On Theories of Unemployment." *American Eeconomic Review*, 70, 1–11.

——— 1985. "Insiders and Outsiders in Wage Determination." *Scandinavian Journal of Economics*, 87, 411–428.

——— 1990. *The Labor Market as a Social Institution*. Cambridge, Mass.: Basil Blackwell.

Spitz, Janet. 1993. "Work Force Response to an Efficiency Wage: Productivity, Turnover, and the Grievance Rate." *Proceedings of the Forty-fifth Annual Meeting*, Industrial Relations Research Association, 142–150.

Stagner, Ross. 1987. *Psychology of Industrial Conflict*. New York: Garland.

Staiger, Douglas, James H. Stock, and Mark W. Watson. 1997. "The NAIRU, Unemployment, and Monetary Policy." *Journal of Economic Perspectives*, 11 (Winter), 33–49.

Staw, Barry M. 1984. "Organizational Behavior: A Review and Reformulation of the Field's Outcome Variables." *Annual Review of Psychology*, 35, 627–666.

Staw, Barry M., Nancy E. Bell, and John A. Clausen. 1986. "The Dispositional Approach to Job Attitudes: A Lifetime Longitudinal Test." *Administrative Science Quarterly*, 31, 56–77.

Staw, Barry M., Robert I. Sutton, and Lisa H. Pelled. 1994. "Employee Positive Emotion and Favorable Outcomes at the Workplace." *Organization Science*, 5, 51–71.

Steers, Richard M., and Susan R. Rhodes. 1978. "Major Influences on Employee Attendance: A Process Model." *Journal of Applied Psychology*, 63, 391–407.

Stephenson, Stanley P. 1976. "The Economics of Youth Job Search Behavior." *Review of Economics and Statistics*, 58, 104–111.

Stern, David, and Daniel Friedman. 1980. "Short-Run Behavior of Labor Productivity: Tests of the Motivation Hypothesis." *Journal of Behavioral Economics*, 9 (Winter), 89–105.

Stevens, David W. 1978. "A Reexamination of What Is Known about Jobseeking Behavior in the United States." In *Labor Market Intermediaries*, Special Report no. 22 of the National Commission for Manpower Policy. Washington, D.C.

Stiglitz, Joseph E. 1974. "Alternative Theories of Wage Determination and Unemployment in LDC's: The Labor Turnover Model." *Quarterly Journal of Economics*, 88, 194–227.

——— 1986. "Theories of Wage Rigidity." Chapter 4 in James L. Butkiewicz et al., eds., *Keynes' Economic Legacy*, New York: Praeger.

——— 1992. "Capital Markets and Economic Fluctuations in Capitalist Economies." *European Economic Review*, 36, 269–306.

Stoikov, Vladimir, and Robert L. Raimon. 1968. "Determinants of Differences in the Quit Rate among Industries." *American Economic Review*, 58, 1283–98.

Stole, Lars A., and Jeffrey Zwiebel. 1996. "Organizational Design and Technology Choice under Intrafirm Bargaining." *American Economic Review*, 86, 195–222.

Stouffer, Samuel A., Edward A. Suchman, Leland C. DeVinney, Shirley A. Star, and Robin M. Williams, Jr. 1949. *The American Soldier*. Princeton, N.J.: Princeton University Press.

Straka, John W. 1993. "Is Poor Worker Morale Costly to Firms?" *Industrial and Labor Relations Review*, 46, 381–394.

Strong, John S., and John R. Meyer. 1990. "Sustaining Investment, Discretionary Investment, and Valuation: A Residual Funds Study of the Paper Industry." Chapter 5 in R. Glenn Hubbard, ed., *Asymmetric Information, Corporate Finance, and Investment*. Chicago: University of Chicago Press.

Stulz, René M. 1984. "Optimal Hedging Policies." *Journal of Financial and Quantitative Analysis*, 19, 127–140.

——— 1996. "Rethinking Risk Management." *Journal of Applied Corporate Finance*, 9 (Fall), 8–24.

Summers, Lawrence. 1988. "Relative Wages, Efficiency Wages, and Keynesian Unemployment." *American Economic Review, Papers and Proceedings*, 78, 383–388.

Sundstrom, William A. 1990. "Was There a Golden Age of Flexible Wages? Evidence from Ohio Manufacturing, 1892–1910." *Journal of Economic History*, 50, 309–320.

Svejnar, Jan. 1986. "Bargaining Power, Fear of Disagreement, and Wage Settlements: Theory and Evidence from U.S. Industry." *Econometrica*, 54, 1055–78.

Swaim, Paul L., and Michael J. Podgursky. 1991. "Displacement and Unemployment." Chapter 5 in John T. Addison, ed., *Job Displacement, Consequences and Implications for Policy*. Detroit: Wayne State University Press.

Tajfel, Henri. 1970. "Experiments in Intergroup Discrimination." *Scientific American*, 223 (November), 96–102.

Taylor, John B. 1979. "Staggered Wage Setting in a Macro Model." *American Economic Review, Papers and Proceedings*, 69, 108–113.

———— 1980. "Aggregate Dynamics and Staggered Contracts." *Journal of Political Economy*, 88, 1–23.

———— 1986. "Improvements in Macroeconomic Stability: The Role of Wages and Prices." Chapter 11 in Robert J. Gordon, ed., *The American Business Cycle*. Chicago: University of Chicago Press.

Telly, Charles S., Wendell L. French, and William G. Scott. 1971. "The Relationship of Inequity to Turnover among Hourly Workers." *Administrative Science Quarterly*, 16, 164–172.

Theodore, Rose. 1957. "Layoff, Recall, and Work-Sharing Procedures, II—Union Participation in Layoff Procedures; Advance Notice of Layoffs." *Monthly Labor Review*, 80, 1–7.

Thibaut, J. R., and L. Walker. 1975. *Procedural Justice: A Psychological Analysis*. Hillsdale, N.J.: Erlbaum.

Thomas, Jonathan, and Tim Worrall. 1988. "Self-Enforcing Wage Contracts." *Review of Economic Studies*, 55, 541–554.

Tillery, Winston L. 1971. "Layoff and Recall Provision in Major Agreements." *Monthly Labor Review*, 94, 41–46.

Tobin, James. 1972. "Inflation and Unemployment." *American Economic Review*, 62, 1–18.

———— 1975. "Keynesian Models of Recession and Depression." *American Economic Review, Papers and Proceedings*, 65 (May), 195–202.

Topel, Robert. 1986. "Local Labor Markets." *Journal of Political Economy*, 94, S111–S143.

———— 1990. "Specific Capital and Unemployment: Measuring the Costs and Consequences of Job Loss." *Carnegie-Rochester Conference Series on Public Policy*, 33, 181–214.

Townsend, Robert. 1995. "Financial Systems in Northern Thai Villages." *Quarterly Journal of Economics*, 110, 1011–46.

Tracy, Joseph. 1986. "An Investigation into the Determinants of U.S. Strike Activity." *American Economic Review*, 76, 423–436.

———— 1987. "An Empirical Test of an Asymmetric Information Model of Strikes." *Journal of Labor Economics*, 5, 149–173.

———— 1988. "Testing Strategic Bargaining Models Using Stock Market Data." National Bureau of Economic Reseach Working Paper no. 2754. Cambridge, Mass.

Trevithick, J. A. 1976. "Money Wage Inflexibility and the Keynesian Labour Supply Function." *Economic Journal*, 86, 3237–32.

Tufano, Peter. 1996. "Who Manages Risk? An Empirical Examination of Risk Management Practices in the Gold Mining Industry." *Journal of Finance*, 51, 1097–1137.

Turnbull, Peter J. 1988. "Industrial Relations and the Seniority Model of Union Behavior." *Oxford Bulletin of Economics and Statistics*, 50, 53–70.

Turner, John C. 1987. *Rediscovering the Social Group: Self-Categorization Theory*. Oxford: Basil Blackwell.

Tyler, Tom R., and Robert J. Bies. 1990. "Beyond Formal Procedures: The Interpersonal Context of Procedural Justice." Chapter 4 in John S. Carroll, ed., *Applied Social Psychology and Organizational Setting*. Hillsdale, N.J.: Lawrence Erlbaum Associates.

Udry, Christopher. 1994. "Risk and Insurance in a Rural Credit Market: An Empirical Investigation in Northern Nigeria." *Review of Economic Studies,* 61, 495–526.

—— 1995. "Risk and Saving in Northern Nigeria." *American Economic Review,* 85, 1287–1300.

Ullman, J. C. 1966. "Employee Referrals: Prime Tool for Recruiting Workers." *Personnel,* 43, 30–35.

Ulman, Lloyd. 1965. "Labor Mobility and the Industrial Wage Structure in the Postwar United States." *Quarterly Journal of Economics,* 79, 73–97.

Ulph, A., and D. Ulph. 1990. "Union Bargaining: A Survey of Recent Work." In D. Sapsford and Z. Tzannatos, eds., *Current Issues in Labour Economics,* 86–125. Basingstoke: Macmillan.

Valenzi, E. R., and I. R. Andrews. 1971. "Effect of Hourly Overpay and Underpay Inequity When Tested with a New Induction Procedure." *Journal of Applied Psychology,* 55, 22–27.

Viteles, Morris S. 1953. *Motivation and Morale in Industry.* New York: W. W. Norton.

Vroman, Susan B. 1989. "A Longitudinal Analysis of Strike Activity in U.S. Manufacturing: 1957–84." *American Economic Review,* 79, 816–826.

Vroom, Victor H. 1964. *Work and Motivation.* New York: John Wiley.

Wachter, Michael L., and Oliver E. Williamson. 1978. "Obligational Markets and the Mechanics of Inflation." *Bell Journal of Economics,* 9, 549–571.

Wadhwani, Sushil B., and Martin Wall. 1991. "A Direct Test of the Efficiency Wage Model Using UK Micro-Data." *Oxford Economic Papers,* 43, 529–548.

Wadsworth, Jonathan. 1991. "Unemployment Benefits and Search Effort in the UK Labour Market." *Economica,* 58, 17–34.

Walton, Richard E., and Joel E. Cutcher-Gershenfeld. 1994. *Strategic Negotiations.* Boston: Harvard Business School Press.

Walton, Richard E., and Robert B. McKersie. 1965. *A Behavioral Theory of Labor Negotiations.* New York: McGraw-Hill.

Wanous, John P. 1992. *Organizational Entry: Recruitment, Selection, Orientation, and Socialization.* Reading, Mass.: Addison-Wesley.

Ward, Virginia L. 1980. "Measuring Wage Relationships among Selected Occupations." *Monthly Labor Review,* 103, 21–25.

Warner, John T., J. Carl Poindexter, Jr., and Robert M. Fearn. 1980. "Employer-Employee Interaction and the Duration of Unemployment." *Quarterly Journal of Economics,* 94, 211–233.

Wedderburn, Dorothy. 1965. *Redundancy and the Railwaymen.* Cambridge: Cambridge University Press.

Weibull, Jürgen. 1987. "Persistent Unemployment as Subgame Perfect Equilibrium." Seminar Paper no. 381, Institute for International Economic Studies, Stockholm.

Weiss, Andrew. 1980. "Job Queues and Layoffs in Labor Markets with Flexible Wages." *Journal of Political Economy,* 88, 526–538.

—— 1990. *Efficiency Wages, Models of Unemployment, Layoffs, and Wage Dispersion.* Princeton, N.J.: Princeton University Press.

Weitzman, Martin L. 1983. "Some Macroeconomic Implications of Alternative Compensation Systems." *Economic Journal,* 93, 763–783.

—— 1984. *The Share Economy.* Cambridge: Harvard University Press.

—— 1985. "The Simple Macroeconomics of Profit-Sharing." *American Economic Review,* 75, 937–953.

—— 1986. "Macroeconomic Implications of Profit-Sharing." *NBER Macroeconomics Annual, 1986,* 291–335.

—— 1988. "Comment on 'Can the Share Economy Conquer Stagflation?' " *Quarterly Journal of Economics,* 103, 219–223.

Weitzman, Martin L., and Douglas L. Kruse. 1990. "Profit Sharing and Productivity." In Alan S. Blinder, ed., *Paying for Productivity,* 95–140. Washington, D.C.: Brookings Institution.

Wheeler, Hoyt N. 1976. "Punishment Theory and Industrial Discipline." *Industrial Relations,* 15, 235–243.

—— 1985. *Industrial Conflict.* Columbia: University of South Carolina Press.

Wheeler, Hoyt N., Brian S. Klaas, and Jacques Rojot. 1994. "Justice at Work: An International Comparison." *Annals of the American Academy of Political and Social Sciences,* 536, 31–42.

White, Michael. 1983. *Long-Term Unemployment and Labour Markets.* London: Policy Studies Institute.

—— 1991. *Against Unemployment.* London: Policy Studies Institute.

White, Michael, and Susan McRae. 1989. *Young Adults and Long-Term Unemployment.* London: Policy Studies Institute.

Whyte, William Foote, et al. 1955. *Money and Motivation.* New York: Harper and Brothers.

—— 1961. *Men at Work.* Homewood, Ill.: Corsey Press.

Wial, Howard. 1991. "Getting a Good Job: Mobility in a Segmented Labor Market." *Industrial Relations,* 30, 396–416.

Wilcock, Richard C., and Walter H. Franke. 1963. *Unwanted Workers, Permanent Layoffs, and Long-Term Unemployment.* London: Collier-Macmillan.

Williamson, Oliver E. 1985. *The Economic Institutions of Capitalism.* New York: Free Press.

Wilson, Beth Ann. 1996. "Movement of Wages over the Business Cycle: An Intra-Firm View." Federal Reserve Board, Discussion Paper.

Wilson, S. H., and G. M. Walker. 1993. "Unemployment and Health: A Review." *Public Health,* 107, 153–162.

Winkelmann, Liliana, and Rainer Winkelmann. 1995. "Happiness and Unemployment: A Panel Data Analysis for Germany." *Konjunkturpolitik,* 41, 293–306.

Wood, Stephen. 1985. "Recruitment Systems and the Recession." *British Journal of Industrial Relations,* 23, 103–120.

Woodbury, Stephen A., and Robert G. Spiegelman. 1987. "Bonuses to Workers and Employers to Reduce Unemployment: Randomized Trials in Illinois." *American Economic Review,* 77, 513–530.

Wright, Randall. 1986. "Job Search and Cyclical Unemployment." *Journal of Political Economy,* 94, 38–55.

Yoon, Bong Joon. 1981. "A Model of Unemployment Duration with Variable Search Intensity." *Review of Economics and Statistics,* 63, 599–609.

Young, Anne McDougall. 1979. "Job Search of Recipients of Unemployment Insurance." *Monthly Labor Review,* 102 (February), 49–54.

Young, Madelyn V., and Bruce E. Kaufman. 1997. "Interfirm Wage Differentials in a Local Labor Market: The Case of the Fast-Food Industry." *Journal of Labor Research*, 18, 463–480.

Index